D1444754

SAP PRESS is issued by
Bernhard Hochlehnert, SAP AG

SAP PRESS is a joint initiative of SAP and Galileo Press. The know-how offered by SAP specialists combined with the expertise of the publishing house Galileo Press offers the reader expert books in the field. SAP PRESS features first-hand information and expert advice, and provides useful skills for professional decision-making.

SAP PRESS offers a variety of books on technical and business related topics for the SAP user. For further information, please also visit our website: *www.sap-press.com.*

Sigrid Hagemann, Liane Will
SAP R/3 System Administration
2003, approx. 450 pp., ISBN 1-59229-014-4

Helmut Stefani
Archiving Your SAP Data
A comprehensive guide to plan and execute archiving projects
2003, 360 pp., ISBN 1-59229-008-6

A. Rickayzen, J. Dart, C. Brennecke, M. Schneider
Practical Workflow for SAP
2002, 504 pp., ISBN 1-59229-006-X

Horst Keller, Joachim Jacobitz
ABAP Objects. The Official Reference
2003, 1094 pp., 2 Volumes and CD Set
ISBN 1-59229-011-6

Frédéric Heinemann, Christian Rau
The complete guide for ABAP and web developers
SAP Web Application Server
2003, approx. 600 pp., ISBN 1-59229-013-2

SAP® BW Professional

Norbert Egger

SAP® BW Professional

Tips and tricks for dealing with SAP Business Information Warehouse

SAP PRESS is an imprint of Galileo Press, Fort Lee, NJ, Bonn.
German Edition first published 2003 by Galileo Press.

Translation: Lemoine International, Inc., Salt Lake City, UT
Copy Editor: Nancy Etscovitz, UCG, Inc., Boston, MA
Cover Design: department, Cologne, Germany

Printed in the Netherlands
ISBN 1-59229-017-5

Contents

Appendix

Foreword

The commercial use of electronic data processing also marked the beginning of an attempt to use the increasingly comprehensive and detailed data in decision-making. Soon, one conceptual design followed another; little by little, IT tools that supported or claimed to support various concepts came into existence.

However, until the end of the last decade, the attempt to use these types of concepts and designs carried with it a high risk of failure. Even if the implementation of these concepts and designs itself did not collapse, the operation of such solutions often ultimately failed. This situation became even more dramatic as economic developments required the appropriate (that is, IT-supported) use of information for management activities.

The significance of the IT-supported availability of information for management soon reached a new level of quality: successful strategic management became a global, core competency with a geographic aspect, a cross-industry aspect, and an aspect independent of the size of the company involved. This development was concurrent with and had an effect on additional processes which, when viewed as a whole, meant new opportunities and risks. These processes included:

- Dramatic changes to the framework of business activity in general
- Continuing standardization of business processes
- Implementation of standard software that supported business processes in an integrated manner
- Development of IT (particularly the Internet and Web technology)
- Some consolidation of the concept of providing information (particularly the concepts of data warehousing and online analytical processing (OLAP))
- Appearance of a new supplier that fundamentally changed the market in the area of business intelligence software—SAP

While the competition and business analysts were skeptical about ERP-based data warehouse solutions, the SAP customers increasingly demanded it, and in 1997-98, SAP introduced its main business intelligence product—*SAP Business Information Warehouse (SAP BW)*—to the market. After its initial growing pains, SAP BW 1.2B was a serviceable and high-performance tool for analytical applications by mid-1998.

Then, after a period of initial reluctance among customers, SAP and most consulting firms were ultimately overwhelmed with an outright boom in demand by the time that SAP BW 2.0B and 2.1B appeared. In the business intelligence market, SAP moved from being a non-starter to a leading position; the success of SAP left its competitors' jeering far behind.

With SAP BW 3.0B, SAP succeeded in advancing development another step forward. The software now reached the level of "Best Practices" in its presentation of information. Although Web reporting in SAP BW had been strong since Release 2.0B, most consultants ignored this powerful tool completely, just as they had so many other new developments.

Given the often poor quality of implementations (due to inadequate design and resulting performance problems; reports viewed as inadequate by their intended audience; and the problems and high costs of operating such solutions), the need for a presentation of design knowledge in book form became ever more apparent. However, both the volume of work demanded by the scope of such a project and the short half-life of each version of SAP BW struck me as impossible to tackle in a reasonable period. Therefore, I must thank the tenaciousness of this book's editor for convincing me that this project could be undertaken.

Now that I've experienced and survived the production of this book, I'd like to thank all those who contributed for their cooperation and patience:

- The editor, Wiebke Hübner, for her assistance and patience during our collaboration
- The employees of *CubeServ AG (Switzerland)* and *CubeServ GmBH* (Germany) for their understanding of my drastically reduced management and consulting activity and for their numerous tips, which have become part of this work
- My management colleagues, Roland Merz and Jens Rohlf, for serving as editors and advisers when needed

Above all, I'd like to thank my family and especially my wife, Margot, for their understanding, enormous assistance, and handling of all the tasks that fell victim to this work. Without Margot, this work would have been impossible, and therefore, I dedicate this book to her with gratitude.

Norbert Egger
Jona (Switzerland), December 2003

Preface

This book is divided into four parts:

Part 1

Chapter 1 addresses classification and provides a conceptual overview of it. In this first part of the book, the need for successful strategic information management is discussed and the most important conceptual designs are outlined—data warehousing, OLAP, and the balanced scorecard method of management.

Part 2

The second part of this book provides an overview of SAP BW. Chapter 2 presents a general overview of the architecture and functions of SAP BW. Based on an implementation guide for profitability analysis in SAP BW, Chapter 3 examines all the steps required to create an application in SAP BW: extraction in SAP R/3, data retrieval from SAP R/3 and interface files, data modeling, and Web reporting.

Part 3

Chapters 4 and 5 examine aspects of data modeling and data retrieval. Chapter 4 shows the modeling and conversion of a column-oriented InfoSource into an account-oriented InfoCube; Chapter 5 addresses the appropriate mapping of the SAP product hierarchy in data modeling, data retrieval, and reporting.

Part 4

Chapters 6 to 8 deal with reporting tools. Chapter 6 explains the Business Explorer—Query Designer (especially its operations, its basic functions, and the important changes in SAP BW 3.x). Chapter 7 introduces the Business Explorer—Web Application Designer, a new component of SAP BW 3.0, which can be used to generate professional Web applications directly in the development environment of SAP BW. Chapter 8 provides examples of some of the options of Query Designer and Web Application Designer in SAP BW, which are based on a tutorial for a Web application with an expandable and quickly adaptable Management Cockpit.

Using This Book

Users with different levels of expertise and varying specific needs can easily use this book:

- Readers who want to understand SAP BW from its theoretical foundation should begin by looking at its strategic and conceptual design in Chapter 1, *Successful Strategic Information Management*.
- Readers who are primarily interested in a quick overview of SAP BW and the enhancements in SAP BW 3.0 and 3.1 should concentrate on Chapter 2, *SAP Business Information Warehouse—Overview*, and Chapter 3, *Step-by-Step: Profitability Analysis with SAP BW.*

- Readers who are interested in broadening and updating their knowledge of SAP BW can find an introduction and orientation in Chapter 2, *SAP Business Information Warehouse—Overview*, and then peruse the respective individual topics, beginning with Chapter 4.
- Readers with a basic knowledge of SAP BW and a particular interest in reporting can begin directly with Chapter 6, *Important Functions of the Query Designer SAP BW 3.x Based Upon a Sample Solution*; Chapter 7, *Selected Functions of SAP BW Web Application Designer in SAP BW 3.x*; and Chapter 8, *Sample Solution for an Expandable Web Cockpit in SAP BW*.

Part 1
Conceptual Overview

1 Successful Strategic Information Management

Successful management of information is becoming increasingly important—it is now a global core competency of all enterprises. However, given the flood of information that we must navigate through on a daily basis, this task has become ever more daunting. A solid concept of this core competency and the appropriate tools with which to implement this concept provide us with an opportunity to meet this challenge.

1.1 Foundations of Management Decision-Making

In the 1990's, during a discussion of the possible implementation of the balanced scorecard method of management, a very successful CEO confronted me with his unvarnished credo: "You know, I don't need a balanced scorecard. My traffic lights are in my gut."[1]

Intuition or information?

As it has done before, the quarrel over successful management decision-making pits "intuitive decisions" directly against "decisions based upon information." And with every public disclosure of the failure of highly vaunted decision-makers who go with their guts, the scale moves a bit further in the direction of "decisions based upon information."

Do those who insist upon intuition—as the foundation for successful management decision-making—conceal only personal acquisitiveness, or their inability to decide rationally? Although such an assessment might appear obvious, it also disregards several important aspects:

- A correlation exists between the hierarchical level of managers and the probability that they rely on intuition as the basis of successful management decision-making. The more successful these managers were (and are?), the more they appear to believe in intuition. Even this aspect forces us to seriously examine the conflict between intuition and information.
- Does the belief in intuition rest on the ability of earlier information systems to provide only an inadequate or unusable basis for management decisions?

1 See Robert S. Kaplan and David P. Norton 1996.

- Is intuition possibly a web of highly complex management information that is available only to its "owner"? And might not the "owner" have a good reason to ensure that no one else can reproduce the web?

Regardless of the position taken, it's apparent that there's a problem. The risk that leading managers will fail (as will their respective previously successful companies) has never been greater than it is today. Many places continue to report new bankruptcies and record negatives. Has intuition reached its limits, or does the information that is available as the basis for management decisions still lack the necessary precision?

Call for action

The call for action is obvious and it demands that we examine the conceptual foundations, the methodological considerations, and the required technologies.

1.2 Changed Demands on Information Management

The economic trends of the last few years are characterized by developments that are almost dramatic: takeover battles, restructuring, high volatility of the international financial markets, and so on.

In the last decade, it seems that every law of economics has been repealed or changed. How many publications opined that the New Economy and the Internet would eliminate economic crises once and for all? And how many of today's publications claim that nothing has really changed, except that a downturn has started—a downturn which will likely last as long as the boom that just ended?

It will probably be reserved for future generations of historians and economists to caricature these kinds of mechanical positions. For strategic information management to be successful, two things are clear:

- The question of whether there are connections between the increasing number of failed management decisions based on intuition and general developments. If connections do exist, what are they?
- A (decisive) level of triteness. The general framework of enterprise activity has fundamentally changed and demands a better basis for management decisions.

New opportunities, risks, and difficulties

These changes present a mixture of new opportunities, but they also include risks and difficulties. Simply continuing with earlier company policies will no longer ensure survival, at least in the medium- and long-term. Companies of any size that cannot deal successfully with the challenges of increasingly global and cross-industry competition will lose terrain, or simply disappear from one type (or another) of "economic soil."

Companies that face the challenge must implement more frequent and often dramatic adjustments to map their business processes to new conditions. Accordingly, cost-reduction programs, diversification, concentration on core business, mergers and acquisitions, and so on, can turn organizational structures into transactional data.

Integrated standard software

In the 1990's, many companies recognized that traditional methods of data processing would not meet these challenges. Adequate, flexible, and integrated IT tools were recognized as a compelling precondition for proper support. The unavailability of this support resulted in a lack of flexibility in the design of business processes and therefore posed a significant disadvantage over and against the competition. Once common individual solutions now proved to be inappropriate, insufficiently expandable, and too inflexible. Accordingly, the recognition of the necessity of flexible and integrated standard software prevailed to a large extent in the area of transactional software (software to support financial accounting, the processing of customer orders, and so on).

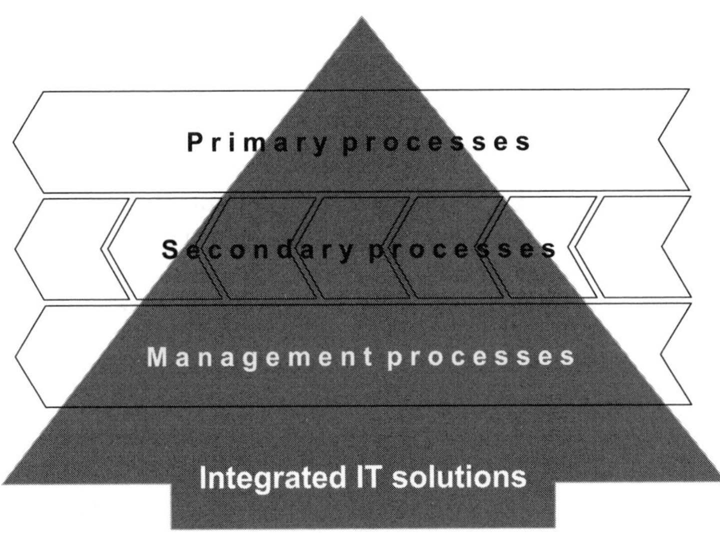

Figure 1.1 Business Processes and Integrated IT Solutions

In this regard, an unparalleled boom in various standard software products characterized the 1990's. Gigantic projects to implement standard business software often determined the agenda of many companies for years.

The triumph of SAP R/3

In this phase, SAP R/3, a product of SAP in Walldorf, Germany, triumphed in an area of business software that had never existed before. Although many locations reported significant problems with the implementation and operation of this solution, most of the companies acquired appropriate IT tools with the functions and flexibility necessary to support their business processes for the very first time. A careful examination clearly reveals that problems would have to appear here and there with such a large number of implementation projects: entire armies of SAP consultants were created in often skeletal training programs, which emerged out of the blue, inadequate and ill prepared. Experience with projects and the ability to provide business and IT **advice** were unfortunately often relegated to the background. The high rate of success in implementing SAP R/3 speaks well for the product.

Improving business processes

Many companies implemented SAP R/3 to handle their operating processes. Doing so enabled them to adjust the processes to reflect changing market conditions with appropriate integration, limited risk, and reasonable effort. It's also interesting that during this phase of the revolution of the "transactional world," the implementation of SAP R/3 as standard software often resulted in smaller or greater improvements to the actual business processes. Use of the software recommended standard structures and standard processes that were often superior to those of the previous, individual solutions—even if this conclusion was not often recognized during the implementation phase.

In contrast to the support of operative processes, the actual situation regarding comprehensive and continuous IT support of management processes almost seems disillusioning. Although this kind of support has been required for some time, in most companies it simply does not exist. Even less common are integrated IT solutions for bidirectional communication between management processes and operative processes. The more critical and frequent it is that radical management decisions must be made, the more critical this situation (i.e., the lack of continuous IT support for management processes) becomes for the practice of management.

IT support of management processes

It should be noted that mapping requirements for reporting, analysis, and planning, which involve unjustifiable efforts, are woefully inadequate. It is precisely those new challenges, which are created by management activities, that lack adequate support—even after the implementation of transactional SAP components.

Standard solutions not yet typical

Contrary to the implementation of software business processes in the transactional world, the need for a comprehensive and integrated standard solution for management processes has not yet achieved recognition. In view of the rare adaptation of comprehensive information systems, a widely-present deficit can be seen here. And so, many companies today still use the most varied types of insular solutions and expend incomprehensible amounts of manual effort to use PC software (usually Microsoft Excel) to format the vast amounts of data produced by standard software into a form that meets the information needs of management.

But to follow the approach of management decision-making based on information, these kinds of solutions would have to satisfy the increasing demands of management information for precision, availability, and timeliness. Information systems that are not comprehensive and integrated, that reach their limits given the media breaks and interfaces involved, and that require a great deal of effort to operate, already cover the requirements only inadequately or with unreasonable effort. Without the use of appropriate solutions, this trend (i.e., the trend towards information systems that are comprehensive and integrated) will become even more prevalent in the future.

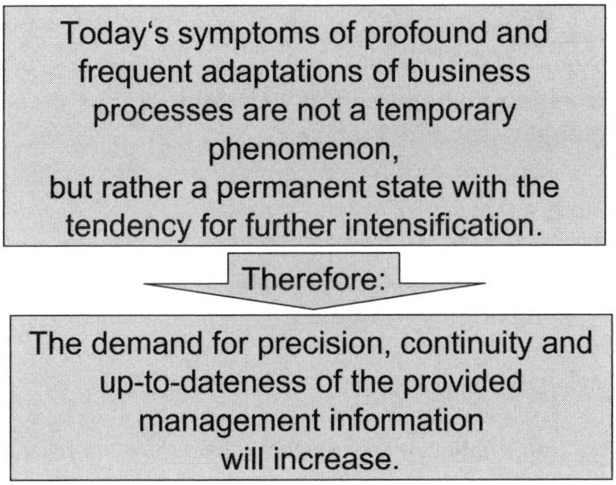

Today's symptoms of profound and frequent adaptations of business processes are not a temporary phenomenon,
but rather a permanent state with the tendency for further intensification.
Therefore:
The demand for precision, continuity and up-to-dateness of the provided management information will increase.

Figure 1.2 New Requirements of Information Systems

If those who advocate for information-based management decisions criticize the intuitive approach, the problems inherent in providing information today explain why many managers refuse to join their camp. Managers or project leaders have intuitions and many people cannot comprehend these intuitions. Nonetheless, for the respective manager, these intuitions can be regarded as comprehensive, integrated, and extremely up-to-date, in the context of the manager's experience. The obvious weaknesses of many information systems don't allow for a hasty argument—even with regard to the precision of a manager's intuition.

This situation, however, does not reflect the superiority of the intuitive approach. The weaknesses and increasing problems of that method have become evermore apparent. In fact, these considerations indicate the problems that the development and implementation of the information system must solve.

Extracting and using information

All these problems can be reduced to two principal elements: the adequate extraction of information and the use of information. If opportunities and risks are recognized too late or not at all—based on the information available—a company cannot maintain its market position and, in some circumstances, cannot develop further.

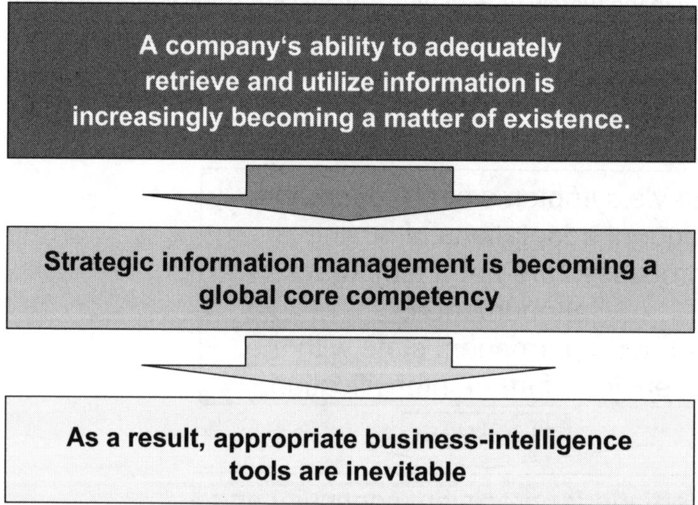

A company's ability to adequately retrieve and utilize information is increasingly becoming a matter of existence.
Strategic information management is becoming a global core competency
As a result, appropriate business-intelligence tools are inevitable

Figure 1.3 Strategic Information Management as a Global Core Competency

This kind of strategic information management is becoming more and more of a global core competency. Here the term *global core competency* stands for a geographical dimension and an aspect that goes beyond the boundaries of a company, and even an entire industry.

Most past attempts at IT-supported extraction and use of information have failed or have proven to be inadequate, as the significance of the intuitive approach has shown. Accordingly, particular attention must be paid to suitable business intelligence tools, where business intelligence is understood as the transformation of operative data into decision-relevant knowledge. These kinds of tools provide the following core abilities:

- They permit comprehensive solutions that are sufficiently precise, continuous, and timely.
- They are integrated, standard solutions that ideally enable not only the integrated use of information, but also the integrated extraction of information. They integrate the various relevant source systems and advanced tools to support planning processes or the balanced scorecard method of management.
- They are standard solutions—the greater the portion of individual development, the greater the probability of inadequate or improperly expandable implementation and unmanageable operation.
- They enable simultaneous access by many users.

Software products for business intelligence solutions

In the past few years, various tools have established themselves and claim to meet the requirements stated above. An examination of market position (depending on the method of comparison) reveals various relevant tools. Products in the business intelligence market include products of the following companies: Hyperion, SAS, PeopleSoft, and Oracle. SAP entered this market with a series of attempts based on different designs and ultimately offered SAP Business Information Warehouse (SAP BW) and additional products based on it. SAP began a market penetration that recalled the success of SAP R/3 and gave SAP a correspondingly significant market position.

The choice of an adequate business intelligence tool follows the traditional procedure for systematic selection of any software product. However, during the selection of this type of software product, companies must not forget that they are selecting a tool that is simply that: a tool or a utility. If used improperly, even the right tool can create more damage than benefit for the user.

Consequently, considerations of the implementation and operation of a business intelligence solution lead to questions on conceptual foundations, tools, and implementation methods.

1.3 Conceptual Foundations

Just because you select the appropriate tool, the solution for which the tool was selected is not automatically guaranteed—the correct solution is not determined by the selection of the tool. From the very beginning of scientific processing of various aspects of the extraction and use of information, a series of concepts, some of which build on each other, has been developed. The development can be summarized in the following main stages.

The development of concepts to provide IT systems that support decision-making ultimately rests on centuries-old experience and reflection. From the development of mechanical data processing to the development of electronic data processing, new possibilities of mass data processing and analysis of the data have opened up.[2]

These developments can be summarized in the following three principal concepts:

Management Information System (MIS)

The concept of a *management information system (MIS)* was developed in the 1960's to provide management with information in a helpful form: standard reports created from heterogeneous transactional systems. This attempt failed for several reasons, particularly, the lack of integrated databases, opportunities for online processing, and appropriate visualization tools.

Decision Support System (DSS)

In the 1970's, a new approach that considered the experience honed from the use of MIS and the new technological possibilities offered by emerging databases and dialog process led to the development of *decision support systems*. This method focused on analyses, simulations, and trends for controllers and database specialists.

Executive Information System (EIS)

In the 1980's, technological advances, including the appearance of PC-based solutions, led to a renewed orientation to management as the primary target group. Despite the euphoric expectations, these systems generally failed as well, primarily because of the inadequate quality of the data, poor performance, user-unfriendly analysis tools, and the target group's insufficient mastery of PCs and the software.

All of these methods have the following common elements:

1. They all look at the problems of strategic information management from the viewpoint of those technologies (or parts of those technologies) that were available. Interestingly, as the development of these

2 See the brief sketch in Rudy Rucker 1996.

technologies advanced, people failed to consider that fundamental aspects of earlier concepts had hardly been applied or used by a broad public.

2. In the past, the implementation and success rates of attempted implementations were disappointingly low.

Previous attempts teach us that successful implementation and operation does not primarily depend on implementing the most recent conceptual breakthrough; rather, it depends on the ability to consider the conceptual foundation in the context of the actual problems to be solved.

Two concepts developed in the 1990's that considered the essential elements and experiences of earlier attempts are relevant: the concept of data warehousing developed by William H. Inmon[3] and considerations on online analytical processing (OLAP) by Edgar F. Codd.[4]

The data warehouse concept

Inmon defines the term *data warehouse* as follows: "The data warehouse is...the foundation of all DSS processing.... A data warehouse is a subject-oriented, integrated, nonvolatile, and time-variant collection of data in support of management's decisions. The data warehouse contains granular corporate data."[5]

The essential attributes include the following:

- Subject orientation
- Integration
- Nonvolatility and time-variability
- Durability
- Data granularity

Therefore, the term *data warehouse* means a comprehensive information architecture and the related support-processes for strategic and operative decisions in the company. A data warehouse is not a ready-made product. Rather, data warehousing is a combination of various organizational, technical, software, and hardware components. It summarizes data from various sources in a special information database.

The ETL process

One important problem that we must not underestimate is the necessity or the requirement to process data that is asynchronous. Apart from this issue, we also need to consider the following: the technical requirements

3 See William H. Inmon 2002.
4 See Nigel Pendse 2002. See also: *http://www.olapreport.com/fasmi.htm*
5 See William H. Inmon 2002, p. 31.

of extracting data from the most varied types of source systems and storing the data in a target database of significant size.

This process is known as the *ETL process*: extraction, transformation, and loading. It requires a terminology that is company-wide, considers all the affected systems, and that is used in the process of transforming heterogeneous source data. The ETL process must also consider every data element and key that expands the source systems. Inmon's notes on this process contain both the task of implementing this process, with all its technical and organizational elements, and the no less problematic aspect of operating a data warehouse.

Transformation of data into information

The use of a data warehouse is often discarded with a reference to the futility of simply providing data. The mere provision of data is, in fact, useless because it's unmanageable and cannot be utilized. This is a significant risk to these types of projects. Therefore, stating the actual purpose of the data warehouse is of primary significance: offering decision-support or support of management's decisions. The data warehouse must present the stored data to the target group in the form of usable information. However, the conversion of data into information is no trivial task.

Figure 1.4 Main Process of the Data Warehouse

OLAP: online analytical processing

The concept of *online analytical processing (OLAP)* supplements the data warehouse concept and defines the characteristics required of a serviceable business intelligence system.

Codd proposes the following 12 rules:[6]

1. Multidimensional conceptual view
2. Transparency
3. Accessibility
4. Consistent reporting performance
5. Client/server architecture
6. Generic dimensionality

6 See Edgar Frank Codd, et al. 1993. See also: *http://www.fpm.com/refer/codd.html.*

7. Dynamic sparse matrix handling
8. Multiuser support
9. Unrestricted cross-dimensional operations
10. Intuitive data manipulation
11. Flexible reporting
12. Unlimited dimensions and aggregation levels

Flexible provision of information

Despite the importance of all these criteria to the enhancement of the data warehouse concept with an OLAP design, other aspects must be highlighted as well. One significant consequence occurs due to the fundamental difference between the operative display of data in a transactional system and the analysis of data in an information system. Reports must be created in light of what the target group is used to receiving. The suitability of this type of tool therefore rises and falls with its ability to provide information flexibly.

Requirements of multidimensional databases

In addition, the criteria pertaining to the multidimensional aspects (slice and dice, performance, and so on) are of special importance. Without an adequate form of data storage and relatively simple and high-performance access to the data, these kinds of solutions are not viable.

1.4 Required Enhancements

1.4.1 Integration of Systems and Applications

As the aforementioned concepts were being developed, homogeneity of the source systems and the integration of transactional and data warehouse systems was unthinkable (see Codd's third OLAP criterion—accessibility). A data warehouse system required manual redefinition of all data elements (even the structure of objects that carried master data, for example). In addition, all the interfaces between the source systems and the data warehouse system had to be explicitly defined; extraction, transformation, and load programs had to be created. The complexity and volume of this task cannot be overstated. To arrive at even a relatively small solution between a single source system and one data warehouse, experience has shown that several hundred data elements and at least as many interfaces for transaction and master data (attributes, texts, and hierarchies) are involved.

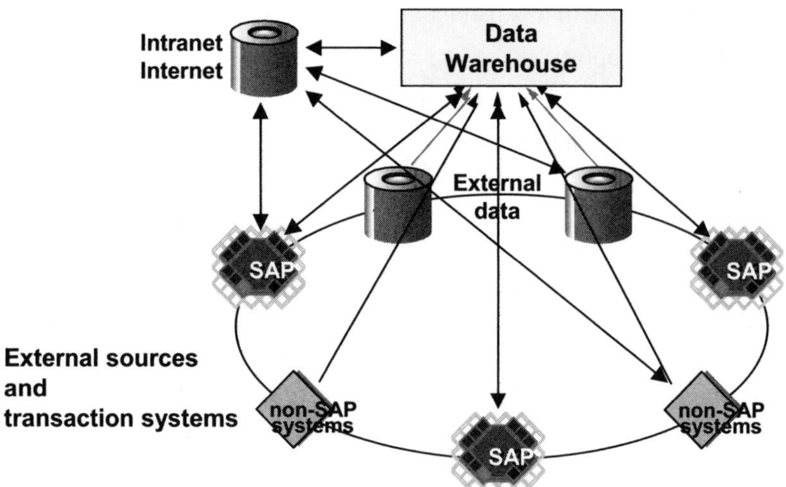

Figure 1.5 System Landscape: Transactional Systems and Data Warehouse

When a relatively small solution that involves only a few sources and systems is added to the system landscape and thereby expands it (as discussed above, see Figure 1.5), it quickly becomes apparent that the expansion multiplies the complexity of the effort involved. The greater the number of extraction programs (and possibly transformation programs for each source system) that must be created, the lower the probability of successful implementation and operation of such a system. If the data warehouse system is to be used as a data source for transactional systems (as a result of central planning and the return of the input data to the operative systems, for example), the complexity increases even further. In an actual system environment that involves dozens or even hundreds of systems, the situation can become completely unmanageable—at least during the operation of the data warehouse.

Technical and application integration

The reverse is obvious. If the source system and data warehouse systems can be integrated technically (over implicit, standard interfaces) and if the applications can be integrated, the effort involved in implementation and operation is dramatically reduced. This insight shows that in addition to considering the concepts of data warehouse and OLAP, the integration of operative processes and analytical applications must be realized.

The significant market share of SAP R/3 as a transactional system, the increasing attempt of companies to harmonize these systems, and the ability of SAP R/3 to support technical and application integration (even to other transactional software products) mean that a suitable tool is present for the first time in SAP Business Information Warehouse (SAP BW).

1.4.2 Providing and Distributing Information

The previous section, which dealt with the concept of a data warehouse, noted the problems inherent in transforming data into information. Such a conversion can occur in steps only when good reporting functions (comparisons and analysis of deviations from the plan or the previous year, with exceptions noted in color or with graphics for visualization, for example) are available.

Problem: providing information

If the transformation of data into information is successful, the problem of providing the information in the proper form quickly arises. A simple pool of reports and analyses is inadequate because a solution of even medium complexity often produces several hundred or even thousands of reports and analyses after one or two years. A pool of this size increasingly creates the problem of not being able to find ready-made reports, so that new, redundant reports are created in addition to the existing reports and analyses. Furthermore, the new reports magnify the problem of finding the right information. Simultaneously, existing reports might not be updated, so that a growing number of reports and analyses include erroneous and deceptive statements, thereby endangering the ability to make well-informed decisions.

Role-based menu structures

Role-based menu structures are an attempt to provide information in manageable groupings. This approach demands a great deal of discipline, documentation, and assertiveness from the team implementing the information system. However, because this function does not always follow the traditional means of management to get information, it is often inadequate.

Management Cockpits

The attempt to provide a *management cockpit* represents another step in the right direction. Primarily graphical material is summarized for specific target groups. Advanced solutions also enable you to navigate to other reports, thereby offering a *single point of entry* to information relevant to a target group. The problem with this design is that the significant effort involved in realizing and maintaining it generally hinders development of a solution that covers an entire area. Additionally, the definitions of the target groups are often too rough and do not reach the level of personalized solutions tailored to the tasks of a particular manager.

With both concepts, consider that providing information in this manner within a proprietary environment partially negates a single-point-of-entry design and requires specific tool-handling from users.[7] However, the readiness to learn how to handle such tools was and is limited.

7 Designs widely used in the past include the interface for SAP R/3, the SAP GUI, and the interfaces of frequently used PC tools such as Excel or inSight/dynaSight.

Portal technology

Technologies that include all the essential aspects of portals can also adequately cover the personalization needs for the designs addressed above. The use of the executable reporting tools in HTML browsers (Microsoft Internet Explorer or Netscape Navigator) can also leverage existing knowledge of the tool. Many managers have sufficient experience with the tools because of their (sometimes non-professional) use of the Internet. Familiarity with HTML browsers as a basic technology makes using solutions that employ this technology easier and therefore more likely to find greater acceptance among users.

Solutions that combine the design or concept of providing information can, to a large degree, fulfill the expectations of the target groups, and therefore be used efficiently. However, if an additional step moves from passive provision of information to active distribution of information, the usability and implementation of the solutions increase significantly.

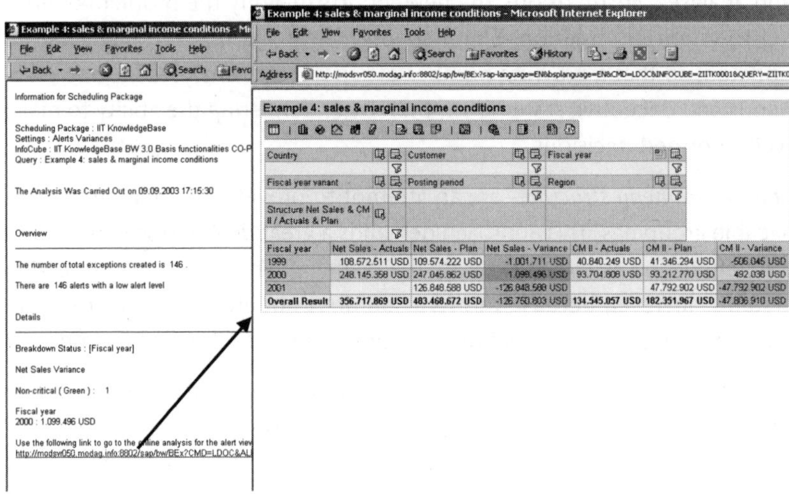

Fiscal year	Net Sales - Actuals	Net Sales - Plan	Net Sales - Variance	CM II - Actuals	CM II - Plan	CM II - Variance
1999	108.572.511 USD	109.574.222 USD	-1.001.711 USD	40.840.249 USD	41.346.294 USD	-506.045 USD
2000	248.145.358 USD	247.045.862 USD	1.099.496 USD	93.704.808 USD	93.212.770 USD	492.038 USD
2001		126.848.588 USD	-126.848.588 USD		47.792.902 USD	-47.792.902 USD
Overall Result	**356.717.869 USD**	**483.468.672 USD**	-126.750.803 USD	**134.545.057 USD**	**182.351.967 USD**	-47.806.910 USD

Figure 1.6 Reporting Agent: E-mail with a Link to a Detailed Report

The next step: distribution of information

Personalized distribution of information can use technologies that are already available. Alert monitors automatically determine deviations from threshold values and electronically create information for these situations that are exceptional. Users receive an overview of all essential information as soon as they log on to the portal and can, if necessary, easily navigate to view the details. The same design enables sending e-mail with links to detailed reports about problems that have developed (see Figure 1.6). Message recipients therefore have all the information they need without having to know how to navigate the system. This technology automatically opens the right report in the underlying information system. Recent developments in mobile computing can also be used in the same way.

1.4.3 Internal and external data

Most information systems implement comparative analyses (e.g., with the previous year and plan–actual). The analyses often provide valuable information on current conditions and developments. But the limitations of this method can be found in its introspective view. Are costs remaining within the budget? Could per capita revenue be increased? Even analysis of revenue developments enables only a highly limited and dangerous (and therefore deceptive) view of a company's market position. The cause? Many information systems offer a view of only internal data.

Internal data in information systems

For example, consider that increased revenue of 10% is, under certain circumstances, regarded as an outstanding development. A management decision based on this purely internal view might well be to "stay the course and stabilize the development." However, if the competition shows growth of 20–30% in the same period, the company has actually lost market share!

This example clearly shows that only after a careful consideration of internal *and* external data, can one glean truly meaningful information. Only the comparison of internal with external developments can prevent erroneous prognostications.

Freely available data and information providers

Of course, the extraction of external data is not easy in each case and for every purpose. Generally, both available data and data purchased from information providers can form the basis for the required benchmarking. Media companies and public agencies are responsible for making a great deal of data available free of charge. Other companies' publications can enhance this data: annual reports, general publications, investor relationship information, homepages, and so on.

1.5 Translating Strategy into Action – The Balanced Scorecard Method of Management

A management method to realize a strategy

All the concepts that we addressed focus on analyzing data; however, all these concepts were limited. The development of the *balanced scorecard method of management* by Robert S. Kaplan and David P. Norton overcomes this restriction. The real significance here is that it is not a controlling method, but a management method. "The Balanced Scorecard is more than a...measurement system. Innovative companies are using their scorecard as a strategic management system—to manage their strategy over the long run."[8]

According to Kaplan and Norton, the core of this method lies in the successful realization of its strategy. "The Balanced Scorecard translates an organization's mission and strategy into a comprehensive set of performance measures that provides the framework for a strategic measurement and management system.[9]

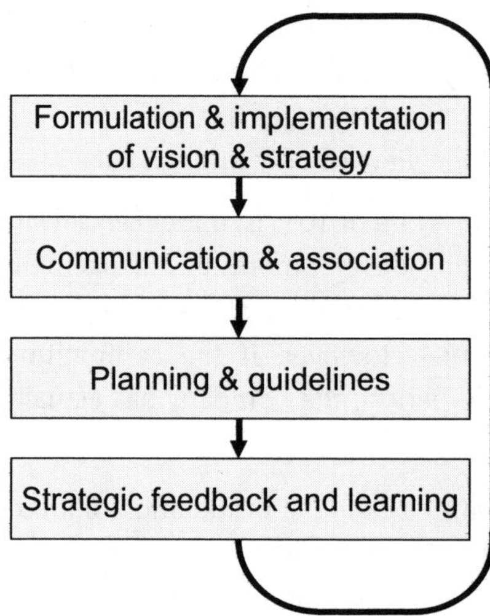

Figure 1.7 The Balanced Scorecard Method of Management

Starting with the strategy

In the first step, an explicit strategy is defined from the company's vision. The ability to find a consensus while formulating the strategy is an essential element of this method. The second step of implementing a balanced scorecard communicates the scorecard, sets goals, and links the goals to incentives. The third step determines planning and standards: strategic actions are agreed upon, resources distributed, and milestones set. Finally, in the fourth step, strategy reviews and feedback provide the basis for strategic learning, which then becomes part of further development and optimization of the management method.

Permeating the entire company

According to Kaplan and Norton, the success of this management method depends (at least partly) upon its ability to permeate the entire company from top to bottom—in terms of both organization and management processes.

8 See Robert S. Kaplan and David P. Norton 1996, p. 10.
9 See Robert S. Kaplan and David P. Norton 1996, p. 2.

Regarding the organizational dimension, Kaplan and Norton state that the method should not be limited to upper management, but used at all management levels:

> *Formulating a Balanced Scorecard that links a business unit's mission to explicit objectives and measures is only the start of using the scorecard as a management system. The Balanced Scorecard must be communicated to a variety of organizational constituents, especially employees, corporate-level managers, and boards of directors. The goal of the communication process is to align all employees within the organization...to the strategy.*[10]

Regarding the process, they explain the required integration:

> *Managers should use their Balanced Scorecard to implement an integrated strategy and budgeting process. The organizational, team, and individual employee processes, described...align human resources to the...strategy. The business must also align its financial and physical resources to the strategy. Long-run capital budgets, strategic initiatives, and annual discretionary expenses must all be directed to achieving ambitious targets for the objectives and measures on the business's scorecard. We have found that four steps are needed to use the scorecard in an integrated long-range strategic planning and operational budgeting process:*
> *1. Set stretch targets.*
> *2. Identify and rationalize strategic initiatives.*
> *3. Identify critical cross-business initiatives.*
> *4. Link to annual resource allocation and budgets.*[11]

Perspectives—meaning and misunderstandings

A second important point often leads to misunderstandings: The balanced scorecard method of management surmounts an examination of financial perspectives only—that's what makes it balanced. According to Kaplan and Norton, the financial perspective, along with the *learning-and-growth perspective*, the *internal-business-process perspective*, and the *customer perspective* (see Figure 1.8), should all drive the added-value of the company as part of an overall method of management. In many places, however, the perspectives are misunderstood and the balanced scorecard is reduced to key numbers that join the controlling of financial and non-financial key figures.[12]

10 See Robert S. Kaplan and David P. Norton 1996, p. 222.
11 See Robert S. Kaplan and David P. Norton 1996, pp. 224-26.
12 See also: *http://www.balancedscorecard.org/.*

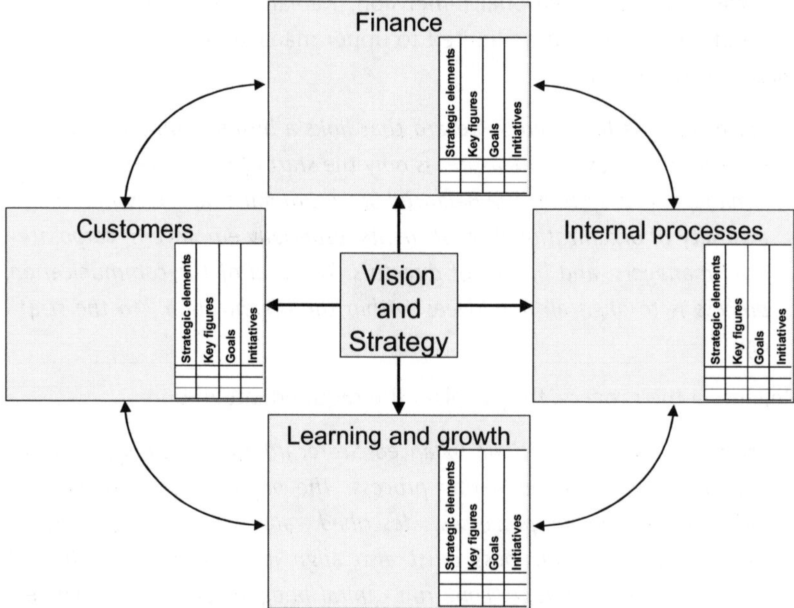

Figure 1.8 The Perspectives of the Balanced Scorecard

Regarding supplementing the strategic key figures of a balanced scorecard, the authors note: "The BSC is not a replacement for an organization's daily measurement system."[13] Successful implementation of the BSC and use of this management method requires special attention to this type of integration.

Ultimately, the expected dependencies of the elements of the balanced scorecard are linked with a *strategy map* that shows a cause–effect relationship:

> *A properly constructed scorecard should tell the story of the business unit's strategy through...a sequence of cause-and-effect relationships.... The measurement system should make the relationships (hypotheses) among objectives (and measures) in the various perspectives explicit so that they can be managed and validated. It should identify and make explicit the sequence of hypotheses about the cause-and-effect relationships between outcome measures and the performance drivers of those outcomes. Every measure selected for a Balanced Scorecard should be an element of a chain of cause-and-effect relationships....*[14]

13 See Robert S. Kaplan and David P. Norton 1996, p. 164.
14 See Robert S. Kaplan and David P. Norton 1996, p. 149.

The use of the balanced scorecard method of management does not have to involve IT tools. As already noted regarding concepts that are oriented solely to data processes, however, appropriate software products improve the realization and usability of the balanced scorecard.

1.6 Successful Implementation and Operation of Business Intelligence Solutions

The problem of adequate information extraction and use can be resolved on the basis of the right concepts. Nonetheless, many data warehouse projects fail during the implementation phase, during the go-live, or even in the first phase when the concept is implemented in production.

An analysis shows that three primary risks exist for data warehouse projects:

1. Selection of unsuitable software products
2. Grievous errors in project management
3. Insufficient knowledge of tools

Because this book is intended as an aid in the implementation of SAP BW, the following doesn't compare the various products available in detail; rather, it offers an overview of their market position and functions and provides tips and tricks on tasks that occur in many projects.

If the right concept is realized with the right tools and the right procedures, the most important elements for a successful implementation and efficient operation of business intelligence solutions are in place.

Part 2
Introduction to SAP BW

2 SAP Business Information Warehouse—Overview

SAP Business Information Warehouse (SAP BW) offers the first comprehensive tool for analytical applications and all the required data warehouse components: tools for the ETL (extraction, transformation, and loading) process, a flexible tool for data modeling, and powerful reporting tools.

2.1 Architecture of SAP BW

A comprehensive data warehouse solution

SAP Business Information Warehouse (SAP BW), which corresponds to the concept developed by William H. Inmon, is a comprehensive data warehouse solution. As such, it contains all the components required for data warehouse processes.[1] The processes include:

- Functions for the ETL process (extraction of data from a source system and the related data processing)
- Components for storing data (complex master and transaction data)
- Tools for analyses and reports (SAP Business Explorer with browser-based SAP Web Reporting and Microsoft Excel)

Additional components are related to these core elements, including tools for customizing (to set up and configure a customer-specific application), administration (monitoring, scheduling, and performance optimization), open hub components, and so on. All elements of SAP BW are based on consistent metadata, which is managed with the *Administrator Workbench*.

SAP BW works on its own dedicated installation, which usually means its own client/server architecture. Accordingly, it also contains functions that enable SAP BW to communicate with other systems. Various technologies are used for this purpose: application link enabling (ALE: proprietary SAP technology similar to Electronic Data Interchange (EDI) for communication between various systems) for the exchange of metadata and data retrieval; and transactional remote function calls (RFC: the SAP interface protocol) for the extraction of data from SAP R/3. Connections to non-SAP source systems are also available: the XML protocol for the exchange

1 SAP online documentation SAP BW 3.0B, SAP 2002, Business Information Warehouse: overview at *http://help.sap.com/saphelp_bw30b/helpdata/en/e3/e60138fede083de10000009b38f8cf/frameset.htm*.

of metadata and/or third-party extraction tools. Data can be retrieved from interface files over third-party extraction tools of the XML protocol.

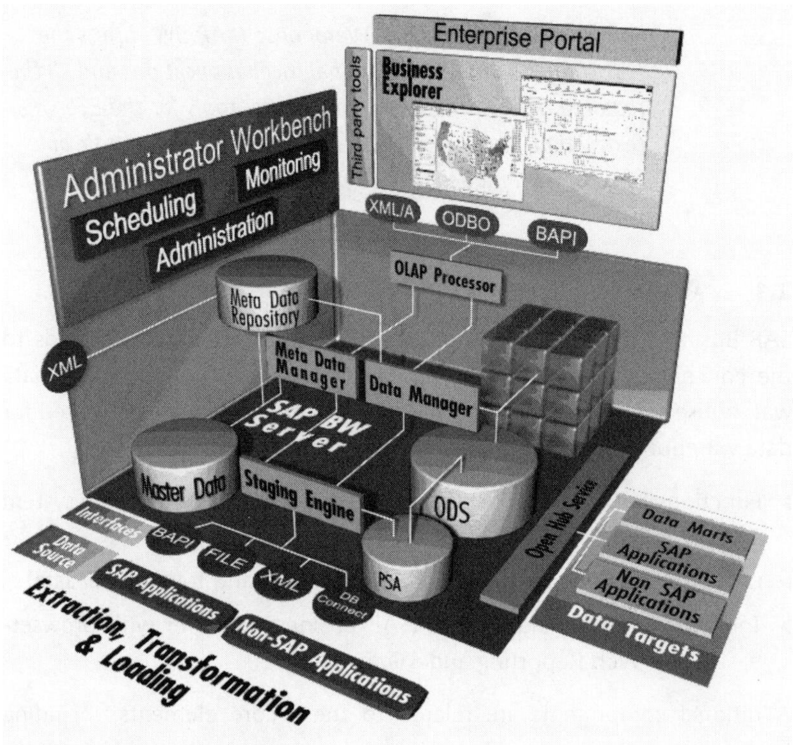

Figure 2.1 Architecture of SAP Business Information Warehouse

Third-party tools for analysis (reporting, for example) can also be connected by various technologies such as business application programming interfaces (BAPIs), standard program interfaces that enable external access to the business processes and data of an SAP R/3 system.

SAP BW enables analytical applications in terms of the data warehouse and *online analytical processing (OLAP)* concepts: it is the foundation for mySAP Business Intelligence components.

2.2 Storing Data in SAP BW

2.2.1 InfoObjects as the Foundation

InfoObjects build the foundation for the data model in SAP BW. You can edit InfoObjects in the *Administrator Workbench*, the SAP BW tool for configuration, control, and monitoring, and maintenance of all the processes associated with data retrieval and storage, under "modeling" in the "InfoObjects" view. SAP defines these objects as *business evaluation objects*. InfoObjects are divided into key figures and characteristics.

- *Key figures* provide the values (amounts, quantities, counters, dates, and times) to be analyzed. **Key figures**
- *Characteristics* describe the business event and create relationships. SAP provides the following types of characteristics: **Characteristics**
  - Business characteristics (customer, cost center, and company code)
  - Units (currency and quantity)
  - Time characteristics (calendar day, calendar year, and fiscal year)
  - Technical characteristics (the number of a data-load procedure, for example)

Master data and texts

Master data, texts, and hierarchies can be stored for InfoObjects typed as "characteristics." This data is available for reporting on master and transaction data.

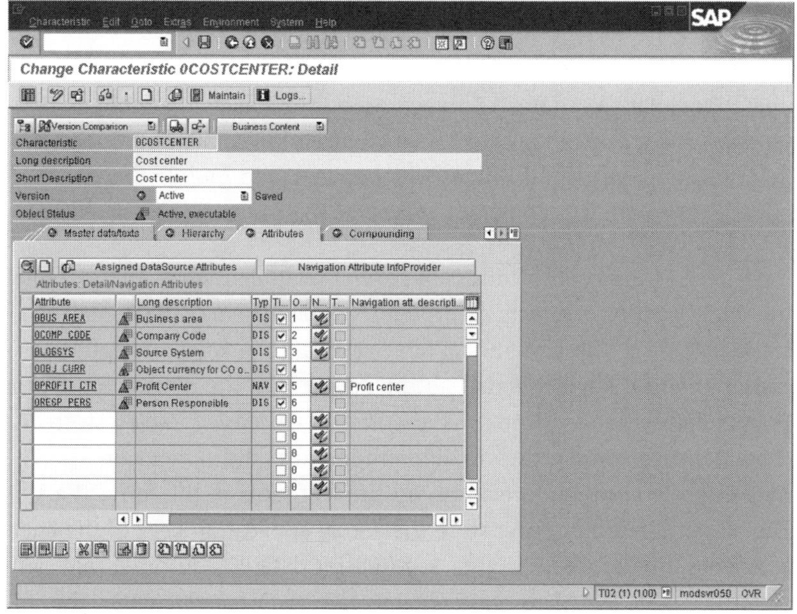

Figure 2.2 InfoObjects Create the Foundation of the SAP BW Data Model

Complex key figures and characteristics

SAP BW enables you to map very powerful key figures and characteristics. Examples include the following:

- non-cumulative key figures mapped by opening and supportive postings
- complex, time-dependent texts (short and medium-length texts), attributes (profit center and person responsible),

InfoObject catalogs

InfoObject catalogs group InfoObjects; *InfoAreas* can group the catalogs.

2.2.2 InfoProviders

InfoProviders

All objects related to reports, objects that can be analyzed with *SAP Business Explorer (SAP BEx)*, and the standard reporting tool in SAP BW are characterized as *InfoProviders* and can be found in the Administrator Workbench under "modeling" in the same view. InfoProviders consist of the following:

- Objects that physically contain data—the data in the database tables for these objects is stored in SAP BW.
- Logical views—objects whose data is stored in another system (such as SAP R/3) or in other physical objects.

The group of objects that physically contains data includes InfoCubes, operational data store (ODS) objects, and InfoObjects that contain master data. The group of logical views includes InfoSets, RemoteCubes, SAP RemoteCubes, virtual InfoCubes with services, and MultiProviders.

InfoAreas

InfoProviders are grouped into *InfoAreas,* much as are InfoObject catalogs.

BasicCubes and star schema

Data-bearing *BasicCubes* consist of several relational tables that organize the underlying InfoObjects according to a star schema. The central table is the *fact table*. These relational tables contain the key figures, the summary numerical key generated automatically, and the dimension ID, for characteristics summarized as dimensions. *Dimension tables* store the characteristics summarized as dimensions and the dimension ID. The dimension tables therefore surround the fact table in the form of a star. The dimension tables don't store the actual application keys of the characteristics, but another number key (master data ID), automatically generated by SAP BW. The *master data table (SID table)* creates the link between the master data ID and the value of the characteristic. This form of organization, which is enhanced by using master-data-bearing characteristics, enables very powerful and complex data models.

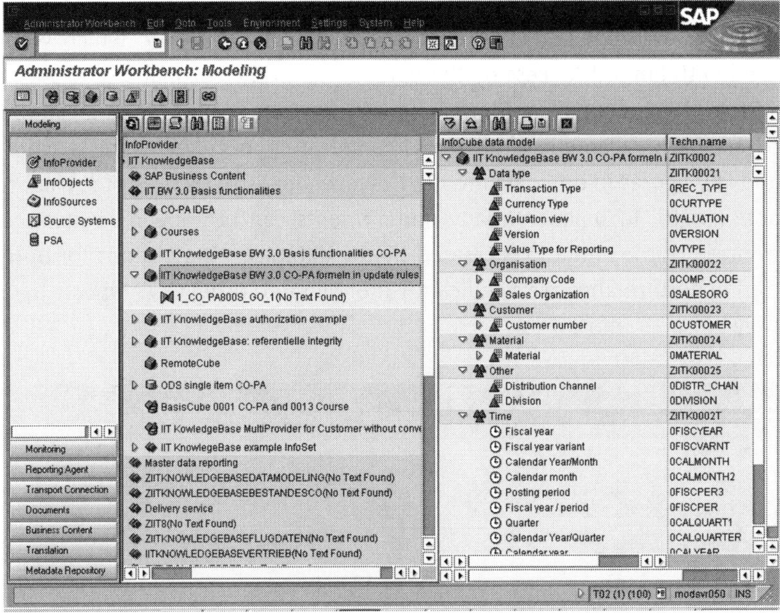

Figure 2.3 InfoCubes Create a Suitable Foundation for Queries with OLAP Functions

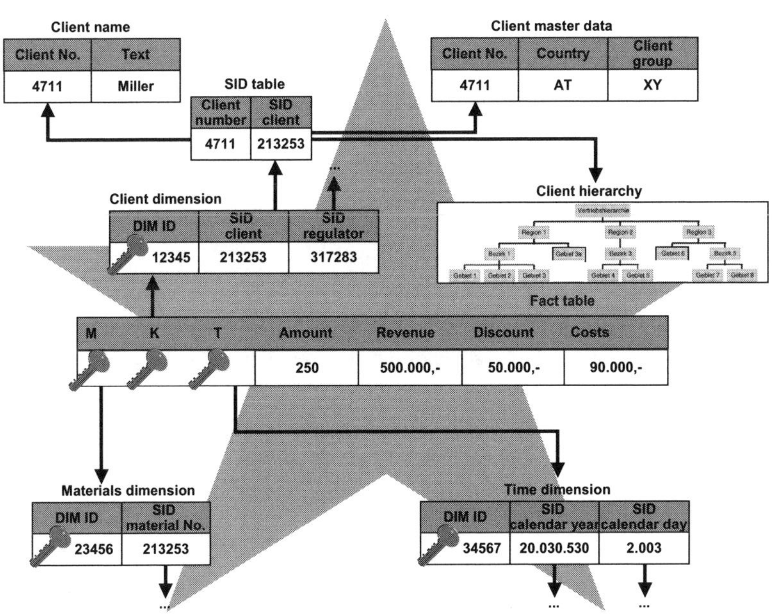

Figure 2.4 The Enhanced Star Schema of SAP BW Permits Mapping of Complex Data Models

The problems of ODS objects

Technically, *operational data store (ODS) objects* are simple tables that contain key fields and data fields. ODS objects, however, which were used with limited success by the data model in the original SAP R/3 Info system, have a significant limitation—the number of key fields is limited to 16. The placement of all key characteristics, non-key characteristics, and key figures in one data record, however, leads to records of considerable length. In practice, many requirements can no longer be mapped because of the limitations created by the database. The options for optimizing performance are significantly more limited using ODS objects than they are with InfoCubes.

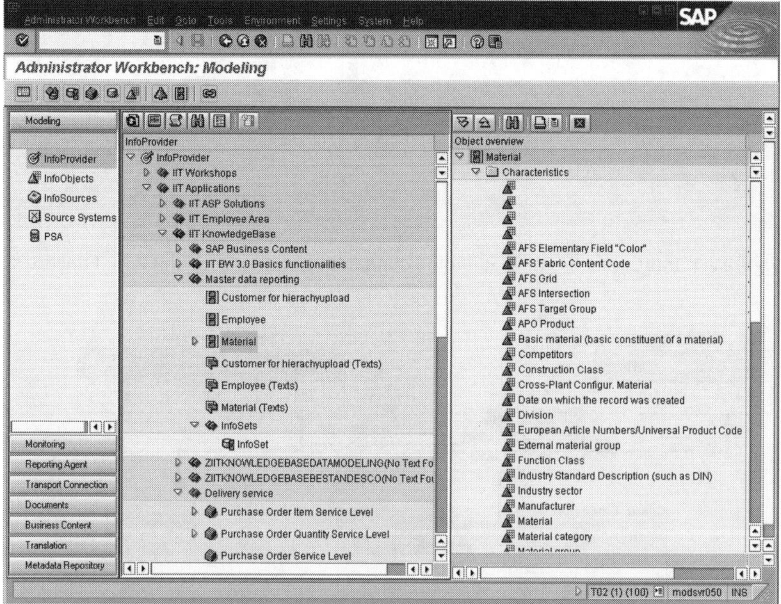

Figure 2.5 ODS objects, InfoObjects, and InfoSets Supplement InfoProviders and Enable the Mapping of Additional Reporting Requirements and Functions

Using ODS objects

Why would you use ODS objects despite all their problems? Because it makes sense to store data at the document level in ODS objects if you think of this storage as a kind of archive that can be directly accessed with key fields that lead to it directly, such as "document number" or "item number." However, mapping the last requirement with InfoCubes (with line items) offers better performance.[2] Configurations that the InfoCube

2 Line items are created for InfoObjects whose fact tables contain only a few facts. Because the dimension table of line item InfoObjects would be approximately as large as the fact table, no dimension table is created for this type of InfoObject.

cannot map exist only when the characteristics in the table are to be overwritten (such as is the case with order status). Once again, this raises the data-modeling questions of whether the order status isn't simply a time-dependent attribute of the basic characteristic, "document number."

InfoObjects as InfoProviders

Master-data-bearing characteristics as InfoProviders provide reporting with the master data tables of the attributes and texts of the particular characteristic involved.

MultiProviders

MultiProviders combine data from various InfoProviders. One option for their use would combine an InfoCube that contains revenues with an additional InfoCube that contains head-count data. Doing so would enable a report that calculates per capita revenue. Another example would combine the InfoCube that contains revenues with an InfoProvider of type "InfoObject material" to display materials without revenues. Note that MultiProviders work with a UNION operation (collated from the tables involved) rather than with a JOIN operation.

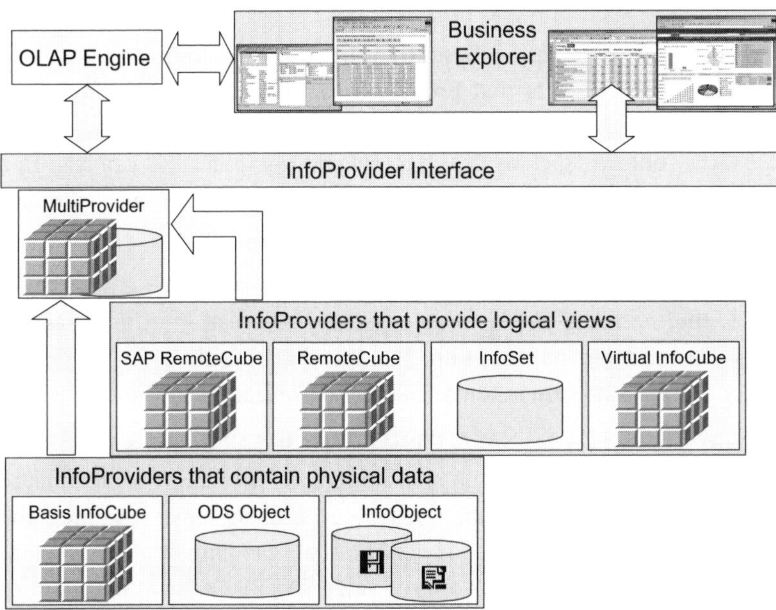

Figure 2.6 MultiProviders Make Physical Data-Bearing Objects and Logical Views Available for Reporting

InfoSets

InfoSets form a semantic layer over the data sources, such as ODS objects and master data. Here you can use all database techniques (including JOINs). The usability of this technology in SAP Business Explorer significantly enhances flexibility. Given the problematic nature of the source objects (see ODS object), it is advisable that you limit using these objects to special cases.

SAP RemoteCube, RemoteCube, and virtual InfoCube

Objects in SAP BW that don't contain data are additional InfoProviders that enable very flexible reports. These objects include the *SAP RemoteCube* (access to transaction data in other SAP systems, based on flexible updates: see also the following comments), the *RemoteCube* (access via a BAPI to data from another system), and the *virtual InfoCube* (access to data from non-SAP BW data sources via user-defined function modules). Naturally, however, you cannot enforce system behavior for all objects (i.e., influence performance) by storing data in other systems, or via remote access to other systems. Note that these objects should be used only after careful consideration. One successful use of these objects, which has proven itself in practice, is that of data checking: an SAP RemoteCube enables access to a data-delivery system and a MultiCube links the SAP RemoteCube with a BasicCube. A variance analysis then verifies whether the data in the source system matches the data in SAP BW.

Recommendation

In the author's experience, basic InfoCubes and MultiProviders are the most important objects that provide a foundation for reporting. Only these objects have the potential for performance optimization of SAP BW. Other objects, such as ODS objects and RemoteCubes can lead to a significant degradation of performance—even with medium-sized quantity structures (10–100 million data records).

Performance optimization and aggregates

Various functions are available to optimize performance. The main function is the modeling ability of *aggregates*. Much like InfoCubes, aggregates are modeled objects with a reduced data volume or improved access options; they are automatically synchronized by SAP BW.

Significant improvements since SAP BW 3.0

Of course, earlier versions of SAP BW could use SAP Business Explorer to analyze InfoCubes and ODS objects along with *InfoSet queries* to analyze tables (master data, for example). However, users never accepted the InfoSet query tool because of its unusual handling and insufficient options. The new possibilities offered since SAP BW 3.0—to link all InfoProviders in MultiProviders, and to analyze all types of InfoProviders with the same reporting tool (SAP BEx)—are important advances in SAP BW's development.

Best-practice solution for data modeling

SAP BW offers high-performance components to map complex data models and large sets of data. Given its options for data modeling, SAP BW can easily be called a best-practice data warehouse.

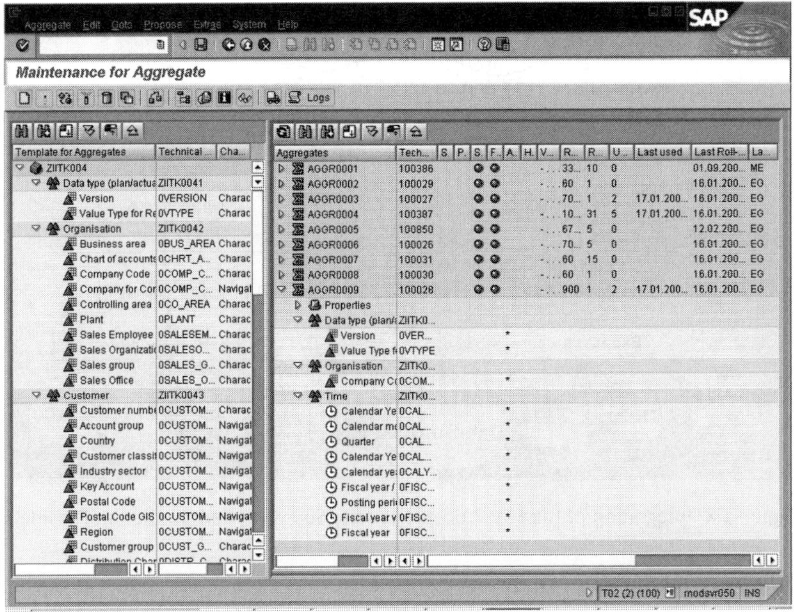

Figure 2.7 Aggregates, in Addition to Other Functions, Can Optimize Performance

2.3 Data Retrieval

2.3.1 Components of the Data-Retrieval Process: DataSources

Types of source systems

Data from almost any source can be used to retrieve data into SAP BW. The main groups of sources include the following:

- SAP systems: SAP R/3, SAP CRM, SAP APO, and SAP SEM
- Structured interface files: *flat files*
- XML files
- Database systems that allow the use of DBConnect
- Non-SAP systems that can use staging BAPIs to load data and metadata into SAP BW (third-party data integration tools such as Ascential or Informatica's PowerCenter, for example)

Each source system makes its own data available, usually with DataSources. Upon request, SAP BW starts to transfer the data. The connection is highly integrated for the following source systems: SAP systems, database systems via DBConnect, and non-SAP systems linked via BAPIs. SAP BW reads the data directly in the source system and then imports it according to the selected procedure.

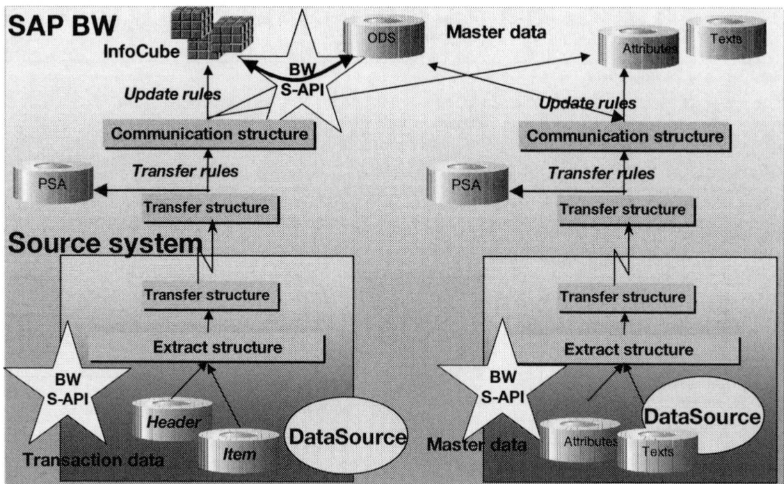

Figure 2.8 Integration of the ETL Process from the Source System to the InfoProviders

You can maintain source systems in the Administrator Workbench under "modeling" and in the same view. The known DataSources can be displayed for each source system. Each DataSource has a *transfer structure* to transfer data to SAP BW. If new DataSources are added, they are available with a metadata upload. SAP R/3 systems offer a number of SAP Business Content DataSources that you can use immediately.

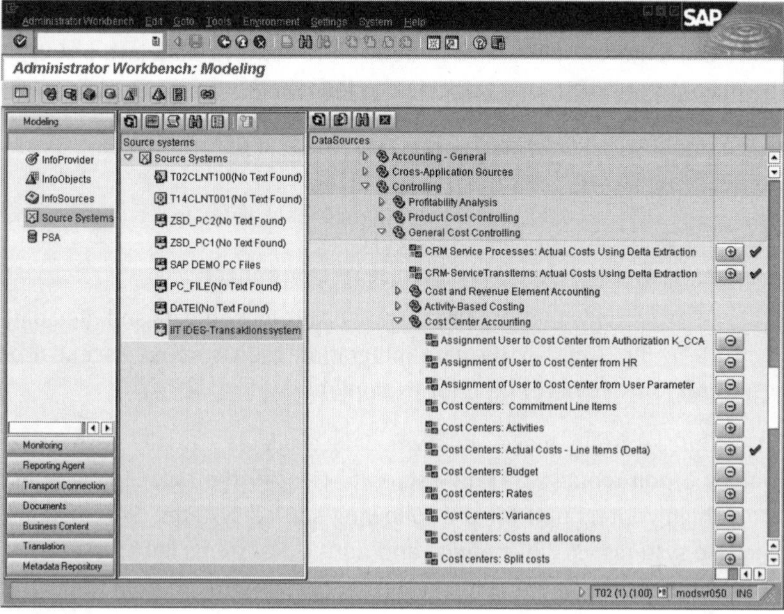

Figure 2.9 DataSources of SAP and Non-SAP Systems in the Administrator Workbench

DataSources can be used for all data-bearing objects: master data (texts, attributes, and hierarchies on InfoObjects) and transaction data.

DataSources and transfer structure

2.3.2 Components of the Data Retrieval Process: InfoSources

Communication structure

An *InfoSource* is a set of logically related information collected into a unit. A communication structure houses the InfoObjects into which an InfoSource is to transfer data (for master data, characteristic values, language key, and long text, for example).

You maintain InfoSources in the Administrator Workbench under "modeling" in the view of the same name. One or more DataSources for a selected source system are assigned to an InfoSource, which means that the transfer structure for the InfoSource is available from every DataSource.

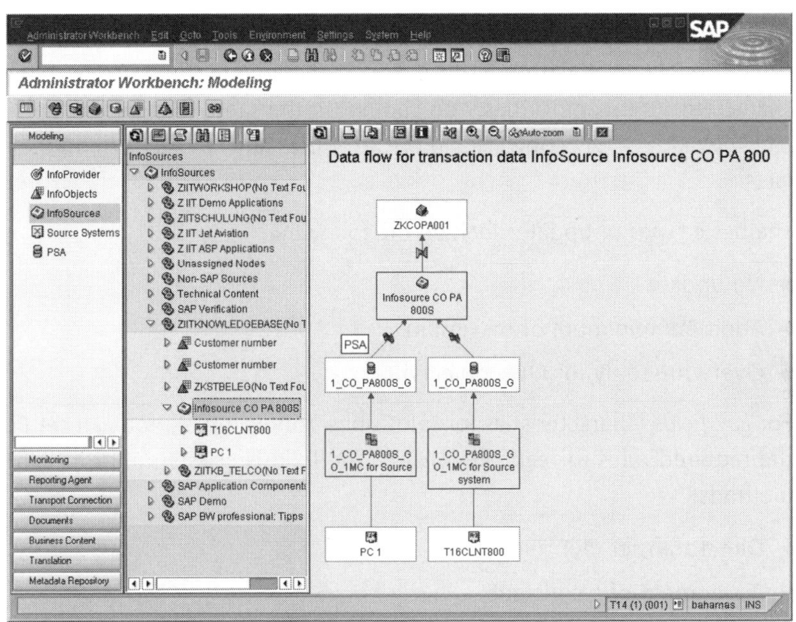

Figure 2.10 Configuration of Data Retrieval from the Connection of a DataSource to Posting the Target Data (InfoCubes) in the Administrator Workbench

Transfer rules

Transfer rules handle the connection between the data delivered in the transfer structure and conversion of data according to the requirements of SAP BW in the communication structure. The transfer can occur as follows:

- Direct transfer (1:1 rule)
- Assignment of a constant value
- Routines (ABAP program coding)
- Formulas

Master data can be updated directly to the InfoObjects with the mechanism described. Posting InfoProviders (master data and an option for InfoObjects as of SAP BW 3.0) involves a second step—update rules.

2.3.3 Components of the Data Retrieval Process: Update Rules

Update rules

Update rules specify how the data from the communication structures of the assigned InfoSources is updated to an InfoProvider. You maintain update rules in the Administrator Workbench under "modeling" in the "InfoProvider" view.

Processing differs for each of the different types of InfoProviders. You should define an update rule for every key figure and the corresponding characteristics for InfoCubes. You should do the same for the data fields and key fields of ODS objects and the attributes and key fields of InfoObjects.

Rules for each data field

The basic types of updates include the following:

- No update
- Addition: minimum or maximum
- Overwrite (only for ODS objects)

Rules for each key field

For *key fields* (characteristics for InfoCubes, for example), you can set up the required rules for each key figure. The following lists the processing methods:

- Direct transfer (1:1 rule)
- Assignment of a constant
- Routines (ABAP program coding)
- Formulas

2.3.4 Components of the Data Retrieval Process: Requesting the Data Transfer and Monitoring

InfoPackage

A request for transferring data into SAP BW occurs with the Scheduler. Configuration occurs in InfoPackages, which you can maintain in the Administrator Workbench under "modeling" in the "InfoSources" view.

InfoPackages determine selection, processing criteria, and scheduling criteria for a DataSource assigned to an InfoSource (using the functions of SAP job control). Customizing InfoPackages offers the required settings for the DataSources of various types of source systems: the selection of localization of flat files for interface files, an option for full or delta upload for delta-capable SAP R/3 DataSources, and tool-specific limits for third-party tools.

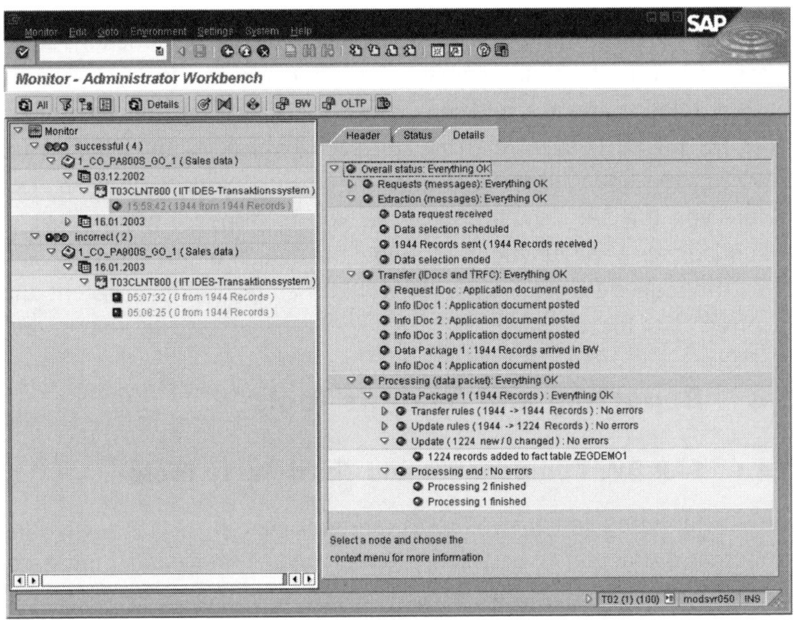

Figure 2.11 Monitoring Permits Cross-System Tracing of Data Retrieval and Supports Error Analysis

Process chains

Process chains configure complex controls (the sequence and the criteria used to process requests for data) as of SAP BW 3.0.

Monitor

You can keep an eye on the processing procedure with the *Monitor*. The Monitor has an overview screen and provides detailed information on the current status or result of the loading procedure.

2.3.5 Components of the Data Retrieval Process: Persistent Staging Area (PSA)

PSA

When using an update method, the *Persistent Staging Area (PSA)* enables you to store data in SAP BW as it was delivered by the source system, except for technical conversions such as those of type date. This data is stored in transparent tables.

Recommendation: systematic reorganization of the PSA

Note that data is stored in the PSA by default when using the PSA transfer method. This feature enables the PSA to quickly reach a size many times larger than that of the actual reporting-relevant objects. Therefore, we strongly recommend that you monitor both the size of the PSA and an appropriate reorganization of it.

2.3.6 The ETL Process

In relation to the entire ETL process, SAP BW offers many functions and a great deal of flexibility. In general, we can recommend that you use the transfer rules to create a sufficient level of data hygiene, and the update rules for logical conversion. This approach (which is non-standard for SAP) has the added benefit of enabling you to work with clean data before you use SAP BW. It also allows you to dispense with (possibly) redundant cleansing functions and avoid the danger of not cleansing data at all the required locations, which would then lead to inconsistent and incorrect data for reporting.

2.4 Reporting and Analysis Tools

2.4.1 SAP BW Components and Third-Party Tools

Various reporting and analysis tools can be used with SAP BW. The fundamental distinction is between proprietary SAP tools and third-party tools.

SAP Business Explorer

SAP BW reporting and analysis tools are various components of SAP Business Explorer, which consists of the following components:

- **Query Designer**
  The tool used to define queries of SAP BW InfoProviders
- **Web Application Designer**
  The tool used to create Web-reporting applications

- **Web Applications**
  The executing environment of reports and analyses in an HTML browser
- **Analyzer**
  The executing environment of queries in Microsoft Excel
- **Additional functions**
  Personalization, mobile reporting components, and functions necessary to integrate SAP BEx Web Applications into SAP Enterprise Portal

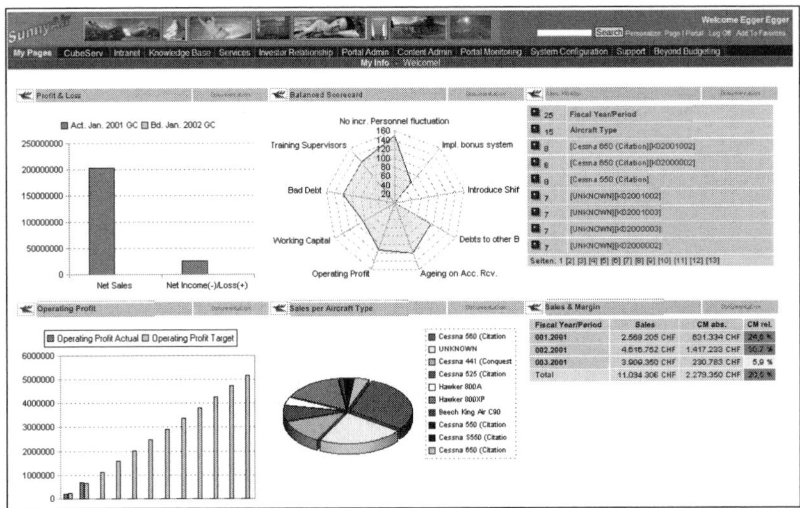

Figure 2.12 Standard Functions of SAP BW 3.0 Include the Creation of Web Reports Linked to SAP Enterprise Portal

The *Reporting Agent* enhances the functions of SAP BEx. It offers both background and supplemental functions: **Reporting Agent**

- Evaluation of exceptions with alternative follow-up actions: sending messages (e-mails) or generating entries in the Alert Monitor
- Printing queries
- Precalculation of Web templates and value sets for characteristic variables
- Managing bookmarks
- Functions for third-party tools

Third-party tools

You can also access the data of SAP BW with several third-party tools. The traditional primary method for executing an SAP BEx query has long been a front-end tool manufactured by a third party. Various SAP interfaces are available to use queries: the OLE DB-for-OLAP interface and the BAPI interface.

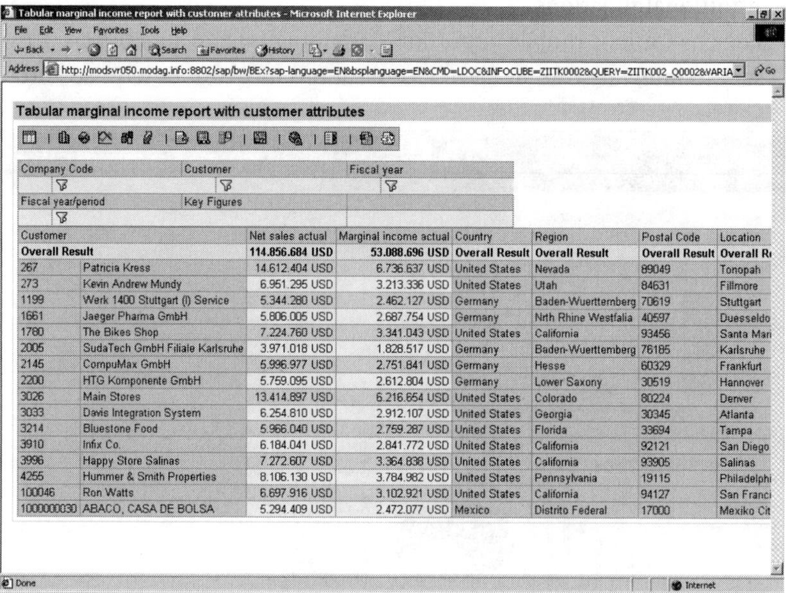
Tabular marginal income report with customer attributes

Customer		Net sales actual	Marginal income actual	Country	Region	Postal Code	Location
Overall Result		**114.856.684 USD**	**53.088.696 USD**	**Overall Result**	**Overall Result**	**Overall Result**	**Overall R**
267	Patricia Kress	14.612.404 USD	6.736.637 USD	United States	Nevada	89049	Tonopah
273	Kevin Andrew Mundy	6.951.295 USD	3.213.336 USD	United States	Utah	84631	Fillmore
1199	Werk 1400 Stuttgart (I) Service	5.344.280 USD	2.462.127 USD	Germany	Baden-Wuerttemberg	70619	Stuttgart
1661	Jaeger Pharma GmbH	5.806.005 USD	2.687.754 USD	Germany	Nrth Rhine Westfalia	40597	Duesseldo
1780	The Bikes Shop	7.224.760 USD	3.341.043 USD	United States	California	93456	Santa Mari
2005	SudaTech GmbH Filiale Karlsruhe	3.971.018 USD	1.828.517 USD	Germany	Baden-Wuerttemberg	76185	Karlsruhe
2145	CompuMax GmbH	5.996.977 USD	2.751.841 USD	Germany	Hesse	60329	Frankfurt
2200	HTG Komponente GmbH	5.759.095 USD	2.612.804 USD	Germany	Lower Saxony	30519	Hannover
3026	Main Stores	13.414.897 USD	6.216.654 USD	United States	Colorado	80224	Denver
3033	Davis Integration System	6.254.810 USD	2.912.107 USD	United States	Georgia	30345	Atlanta
3214	Bluestone Food	5.966.040 USD	2.759.287 USD	United States	Florida	33694	Tampa
3910	Infix Co.	6.184.041 USD	2.841.772 USD	United States	California	92121	San Diego
3996	Happy Store Salinas	7.272.607 USD	3.364.838 USD	United States	California	93905	Salinas
4255	Hummer & Smith Properties	8.106.130 USD	3.784.982 USD	United States	Pennsylvania	19115	Philadelphi
100046	Ron Watts	6.697.916 USD	3.102.921 USD	United States	California	94127	San Franci
1000000030	ABACO, CASA DE BOLSA	5.294.409 USD	2.472.077 USD	Mexico	Distrito Federal	17000	Mexiko Cit

Figure 2.13 Tabular Report in SAP BW 3.0

Since the release of SAP BW 3.0, SAP delivers components by Crystal Reports for *formatted reporting*, which contain only runtime components. Accordingly, with Crystal Reports and all other third-party tools, company-specific reports can be created only with the licensed definition tools of a given supplier.

2.4.2 SAP Business Explorer—Query Designer

New functions

As of release of SAP BW 3.0, you can use the standalone tool, *Query Designer*, to define queries of SAP BW InfoProviders. Since this release and as a result of enhancing the reporting-relevant objects with InfoObjects, SAP supports reporting on transaction data and the analysis of master data. In addition to the OLAP reporting that exists in all releases, SAP BW 3.0 also offers tabular reporting (see Figure 2.14).

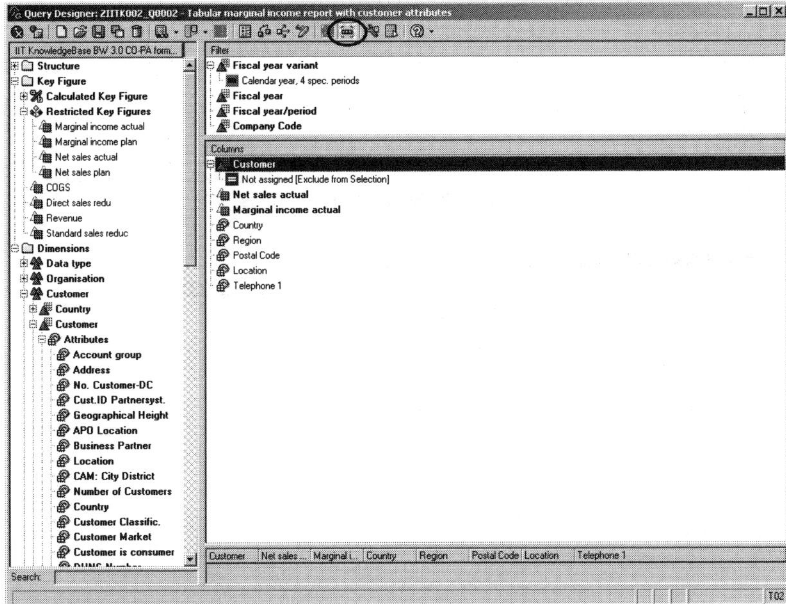

Figure 2.14 Creating Tabular Reports in Query Designer

Query Designer enables you to define the components of an SAP BEx query: general characteristics, filters, free characteristics, rows, and columns.

Building complex report elements

You can select and assign the objects of an InfoProvider in various ways. The characteristics of an InfoCube can be output as a list or a group change criterion, used for selection, or used as free characteristics for slice and dice or to build complex group structures.

You can use the key figures of an InfoCube to display, build, and reuse formulas. You can use combinations of characteristics and key figures to configure reusable, limited key figures and structures. Hierarchies can be depicted flexibly or used for selection in query definitions.

Variables

You can define variables for optimal selection. The variables populate various query elements: characteristic values can be selected with parameter variables (to select individual values), interval variables, or select-option variables, which support selection based on a characteristic. You can statically or variably select entire hierarchies (via hierarchy variables) or portions of hierarchies (via hierarchy node variables). Formula variables can be used for formula functions. Text variables enable dynamic and multilingual labeling of query elements, such as those dependent on current selections (i.e., selections are mapped to certain query elements).

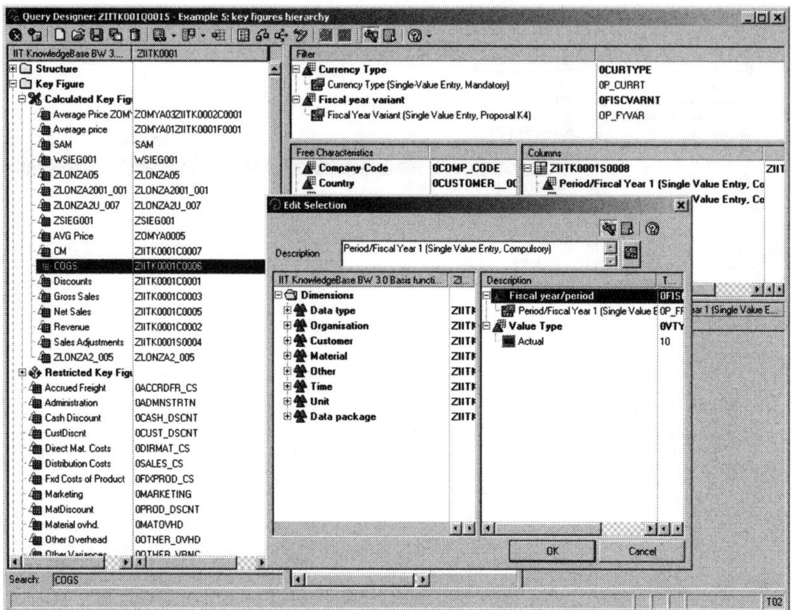

Figure 2.15 Definition of Query Elements: Hierarchy of Key Figures, Variable Selection of Columns with Dynamic Texts, and Variable Filtering

You can process variables via manual entries that contain possible proposed values (selection of a company, for example), substitute paths (such as a column header "2003 Actual," depending on the selection of a fiscal year and the value type "actual"), an SAP user exit or customer exit (with flow logic in ABAP to determine values), and authorizations (automatic population of variables with the authorizations of the user).

Exceptions

Exceptions in the Query Designer enable color highlighting of conditions defined as critical, such as a negative deviation in current revenues over and against the previous year or budget, or in a relative profit margin smaller than a given percent. You can use the exceptions defined in the Query Designer in the Reporting Agent for the Alert Monitor (see Section 2.4.7).

The Query Designer also enables you to define conditions, which can limit the results of a query to include only such relevant criteria as, for example, determining which customers show a decline in current-year revenues. Both the exception and condition functions in SAP BW 3.0 have been significantly improved.

Queries defined in the Query Designer can be executed immediately after saving them. The **Display Query on the Web** button starts the query directly in the Web browser (such as Microsoft Internet Explorer). Queries can also be executed in SAP BEx.

2.4.3 Web Application Designer

A *standard Web template* is used during the direct execution of queries; that is, a system-wide template standardizes the functions and layout of the query. This layout is usually adequate only for ad hoc queries; therefore, the *Web Application Designer* enables you to implement any layout and reporting functions.

Web templates and standard HTML functions

The Web Application Designer supports all options from the creation of OLAP reports according to targeted defaults to complex reports in the Management Cockpit integrated into the portal. The *Management Cockpit* contains all the required functions, such as professional navigation components, selection and display objects, and the entire width of layout options offered by HTML technology. These types of reports are stored as Web templates in SAP BW in the form of HTML code. Web templates offer all the options of Web technology, such as standard HTML functions and the use of formulas, style sheets, JavaScript, and so on.

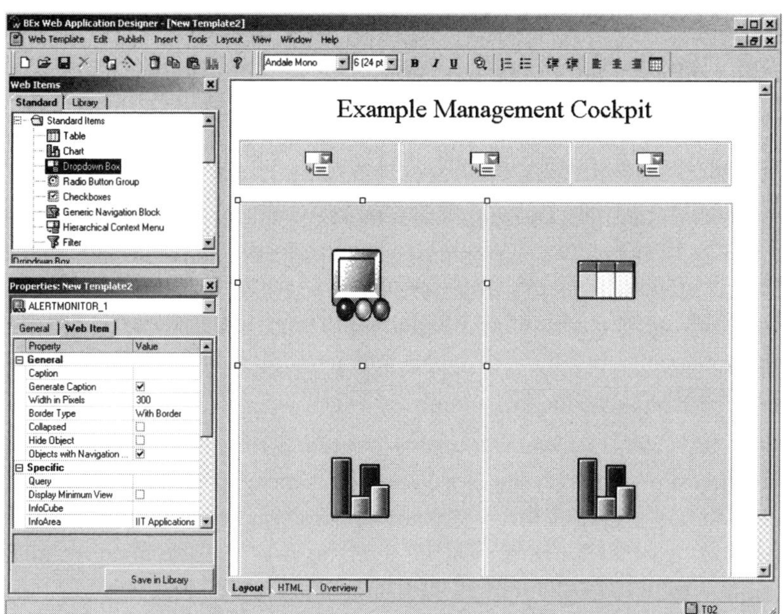

Figure 2.16 Web Templates Are Defined in the Web Application Designer of SAP BW

The Web Application Designer is used to insert object tags specific to SAP BW into all SAP BW objects; the tags can contain control information on the following:[3]

- Characteristics of Web templates
- Data providers
- Web items

Data providers *Data providers* make available information that is specific to SAP BW; the information provides queries or query views (the stored navigational status of an SAP BW query) as a data source in the corresponding Web template.

Web items Objects that display visual content (or graphics) specific to SAP BW are called *Web items*. They include the following:

- Tables (displaying query results as tables)
- Charts (displaying query results as navigable, online graphics, such as bar diagrams)
- Drop-down boxes (objects to filter characteristics)
- Text elements (general query information, such as the timeliness of the data)
- Alert Monitor (list of the exceptions defined for the Reporting Agent)
- Role-based menu (SAP menu tree with favorites and roles)
- Maps (map graphics with data analyzed by SAP BW)

The Web Application Designer also offers several other functions, including URLs to call another Web template or to insert language-dependent ABAP text elements); and URLs specific to SAP BW and the Web Design API (Web Design application programming interface), which can change the display and functions of tables and navigation blocks with support from ABAP.

Web Application Server As of SAP BW 3.0, Web templates created with the Web Application Designer are stored on the SAP Web Application Server (SAP Web AS). This feature is one of the essential technological improvements in SAP BW 3.0 because it overcomes the limitations of the less than optimal technology of the SAP Internet Transaction Server (SAP ITS). The technology of SAP Web AS provides SAP Web reporting with improved functions, especially in terms of interactivity.

3 HTML uses tags to define controlling code. For example, *<a href ...>* ... *</a>* defines a hyperlink to another document or to a specific location in a document.

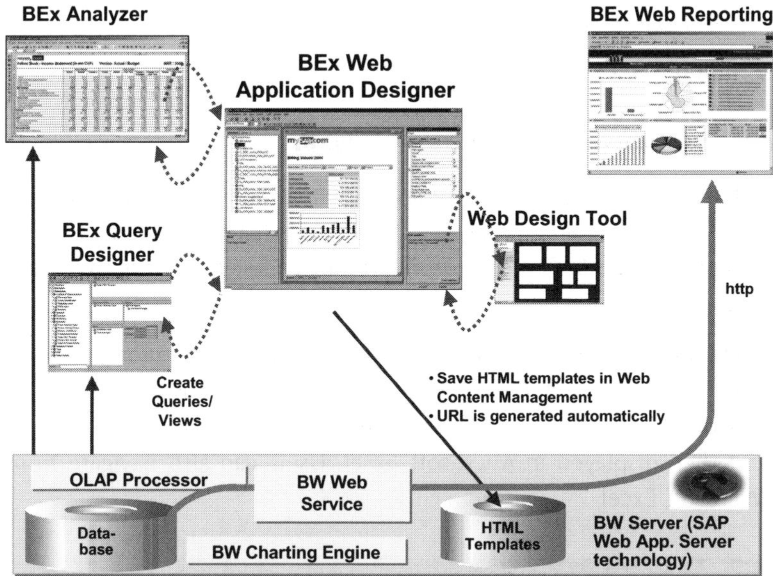

Figure 2.17 Architecture of SAP BW Reporting Components

2.4.4 The Runtime Environment of Web Applications

Executing Web reports

Once queries and query views have been defined, they can be executed as Web applications. As of SAP BW 3.0, queries can be stored directly in SAP roles, which allow end users to execute queries without performing additional activities. The same is true of Web templates designed with Web Application Designer. After the Web templates have been assigned to roles, powerful and complex reports can be started from the role-based menus. When a report is started, the reporting data in the InfoProviders is presented online. Users can navigate (filters, drilldown, and going to other reports) from the displayed query results.

Ad hoc Query Designer

As of SAP BW 3.0, Web reporting functions include an option to define ad hoc queries at runtime. The *ad hoc Query Designer* provides the following options:

- Queries can be created by assigning the characteristics of an InfoProvider in rows, columns, filters, and free characteristics; and by recording the key figures of an InfoProvider in the key figure structure.
- Key figures and characteristics can be limited.
- Queries can use predefined key figure structures and limited or calculated key figures.

- ▶ Query characteristics and the characteristics of key figures in the query can be created and changed.
- ▶ Conditions and exceptions can be created and changed.

2.4.5 SAP Business Explorer Analyzer

SAP defines the execution of queries and views from Microsoft Excel via the *SAP Business Explorer Analyzer (SAP BEx Analyzer)*. Microsoft Excel is enhanced with an SAP BW add-on. SAP BEx Analyzer offers two basic options for its use:

Queries in Business Explorer Analyzer

- ▶ Once the tool is opened, a toolbar specific to SAP BW allows users to select and start predefined SAP BEx queries. As discussed in the context of Web Reporting, query data in the InfoProviders is read online and then displayed in Microsoft Excel. Users can also navigate from Microsoft Excel.

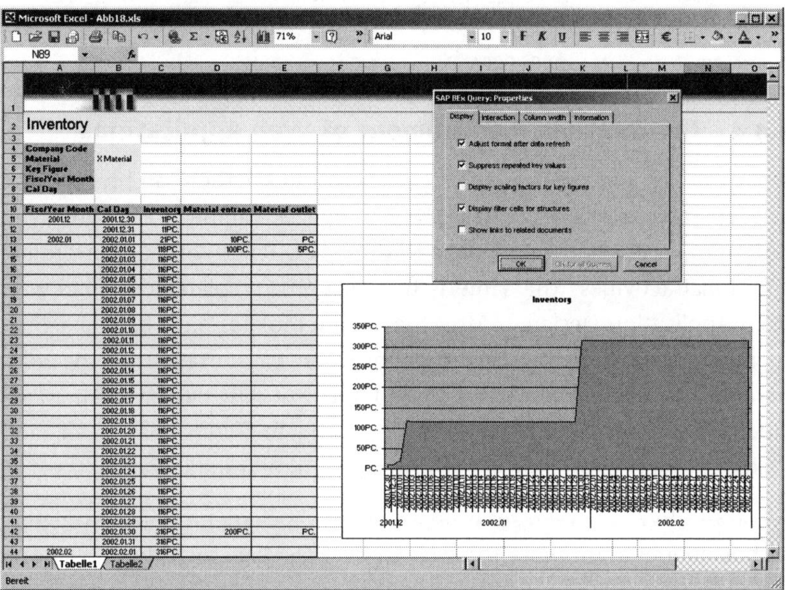

Figure 2.18 SAP Business Explorer Analyzer Joins Microsoft Excel and OLAP Functions for Selected Tasks

Queries in Workbooks

- ▶ The second option opens workbooks with embedded queries in Microsoft Excel. This option enables report-specific formatting, the linking of graphics, and more in certain contexts. The workbooks can also be assigned to role-based menus, which make them available to users for direct execution. SAP BEx workbooks offer end users another way to present queries; however, this method, when compared with SAP BEx Web Applications, offers limited functions and layout options.

2.4.6 Additional SAP BW Reporting Functions

SAP BW has several other reporting functions.

Personalization

The most important additional function is *personalization*, available as of SAP BW 3.0. This function enables user-specific population of variables, stores user-specific start-views of Web Applications, and offers a user-specific history of the last-opened reporting objects.

Integration into SAP Enterprise Portal

SAP responded to the growing importance of portals by integrating SAP BEx Web Applications into SAP Enterprise Portal. These applications can be stored as *iViews* during the creation of Web Templates. An *iView* is a component of the portal solution. It can extract and display data from applications, documents, and the Internet. It enables Web Reporting functions to leverage the features of portal technology (single sign-on (SSO), for example).

Mobile Reporting

SAP BEx Mobile Intelligence functions allow the execution of Web reports on mobile devices, for example, mobile telephones and PDAs. The SAP BW server automatically recognizes the type of mobile device and generates a device-specific HTML or WML (Wireless Markup Language) page.

2.4.7 Reporting Agent

The *Reporting Agent* expands SAP BW's functionality by offering such additional functionality as background, administrative, and Alert Monitor features.

Precalculating query results

The background functions of the Reporting Agent enable the precalculation of query results. The precalculated results can be used during the execution of Web reports that use the DATA_MODE=STORED mode. Using precalculated results significantly improves the response time, because executing the query no longer requires access to the large volume of data of the InfoProvider on which the query rests. Additional functions enable background printing of queries based on SAP BEx. The Reporting Agent can also administer the bookmarks of all users of SAP BW.

Exception reporting and Alert Monitor

Exception reporting and the *Alert Monitor* are especially important. These components analyze exceptions in the background and trigger follow-up actions that users can configure to meet their needs. Follow-up actions include messages (e-mail with information on the exception) or Alert Monitor entries (with traffic-light icons that contain hyperlinks to the reports).

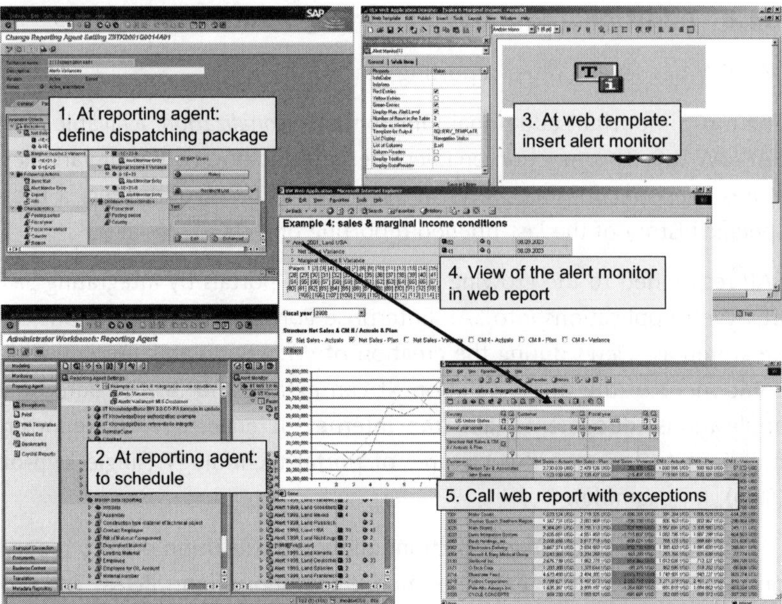

Figure 2.19 Information Distribution with Alert Monitor in Web Reporting

2.4.8 Reporting Functions and Frontends for SAP BW

SAP BW 3.0 offers significant enhancements and improvements in reporting functions. Here, SAP has taken a step toward a best-practice OLAP and a data warehouse solution.

This area exhibits clear differences between the reporting components offered by SAP. Until SAP BW 1.2, SAP BEx Analyzer was the only tool available for OLAP reporting. Despite the availability of Web Reporting in SAP BW 2.0, no fundamental shift had occurred. With SAP BW 3.x, however, Web Reporting became the primary technology of reporting in SAP BW, as is evident in the following:

- Standard calls of queries could now be exhibited in an HTML browser instead of having to use Microsoft Excel.
- Reporting functions were significantly enhanced in Web Reporting from the BEx Analyzer based on Microsoft Excel.
- There are significantly more functions and enhanced options for Web Reporting

The use of third-party front-end tools played an important role during the implementation of earlier releases of SAP BW. The author led some 40 projects with SAP BW 2.1B, 35 of which used the same third-party front-end tools: inSight/dynaSight by arcplan Inc. The remaining projects used SAP BEx, products from Cognos Incorporated, and products from Business Objects. The author also led 60 projects with SAP BW 2.x, of which more than 50% used proprietary SAP reporting tools. More than 10 of these projects used SAP Web Reporting. The author's experience with projects involving SAP BW 3.x shows even more of a shift of standard SAP functions toward Web Reporting.

Third-party front-end tools

The search for causes and the probable direction of future development is interesting from the investment security perspective. While SAP had to undergo all the development steps of an OLAP front-end tool with SAP BEx, and the development of SAP BW was restricted because of the limitations of Microsoft Excel and the paradigm shift to Web technology, other manufacturers already offered mature products. However, the partner companies (inSight/dynaSight, Cognos Inc., and Business Objects) were apparently unwilling or unable to keep up with the burgeoning developments at SAP, so that by the time SAP BW 3.x was available, no third-party reporting tool could support all the reporting functions of SAP BW. Therefore, SAP BW users should be skeptical of third-party front-end tools.

Significance of third-party frontends

2.5 Additional Functions and Components

The functions of SAP BW that have been outlined are limited to the core processes of analytical applications: data retrieval, data storage, and reporting. Numerous additional components are available that exceed the limits of this introduction. Accordingly, the following can only be mentioned briefly:

- SAP R/3 Basis technology offers powerful and mature Basis functions: job control, role and print functions, user management, and so on
- Additional SAP BW components such as Open Hub Services, SAP BW-specific functions based on core SAP R/3 functions to control authorizations, and linking documents suitable to reporting

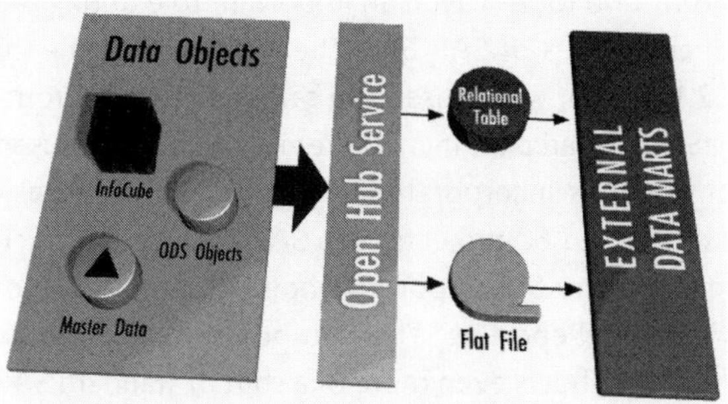

Figure 2.20 As of SAP BW 3.0, Open Hub Services Can Distribute Data from SAP BW to Other SAP and Non-SAP Systems

2.6 SAP Business Content

Defining Business Content

SAP Business Content has a special place in the marketing of SAP BW. SAP BW documentation describes Business Content as follows:

> *Business Content is a preconfigured set of role and task-relevant information models based on consistent metadata in SAP Business Information Warehouse. Business Content provides selected roles within a company with the information they need to carry out their tasks.*[4]

Note that, unlike SAP R/3 application components, Business Content is expressly not positioned as an SAP standard.

Components of SAP Business Content

SAP Business Content contains all the components necessary for an analytical application. The components include extractors in SAP R/3 and contain the required elements of the data model (such as key figures, characteristics, InfoCubes, and ODS objects), components to load data into SAP BW (InfoSources and update rules), reporting components (queries, Web templates, and workbooks), and Basis components (roles and types of currency exchange).

Because SAP Business Content is not an SAP standard, the following applies:

- It can be used without any modifications.
- It can be modified to meet customer-specific needs.
- It can be used as a template for customer-specific business content.

The advantage of SAP over its competitors

The scope of SAP Business Content places SAP far ahead of its competition. As a leading supplier of business software, the high level of knowledge at SAP benefits the company's ability to offer its business warehouse

4 Documentation on SAP BW 3.0, SAP 2002, "Business Content."

solution. However, you must be careful when differentiating SAP Business Content—careless adoption of content can lead to unwelcome surprises, namely, missing functions, errors, or unacceptable handling. Therefore, you should examine SAP Business Content carefully during the business blueprint phase of a project. It is imperative that you compare the functions that you want with the functions that are offered. Tests that ensure intensive quality control must follow during the implementation phase.

Experience with SAP Business Content indicates the following two dimensions of its usability.

Usability regarding object type

When looking at the core processes of analytical applications, the usability of SAP Business Content is significantly higher in the first half of the process (data retrieval and data modeling). The extractors of SAP Business Content can be used to a great extent in transactional SAP components. Only a portion of the data model within SAP BW is appropriate for productive use: a large portion of the InfoObjects and selected InfoProviders, such as InfoCubes and ODS objects. The situation is less optimal for the reporting components (queries, workbooks, and so on). Reports from SAP Business Content could not be used in any of the 100 plus projects led by the author.

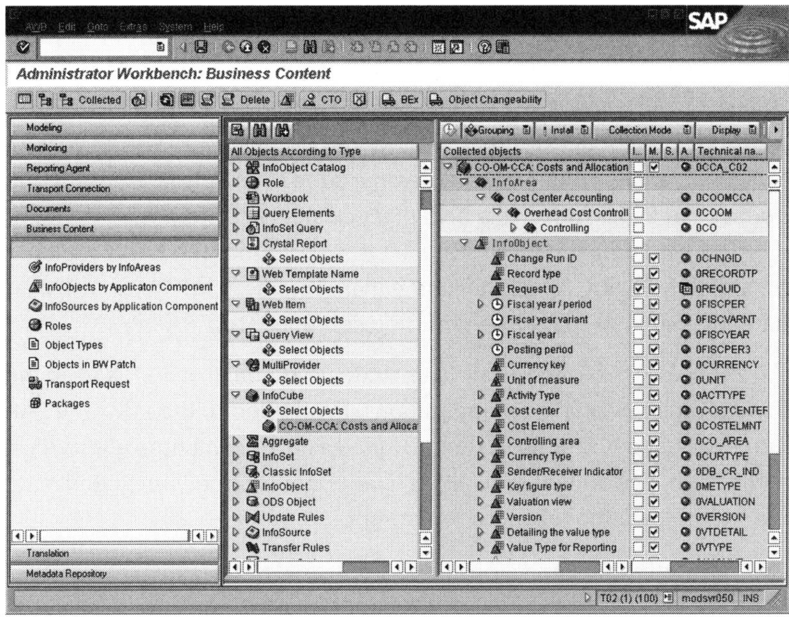

Figure 2.21 SAP Business Content Contains All the Components Required for an Analytical Application

Usability with analytical applications

Significant differences also appear when looking at the various analytical applications and comparing the business application areas. In the area of financial accounting and controlling in SAP BW applications, SAP Business Content's high level of quality allows for the frequent use of the greater portion of the extractors, data retrieval, and data model. A notable number of projects could use SAP Business Content here and with InfoCubes that have undergone significant enhancements. The situation is less satisfactory with SAP Business Content for logistics. Some of the extractors contain errors and the InfoCubes are often inadequate, which requires the creation of a customer-specific data model. The same situation occurs with HR. Solutions with SAP Business Content are often not available for analytical applications that are created for the highest levels of management. The reason? According to the author's experience, it's because requirements become increasingly more specific to a company the more you look at the enterprise as a whole, or even if you look beyond the scope of your company.

2.7 The Position of SAP Business Information Warehouse

SAP BW as a best-practice solution

Thus far, our discussion of the individual components of SAP Business Information Warehouse have helped us to evaluate the efficacy of SAP BW. A general overview shows that, with SAP BW, SAP has for the first time offered a product that appropriately considers the conceptual foundations of a data warehouse and OLAP. SAP BW 1.2B offers sufficient functions for productive use. The new developments in SAP BW 2.0B, 2.1C, 3.0B, and 3.1C reflect considerable added functionality, so that the product can be classified as a best-practice solution. From the viewpoint of reporting, companies that use SAP R/3 show that the effort required for implementation, operation, and enhancement of SAP BW is less than the effort required to use the reporting components in SAP R/3.

Advantages over competitors' products

SAP BW has established itself as a strategic product of SAP and is the foundation for all analytical applications. In addition to the power of SAP Business Content, SAP BW offers advantages over competitors' products in the high performance of all its components: from integrated data retrieval, to data modeling, to reporting.

Market development

The high performance of SAP R/3 Basis increases the functional prominence of SAP BW, which gives it a strong market position. With more than 6,500 installations (as of January 2003), the SAP solution has already reached a significant portion of the market with a product that has been available only since 1998. SAP is in the process of displacing other suppliers in the market for data warehouses and OLAP tools.

SAP BW is also a core component of many new SAP applications, including the following:

- *SAP Advanced Planner & Optimizer (SAP APO)*, a software solution for dynamic supply chain management. This application enables precise and global monitoring and control of the supply chain beyond the boundaries of a company. It is part of the SAP Supply Chain Management and includes the Supply Chain Cockpit, sales planning, supply network planning and deployment, production and detailed scheduling, and global availability check.
- *mySAP Customer Relationship Management (mySAP CRM)* is the application that supports all business processes involving customers and external business partners. As a comprehensive product for all users who have contact with customers, mySAP CRM contains solutions for sales (SAP Sales), service (SAP Service), and marketing (SAP Marketing). These solutions involve existing functions of SAP R/3 (such as customer service) and new components (such as mobile sales, mobile service, customer interaction center, and Internet sales).
- *SAP Strategic Enterprise Management (SAP SEM)* consists of the following components: Strategy Management (especially the balanced scorecard), Performance Measurement (especially the Management Cockpit), Business Consolidation, Business Planning & Simulation, and Stakeholder Relationship Management. In many areas, SAP SEM is the direct enhancement to SAP BW (balanced scorecard, Management Cockpit, and Business Planning & Simulation, for example) and is recommended in combination with SAP BW.

With its offerings that include a wide coverage of tools for transactional tasks and a business intelligence solution, SAP has a considerable advantage in the market. Now that transactional SAP R/3 has already reached a leading market position, SAP is poised to become the market leader for business intelligence solutions as well.

3 Step-by-Step: Profitability Analysis with SAP BW

This "SAP BW Walk Through" provides you with all the steps you'll need to create an SAP BW application—one with an application-specific DataSource, customer-specific InfoCubes, data retrieval, and the required reporting components.

3.1 Introduction

DataSource

In this section, we'll take a detailed look at the steps required to implement an SAP BW application. Because almost all projects require customer-specific components, SAP Business Content here is used in the context of the author's experience with projects. It is used only partially and supplemented with self-defined objects as examples. This process begins with the creation of a customer- and application-specific DataSource to extract data incrementally from SAP R/3 CO-PA. The next step includes configuration of ETL (extraction, transformation, and loading) components (InfoSource, transfer and update rules, and InfoPackages) on the SAP BW side for the SAP DataSource and flat files. The data is stored in a customer-specific data model (with InfoCubes and MultiProviders) that serves as the foundation of sample reporting (with *SAP Business Explorer (SAP BEx)* Web Reporting and Analyzer)). Scheduling and monitoring are addressed in the section on data retrieval (i.e., Section 3.3.5).

The following example covers profit margin reporting that compares plan and actual values and values of the current and preceding years. Master and actual data is loaded from the operative SAP R/3 system; plan data is loaded from an interface file.

The procedure:

1. Data modeling (InfoObjects, InfoProviders, and aggregates)
2. Creating the DataSource (for SAP R/3)
3. Creating the InfoSources with transfer rules
4. Creating the update rules
5. Creating the InfoPackages
6. Retrieving data: scheduling and monitoring

7. Creating the BEx query

8. Calling the query with SAP BEx Web Reporting and Analyzer

3.2 Data Modeling

3.2.1 Sample Creation of an InfoObject of Type "Characteristic"

The definition and modification of InfoObjects (characteristics and key figures) lay the foundation on which the data model is to be created. These tasks include setting up customer-specific InfoObjects.

You will need to create a customer-specific key figure for gross revenues. You perform this setup in the **InfoObjects** view of the Administrator Workbench. You can open the view with Transaction RSA14 (or with RSA1 and some navigation).

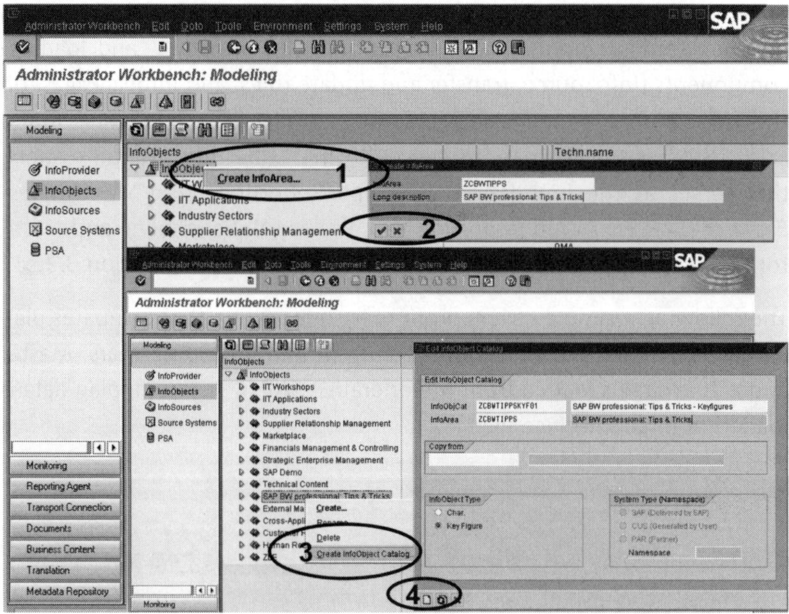

Figure 3.1 Creating an InfoArea and InfoObject Catalog

Creating an InfoArea

The application is created in its own InfoArea. In the **InfoObjects** view of the Administrator Workbench (Transaction RSA14), right-click on the top node, **InfoObjects.** Select **Create InfoArea** to create an InfoArea and to query the required information (see Figure 3.1, Step 1). Enter the technical name and description. Once you confirm the entry, the InfoArea is created (see Figure 3.1, Step 2).

InfoObjects are grouped into InfoObject catalogs. Right-click on InfoArea **SAP BW Professional: Tips & Tricks** to display the context menu. Select the menu entry **Create InfoObject Catalog** (see Figure 3.1, Step 3). In the **Edit InfoObject Catalog** popup, enter the technical name and description of the InfoObject and select the type of catalog (here: "Key Figure"). Click on the **Create** button to complete the operation (see Figure 3.1, Step 4).

Creating an InfoObject catalog

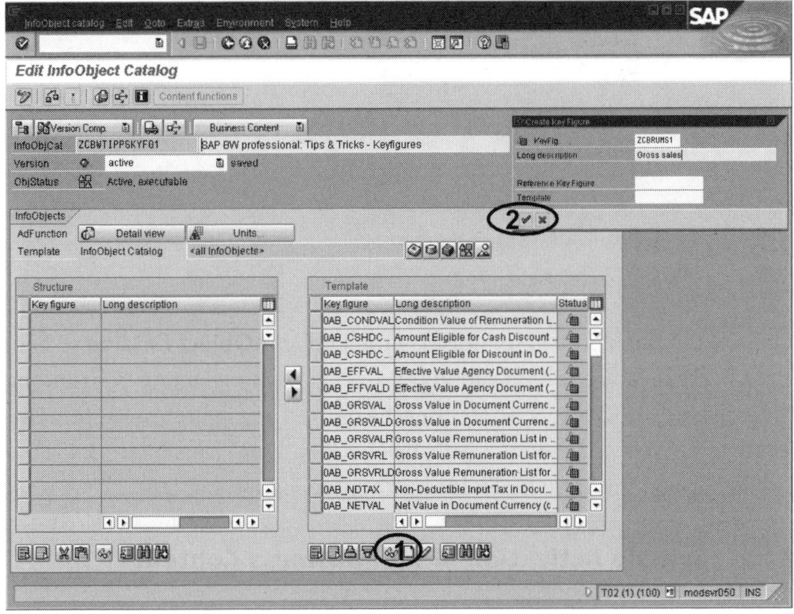

Figure 3.2 Calling "Create Key Figure"

Use the **Create InfoObject(s)** button in the **Edit InfoObject Catalog** screen to create a key figure (see Figure 3.2, Step 1). Enter the technical name and description in the **Create Key Figure** popup. Click on the **Continue** button (see Figure 3.2, Step 2) to open the **Detail** screen for creating a key figure.

InfoObject "create key figure"

In the **Create Key Figure** screen in the **Type/unit** tab, select the type/data type ("Amount") and the unit/currency ("0CURRENCY", see Figure 3.3, Steps 1 and 2). In the **Additional Properties** tab, set the default for the number of decimal places ("0") and the display ("in 1"). Then, click on the **Activate** button to create the InfoObject (see Figure 3.3, Steps 3 and 4).

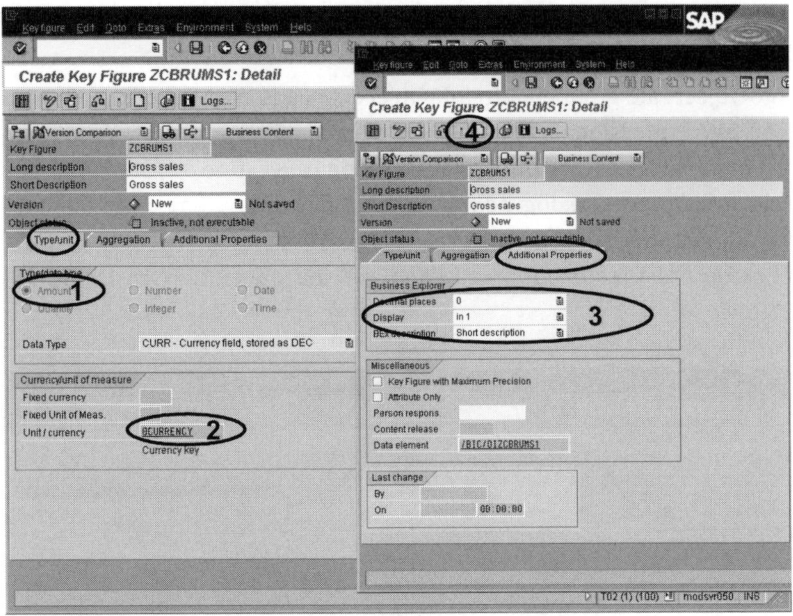

Figure 3.3 Creating a Key Figure

InfoObject "record key figure in InfoObject catalog"

Click on the **Back** button to redisplay the **Edit InfoObject Catalog** screen. You can create any additional required key figures by selecting from among the available InfoObjects. To transfer the desired key figures to the InfoObject catalog, select the InfoObjects by checking them (see Figure 3.4, Step 1) and click on the **Transfer Fields** button (see Figure 3.4, Step 2).

3.2.2 Sample Activation of SAP Business Content

You can use some of the InfoObjects of SAP Business Content for the components of the ETL process in SAP BW and the InfoCube. To do so, you must activate the required portions of SAP Business Content. Start the Administrator Workbench with the **Business Content** view. You can use the **Grouping button** to make selections (see Figure 3.5, Step 1). Doing so activates both the InfoObjects from SAP Business Content and the data-retrieval components (InfoSource and transfer rules).

Next, select **Object Types** in the selection list in the left frame (see Figure 3.5, Step 2). The InfoObject directory is opened in the list of **all objects according to type**. Double-click on the **Select Objects** entry to begin selecting the InfoObjects to be transferred (see Figure 3.5, Step 3). Your personal settings will determine which objects are listed in the InfoObject directory.

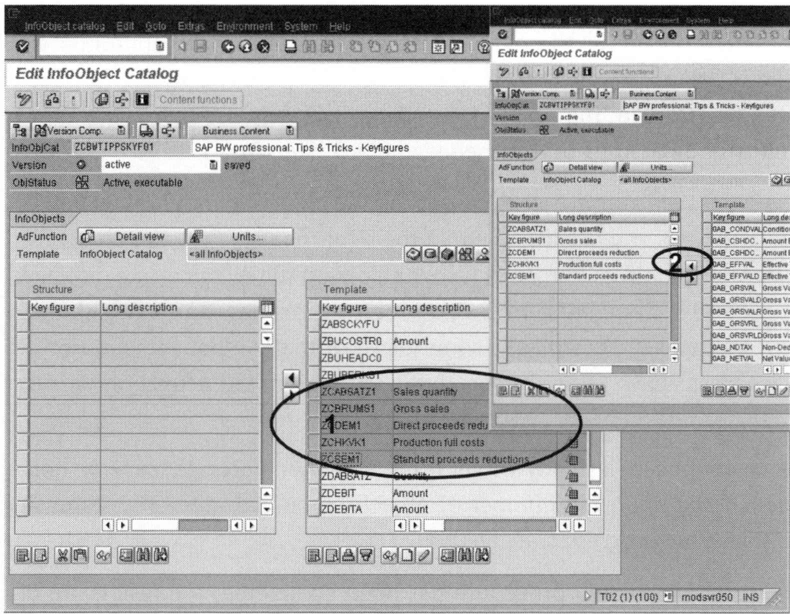

Figure 3.4 Recording Key Figures in the InfoObject Catalog

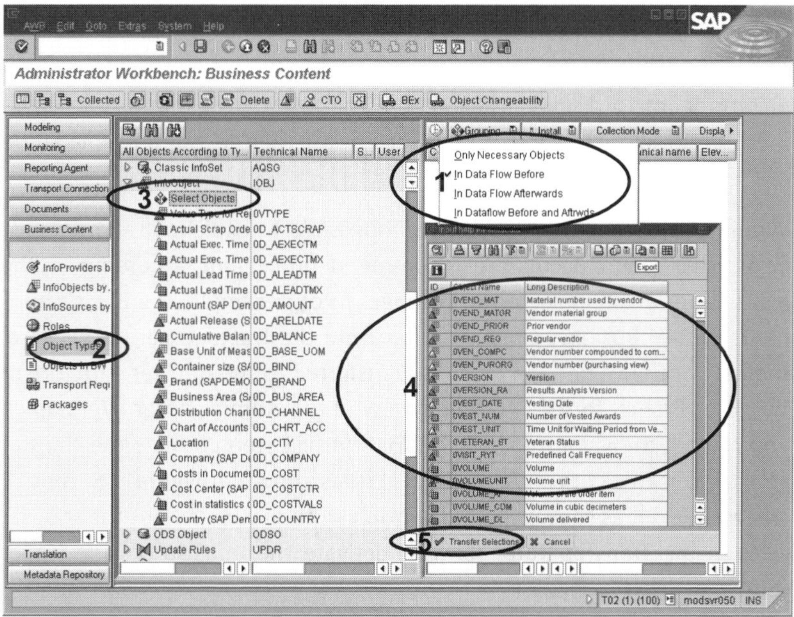

Figure 3.5 Activation of Usable SAP Business Content Objects

Selecting SAP Business Content objects

Next, the Input Help for Metadata popup opens. To ensure that the selection list contains all the objects that you want, select the appropriate filters. Click on an object to be transferred (or use **CTRL + click** for several objects) to mark the object (see Figure 3.5, Step 4). Then, click on the **Transfer Selections** button (see Figure 3.5, Step 5).

SAP BW then automatically collects all the objects and the associated ETL components and displays them in the right frame. When the object hierarchy is opened, all the objects that belong to the hierarchy are displayed. Unlike the screen in Figure 3.6, the objects in a new SAP BW system are not yet active. Accordingly, some or all of the components are not displayed as active with a green traffic light. You start activation with the **Transfer** button.

Activating SAP Business Content

Activation can last anywhere from a few minutes to several hours, depending upon the number of objects to be activated. The status line displays the progress of activation.

Once the activation procedure has been completed, the results are displayed (see Figure 3.7). If all the objects and the associated ETL components could be activated correctly, the overview frame (see Figure 3.7, Step 1) displays all the results with a green traffic light. If the entire activation or part of it was unsuccessful (as shown in the example), individual components are marked with yellow or red traffic lights. Double-click on a component to display a message in the lower right frame (see Figure 3.7, Step 2). Double-click on the icon for the long text or an explanation of the error.

Within this short introduction, it's impossible to explain all the possible errors that might occur. We recommend proceeding according to the instructions given in the error message. In our example, the ETL components of SAP Business Content differ from the DataSource. In this case, the key for the value type must be transferred to the transfer structure of SAP BW. Branch to the **Modeling** view in the Administrator Workbench and rework the value type (0VTYPE). The first step corrects the transfer structure. It marks the VALUETYPE field as shown in Figure 3.8, Step 1, and transfers it as shown in Step 2. You can then supplement the transfer rules in the **Transfer Rules** tab and activate the InfoSource (see Figure 3.9).

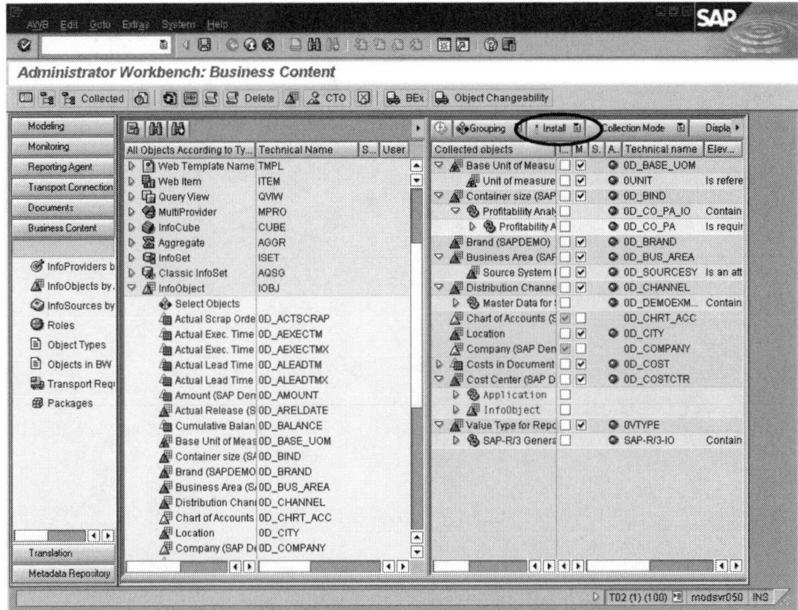

Figure 3.6 Activation of Selected Objects of SAP Business Content

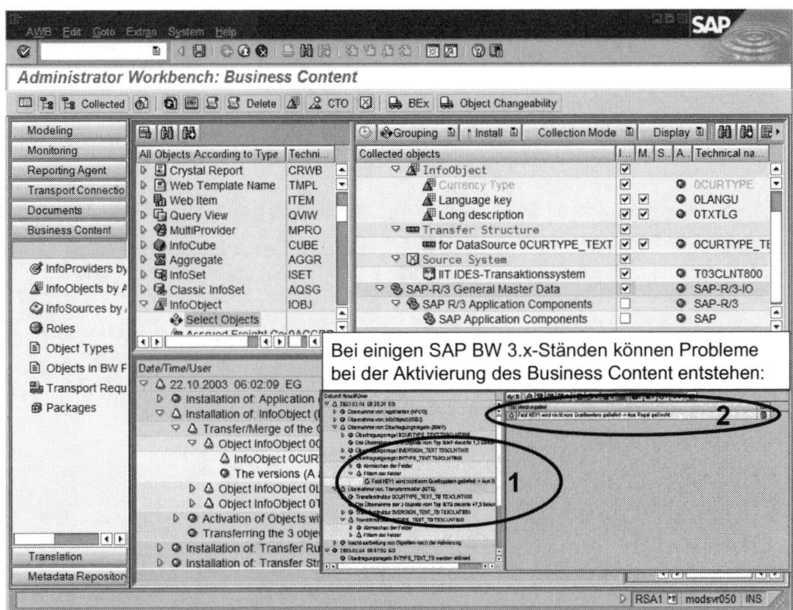

Figure 3.7 Results of Activation: Errors Might Occur for One or Another Portion of the Objects

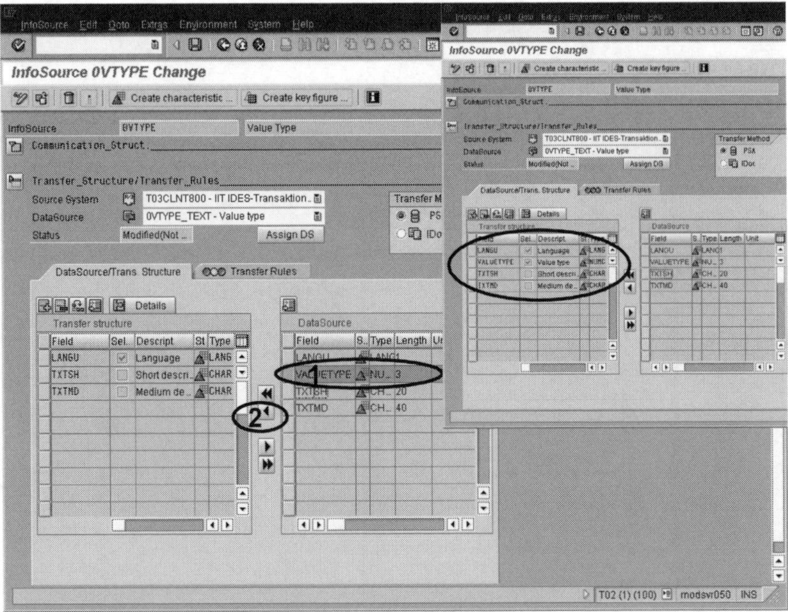

Figure 3.8 Reworking SAP Business Content Objects That Have Been Activated Incorrectly (Correction of the Transfer Structure)

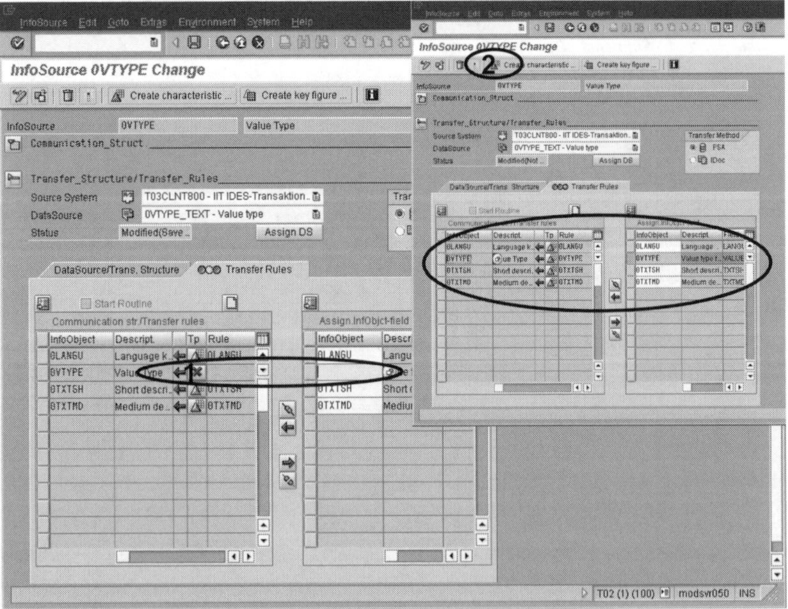

Figure 3.9 Reworking SAP Business Content Objects That Have Been Activated Incorrectly (Supplementing the Transfer Rules)

3.2.3 Sample Creation of an InfoObject: "Characteristic" Type

In our sample company, plan data is delivered at the "product group" level. Product groups are summarized in product main groups in reporting. The actual data is delivered at the document level with "customer/material." Plan–actual comparisons are to occur at the level of "product group" and "product main group." To meet these requirements, these objects must be mapped as navigational attributes for the material.

An InfoObject catalog is also required to create InfoObjects of "characteristic type" (see Figure 3.10). As noted in Section 3.2.1, InfoObject catalog **ZCBWTIPPSCHA01** (characteristic type) is created in InfoArea **ZCBWTIPPS** (similar to the process described in Section 3.2.1).

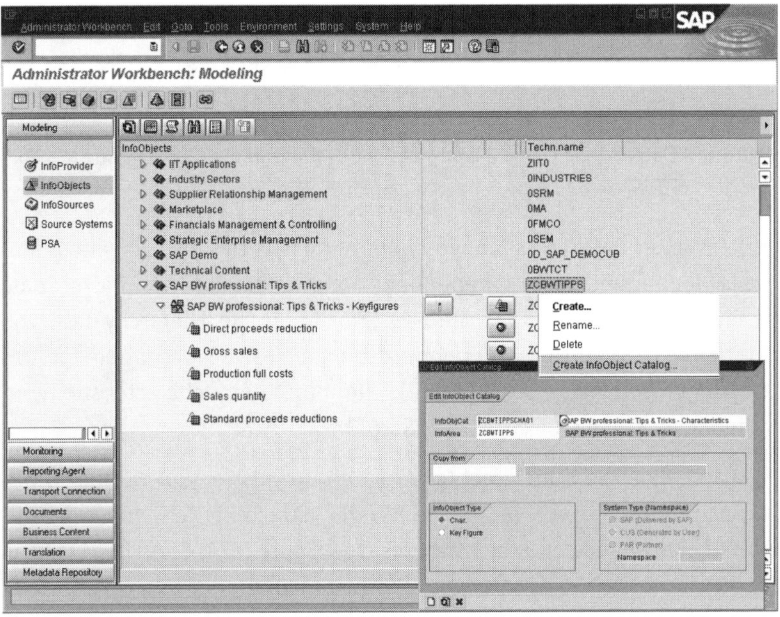

Figure 3.10 Creating an InfoObject Catalog for Characteristics

Creating a characteristic

You can create the InfoObject for "Product main group" from the InfoObject catalog for characteristics as shown in Figure 3.2. In the maintenance dialog for the material to be created, use the **General** tab for settings such as data type, length, and conversion exit (see Figure 3.11, Steps 1–3). Define the presentation in SAP Business Explorer and behavior during selection in the **Business Explorer** tab (see Figure 3.11, Step 4).

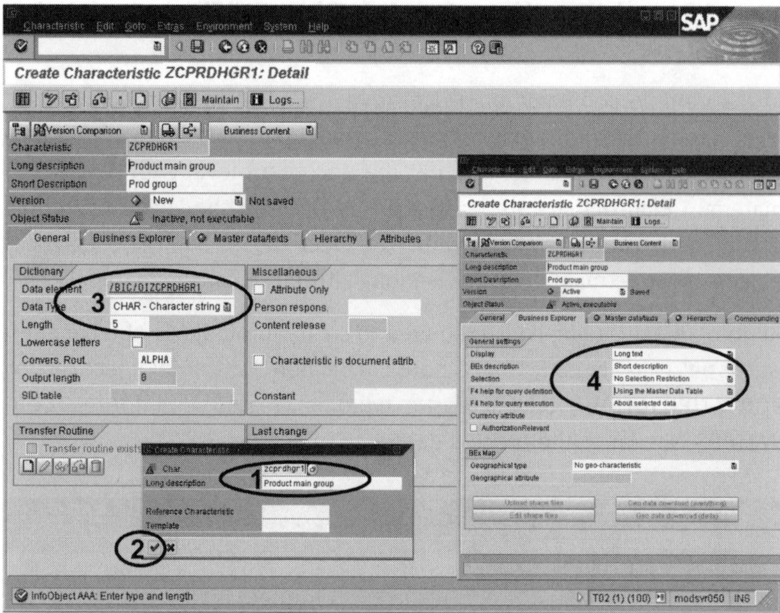

Figure 3.11 Determining General Properties and Settings of the Characteristic for SAP Business Explorer

In the **Master data/texts** tab, you determine that this InfoObject has language-dependent, time-independent long texts but no master data attributes (see Figure 3.12, Step 1). Finally, in the **Hierarchy** tab, you determine that non-time-dependent hierarchies are permitted for this InfoObject (see Figure 3.12, Step 2). The InfoObject "characteristic type" is then activated (see Figure 3.12, Step 3).

Setting up navigational attributes

You can create the InfoObject "product group" just as you did the "product main group." However, in the **Master data/texts** tab, you have this InfoObject use master data attributes (see Figure 3.13, Step 1). Finally, in the **Attributes** tab, you enter the "Product main group" as an attribute of the product group (see Figure 3.13, Step 2) before activating the InfoObject.

Because the actual data from SAP R/3 CO-PA is available on the basis of "document/material/customer," the characteristics "Product main group" and "Product group" are set up as navigational attributes for the material. The InfoObject "material" (0MATERIAL) is an SAP Business Content object, which will now be modified.

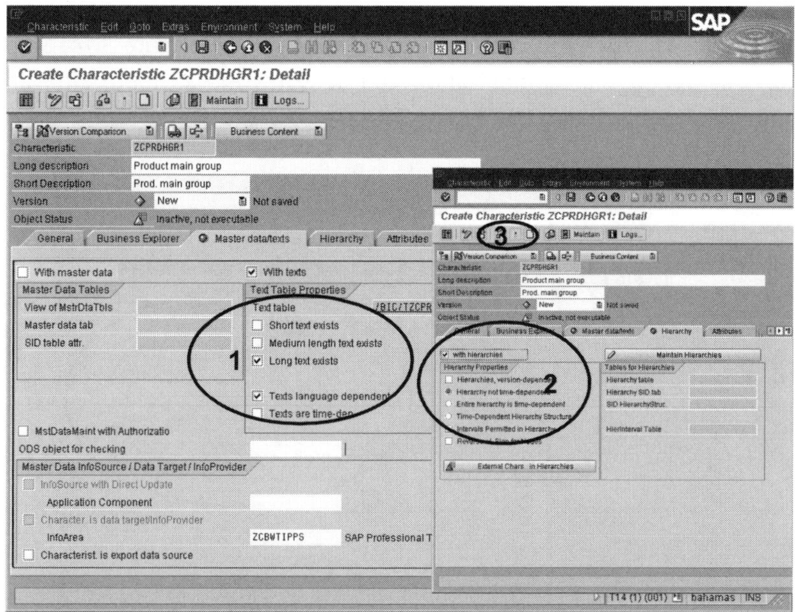

Figure 3.12 Setting the Properties of the Characteristic for Master Data and Hierarchies

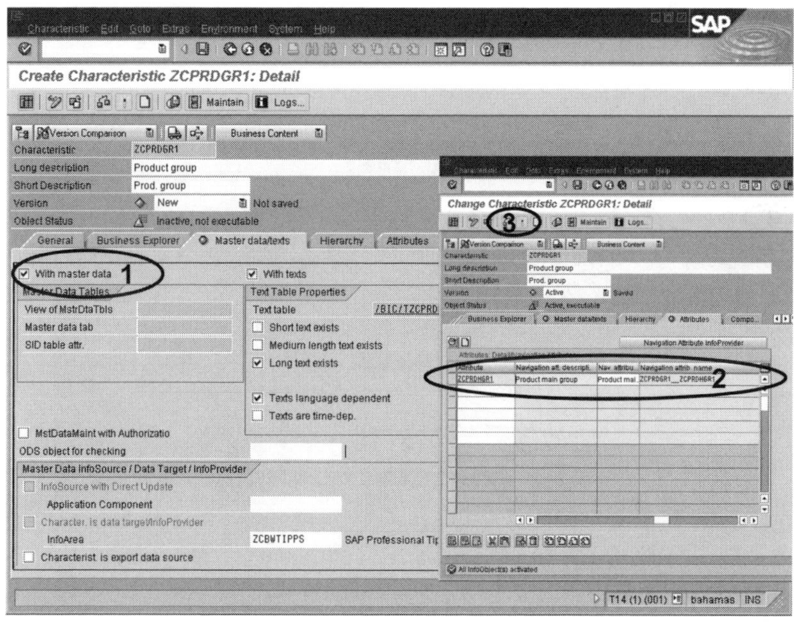

Figure 3.13 Setting Up a Navigational Attribute

Modifying SAP Business Content objects

As noted, navigational attributes are set in the **Attributes** tab (see Figure 3.14, Step 1). After you click the **Activate** button (see Figure 3.14, Step 2), SAP BW logs the modification and activates the attribute after an additional confirmation (see Figure 3.14, Steps 3 and 4).

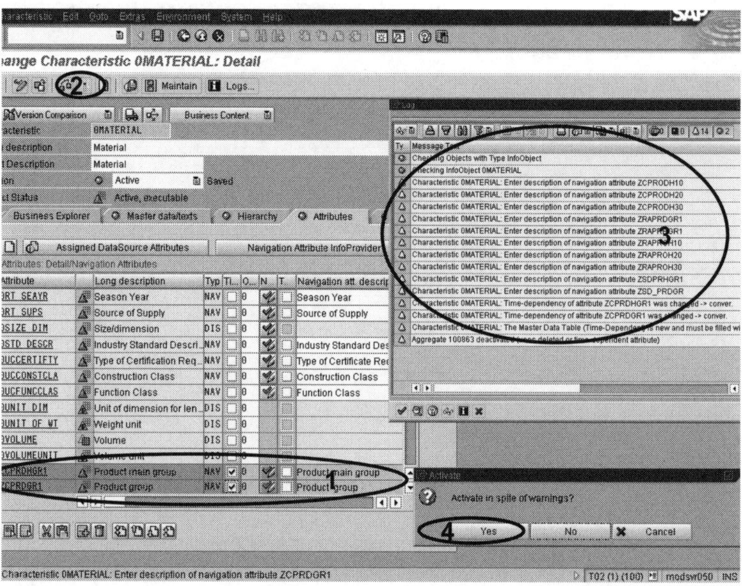

Figure 3.14 Enhancing the SAP Business Content Object "Material"

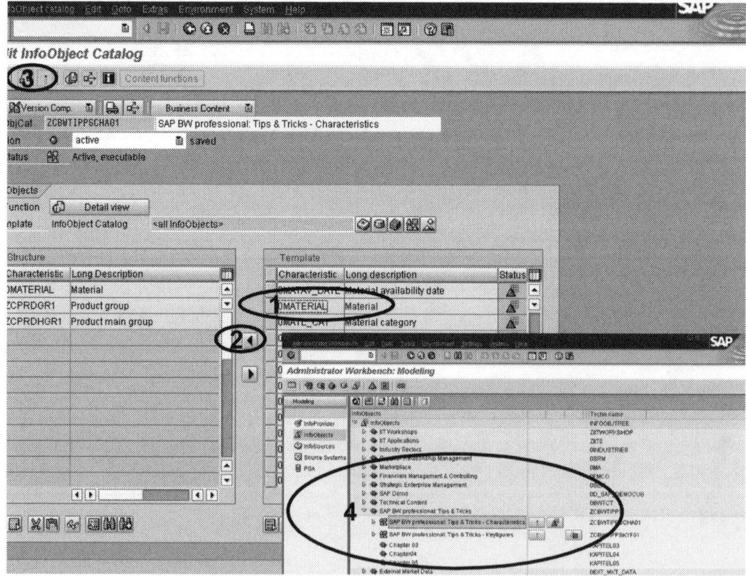

Figure 3.15 Recording the Characteristic in the InfoObject Catalog

After you return to maintenance of the InfoObject catalog, you can transfer the created and edited characteristics just as you transferred key figures in the InfoObjects catalog (see Figure 3.15).

3.2.4 Creating InfoCubes and a MultiProvider

After you create the foundation as InfoObjects (characteristics and key figures), you can set up the data model to store transaction data.

Three InfoProviders are required for the model. One InfoCube stores the actual data from SAP R/3 CO-PA; a second InfoCube stores the plan data. Both Basic InfoCubes are joined by a MultiProvider for reporting. The structure of the InfoCubes is given in list format in Appendix A.1, A.2, and A.3).

Creating the InfoCube for actual data

You select the appropriate InfoArea in the **InfoProvider** view of the Administrator Workbench (Transaction RSA11) by clicking on it. To open the context menu, right-click in the **InfoProvider** view (see Figure 3.16, Step 1). Select **Create InfoCube** (see Figure 3.16, Step 2).

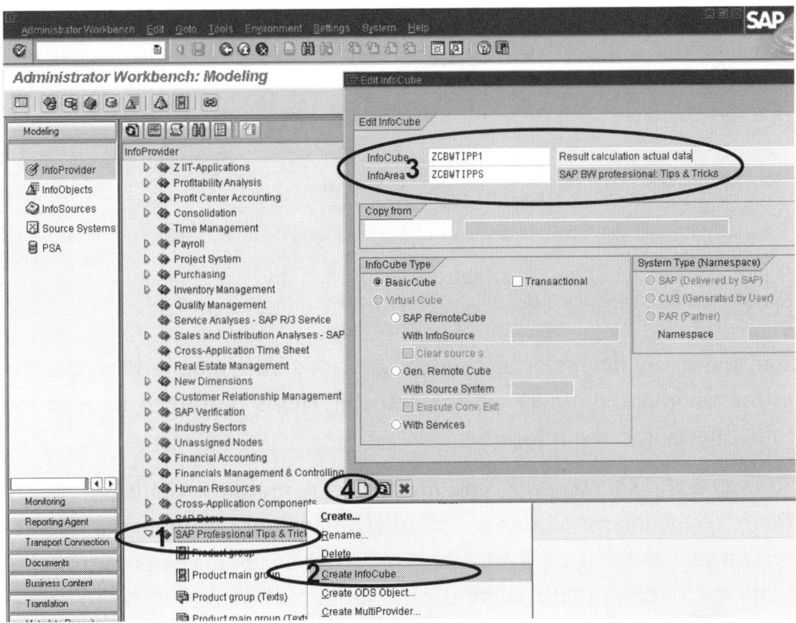

Figure 3.16 Opening the Create InfoCube Command

SAP BW then opens the **Edit InfoCube** popup. Enter the technical name and description (see Figure 3.16, Step 3) and select the **InfoCube Type**: **BasicCube**. Click on the **Create** button to confirm the entries (see Figure 3.16, Step 4).

Select characteristics

SAP BW then opens the **Edit InfoCubes: Characteristics** screen; the template offers InfoObjects of "characteristic type." Mark a required object and click on the **Transfer Fields** button to transfer the InfoObjects into the InfoCube (see Figure 3.17, Steps 1 and 2). Then, toggle to the **Time characteristics** tab (see Figure 3.17, Step 3), where you can use the same procedure to transfer all the InfoObjects offered by SAP as standard.

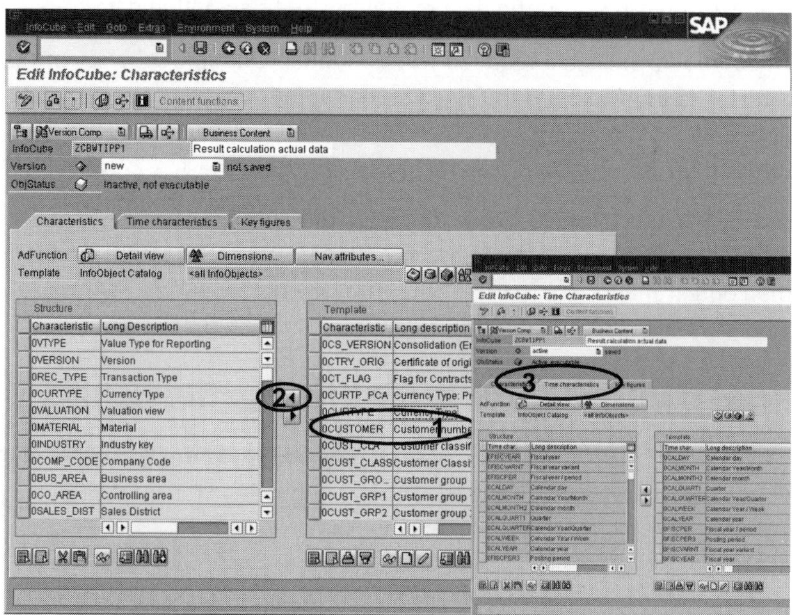

Figure 3.17 Transfer of the Characteristics Required for the Time Dimension and InfoObjects into the InfoCube

Selecting key figures

Transfer of key figures occurs similarly. Mark all the required InfoObjects in the template and click on the **Transfer Fields** button to transfer the InfoObjects into the InfoCube.

Creating and defining dimensions

To define the star schema, you must then name dimensions and assign them to characteristics. Begin with the **Dimensions** button in the **Characteristics** tab (see Figure 3.18, Step 1). Do not create dimensions from the template in the **Create Dimensions** popup: when prompted to create dimensions from the template, click on the **No** button (see Figure 3.18, Step 2). Instead, create the required dimensions in the **Define** tab in the **Define Dimensions** popup (see Figure 3.18, Step 3).

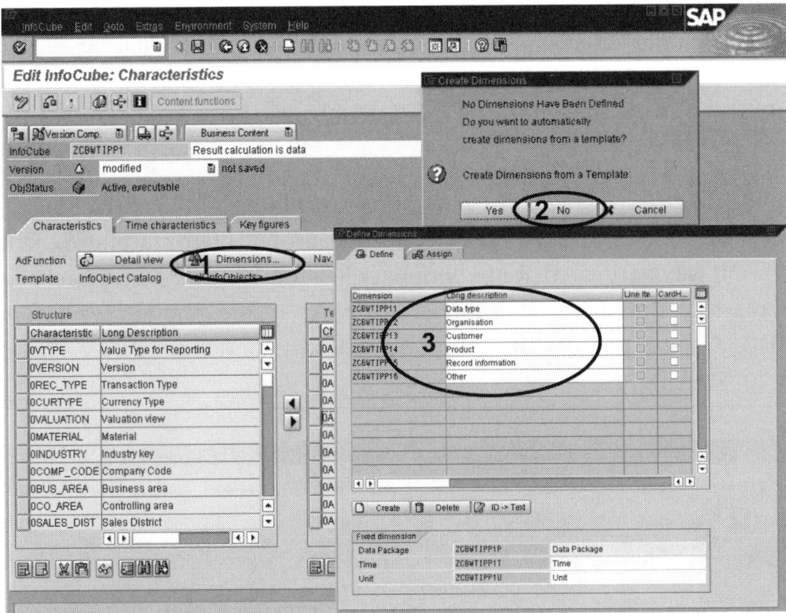

Figure 3.18 Creating Dimensions for the Star Schema

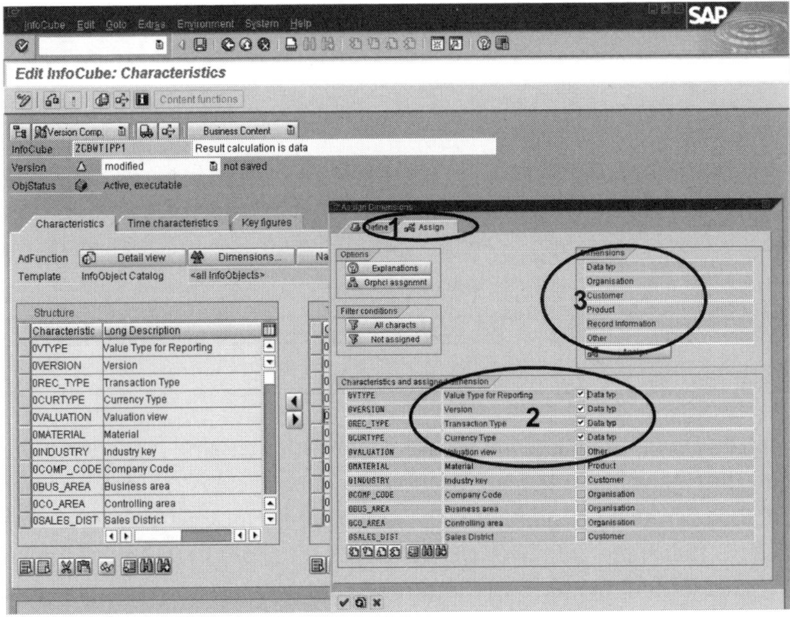

Figure 3.19 Assigning Characteristics to the Dimensions

Assigning characteristics to the dimensions

After you define the dimensions, select the **Assign** tab (see Figure 3.19, Step 1). In the list of characteristics, now mark all the characteristics that are to be combined into a dimension (see Figure 3.19, Step 2). Then double-click on the dimension to execute the assignment (see Figure 3.19, Step 3).

Activating navigational attributes

In the next step, activate the navigational attributes of the characteristics for the InfoCube. Use the **Nav. Attributes** pushbutton to start the **Switch On/Off Navigation Attribute** popup (see Figure 3.20, Step 1). Select and confirm the required navigational attributes in the popup (see Figure 3.20, Steps 2 and 3). The InfoCube can now be activated (see Figure 3.20, Step 4).

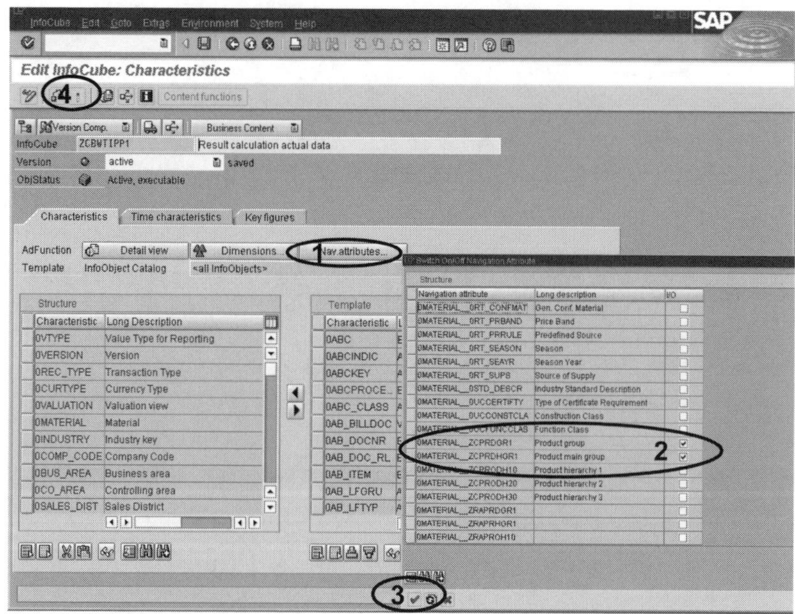

Figure 3.20 Selecting Navigational Attributes

Creating an InfoCube for plan data

You can create the InfoCube for plan data with the same procedure. The only difference lies in the smaller number of characteristics (no customer number, no material number, and no document information, for example), so that there are fewer characteristics to record in the InfoCube. In the customer dimension, the InfoCube contains only the characteristics for "country/region"; in the material dimension, the InfoCube contains only the characteristic "product group", with "product main group" as the navigational attribute. Because of the smaller number of characteristics, fewer dimensions are needed (see Figure 3.21).

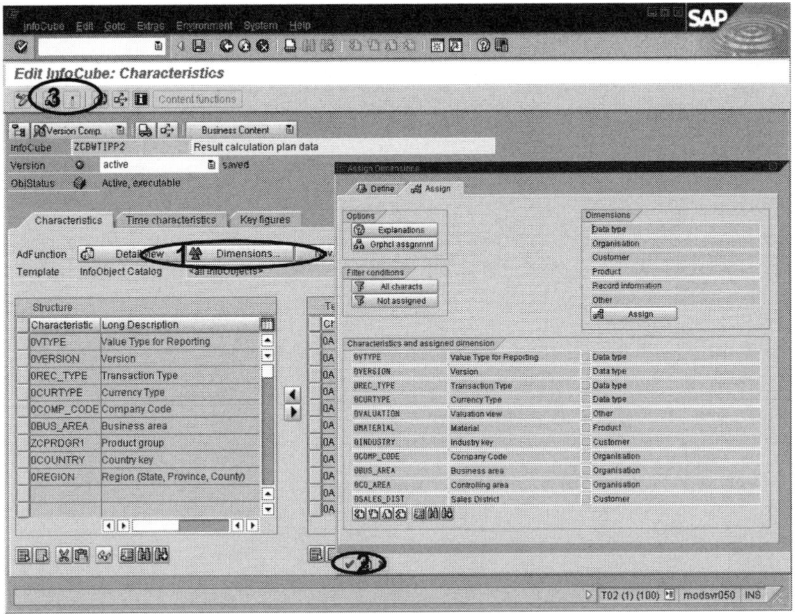

Figure 3.21 Country, Region, and Product Group as Basic Characteristics for Plan Data in the InfoCube

MultiProvider for plan–actual comparisons

Actual and plan data are combined for reporting with a MultiProvider. The special (and usual) starting situation for the creation of this MultiProvider is that actual and plan data are available in different granularities. The actual data exists at the document level with "customer/material/calendar day"; however, planning is much less detailed and uses only "product main group," "customer country," and "period." A MultiProvider offers functions to link the basic characteristics and navigational attributes of different InfoCubes to each other. For example, these functions enable you to link the basic characteristic "planned country" of the plan data InfoCube to the navigational attribute "customer country" of the actual data InfoCube.

For the plan–actual comparison, the characteristics and navigational attributes displayed in Table 3.1 are linked. The key figures of both InfoCubes are available automatically.

Actual Data InfoCube	Plan Data InfoCube
Fiscal year variants	Fiscal year variants
Fiscal year	Fiscal year

Table 3.1 Characteristics to Be Linked in the MultiProvider

Actual Data InfoCube	Plan Data InfoCube
Fiscal year/period	Fiscal year/period
Posting period	Posting period
Calendar year	Calendar year
Mid-year	Mid-year
Calendar year/quarter	Calendar year/quarter
Quarter	Quarter
Calendar year/month	Calendar year/month
Calendar month	Calendar month
Version	Version
Value type	Value type
Currency type	Currency type
Type of procedure	Type of procedure
Company code	Company code
Business area	Business area
Navigational attribute "product group of the material"	Product group
Navigational attribute "product main group of the material"	Navigational attribute "product main group of the product group"
Navigational attribute "customer country"	Country
Navigational attribute "customer region"	Region

Table 3.1 Characteristics to Be Linked in the MultiProvider (Cont.)

Select the corresponding InfoArea in the **InfoProvider** view of the Administrator Workbench (Transaction RSA11). Right-click to open the context menu (see Figure 3.22, Step 1). Select **Create MultiProvider** (see Figure 3.22, Step 2).

SAP BW opens the **Edit MultiProvider** popup. Enter the technical name and description (see Figure 3.22, Step 3). Use the **Create** button to confirm the entries (see Figure 3.22, Step 4).

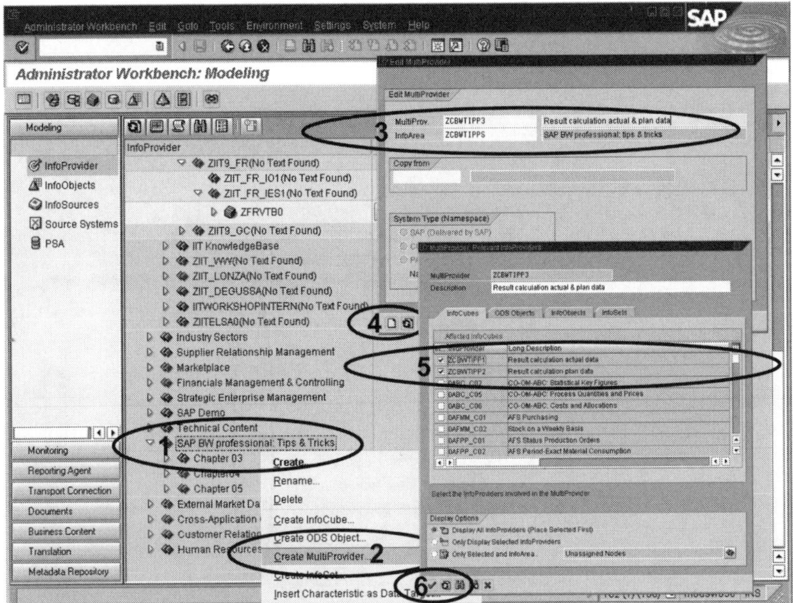

Figure 3.22 Creating a MultiProvider

SAP BW then opens a popup, **MultiProvider: Relevant InfoProviders**; here you select the InfoCubes for actual and plan data. Click on the **Continue** button to confirm your selection (see Figure 3.22, Steps 5 and 6).

Creating a MultiProvider

You can define the MultiProvider in the **Edit MultiProvider** screen, using the same procedure as noted above to define InfoCubes. Select key figures, time characteristics, characteristics, and the required navigational attributes. Similarly, you can select dimensions and assign characteristics. If desired, you can define the dimensions by using the template, such as the dimensions of the plan data InfoCube.

For a MultiProvider, you must also identify the characteristics and key figure involved, which define the InfoCubes from which they come. For example, the country of the customer defines that the basic characteristic "country" in the plan data InfoCube and the navigational attribute "customer country" in the actual data InfoCube should be linked in the MultiProvider.

Identifying characteristics

Begin with the **Identification** pushbutton (see Figure 3.23, Step 1). Then, specify the source in the **Identification of Characteristics Involved** popup. Confirm the entry by clicking on the **Continue** button (see Figure 3.23, Steps 2 and 3).

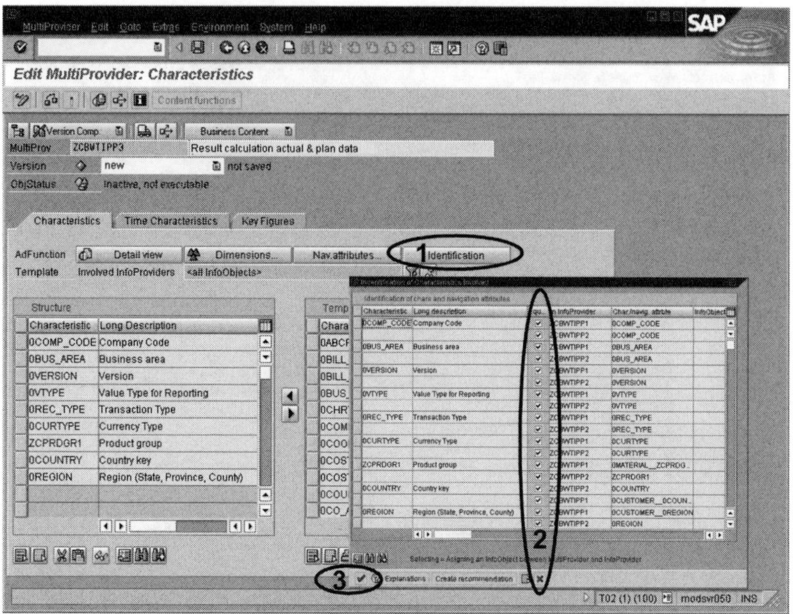

Figure 3.23 Identifying the Participating Characteristics

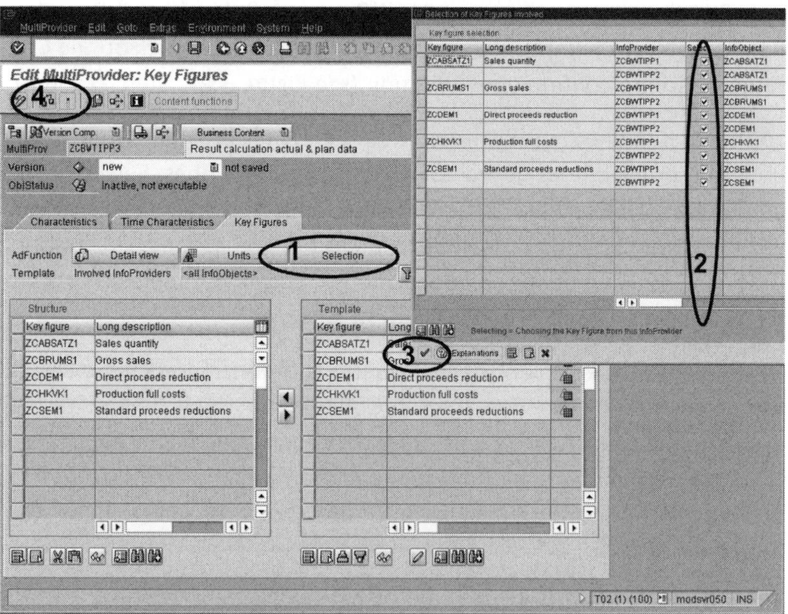

Figure 3.24 Selecting Key Figures

Define the source of key figures with the **Selection** pushbutton (see Figure 3.24, Step 1). In the **Selection of Key Figures Involved** popup that opens, select all the key figures from both InfoCubes for our model (see Figure 3.24, Steps 2 and 3). The MultiProvider can now be activated (see Figure 3.24, Step 4).

Selecting key figures

3.3 Setting Up the Retrieval of Master Data

3.3.1 General Comments

After the data model has been created, data retrieval can be configured. Appropriate ETL processes are defined for master and transaction data.

This section shows you how to combine data from various source systems in SAP BW. The scenario here supplements material master data from SAP R/3 with master data ("product group" and "product main group") from interface files.

3.3.2 Master Data Texts for the Product Group from Interface Files

Creating application components

An individual application component is set up in the **InfoSources** view of the Administrator Workbench for the supplemental master data: "product group" and "product main group." Open the view with Transaction RSA12 or the **Administrator Workbench** (Transaction RSA1) menu and selection of the **InfoSources** view. In the **InfoSources** view, open the context menu by right-clicking on the uppermost node of **InfoSources** and select **Create application component** (see Figure 3.25, Steps 1 and 2). Enter the technical name and description of the application component in the popup that appears, then confirm the entries (see Figure 3.25, Steps 3 and 4).

Creating an InfoSource

You can select the new application components and right-click to open the context menu (see Figure 3.25, steps 5 and 6). Select the **Create InfoSource** command. A popup with the same name opens, in which you can specify the type of InfoSource (here: **Direct Update of Master Data**) and the technical name of the InfoObject. You can then confirm the entries (see Figure 3.25, Steps 7 and 8). The notification, **"InfoSource...(Master Data) assigned to application component..."** then serves as confirmation (see Figure 3.25, Step 9).

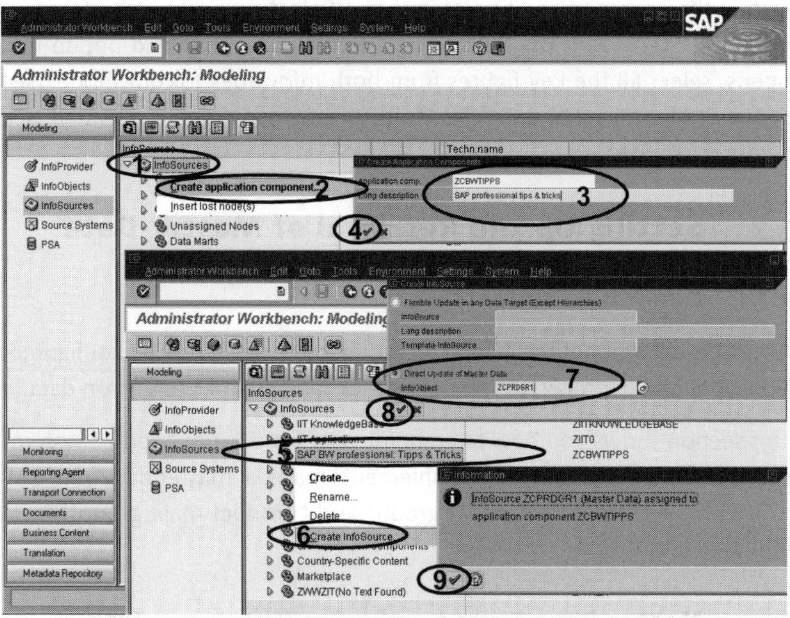

Figure 3.25 Creating an Application Component and InfoSource for Direct Updating of Master Data

Assigning the DataSource

You must now assign the source system for interface files to the newly created InfoSource (after a refresh, the screen appears as in Figure 3.26, Step 1). Right-click to open the context menu and select the **Assign DataSource** command (see Figure 3.26, Step 2). Use **SAP_DEMO** as the source system and confirm the entry (see Figure 3.26, Steps 3 and 4). In actual practice, an individual source system is set up and used here. Then, confirm the entries in the **Save changes?** popup (see Figure 3.26, Step 5).

Setting up a transfer structure and transfer rules

Now, you must define the structure of the interface file (transfer structure) and the transfer rules. The interface file to be used has the following structure:

- Column1: Language key (D for German and E for English, for example)
- Column2: Product group key
- Column3: Description of the product group

Table 3.2 provides an excerpt from the interface file for the product group texts.

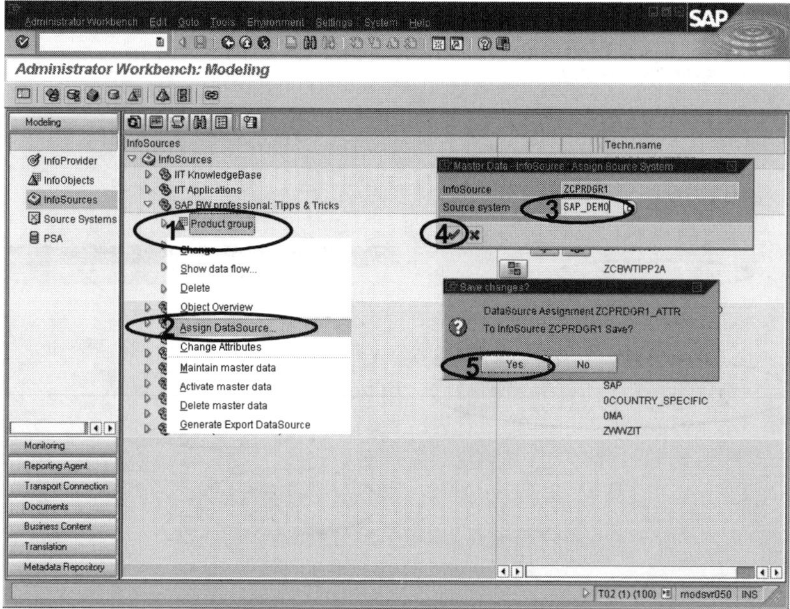

Figure 3.26 Assigning the DataSource to the InfoSource

Language	Key	Description
E	A10	Colors
E	A20	Electric-powered
E	B10	Seats

Table 3.2 Excerpt from the Interface File for the Product Group Texts

You now set up the structure of the interface file in the **InfoSource...Change** function and the **DataSource/Trans. Structure** tab (see Figure 3.27, Steps 1 and 2). Here, you use the **InfoObject** column to specify the technical descriptions of the fields (as InfoObjects) in the same as order as the columns of the interface file:

- 0LANGU
- ZCPRDGR1
- 0TXTLG

Transfer rules are set up based on the transfer structure. Branch to the **Transfer Rules** tab (see Figure 3.27, Step 3). The fields of the transfer structure in their entirety are transferred by clicking on the **Propose Transfer Rules** button (see Figure 3.27, Step 4).

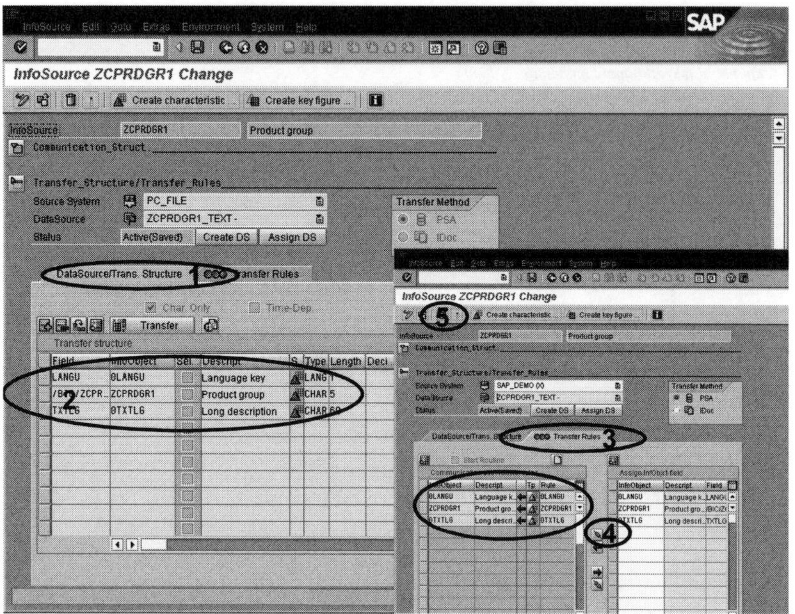

Figure 3.27 Setting Up the InfoSource: Defining the Transfer Structure and Transfer Rules

Doing so also defines the structure of the InfoSource (and therefore, the communications structure). You can then activate the InfoSource with the transfer rules (see Figure 3.27, Step 5).

Creating an InfoPackage

Once you have returned to the **InfoSources** view of the Administrator Workbench with the **F3** key or with the **Back** button, you can set up the InfoPackage to execute data retrieval. Select **SAP Demo(No Text Found)** (see Figure 3.28, Step 1). Right-click to open the context menu and select **Create InfoPackage** (see Figure 3.28, Step 2). A popup of the same name appears in which you enter the description of the InfoPackage: mark the DataSource ("Product group (Texts)," and confirm the entries (see Figure 3.28, Steps 3–5).

Detailed specifications of the InfoPackage are entered in the **Scheduler (Maintain InfoPackage)** screen. In the **External data tab** (see Figure 3.29, Step 1), specify the location of the interface file (see Figure 3.29, Steps 2 and 3), the **File Type** (here: "CSV"), separator, and the **Number of Header Rows to be Ignored** (see Figure 3.29, Steps 4 and 5).

Now you can branch to the **Processing** tab (see Figure 3.29, Step 6). You don't have to store the data in the Persistent Staging Area (PSA); rather, you can select the **Update Data Only InfoObject** option(see Figure 3.29, Step 7).

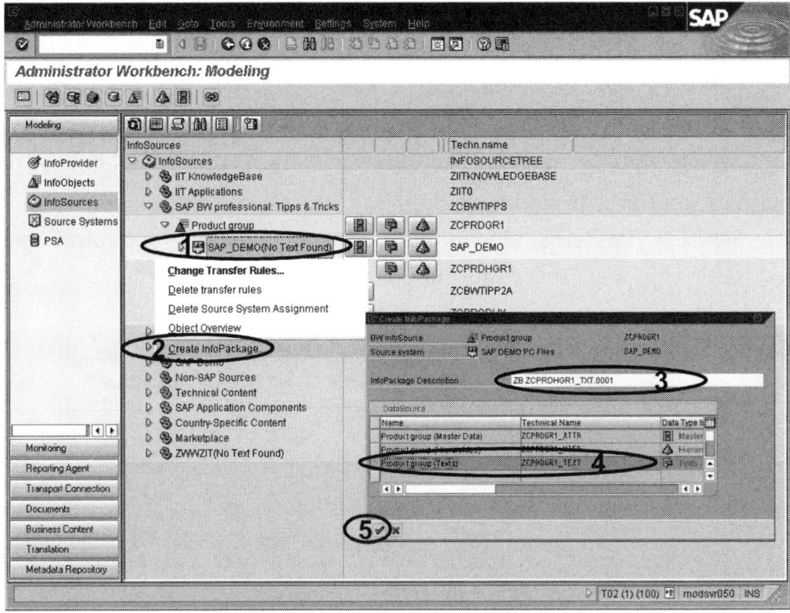

Figure 3.28 Creating an InfoPackage for the Interface file (texts)

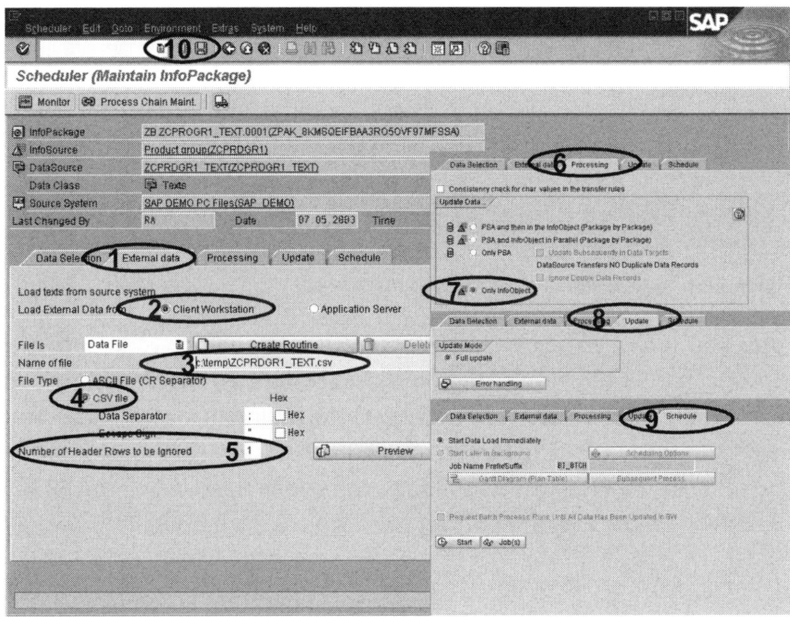

Figure 3.29 Detailed Entries for an InfoPackage

Store the default settings in the **Update** and **Schedule** tabs (see Figure 3.29, Step 8 and 9), and save the definition of the InfoPackage (see Figure 3.29, Step 10).

Scheduling and Monitoring

Click on the **Start** button in the **Schedule** tab to upload the master data texts (see 3.30, Steps 1 and 2). To display the results of the update, click on the **Monitor** button in the **Scheduler (Maintain InfoPackage)** screen. (see Figure 3.30, Step 3). The monitor displays "incorrect" updates with a red traffic light and "successful" updates with a green traffic light.

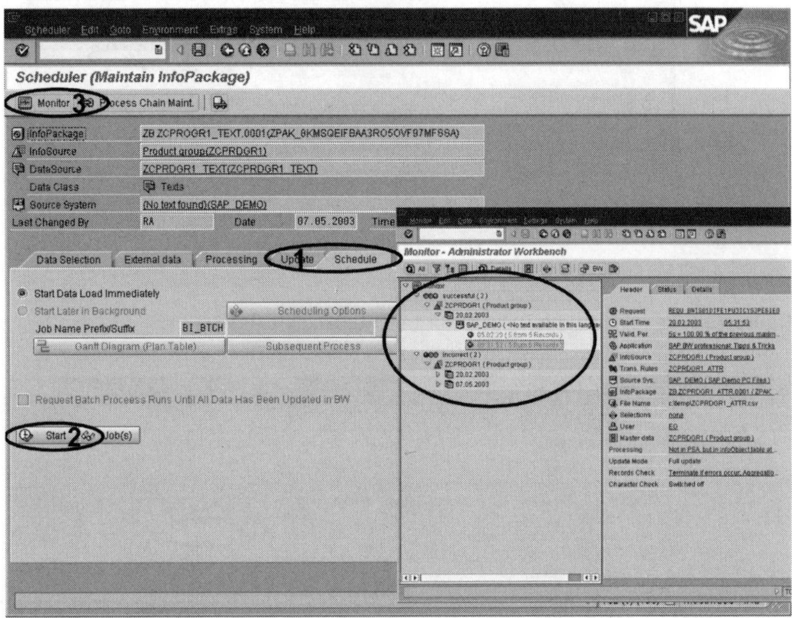

Figure 3.30 Starting and Monitoring the InfoPackage

After you return to the overview in the Administrator Workbench (by pressing the **F3** key or clicking on the **Back** button), open the context menu in the **InfoSources** view and select the **Maintain master data** command to display the data that has been loaded (see Figure 3.31, Steps 1 and 2). Start the display from the selection screen (by pressing the **F8** key or clicking on the **Execute** button) (see Figure 3.31, Step 3).

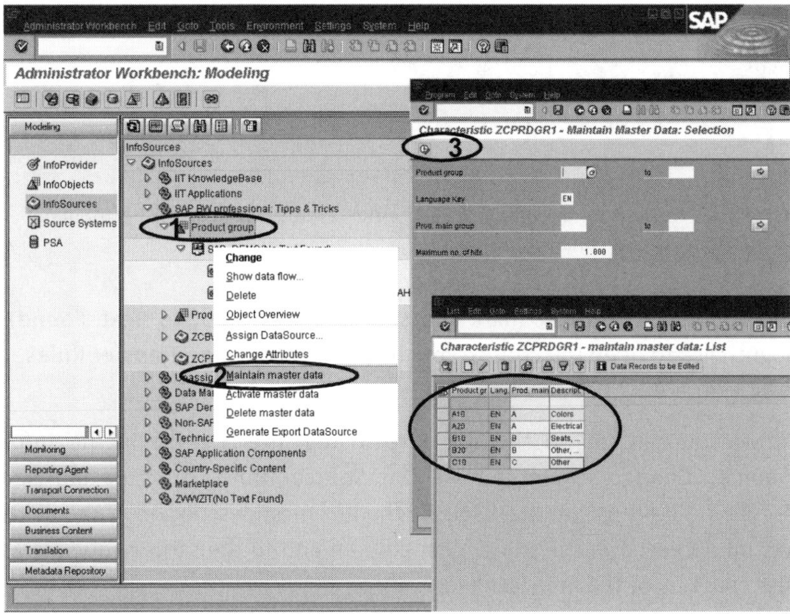

Figure 3.31 Displaying the Master Data Texts That Have Been Loaded

3.3.3 Master Data Texts for the Product Main Group from Interface Files

You set up and retrieve data for the master data texts of product main group ZCPRDHGR1 just as you did for the master data texts of the product group (see Section 3.3.1).

3.3.4 Master Data Attributes for the Product Group from Interface Files

Now you can retrieve the data for the product group and its attribute—product main group. Just as you did when you retrieved the master data texts, define the structure of the interface file (transfer structure) and the transfer rules here. The file that you will use has the following structure:

- Column1: Key of the product group
- Column2: Key of the product main group, which is assigned to each product group

Table 3.3 provides an excerpt from the interface file for the product group and the associated product main groups. The setup of data retrieval for master data attributes occurs in the same maintenance function you used for master data texts.

Key: Product Group	Key: Product Main Group
A10	A
A20	A
B10	B

Table 3.3 Excerpt from the Interface File for the "Product Main Group" Attribute of the "Product Group" Characteristic

Once again, you must mark the source **SAP Demo(No Text Found)**. Right-click to open the context menu and select **Change Transfer Rules...** (see Figure 3.32, Steps 1 and 2).

Transfer structure and transfer rules for master data attributes

Now, you can set up the structure of the interface file in the **InfoSource...Change** screen and the **DataSource/Trans. Structure** tab (see Figure 3.33, Steps 1 and 2). Specify the technical description of the fields (as InfoObjects) in the InfoObject column and in the same sequence as the columns of the interface file:

- ZCPRDGR1
- ZCPRDHGR1

Then branch to the **Transfer Rules** tab, where you can accept the proposed transfer rules and activate data retrieval, just as you did to retrieve the master data texts (see Figure 3.33, Steps 3–5).

You must also set up an InfoPackage to retrieve the master data attributes. Just as you created the InfoPackage for the master data texts, you can select the **Create InfoPackage...** command from the context menu, enter a description of the InfoPackage, and select the corresponding DataSource ("Product group (Master Data)") by marking it (see Figure 3.34, Steps 1–5). As you did with InfoPackages for master data texts, make and save your settings in the **External data** and **Processing** tabs (see Figure 3.35, Steps 1–5).

You can retrieve data for the InfoPackage of master data attributes just as you uploaded the master data texts (see Section 3.3.2). After the update, the attributes of the "Product main group" are assigned to the product groups (see Figure 3.36).

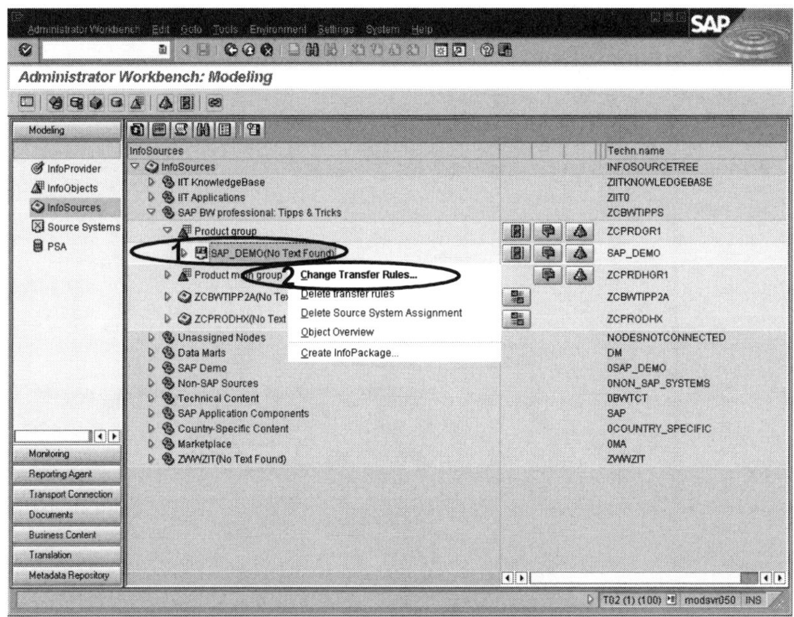

Figure 3.32 Setting Up Retrieval of the Master Data Attributes

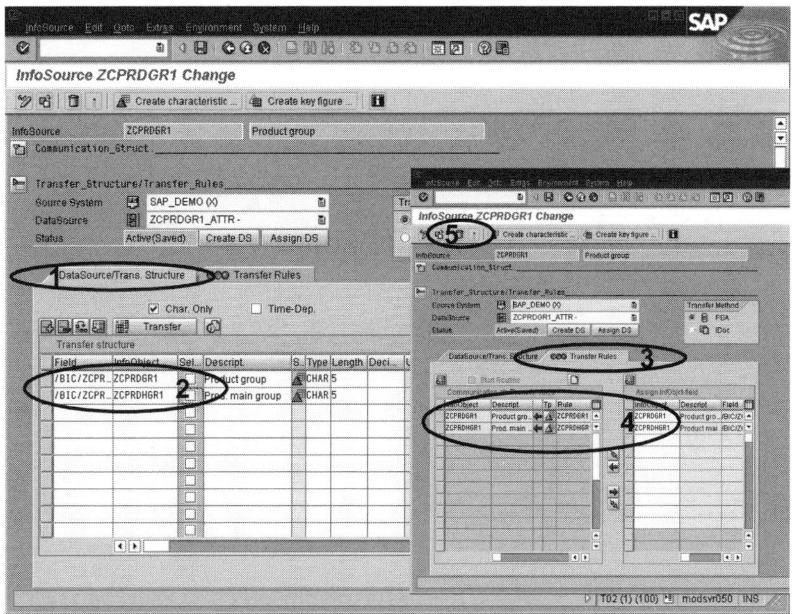

Figure 3.33 Transfer Structure and Transfer Rules for Master Data Attributes

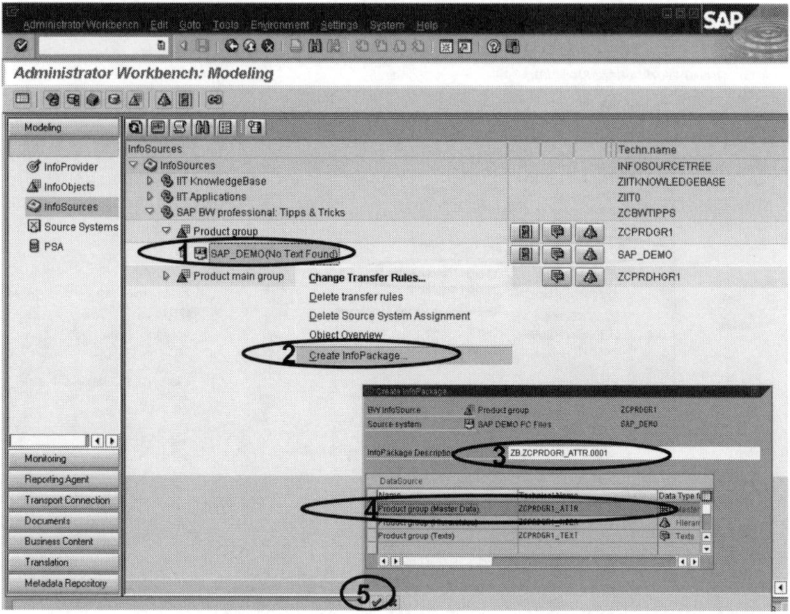

Figure 3.34 Creating an InfoPackage for an Interface File (Attributes)

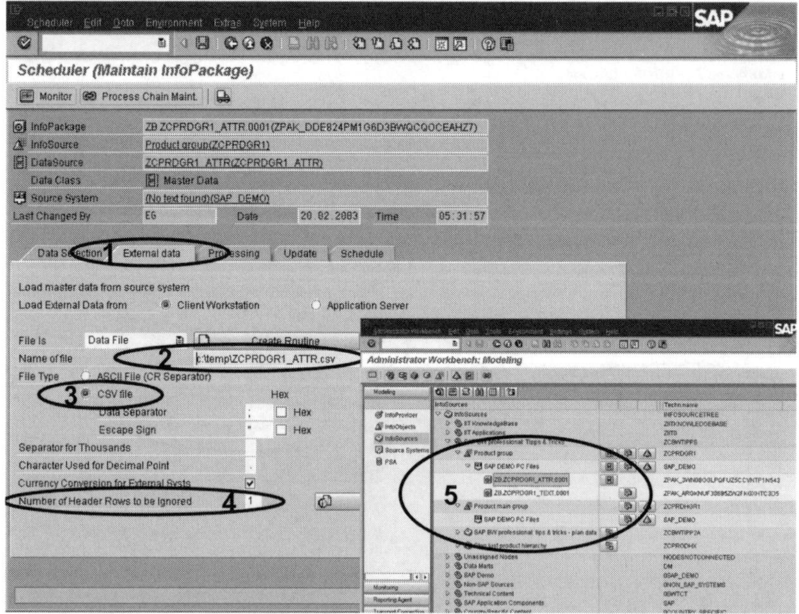

Figure 3.35 Making Settings for the InfoPackage Attribute

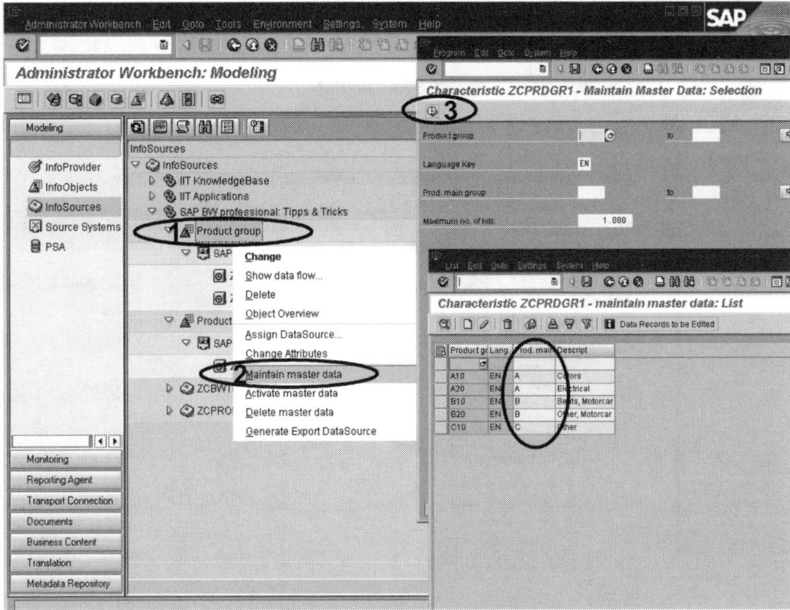

Figure 3.36 Results of the Upload of Master Data Attributes

3.3.5 Master Data Texts and Attributes for Materials from SAP R/3 and Retrieving Data with SAP R/3 Data-Sources and Interface Files

You can retrieve material master data from various sources. Attributes and texts specific to SAP R/3 are loaded from the corresponding SAP R/3 source systems; however, you retrieve data for the customer-specific material attributes "product group" and "product main group" (data that is not stored in an SAP R/3 system) from an interface file that you must provide.

Using the Data-Sources in SAP Business Content

After SAP Business Content has been activated, an InfoSource for the InfoObject **Material** (0MATERIAL) and the InfoProvider **Material (attributes)** (0MATERIAL_ATTR) are available. DataSource **Material** (0MATERIAL_ATTR) is assigned to the selected InfoSource (0MATERIAL); in this case, it is a direct update of the InfoObject "Material" (see Figure 3.37, Steps 1–6). Next, you accept the proposed transfer rules and activate the transfer rules (see Figure 3.37, Steps 7 and 8).

You create the InfoPackage and update the material attributes as shown in detail in Figures 3.28–30. Figure 3.38 provides you with an overview.

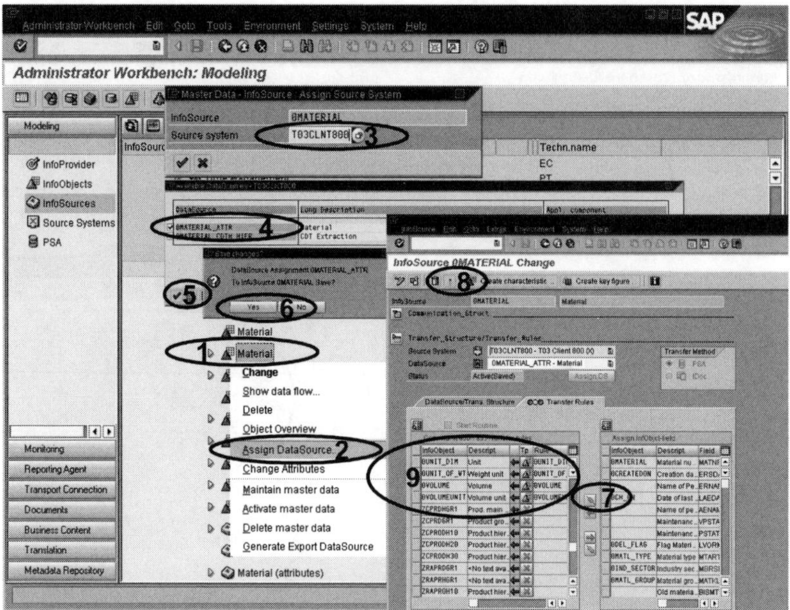

Figure 3.37 Setting Up Data Retrieval from SAP R/3 for Material Attributes

You can create the link between SAP Business Content (depending on its level of activation) and the (required) DataSource for the material texts (0MATERIAL_TEXT) from SAP R/3 just as you linked the DataSource for the attribute Material (see Figure 3.37). Here too, you set up an InfoPackage based upon the InfoSource, the assigned DataSource, and the transfer rules accepted from the list proposed by SAP BW. You can use the InfoPackage to upload material texts from SAP R/3 into SAP BW.

Supplemental data retrieval

These steps load all the SAP R/3 master data for the material into SAP BW. However, the attributes "Product main group" and "Product group" are not mapped in SAP R/3 and therefore have not (yet) been loaded into SAP BW: see Figure 3.37 (Step 9). Because the SAP R/3 DataSource does not provide any corresponding attributes, no transfer rules for these attributes are proposed.

Accordingly, you must load a supplemental file that contains the related assignments into SAP BW, just as you did for the "Product group" and "Product main group" InfoSources.

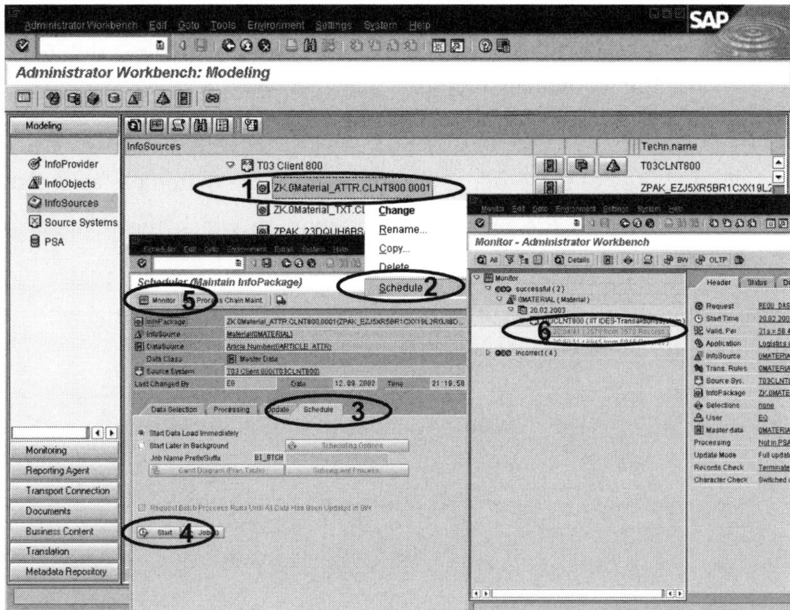

Figure 3.38 Uploading Material Attributes from SAP R/3

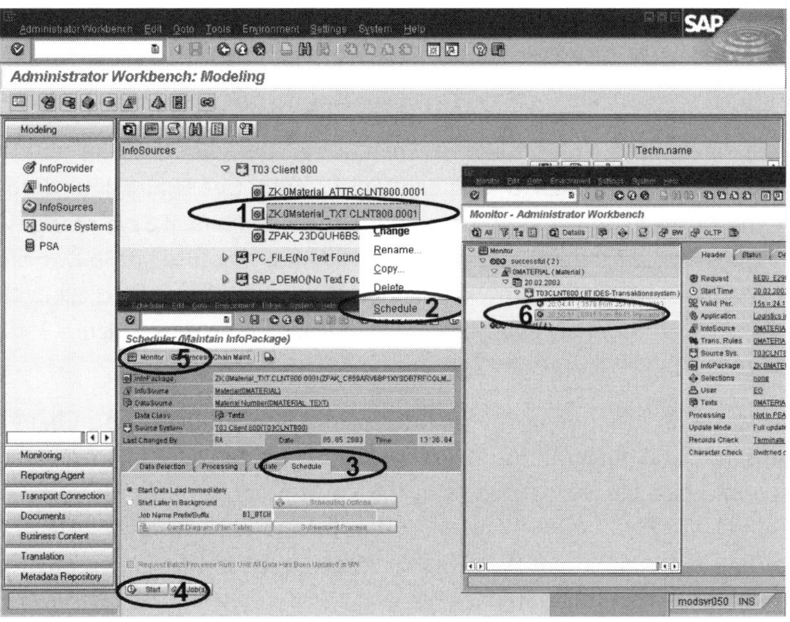

Figure 3.39 Uploading Material Texts from SAP R/3

Similar to the retrieval of master data texts, you must define the structure of the interface file (transfer structure) and the transfer rules. The interface file has the following structure:

- Column1: Material number
- Column2: Key of the product group to which the material is assigned
- Column3: Key of the product main group to which the material is assigned

Table 3.4 provides an excerpt of the interface file for the material with its attributes "Product group" and "Product main group."

Material	Product Main Group	Product Group
100-410	B	B20
100-420	A	A20
100-430	C	C10
100-431	A	A20

Table 3.4 Excerpt from the Interface File for the Material and Its Attributes: "Product Group" and "Product Main Group"

In the **InfoSources** view, right-click on the **InfoSource "Material"** (0MATERIAL) to open the context menu and select **Assign DataSource...** (see Figure 3.40, Steps 1 and 2). Then, assign the source system for the interface file, **SAP_DEMO**, and confirm the entry (see Figure 3.40, Steps 3 and 4). Next, you answer the prompts in the sequential **Save changes?** popups for attributes, texts, and hierarchies. Because attributes are loaded as supplements, answer the question on attributes by clicking on **Yes**; answer the other two questions by clicking on **No** (see Figure 3.40, Steps 5–7).

Now, set up the structure of the interface file in the **InfoSource...Change** screen, **DataSource/Trans. Structure** tab. Fields that aren't contained in the interface file are deleted from the list of proposed fields in SAP BW (see Figure 3.40, Steps 8 and 9). In the **InfoObject** column, specify the technical description of the fields (as InfoObjects) in the same sequence as the columns of the interface file:

- 0MATERIAL
- ZCPRDHGR1
- ZCPRDGR1

Based on these entries, the **Transfer Rules** tab contains assignments only for the remaining fields of the transfer structure. Activate the rules to complete the maintenance of the InfoSource (see Figure 3.40, Steps 10–12).

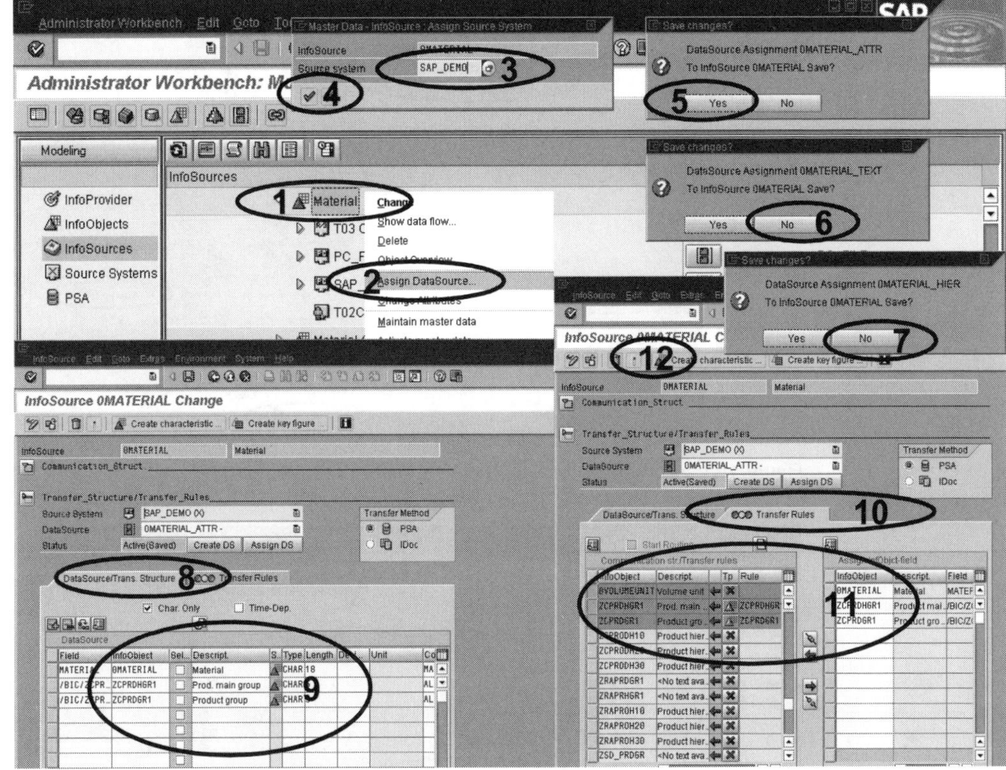

Figure 3.40 Setting Up Data Retrieval for Supplemental Material Attributes

You can set up and start the upload of the supplemental material attributes according to the procedure documented for an InfoPackage (see Figure 3.41, Steps 1–9).

The data loaded into SAP BW by the two retrievals from SAP R/3 (material texts and SAP R/3 attributes) and from supplemental retrieval (the material attributes "Product group" and "Product main group") can be displayed in the **Maintain Master Data** screen by clicking on the **Execute** button or pressing the **F8** key (see Figure 3.42, Steps 1–3).

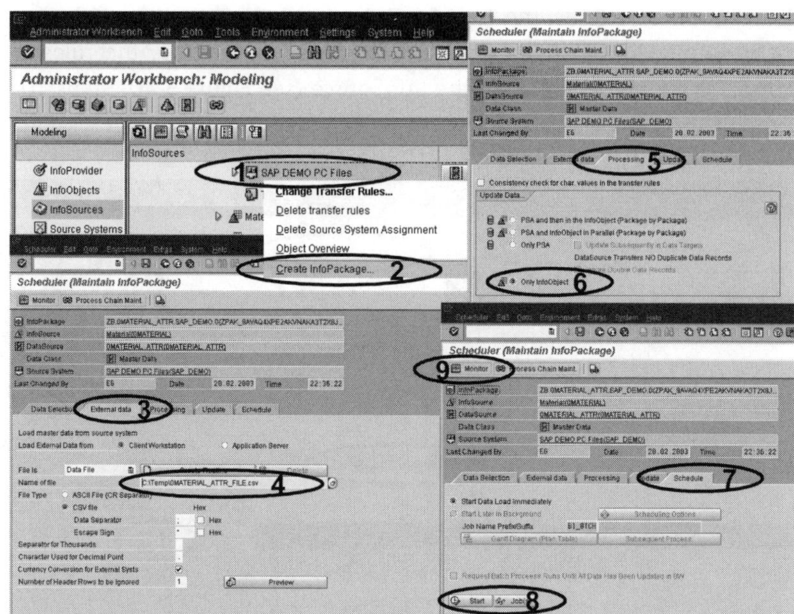

Figure 3.41 InfoPackage for Supplemental Material Attributes

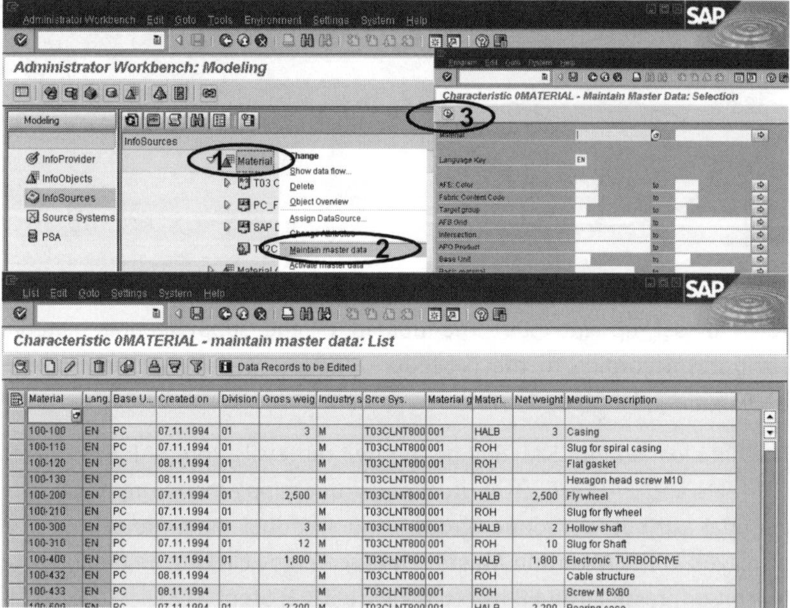

Material	Lang.	Base U...	Created on	Division	Gross weig	Industry s	Srce Sys.	Material g	Materi.	Net weight	Medium Description
100-100	EN	PC	07.11.1994	01	3	M	T03CLNT800	001	HALB	3	Casing
100-110	EN	PC	07.11.1994	01		M	T03CLNT800	001	ROH		Slug for spiral casing
100-120	EN	PC	08.11.1994	01		M	T03CLNT800	001	ROH		Flat gasket
100-130	EN	PC	08.11.1994	01		M	T03CLNT800	001	ROH		Hexagon head screw M10
100-200	EN	PC	07.11.1994	01	2,500	M	T03CLNT800	001	HALB	2,500	Fly wheel
100-210	EN	PC	07.11.1994	01		M	T03CLNT800	001	ROH		Slug for fly wheel
100-300	EN	PC	07.11.1994	01	3	M	T03CLNT800	001	HALB	2	Hollow shaft
100-310	EN	PC	07.11.1994	01	12	M	T03CLNT800	001	ROH	10	Slug for Shaft
100-400	EN	PC	07.11.1994	01	1,800	M	T03CLNT800	001	HALB	1,800	Electronic TURBODRIVE
100-432	EN	PC	08.11.1994			M	T03CLNT800	001	ROH		Cable structure
100-433	EN	PC	08.11.1994			M	T03CLNT800	001	ROH		Screw M 6X60

Figure 3.42 Display of the Material Attributes and Texts That Have Been Loaded

3.4 Retrieving Actual Data from SAP R/3 CO-PA

3.4.1 General Comments

After uploading master data into SAP BW, configure the data retrieval for transaction data: actual and plan. In the following example, the actual data is retrieved from SAP R/3 with higher granularity; the plans data is retrieved from an interface file with lower granularity.

3.4.2 Setting Up the DataSource in SAP R/3

SAP R/3 CO-PA requires customer and application-specific DataSources. This requirement stems from the flexibility of profitability analysis, because every company can set up the structures to meet to its own needs.

Accordingly, you must set up a specific DataSource in the SAP R/3 source system. To do so, you can branch from the **Source System** view of the Administrator Workbench (Transaction RSA13) in SAP BW to the SAP BW-specific implementation guidelines in SAP R/3. Alternatively, you can open the menu after logging on directly to SAP R/3 with **Transaction SBIW**. In the Implementation Guide (IMG), use the menu path **Settings for Application-Specific DataSources Profitability Analysis Create Data-Source** to start the function (see Figure 3.43, Step 1).

Setting Up the DataSource

In the initial screen, select the **Operating concern** (S_GO) and the type (here: **Costing-based**), the technical name of the DataSource, and the **Function** ("Create," see Figure 3.43, Steps 2–4), before you activate the settings (see Figure 3.43, Step 5).

Specify a descriptive text and select the fields in the maintenance screen (see Figure 3.44, Steps 1–3). The next step involves the alignment of the InfoObjects (see Figure 3.44, Step 4). Depending on the system settings, creating the required ABAP Workbench objects requires that you assign each object to a development class and create a transport request. The assignment is relevant for a possible transport of the settings from an SAP R/3 development system into an SAP R/3 production system (see Figure 3.44, Steps 5–10).

Next, you can set up selection fields for the DataSource. Select the fields in the **DataSource: Customer version Edit** screen (see Figure 3.45, Steps 1–3).

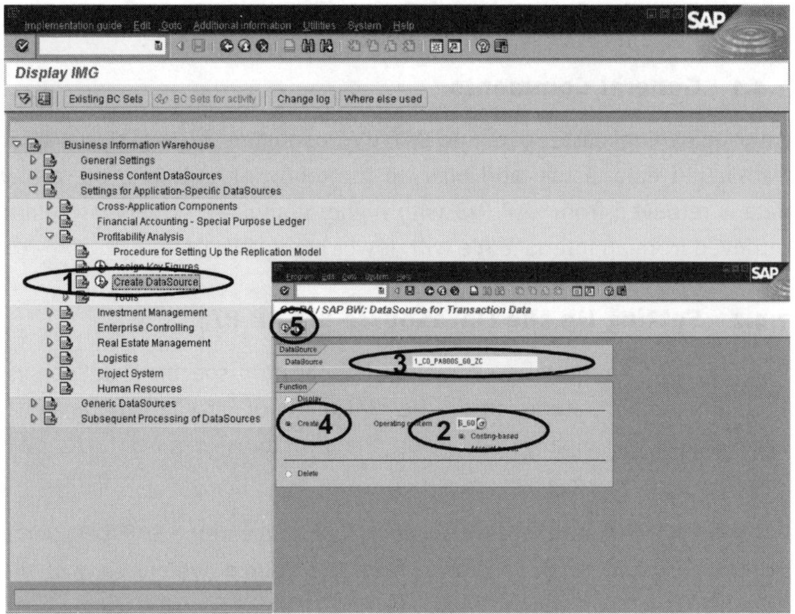

Figure 3.43 Creating Application-Specific DataSources

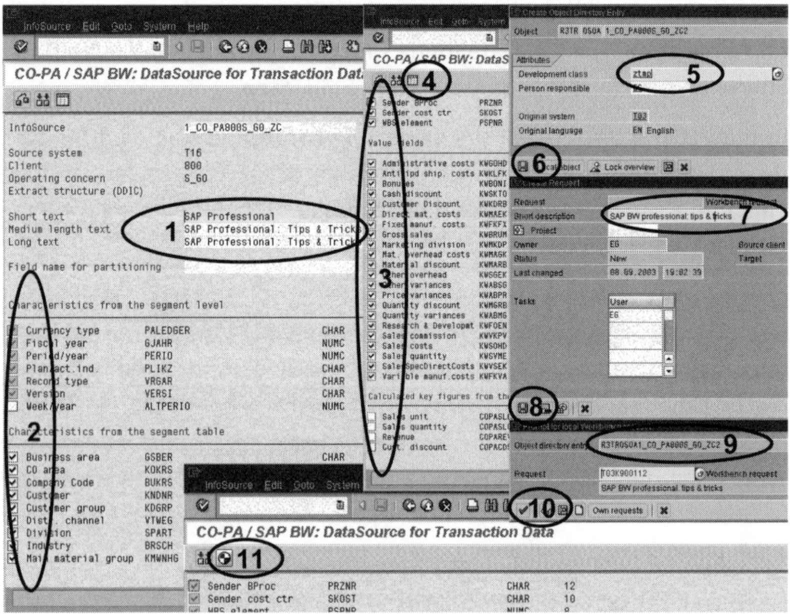

Figure 3.44 Selecting the Fields of the DataSource

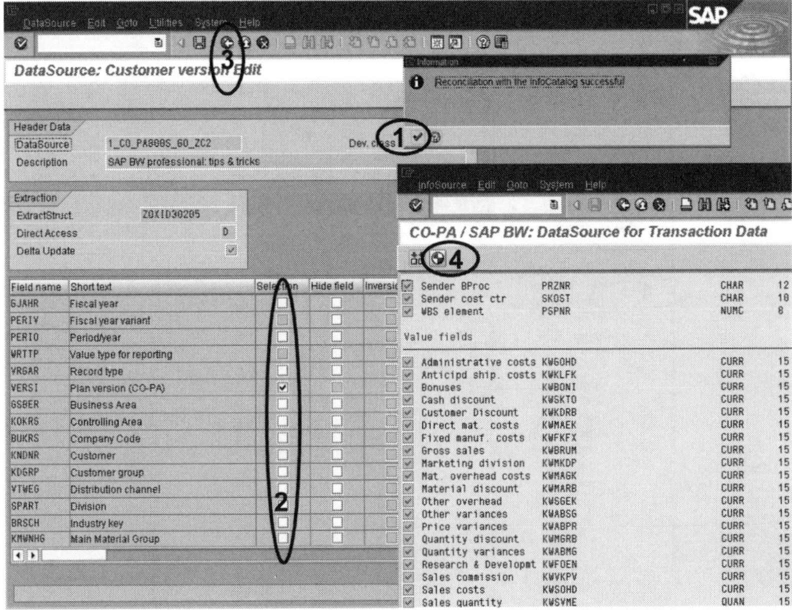

Figure 3.45 Selecting the Selection Fields

After you return to the field selection screen, the **Generate** button is displayed. Click on the button to complete the creation of the application-specific DataSource (see Figure 3.45, Step 4). After you click on the button, the DataSource is set up in the source system. Click on the **Back** button several times (or use the **F3** key) to return to SAP BW.

3.4.3 Replicating the DataSource in SAP BW

DataSource replication

The DataSource that you just created in SAP R/3 is, as yet, unknown to SAP BW. To use the DataSource, the DataSources in the source systems must be replicated in SAP BW. You can do this in the **Source systems** view of the Administrator Workbench (Transaction RSA13). Right-click on "IIT IDES transaction system" to open the context menu; then, select **DataSource Overview** (see Figure 3.46, Step 1). You can now open the hierarchy of DataSources to **Profitability Analysis**. Right-click on **Profitability Analysis** to open the context menu and select **Replicate DataSources** (see 3.46, Steps 2 and 3). After replication is finished, the DataSource hierarchy is updated and the newly created DataSource is available in SAP BW (see Figure 3.46, Step 4).

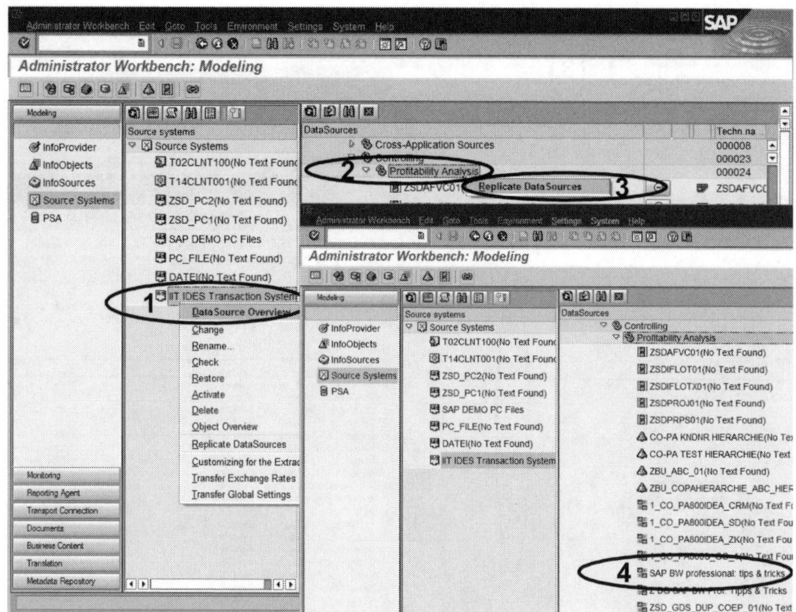

Figure 3.46 Replication of the DataSource

3.4.4 Creating the InfoSource with Transfer Rules

You must assign the newly created DataSource to an InfoSource in SAP BW. The following sample application also creates a new InfoSource for the assignment.

Assigning the InfoSource

From the **Source systems** view (Transaction RSA13 or RSA1O in the Administrator Workbench), select the overview of **DataSources** of the corresponding SAP R/3 source system (see Section 3.4.3): the DataSource tree is positioned to display the previously created and replicated CO-PA DataSource. Use the content menu or button (see Figure 3.47, Step 1) to select **InfoSource Assignment**.

The **InfoSource for DataSource** popup opens. SAP BW proposes an InfoSource of the same name as the DataSource. Confirm the proposal (see Figure 3.47, Step 2). Then, in the following **Save Changes?** Popup, click on **Yes** when prompted to confirm the assignment (see Figure 3.47, Step 3).

Proposing transfer rules

SAP BW then creates an InfoSource and records the transfer structure of the DataSource in the InfoSource. You must now maintain the transfer rules in the **InfoSource...Change** maintenance screen based upon this foundation: use the **Propose Transfer Rules** button (see Figure 3.48, Step 1). You must accept the note about the warning message (see Figure

3.48, Step 2) before you can activate the InfoSource with the proposed transfer rules (see Figure 3.48, Step 3).

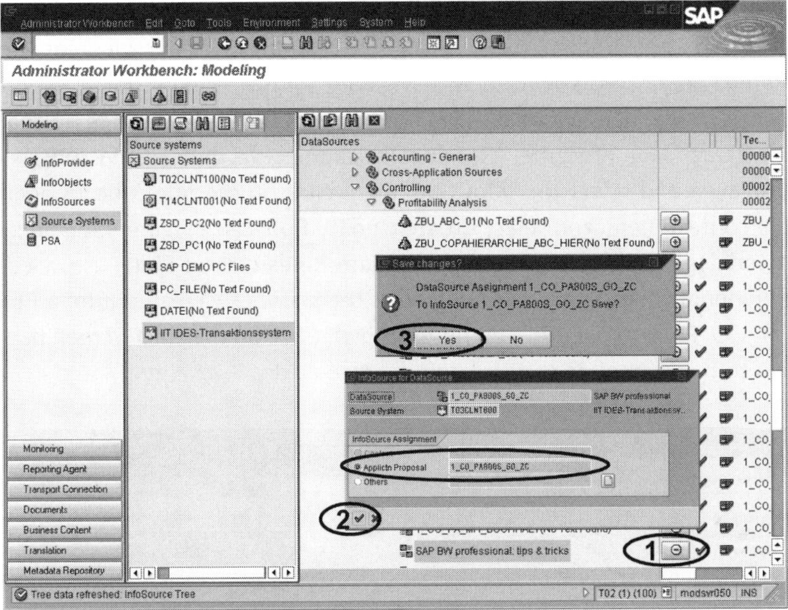

Figure 3.47 Assigning a DataSource to an InfoSource

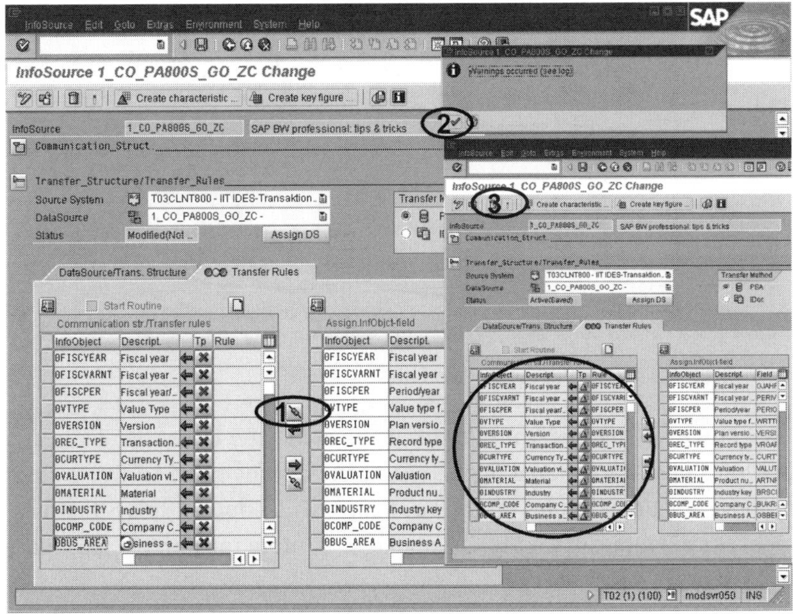

Figure 3.48 Creating the Transfer Rules and Activating the InfoSource

3.4.5 Creating the Update Rules

Update rules must be created to update an InfoCube. The following sample application creates identical rules, each with a user exit and a formula.

Creating update rules

To set up the update rules, change to the **InfoProvider** view of the Administrator Workbench (by navigating in the Administrator Workbench or via Transaction **RSA11**). Position the InfoProvider tree so that the actual data InfoCube, "Result calculation actual data (ZCBWTIPP1) is displayed and select the InfoCube. Right-click on the InfoCube to open the context menu and select **Create Update Rules** (see Figure 3.49, Steps 1 and 2). In the selection screen, **Update Rules create: Start**, use selection help to select or type the name of the previously created InfoSource ("1_CO_PA800S_GO_ZC" in this example). Click on the **Next Screen** button to begin creating the update rules (see Figure 3.49, Steps 3 and 4).

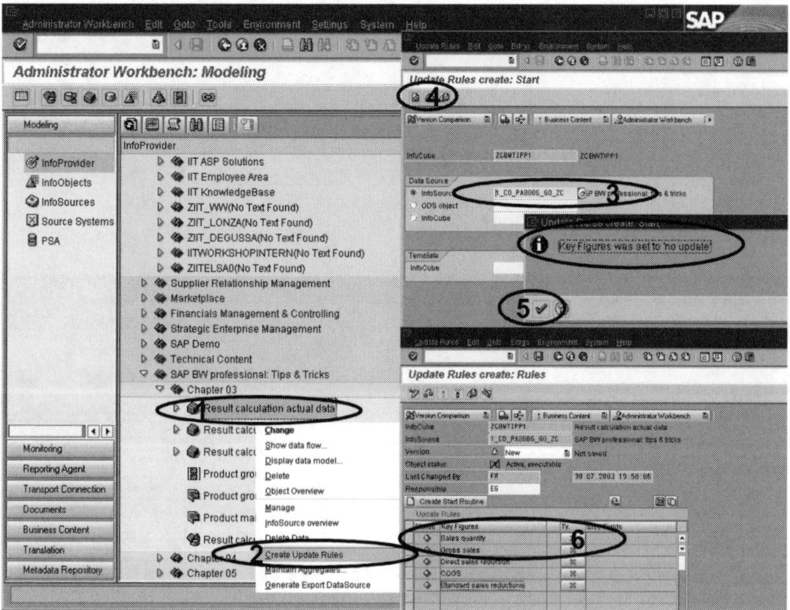

Figure 3.49 Calling Creation of Update Rules

The source key figures from the InfoSource and the target key figures in the InfoCube are unequal in the example. Accordingly, SAP BW cannot propose any update rules for the key figures. The popup displays the message, "Key Figures was set to 'no update:'" confirm the popup (see Figure 3.49, step 5).

The maintenance screen, **Update Rules create: Rules**, is displayed next. Double-click on a key figure to create an update rule (see Figure 3.49, Step 6).

Update method: source key figure

Double-click on the key figure "sales quantity" (see Figure 3.50, Step 1) to display the **Update Rule: Detail** popup. Set the type of update rule in this popup by selecting the radio button **Addition** (see Figure 3.50, Step 2). Doing so makes the key figure relevant to the update. The next step sets the foundation of which source the update is to follow. Select the update method with the **Source Key Fig** radio button (see Figure 3.50, Step 3). Now you can select the source key figure. Open the drop-down list for **Source Key Fig** (see Figure 3.50, Step 4) and double-click on the key figure "Sales quantity" in the selection list that appears in the InfoObject popup (see Figure 3.50, Step 5). The source key figure is then transferred into the corresponding field.

For the sample application, accept the proposed update rules for the characteristic. Every characteristic from the InfoSource is thus assigned to the identical characteristic in the InfoCube (see Figure 3.50, Step 6).

Update rules: time reference

Transfer of the proposed rules is insufficient for the time characteristic. As you can see in the **Time Ref.** tab, no update rules are proposed for several time characteristics (see Figure 3.51, Step 3).

You must set up the rules manually: use the **Initial** button. In the **Change Source** popup, click on the **Source Chars** radio button in the source field to set it to a source characteristic (see Figure 3.51, Step 4). Next, select the source field: use the drop-down box for the source field (see Figure 3.51, Step 5) and double-click on characteristic 0BILL_DATE in the selection list in the **Source InfoObject** popup (see Figure 3.51, Step 6). The source field is then transferred to the corresponding field (see Figure 3.51, Step 7). Then, transfer the setting by clicking on the **Execute** button (see Figure 3.51, Step 8).

In the **Copy Source Characteristic** popup, confirm the question "Do you want to transfer the source characteristic for this characteristic to all key figures rules?" (see Figure 3.51, Step 9) by clicking on **Yes**. The source characteristic is transferred into the update rules (see Figure 3.51, Step 10).

You must make these settings for all default time characteristics (see Figure 3.52, Step 1). The settings are then transferred (see Figure 3.52, Step 2).

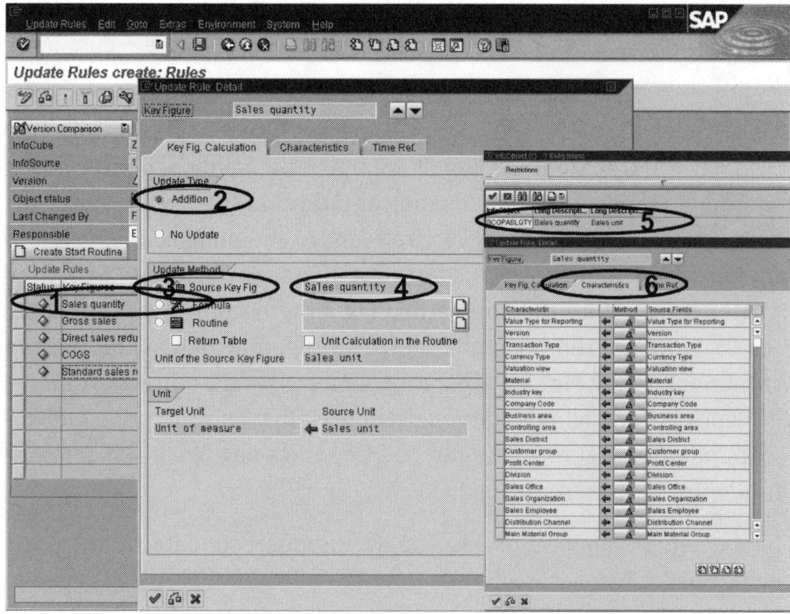

Figure 3.50 Assigning the Source Key Figure to the Target Key Figure and Transferring the Proposed Rules for the Characteristics Combination to the Key Figure

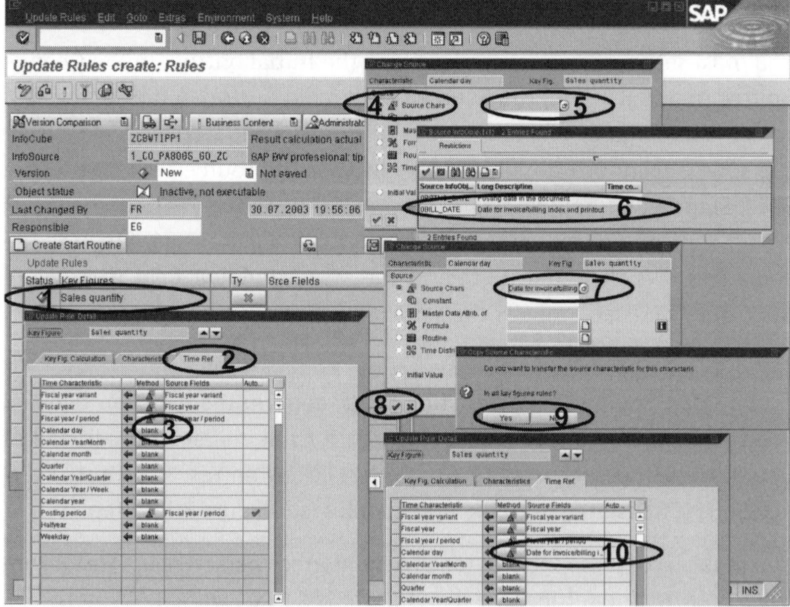

Figure 3.51 Supplementing the Update Rules for the Time Characteristic

The key figure "Sales quantity" is now set up completely. A green traffic light is displayed if all the characteristics for the identical units (currencies and quantity units) are updated correctly. Otherwise – as in the example – a yellow traffic light is displayed (see Figure 3.52, Step 3): The source and target units differ in the example (see Figure 3.50). You work with the key figure "net sales" in the same way: here the source key figure "revenue" (0COPAREVEN) is assigned.

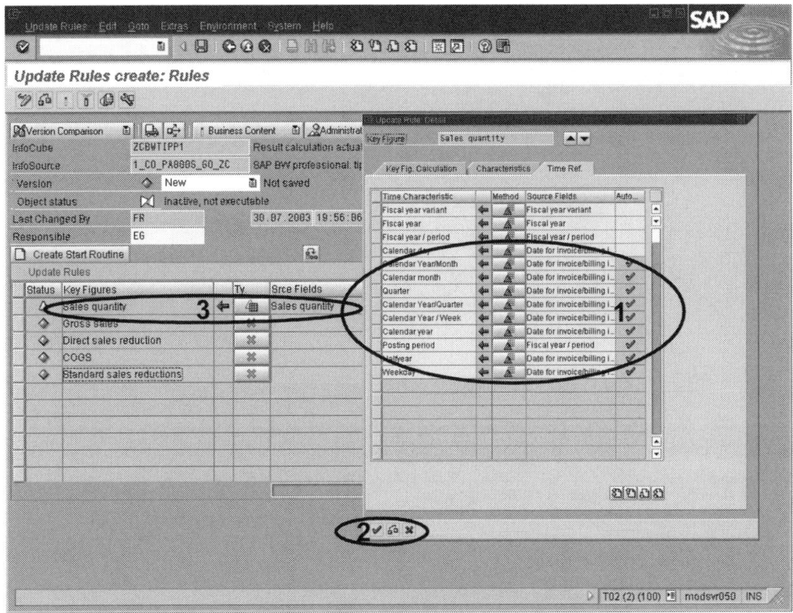

Figure 3.52 Complete Setup of the Update for the Key Figure "Sales Quantity"

Various discounts must be added up and negated for direct revenue losses. You can do so with the formula function. Start maintenance of the update rules by double-clicking on the key figure "Direct sales reduction" (see Figure 3.53, Step 1).

Update method: formula

In the **Update Rule Detail** popup, set the update method to formula and then select the **Formula** radio button (see Figure 3.53, Steps 2 and 3). Enter a description of the formula in the **Form Create** popup and then confirm your entry (see Figure 3.53, Step 4).

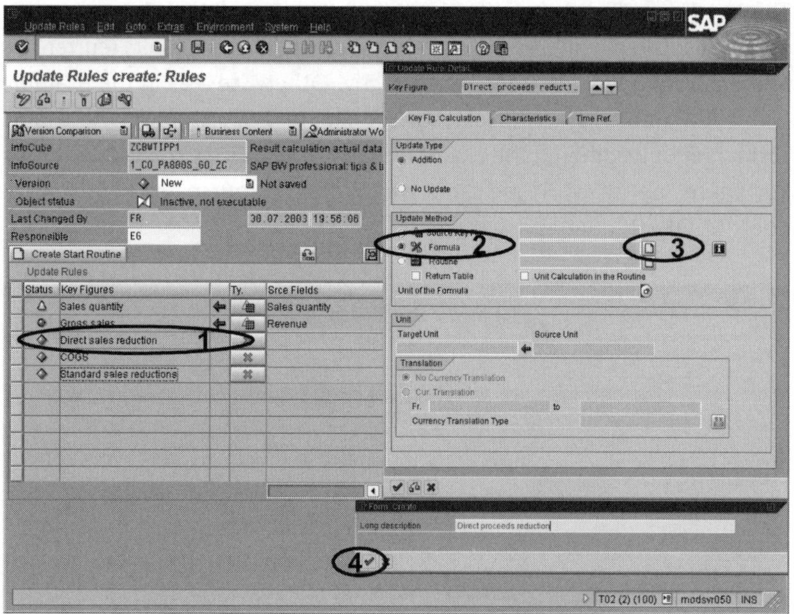

Figure 3.53 Formula Maintenance

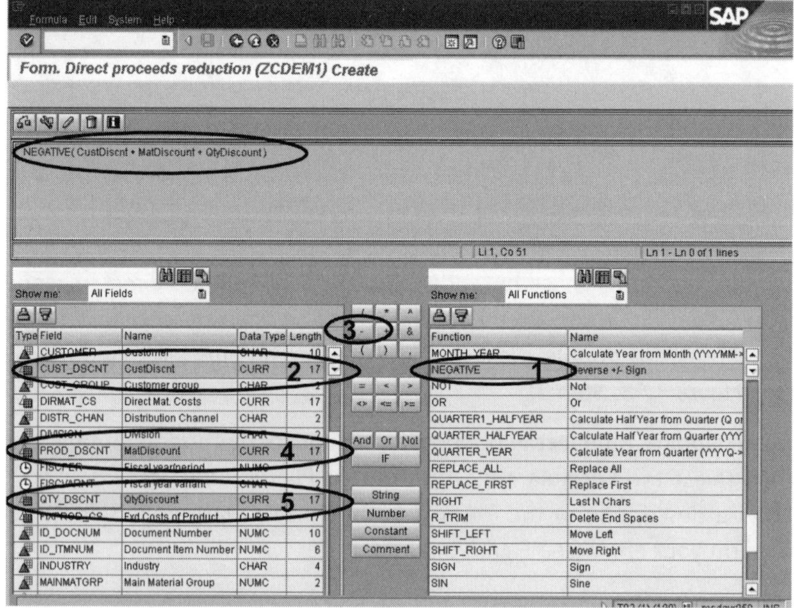

Figure 3.54 Formula: Negating the Sum of the Discounts

In the **Form. Direct proceeds reduction...Create** maintenance screen, you can now combine various functions. To negate the amounts, double-click on the **NEGATIVE** function (see Figure 3.54, Step 1). The formula window then displays:

NEGATIVE ( )

Double-click on the key figure "CustDiscnt" (see Figure 3.54, Step 2). The formula window then displays:

NEGATIVE (CustDiscnt)

To add the various discounts, click on the addition function. (see Figure 3.54, Step 3). The formula window then displays:

NEGATIVE (CustDiscnt +)

Continue as above for the key figures "MatDiscount" and "QtyDiscount" until you have defined the complete discount (see Figure 3.54, Steps 4 and 5).

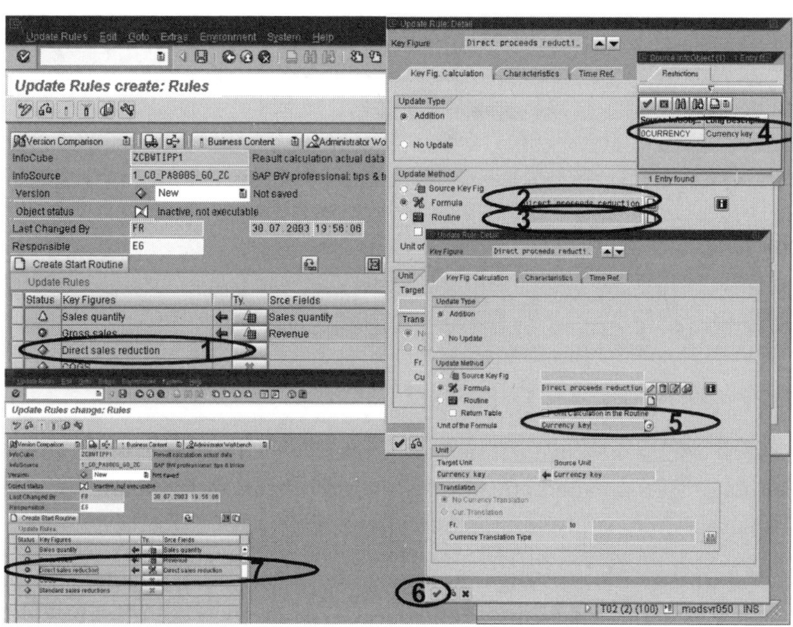

Figure 3.55 Assigning the Currency Key

Use the **Back** button (or **F3**) to transfer the formula into the update rules (see Figure 3.55, Step 2). The definition of the formula has not yet determined a unique currency key. To do so, open the drop-down box for the unit of the formula (see 3.55, Step 3). Select the currency key, 0CURRENCY, in the **Source InfoObject** popup (see Figure 3.55, Step 4). Then, transfer this selection into the update rules (see Figure 3.55, Step 5).

You can now confirm and transfer the completely defined update rule (see Figure 3.55, Steps 6 and 7).

You can create a formula for the "production full costs" in a similar manner (see Figure 3.56):

NEGATIVE (Fxd Costs of Product + Var. Production Cost)

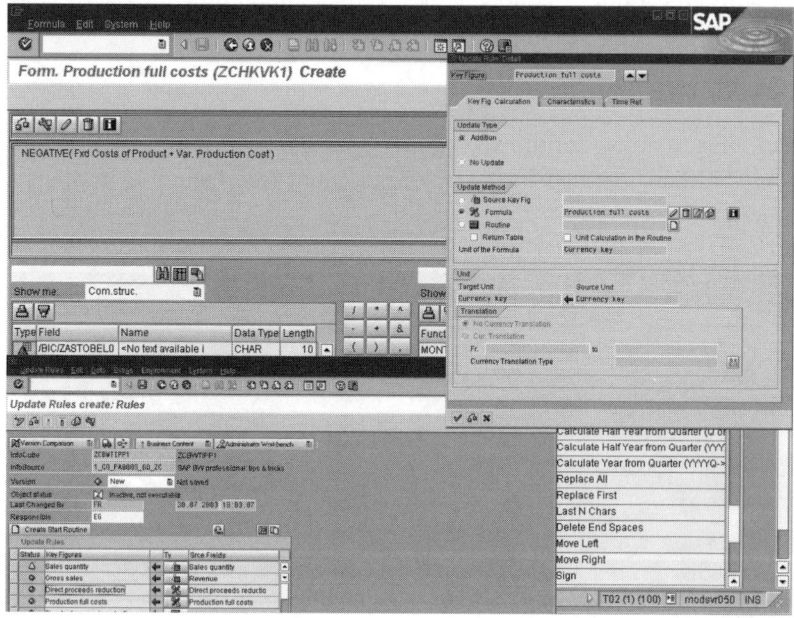

Figure 3.56 Formula for Production Costs

Several source key figures must also be totaled for standard proceeds reductions. As an alternative to the solution that uses formulas, you can also use a user exit. An example follows.

In the **Update Rules change: Rules** maintenance screen, double-click on the key figure **Standard proceeds reductions** to open the **Update Rule: Detail** popup. Select the **Addition** radio button for the update type (see Figure 3.57, Steps 1 and 2).

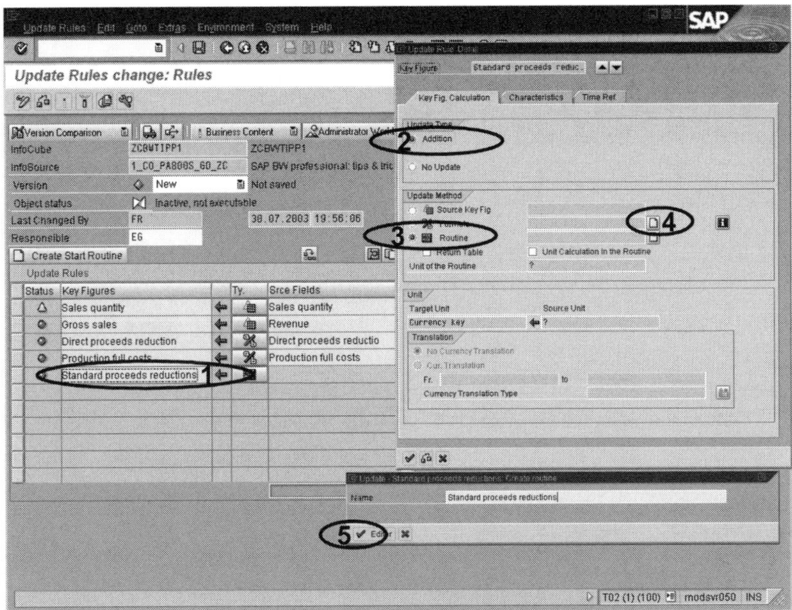

Figure 3.57 Preparation for the Creation of a User Exit

Update method: routine

Select the **Routine** radio button and **Routine** button for the update method (see Figure 3.57, Steps 3 and 4). Enter the description of the routine in the **Update...Create Routine** popup and then click on the **Editor** button to start the routine editor (see Figure 3.57, Step 5).

Both standard proceeds reductions noted in the example, the key figures "cash discount" and "freight costs," are added (as negatives) in the editor:

```
RESULT = – COMM_STRUCTURE-CASH_DSCNT –
COMM_STRUCTURE-ACCRDFR_CS.
```

According to SAP ABAP, the technical names of the fields are created from the name of the structure (here: COMM_STRUCTURE for the communication structure) and the field names – separated by a hyphen. You can determine the relevant field names by double-clicking on the name of the Dictionary structure (/BIC/CS1_CO_PA800S_GO_ZC in the example).

Now you enter the formula into the Routine Editor and save the routine (see Figure 3.58, Steps 1 and 2). Doing so closes the Routine Editor and returns you to the **Update Rule: Detail** popup: enter the routine there (see Figure 3.58, Step 3). Confirm the settings with the **Transfer** button; the **Update Rules change: Rules** screen is redisplayed. Then, you can activate the update rules (see Figure 3.58, Steps 4–6).

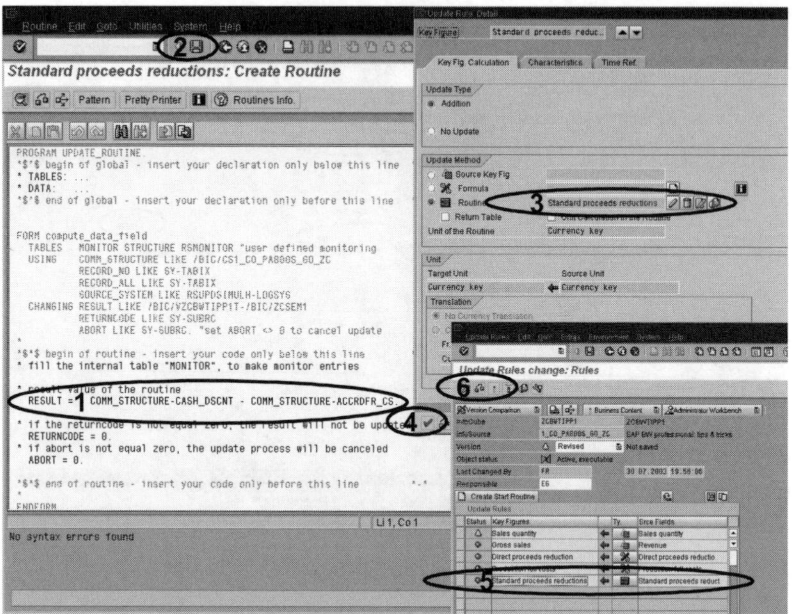

Figure 3.58 Creating a Routine in the Update Rules

3.4.6 Creating and Executing the InfoPackage for the Actual Data

After you return to the **InfoProvider** view of the Administrator Workbench with the **F3** key or the **Back** button, you can change to the **InfoSources** view to set up the InfoPackage to execute retrieval of transaction data.

Creating an InfoPackage for SAP R/3 data

Highlight the SAP R/3 source system beneath the transaction data InfoSource (see Section 3.4.4). Then, right-click to open the context menu and select **Create InfoPackage...** (see Figure 3.59, Steps 1 and 2). Specify the description of the InfoPackage in the **Create InfoPackage** popup and click on the **Save** button (Figure 3.59, Steps 3 and 4).

If necessary, you must select the data to be requested: you can use a field value to do so. This particular example sets up a complex request. Because the SAP R/3 CO-PA data is to provide only actual data, select the "version" source field. However, the version for actual data in SAP R/3 CO-PA is "empty" (it contains three spaces). But you cannot select spaces by entering the value directly because no selection and the selection of the value would be identical). Accordingly, you must make your selection with a routine in this case.

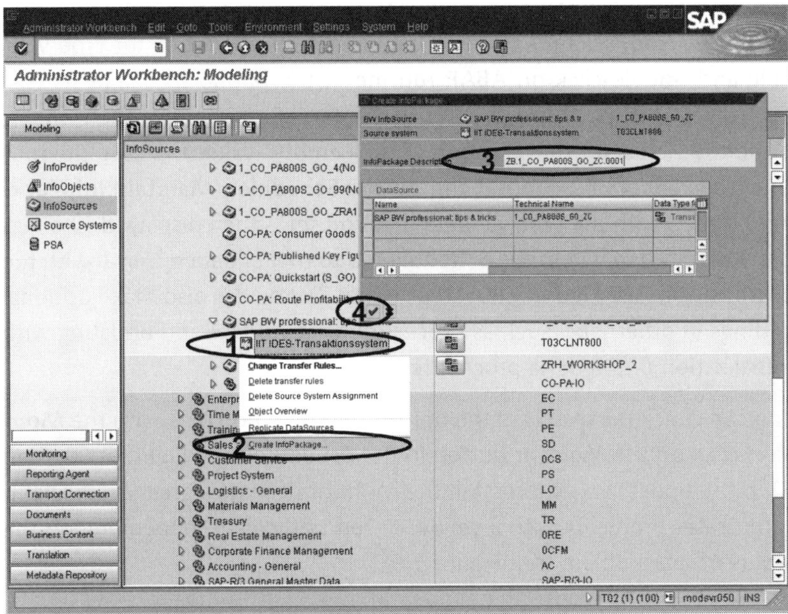

Figure 3.59 Creating an InfoPackage for Transaction Data

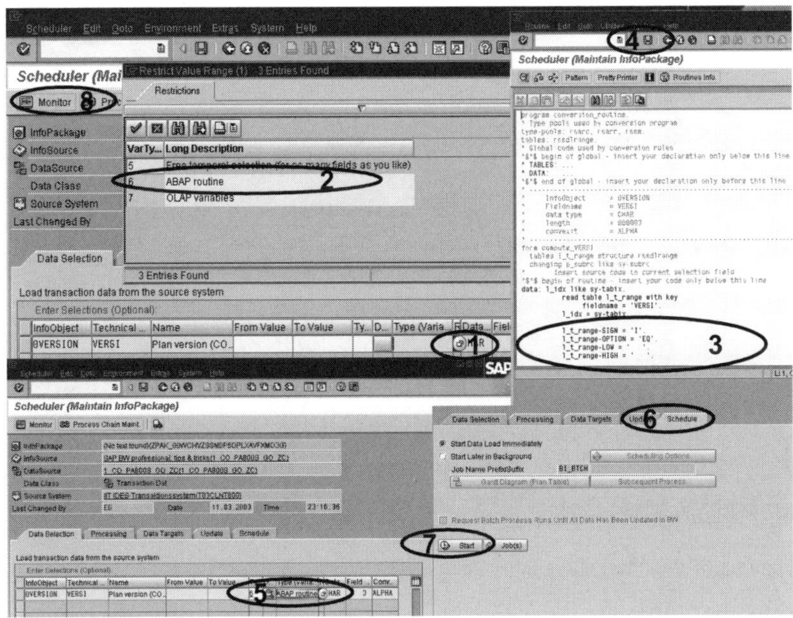

Figure 3.60 Definition of an InfoPackage with Selection via a User Exit

InfoPackage: selecting data via an ABAP routine

You set up the selection from the **Data Selection** tab in the **Scheduler (Maintain InfoPackage)** screen. Open the drop-down box for type variable and double-click on **ABAP routine** in the popup that appears (see Figure 3.60, Steps 1 and 2). The Editor for ABAP routines then opens. Code the syntax for the selection of the "empty" value and save the routine (see Figure 3.60, Steps 3 and 4). The **Scheduler (Maintain InfoPackage)** screen with the type variable that you set is then displayed (see Figure 3.60, Step 5). Go to the **Schedule** tab to trigger data retrieval with the **Start** button (see Figure 3.60, Steps 6 and 7). You can also make optional settings in other tabs, such as processing without PSA and updating with initialization of the delta procedure.

You can check the results of the upload of transaction data with the **Monitor**: click on the **Monitor** button in the **Scheduler** (see Figure 3.60, Step 8). If the update was successful, the Monitor displays a green traffic light. It indicates problems with a yellow or red traffic light, depending on the status of the problem (see Figure 3.61).

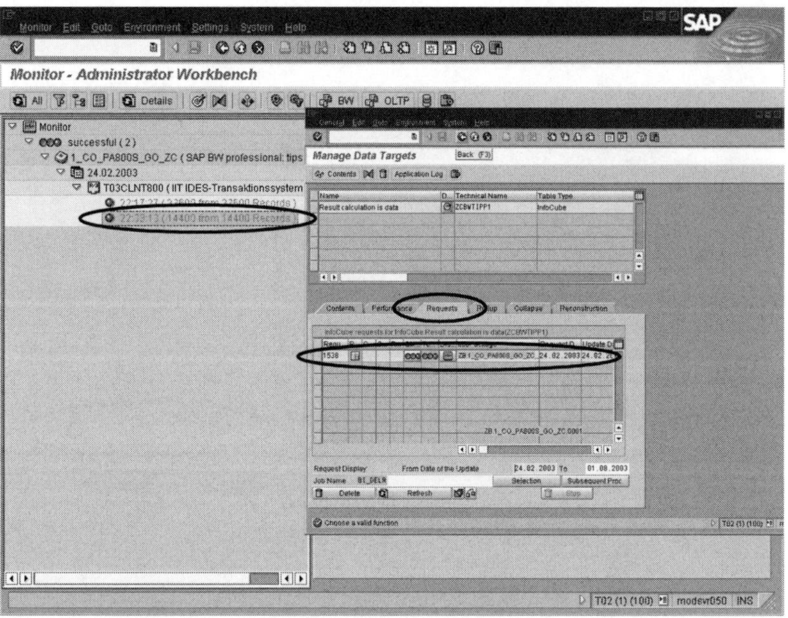

Figure 3.61 Monitoring for Transaction Data

Managing the data targets

The results of the update are also displayed in the InfoCube into which the data has been loaded. Select the InfoCube in **InfoProvider** view of the **Administrator Workbench**. Right-click to open the context menu and select **Manage**. The result is indicated by a traffic light in the **Requests** tab of the **Manage Data Targets** screen (see Figure 3.61).

3.5 Uploading Plan Data from a File

3.5.1 Creating the InfoSource with a Transfer Structure and Transfer Rules for the Plan Data

The following example makes plan data available with an interface file. You must update the InfoCube for the plan data. Table 3.5 illustrates the structure of the interface file.

Column	Field
1	Fiscal year variant constant K4
2	Fiscal year/period as YYYYPPP: 2000001, for example
3	Calendar year/month as YYYYMM: 200001, for example
4	Version, here: plan version 000
5	Value type, here plan 020
6	Currency type, here company code currency B0
7	Company code
8	Business area
9	Country
10	Region
11	Product group
12	Gross revenues
13	DEM
14	SEM
15	HKVK
16	Sales quantity
17	Currency
18	Quantity unit

Table 3.5 Structure of the Interface File for Plan Data

Transaction data InfoSource: assigning the source system

As in the procedure you followed to retrieve master data from interface files (see Section 3.3.2), open the context menu in the **InfoSources** view of the Administrator Workbench (Transaction RSA12) by right-clicking on the application component and select **Create InfoSource** (see Figure 3.62, Steps 1 and 2). Enter the technical name and description in the **Create InfoSource** popup for flexible updating. After the entry has been transferred (see Figure 3.62, Step 3), the InfoSource is created in the Administrator Workbench (see Figure 3.62, Step 4). Right-click on the InfoSource you just created to open the context menu, and then select **Assign DataSource** (see Figure 3.62, Step 5). Enter the source system, **SAP_DEMO**, once again in the **Transaction Data—InfoSource: Assign Source System** popup and confirm the entry (see Figure 3.62, Steps 6 and 7). Click on **Yes** in the **Save Changes?** popup (see Figure 3.62, Step 8).

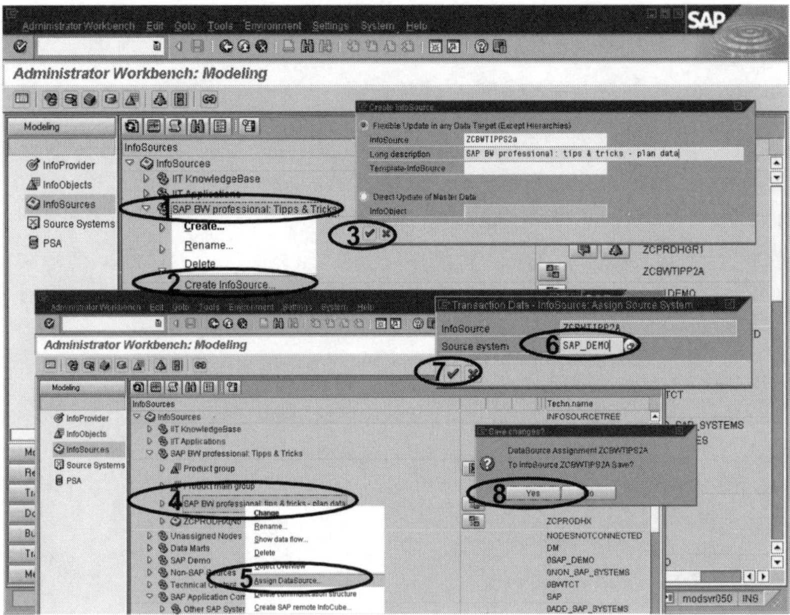

Figure 3.62 Creating an InfoSource for the Upload of Transaction Data and Assigning a DataSource

Defining a transfer structure for transaction data

Because the source system of type "file interface" with manually defined metadata does not contain any information on the file and the transfer structure, you must define the structure manually in the InfoSource. After you confirm the last popup in the assignment of the DataSource, the **InfoSource...Change** maintenance screen is displayed. You can set the column structure of the interface file there by listing the InfoObjects (see Figure 3.63, Steps 1 and 2).

Once you have entered all the InfoObjects, you can confirm the entries with the Return key. Reference InfoObjects are inserted automatically: accept them (see Figure 3.63, Steps 3 and 4). The transfer structure is now defined completely (see Figure 3.63, Step 5). Now you can go to the **Transfer Rules** tab (see Figure 3.64, Step 1).

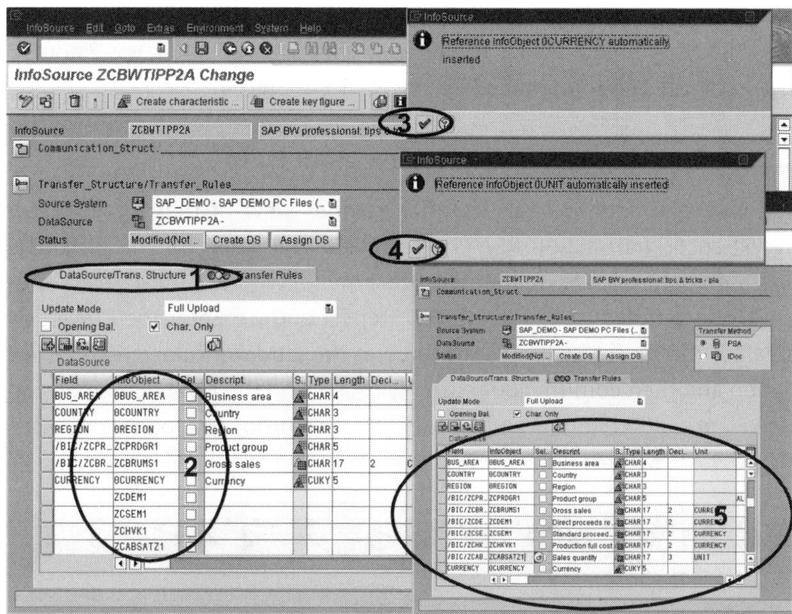

Figure 3.63 Definition of the Transfer Structure for a File

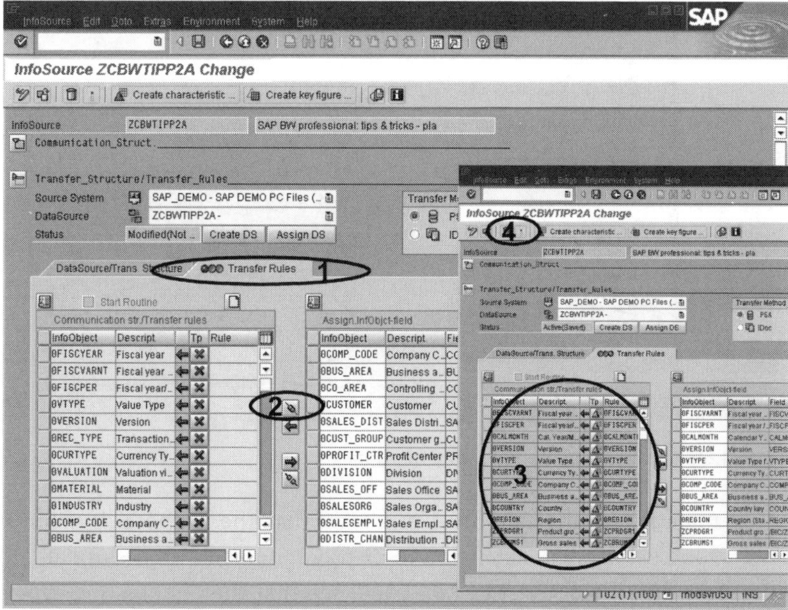

Figure 3.64 Defining Transfer Rules for Transaction Data

After you click on the **Propose Transfer Rules** button, SAP BW generates the rules "target field equals source field" (see Figure 3.64, Steps 2 and 3). Then activate the InfoSource (see Figure 3.64, Step 4).

3.5.2 Creating Update Rules for Plan Data

Creating update rules for plan data

You create update rules in the **InfoProvider** view of the Administrator Workbench (Transaction RSA11). Select the InfoCube for the plan data and then right-click to open the context menu, where you can select **Create Update Rules** (see Figure 3.65, Steps 1 and 2). Enter the previously created InfoSource as the data source in the **Update Rules create: Start** screen and then confirm your entry by clicking on the **Next Screen** button (see Figure 3.65, Steps 3 and 4). SAP BW then proposes update rules (see Figure 3.65, Step 5).

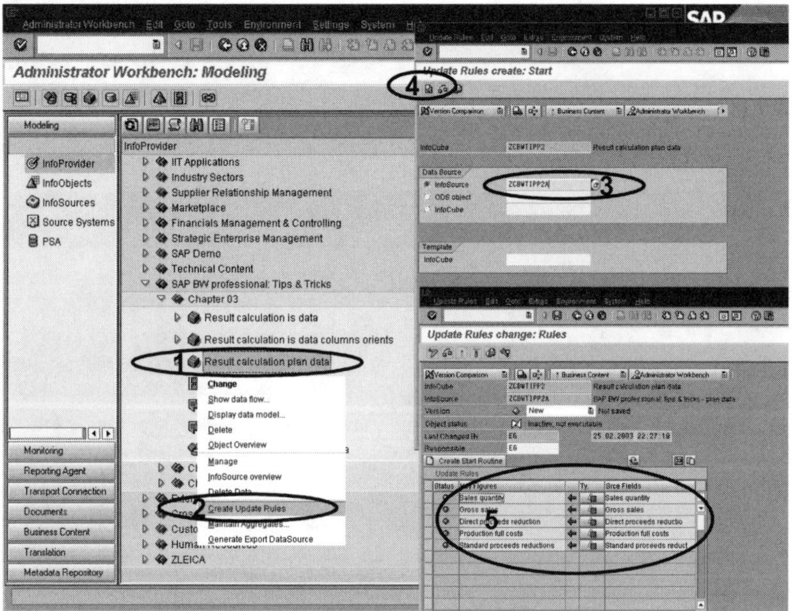

Figure 3.65 Creating Update Rules for Plan Data

Update rules: changing the source

An examination of the update rules shows that the proposal is incomplete. Double-click on a key figure to display the details on the update. If you select the **Characteristics** tab, you'll see that the "Transaction Type" characteristic lacks an update (see Figure 3.66, Steps 1 and 2). Use the **Initial** button to display the **Change Source** popup. Because the interface file in the example contains only billing data, you can select the **Constant** radio button in the popup (see Figure 3.66, Step 3). Open the drop-down box (see Figure 3.66, Step 4) to InfoHelp for the transaction type.

Select Transaction Type **F** and confirm the selection (see 3.66, Steps 5 and 6). The selection is transferred into the **Change Source** popup: confirm the change (see Figure 3.66, Steps 7 and 8). After you answer **Yes** to the question in the **Copy Source Characteristic** popup, the update rules are complete (see Figure 3.66, Steps 9 and 10). You must also confirm the **Update Rule: Detail** popup, after which you can activate the update rules (see Figure 3.66, Step 11).

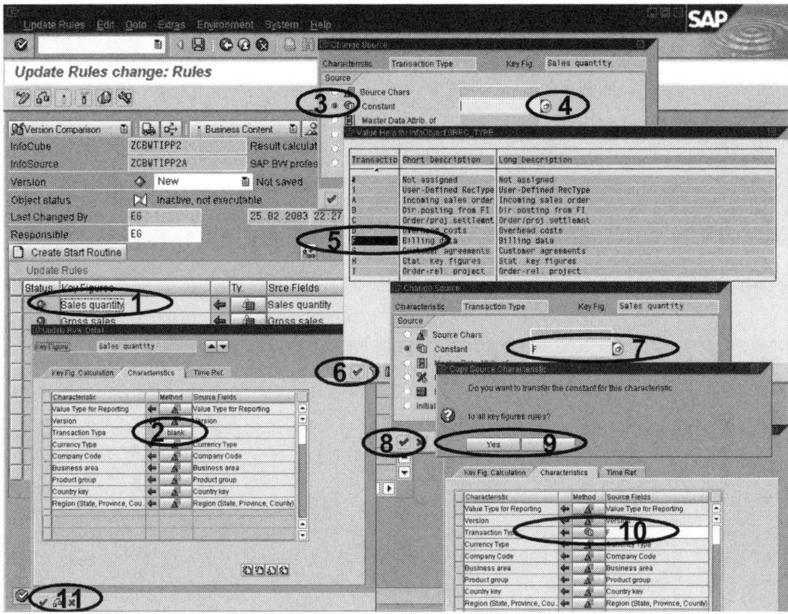

Figure 3.66 Enhancing the Update Rules

3.5.3 Creating and Executing the InfoPackage for Plan Data

As was the case for data retrieval, the InfoPackage is created from the **InfoSources** view of the Administrator Workbench, (Transaction RSA12).

Creating the InfoPackage for plan data

Select the DataSource and then open the context menu for the InfoSource for the plan data. Then select **Create InfoPackage** (see Figure 3.67, Steps 1 and 2). Enter a description in the **Create InfoPackage** popup and then activate it (see Figure 3.67, Step 3). In the **Scheduler (Maintain InfoPackage)** screen, select the **External data** tab, where you enter specifications of the interface file (see Figure 3.67, Steps 4–7).

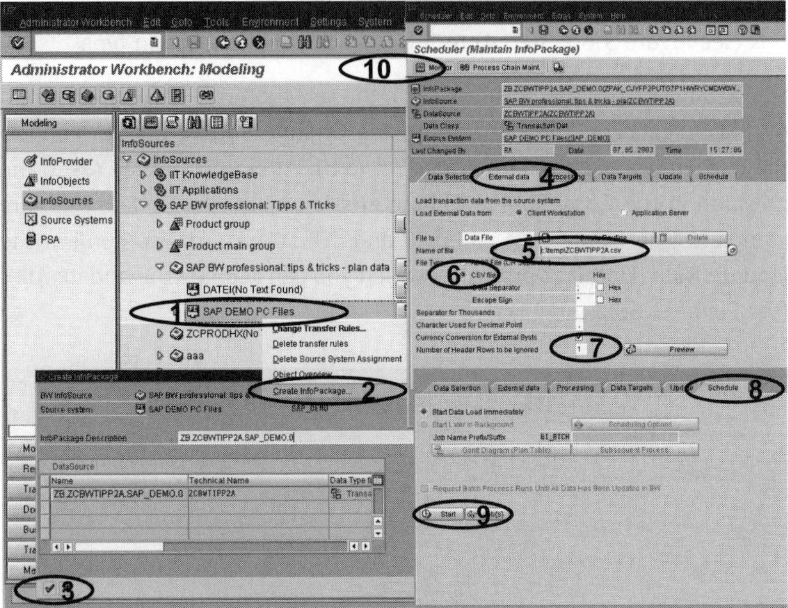

Figure 3.67 Creating an InfoPackage for Plan Data

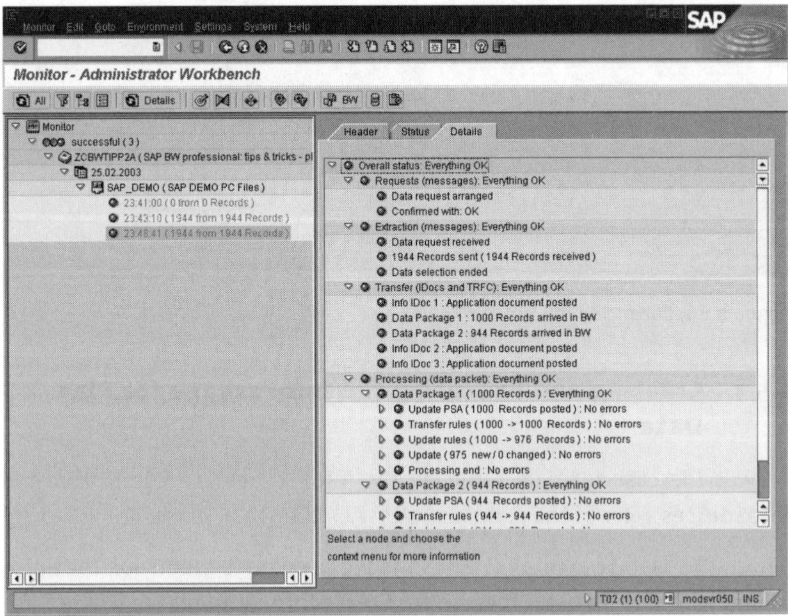

Figure 3.68 Monitoring the Update of the Plan Data

Switch to the **Schedule** tab (see Figure 3.67, Step 8), where you begin the upload with the **Start** button (see Figure 3.67, Step 9). You can check the success of the update with the **Monitor** (see Figure 3.67, Step 10, and Figure 3.68).

Starting an InfoPackage for plan data

3.6 Creating an SAP Business Explorer Query

Once data been retrieved and after it has been stored in SAP BW, you can analyze the data with queries from SAP Business Explorer (SAP BEx). You create queries with the BEx–Query Designer.

This tool is a PC application that you can start from the menu, as a link, or directly (executable file: **wdbrlog.exe**: see Figure 3.69, Step 1). First, you must log on to SAP BW: enter your user ID and password, then click on the **OK** button (see Figure 3.69, Steps 2 and 3).

Starting the Query Designer

You then start the Query Designer. To configure a new query, select the button with the same name (see Figure 3.69, Step 4). In the **Open Query** popup, select **InfoAreas**. Doing so displays the InfoArea tree and the associated InfoProviders. Expand the tree to display the InfoProvider that you want to use and then select the InfoProvider. Confirm your selection by clicking on the **OK** button (see Figure 3.69, Steps 5–7).

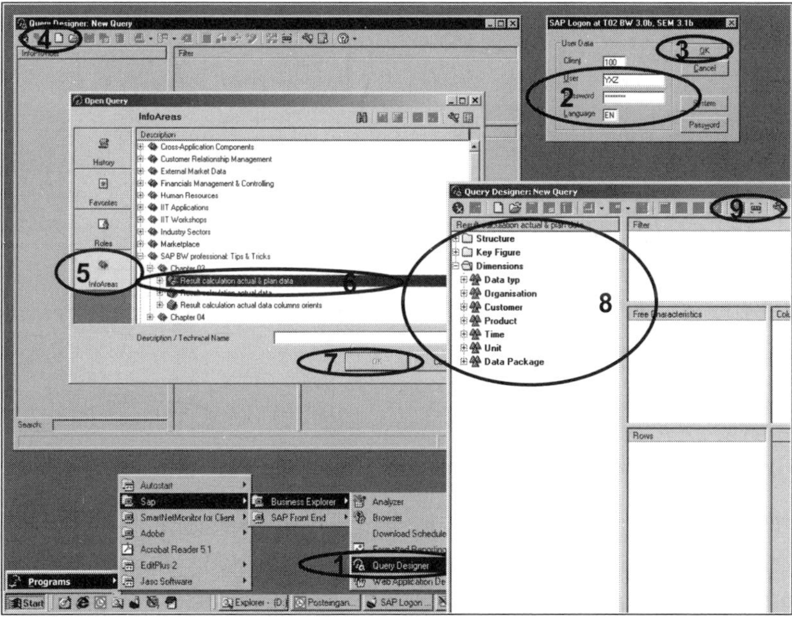

Figure 3.69 Starting SAP Business Explorer–Query Designer

Query Designer: technical name

The InfoProvider is then displayed in the Query Designer (see Figure 3.69, Step 8). Select the Technical Name button to display the SAP BW key (see Figure 3.69, Step 9 and the following figures).

Transferring InfoObjects into the Query

To select the InfoObject, click on the exclamation point icon (!) to open the object tree in the left frame (see Figure 3.70, Step 1). You can drag and drop the required InfoObjects into the frames for filter values, free characteristics, rows, and columns (see Figure 3.70, Steps 2–5).

Formulas

To calculate the net sales ("gross sales ./. direct sales reductions") and marginal income ("net sales ./. standard sales reductions ./. COGS"), you must define formulas. Right-click on the key figures node to open the context-sensitive menu. Then, select **New Formula** (see Figure 3.70, Step 6).

You then use drag and drop to select the key figures and the operator in the **Edit Formula** popup (see Figure 3.70, Steps 7–10). Click on the **OK** button to close the definition (see Figure 3.70, Step 11).

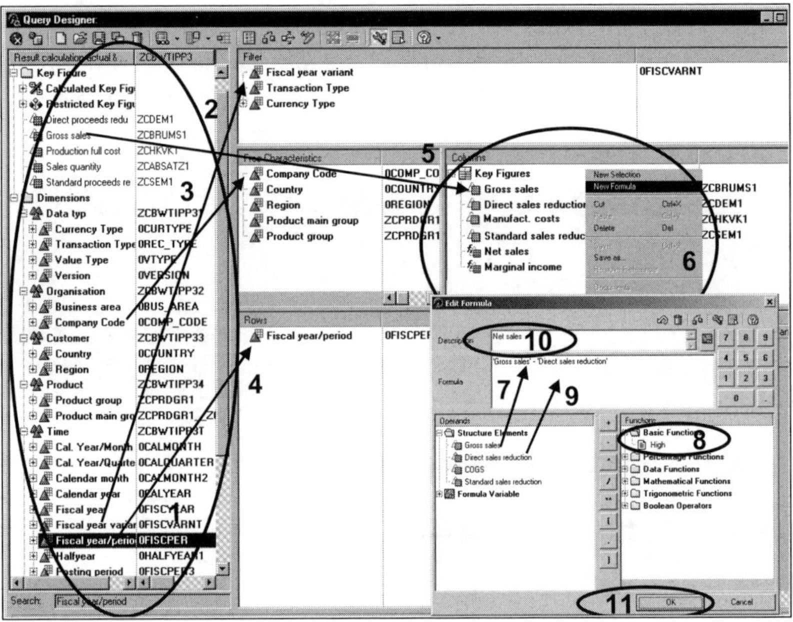

Figure 3.70 Configuration of the Query, Part 1: Defining Elements

The procedure is repeated for the "marginal income" formula. Now two calculated key figures are available for the query, along with the key figures from the InfoCube.

The sample query should not display the key figures from the InfoCube. Right-click on the key figure that you want to hide, and in the context menu that opens, select **Properties** (see Figure 3.71, Step 1). In the **Properties of the Selection/Formula** popup, check the **Hide** box and confirm your choice by clicking on the **OK** button (see Figure 3.71, Steps 2 and 3). Repeat the procedure for the other key figures: DEM, HKVK, and SEM.

Hiding a key figure

When you return to the overview of the Query Designer, the hidden key figures are marked accordingly (see Figure 3.71, Step 4).

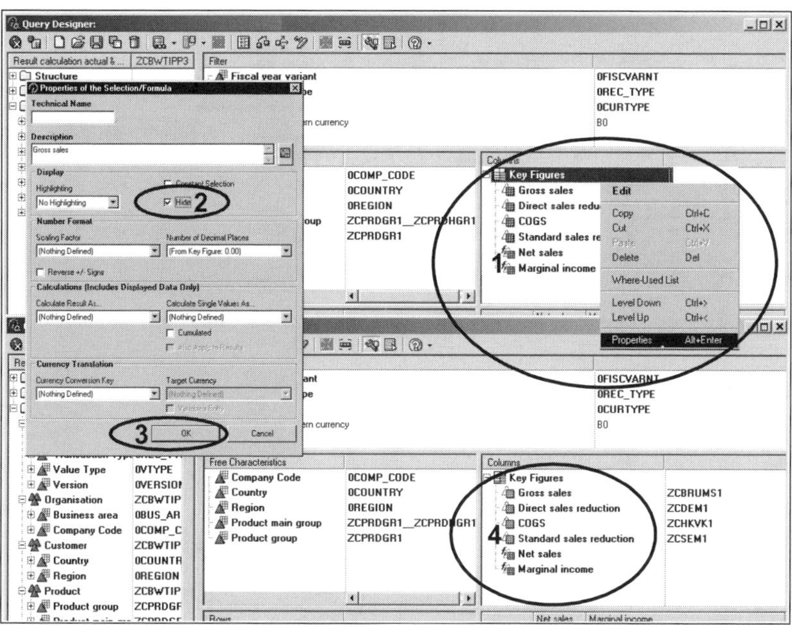

Figure 3.71 Configuration of the Query, Part 2: Hiding Elements

Because we need to enable a plan–actual comparison for the remaining key figures, we will require a structure with selections of the value type. Right-click on the **Columns** title to open the context menu and select **New Structure** (see Figure 3.72, Step 1).

Structure

The query definition then displays an empty structure (see Figure 3.72, Step 2). Here too, you open the context menu and select **New Selection** (see Figure 3.72, Step 3). In the **New Selection** popup, you can drag and drop the "Value Type" characteristic into the **Description** frame and then start the characteristic with the **Restrict** command in the context menu (see Figure 3.72, Steps 4 and 5).

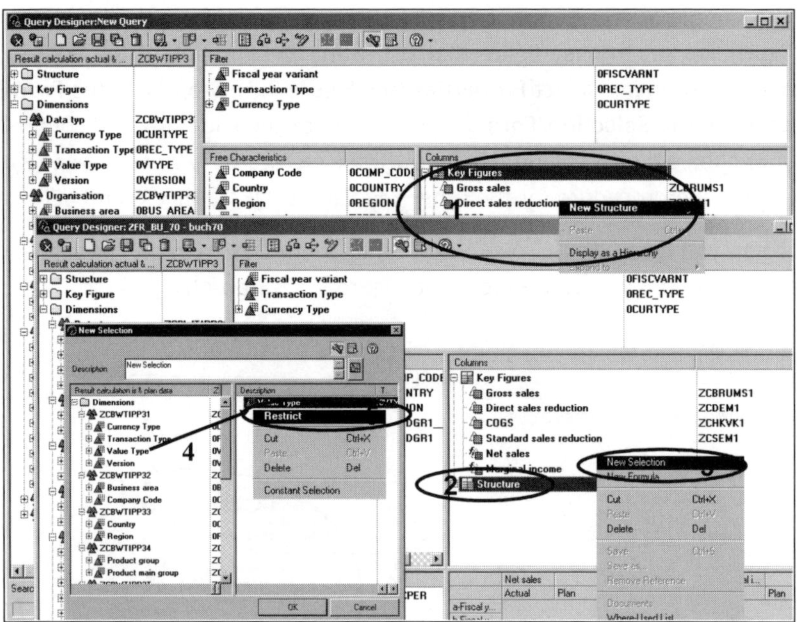

Figure 3.72 Configuration of the Query, Part 3: Structure and Selection

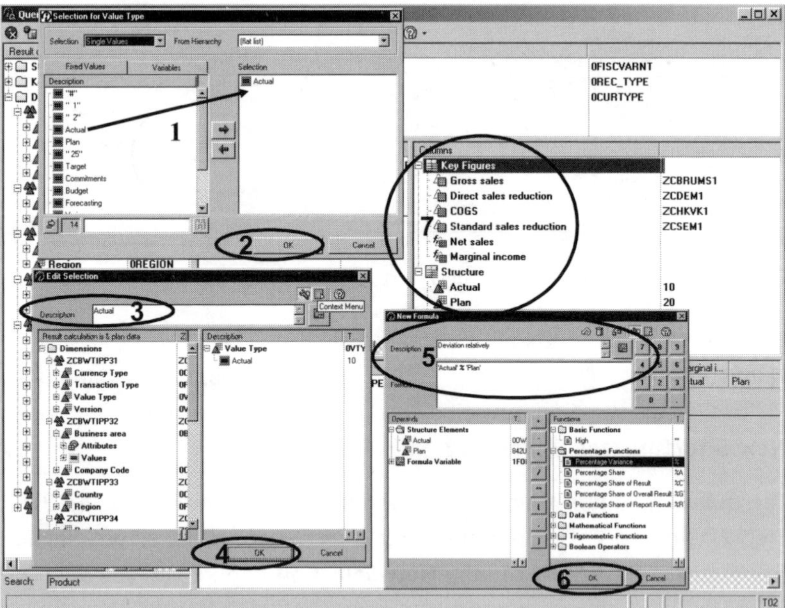

Figure 3.73 Configuration of the Query, Part 4: Formulas (Absolute and Relative Deviation) for the "Actual" and "Plan" Structure Elements

Restricting

In the **Selection for Value Type** popup, drag and drop the selection of the "Actual" value type into the **Selection** frame and confirm the selection with the **OK** button (see 3.73, Steps 1 and 2). The restriction is then transferred to the **Edit Selection** popup, where you can describe the selection and close the entire definition with the **OK** button (see Figure 3.73, Steps 3 and 4). Create a second selection for the "plan" of InfoObject "value type."

Formula: percentage variance

You calculate the absolute and relative plan–actual variance by defining formulas in the structure and using the selections. To calculate the relative deviation, right-click on the structure to open the context menu and select **New Formula**. Then, drag and drop the "Actual" and "Plan" elements and the "Percentage variance" operand into the new formula. Describe the formula and then click on the **OK** button to transfer the query definition (see Figure 3.73, Steps 5 and 6).

Use a similar procedure for the absolute plan–actual comparison. A minus sign (-) is used as the operand. Now, all the elements of the column have been defined. Because the "Net sales" and "Marginal income" formulas are to be displayed directly next to the absolute and relative deviation, you must drag and drop the structure under the key figures (see Figure 3.73, Step 7).

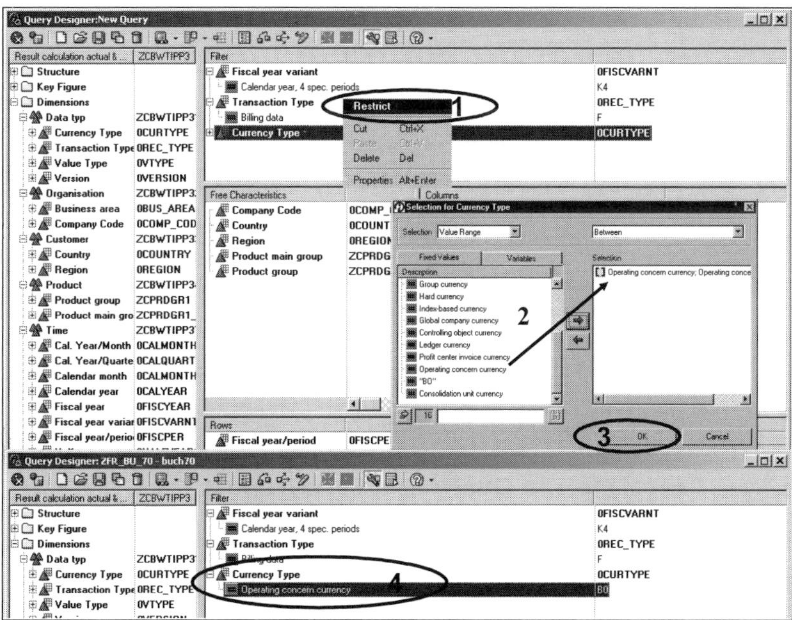

Figure 3.74 Configuration of the Query, Part 5: Filters

Filters You can make preselections for the query as restrictions on the InfoObjects in the **Filter** frame. Right-click to open the context menu and select **Restrict**. You now work just as you did with the restrictions described previously. After configuration, the restrictions are displayed in the **Filter** frame beneath the InfoObjects (see Figure 3.74, Steps 1 and 4).

Saving the query Saving and storing the query in a role completes its configuration. Save the query with the **Save** button (see Figure 3.75, Step 1). Select the role into which you want to insert the query in the **Save Query As...** popup (see Figure 3.75, Steps 2 and 3). Enter the description and technical name of the role and then complete the definition by clicking on the **Save** button (see Figure 3.75, Steps 4 and 5). All authorized users of SAP BW can now use the query.

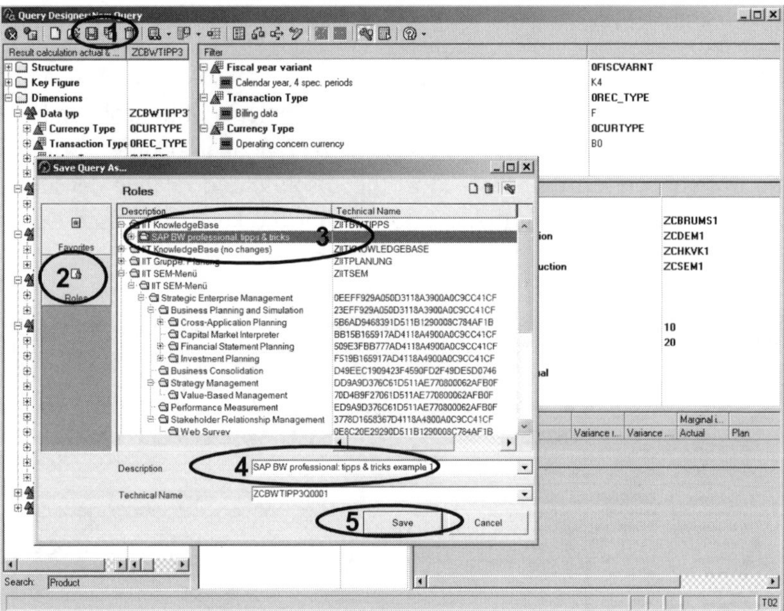

Figure 3.75 Configuration of the Query: Part 6: Saving

3.7 Executing the Query

3.7.1 Executing the Query as a Web Report

The queries are available for use as Business Explorer (BEx) Web Reports and in the Excel-based BEx Analyzer. As of SAP BW 3.0, Web Reporting is the standard medium.

You can call a report in various ways: consider the following two examples. First, the query definition is started in the HTML browser with the **Display Query on the Web** button (see Figure 3.76, Step 1). Secondly, you can produce the same result by selecting the query in the corresponding role in the **SAP GUI** and double-clicking on it (see Figure 3.76, Step 2).

Display the query in the browser

When you start the query directly, it automatically uses the default template stored in SAP BW for the layout (see the depiction of the query in the HTML browser in Figure 3.76).

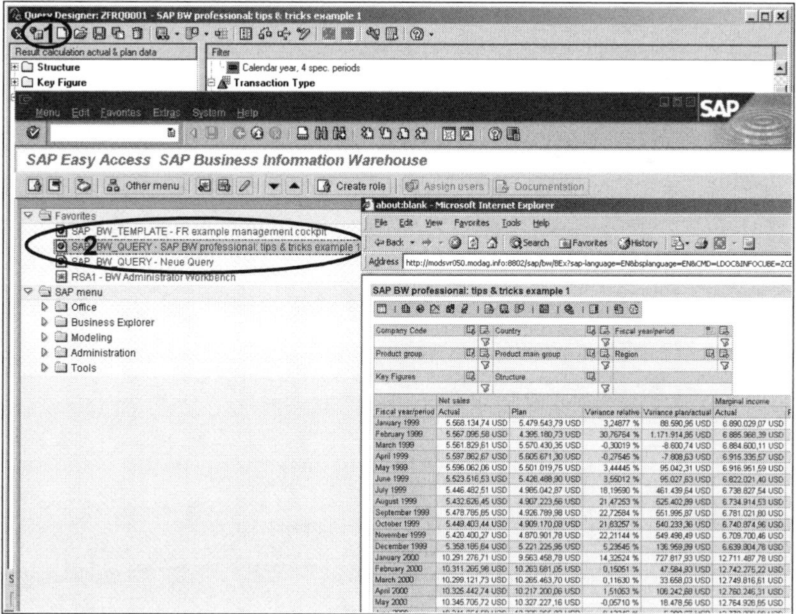

Figure 3.76 Calling the Query from the Query Designer and from the SAP GUI

The standard template already offers several functions. When displaying the query, you can select the **Filter Value for...** popup by using the **Select Filter** button to select a complex set of filter values (see Figure 3.77, Steps 1 and 2). Make your selections and transfer them with the **Transfer** button. When using dynamic selection, the query will be updated (see Figure 3.77, Steps 3 and 4).

Selecting filter values

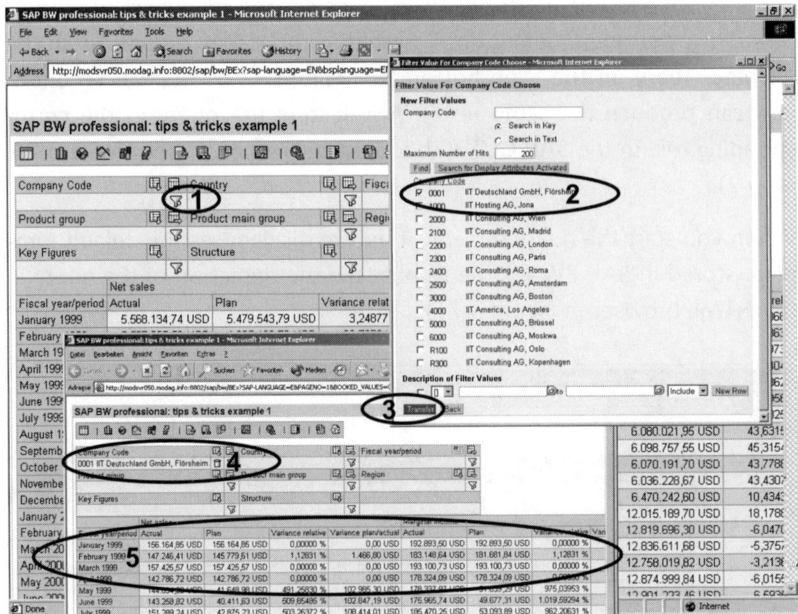

Figure 3.77 Filter of Characteristics Properties

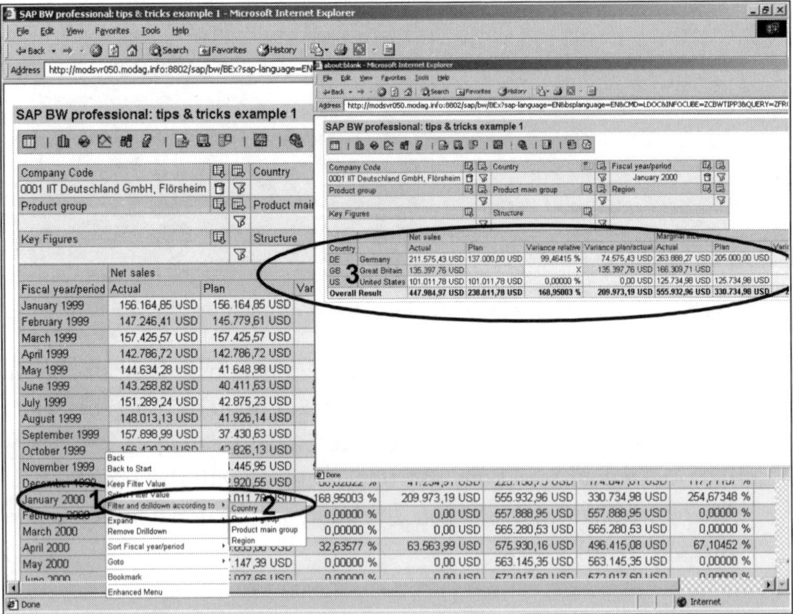

Figure 3.78 Filter and Drilldown

You can also filter the displayed values dynamically by drilling down according to free characteristics. Select the value to be filtered and open the context menu (see Figure 3.78, Step 1). Select the **Filter and drill-down according to** command in the context menu and then select the new drilldown characteristic from the list of available characteristics in the submenu (see Figure 3.78, Step 2). The query is then updated according to the new entries (see Figure 3.78, Step 3).

Filter and drill-down according to...

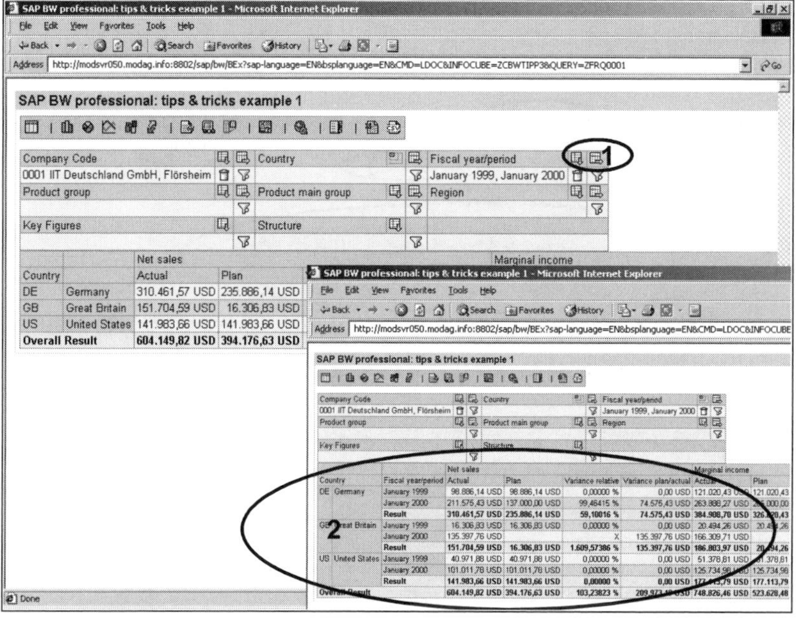

Figure 3.79 Several Leading Columns

Several leading columns

Click on the Drill Down Into Rows button to insert additional leading columns (see Figure 3.79, Step 1).

Currency translation

In addition to the basic commands available in the simple **Functions** menu, you can use additional commands in the expanded menu. Consider dynamic currency translation as an example. To do so, open the context menu and select **Enhanced Menu** (see Figure 3.80, Steps 1 and 2). SAP BW opens the enhanced menu, where you can select **Currency Translation** (see Figure 3.80, Step 3).

You can then select the target currency and the translation type in the **Currency Translation** popup. When you transfer the settings by clicking on the **Transfer** button, the display is updated with the new settings (see Figure 3.80, steps 4–6).

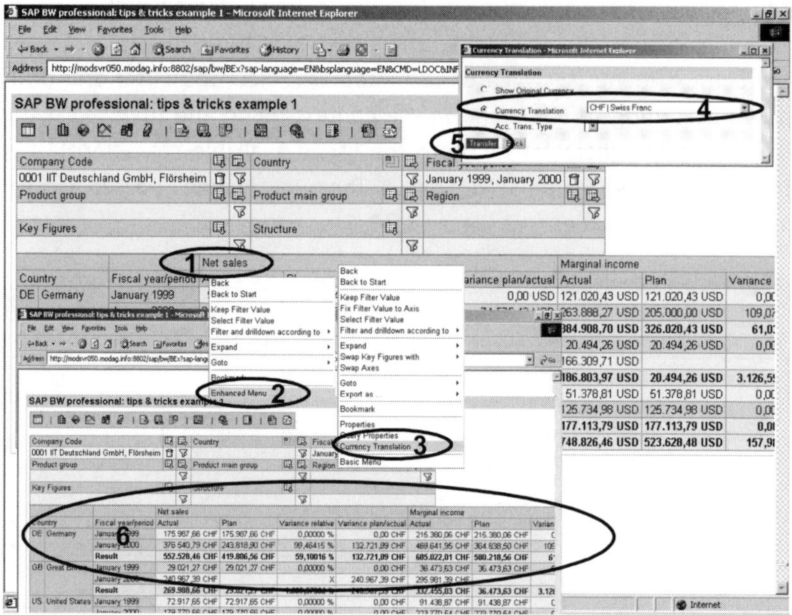

Figure 3.80 The Enhanced Menu: Sample Currency Translation

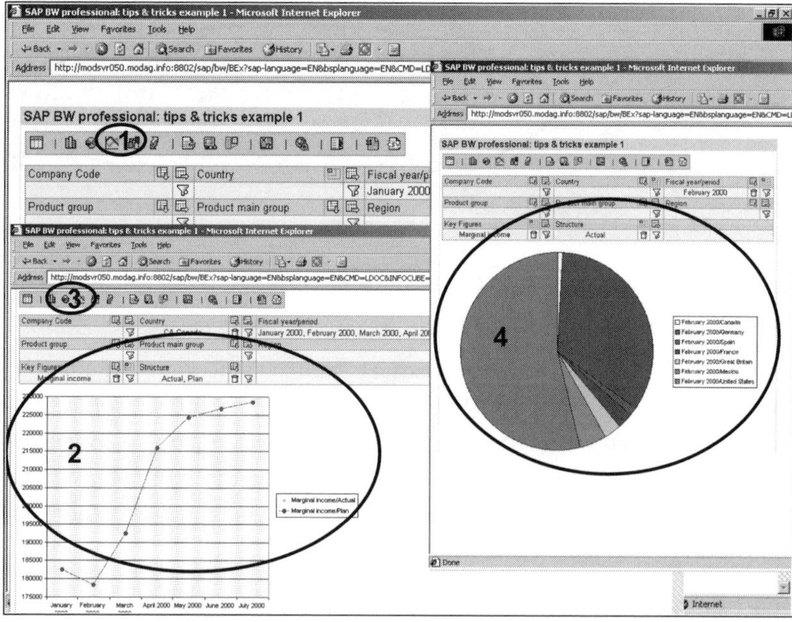

Figure 3.81 Charts with Dynamic Navigation

You also have additional options with the use of graphics. Use the **Chart** button to display the current selection (the selected filters, characteristics, and key figures) as a chart (see Figure 3.81, Step 1 or 2). As with most navigation options in tables, right-click to trigger filters and navigation. Graphics

3.7.2 Executing the Query in Microsoft Excel

When you call Microsoft Excel, SAP BEX Analyzer starts proprietary SAP macros that enable you to access SAP BW.

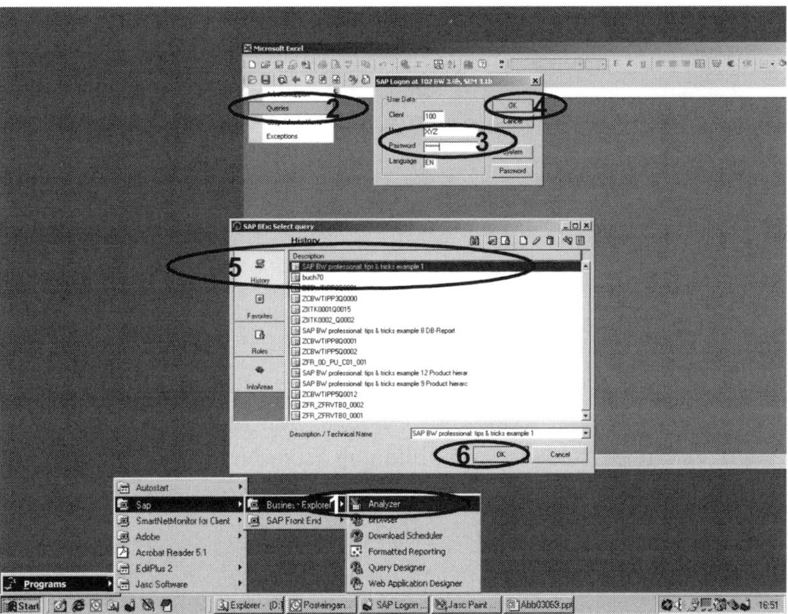

Figure 3.82 Starting SAP Business Explorer Analyzer

This tool is a PC application that you can start from the menu, as a link, or directly (executable file: **sapbex.xla**: see Figure 3.82, Step 1). Click on the **Open** button and select **Queries** from the popup menu (see Figure 3.82, Step 2). Then log on to SAP BW: enter your user ID and password and then confirm the logon by clicking on the **OK** button (see Figure 3.82, Steps 3 and 4). Mark the query that you want to execute in the **SAP BEx: Select query** popup (see Figure 3.82, Step 5). The query starts after you click on the **OK** button (see Figure 3.82, Step 6).

The navigation options in BEx Analyzer are similar to those options for Web Reporting, without the limitations of the MS Excel solution. Executing a query in SAP BEx

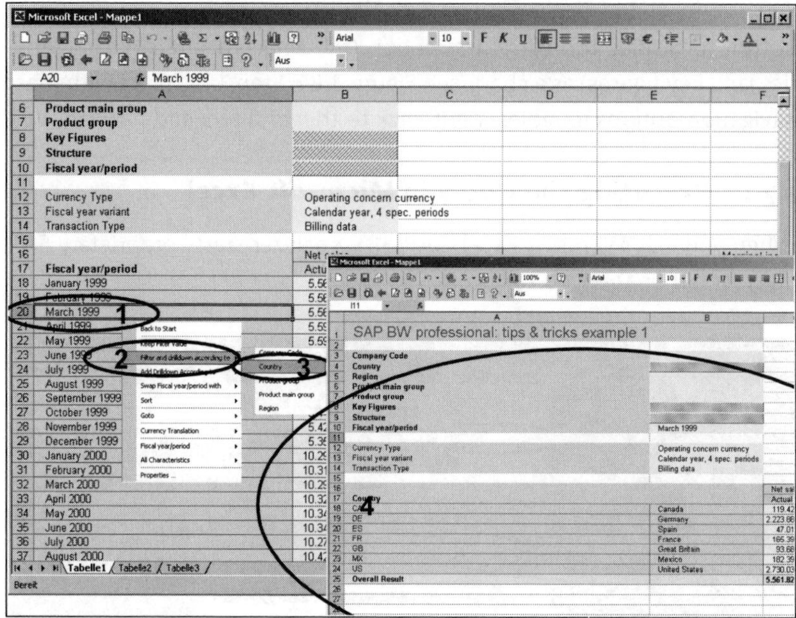

Figure 3.83 Displaying the Query in BEx Analyzer

The essential difference is that you generally activate context-sensitive navigation via right- clicking. For example, you right-click to open the context menu for the **Filter and drilldown according to...** command, just as you did with Web Reporting (see Figure 3.83, Steps 1–3). The display is then updated (see Figure 3.83, Step 4).

Part 3
Data Modeling and Data Retrieval

4 Data Modeling and Conversion from a Column-Oriented Info-Source to an Account-Oriented InfoCube

The mapping of facts in account-oriented data models offers greater flexibility than the column-oriented approach and can enable OLAP-compatible data modeling. In this chapter, we'll discuss the advantages and disadvantages of both methods, and outline a solution—from data retrieval to data storage to reporting.

4.1 The Account-Oriented Data Model Versus the Column-Oriented Data Model

The following section describes the account- and column-oriented data modeling methods, compares the advantages and disadvantages of each, and instructs you on how to use them.

4.1.1 Problems Associated with the Column-Oriented Data Model

Problems associated with the column-oriented data model

In many data warehouse transaction-data tables, for example, InfoCubes in SAP Business Information Warehouse (SAP BW) systems, there are *fact tables* with extensive record lengths, frequently linked with a high percentage of *non-posted cells* (that is to say, many initial or null cells). In tables with many data records and also a frequently low use of capacity, these characteristics can result in system degradation and needlessly high usage of hard drive capacity. The reason for this problem often lies with the underlying column-oriented (or even key figure-oriented) data model.

These models work in accordance with the following principle: To simplify the work of report designers, key figures of various different types are grouped together in a (flat) fact table. This solution is often used to map the profitability analysis and financial statement.

Record type-dependent updating

A data source, for example, based on the SAP R/3 CO-PA, provides, among other things, data for the record types "Incoming sales orders" (A),

"Billing document" (F), "Overhead costs" (D), and "Order/project settlement" (C). This generates the posting of very different characteristics and key figures (see Table 4.1).

InfoObject	SAP name	A	C	D	F
0CURTYPE	Currency type	X	X	X	X
0MATERIAL	Material	X	X	–	X
0CUSTOMER	Customer	X	–	–	X
0PROFIT_CTR	Profit center	X	–	X	X
0ID_DOCNUM	Document number	X	X	X	X
0COPASLQTY	Sales quantity	X	–	–	X
0COPAREVEN	Sales revenue	X	–	–	X
0QTY_DSCNT	Quantity discount	X	–	–	X
0CASH_DSCNT	Cash discount	X	–	–	X
0VARPROD_CS	Various production costs	X	–	–	X
0FIXPROD_CS	Fixed production costs	X	–	–	X
0QUANT_VRNC	Quantity variance	–	X	–	–
0PRICE_VRNC	Price variance	–	X	–	–
0RSRCH_DEV	R&D	–	–	X	–
0MARKETING	Marketing	–	–	X	–
0SALES_CS	Sales & dist. costs	–	–	X	–
0ADMNSTRTN	Administration	–	–	X	–

Table 4.1 Examples of How Characteristics and Key Figures Are Posted, Depending on the Record Type

Generating empty cells

Key figures such as "Sales quantity," "Sales revenue," "Direct reduction in revenue" (for example, discounts), "Standard reduction in revenue" (for example, cash discount), and "Production costs" (for example, variable production costs) can be posted only with the record types "Incoming sales orders" and "Billing document." The variance key figures (for example, "Quantity variance") are posted only in the context of "Order/project settlement." Overhead expenses (for example, administration) are posted only in the context of "Overhead costs." Based on the basic characteristic "record type," posting is automatically done in different data records, and the key figures that are irrelevant from the point of view of a record type remain initial.

This effect is intensified when characteristics are posted, something that is also record- type-dependent. Whereas in the context of the record types "Incoming sales orders" (A), "Billing document" (F) and "Order/project settlement" (C) the characteristic Material is updated, it remains unchanged for the record type "Overhead costs." The Profit Center, in turn, is updated for the record types "Incoming sales orders" (A), "Billing document" (F) and "Overhead costs" (D), but remains initial for "Order/ project settlement" (C). This results in empty cells in the dimensions.

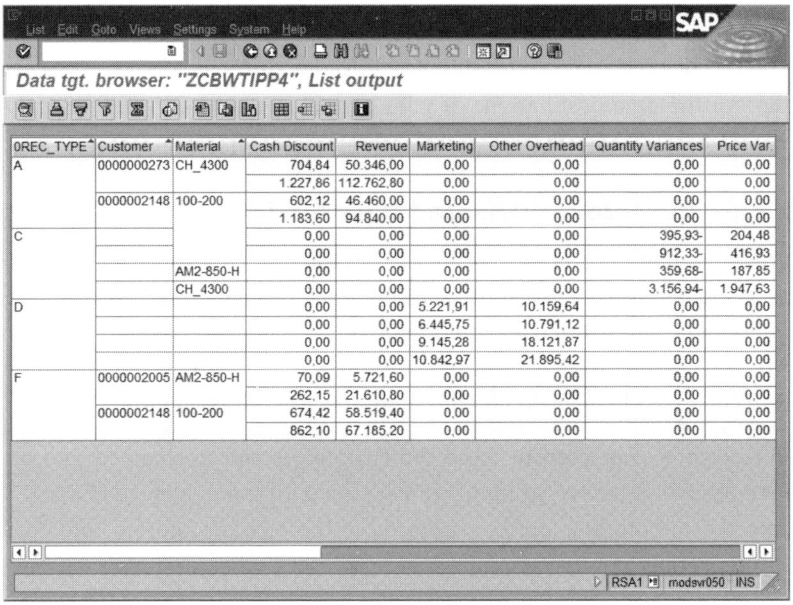

Data tgt. browser: "ZCBWTIPP4", List output

0REC_TYPE	Customer	Material	Cash Discount	Revenue	Marketing	Other Overhead	Quantity Variances	Price Var.
A	0000000273	CH_4300	704,84	50.346,00	0,00	0,00	0,00	0,00
			1.227,86	112.762,80	0,00	0,00	0,00	0,00
	0000002148	100-200	602,12	46.460,00	0,00	0,00	0,00	0,00
			1.183,60	94.840,00	0,00	0,00	0,00	0,00
C			0,00	0,00	0,00	0,00	395,93-	204,48
			0,00	0,00	0,00	0,00	912,33-	416,93
		AM2-850-H	0,00	0,00	0,00	0,00	359,68-	187,85
		CH_4300	0,00	0,00	0,00	0,00	3.156,94-	1.947,63
D			0,00	0,00	5.221,91	10.159,64	0,00	0,00
			0,00	0,00	6.445,75	10.791,12	0,00	0,00
			0,00	0,00	9.145,28	18.121,87	0,00	0,00
			0,00	0,00	10.842,97	21.895,42	0,00	0,00
F	0000002005	AM2-850-H	70,09	5.721,60	0,00	0,00	0,00	0,00
			262,15	21.610,80	0,00	0,00	0,00	0,00
	0000002148	100-200	674,42	58.519,40	0,00	0,00	0,00	0,00
			862,10	67.185,20	0,00	0,00	0,00	0,00

Figure 4.1 In the Column-Oriented Data Model, There Can Often Be Many Non-Posted Cells

Waste of hard-drive capacity

In this example, which is based on a transfer of key figures from SAP R/3 CO-PA to SAP BW, this means that 40.9% of the cells are posted. In other words, almost 60% of the cells are initial and the data volume for storing the key figures is therefore 2.5 times too high! In a productive data model with only 50 key figures and 10 million entries in the fact table, this would mean a memory requirement (for the key figures only) of 4 gigabytes (GB); however, approximately 2.4 GB of this memory space would comprise empty cells. Because the costs of hard-drive memory space are plummeting, this may not appear to be a serious problem. However, in productive systems, this figure does grow exponentially. The need for aggregates and indexes multiplies the actual memory space requirement. Consequently, this issue of hard-drive capacity should not be neglected for the medium- and long-term.

Performance problems

This waste of memory space often has direct problematic consequences: when processing the data, the Data Warehouse must read the fact tables in different situations. Consequently, in order to run a report for such an InfoCube, there could be a main memory requirement of 4 GB (just for the key figures), which, in turn, would result in weak storage/retrieval processes if the main memory available is insufficient. These storage/retrieval processes can contribute to very poor response times because of temporary storage on the hard drive.

Such a phenomenon can result if SAP Business Content is used, for example, for the data destinations of sales and stock control. In this case, the share of empty cells in productive systems can be as high as 85 to 90%!

4.1.2 The Account-Oriented Data Model

Key figures with a qualifying characteristic

Precisely the opposite path is pursued in the mapping of an account-oriented data model. At its most extreme, for example, only a physical key figure "amount" is used. By adding a qualifier ("account," better characteristic "key figure"), you can restrict whether or not revenues or administration costs should be presented in a context with the key figure "amount."

Initially, the characteristics and dimensions remain unchanged and are extended with a new "account" dimension with the qualifying characteristic. All amount key figures are stored in the one key figure—"amount." If the posting of initial key figures is suppressed when updating the InfoCube, no empty cells will appear in the key figures. When updating data records, for each non-initial key figure of a source data record, there is a data record with said "amount" key figure. Therefore, the number of data records is multiplied!

In the example in Section 4.1.1, from ten million source data records with 50 physical key figures and an update density of 40.9%, there would be 204,500,000 data records. The advantage of a low main-memory requirement per data record is coupled with the disadvantage of a possibly problematic quantity structure regarding the number of data records. Concurrently, in this first approximation, the problem of the empty cells in dimensions still remains.

Use of the account-oriented data model

Therefore, use of the account-oriented data model requires that you carefully consider the number of source data records, the number of key figures, the update density, and the context. You also need to ask the following questions: Which characteristics and key figures are connected in a business sense? What quantity structures can arise from which business transactions or events (or in the example given, record types)?

These questions must be answered upon following the appropriate practical and technical deliberations.

- Is the record type relevant to "Incoming sales orders"? If the evaluations should be on the basis of SAP R/3 sales documents, the additional filing to a profit and loss statement InfoCube is irrelevant. This record type is not necessary to calculate the profit margin and is therefore either not useful or, at best, applicable only in another InfoCube.
- Which characteristics and key figures can be updated in "Billing document," "Overhead costs," and "Order/project settlement"? Separating the InfoCubes for these record types is a good solution.
- The quantity structure of "Billing document" (the CO-PA line items here correspond to the billing document items) is usually substantial, to the extent that mapping the account-oriented data model for billing documents is not recommended in this case. In the "Billing document" InfoCube, only the relevant characteristics and key figures are used.
- The quantity structure for "Overhead costs" is small, as is the number of key figures posted. Therefore, here, it would be advisable to use the account-oriented data model for mapping. In the "Overhead costs" InfoCube, only the relevant characteristics and key figures are used.
- For "Order/project settlement," you should proceed as described in the cases mentioned above.

4.1.3 Comparing the Data Models

- Whereas the column-oriented data model generated many empty cells for many configurations, with the account-oriented data model, there can sometimes be a one-to-one correspondence between the number of data records and the number of cells in the data model. It is therefore not possible to make an across-the-board recommendation for the data model that should be used. Rather, each actual case must be considered. This question is closely related to the InfoCube grouping, that is to say, what data is appropriately grouped in InfoGroups. The question of physical data management in data destinations is, for the most part, not subject-related; rather, it is a technical question. Based on this, MultiProviders can be provided for the appropriate semantics.

- A column-oriented data model is advantageous if the key figures are primarily posted together (i.e., initial key figures are not the norm).
- An account-oriented data model, on the other hand, can be beneficial in the following cases:
  - If the key figures are often initial
  - If key figures must later be extended or removed

Combination of approaches

Similarly, there is also an InfoCube design in which the posting depth is relatively homogenous (i.e., the characteristics are generally filled to a similar granularity).

Consequently, in many cases, the solution lies in having different base InfoCubes, in which (depending on the data segment) either the account-oriented or the column-oriented approach can be used as deemed appropriate.

4.2 Practical Example: Combination of the Account-Oriented and the Column-Oriented Data Model

The following section presents a solution for mapping a profitability analysis and profit and loss statement.

4.2.1 Analyzing the Source Data

The logical and empirical analysis of source data helps you to determine which approach to use. The main focus of the analysis is to consider the different types of records.

Data of the record type "Incoming sales orders"

Irrelevant data

In the previous example, we want to create a turnover and profit margin report. Analyses of sales orders should be created via another sub-project based on sales documents. Therefore, data of record type "Incoming sales orders" is irrelevant and is eliminated during data retrieval.

Data of the record types "Billing document," "Order/project settlement," and "Overhead costs"

Relevant data

The data in these record types should be used. You can verify which characteristics and value fields from SAP R/3 CO-PA should be posted in the implementation guide (transaction SPRO) of the underlying SAP R/3 source system. Mapping characteristics and key figures in the transfer and update rules results in the grouping of relevant characteristics and key figures for each record type.

Relevant characteristics

The analysis shows that currency type, record type, valuation view, version, value type, time attributes, and units are relevant for all record types. In addition, for the record type "Billing document," the analysis shows that, for the example application, the characteristics and key figures shown in Table 4.2 are relevant.

Characteristics	Key figures
Company code	Accrued shipment costs
Controlling area	Cash discount
Sales organization	Sales revenue
Sales office	Sales quantity
Division	Customer discount
Distribution channel	Individual material costs
Customer number	Fixed production costs
Material	Material discount
Quantity	Quantity discount
Document number	Sales commission
Profit center	Special one-off sales costs
Posting date in the document	Variable production costs
	Bonus

Table 4.2 Characteristics and Key Figures for Record Type F ("Billing Document")

For the record type "Order/project settlement," the analysis shows that for the example application, the characteristics and key figures shown in Table 4.3 are also relevant.

Characteristic	Key figure
Division	Other variances
Material	Price variances
Document number	Quantity variances
Posting date in the document	

Table 4.3 Characteristics and Key Figures for Record Type C ("Order/Project Settlement")

For the record type "Overhead costs," the analysis shows that for the example application, the characteristics and key figures shown in Table 4.4 are also relevant.

Characteristic	Key figure
Company code	Administration
Controlling area	Marketing
Sales organization	Other overhead costs
Distribution channel	Research and development
Document number	Distribution costs
Profit center	
Posting date in the document	

Table 4.4 Characteristics and Key Figures for Record Type D ("Overhead Costs")

4.2.2 Data Model

InfoCube for "Billing Document"

The data model is developed based on the analysis of the source data. The analysis shows that in our example application, the record type "Billing document" provides over 50% of the key figures (in practice, this may account for up to 90% of data volume). When considering the quantity structure arising from the "Order number" granularity (in this example the record type "Billing document" provides most of the data) for this record type, it becomes apparent that the best approach would be to use a special InfoCube with a column-oriented data model.

InfoCube for "Order/project settlement"

Alternatively, the record type "Order/project settlement" contains only three key figures in this model. At the same time, characteristics such as "customer," "sales organization," and "distribution channel" are missing. This omission of these characteristics results in a significantly smaller quantity structure. For this record type, the best solution is an InfoCube based on the account-oriented approach.

InfoCube for "Overhead costs"

For the record type "Overhead costs," only five key figures are relevant in this model. At the same time, compared with other record types, granular characteristics are lacking. For this record type also, provision is made for an InfoCube based on the account-oriented approach.

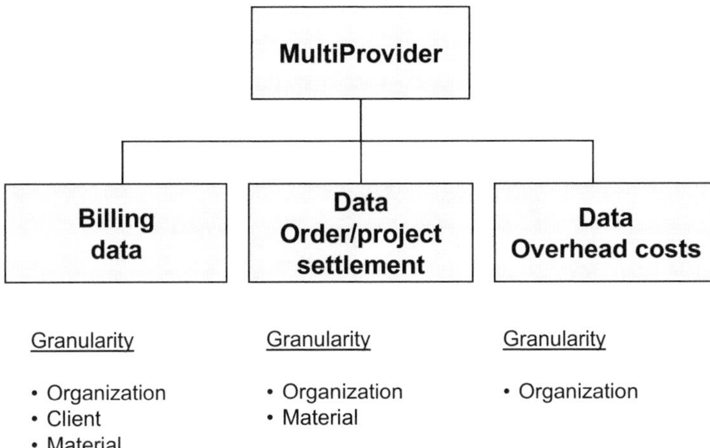

Figure 4.2 Combination of the Account-Oriented and Column-Oriented Data Model

MultiProvider for reporting

To simplify reporting, a MultiProvider is provided—on the basis of the three primary characteristics—which combines the base InfoCubes.

4.3 Implementation: InfoCubes

The structure of the InfoCubes is provided in list form in the Appendix (see Appendices B.1, B.2, B.3, and B.4). The InfoCube for "Billing document" contains all characteristics and key figures relevant to record type F.

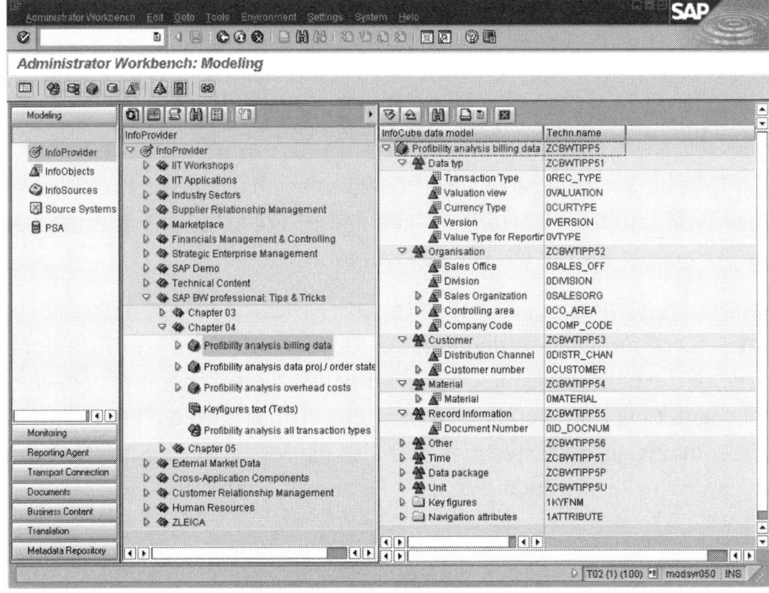

Figure 4.3 InfoCube ZCBWTIPP5 for "Billing Document"

"Key figure" characteristic for account-oriented InfoCubes

When defining the account-oriented InfoCubes, a "key figure" characteristic (ZCTYPKYF1) is generated. In the InfoCube, this characteristic assumes the role of the accounts and qualifies a general key figure (0AMOUNT).

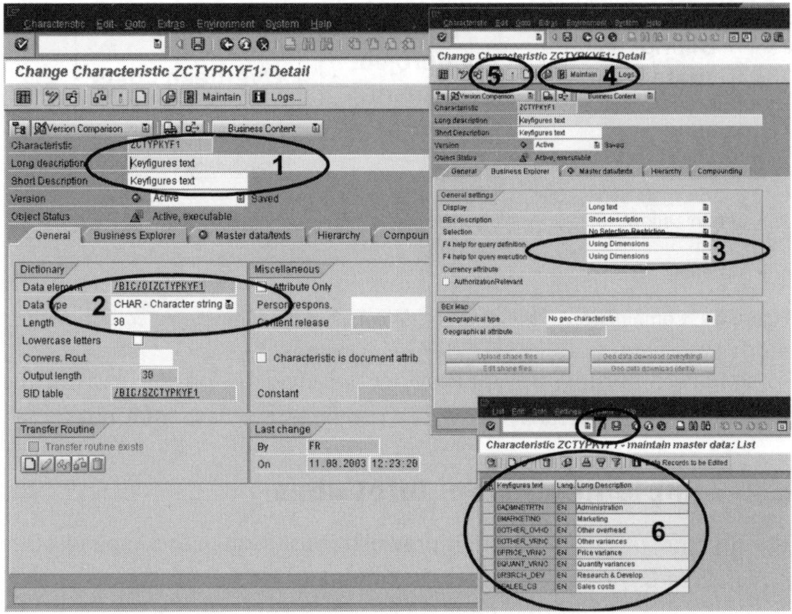

Figure 4.4 Defining the Characteristic "Key Figure" and Recording the Permissible Values

The InfoCube for "Order/project settlement" contains all characteristics relevant to record type C, the characteristic "key figure" (ZCTYPKYF1) and the key figure "amount" (0AMOUNT) (see Figure 4.5).

The InfoCube for "Overhead costs" contains all characteristics relevant to record type D, the characteristic "key figure" (ZCTYPKYF1) and the key figure "amount" (0AMOUNT) (see Figure 4.6).

MultiProvider for mapping complete profit and loss statement

Dedicated reporting on just one of the three record types—"Billing document," "Order/project settlement," or "Overhead costs"—can be done on one of the base InfoCubes. If the entire key-figure scheme is necessary to calculate the profit margin, then a MultiProvider is used. This MultiProvider contains all characteristics and key figures of the base InfoCubes and assembles their InfoObjects (see Figures 4.7 and 4.8).

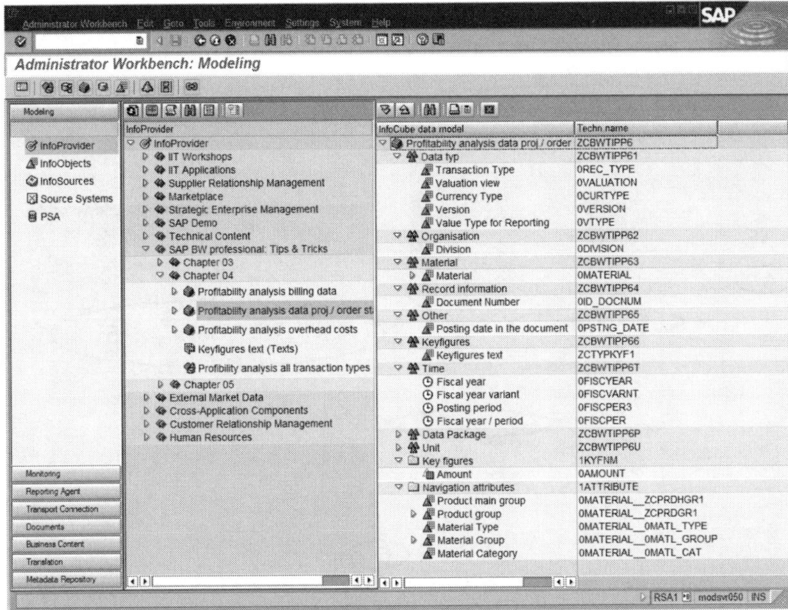

Figure 4.5 InfoCube ZCBWTIPP6 for "Order/Project Settlement"

Figure 4.6 InfoCube ZCBWTIPP7 for "Overhead Costs"

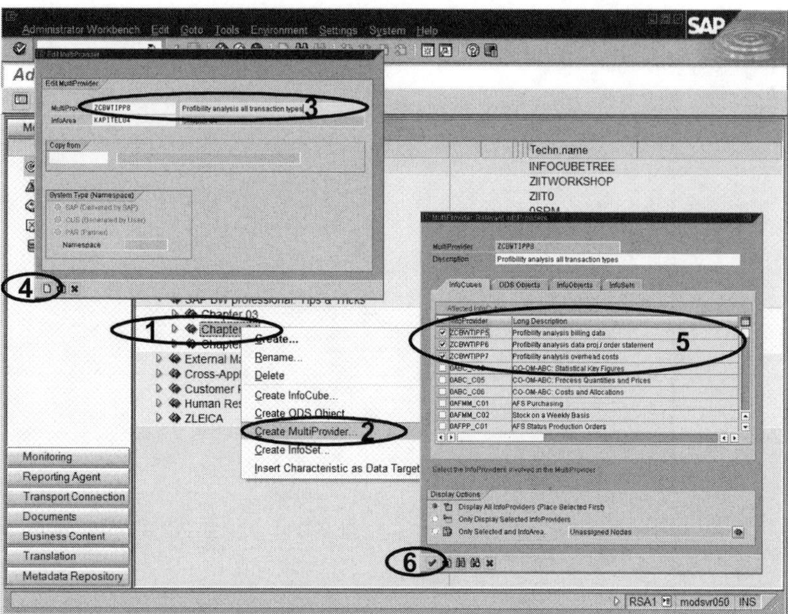

Figure 4.7 MultiProvider for Base InfoCubes

Figure 4.8 Identifying the Characteristics and Selecting the Key Figures

In addition, in the MultiProvider, the characteristics of the base InfoCubes must be identified (all base characteristics, where available, are used and merged with the same InfoObjects of the other base InfoCubes) and all key figures of the base InfoCubes must be selected (see Figure 4.8).

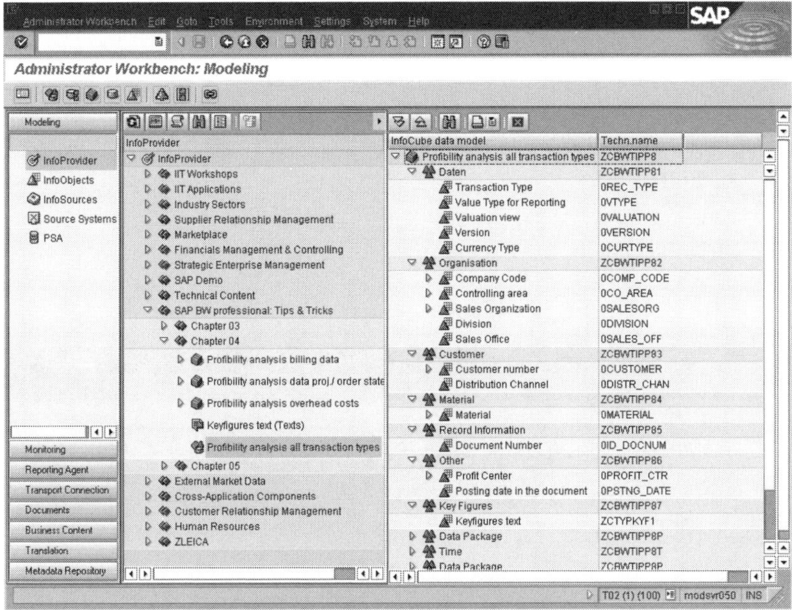

Figure 4.9 MultiProvider for Reporting with all Record Types

4.4 Implementation: Data Retrieval

Data retrieval for the InfoCubes, which is described in Sections 4.2 and 4.3, is based on the data source and the InfoSource discussed in Chapter 3 (SAP BW Professional: Tips & Tricks: 1_CO_PA800S_GO_ZC). Based on this InfoSource, the updating rules for the InfoCubes mentioned in Sections 4.2 and 4.3 must be created.

4.4.1 Setting Up the Update Rules for the InfoCube "Billing Document"

Data retrieval for "Billing document" is done as described in the example in Chapter 3. The only difference is that record type F is selected in such a way that all source data from other source record types is discarded.

Selection of record type F via a user exit

To select the data of record type F, a user exit is inserted in the update rules. The source value "record type" is transferred to the result field RESULT. For record type F only, the RETURNCODE field—which controls updating—is left at the update value 0. For all other record types, this value is set to 4. Because the logic of SAP BW only updates data with record type 0, the other record types A, C, and D are discarded:

```
* result value of the routine
  RESULT = COMM_STRUCTURE-REC_TYPE.

* if the returncode is not equal zero, the result will
not be updated
  if RESULT = 'F'.
    RETURNCODE = 0.
  else.
    RETURNCODE = 4.
  endif.
```

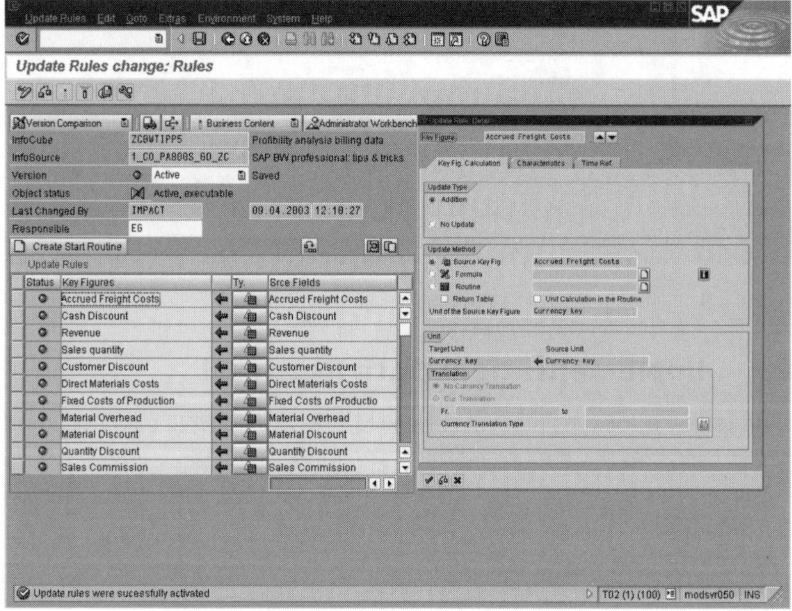

Figure 4.10 All Key Figures Are Updated from the InfoSource 1:1 in the InfoCube

With the exception of the source field "record type," all characteristics (including time characteristics) and key figures are updated exactly as they appear in the InfoCube (see Figures 4.10 and 4.11), in accordance with the SAP recommendation. The subroutine for the record type is created in the pop-up characteristic subroutine and must be transferred to all key figures (see Figure 4.11, Step 1 to 3).

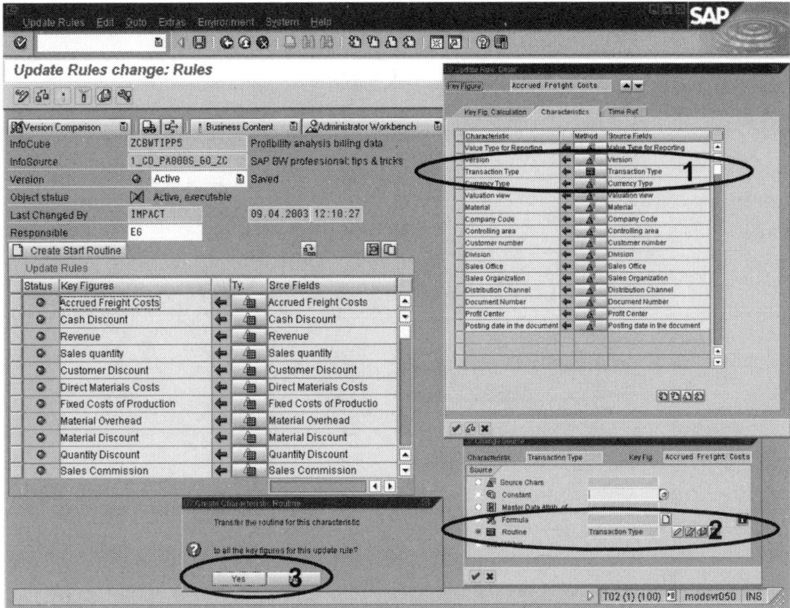

Figure 4.11 Updating the Key Figures, with the Exception of the "Record Type" Characteristic, which Is Updated by the Subroutine

4.4.2 Setting Up the Update Rules for the InfoCube "Order/Project Settlement"

Also for the InfoCube "Financial statement data Order/project settlement" (ZCBWTIPP6), update rules are created for InfoSource 1_CO_PA800S_GO_ZC. For the single key figure "amount," SAP BW cannot create any update recommendations from the InfoSource. Consequently, the pop-up, **Create update rules: Initial screen,** must be confirmed (see Figure 4.12, Step 4).

To manually create update rules, you must double-click on the key figure (see Figure 4.13, Step 1); in the pop-up **Update rule: Detail**, you must select the update type **Addition** (see Figure 4.13, Step 2). The update method is **Routine** with **Return table** (see Figure 4.13, Step 3).

Finally, you must press the button **Create routine** (see Figure 4.13, Step 4). Enter the name and confirm it (see Figure 4.13, Steps 5 and 6).

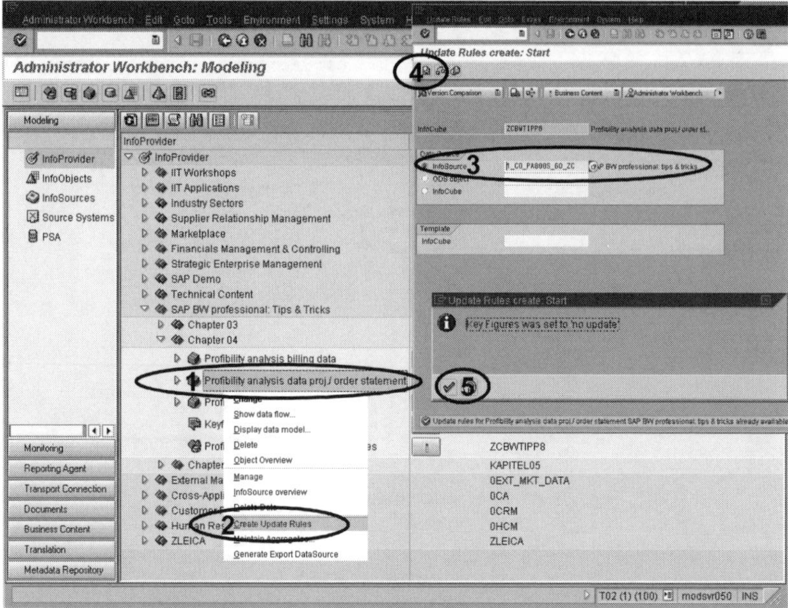

Figure 4.12 No Rules Can Be Proposed for the Key Figure 0AMOUNT

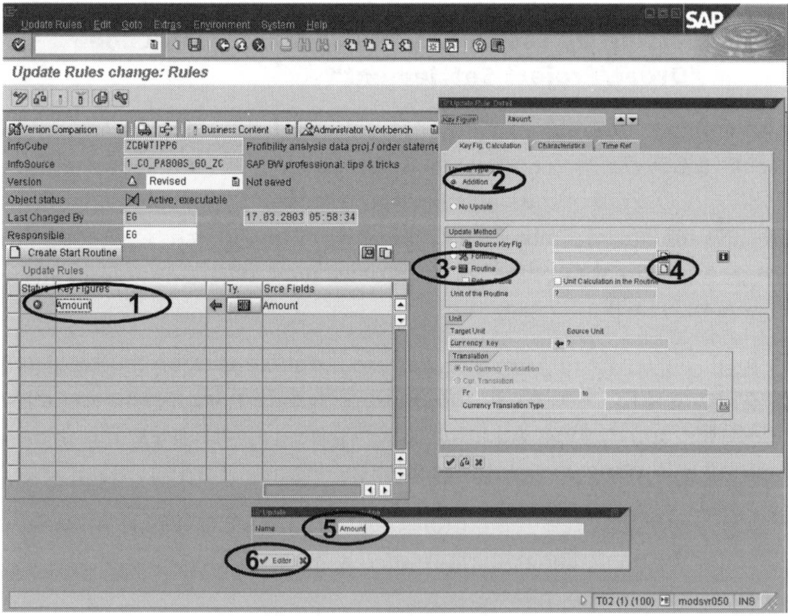

Figure 4.13 Creating the Update Rules for the Key Figure

The subroutine for the key figure is subsequently created. Key figures that are column-oriented from the InfoSource must be converted to the account model using this subroutine. For the record type C, the relevant key figures are transferred to 0AMOUNT and the characteristic "key figure" (ZCTYPKYF1) is set accordingly:

Result table technique for converting to the account model

```
if COMM_STRUCTURE-REC_TYPE = 'C'.
  RETURNCODE = 0.
  move-corresponding COMM_STRUCTURE to RESULT_TABLE.
  if COMM_STRUCTURE-OTHER_VRNC <> 0.
    RESULT_TABLE-/BIC/ZCTYPKYF1 = '0OTHER_VRNC'.
    RESULT_TABLE-AMOUNT = COMM_STRUCTURE-OTHER_VRNC.
    append RESULT_TABLE.
  endif.
  if COMM_STRUCTURE-PRICE_VRNC <> 0.
    RESULT_TABLE-/BIC/ZCTYPKYF1 = '0PRICE_VRNC'.
    RESULT_TABLE-AMOUNT = COMM_STRUCTURE-PRICE_VRNC.
    append RESULT_TABLE.
  endif.
  if COMM_STRUCTURE-QUANT_VRNC <> 0.
    RESULT_TABLE-/BIC/ZCTYPKYF1 = '0QUANT_VRNC'.
    RESULT_TABLE-AMOUNT = COMM_STRUCTURE-QUANT_VRNC.
    append RESULT_TABLE.
  endif.
else.
  RETURNCODE = 4.
endif.
```

Finally, the update rules are activated.

4.4.3 Setting Up the Update Rules for the InfoCube "Overhead Costs"

Also for the InfoCube "Profit and loss statement overhead costs" (ZCBWTIPP7), the update rules are created for InfoSource 1_CO_PA800S_GO_ZC. This is done in the same way as described in Section 4.4.2. Here also, you must create a subroutine with a return table for the key figure "amount." Key figures that are column-oriented from the InfoSource must be converted to the account model using this subroutine.

For the record type D, the relevant key figures are transferred to 0AMOUNT and the characteristic "key figure" (ZCTYPKYF1) is set accordingly (see Figure 4.14, Step 1). The subroutine must once again be checked (see Figure 4.14, Step 2), then the updating of the key figure is confirmed (see Figure 4.14, Step 4). Finally, the update rules are activated (see Figure 4.14, Step 6).

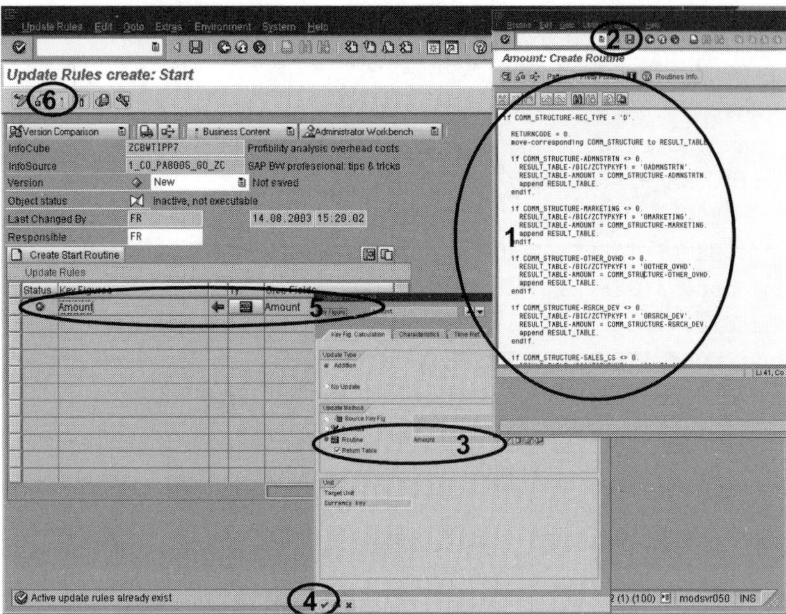

Figure 4.14 Updating the InfoCube "Overhead Costs"

4.5 Executing Data Retrieval

An InfoPackage is created to execute data retrieval that posts precisely the three basic InfoCubes needed for this application. An InfoPackage is created in the Administrator Workbench, in the InfoSources view, based on InfoSource 1_CO_PA800S_GO_ZC, and following the procedure described in Chapter 3. The subroutine for selecting actual data is once again used for the data selection. The entire extraction, transformation, and loading (ETL) process is therefore set up (see Figure 4.15).

Updating according to data destination

When you start the InfoPackage, updating is done depending on the data destination. Using the update rules, 3,600 data records are inserted into the fact table of the billing data InfoCube. The effect of using the account-oriented model approach can be seen in the "Order/project settlement" and "Overhead costs" InfoCubes: from 3,600 source records each in the example application, three records are updated in the "Order/project settlement" InfoCube and five records are updated in the "Overhead costs" InfoCube, resulting in two fact tables that have 10,800 and 18,000 data records respectively (see Figure 4.16).

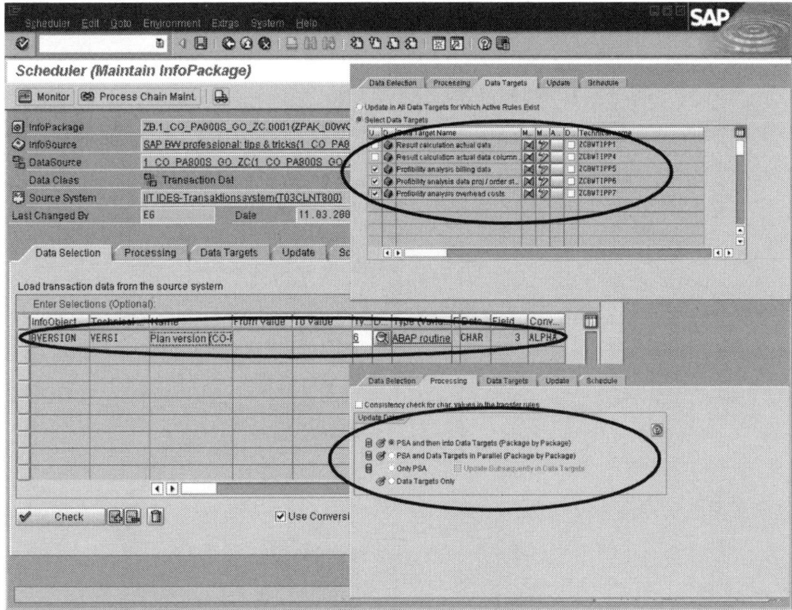

Figure 4.15 InfoPackage for Updating the Base InfoCubes

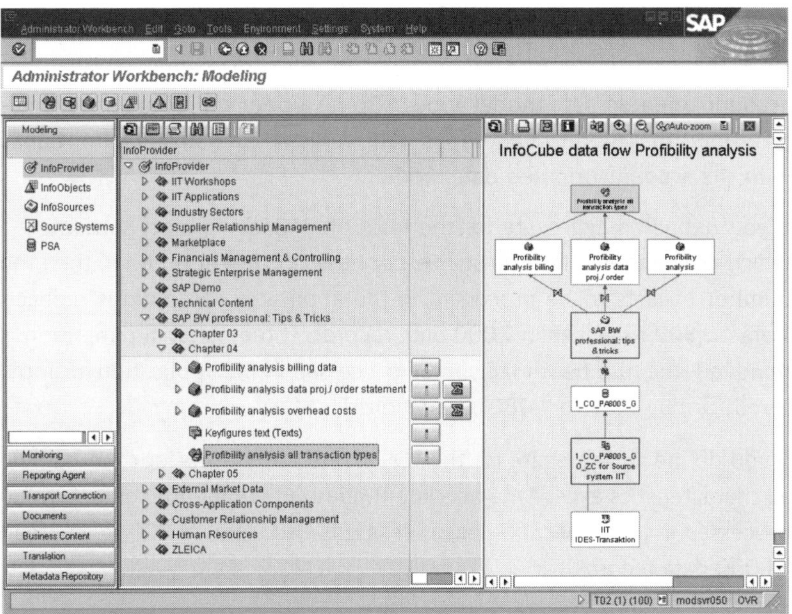

Figure 4.16 Presentation of the Data Flow from the Source System to the Base Info-Cubes and the Corresponding MultiProvider

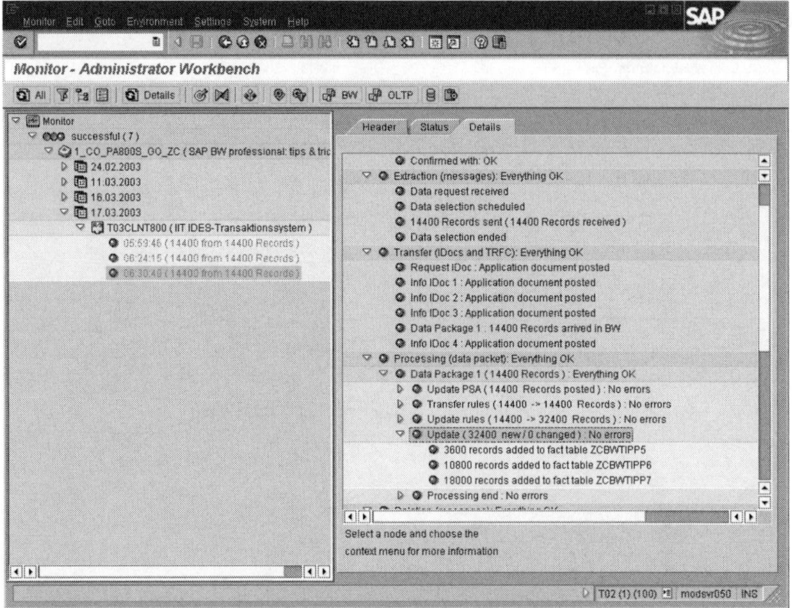

Figure 4.17 Update Depending on Data Destination

4.6 Performance Optimization and Reporting

From the perspective of performance and the complexity of design, the account-oriented data model appears to be a poor solution. A data analysis shows that there are additional requirements for managing InfoCubes with the account-oriented data model.

Reducing data records using aggregates

If you define an aggregate for the InfoCube "Order/project settlement," which contains all characteristics except the document number, then the number of facts to be processed in the application example is reduced from 10,800 to less than 7,000 data records. If the material dimension is removed, the number of facts to be processed in the application example is reduced by 90% to 1,080 data records!

If you define an aggregate for the "Overhead costs" InfoCube, containing all characteristics except the document number, the number of facts to be processed in the application example is reduced from 18,000 to less than 11,000 data records.

Therefore, if you devise the content-oriented modeling of InfoCubes in combination with an optimal configuration of aggregates, it will result in very high-performance data models (see Figure 4.18).

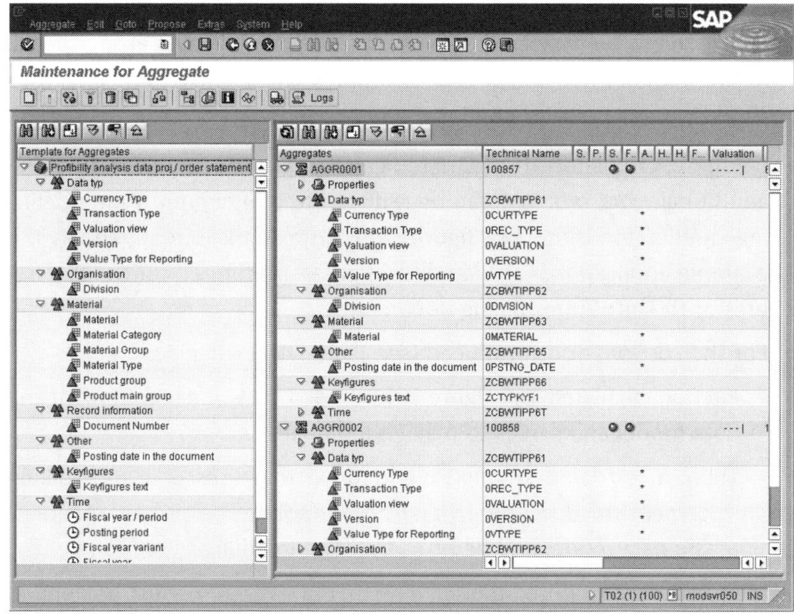

Figure 4.18 Optimal Access to the Account-Oriented InfoCube "Order/Project Settlement" Using Aggregates

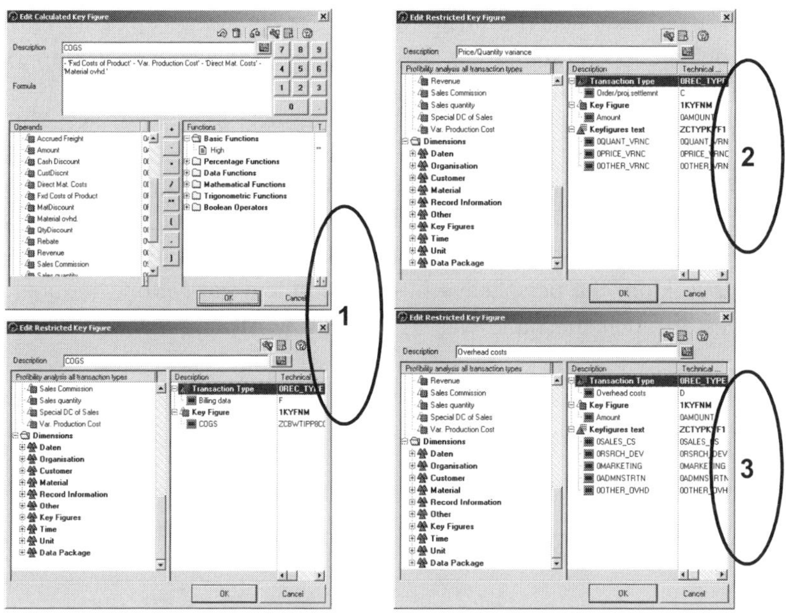

Figure 4.19 Limited and Calculated Key Figures Allow for a Flexible Combination of Column- and Account-Oriented InfoCubes

The question as to whether it is possible to manage such complex data models is yet to be answered. Will this type of model cover absolutely all reporting requirements? If so, how complex will such solutions need to be?

Calculated and restricted key figures

- If you use calculated and restricted key figures for query definition, the additional work required can be reduced to a minimum. When defining queries for these key figures, no extra work is required. In the example application, calculated key figures are formed for the key figures of the InfoCube "Billing document":
- For the cost of goods produced (see Figure 4.19, Step 1):
  - First, a calculated key figure is formed. This is independent of the data model and serves to make handling easier.
  - Then, a restricted key figure is defined that uses only the "Billing document" record type. This part of the solution is also independent of the data model and helps to facilitate handling.
- In the account-oriented model, a restricted key figure must be defined for the sum of the price/quantity variances (see Figure 4.19, Step 2). This is different from a solution in a column-oriented model, for which a calculated key figure would be required.
- Similarly, in the account-oriented model, a restricted key figure must be defined for the sum of the overhead costs (see Figure 4.19, Step 3). This is also different from a solution in a column-oriented model, for which a calculated key figure would also be required.

The restricted key figures are used to define queries to the MultiProvider. Using these elements, the complexity and work inherent in generating queries is no greater than it is with the column-oriented model (see Figure 4.20). From the perspective of execution and navigation, the query behaves in much the same way as would any other query (see Figure 4.21).

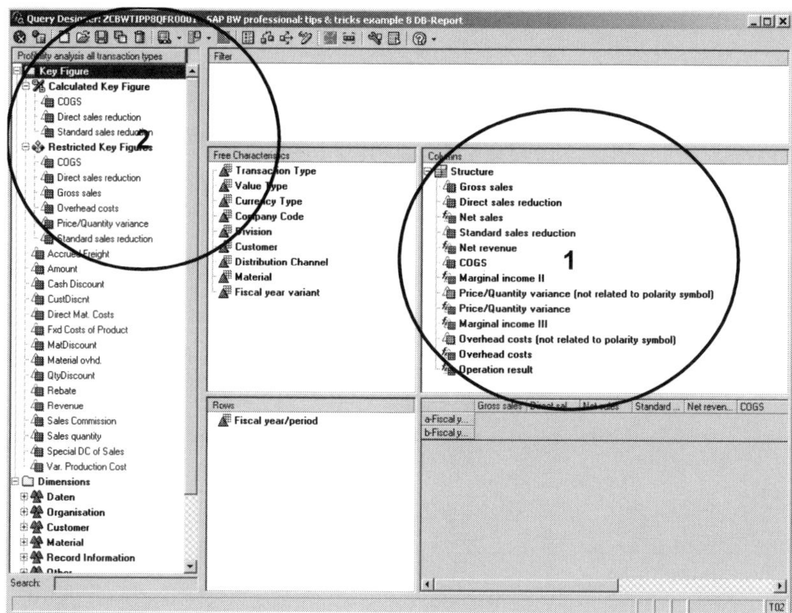

Figure 4.20 Query to the MultiProvider Regarding Column- and Account-Oriented InfoCubes Using the Restricted Key Figures

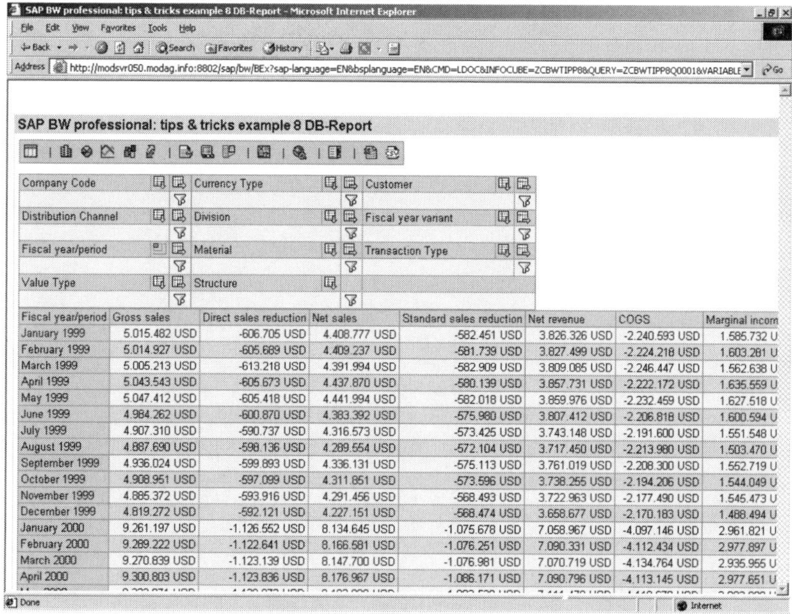

Fiscal year/period	Gross sales	Direct sales reduction	Net sales	Standard sales reduction	Net revenue	COGS	Marginal incom
January 1999	5.015.482 USD	-606.705 USD	4.408.777 USD	-582.451 USD	3.826.326 USD	-2.240.593 USD	1.585.732 U
February 1999	5.014.927 USD	-605.689 USD	4.409.237 USD	-581.739 USD	3.827.499 USD	-2.224.218 USD	1.603.281 U
March 1999	5.005.213 USD	-613.218 USD	4.391.994 USD	-582.909 USD	3.809.085 USD	-2.246.447 USD	1.562.638 U
April 1999	5.043.543 USD	-605.673 USD	4.437.870 USD	-580.139 USD	3.857.731 USD	-2.222.172 USD	1.635.559 U
May 1999	5.047.412 USD	-605.418 USD	4.441.994 USD	-582.018 USD	3.859.976 USD	-2.232.459 USD	1.627.518 U
June 1999	4.984.262 USD	-600.870 USD	4.383.392 USD	-575.980 USD	3.807.412 USD	-2.206.818 USD	1.600.594 U
July 1999	4.907.310 USD	-590.737 USD	4.316.573 USD	-573.425 USD	3.743.148 USD	-2.191.600 USD	1.551.548 U
August 1999	4.887.690 USD	-598.136 USD	4.289.554 USD	-572.104 USD	3.717.450 USD	-2.213.980 USD	1.503.470 U
September 1999	4.936.024 USD	-599.893 USD	4.336.131 USD	-575.113 USD	3.761.019 USD	-2.208.300 USD	1.552.719 U
October 1999	4.908.951 USD	-597.099 USD	4.311.851 USD	-573.596 USD	3.738.255 USD	-2.194.206 USD	1.544.049 U
November 1999	4.885.372 USD	-593.916 USD	4.291.456 USD	-568.493 USD	3.722.963 USD	-2.177.490 USD	1.545.473 U
December 1999	4.819.272 USD	-592.121 USD	4.227.151 USD	-568.474 USD	3.658.677 USD	-2.170.183 USD	1.488.494 U
January 2000	9.261.197 USD	-1.126.552 USD	8.134.645 USD	-1.075.678 USD	7.058.967 USD	-4.097.146 USD	2.961.821 U
February 2000	9.289.222 USD	-1.122.641 USD	8.166.581 USD	-1.076.251 USD	7.090.331 USD	-4.112.434 USD	2.977.897 U
March 2000	9.270.839 USD	-1.123.139 USD	8.147.700 USD	-1.076.981 USD	7.070.719 USD	-4.134.764 USD	2.935.955 U
April 2000	9.300.803 USD	-1.123.836 USD	8.176.967 USD	-1.086.171 USD	7.090.796 USD	-4.113.145 USD	2.977.651 U

Figure 4.21 Execution of the Query from Figure 4.20

5 Appropriate Mapping of the SAP Product Hierarchy in Data Modeling, Data Retrieval, and Reporting

The material attribute "product hierarchy" is a very important grouping criterion for many analytical applications. In SAP BW implementations, the mapping of the SAP product hierarchy is often done in the context of the standard solution supplied by SAP. However, this can cause significant problems in analysis and reporting. This chapter presents various solutions and outlines the strengths and weaknesses of each.

5.1 The Material Attribute "Product Hierarchy" in SAP R/3

The material attribute "product hierarchy" in SAP R/3 is an alphanumeric character string used to group materials by combining various characteristics. It is frequently used for analysis and for pricing purposes. There are two product hierarchy characteristic values, available in two material views: in **Basic data 1** and in the tab **Sales: sales org. 2**.

Although no distinction is made between these two attributes in many enterprises, in SAP R/3 they represent different properties (compare SAP R/3 documentation). **Basic data 1** is stored in the table MARA, which contains the keys "client" and "material number" only. Alternatively, the **Sales: sales.org 2** tab has the keys "client," "material number," "sales organization," and "distribution channel." Therefore, the product hierarchy in the basic view is valid for a single client (and thus generally for the entire enterprise), whereas for a single material, there may be a different product hierarchy for each sales organization and distribution channel. If both attributes are used, it is often necessary to map both attributes in SAP Business Information Warehouse (SAP BW) so that they can be used appropriately in reporting.

In SAP R/3, this attribute is, from the software point of view, treated like a hierarchy, although, technically speaking, a *product hierarchy* is a flat 18-character alphanumeric field (field type or data element PRODH_D with the domain PRODH).

The Help system in SAP R/3 (for example, using the function key **F4**) opens a selection list of the highest level of the product hierarchy. After you click on the **Next level** button, the next level, based on the preselection (in the example, "Main group 00105, Vehicles"), is offered for selection, until at the lowest level (in the example "Subgroup 00000105 Components"), the final characteristic value of the product hierarchy is incorporated into the material master data by clicking on the **Choose** button (see Figure 5.1).

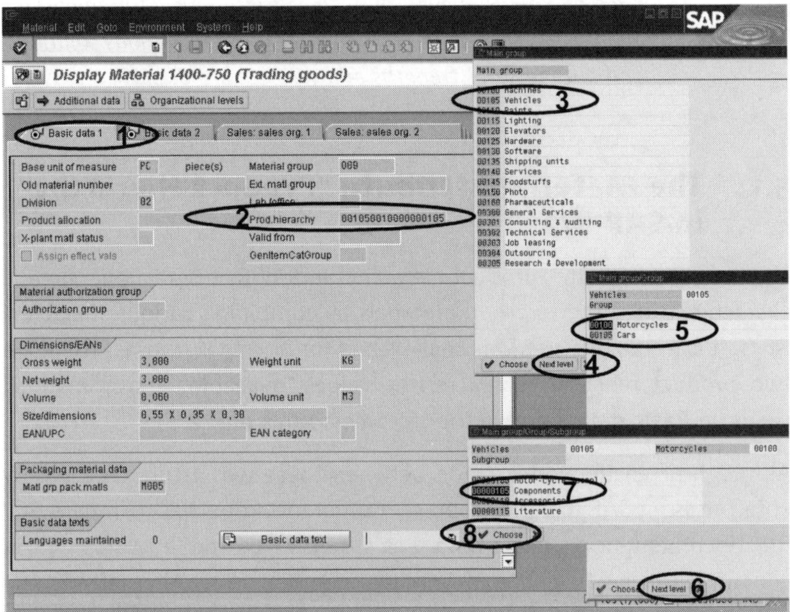

Figure 5.1 The Product Hierarchy as an Attribute in the View **Basic Data 1** of Material Master Maintenance in SAP R.3

The procedure is the same in the tab **Sales: sales org. 2** (see Figure 5.2, Steps 1 and 2). In both cases, the product hierarchy is based on the domains mentioned above. The value range of these domains is shown in table T179 (Materials: product hierarchies"). The corresponding texts are stored in table T179T ("Materials: product hierarchies: texts").

The number of product hierarchy levels and their technical length is configured in the R/3 customizing-implementation guide (Transaction SPRO, then **General logistics · Material master · Settings for central fields · Sales-related data · Define product hierarchies**).

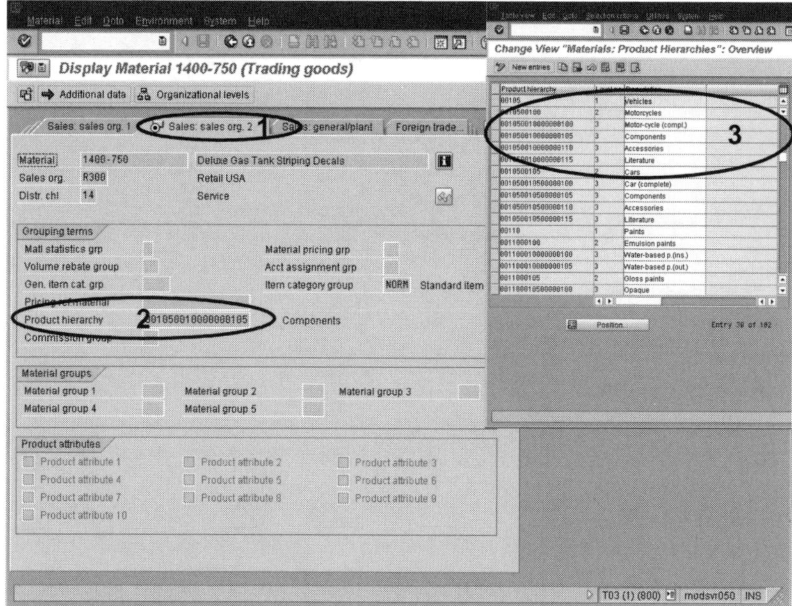

Figure 5.2 The Product Hierarchy in the View **Sales: sales org. 2**

The structure of the product hierarchy is represented by the level number (see Figure 5.2, Step 3). This ensures that the product hierarchy is used correctly in transactional SAP R/3. In reporting, however, there is usually an unsatisfactory mapping that may often cause a malfunction.

5.2 Storing the Material Attribute "Product Hierarchy" in SAP BW Using the SAP Business Content Navigation Attribute

5.2.1 The SAP Business Content InfoObject "Product Hierarchy" and The Associated Data Retrieval from SAP R/3

The characteristic "product hierarchy" (0PROD_HIER) is provided as an InfoObject in the context of the SAP Business Content. Once it has been activated, it can be viewed or edited in the Administrator Workbench, **InfoObjects** view (see Figure 5.3). In SAP BW, as in SAP R/3, the product hierarchy is represented technically as an 18-character alphanumeric domain. The level number, however, which is used in SAP R/3 for the software-based hierarchy mapping (compare SAP R/3 table T179), is not available in SAP BW.

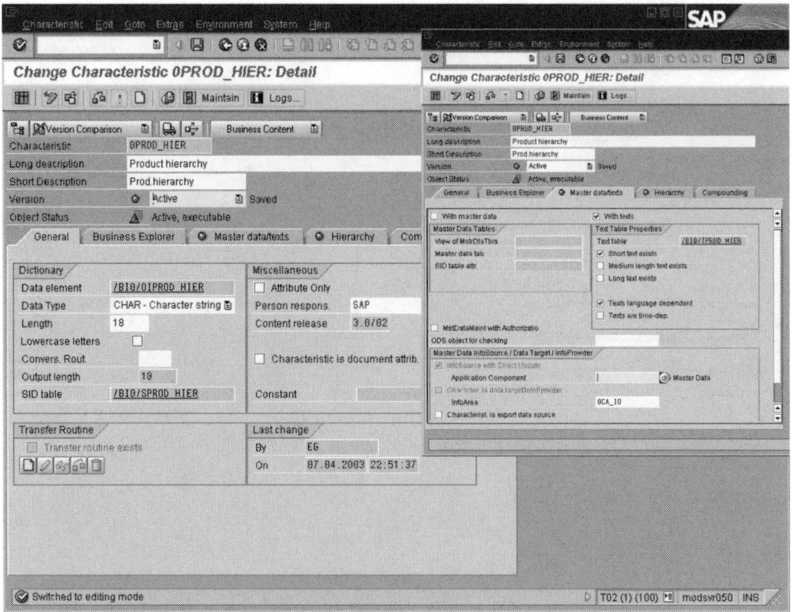

Figure 5.3 The Business Content InfoObject "Product Hierarchy"

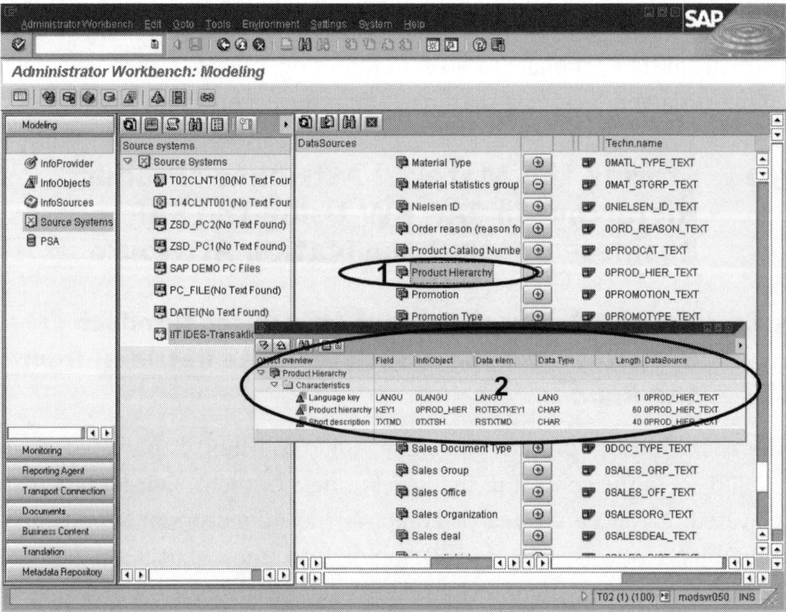

Figure 5.4 The Business Content DataSource "Product Hierarchy"

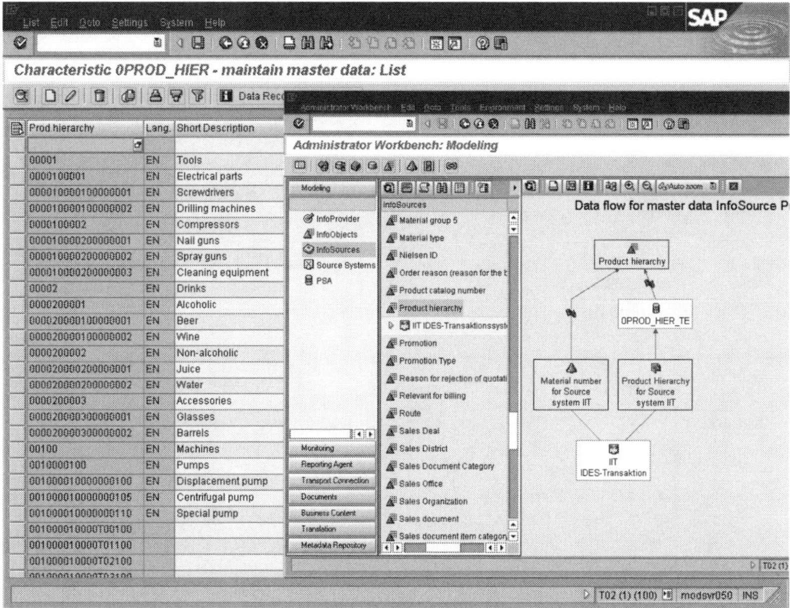

Figure 5.5 Texts of the Characteristic "Product Hierarchy" in SAP BW

The SAP Business Content also provides a DataSource for the texts of the product hierarchy (see Figure 5.4) and additional components for the extraction, transformation, and loading (ETL) process. If data retrieval is set up and executed using the SAP Business Content components, the texts are available as mapped (see Figure 5.5). In various patches of SAP BW 3.x, some parts of the ETL components may be missing. In this case, you may need to customize the present setup of data retrieval to meet your needs.

5.2.2 The SAP Business Content InfoObject "Material" and the Associated Retrieval of Material Attributes from SAP R/3

The InfoObject "product hierarchy" is also available in the SAP Business Content as a navigation attribute for the InfoObject "material" (0MATERIAL). This is also available in the Administrator Workbench, **InfoObjects** view, once it has been activated, and, if necessary, it can be edited there (see Figure 5.6).

The SAP Business Content also provides a DataSource for the attributes of the material (see Figure 5.7) and additional components for obtaining material master data.

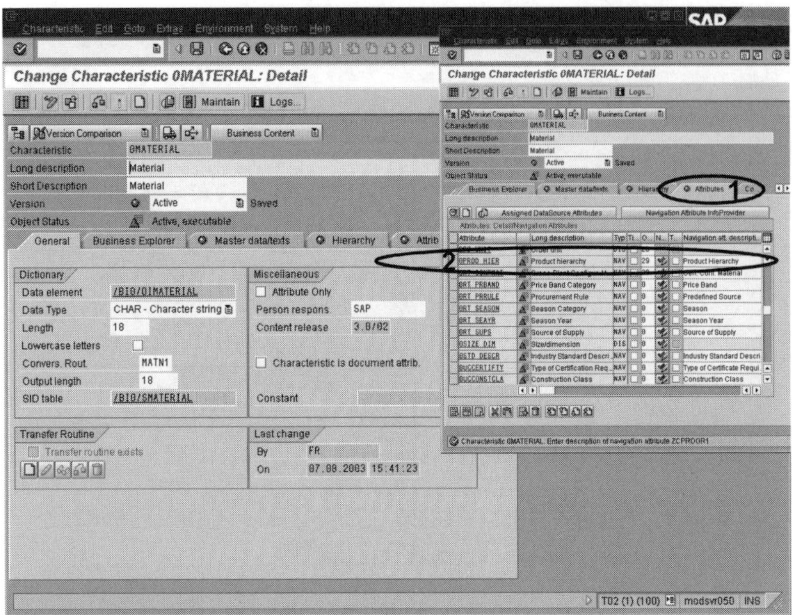

Figure 5.6 The Business Content InfoObject "Material" (0MATERIAL)

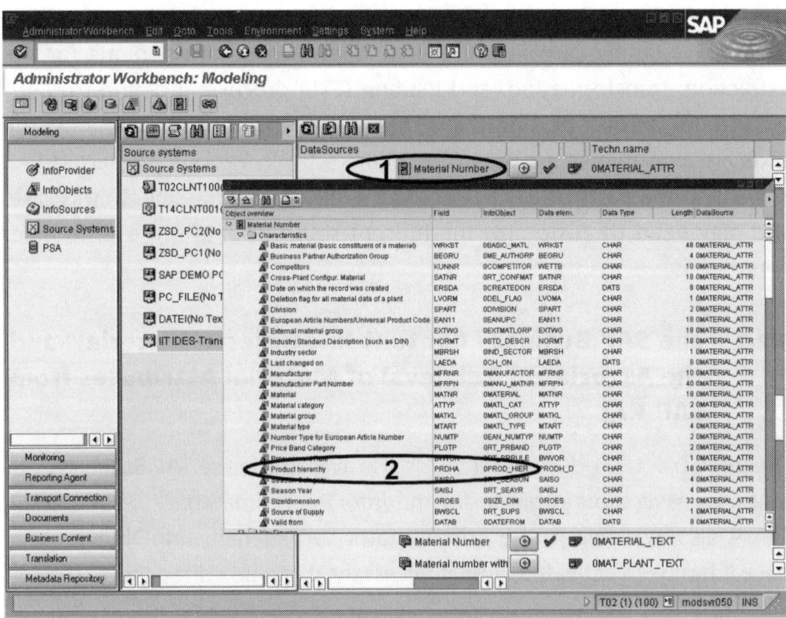

Figure 5.7 The DataSource for the Material Attributes

If data retrieval is set up and executed using the SAP Business Content components, the attributes are available as mapped (see Figure 5.8).

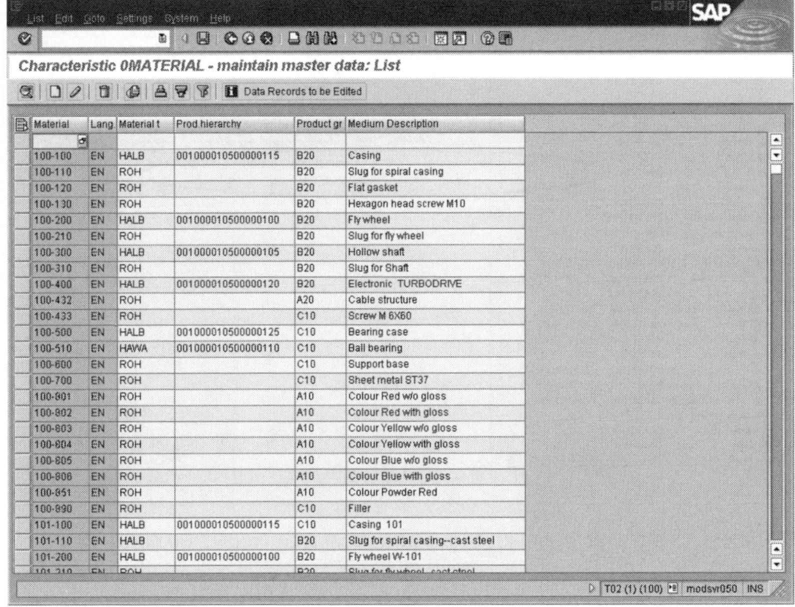

Figure 5.8 The Product Hierarchy as an Attribute of the Material

5.2.3 Problems with Using the SAP Business Content Material Attribute "Product Hierarchy" in Reporting

The SAP Business Content material attribute "product hierarchy" can be used in reporting based on the SAP Business Explorer (SAP BEx) query. In the example query, revenues are added to the values in the product hierarchy. To add revenues, you must transfer the navigation attribute "product hierarchy" from the hierarchy of usable objects to the rows by dragging and dropping (see Figure 5.9).

When executing the query, SAP BW determines the sums for each product hierarchy value in the material attributes. After you call the query and click on the **Execute** button in the selection screen **Variables for Ad Hoc Report** (see Figure 5.10, Step 1), the results list is displayed (see Figure 5.10, Step 2).

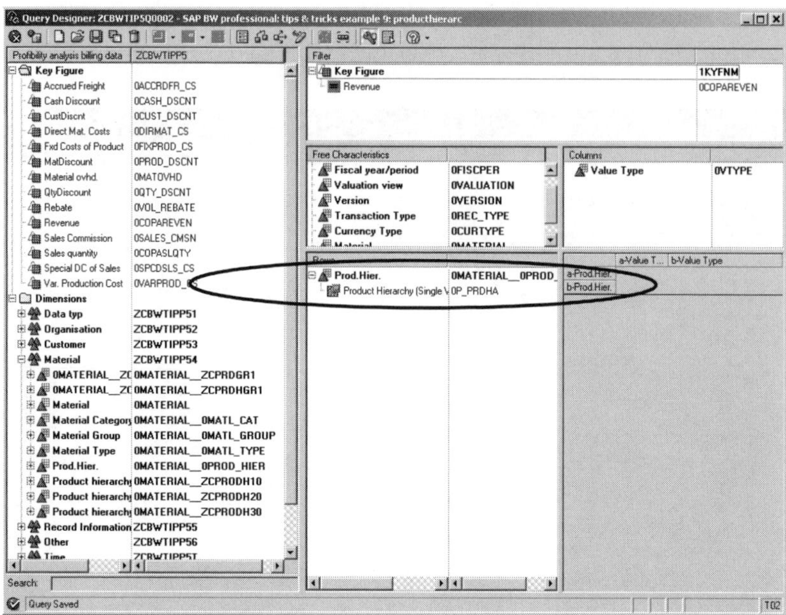

Figure 5.9 Query with Revenues, Grouped According to Product Hierarchy Values

Problems with use in reporting

In the results list in the HTML browser (presented via the SAP BEx), you should note that the total list of results shown is correct, as is the revenues total. The problem with the results table, however, is that the totals are calculated in accordance with the values found, which are partly on the second level of the product hierarchy and partly on the third level. Depending on the master data values, non-comparable totals may also occur on all levels of the product hierarchy (for example, the materials that are validly and directly assigned to value 00125 of level 1 in the product hierarchy produce a list structure that is difficult to comprehend). Therefore, when listing the values it is not possible to give a total that is compatible with reporting and that follows the structure of the product hierarchy, such as: Total → all subtotals of the first level → all subtotals of the second level → and so on → all totals on detail level (level 3 in our example). Mapping of this nature would require fixed structures, which would either be very costly, or obstruct many popular reporting functions.

Even more problematic, and in this case, actually erroneous, is how the query functions when the abovementioned characteristic value is being selected: If the user guidance is activated (see Figure 5.11, Step 1), then the posted values are shown in the form of a selection list (see Figure 5.11, Step 2).

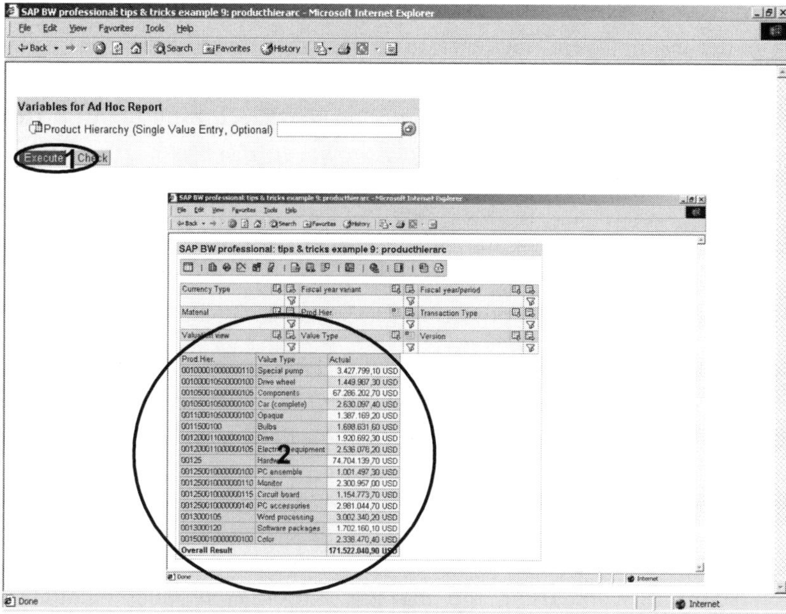

Figure 5.10 Adding Up Values to Reflect the Specifications in the Product Hierarchy

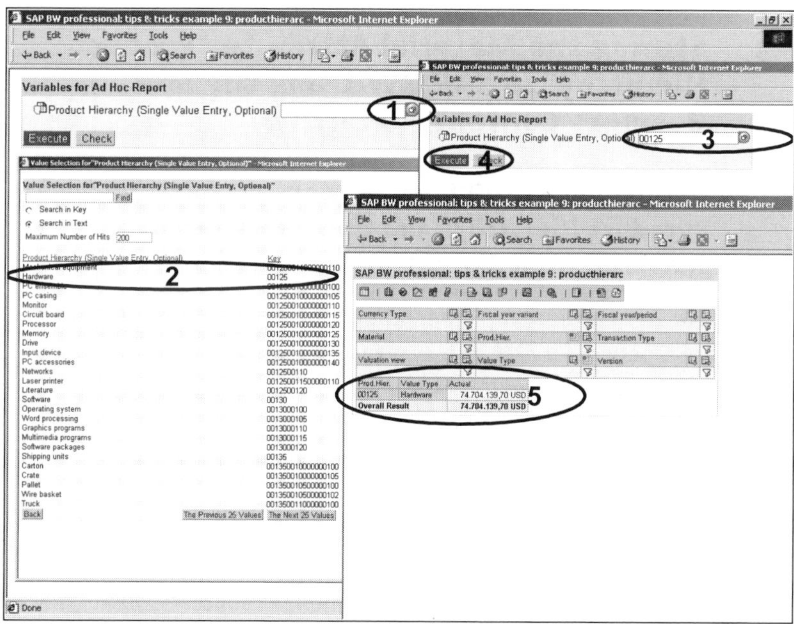

Figure 5.11 Misleading or, from the User's Point of View, Incorrect Result for the Query Based on the Material Attribute "Product Hierarchy"

In this case, this is the best possible reporting-related setting in SAP BW. If, in the example, we now click to select value 00125 at level 1 of the product hierarchy (see Figure 5.11, Step 3), it will be correctly transferred to the selection screen. After clicking on the **Execute** pushbutton (see Figure 5.11, Step 4), the query now, however, displays a value that is incorrect from the user's point of view (see Figure 5.11, Step 5).

Instead of displaying the sum of the values on the would-be selected value 00125 at level 1 of the product hierarchy, of course, only those amounts that are directly posted to this specification are displayed.

Solution for the view "Material (sales)"

As with the characteristic "material" (0MATERIAL), the attribute "product hierarchy" is available in the **Material (sales)** view (0MAT_SALES) with all components, from the DataSource to the sales material attribute. The solution for the sales view and the basic view is the same as the problems that occur.

Unsuitable solution

Consequently, this variant of the Business Content solution is not suitable for reporting when using the material attribute "product hierarchy," because of the problematic presentation and the misleading or even erroneous statements.

5.3 Storing the Material Attribute "Product Hierarchy" in SAP BW Using the SAP Business Content Hierarchy

5.3.1 Adjusting the SAP Business Content InfoObject "Product Hierarchy" and the Associated Data Retrieval from SAP R/3

In the SAP BW-specific Implementation Guide in the SAP R/3 system, there is a function for the characteristic "product hierarchy" (0PROD_HIER) for generating a true product hierarchy (from an SAP BW point of view), together with the corresponding ETL components. In it, the hierarchy structure is based on the SAP R/3 hierarchy-level settings.

To access it, go to the SAP BW-specific Implementation Guide in the SAP R/3 system:

- Variant 1: Call the Administrator Workbench, **Source system** view or Transaction RSA13; once there, right-click on the SAP R/3 source system and select the function **Customizing the Extractors ....** . Then, log on to SAP R/3, after which you can open and execute the menu entry **Modify Product Hierarchies for Transfer into SAP BW**.

- Variant 2: Log on directly to the corresponding SAP R/3 source system, call the SAP BW-specific Implementation Guide using Transaction SBIW, and then open and execute the menu entry **Modify Product Hierarchies for Transfer into SAP BW** (see Figure 5.12, Steps 1 and 2).

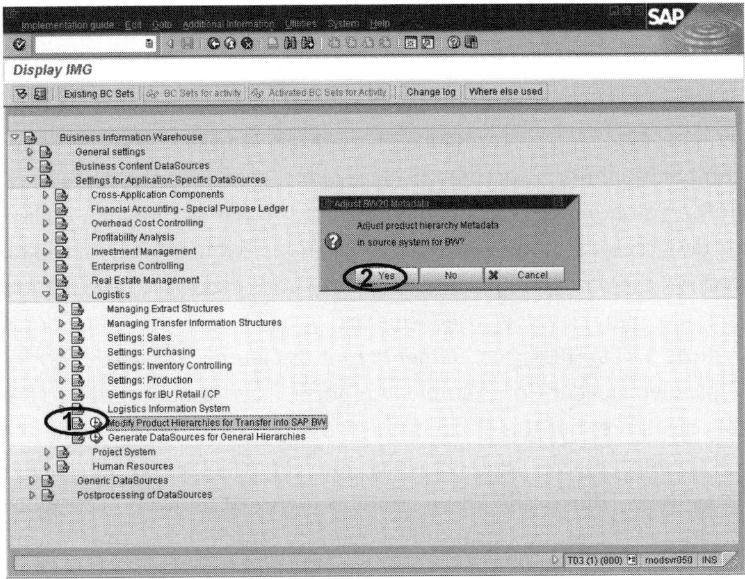

Figure 5.12 Adjusting the Metadata in the Source System to the Settings for Product Hierarchy on the SAP R/3 Side

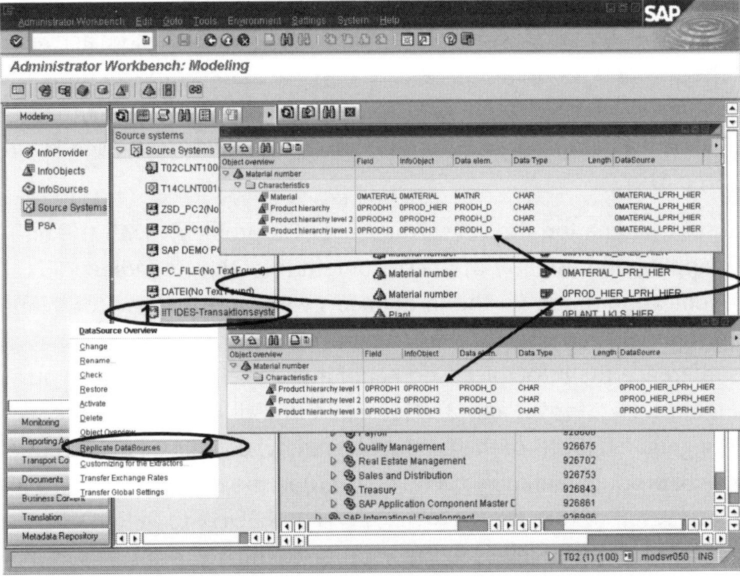

Figure 5.13 Replicated DataSources for the Product Hierarchy

You must then replicate the metadata for the DataSources. To do this, in the SAP BW, in the Administrator Workbench, **Source system** view (or Transaction RSA13), right-click to execute the function **Replicate DataSources** on the SAP R/3 source system. Two DataSources are available for the product hierarchy: "material number (0PROD_HIER_LPRH_HIER)" and "material number (0MATERIAL_LPRH_HIER)" (see Figure 5.13).

DataSources for SAP BW-compatible product hierarchies

The generation of two DataSources in the context of SAP Business Content is based on considerations regarding the quantity structure and the load time or reporting performance. In many SAP installations, the material number quantity structure (here, even considering the base view 0MATERIAL alone) ranges from a few tens of thousands to over a million master data records. If, in analytical applications (which mostly evaluate summaries), the complete product hierarchy from material to the highest product hierarchy level is used (hierarchy based on the DataSource 0MATERIAL_LKLS_HIER, see elements of it in Figure 5.13), then considerable problems occur (for example in reporting performance) due to the quantity structure. For this situation, SAP offers a shorter variant—in the form of the Business Content—in which the hierarchy based on the DataSource 0PROD_HIER_LPRH_HIER contains the most detailed occurrence of the product hierarchy. Because the quantity structure can usually vary between a few hundred values to tens of thousands of values, performance in reporting can be significantly improved in the most reasonable variants. (For more information, see the explanation in the OSS Note 407033: Extractor product hierarchy.)

The SAP Business Content InfoObject 0PRODHx

In the SAP BW, the product hierarchy level InfoObjects must be activated from the Business Content, as per the message, after implementing the adjustments in SAP R/3 (see Figure 5.12). These adjustments will then be available in the Administrator Workbench, **InfoObjects** view (see Figure 5.14, Step 1).

Problems with InfoObjects for the product hierarchy

On closer examination, however, there are also problems with the technical mapping of these SAP Business Content InfoObjects. When you call the modification mode (in the InfoObjects view in Administrator Workbench, right-click and select the function Modify), you will see that all levels reference the InfoObjects domain for the overall product hierarchy (see Figure 5.14, Steps 2 and 3). Consequently, all levels (even the very highly aggregated levels of the product hierarchy) contain all the values of the overall product hierarchy (0PROD_HIER) in the check table. Furthermore, as a result of this, for the lower levels 0PRODH2 to 0PRODHn, the compounding of lower levels to the appropriate higher levels, ensured by the software in SAP R/3, does not occur.

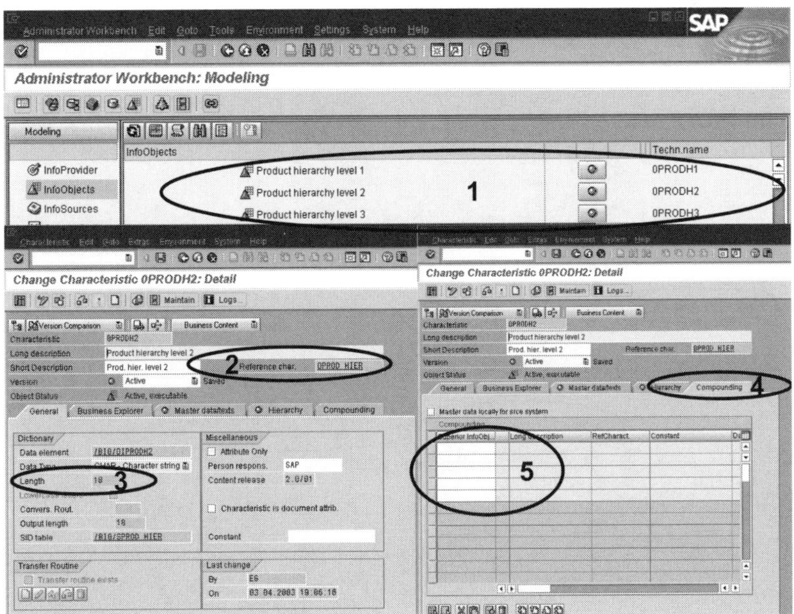

Figure 5.14 The SAP Business Content InfoObjects for the Levels of the Product Hierarchy

In order to ensure that SAP Business Content InfoObjects 0PRODHx are of use to the product hierarchy, you must enter the levels in the InfoObjects as characteristics for the hierarchy, in accordance with the SAP R/3 settings. Accordingly, you must navigate in the **Hierarchy** tab of InfoObject maintenance for "material" (0MATERIAL) and/or "product hierarchy (0PROD_HIER) (see Figure 5.15, Step 1). Once there, click on the pushbutton **External Chars. In Hierarchies** (see Figure 5.15, Step 2). In the pop-up **External Characteristics**, you must adopt the product hierarchy levels 0PRODH1 to 0PRODH3 (see Figure 5.15, Steps 3 through 5).

Based on the preceding settings, the DataSources can henceforth be assigned to SAP BW InfoSources. The DataSource "material number" (0MATERIAL_LPRH_HIER) is assigned to the InfoSource "material" (0MATERIAL). In the **Transfer structure** for the hierarchy, apart from the basic characteristic 0MATERIAL, the InfoObjects for the product hierarchy levels are also specified. These settings must then be saved (see Figure 5.16, Steps 1 and 2). An InfoPackage is set up for retrieving this hierarchy data, in which the hierarchy prepared by the DataSource is selected (see Figure 5.16, Steps 3 and 4).

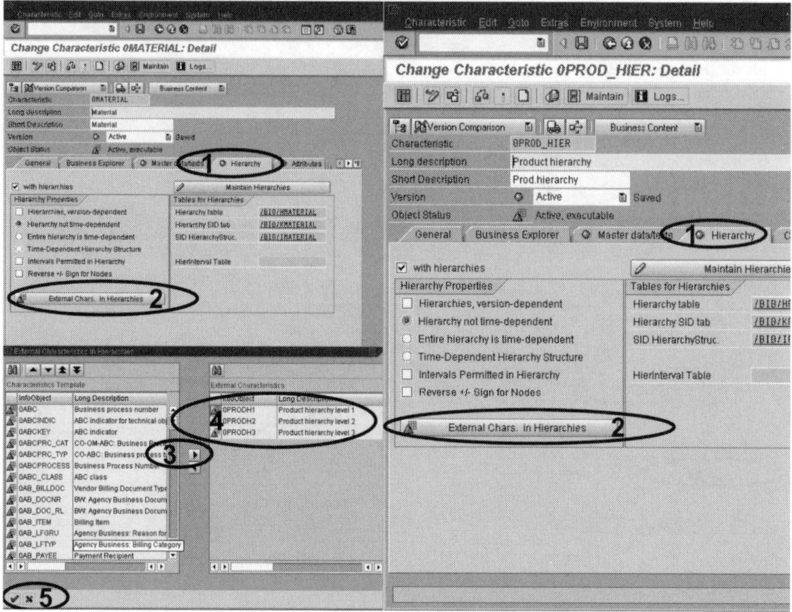

Figure 5.15 Incorporating the Product Hierarchy Levels as External Characteristics for the Hierarchies Based on 0MATERIAL and 0PROD_HIER

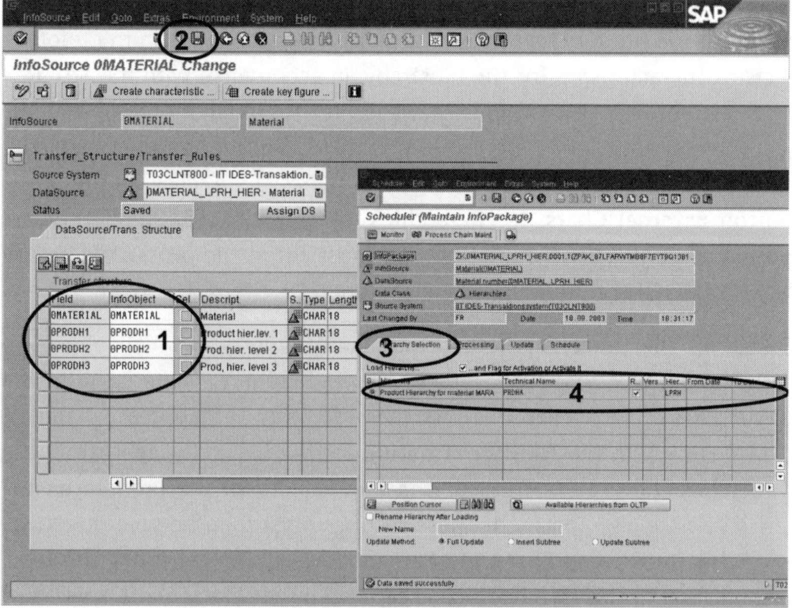

Figure 5.16 Data Retrieval for the Product Hierarchy for 0MATERIAL

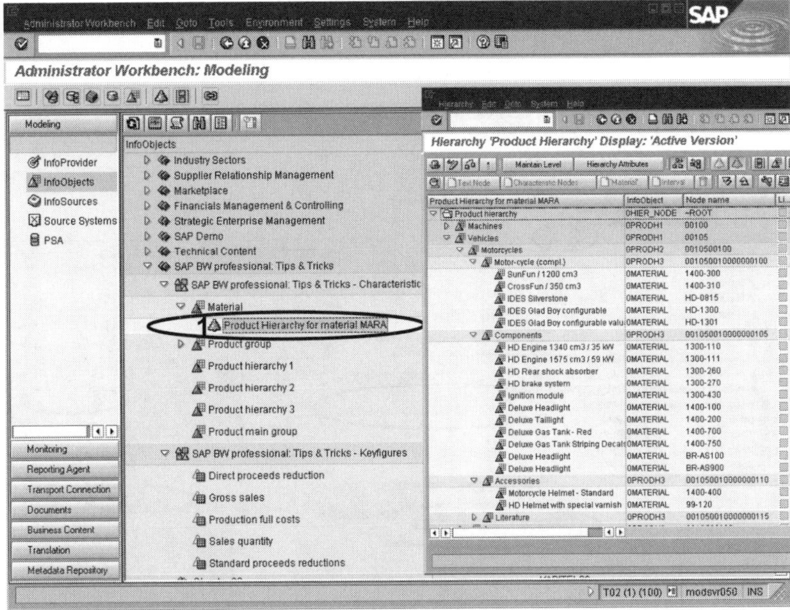

Figure 5.17 Product Hierarchy Based on 0MATERIAL

After updating, in the InfoObject Material (0MATERIAL), a hierarchy called **Product Hierarchy for material MARA** (PRDHA) is available (see Figure 5.17). As you can see, apart from values for the material (in the example material number 1400 – 300, 1400 – 310, and so on) and the text nodes (~ROOT), there are also hierarchy nodes based on the product hierarchy level values (in the example 0PRODH1: 00105, 0PRODH2: 0010500100, and so on).

5.3.2 Using the Adjusted SAP Business Content Product Hierarchy in Reporting

This hierarchy can be used in the query definition. For this hierarchy, the InfoObject "material" (0MATERIAL) is used, for example, to define the query rows, by dragging it from the frame on the left and dropping it in the Rows frame. Then, in the entry "material" (see Figure 5.18, Step 1), right-click to open the context-sensitive menu and select **Properties**. In the pop-up **Characteristic Properties for Characteristic Material**, activate the drop-down box (see Figure 5.18, Step 2) to open the pop-up **Select Hierarchy.** Confirm the hierarchy transfer by clicking on **OK** (see Figure 5.18, Step 3). The hierarchy name is then transferred to the pop-up **Characteristic Properties for Characteristic Material**, where you can set the drilldown level (see Figure 5.18, Step 4) and click on **OK** to adopt the settings (see Figure 5.18, Step 5).

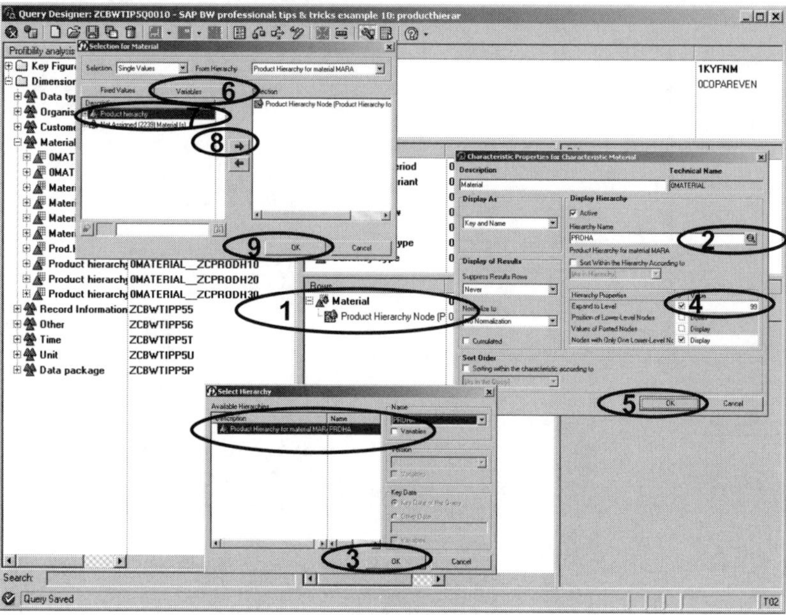

Figure 5.18 Using the Product Hierarchy Based on the InfoObject 0MATERIAL in the Query

If not all of the hierarchy should be displayed, you must use a variable in the query to select which hierarchy nodes should be displayed. Once again, in the entry "material" (see Figure 5.18, Step 1) right-click to open the context-sensitive menu and select the function **Restrict**. In the pop-up **Selection for Material,** you must now click on the **Variables** pushbutton (see Figure 5.18, Step 6). In the list of hierarchy variables, click on the variable 0N_PRDHA to select it and then click on **Add** to include it (see Figure 5.18, Steps 7 and 8). Click on **OK** to implement the settings (see Figure 5.18, Step 9). Once you have saved it, the query is available for reporting with the hierarchy and the hierarchy node selection.

After you start the query, the page for entering variables opens. Activate the drop-down box (see Figure 5.19, Step 1) to open a new window in which you can choose the desired hierarchy nodes. Click on the entry you want (see Figure 5.19, Step 2) and it will then be put into the variable entry page (Figure 5.19, Step 3). After you click on the **Execute** button, the result is displayed, including the selected hierarchy sub-tree (see Figure 5.19, Steps 4 and 5).

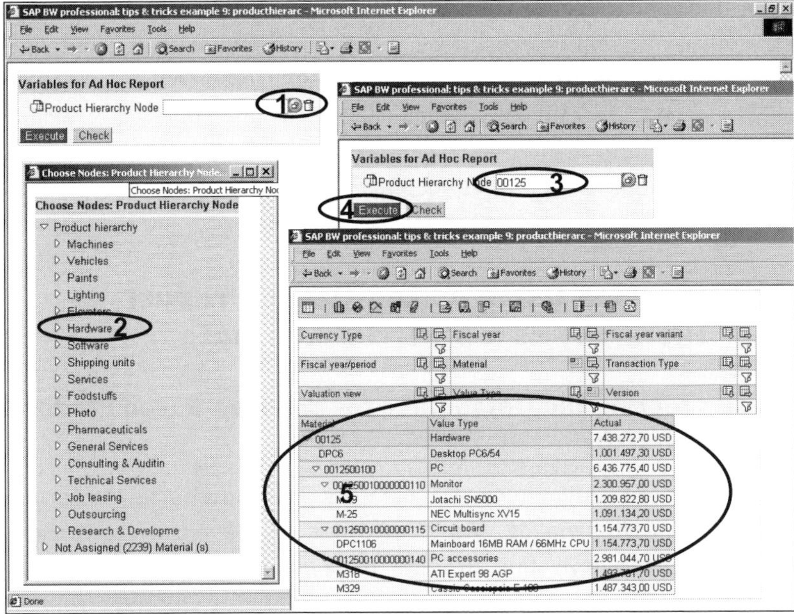

Figure 5.19 Executing the Query with Product Hierarchy and Selection Variables for Hierarchy Nodes

You can easily distinguish the query in the presentation, because (in contrast to the SAP Business Content attributes) the solution works correctly with the SAP Business Content hierarchy. Both the lower level values and the material appended directly under the product hierarchy 1—Characteristic value 00125—are shown correctly with their values (compare Figure 5.19 with Figure 5.11).

Alternative

If, as outlined above, the quantity structure is too large to use the hierarchy based directly on the material because there are too many materials, you can alternatively use the hierarchy based on the navigation attribute "product hierarchy" (0PROD_HIER).

If data retrieval for the hierarchy using the InfoObject 0PROD_HIER is done in the same way (for configuration and execution) as the product hierarchy using the characteristic "material" (0MATERIAL), you can also use this hierarchy in reporting.

In this way, the SAP Business Content hierarchy variant solves some of the problems associated with the attribute variant. However, two problem areas remain. Not optimally resolved, but of lesser consequence, is the problem that the same domain—and therefore also check and text tables—exists for the different product hierarchy levels. The second problem—it may no longer be possible to control performance with medium- or large-sized quantity structures—is the more serious issue. For aggregates based on hierarchies, no generic or fixed value selections are available. A generic or fixed value selection is necessary, however, to enable an adequate performance with a possibly large drill-down depth. For this reason, additional variants with material attributes based on a step-based product hierarchy must be taken into account.

5.4 Solution Using a Step-Based Product Hierarchy as a Material Attribute

5.4.1 Creating the DataSource for the Step-Based Product Hierarchy

The use of product hierarchy as a hierarchy offers advantages and disadvantages vis-à-vis handling. Many enterprises favor the use of this material property as a navigation attribute. In Section 5.2, the problems associated with the non-step-based mapping of the SAP Business Content attribute were explained. If the solution using the navigation attribute is preferred, then a correctly functioning customer-specific solution must be implemented.

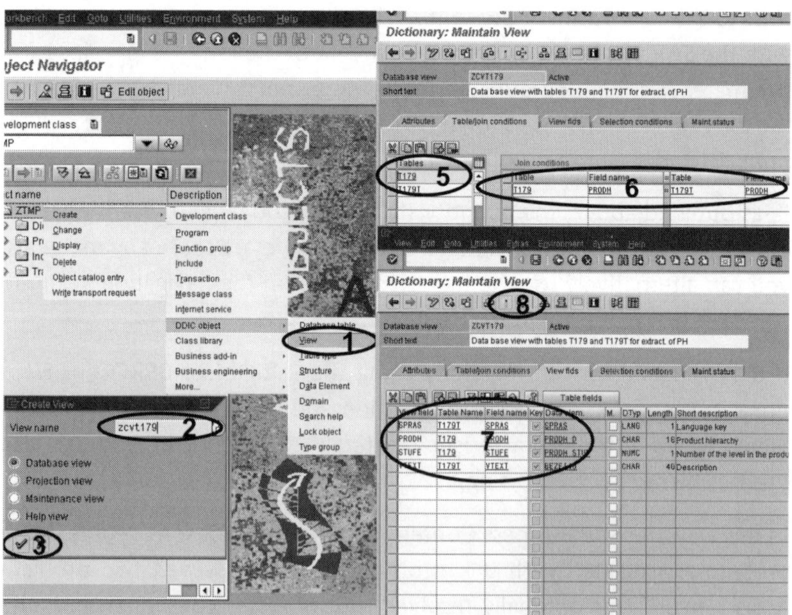

Figure 5.20 Creating a View for the Generic Product Hierarchy DataSource

Generic product hierarchy DataSource

To provide the values of the product hierarchy with the necessary information on hierarchy level for the SAP BW, a generic DataSource must be configured in the source system. This generic DataSource is based on a view that links the product hierarchy text table (T179T) with the level information in check table T179.

Creating a view

You define the view in the Object Navigator in the ABAP/4 Workbench (Transaction SE80). In the context of a customer-specific development class, right-click on the object name of the development class in the object tree to open the context-sensitive menu. In the menu tree, select the function **Create DDIC object View** (see Figure 5.20, Step 1). In the **Create View** pop-up, enter the technical name of the view (see Figure 5.20, Step 2) and select the type **Database view**. After confirming the entry (see Figure 5.20, Step 3), in the maintenance screen **Dictionary: Maintain View**, enter the short description of the view (see Figure 5.20, Step 4). In the **Table/join conditions** tab, tables T179 and T179T and the **join condition via field PRODH** must be entered for both tables (see Figure 5.20, Steps 5 and 6). In the **View flds** tab, enter the view fields SPRAS (table T179T), PRODH (table T179), STUFE (Table T179), and VTEXT (Table T179T) before the view is activated (see Figure 5.20, Steps 7 and 8). The generic DataSource is set up on this basis.

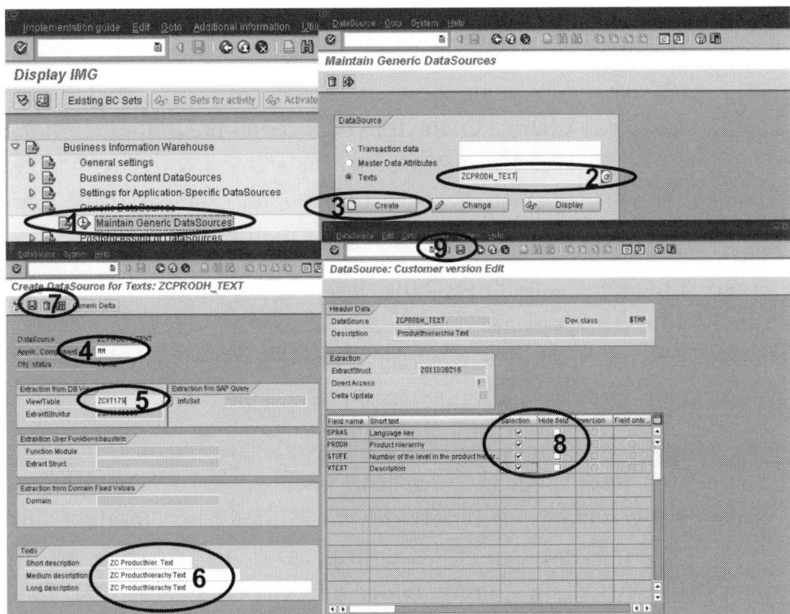

Figure 5.21 Configuration of the Generic DataSource for the Step Just Product Hierarchy

Setting up the generic DataSource

Go to the Implementation Guide in the SAP R/3 source system (transaction SBIW). Start the maintenance function by selecting the menu option **Generic DataSources** (see Figure 5.21, Step 1). In the **Maintain Generic DataSources** selection screen, enter the technical name that you want under type **DataSource Texts** and press the **Create** button (see Figure 5.21, Steps 2 and 3). In the **Create DataSource for Texts: ....** maintenance screen, enter the preferred application components (here: MM), the view configured previously using the ABAP/4-Workbench (here ZCVT179) (with the product hierarchy level information) and the short, medium, and long descriptions, and then press the **Save** button (see Figure 5.21, Steps 4 through 7). In the additional **DataSource: Customer version Edit** screen, check the **Selection** checkboxes for the fields corresponding to language key, product hierarchy, and number of the level in the product hierarchy. Press **Save** to close the DataSource that you just created (see Figure 5.21, Steps 8 and 9).

5.4.2 Creating the InfoObjects and Data Targets for the Step-Based Product Hierarchy

Creating the InfoObject

The InfoObject for the step-based product hierarchy is configured in SAP BW. In the Administrator Workbench, **InfoObjects** view, in a desired Characteristic-InfoObject Catalog, in the context-sensitive menu (right-click to open), select the function **Create InfoObject**. In the pop-up **Create Characteristic**, enter the technical name and description (see Figure 5.22, Step 1). After confirming the entry (see Figure 5.22, Step 2), in the maintenance screen **Change Characteristic ...**, enter the properties of the InfoObject so that level 1 of the product hierarchy is correctly mapped (retaining the SAP R/3 standard value, CHAR 5, for example). Next, activate the InfoObject (see Figure 5.22, Steps 3 through 5).

Proceed in the same way for the other levels in the product hierarchy. In addition to the settings in level 1, however, ensure that each additional level is linked to the next level up. For example, level 2 is compounded to level 1, level 3 is compounded to level 2, and so on (see Figure 5.22, Step 6).

Prerequisites for flexible updates

In order for the DataSource in the step just product hierarchy InfoObjects to be updated, flexible updating, available since SAP BW 3.0, is necessary. To have flexible updates, you must create the InfoObjects (in the example, ZCPRODH10 through ZCPRODH30) as an InfoProvider: In the Administrator Workbench, **InfoProvider** view (Transaction RSA11), open the context-sensitive menu by right-clicking in the desired InfoArea (here: Chapter 05) and select the **Insert Characteristic as Data Target ...** function (see Figure 5.23, Steps 1 and 2).

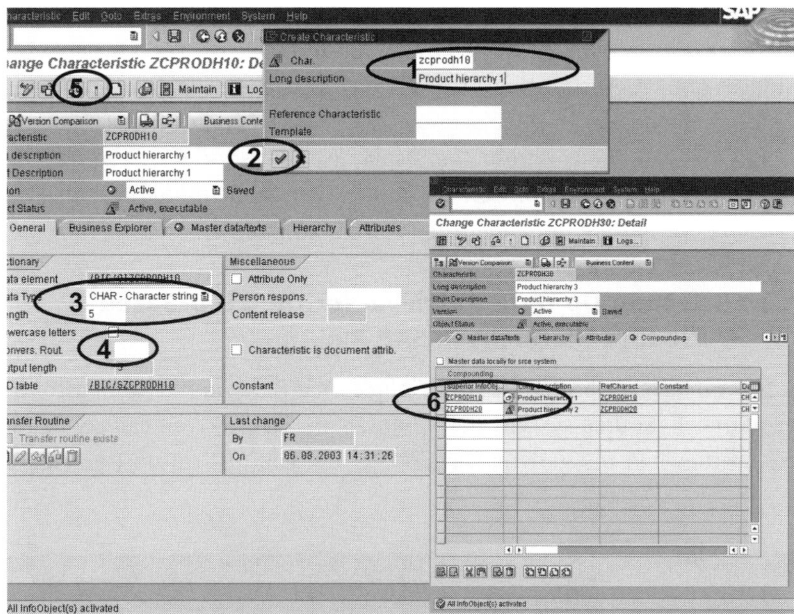

Figure 5.22 InfoObjects for the Step Just Product Hierarchy

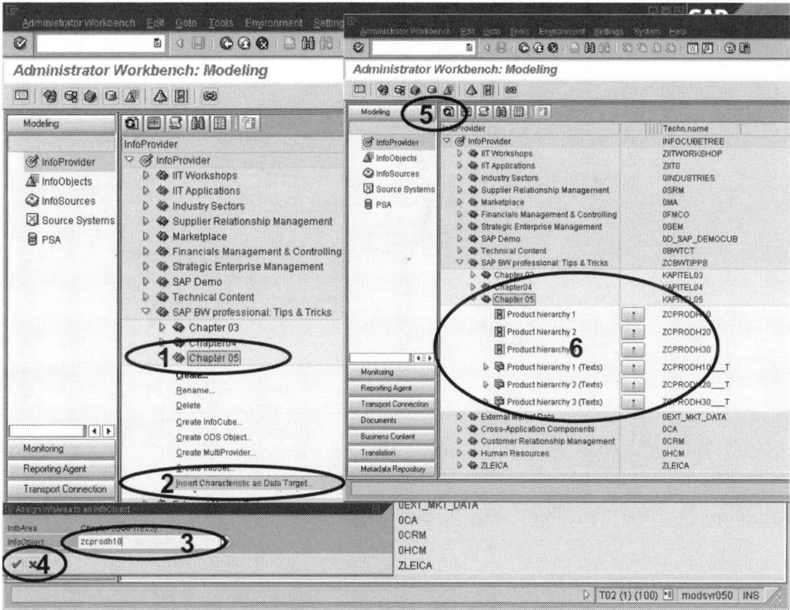

Figure 5.23 Enabling Flexible Updating of the Step-Based Product Hierarchy by Inserting the Product Hierarchy InfoObject as a Data Target

In the **Assign InfoArea to an InfoObject** pop-up, enter the technical name of the InfoObject and click on **Confirm Entry** (see Figure 5.23, Steps 3 and 4). Repeat these steps for all InfoObjects in the step-based product hierarchy (in the example, ZCPRODH10, ZCPRODH20, and ZCPRODH30). Then, refresh the display (see Figure 5.23, Step 5). The InfoObjects are now available as data targets and, therefore, are also available for flexible updating (see Figure 5.23, Step 6).

5.4.3 Setting Up Data Retrieval for the Step-Based Product Hierarchy in SAP BW

Data retrieval in SAP BW

After you have replicated the DataSource in SAP BW in the Administrator Workbench, **Source system** view (Transaction RSA13), you can configure data retrieval in the generic DataSource that you just set up (see Figure 5.24).

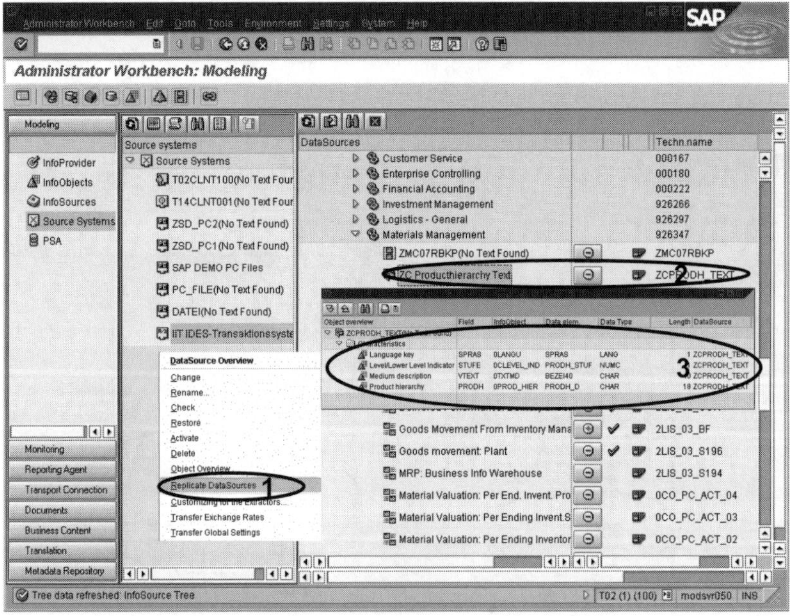

Figure 5.24 Replicating the Generic DataSource for the Step-Based Product Hierarchy in SAP BW

In the Administrator Workbench, **InfoSources** view (Transaction RSA12), an InfoSource is created for the previous DataSource. Right-click on the preferred application components to open the context-sensitive menu, and select the function **Create InfoSource ...** (see Figure 5.25, Steps 1 and 2). Then, in the **Create InfoSource** pop-up, select the type **Flexible**

Update in any Data Target and enter the technical name and description (see Figure 5.25, Step 3). Once you have confirmed your entry (see Figure 5.25, Step 4), the InfoSource will be displayed in the Administrator Workbench (see Figure 5.25, Step 5).

Right-click in this InfoSource to open the context-sensitive menu and select the function **Assign DataSource ...** (see Figure 5.25, Step 6). In the **Transaction Data-InfoSource: Assign Source System** pop-up, you can select and confirm the source system (see Figure 5.25, Steps 7 and 8). From the list of **Available DataSources,** select the generic DataSource for the step just product hierarchy (see Figure 5.25, Steps 9 and 10) and in the **Save Changes** popup, click on **Yes** when prompted with the question **To InfoSource ... Save?** (see Figure 5.25, Step 11).

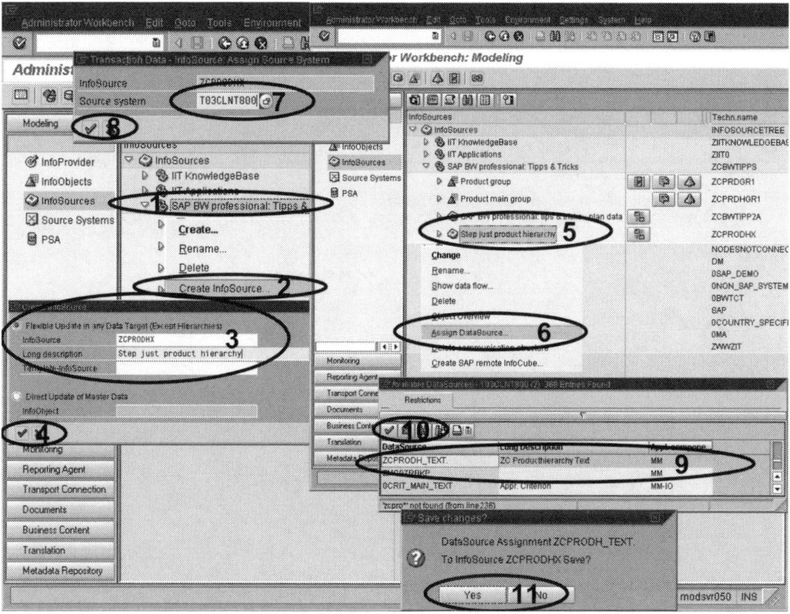

Figure 5.25 Creating the InfoSource and Assigning the DataSource for the Step Just Product Hierarchy

The maintenance screen **InfoSource ... Change** will then open. This is where you must assign InfoObjects to the source fields of the DataSource, as shown in Table 5.1 (see also Figure 5.26, Step 1).

DataSource Field	InfoObject
SPRAS	0LANGU
PRODH	0PROD_HIER
STUFE	0CLEVEL_IND
VTEXT	0TXTMD

Table 5.1 Transfer Rules for Product Hierarchy Texts

After you have clicked on the **Propose Transfer Rules** pushbutton (see Figure 5.26, Step 2), you can activate the InfoSource with the transfer rules (see Figure 5.26, Step 3).

Update rules for master data texts

Based on this InfoSource, in the Administrator Workbench, **InfoProvider** view (Transaction RSA11), you can now create the update rules for the master data texts.

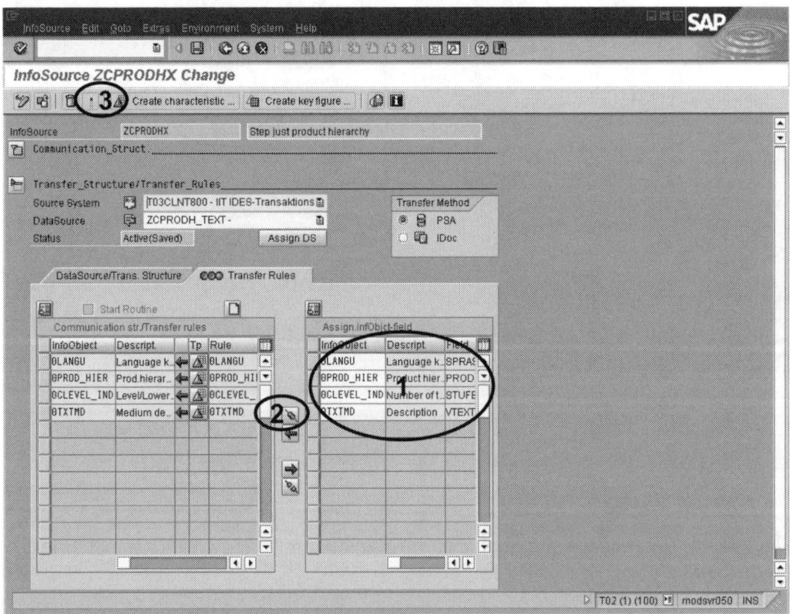

Figure 5.26 Creating the Transfer Rules for the Step Just Product Hierarchy

Right-click on the InfoProvider for product hierarchy 1 (example: ZCPRODH10) to open the context-sensitive menu. Select the function **Create Update Rules** (see Figure 5.27, Steps 1 and 2). In the selection screen **Update Rules create: Start**, enter the InfoSource for the flexible update of the step just product hierarchy and click on the **Next screen** pushbutton (see Figure 5.27, Steps 3 and 4). Depending on the settings of the InfoSource and the InfoObject, the pop-up **Update Rules create: Start** is displayed, containing the information **Attributes were set to "no update"**, which you must confirm (see Figure 5.27, Step 5).

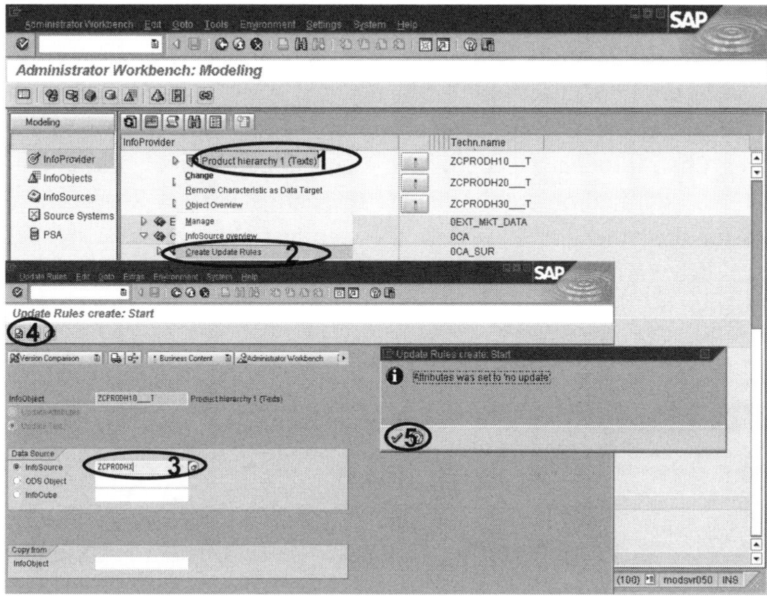

Figure 5.27 Update Rules for the Product Hierarchy, Part 1

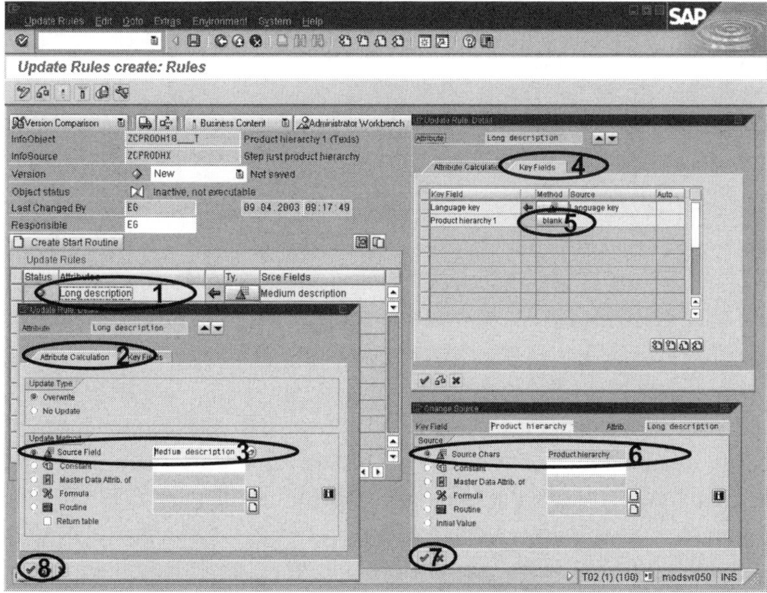

Figure 5.28 Update Rules for the Product Hierarchy, Part 2

In the maintenance screen **Update rules create: Rules**, start rule maintenance by double-clicking on the text attribute (in the example: "Long description") (see Figure 5.28, Step 1). In the **Update Rule: Detail** pop-up, in the **Attribute Calculation** tab, set the update method **Source Field** and select the InfoSource text field (here: "Medium description") (see Figure 5.28, Steps 2 and 3). In the **Key Fields** tab, activate the **blank** pushbutton in the InfoObject product hierarchy 1 (see Figure 5.28, Steps 4 and 5) and in the **Change Source** pop-up, set the source field to the **Source Chars** product hierarchy (see Figure 5.28, Step 6). The entries must be confirmed before the update rules are activated. Repeat these steps for the other InfoObjects in the step just product hierarchy, but with a slight variation: for Steps 2 through n, use the formula function to generate the corresponding partial key (substrings) from the 18 character fully defined key.

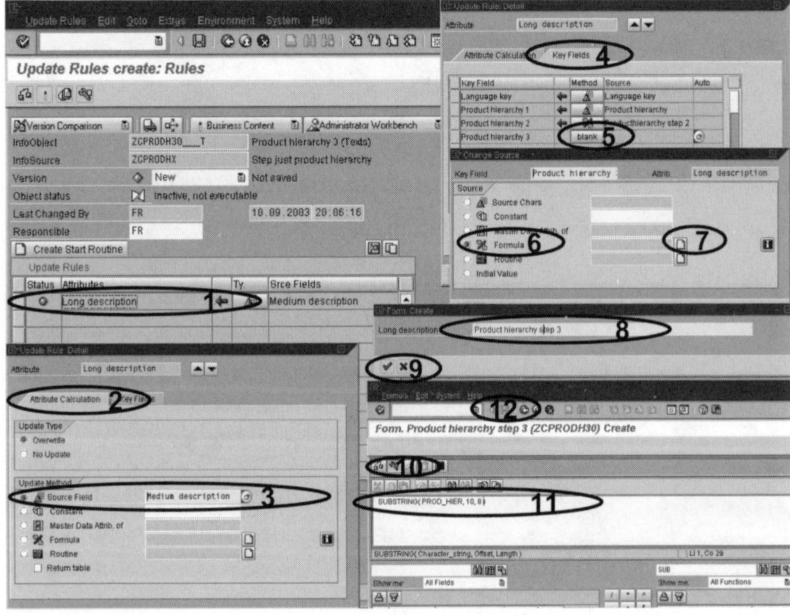

Figure 5.29 Formula for the Substring in the Step Just Product Hierarchy

Formula for the substring

In addition to the general settings listed above, in this case in the InfoObjects "Product hierarchy 2 to n" in the **Update Rule: Detail** pop-up, in the **Key Fields** tab, activate the **blank** pushbutton (see Figure 5.29, Steps 1 through 5). In the **Change Source** pop-up, change the source to **Formula** and then press the **Create** pushbutton [another icon button] (see Figure 5.29, Steps 6 and 7). In the **Form. Create** pop-up, enter the description and confirm your entry (see Figure 5.29, Steps 8 and 9). In the maintenance screen **Form. ... Create** you can activate expert mode (see Figure 5.29, Step 10) and enter the substring function (see Figure 5.29, Step 11). For the standard product hierarchy structure with step lengths 5-5-8, for example, the following substring functions are necessary:

- For Step 2: SUBSTRING(PROD_HIER, 5, 5)
- For Step 3: SUBSTRING(PROD_HIER, 10, 8)

You can then leave formula maintenance using the **Back** button (see Figure 5.29, Step 12) and confirm your entries using the **Transfer** button. The update rules are then activated.

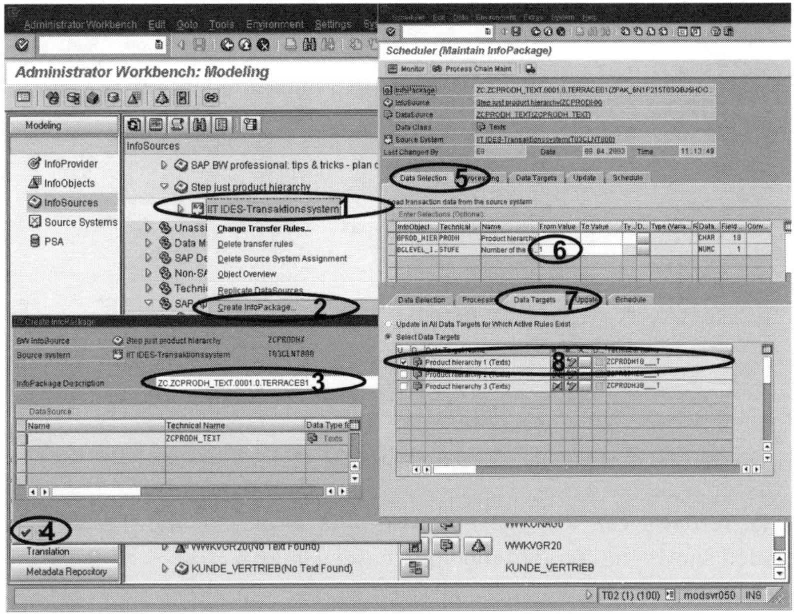

Figure 5.30 InfoPackages for Each Level in the Product Hierarchy

InfoPackages for the step just product hierarchy

The creation of InfoPackages is the last stage in setting up data retrieval. An InfoPackage is created for each level in the product hierarchy. The corresponding level is selected in each InfoPackage. Consequently, the text and check tables, and the configuration of the InfoObject, contain only the product hierarchy values that are correct for the relevant level.

The InfoPackages are created in the Administrator Workbench, **InfoSources** view, for the product hierarchy InfoSource that was previously set up. Right-click on this InfoSource to open the context-sensitive menu and select the function **Create InfoPackage ...** (see Figure 5.30, Steps 1 and 2).

In the **Create InfoPackage** pop-up, enter the InfoPackage description and confirm your entry (see Figure 5.30, Steps 3 and 4). In the **Scheduler (Maintain InfoPackage)** maintenance screen, in the **Data Selection** tab, for each InfoPackage, enter the level for which it should retrieve data (see Figure 5.30, Steps 5 and 6). Similarly, in the **Data Targets** tab, select the data target associated with the level chosen (see Figure 5.30, Steps 7 and 8).

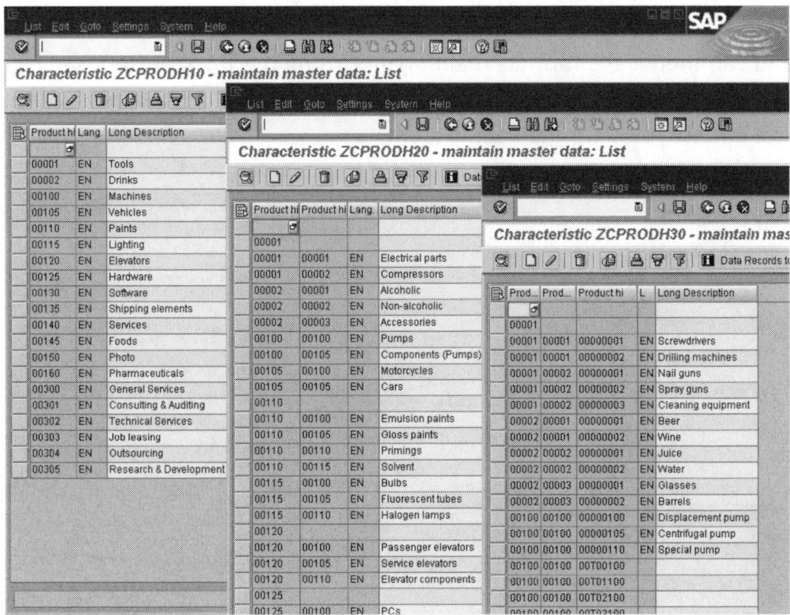

Figure 5.31 Result of the Product Hierarchy Update

Data retrieval can then be executed. The display of the master data loaded shows the result of the update (see Figure 5.31).

5.4.4 The Step-Based Product Hierarchy as a Navigation Attribute for Material and Its Use in InfoCubes

Setting up the step-based product hierarchy

The step-based product hierarchy is available as a navigation attribute for material in reporting. To use the step-based product hierarchy as such, the InfoObjects must be completed as appropriate material attributes. In the Administrator Workbench, **InfoObjects** view, double-click to open and modify the InfoObject "material" (in the example: 0MATERIAL). In the **Change Characteristic ...** maintenance screen, open the **Attributes** tab and press the **Detail/Navigation Attribute** pushbutton (see Figure 5.32, Steps 1 and 2). The InfoObjects for the step-based product hierarchy can now be included in the list of attributes (see Figure 5.32, Step 3).

Activate the button **Navigation Attribute in/out** and enter the description (see Figure 5.32, Steps 4 and 5) to make the attributes available as navigation attributes. Then, activate the "material" InfoObject (see Figure 5.32, Step 6).

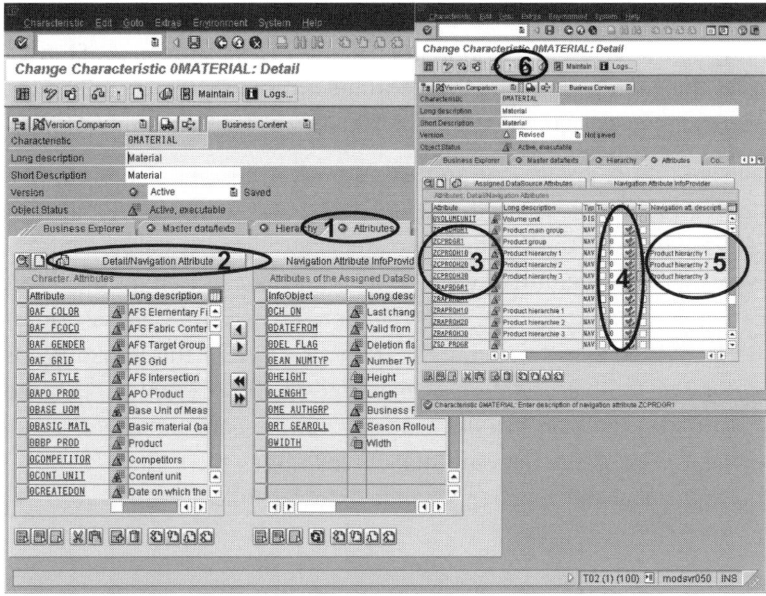

Figure 5.32 Material Attribute: Step-Based Product Hierarchy

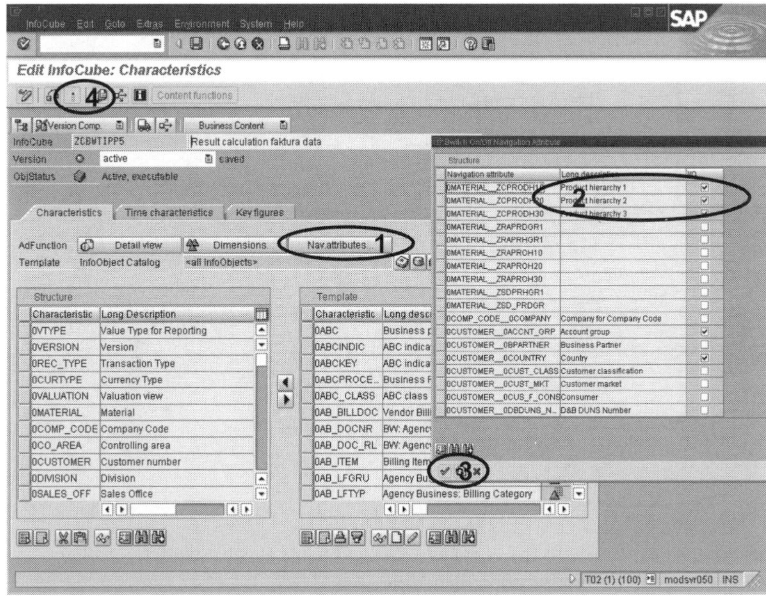

Figure 5.33 Activating the Step-Based Product Hierarchy in the InfoCube

The step-based product hierarchy can be used in reporting if the navigation attributes are activated in the InfoCubes. To activate the navigation attributes, open the **InfoProvider** view in the Administrator Workbench. Double-click on the InfoCube in question to open the maintenance screen **Edit InfoCube: Characteristics.** Once there, press the **Nav. Attributes** pushbutton (see Figure 5.33, Step 1). After switching on the navigation attributes for the step-based product hierarchy (see Figure 5.33, Step 2), transfer the entry by pressing the **Continue** button (see Figure 5.33, Step 3). You can then activate the InfoCube in question (see Figure 5.33, Step 4).

Data retrieval for the material attributes

Finally, you must implement and execute data retrieval of the material attributes for the step-based product hierarchy. To do this, you must extend the InfoSource used for the material attributes in the Administrator Workbench, **InfoSources** view. If the InfoSource is used for the direct updating of master data (0MATERIAL), then the new attributes are automatically available in the communication structure. If the InfoSource is used for the flexible updating of master data (0MATERIAL_ATTR), the new attributes must be manually included in the communication structure. Right-click on the relevant InfoSource to open the context-sensitive menu and select the function **Change Transfer Rules** (see Figure 5.34, Steps 1 and 2).

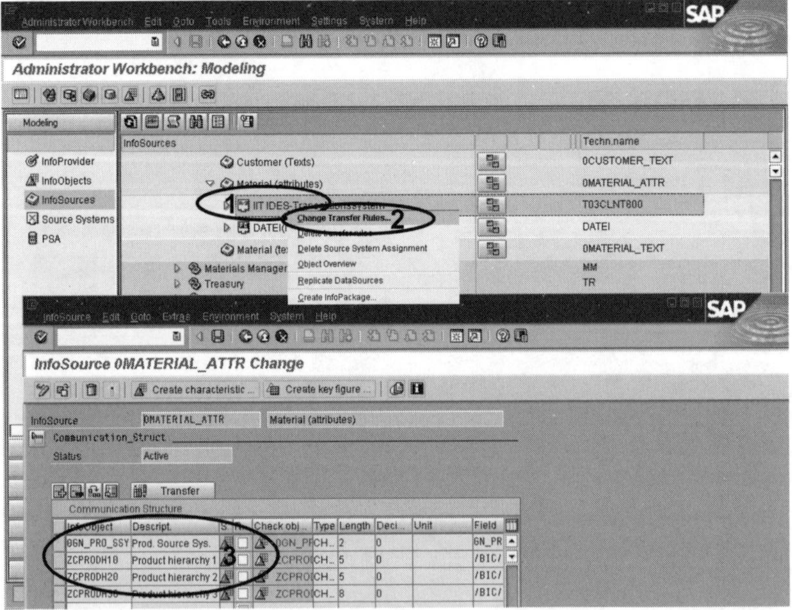

Figure 5.34 Starting to Edit the Transfer Rules and (with Flexible Update) Adding InfoObjects to the Communication Structure

If you have enabled flexible updating, the InfoObjects for the step just product hierarchy are added to the Communication Structure manually (see Figure 5.34, Step 3).

Now, you can maintain transfer rules for the attributes of the step just product hierarchy. In Step 1, you can transfer the SAP source field 0PROD_HIER, because the properties of the step just product hierarchy generate the correct substring.

For additional steps, the corresponding substring must be created using either a user exit or formula. To assign the source field directly, in the **Transfer_Structure/Transfer_Rules** area, position the cursor on the attribute product hierarchy 1 and activate the button **Transfer rule Type** (see Figure 5.35, Step 1). In the **Edit Transfer Rules** pop-up, select the transfer rule **Field as TS** (Transfer Structure) 0PROD_HIER. Confirm your entry by clicking on the **Transfer** button (see Figure 5.35, Steps 2 and 3).

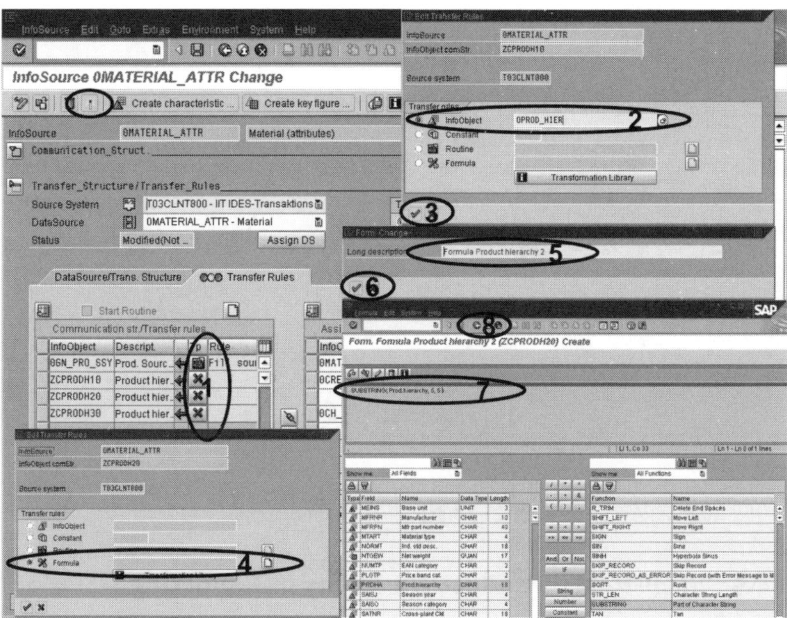

Figure 5.35 Editing the Transfer Rules for the Material Attributes of the Step Just Product Hierarchy

For the other levels in the product hierarchy you must first click the **Type** button, then select the transfer rule formula and click on the **Create** button (see Figure 5.35, Step 4). In the **Form. Change** pop-up, you must enter a description of the formula (see Figure 5.35, Steps 5 and 6). In the maintenance screen **Create Product Hierarchy Formula ...**, apply substring functions just as for the formulae in Section 5.4.3 (see Figure 5.35, Steps 7 and 8). Confirm your entries. Finally, the transfer rules are activated.

Once you have completed the transfer rules (see Figure 5.36, Step 1), data retrieval is started using the InfoPackage. To ensure the flexible update, you must maintain the update rules for the new attributes of the step-based product hierarchy by adopting the corresponding source fields of the InfoSource exactly as they appear (see Figure 5.36, Step 2). After you execute the data retrieval, the additional material attributes are filled step-by-step (see Figure 5.36, Step 3).

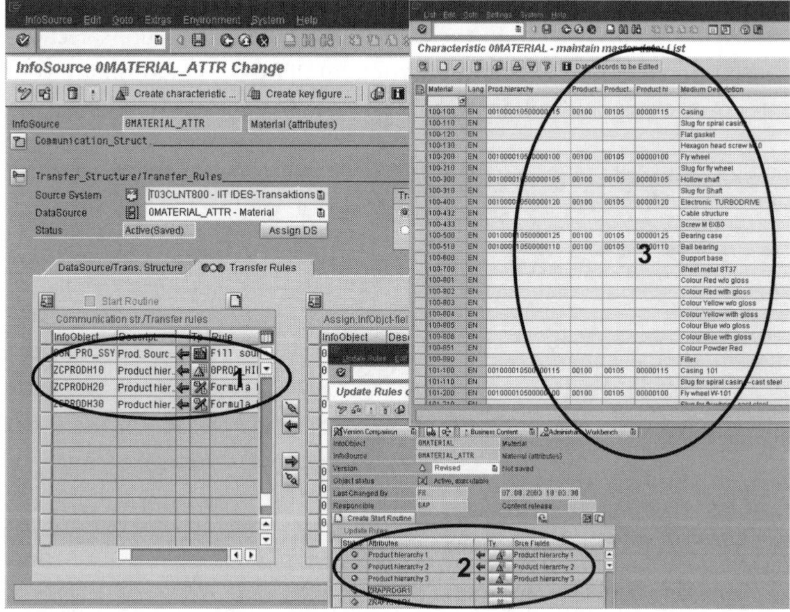

Figure 5.36 The Complete Transfer and Update Rules and the Result of Data Retrieval for the Material Attribute with Step-Based Product Hierarchy

5.4.5 Step-Based Product Hierarchy in Reporting

The navigation attributes

You can use the material attributes with the step-based product hierarchy in query definition. To do this, use the attributes "product hierarchy 1 through n" (for example, 0MATERIAL_ZCPRODHx0) for the InfoObject "material" (0MATERIAL), for example, to define rows or the free characteristics of the query by dragging them from the frame on the left and dropping them in the row frame or the frame with the free characteristics (see Figure 5.37, Steps 1 and 2). These navigation attributes then work correctly when the query is executed (see Figure 5.37, Step 3).

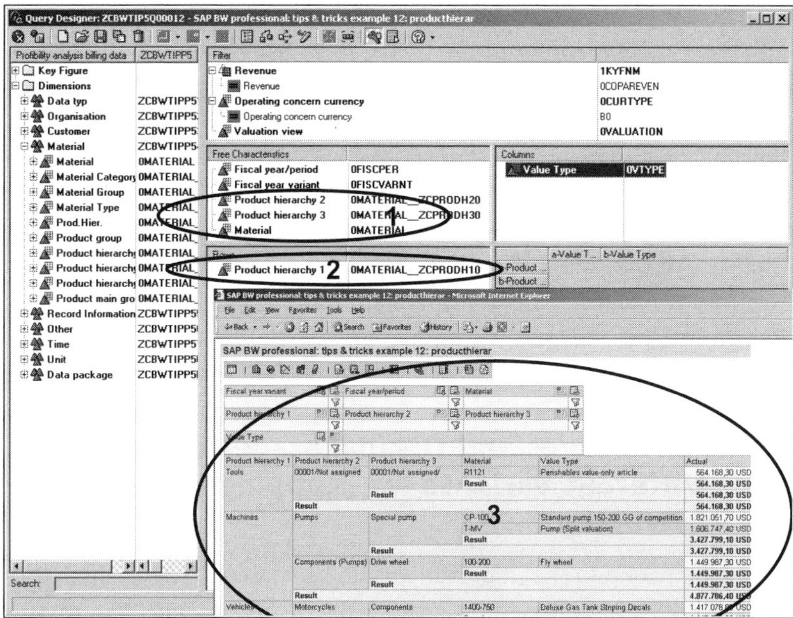

Figure 5.37 Using the Step-Based Product Hierarchy as Drill-down in Reporting

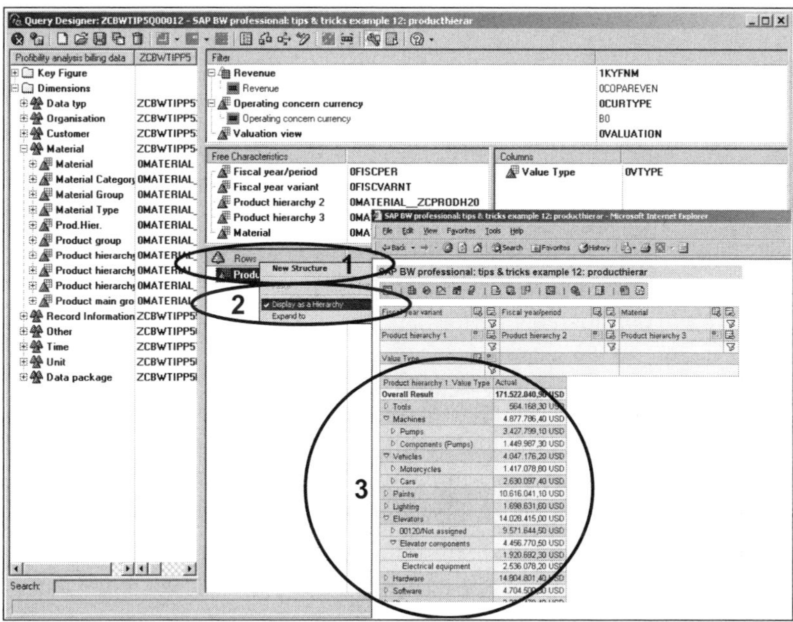

Figure 5.38 The Navigation Attributes of the Step-Based Product Hierarchy and the Material as a Hierarchy in Reporting

Presenting characteristics and attributes as a hierarchy

If the product hierarchy and the material should be treated as a hierarchy, despite attribute mapping of the product hierarchy in reporting, then, as of SAP BW 3.0, the function **Display as a Hierarchy** is available for the query rows. To use this function, in the query definition, right-click on the **Rows** heading to open the context-sensitive menu and select the option **Display as a Hierarchy** (see Figure 5.38, Steps 1 and 2). There will now be a drill-down during the query execution, for example according to characteristics of the step just product hierarchy or the material, and in this way the advantages of the navigation attributes are combined with those of the hierarchy, and both the display and the navigation are correct (see Figure 5.38, Step 3).

5.5 Advantages and Disadvantages of the Different Variants for Mapping the Product Hierarchy

When comparing the solution variants, it is apparent that variant 1 with the SAP Business Content attributes for the product hierarchy is unsatisfactory and does not function correctly. Using the product hierarchy according to variant 2, however, or mapping using step just product hierarchy navigation attributes, is acceptable and functions well.

Advantages and disadvantages of the hierarchy

One advantage of hierarchy mapping is the complete range of functionality of the hierarchy. However, the quantity structure, that is, the size of the hierarchy, can be problematic, because in many enterprises, the number of values in the product hierarchy (including materials) can be tens of thousands, and often even several hundred thousand (sometimes, there can even be more than one million characteristic values and hierarchy nodes). Therefore, hierarchy size can and often does contribute to poor usability and considerable performance problems. Similarly, the non-step based storage of the value tables in a domain, which is referenced by all product hierarchy steps, can result in equally poor performance.

Advantages and disadvantages of the attributes

The main advantage of mapping with step-based attributes is that the check tables are kept to a minimum, which results in the optimal handling of the aggregates (including fixed value aggregates) and therefore contributes to optimal performance. Presenting the drill-down of the navigation attributes and the material as a hierarchy ensures practically optimal handling. It is also possible to obtain hierarchy displays that use only a part of the product hierarchy (for example, "product hierarchies 1 and 2" and "material"); however, not all hierarchy properties are available.

Recommendations for use

Because optimal performance is generally the decisive criterion (to which handling considerations are often subordinated), using attributes is most often recommended. If, however, emphasis is placed on all hierarchy properties, then a combination of the step just product hierarchy with the SAP Business Content hierarchy is suggested. In this way, in addition to achieving optimal performance (using the attributes in aggregates), you also have access to the complete hierarchy properties.

Part 4
Reporting and Web Applications with the SAP Business Explorer

6 Using Sample Solutions to Show the Important Functions of the Query Designer in SAP BW 3.x

Since SAP BW 3.0, SAP also offers a best-practice data warehouse solution in the area of reporting. The optimizations and expansions in the Query Designer represent the core of the improvements. This chapter explains the basic functions and significant changes in SAP BW 3.x.

6.1 Introduction

6.1.1 Calling Up the Query Designer and Creating Queries

Analyses and reports in SAP BW are based on SAP Business Explorer (SAP BEx) queries. You create these queries with the Query Designer, which has been available as a stand-alone PC application since SAP BW 3.0. This application can either be called up via the menu, as a link, or directly (via the executable file wdbrlog.exe) (see Figure 6.1, Step 1). After starting SAP, you must log on to the SAP BW system by entering your user ID and password. Then, you must confirm your logon by clicking on the **OK** button (see Figure 6.1, Steps 2 and 3).

Starting the Query Designer

After logon, the Query Designer is started. To configure a new query, click the **New** button (see Figure 6.1, Step 4). In the **Open Query** pop-up, click the **InfoAreas** button. The InfoArea tree with the respective InfoProviders is displayed. This must then be opened such that the InfoProvider to be used is displayed. Highlight the InfoProvider that you want and select it by clicking on the **OK** button (see Figure 6.1, Steps 5 to 7).

Query Designer: technical name

The selected InfoProvider is then displayed in the **Query Designer: New Query** popup (see Figure 6.1, Step 8). By clicking on the **Technical Name** button, you can display the SAP BW keys (see Figure 6.1, Step 9 and the following figures). This is the starting basis for creating queries.

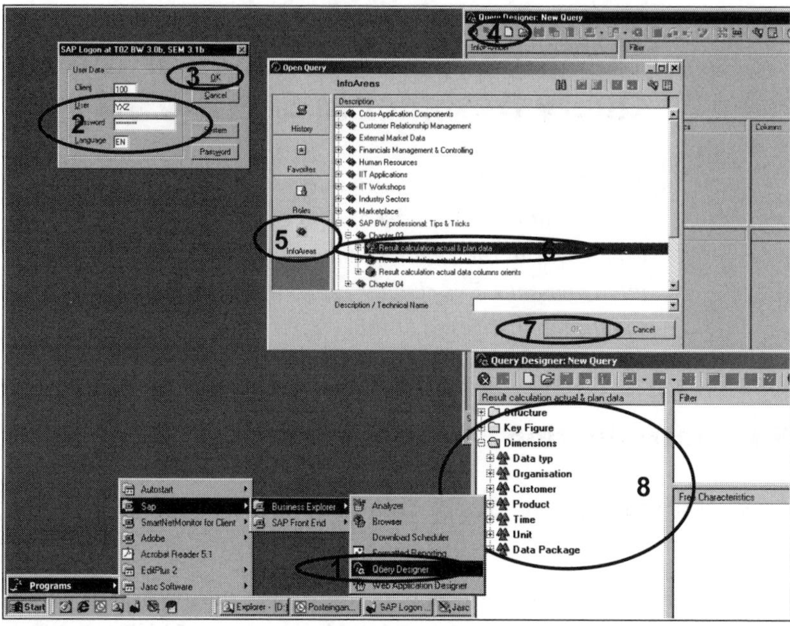

Figure 6.1 Starting the Query Designer with InfoProvider Selection

6.1.2 Including Characteristics and Keys in the Query

Row and column elements

The result of a query is displayed primarily via a table with similarly configured rows and columns. For the respective rows and columns, selections and calculations can be required. For example, this particular table can consist of columns with keys (in the example: "Gross sales," "Direct sales reduction," and "Standard sales revenue," as well as "COGS" and rows (in the example: Fiscal year/period).

Filter Elements

If global selections are necessary, they can be defined as filter elements (in the example, the SAP "Fiscal year variant," the "Currency Type," and the "Value Type" "Actual").

Free Characteristics

If selections or changes to the row or column criteria are necessary, elements of the type "Free Characteristics" can be defined (in the example these are the "Fiscal year," "Country," and "Region").

Including InfoObjects in queries

You should now define the named query elements. In the Query Designer, you can display the relevant components (those to be selected) of the InfoProvider by opening the object tree in the left frame and clicking the ⊞ (see Figure 6.2). Using drag & drop, you can move the necessary InfoObjects (characteristics and keys) into the frames for filter values, free characteristics, rows, and columns (see Figure 6.2).

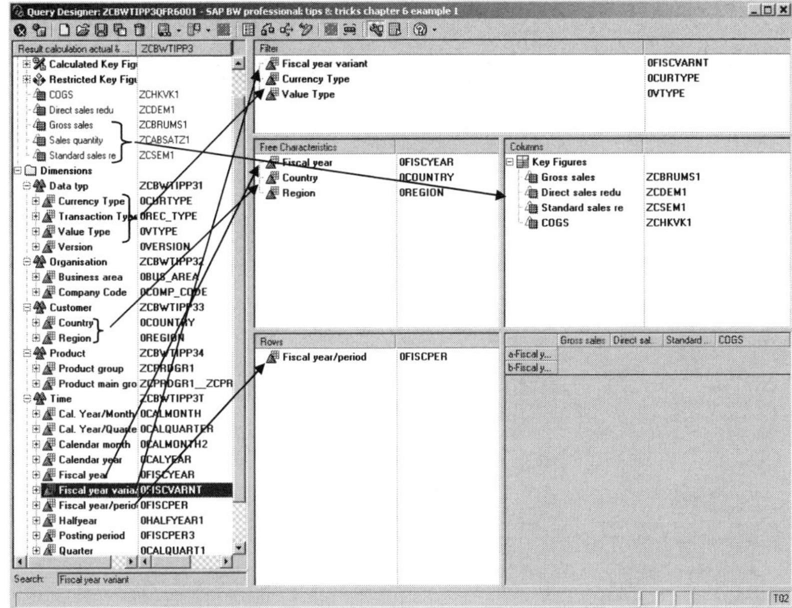

Figure 6.2 Including Characteristics and Keys as Query Elements Using Drag & Drop

6.1.3 Selections (Restricting)

In general, selections are necessary for queries. Selections are required, for example, so that a particular data type is displayed explicitly (in the example: Value Type "Actual"). In addition, selections can be necessary so that no nonsensical summations occur (from SAP R/3, the CO-PA data can also be provided in addition to the result area currency, for example, also in the accounting sector currency; in the example, a nonsensical doubling of the values is avoided using the selection of the currency type "Result area currency"). Finally, technical selections can be necessary in order to achieve better characteristic displays (in the example, the fiscal year variant "Calendar year, 4 spec. periods" is selected, so that the key display of "Periods/year" occurs without the prefix K4).

Selecting filter values

The global restrictions are defined in that on a characteristic in the filter frame the context-sensitive menu is opened using the right mouse button and the function **Restrict** is selected (see Figure 6.3, Step 1). Then, the **Selection for fiscal year variant** pop-up opens. Select the value that you want and click the **Add** button (right-arrow button) to add the value (see Figure 6.3, Steps 2 to 4). After confirming this restriction by clicking on the **OK** button, the restriction is included in the query (see Figure 6.3, Step 5).

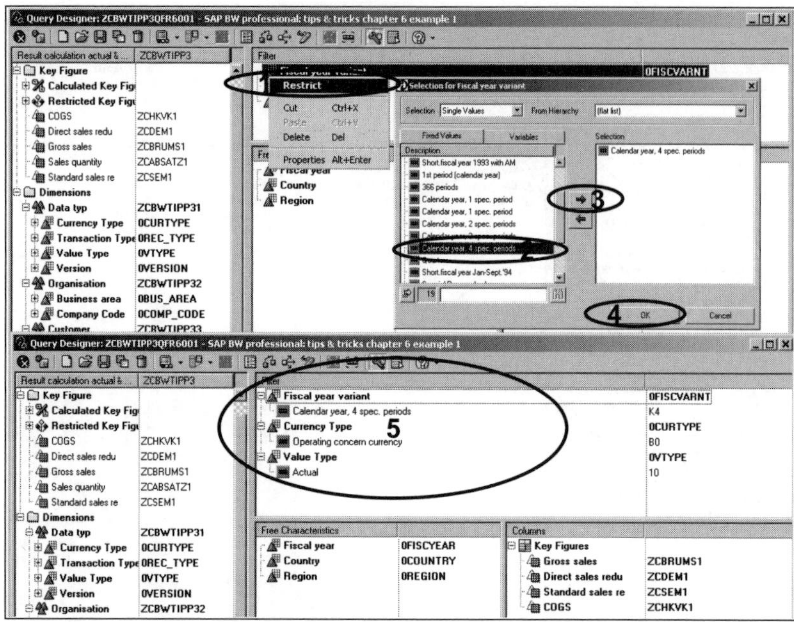

Figure 6.3 Definition of Restrictions for Global Selections

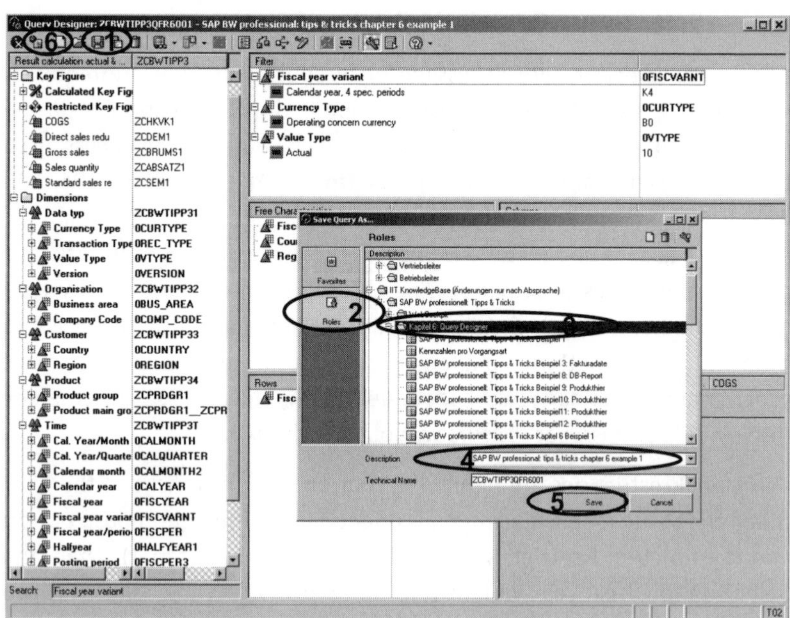

Figure 6.4 Saving the Query

6.1.4 Saving Queries

Saving queries

After you have defined the query, you must save it. To save the query in a role or in Favorites, click on the **Save query** button (see Figure 6.4, Step 1). In the **Save Query As...** pop-up, you must select the storage location (Roles or Favorites) (see Figure 6.4, Steps 2 and 3). After entering the description and technical name, click on the **Save** button (see Figure 6.4, Steps 4 and 5). Now, you can execute the query.

6.1.5 Executing a Query

Executing a query

To start the query in the HTML browser, click on the **Query on the Web** button (see Figure 6.4, Step 6). The SAP default Web template displays the result table (see Figure 6.5).

Displaying filter values

When you click on the **Info** button, the selected filter values are listed in the query configuration (see Figure 6.5, Step 1). To display the result table again, click on the **Table** button to display the result table once again (see Figure 6.5, Step 2).

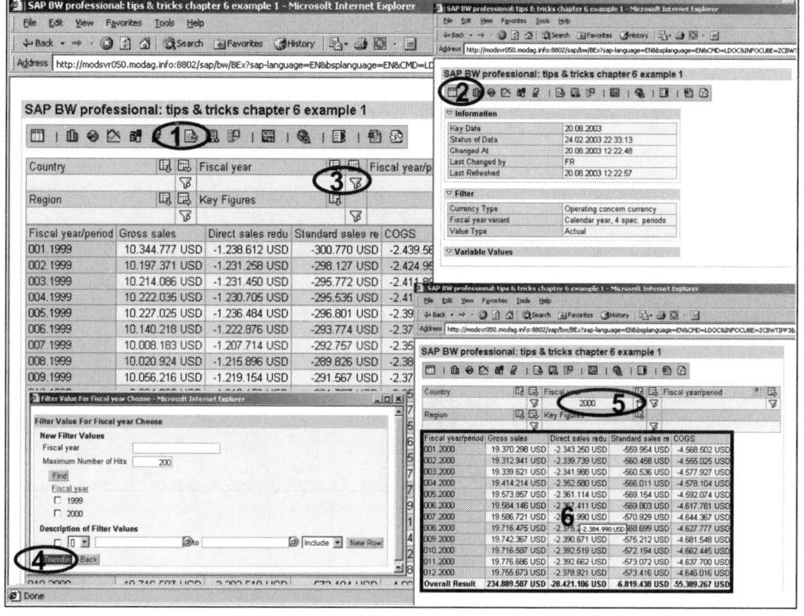

Figure 6.5 Execution of the Query and Navigation: Display of the Filter Values and Selection via Free Characteristics

Selection via free characteristics

If, during the query execution, dynamic selections should occur, in addition to the static filter values, then selection can occur for the corresponding element (characteristic or structural element, for example, a key figure) in the navigation block by clicking on the **Filter value** button (in the example: selection of the fiscal year 2000, so that only the periods 001.2000 to 012.2000 are listed) (see Figure 6.5, Step 3). In the **Filter Value For Fiscal year Choose** pop-up, you can select the value that you want (see Figure 6.5, Step 4). After making your selection, the newly selected data is displayed in the browser (see Figure 6.5, Steps 5 and 6).

Changing drill-down

You can also make selections on the basis of the values in the rows and columns. Open the context-sensitive menu and select the value that you want by highlighting it (see Figure 6.6, Step 1). If you only want to display the selection, you must select **Keep Filter Value**. If in the same step a change of the query drilldown should be made (in the example: display of the countries in the columns for selection of the key "Gross sales"), then you must select the function **Filter and drilldown according to ...** (see Figure 6.6, Steps 2 and 3).

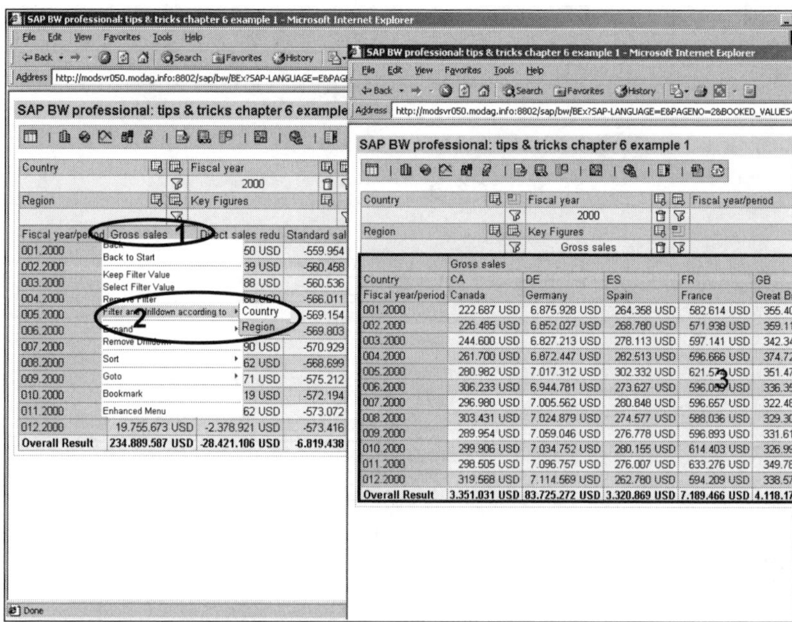

Figure 6.6 Navigation in the Query: Filtering via Free Characteristics and Table Elements with Change of the Drilldown

6.2 Reusable Objects

6.2.1 The Concept

In practice, the same elements are often required in different queries. This axiom holds true for calculations (calculated keys), restricted keys, and structures of keys or characteristics. In order to store these elements without duplicating them, you can save them as reusable objects. Then, these query elements will be available for all queries that use the respective InfoProvider.

6.2.2 Calculated Keys

Formula

If a total should be calculated from different keys, then the formula function is available for the following, for example:

Gross sales
./. Direct revenue reductions
./. Default revenue reductions

./. Full manufacturing costs
= Marginal income II

You can then define this formula directly in the query. Depending on the construction of the query, you must open the context-sensitive menu on the key node on the row or column, using the right mouse button, while concurrently clicking on the **New Formula** function (see Figure 6.7, Steps 1 and 2). In the **Edit Formula** popup, the keys are copied into the **Edit Formula** window using drag & drop and they are linked with the required operators (in the example, the keys are saved according to the plus or minus sign in the InfoCube and therefore per this example must be linked with a plus sign (+)). Then, you can enter the description and complete the formula definition by clicking on the **OK** button (see Figure 6.7, Steps 3 to 5). After that, the formula will be available in the query (see Figure 6.7, Step 6).

During query execution, this formula behaves like the physical keys (see Figure 6.8).

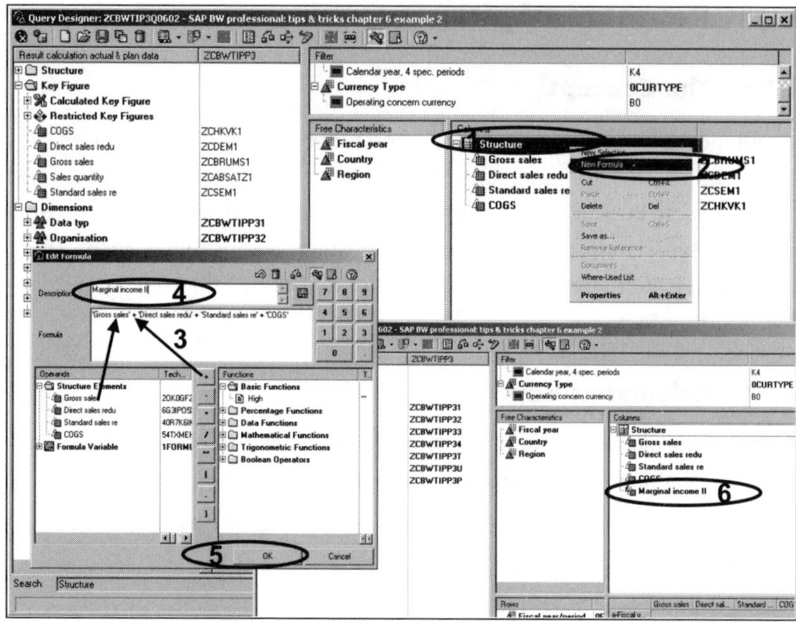

Figure 6.7 Definition of the Formula in the Query

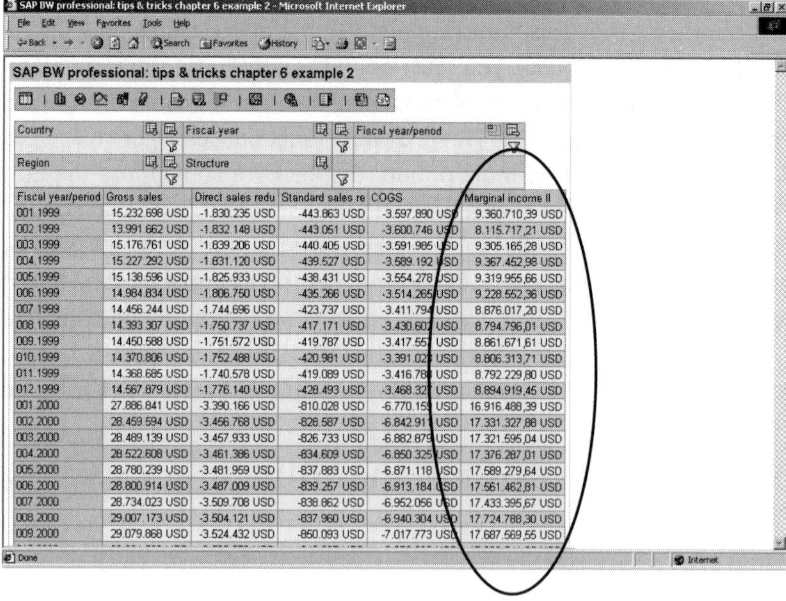

Fiscal year/period	Gross sales	Direct sales redu	Standard sales re	COGS	Marginal income II
001.1999	15.232.698 USD	-1.830.235 USD	-443.863 USD	-3.597.890 USD	9.360.710,39 USD
002.1999	13.991.662 USD	-1.832.148 USD	-443.051 USD	-3.600.746 USD	8.115.717,21 USD
003.1999	15.176.761 USD	-1.839.206 USD	-440.405 USD	-3.591.985 USD	9.305.165,28 USD
004.1999	15.227.292 USD	-1.831.120 USD	-439.527 USD	-3.589.192 USD	9.367.452,98 USD
005.1999	15.138.596 USD	-1.825.933 USD	-438.431 USD	-3.554.278 USD	9.319.955,66 USD
006.1999	14.984.834 USD	-1.806.750 USD	-435.266 USD	-3.514.265 USD	9.228.552,36 USD
007.1999	14.456.244 USD	-1.744.696 USD	-423.737 USD	-3.411.794 USD	8.876.017,20 USD
008.1999	14.393.307 USD	-1.750.737 USD	-417.171 USD	-3.430.602 USD	8.794.796,01 USD
009.1999	14.450.588 USD	-1.751.572 USD	-419.787 USD	-3.417.557 USD	8.861.671,61 USD
010.1999	14.370.806 USD	-1.752.488 USD	-420.981 USD	-3.391.023 USD	8.806.313,71 USD
011.1999	14.368.685 USD	-1.740.578 USD	-419.089 USD	-3.416.788 USD	8.792.229,80 USD
012.1999	14.567.879 USD	-1.776.140 USD	-428.493 USD	-3.468.327 USD	8.894.919,45 USD
001.2000	27.886.841 USD	-3.390.166 USD	-810.028 USD	-6.770.159 USD	16.916.488,39 USD
002.2000	28.459.594 USD	-3.456.768 USD	-828.587 USD	-6.842.911 USD	17.331.327,88 USD
003.2000	28.489.139 USD	-3.457.933 USD	-826.733 USD	-6.882.879 USD	17.321.595,04 USD
004.2000	28.522.608 USD	-3.461.386 USD	-834.609 USD	-6.850.325 USD	17.376.287,01 USD
005.2000	28.780.239 USD	-3.481.959 USD	-837.883 USD	-6.871.118 USD	17.589.279,64 USD
006.2000	28.800.914 USD	-3.487.009 USD	-839.257 USD	-6.913.184 USD	17.561.462,81 USD
007.2000	28.734.023 USD	-3.509.708 USD	-838.862 USD	-6.952.056 USD	17.433.395,67 USD
008.2000	29.007.173 USD	-3.504.121 USD	-837.960 USD	-6.940.304 USD	17.724.788,30 USD
009.2000	29.079.868 USD	-3.524.432 USD	-850.093 USD	-7.017.773 USD	17.687.569,55 USD

Figure 6.8 Query with Formula

Problem of local formula definition

In practice, however, using the (local) formula conceals the problem that this formula must be defined anew in each query. Besides this unnecessary additional effort, there also exists the problem of inconsistent definitions that arise, thereby contributing to the usage of flawed and contradictory information. The person responsible for creating the query must therefore be sufficiently familiar with the (in practice more complex) data model for such a definition – this basic condition is often not fulfilled. Therefore, reusable formulas (= calculated keys) are recommended. This definition also occurs in the Query Designer.

Defining calculated keys

In the left frame, open the context-sensitive menu on the **Key** folder symbol using the right mouse button and select the function **New Calculated Key Figure** (see Figure 6.9, Steps 1 and 2). In the **New Calculated Key Figure** pop-up, make the definition according to the formula (see the definition of the formula) and confirm the entry by clicking on the **OK** button (see Figure 6.9, Steps 3 to 5). In the **Properties of the Calculated Key Figure** pop-up, enter the technical name and also confirm this entry by clicking on **OK** (see Figure 6.9, Steps 6 and 7). In the Query Designer, the calculated key is then available in the **Calculated Key Figure** folder and it can be included in the query definition like a physical key using drag & drop (see Figure 6.9, Steps 8 and 9). During query execution, the calculated key behaves like the physical keys (see Figure 6.9, Step 10).

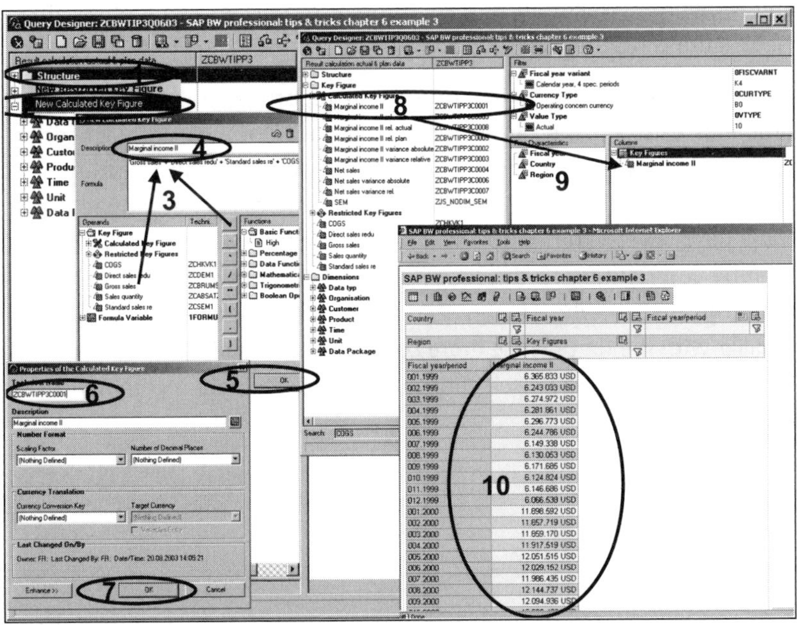

Figure 6.9 Definition and Use of the Calculated Key

6.2.3 Restricted Keys

In productive applications, calculated keys are also usually separate entities. Only in a dedicated context do these receive meaningful contents. For example, actual data is often compared to budgeted data. Calculated keys and global filters are not suited for this kind of data. Such requirements are mapped via restricted keys: a key—in the example "Marginal income II"—is restricted in one column to actual and in another column to budgeted values.

Locally restricted keys

In the Query Designer, such selection combinations (key and characteristic restrictions) can be created as local definitions. To do this—depending on the query construction—open the context-sensitive menu on the title column or row by right-clicking the mouse button and selecting the **New Structure** function in the pop-up menu that displays (see Figure 6.10, Steps 1 and 2). Subsequently, in the corresponding frame, an empty **Structure** appears (see Figure 6.10, Step 3). Again, right-click with the mouse to open a context-sensitive menu and select **New Selection** (see Figure 6.10, Step 4). The **New Selection** pop-up opens, in which, using drag & drop, the required key and characteristic selection occurs (in the example: "Marginal Income II" and Value Type = "Actual") and a description is entered (see Figure 6.10, Steps 5 and 6). After you click on the **OK** button, this definition is available in the query (see Figure 6.10, Steps 7 and 8). During execution, this selection also behaves like a physical key (see Figure 6.10, Step 9).

Problem of the locally restricted keys

This definition also behaves correctly in reporting; however, the same problems exist as when executed for the local formula: in practice, the use of the (local) selection conceals the problem that this selection must be defined anew in each query. Besides the unnecessary additional effort, there also exists the problem of inconsistent definitions that arise, thereby contributing to the usage of flawed and contradictory information. The person who creates the query must therefore be sufficiently familiar with the (in practice more complex) data model for such a definition. Therefore, reusable selections (restricted keys) are recommended.

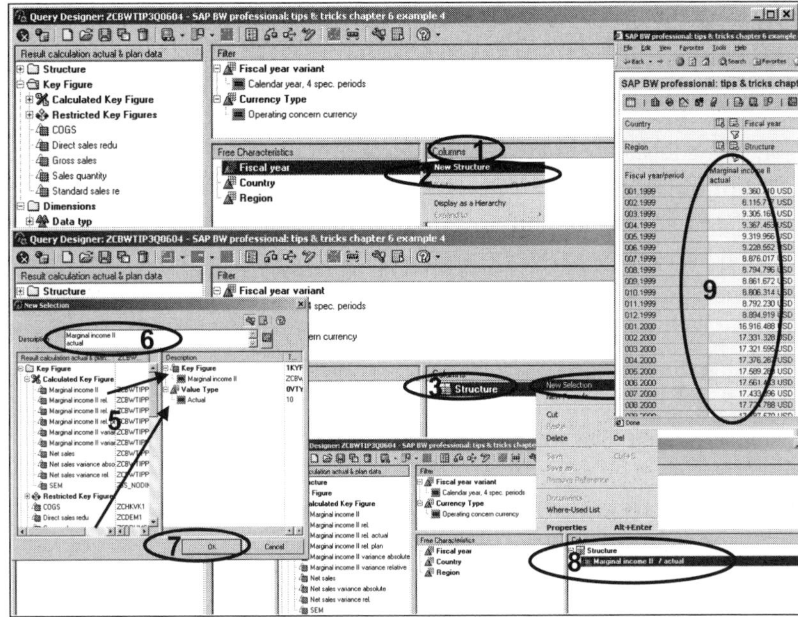

Figure 6.10 Selections of Keys and Characteristic Values in the Query

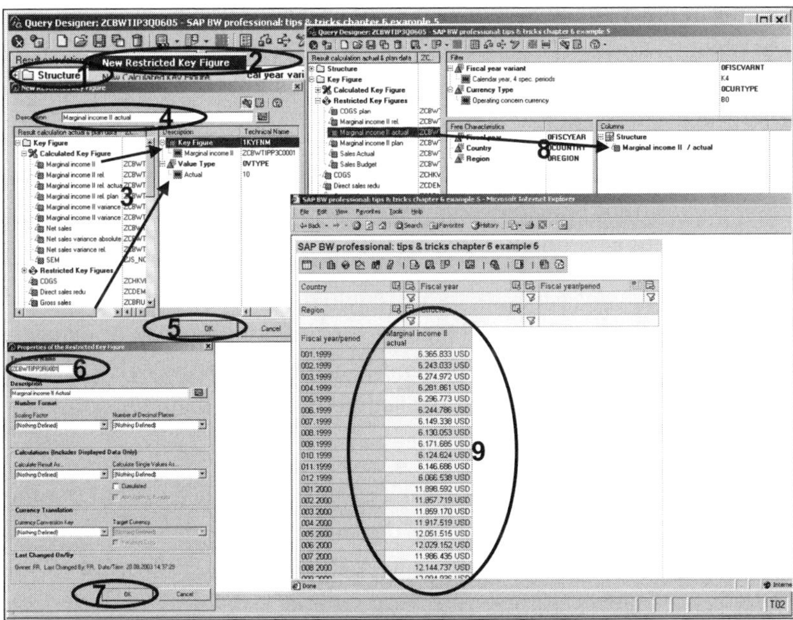

Figure 6.11 Definition and Use of the Restricted Key

Defining the restricted key

In the left frame, right-click to open the context-sensitive menu on the **Key** folder symbol and select the **New Restricted Key Figure** function (see Figure 6.11, Steps 1 and 2). In the **New Restricted Key Figure** pop-up, make the definition according to the local selection (see the definition of the locally-restricted key) and confirm the entry by clicking on the **OK** button (see Figure 6.11, Steps 3 to 5). In the **Properties of the Restricted Key Figure** pop-up, enter the technical name and confirm this entry by clicking on **OK** (see Figure 6.11, Steps 6 and 7). In the Query Designer, the calculated key is then available in the **Restricted Key Figures** folder and you can include it in the query definition like a physical key using drag & drop. It also behaves as physical keys do (see Figure 6.11, Steps 8 and 9). An innovation in SAP BW Release 3.x is the possibility of using calculated keys for the definition of restricted keys and vice versa.

6.2.4 Definition of Calculated and Restricted Keys with Mutual Dependence

Basis: calculated keys

As a rule, during the definition of queries, restricted keys are required (for example, "DB II actual" and "DB II plan," therefore, the key "DB II" with the restriction value type: 020). Both keys are based on a calculation scheme as described in Section 6.2.2, for which the use of calculated keys was recommended (see calculated key "DB II" in Section 6.2.2.). That is, the restricted keys are configured using the definition of the calculated keys (see Section 6.2.3)

This use of calculated and restricted keys minimizes the definition effort, ensures consistent principles—thanks to the common basis—and enables the adjustment of properties in a location.

Basis: restricted keys

Nearly as frequently, calculations are required that are based on restricted keys (in the example, Marginal income variance as difference or percentage variance from "Marginal income II actual" to "Marginal income II plan"). The calculated keys are configured using the definition of either the restricted or other calculated keys.

The procedure for the key "Marginal income II variance absolute" (for the absolute variance) should now be presented here. After the restricted keys "Marginal income II actual" and "Marginal income II plan" are configured in the Query Designer, right-click with the mouse button to open the context-sensitive menu on the **Calculated Key Figure** folder and select the **New Calculated Key Figure** function (see Figure 6.12, Steps 1 and 2). The **New Calculated Key Figure** pop-up opens. Use drag & drop to move the restricted keys "Marginal income II actual" and "Marginal income II plan" into the **Formula** window. By clicking on the [-] button, the operator is inserted (see Figure 6.12, Steps 3 to 5).

After you have entered the description for the restricted key, you can complete the definition by clicking on the **OK** button (see Figure 6.12, Steps 6 and 7). After you enter the technical name and click on the **OK** button in the **Properties of the Calculated Key Figure** pop-up, this key is based on the restricted keys and calculated with the calculated key (see Figure 6.12, Steps 8 and 9).

For the definition of the key "Marginal income II variance relative" (for the relative variance), the same procedure is selected using the operator **Percentage Variance (%)** from the list of functions (**Percentage Functions** folder) in the **New Calculated Key Figure** pop-up (see Figure 6.12, Steps 10 to 16).

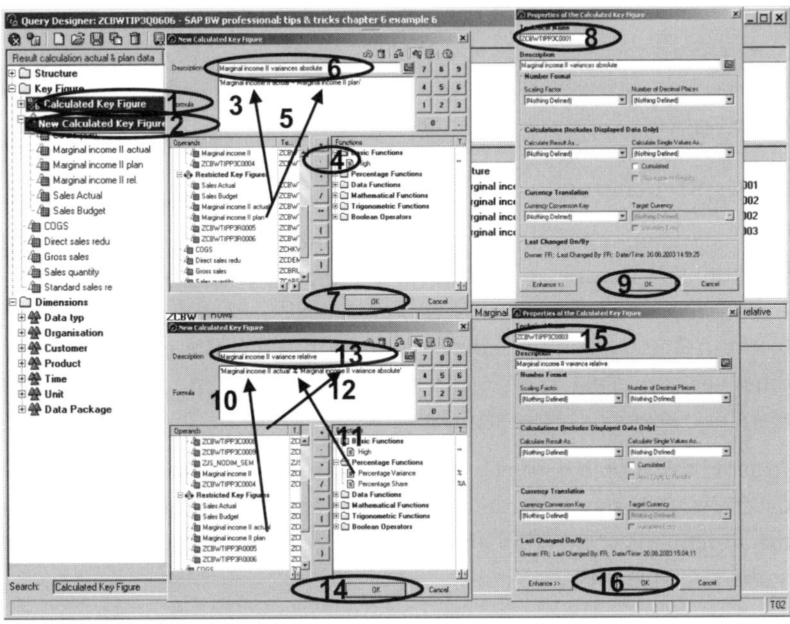

Figure 6.12 Calculated Keys on the Basis of Restricted Keys

Using drag & drop, you can copy the calculated and restricted keys into the query (see Figure 6.13, Steps 1 to 3). A problem that frequently arises from this kind of calculation is the default display of a number of nonsensical decimal places (see Figure 6.13, Step 4). We will address this issue in Section 6.3.1.

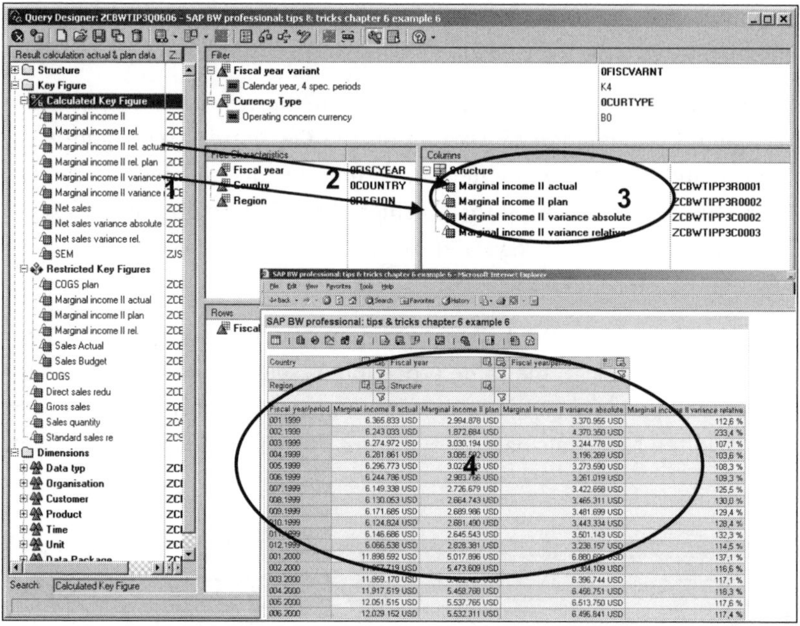

Figure 6.13 Calculated and Restricted Keys in the Query

6.2.5 Structures

Local structures

With the query definition completed according to Figure 6.13, a local structure (in this case: key structure) is formed. This structure is problematic because the definition must be made anew in each query. In addition to the necessary corresponding effort (in practice these structures are often very complex), there is the danger of inconsistent definitions (and therefore, erroneous information).

Reusable structures

To avoid this problem, the Query Designer enables you to create *reusable structures*. Reusable structures can then be copied into various queries. If the structure is changed, then all affected query definitions are changed in the same manner.

To create reusable structures, you would do the following. (Note that the starting point is a structure defined in the Rows or Columns frame in the Query Designer.) Right-click to open the context-sensitive menu on the folder (in the example: **Keys**) and select the function **Save as...** (see Figure 6.14, Steps 1 and 2). In the **Save Structure As...** popup, enter the technical name and description. After you click on the **OK** button to confirm the entries, the structure is stored globally for the InfoProvider (see Figure 6.14, Steps 3 to 5). In the Query Designer, there is a new folder **Structure** for this in the left frame with the inventory elements (see Figure 6.14, Step 6). In the query, the description and technical name are included for this structure (see Figure 6.14, Step 7). In queries to be defined anew, the reusable structure can be copied from the left frame into the query rows and columns using drag & drop.

Characteristic structures

During query execution, reusable structures behave like local definitions. For many reports, in addition to such key structures, it is also necessary to define characteristic structures. The bases for these characteristic structures are, for example, demands for the formation of interim totals, which cannot be mapped using other solution approaches.

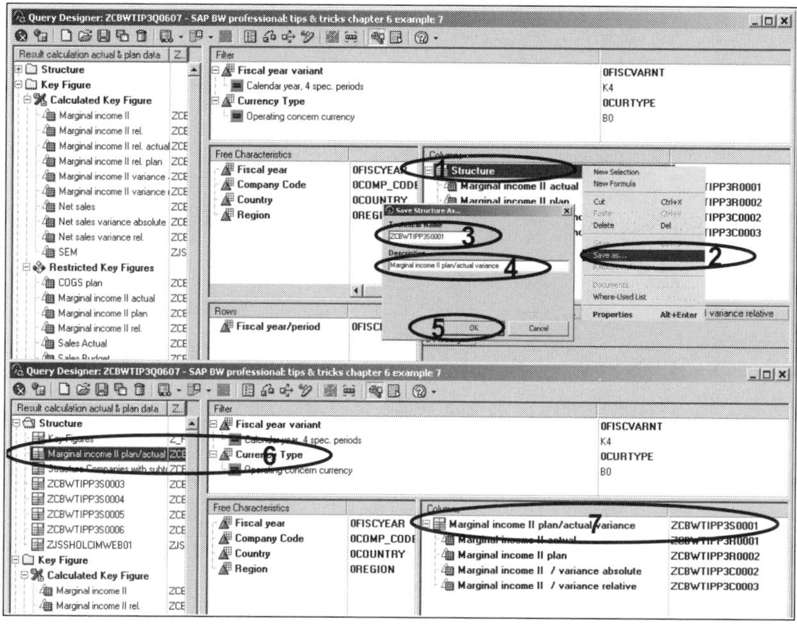

Figure 6.14 Delivery of a Reusable Structure

In the example, interim totals must be formed in addition to a detailed listing and a total row for the European and U.S. companies. In addition, in two footers, the shares of the European and U.S. companies of the total must be displayed as a percentage. While the sum total (i.e., the interim totals) and the total could be displayed alternatively using a hierarchy or using navigation attributes, the simultaneous display of shares without structure cannot be mapped. The detailed specification displayed in Table 6.1 emerges with the master data provided.

Row	Company Code or Formula	Company Code
1	IIT Deutschland GmbH, Flörsheim	Company Code 0001
2	IIT Consulting AG, Vienna	Company Code 2000
3	IIT Consulting AG, Madrid	Company Code 2100
4	IIT Consulting AG, London	Company Code 2200
5	IIT Consulting AG, Paris	Company Code 2300
6	IIT Consulting AG, Rome	Company Code 2400
7	IIT Consulting AG, Amsterdam	Company Code 2500
8	IIT Consulting AG, Brussels	Company Code 5000
9	IIT Consulting AG, Moscow	Company Code 6000
10	IIT Consulting AG, Oslo	Company Code R100
11	IIT Consulting AG, Copenhagen	Company Code R300
12	European companies	Total of rows 1 to 11
13	IIT Consulting AG, Boston	Company Code 3000
14	IIT America, Los Angeles	Company Code 4000
15	U.S. companies	Total of rows 13 to 14
16	Total [Is this right as positioned in the column for Company Code or Formula?]	Total of rows 12 and 15 [???]
17	Share of European companies	Share rows 12 to 16
18	Share of U.S. companies	Share rows 15 to 16

Table 6.1 Construction of the Structure for the Company Overview

Creation of selections as structure elements

A structure must be created as preparatory work. In the Query Designer, right-click the mouse button on the title of the **Rows** frame to open the context-sensitive menu. Select the **New Structure** function (see Figure 6.15, Steps 1 and 2). In the Query Designer, an empty structure is displayed in the **Rows** frame. On this **Structure** folder, open the context-sensitive menu, again using the right mouse button, and select the **New Selection** function (see Figure 6.15, Steps 3 and 4). In the **New Selection** pop-up that opens, select the company code 0001 and use drag & drop to move the code from the template frame into the selection frame (right) (see Figure 6.15, Step 5). Then, enter the description text and confirm the selection by clicking on the **OK** button (see Figure 6.15, Steps 6 and 7).

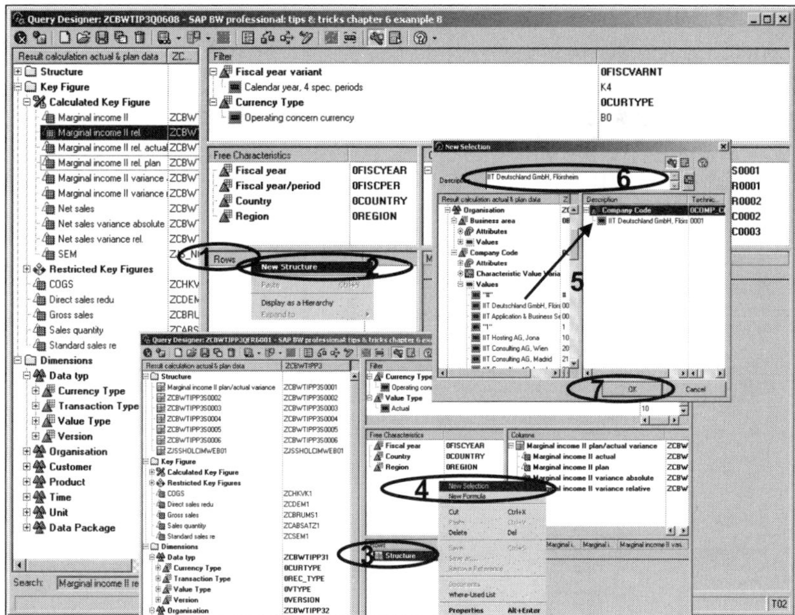

Figure 6.15 Creation of the Elements with Fixed Value Selections

This selection is therefore taken over into the query as a structure element (see Figure 6.16, Step 1). For the additional company codes of the rows 2 to 11, you must repeat Steps 3 to 7 from the detailed specification according to Figure 6.15.

Creation of the total rows

The interim totals are defined as formula. In the Query Designer, right-click on the **Structure** folder in the **Rows** frame to open the context-sensitive menu. Select the **New Formula** function (see Figure 6.16, Steps 2 and 3). In the **New Formula** pop-up, the structural elements (rows 1 to 11) must be taken over into the formula using drag & drop and they must each be linked using the operator **+** (see Figure 6.16, Steps 4 and 5). Then, you must enter the description and confirm the definition by clicking on the **OK** button (see Figure 6.16, Steps 6 and 7). The interim total is taken over into the query definition as a row element (see Figure 6.16, Step 8).

Then, for the example with the company codes 3000 and 4000 (according to the detailed specification, rows 13 to 14), you must repeat Steps 3 to 7 according to Figure 6.15. For the interim total (according to the detailed specification, row 15), you must repeat Steps 2 to 7 according to Figure 6.16. Then, the total line (according to the detailed specification, row 16) must be formed either according to Figure 6.16 via formula (row

12 plus 16) or according to Figure 6.15—which is more reliable with respect to new companies—with a restriction-free row.

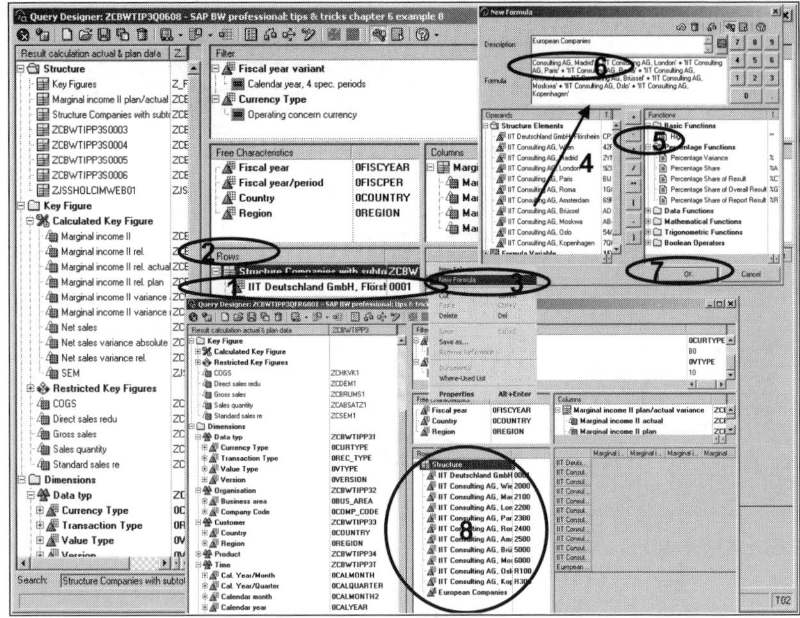

Figure 6.16 Takeover of the Selection of Companies and the Definition of the Interim Total

Mapping of the percentage shares

Thus all required individual positions and total rows are available in the query definition (see Figure 6.17, Step 1). Henceforth, there remains from the detailed specification the mapping of the percentage shares of the interim totals of the total. In the Query Designer, right-click on the **Structure** folder in the **Rows** frame to open the context-sensitive menu. Select the **New Formula** function (see Figure 6.17, Steps 2 and 3). In the **New Formula** pop-up, using drag & drop, ensure that the structural element with the first interim total (row 12) is taken over into the formula. Also using drag & drop, the function percentage share (**%A**) must be taken over into the formula and then into the query element **Total** (see Figure 6.17, Steps 4 to 6).

Then, enter the description and confirm that the definition is taken over by clicking on the **OK** button (see Figure 6.17, Steps 7 and 8). The percentage share of the first interim total is therefore taken over in the query definition. You must repeat this procedure for the second interim total (row 15) (see Figure 6.17, Step 9).

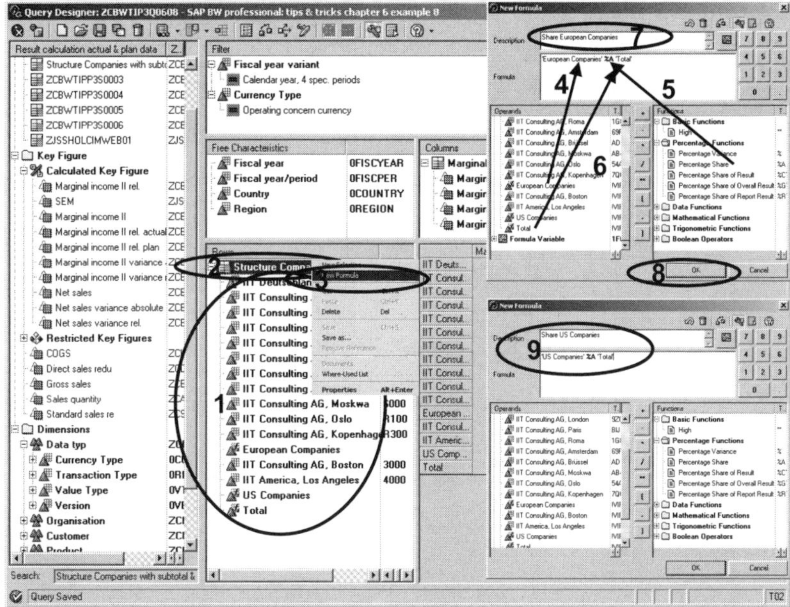

Figure 6.17 Acquisition of the Shares of the Interim Totals for the Total

The detailed specification is mapped in the query as a local structure. In order to make this local structure available as a reusable object, you must right-click on the **Structure** folder in the **Rows** frame to open the context-sensitive menu. Select the **Save as...** function (see Figure 6.18, Steps 1 and 2). In the **Save Structure As...** pop-up, specify the technical name and description. Then, confirm the entries by clicking on the **OK** button (see Figure 6.18, Steps 3 to 5).

Reusable structure

In the inventory frame, the new reusable structure is provided under the **Structure** folder. Similarly, the structure in the **Rows** frame receives the description and the name of the stored object (see Figure 6.18, Steps 6 and 7).

During the query execution, the data of the entire structure is displayed (see Figure 6.18, Step 8). The display of the query result also contains (in the rows with the percentage shares) the problem of display with a nonsensical number of places after the decimal point (see Section 6.3.1 on the display of keys). In addition to the nonsensical display, the formulas produce nonsensical values except in the columns "Marginal income II actual" and "Marginal income II plan." For more information, see Section 6.3.1 on the property "Formula collision."

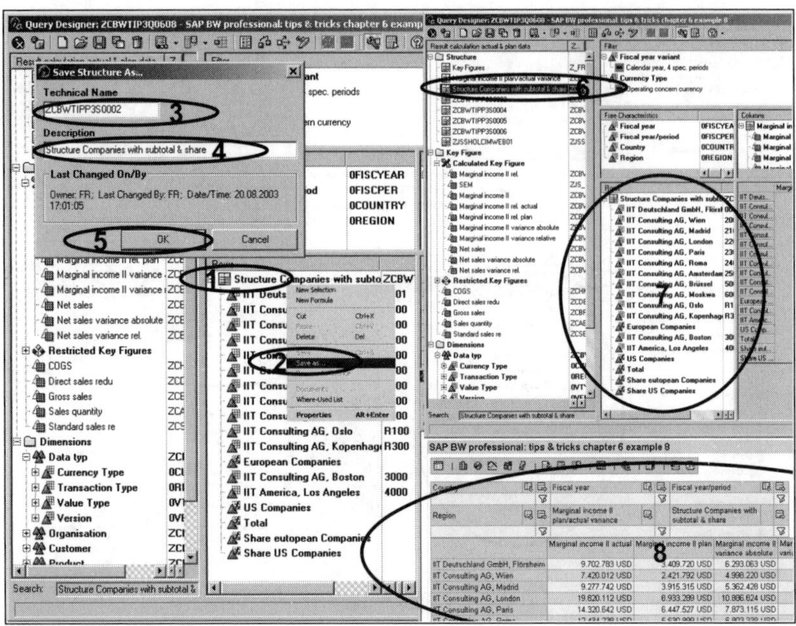

Figure 6.18 Saving a Local Structure as a Reusable Structure

6.3 Properties of Query Elements

6.3.1 Properties of Keys

Local and global properties

The properties of keys can be configured in different places in SAP BW. In queries, the properties of keys can be adjusted in two different places: if the setting occurs in local objects in the **Rows** or **Columns** frame, this setting affects only the changed query. If the setting occurs in global objects in the **Rows** or **Columns** frame, or in the (left) inventory frame, this setting affects all queries that use the changed element.

Changeable properties

On keys, the following properties can be changed:

- The description
- The display (e.g., highlighting)
- The numeric display (e.g., number of decimal places and sign reversal)
- The calculations (e.g., cumulative or non-cumulative)
- The currency conversion

Description

The description can be changed statically or dynamically (for dynamic change see Section 6.7.5). A static change can be necessary if, for example, another text or a multi-line title is required. In the example here, the texts of the Marginal income II variance columns require a greater column width than that of the actual data; however, the table width available for the output is often a problem. With a two-line and abbreviated display, the available space is used more efficiently.

In order to change the column title "Marginal income II variance absolute" to the two-line display

Marginal income II
variance absolute

in the Query Designer, right-click on the **Columns** frame to open a context-sensitive menu and select the **Properties** function (see Figure 6.19, Steps 1 and 2). In the **Properties of the Selection/Formula** pop-up, specify the desired column title in the **Description** field and click on the **OK** button (see Figure 6.19, Steps 3 and 4). The changes are taken over into the query definition (see Figure 6.19, Step 5) and displayed according to the query after saving (see Figure 6.19, Step 6).

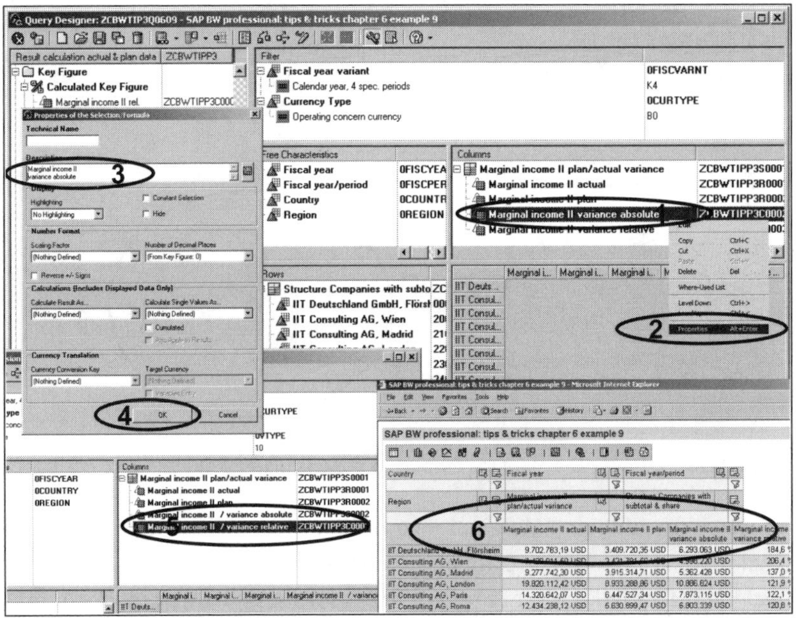

Figure 6.19 Changing the Column Title (Description)

Number display

In the default display of amounts, nearly all currencies are displayed with two decimal places. This type of setting is not practical for many reports. Therefore, you can change the numeric display, for example, in the calculated key "Marginal income II." This has the advantage that you can implement a change that will affect both restricted keys based on this calculated key and therefore the structure itself.

In the Query Designer, right-click on the calculated key "Marginal income II" to open the context-sensitive menu and select the **Properties** function (see Figure 6.20, Steps 1 and 2). In the **Properties of the Calculated Key Figure** pop-up, activate the **Number of Decimal Places** drop-down box and select the value that you want (see Figure 6.20, Step 3). Click on the **OK** button (see Figure 6.20, Step 4) to save the value. The changed setting will now display during the execution of the query: in the example, the columns "Marginal income II actual" and "Marginal income II plan" appear without places after the decimal point (see Figure 6.20, Step 5).

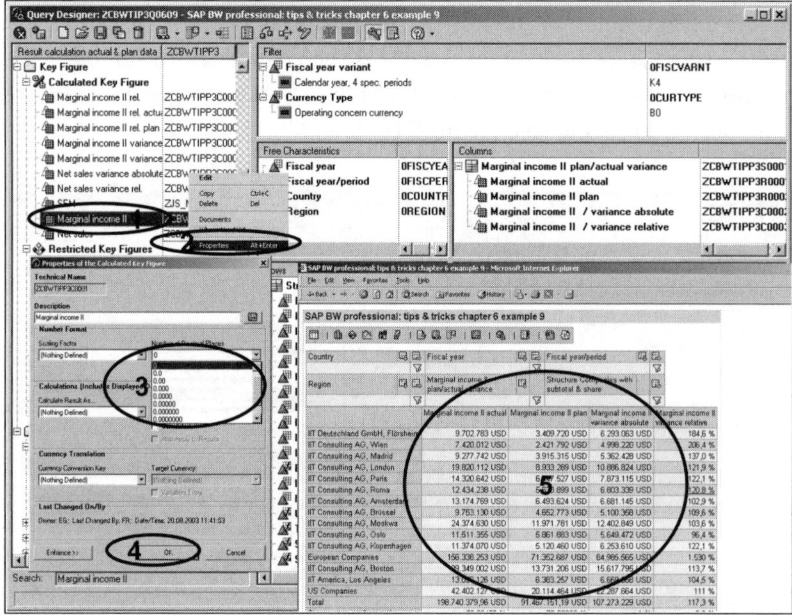

Figure 6.20 Changing the Numeric Display in the Calculated Key

So that the columns "Marginal income II variance absolute" and "Marginal income II variance relative" are displayed with a desired number of decimal places, you can set the properties for these in the same manner—either for the calculated keys or in the structure.

Calculations

If, in a query with a row feature (e.g., "Company code"), you should not display the amount of a physical, calculated, or restricted key, but you should dynamically display the share of the companies of the total, then you can map this information with the property "Calculate individual values as ..." .

In the Query Designer, right-click on the key "Marginal income II actual" in the **Rows** frame to open the context-sensitive menu and select the **Properties** function (see Figure 6.21, Steps 1 and 2). In the **Properties for the Selection/Formula** pop-up, activate the **Calculate Single Values As...** drop-down box and select the setting **Normalize Overall Result** (see Figure 6.21, Step 3). Click on the **OK** button (see Figure 6.21, Step 4) to save the setting. Now, the changed setting will display during the execution of the query: instead of the display of amounts, the display of the percentage shares of the total will appear (see Figure 6.21, Step 5).

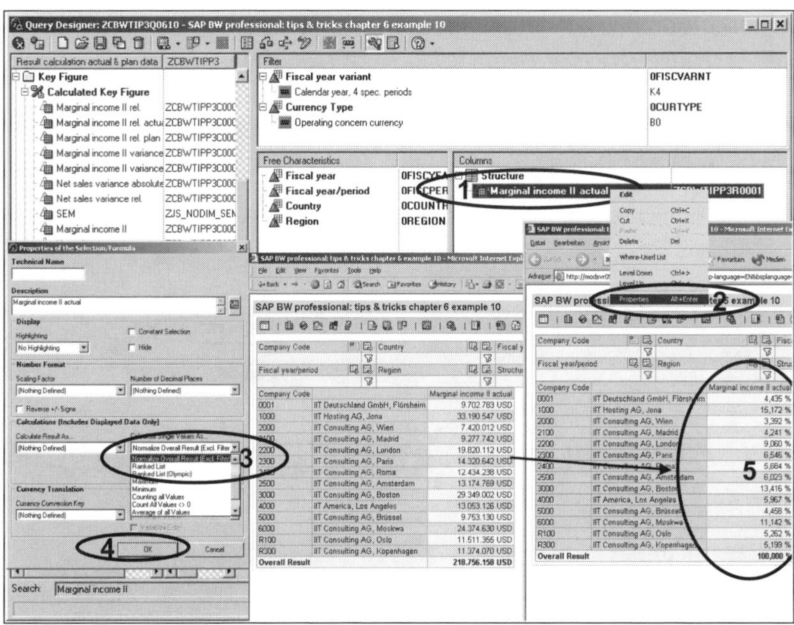

Figure 6.21 Calculation: Normalization of Total Result

Currency conversion

The SAP currency conversion functionality is also available in SAP BW: for example, the currency conversion can occur at the booking time and during query execution. The currency conversion during the query execution can be selected either during the execution or in the query design. In the query design, the configuration of the currency conversion occurs in the course of the properties of keys.

In this example, the amount in the original currency (here: "USD") is contrasted with the amount converted into Euros in an additional key column. Here, two columns with the same data content (here: "Marginal income II actual") must be defined with corresponding column titles.

To set the currency conversion, right-click on the desired column to open the context-sensitive menu and select the **Properties** function (see Figure 6.22, Steps 1 and 2). In the **Properties of the Selection/Formula** pop-up, activate the **Currency Conversion Key** drop-down box and select the desired conversion type (in the example: "Currency Conversion Key ZK03 (ZK03)") (see Figure 6.22, Step 3). Then, in the property's **Target Currency** drop-down list, select the desired currency (in the example: "Euro") (see Figure 6.22, Step 4). Click on the **OK** button to save the setting. The settings are taken over into the query (see Figure 6.22, Step 5). After you save the setting, during query execution, the display of the two currencies occurs on the basis of the set conversion type and the stored conversion exchange rate (see Figure 6.22, Steps 6 and 7).

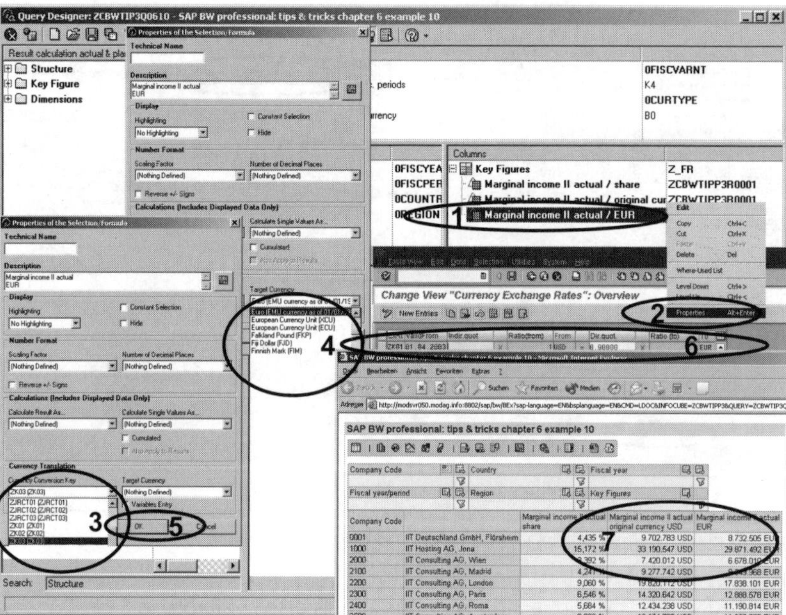

Figure 6.22 Currency Conversion in the Query

6.3.2 Properties of Characteristics and Structural Elements

For characteristics and structural elements, which have no keys, you can set properties regarding display and processing logic.

Characteristic display

For characteristics that contain keys and texts, you can set the characteristic display in the Query Designer. If, for example, the display of company codes should be changed so that only the company code designation appears in a query, proceed as follows: right-click on the desired characteristic to open the context-sensitive menu and select the **Properties** function (see Figure 6.23, Steps 1 and 2). In the **Characteristic Properties for Characteristic Company Code** pop-up, in the **Display As** section, activate the **Key and Name** drop-down box and select the setting **Name** (see Figure 6.23, Step 3).

Click on the **OK** button to save the setting. The settings are taken over into the query (see Figure 6.23, Step 4). After you save the setting, the changed display of the characteristic occurs during query execution (see Figure 6.23, Step 5).

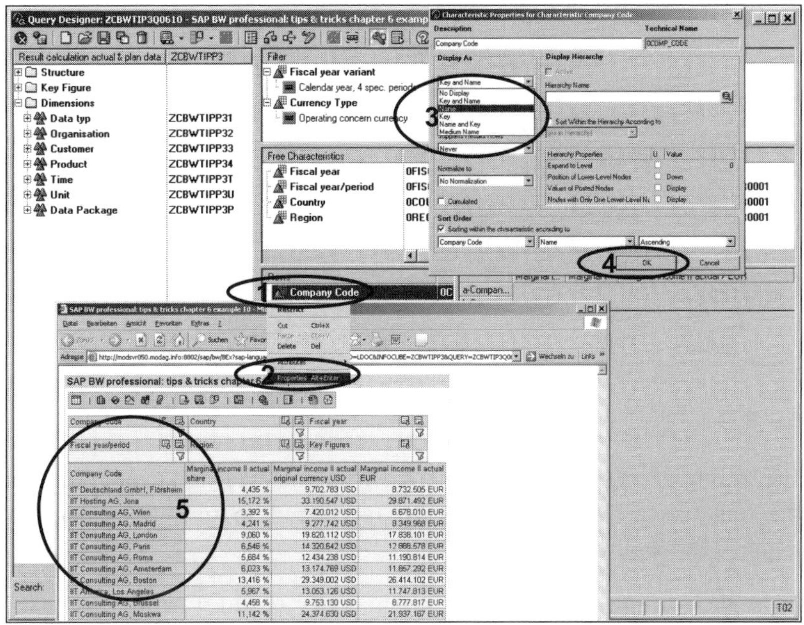

Figure 6.23 Characteristic Display

Sorting

For row and free characteristics, you can set the sorting in the Query Designer. Right-click on the desired characteristic to open the context-sensitive menu and select the **Properties** function (see Figure 6.24, Steps 1 and 2). In the **Characteristic Properties for Characteristic Company Code** pop-up, activate the **Sort Order** checkbox (see Figure 6.24, Steps 3 and 4). As for the characteristic-relevant sorting criterion, select the characteristic or attribute in the left drop-down box (see Figure 6.24, Step 4). Specify in the middle drop-down box whether sorting should occur according to name or key (see Figure 6.24, Step 5). Then, specify whether the sorting direction should be ascending or descending in the right drop-down box (see Figure 6.24, Step 6). Click on the **OK** button to save the settings. The settings are now taken over into the query (see Figure 6.24, Step 7). After you save the settings, the changed sorting settings of the characteristic are applied during query execution (see Figure 6.24, Step 8).

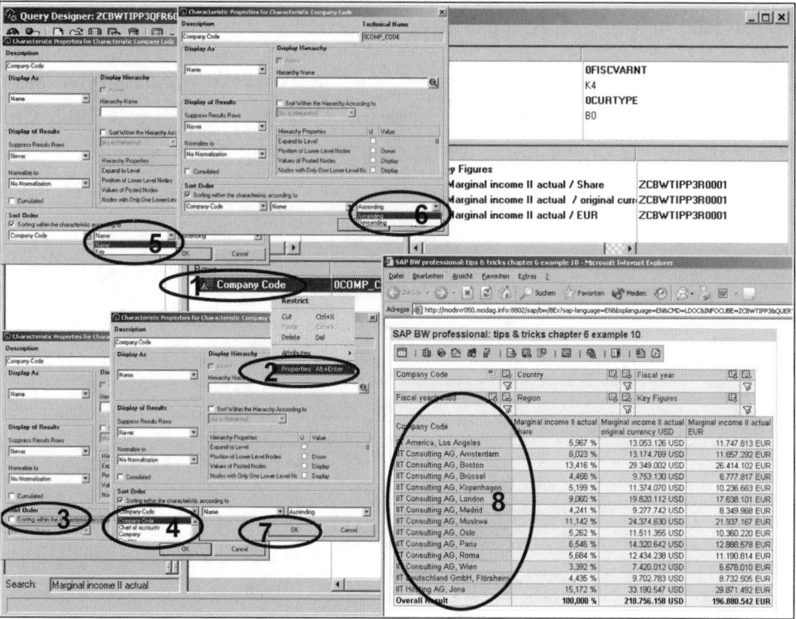

Figure 6.24 Setting the Sorting Properties

Highlighting The setting of properties is also available for characteristic structures. On the one hand, highlighting of total rows, and so forth, is especially required in fixed structures.

Right-click on the desired row or column element to open the context-sensitive menu and select the **Properties** function (see Figure 6.25, Steps 1 and 2). In the **Properties of the Selection/Formula** popup, activate the **Highlighting** drop-down box and select the desired value (see Figure 6.25, Step 3). Click on the **OK** button to save the setting. The settings are taken over into the query (see Figure 6.25, Step 4). After you save the settings, the changed display is applied during query execution (see Figure 6.25, Step 5).

Although the attributes considered for highlighting are difficult to recognize using SAP style sheets, you can use the many offerings of Web technology to assist you (i.e., individual style sheets, color and font attributes, etc.).

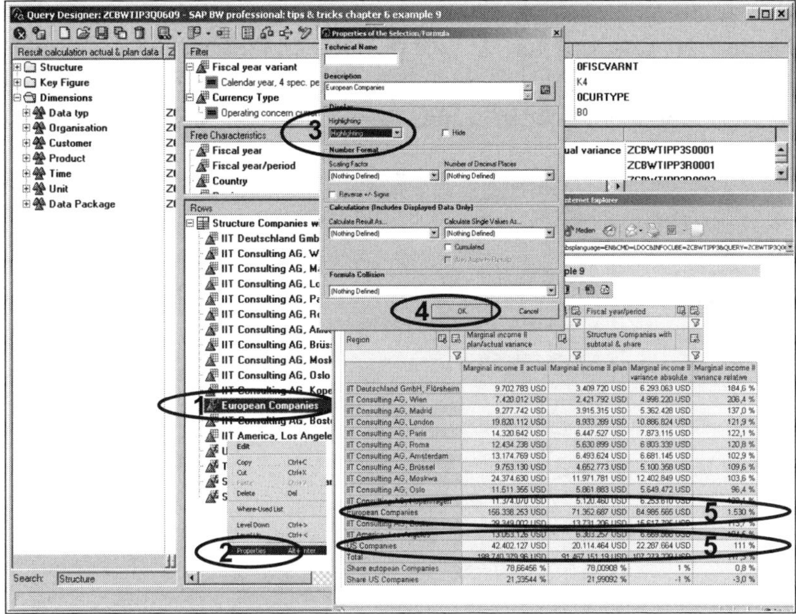

Figure 6.25 Highlighting of Structural Elements (Here: Rows)

As you can discern from Figure 6.25, attributes for customizing key display—such as the number of decimal places to be displayed—are available. These properties are especially relevant if formula collisions arise in queries with structures in rows and columns that produce nonsensical displays (see Figures 6.25 and 6.26). By setting the number of decimal places in the characteristic structure, you can correct this display.

Formula collision

When you examine the result table in Figure 6.25, you'll notice the nonsensical values in both right columns in the two bottom rows—as a result of a formula collision. In the example, instead of the actual share of the European and U.S. companies of the variance in the column "Marginal income II variance absolute," the non-expressive absolute difference of the shares of both company interim totals is displayed as a result of the default formula priority of the column formulas. To realize a correct display, therefore, the formula collision property is available.

Right-click on the desired row or column element (in the example: the rows **Share of European companies** and **Share of U.S. companies**) to open the context-sensitive menu and select the **Properties** function (see Figure 6.26, Steps 1 and 2). In the **Properties of the Selection/Formula** pop-up, activate the **Formula Collision** drop-down box and select the value result from this formula (see Figure 6.26, Step 3). Click on the **OK** button to save the setting. The settings are taken over into the query (see Figure 6.26, Step 4). After you save the settings, the changed formula priority is applied during query execution and the formula is applied (in the example, the sensible **RowFormula** (see Figure 6.26, Step 5).

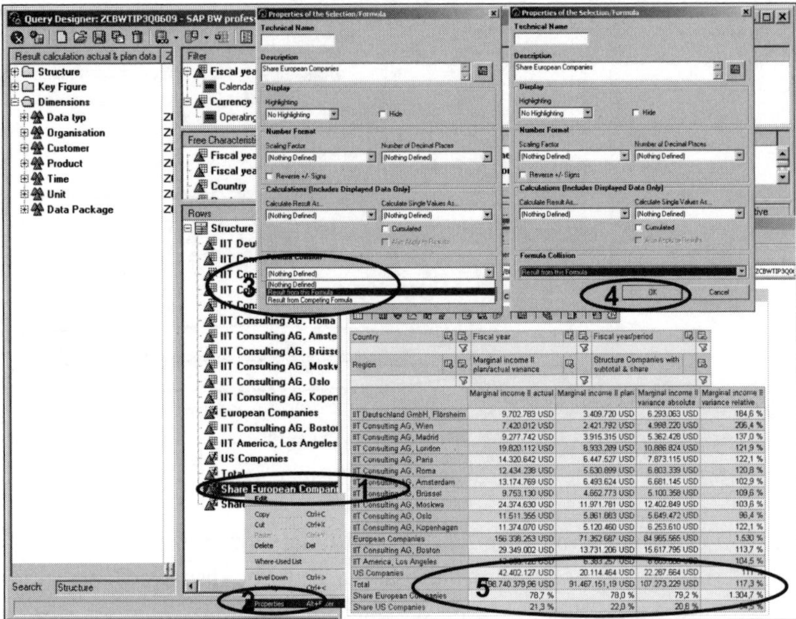

Figure 6.26 Setting of the Query Behavior in Case of Formula Collisions

6.4 Hierarchies

6.4.1 Introduction

The hierarchical display of data is very significant for professional reporting. On the one hand, much reporting-relevant data is organized hierarchically: the aggregation across materials occurs based on the product hierarchy; the aggregation across customers occurs based on the customer hierarchy; the structure of the balance sheet and the income statement follows a hierarchical structure, and so forth.

In many databases, data warehouses, and management information systems, hierarchies are mapped exclusively across attributes or summarizing characteristics. This type of mapping is suitable for only some of the demands. Because most hierarchies are not leveled (that is, not all "leaves" are on the same hierarchical level), the correct mapping of hierarchies is vital for many analytic demands.

With SAP BW, SAP provides a complete solution for the correct mapping and use of hierarchies. This solution organizes the master data object (characteristic "account," "customer," "material," etc.) into hierarchies, which can be used for each evaluation in which a hierarchy-bearing characteristic is used.

6.4.2 The Use of Hierarchies in the Query Designer

Hierarchy display in the leading column

If there are one or several hierarchies for a characteristic, you can set these hierarchies in the Query Designer as a display property. During query execution, the specified hierarchy is displayed.

Right-click on the desired characteristic (in the example: "Country") to open the context-sensitive menu and select the **Properties** function (see Figure 6.27, Steps 1 and 2). In the **Characteristic Properties for Characteristic...** pop-up, click on the button for hierarchy selection (see Figure 6.27, Step 3). The **Select Hierarchy** pop-up opens. Select the desired hierarchy by highlighting it and confirm your selection by clicking on the **OK** button (see Figure 6.27, Steps 4 and 5). Then, enter the selected hierarchy (in this example: "Country") in the **Characteristic Properties for Characteristic...** pop-up and click on the **OK** button to confirm your selection. The settings are taken over into the query definition (see Figure 6.27, Steps 6 and 7).

The setting that displays the characteristic as hierarchy during query execution is visualized in the Query Designer (see Figure 6.28, Step 1). During execution of the query, the hierarchy is displayed according to the customizing settings you applied (see Figure 6.28, Step 2). In addition to the functions possible for lists of characteristic values (navigation and editing of the settings by clicking on a value, etc.) with the hierarchy, there are also additional functions available: by clicking on the hierarchy node symbol (▼ for opened and ▶ for closed partial trees), you can open or close the entire hierarchy and/or a partial tree (see Figure 6.28, Step 3). Also, the context-sensitive menu offers special functions (activate/deactivate hierarchy, expand the entire hierarchy up to a specified level, etc.) for hierarchies on hierarchy nodes or hierarchy leaves (that is, characteristic values).

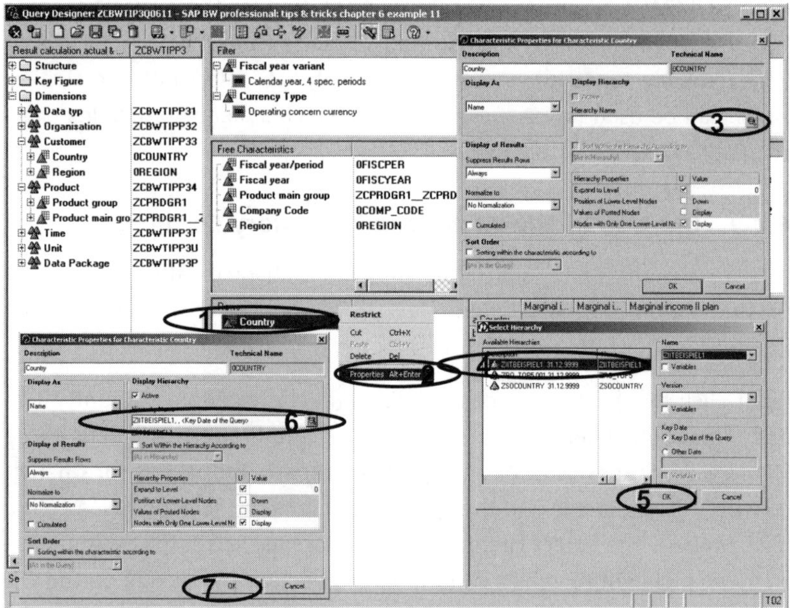

Figure 6.27 Configuration of the Hierarchy Display in the Query Designer

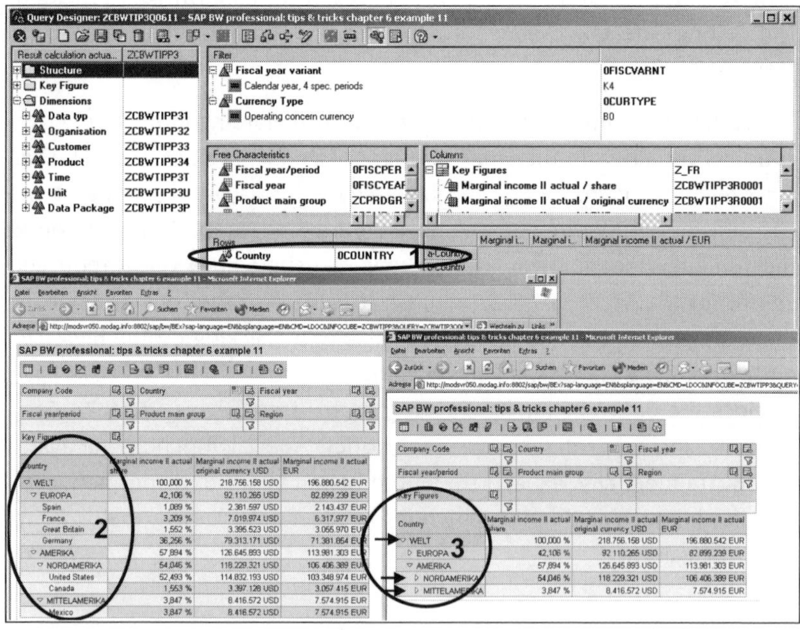

Figure 6.28 Display of the Hierarchy During Query Execution

The same steps are required if you want to display a hierarchy in the columns. During the execution of a query, the same functions are available (see Figure 6.29).

Horizontal hierarchy display

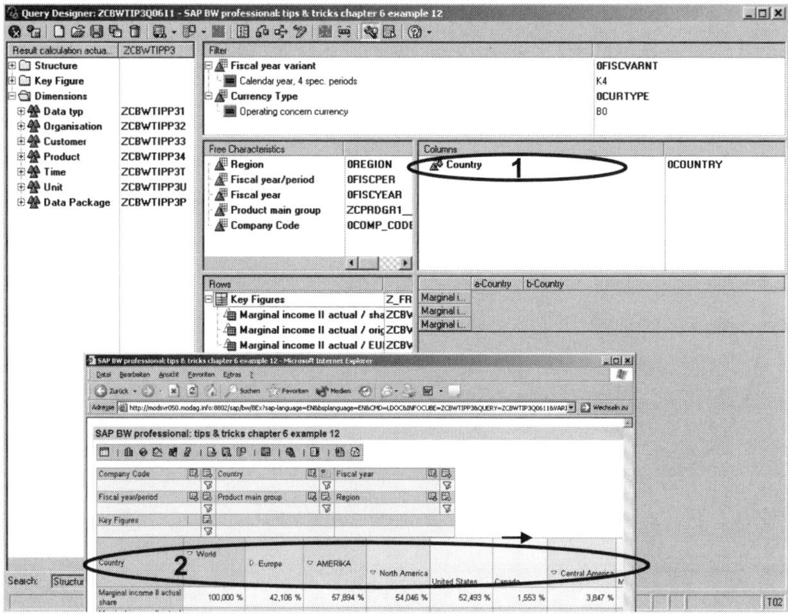

Figure 6.29 Hierarchy Navigation in the Columns

You can also display various hierarchies simultaneously in the rows and columns. The mixed display of hierarchies and characteristics has been supported since SAP BW 3.0. The display can occur without additional settings (see Figure 6.30, variant 1: hierarchy and characteristic, variant 2: characteristic and hierarchy).

Hierarchy and characteristic displayed mixed

If desired, the mixture of hierarchies and characteristic values can also be displayed hierarchically: in the Query Designer, right-click on the title of the **Rows** frame to open the context-sensitive menu and select the **Display as a Hierarchy** function (see Figure 6.31, Steps 1 and 2). Afterwards, the hierarchy symbol is added to the frame title (see Figure 6.31, Step 3). After you save the query, all breakdowns in the row—regardless of whether they are hierarchy or characteristic breakdowns, or a mixture of hierarchies and characteristics—are displayed hierarchically (see Figure 6.31, Step 4, as well as Figure 6.32, Steps 1 and 2).

Displaying hierarchy and characteristic breakdown as hierarchy

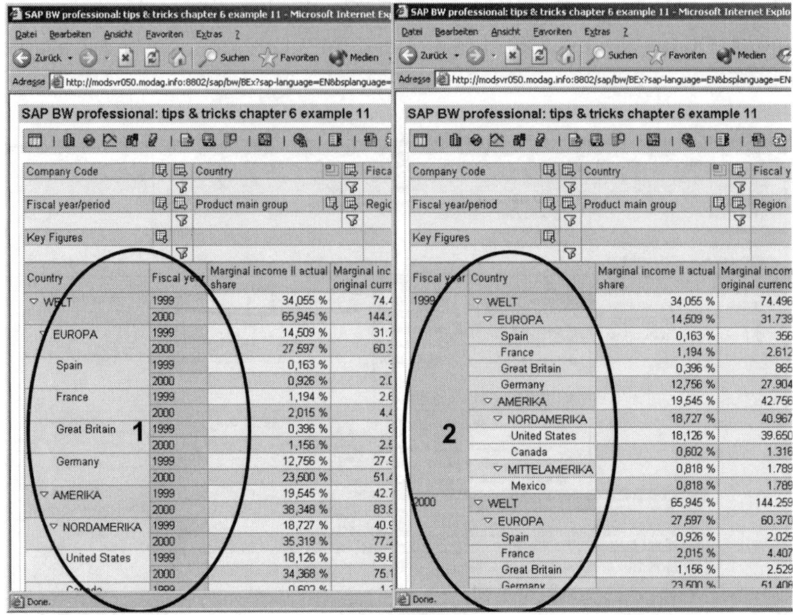

Figure 6.30 Hierarchy and Characteristic Displayed Mixed

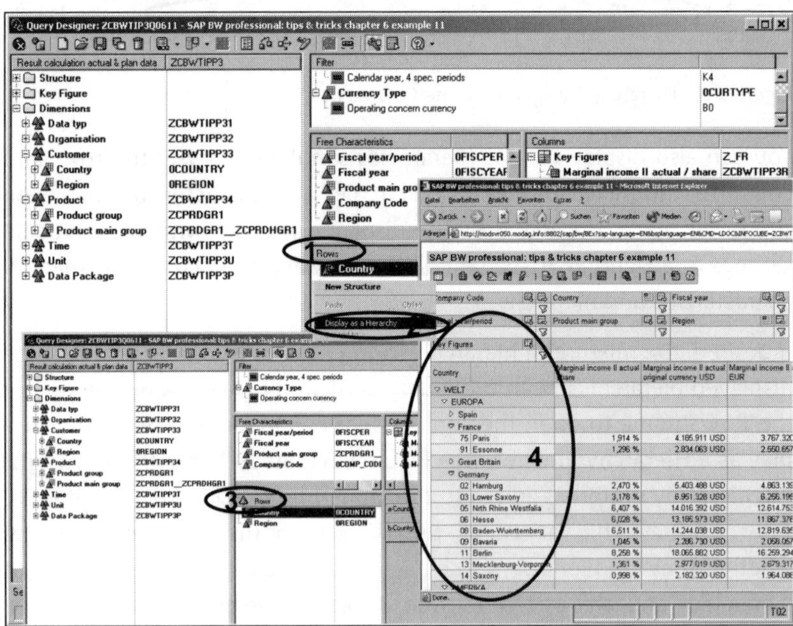

Figure 6.31 Hierarchies and Characteristic Drilldowns as Hierarchy

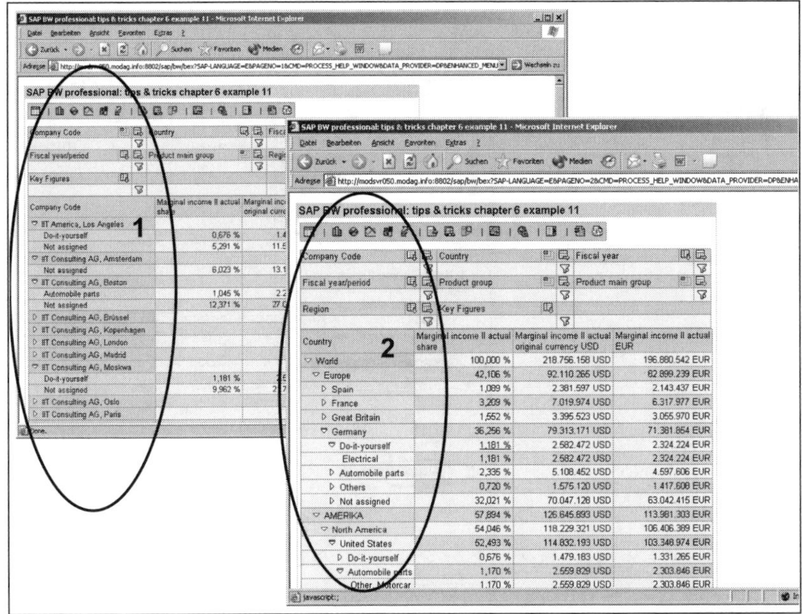

Figure 6.32 Characteristics as Hierarchies and Mixed Hierarchies

Key hierarchy

Key hierarchies can be formed via the function **Display as a Hierarchy** (see Figure 6.33, Step 1) and the option of the hierarchical arrangement of keys (leveling function).

As preparation, you can use drag & drop to copy all desired keys into the Rows frame. After that, you can use the Level Down function as often as necessary to display the keys in hierarchy nodes or hierarchy leaves until these leaves are positioned on the key tree as desired. In the Query Designer, right-click on the key to be positioned and select the Level Up function (see Figure 6.33, Steps 2 and 3). After you save the setting, the keys behave like a hierarchy during query execution (see Figure 6.33, Step 4). Therefore, the aggregation behavior and the calculation of the respective keys is not changed.

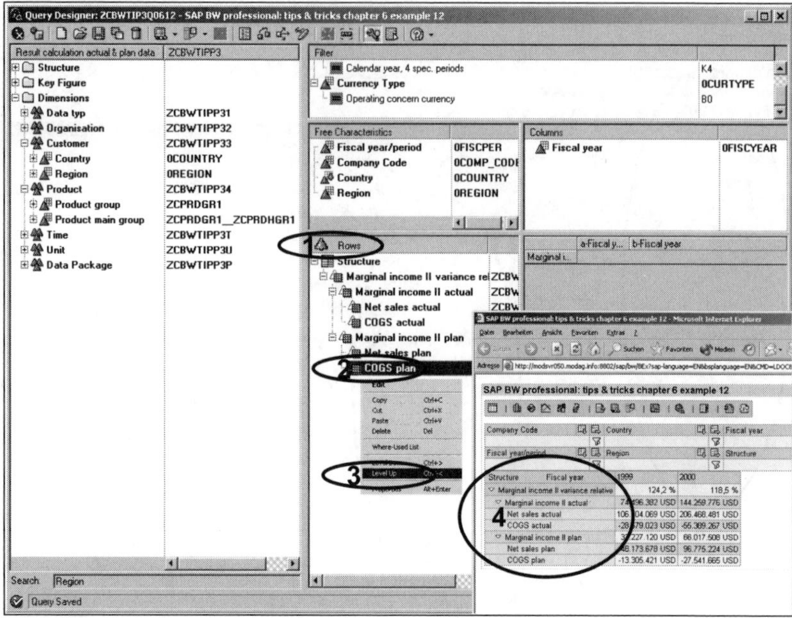

Figure 6.33 Visualization of the Key Hierarchies

6.5 Conditions

6.5.1 The Concept and the Available Types of Conditions in SAP Business Explorer

Principle of the Conditions

Conditions control the restriction of the result area in SAP BW queries; however, they have no influence on result rows—the result row corresponds to the result row of the query without this condition. Several conditions can be defined for a query. They are connected logically with AND; that is, different conditions affect the query simultaneously, insofar as all are active.

Available types of conditions

Using conditions, you can restrict the view of the data of a query as follows:

- Absolute conditions

  A row is filtered independently of the other rows if its reference value exceeds a particular threshold value. The available restrictions are:

  - Equal to/not equal to
  - Less than/greater than
  - Less than or equal to/greater than or equal to
  - Between/not between

- **Ranking lists**
  Here, all rows of the displayed list are considered and their relationship to one another determines whether the row will be displayed. Ranking lists are always sorted automatically. The following operations are available for the creation of ranking lists:
  - Top N, bottom N: the ranking lists reflect a particular number.
  - Top percent, bottom percent: the ranking lists reflect a certain percentage.
  - Top total, bottom total: the ranking lists represent a particular total value.

6.5.2 The Use of Conditions in SAP Business Explorer

Conditions of the type "absolute condition"

An example of the application of an absolute condition is the analysis of the relevant markets by eliminating low-ranked values. In the example, all regions with 5,000,000 Euros and more must be displayed; the other regions must be excluded from the display.

Click on the **Condition** button in the Query Designer and select the **New Condition** function (see Figure 6.34, Steps 1 and 2). In the **Define Condition** pop-up, a description is specified, and via activation or deactivation of the **Active** option, you determine whether or not the condition should be applied automatically during query execution (see Figure 6.34, Steps 3 and 4).

Because this absolute condition is not practical in every drill-down state (if an additional drilldown—for example, according to periods—occurs within the regions), click on the option box under the property **Evaluate the conditions displayed below for single characteristics or combinations of characteristics** and select the desired characteristic (in the example, the "Region") (see Figure 6.34, Steps 5 and 6). Then, click on the **New** button to see the display of drop-down boxes and input fields for specifying the condition (see Figure 6.34, Step 7). Activate the drop-down box for selecting the keys and select the desired key (in the example: "Marginal income II actual EUR") (see Figure 6.34, Step 8). Then, click on the drop-down box for selecting the operator, and select the desired operation (in the example: "Greater than or equal to") (see Figure 6.34, Step 9). Specify the desired threshold value in the **Values** input field, and then click on the **Transfer** button (see Figure 6.35, Steps 1 and 2).

The condition is then adopted into the list. Complete the definition of the condition by clicking on the **OK** button (see Figure 6.35, Steps 3 and 4).

After you save the defined condition, it is applied automatically during query execution (see Figure 6.35, Step 5).

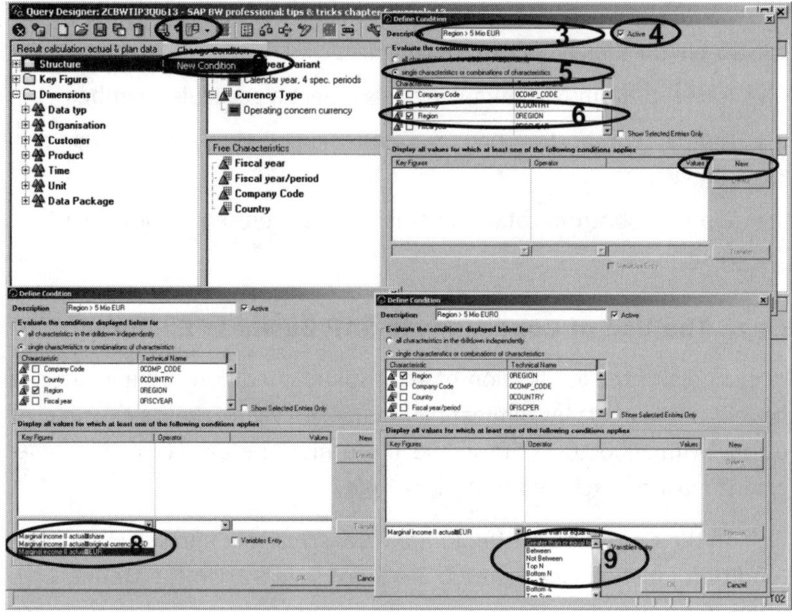

Figure 6.34 Absolute Condition, Part 1

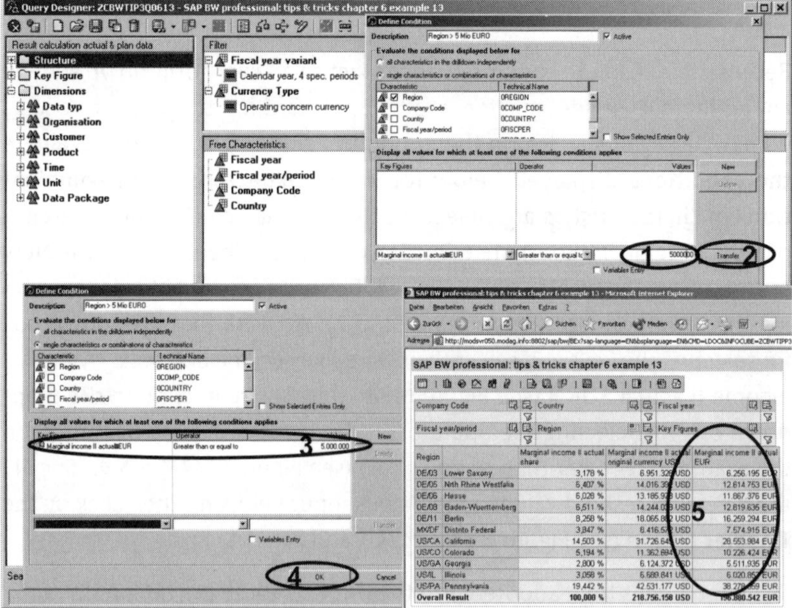

Figure 6.35 Absolute Condition, Part 2

Conditions of the type "ranking list"

An example for the application of a ranking list is the analysis of the relevant values of the drill-down characteristic "Selection" of the respective top values. In the example, those values should be listed independently for all characteristics in the drilldown that collectively represent at least 80% of the total result.

The definition is analogous to that of the absolute condition. Deviating from the example with an absolute ranking list, in the present example, the condition is applied for all characteristics in the breakdown. As operator, **Top %** is selected and the associated percentage value (in the example: 80%) is entered (see Figure 6.36, Steps 1 to 4).

You conclude the definition of the condition by clicking on the **OK** button (see Figure 6.36, Step 5). After you save the definition, the condition is applied automatically during query execution (see Figure 6.36, Step 6). As many values as necessary are displayed in the list (automatically sorted in ascending order) until the threshold value is reached, or it is exceeded for the first time.

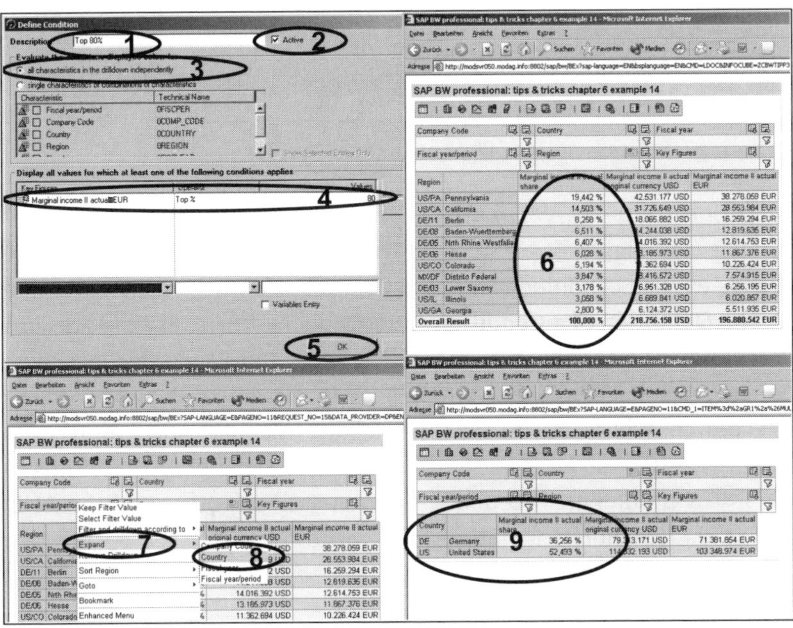

Figure 6.36 Ranking List Condition

If, in the query, you navigate to another list criterion (in the example: via context-sensitive menu to "Country"), then the defined condition is applied to this characteristic as well (see Figure 6.36, Steps 7 to 9).

Definition of conditions during query execution

To ensure that conditions will not simply be defined statically in the Query Designer, you can also define conditions during the execution of a query (see Figure 6.37).

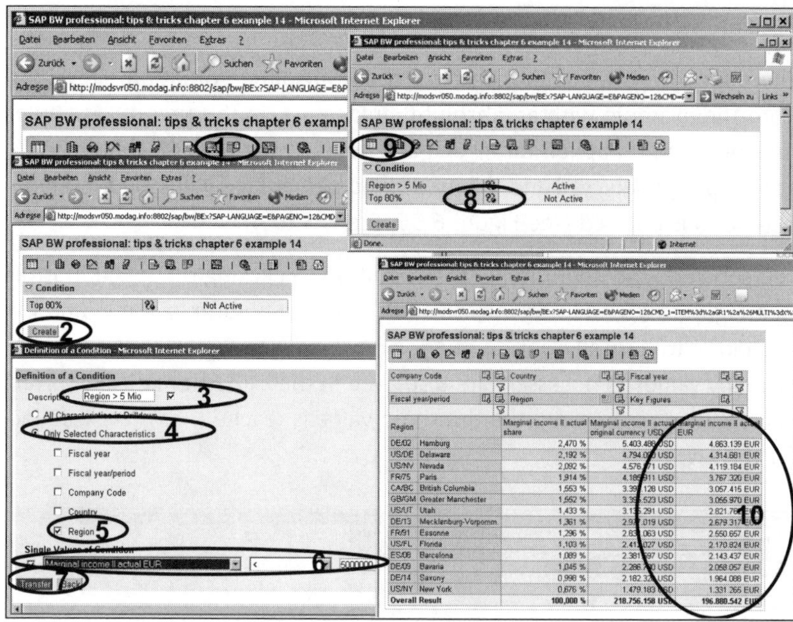

Figure 6.37 Definition of a Condition During Query Execution

In a displayed query, you must select the **Conditions** function by right-clicking (see Figure 6.37, Step 1). Then, the list is displayed with the already existing conditions. Click the **Create** button (see Figure 6.37, Step 2). The **Definition of a Condition** window opens. There, like the previous description of a condition, all required specifications and selections must be made (see Figure 6.37, Steps 3 to 7): in the example, all regions are selected in which fewer than 5 million "Marginal income II" was achieved. After you click on the **Transfer** button, the program returns to the list of conditions. If conditions contradict each other and the AND link of the conditions is not desired, you can simply click on the **Not Active** button (see Figure 6.37, Step 8).

To apply the defined condition in runtime, click on the **Table** button, and the result table is displayed (see Figure 6.37, Steps 9 and 10).

6.6 Exceptions

6.6.1 Visualization of Exception States

In SAP BW queries, you can highlight exception states (that is, query results that exceed or fall short of defined threshold values) using traffic-light colors. This function is called *Exception Reporting*. In addition to highlighted queries, these exceptions also function as the basis for alerts.

6.6.2 The Use of Exceptions in SAP Business Explorer

An example for the application of an exception is the analysis of the colored relative marginal income amounts. In the example, per period, all those countries must be marked as critical (that is, red) that have achieved a relative marginal income II of more than 69%. Those values are designated good (with green) that have achieved a relative marginal income II of greater than or equal to 70%. The remaining values are to be designated with the traffic-light color yellow

Click on the **Exception** button in the Query Designer and select the function **New Exception** (see Figure 6.38, Steps 1 and 2). In the **Defining Exceptions** pop-up, a description is specified, and through activation or deactivation of the **Active** option it is determined whether the exception should be displayed automatically during execution of the query (see Figure 6.38, Step 3). In the drop-down box with the same name, select the key for which the exception should be evaluated (see Figure 6.38, Step 4). On the **Exception Values** tab, click on the **New** button to specify the threshold values and alert levels. For the lower and upper limits of the respective alert level, the corresponding entries occur (see Figure 6.38, Steps 5 to 7). The alert level is selected in the drop-down box (see Figure 6.38, Step 8). After you have completed the definition, the setting is taken over into the list by clicking on the **Transfer** button (see Figure 6.38, Step 9). You must make these settings for all requested alert levels (see Figure 6.38, Step 10).

On the **Cell Restrictions** tab, select the setting **Totals Only (Recommended with Absolute Numbers)** in the drop-down box in order for the example to be realized (see Figure 6.39, Steps 1 and 2). To complete the exception definition, click on the **OK** button (see Figure 6.39, Step 3). After you save the exception definition, it can be applied automatically during the execution of a query (see Figure 6.39, Step 4).

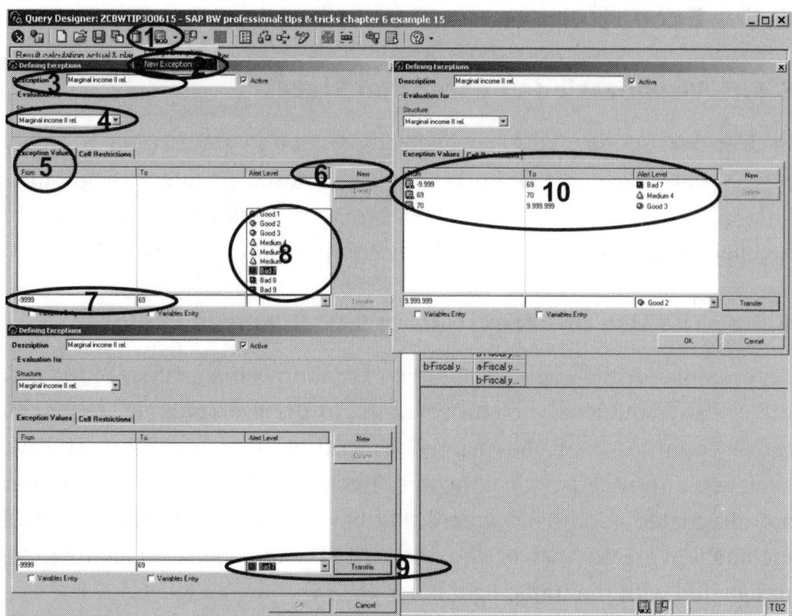

Figure 6.38 Creating an Exception, Part 1

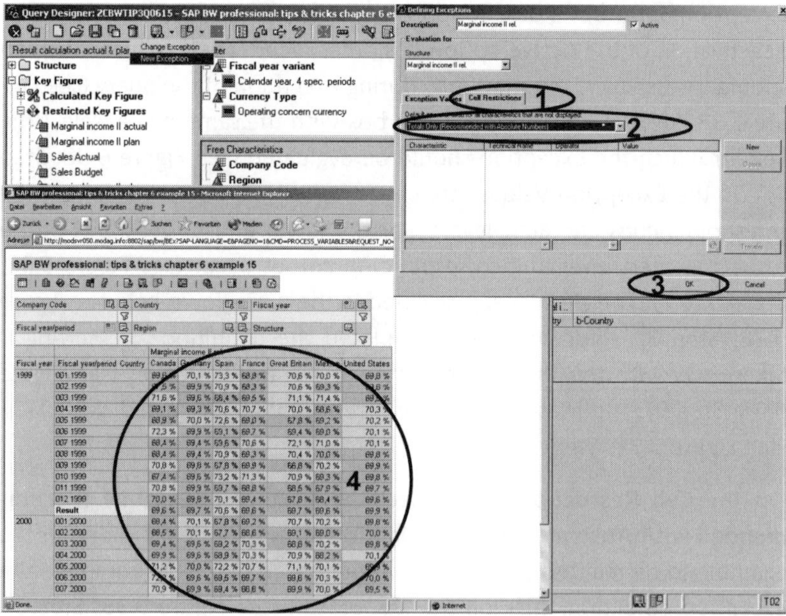

Figure 6.39 Creating an Exception, Part 2

6.7 Variables

6.7.1 Introduction

Queries without variable selections

The queries used until now contain either no selections or static selections. If static selections are used, there exists the problem that for similar demands, duplicates of the queries must be created that significantly increase the maintenance effort required for SAP BW. Note that precisely in this area, in many reviews of productive systems in the years 1998 to 2003, a significant operating cost reduction potential was recognized. If no selections are undertaken, then the query reads more data than is required at the start. This causes drastically increased burdens on the system, which result in extremely bad response times for the query users. In addition, with this approach, significant problems occur regarding authorization controls. Finally, without variable selections, many functional demands cannot be mapped (personalization of query calls, appropriate specifications, which data is actually displayed on the present result list, etc.).

Variable for programming queries

SAP BW makes available various functions for programming queries. The variables play a central role here. They function as placeholders and are filled with values in various ways during the execution of queries.

Variable types

SAP BW recognizes the following variable types:

- **Characteristic variables**
  Characteristic variables represent characteristic values and can always be used where characteristics must be restricted.
- **Hierarchy variables**
  Hierarchy variables represent hierarchies and can be used in places where hierarchies must be selected.
- **Hierarchy node variables**
  Hierarchy node variables represent a node in a hierarchy and can always be used where a hierarchy node must be restricted or partial hierarchies below a hierarchy node must be selected.
- **Text variables**
  Text variables represent a text and can be used in the descriptions of queries, calculated keys, and structural components. The text variables can be used during the creation of calculated keys, restricted keys, selections, and formulas in the description of these objects.
- **Formula variables**
  Formula variables represent numeric values and can be used in formulas. In addition, numeric values are used to restrict exceptions and conditions; here, formula variables can also be used.

Processing types

The processing type of a variable determines how the variable is filled with a value during the runtime of the query or Web application. The following processing types are available:

- **User entry/default value**
  The processing type "User entry/default value" enables the manual entry of the desired value—or the use of the default value specified during the definition of the variables—for the variable during execution of the query or Web application. This processing type is available for all variable types.
- **Replacement path**
  Using the processing type "Replacement path," you can configure the value that the variable should be automatically replaced with during the execution of the query or the Web application. This processing type is available for characteristic variables, text variables, and formula variables.
- **Customer exit**
  If you need to process a variable in a manner different from using the processing types "User entry/default value," "Replacement path," "SAP exit," or "Authorization," use "Customer exit," a customer-specific logic mapped with programming, to get the variable value. All variable types (characteristic, hierarchy nodes, hierarchy, formula, and text variables) can be processed with this type.
- **SAP exit**
  The processing type "SAP exit" is contained in variables that are delivered in the course of the business contents of SAP BW.
- **Authorization**
  The processing type "Authorization" enables the automatic filling of a variable with the values from the authorization of a user. This processing type is available for characteristic variables and hierarchy node variables.

Although variables are created in the Query Designer, they are not available only in a query; they are available system-wide across SAP BW as well. SAP supports the creation of variables with the variable wizard.

6.7.2 Characteristic Variables

Creation of characteristic variables

Characteristic variables are defined in the Query Designer. In the left frame with the elements of the InfoProvider, scroll down the **Structure** folder for an InfoObject to be programmed until the **Characteristic Value**

Variables subfolder is displayed. In the example, a variable selection must be enabled for the InfoObject "Fiscal year" (0FISCYEAR). Right-click on the **Characteristic Value Variables** subfolder to open the context-sensitive menu and select the **New Variable** function (see Figure 6.40, Step 1).

Then, the **SAP BW Variables Wizard** starts and the **General Information** screen is displayed. On the screen, specify the variable names (in the example: ZCFISYP0), the variable description (in the example: "Selection fiscal year (optional)"), and the processing type (in the example: "User Entry/Default Value") (see Figure 6.40, Step 2), and click on the **Next** button to navigate to the next screen—the **Details** screen (see Figure 6.40, Step 3).

In the screen, detailed specifications become the detail characteristics; these are the type of representation (in the example: "Single Value"), the specification of the variable entry (in the example: "Optional", not mandatory), the readiness for input (in the example: "Ready for Input"), the changeability, as well as the personalization setting (in the example both are not relevant) (see Figure 6.40, Step 4). Click on the **Next** button to navigate to the **Default Values** screen (see Figure 6.40, Step 5).

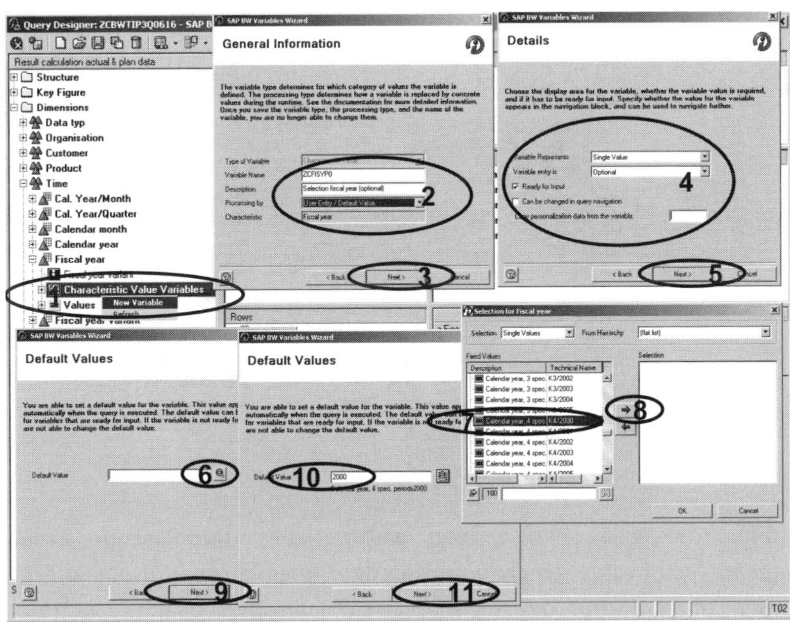

Figure 6.40 Creating Characteristic Variable, Part 1

In the **Default Values** screen, a default value can be provided if desired. If required, through the activation of the selection, the SAP BW selection support is activated, from which the desired value can be selected. After the selection, the value is copied into the **Default Values** screen (see Figure 6.40, Steps 6 to 8). To navigate to the next **Default Values** screen, click on the **Next** button (see Figure 6.40, Steps 9 to 11).

The definition of the variables is complete. On the **Save Variable** screen, click on the **Finish** button to save the variable (see Figure 6.41, Step 1).

Use of Characteristic Variables

Upon restarting the Query Designer or refreshing the list of characteristic variables (right-click on the **Characteristic Value Variables** folder of the corresponding InfoObject to open the context-sensitive menu), a newly defined variable will be incorporated into the list. Using drag & drop, the characteristic value variable can be taken over for the InfoObject in the filter, in the free characteristics, or (as in the example) in the rows (see Figure 6.41, Step 2).

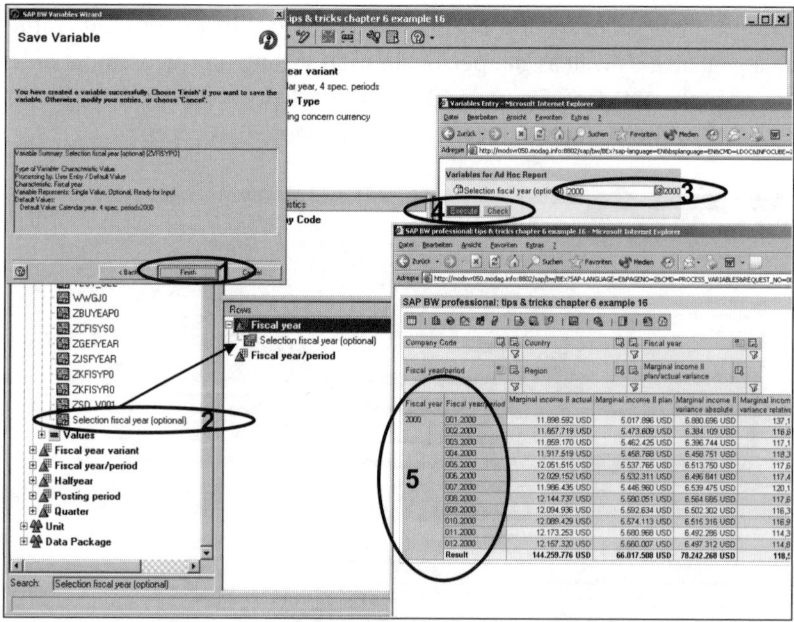

Figure 6.41 Creating Characteristic Variable, Part 2

Characteristic value variable during query execution

During the execution of a query with variables, the selection screen appears first. In this screen, you can either retain a value (if one already exists), enter a value directly, or select a value by activating the drop-down box (see Figure 6.41, Step 3). (Note: For optional variables, no selection needs to occur.) To apply the variable entries and display the query with the given selection, click on the **Execute** button (see Figure 6.41, Steps 4 and 5).

Selection option

Besides individual value selection (parameters), there are additional selection types available in SAP BW. Here, the *selection option* is treated as an example: the definition of a characteristic value variable with this selection type is similar to the Characteristic Value Variables of the selection type "Single Value" (parameter) (see Section 6.7.2). What is different is that in the **Details** screen, you must activate the drop-down box for the property **Variable entry is:** and select the **Selection Option** (see Figure 6.42, Step 4). Then, you must complete the variable definition as described in Section 6.7.2 and copy the variable into the query definition (see Figure 6.43, Step 1).

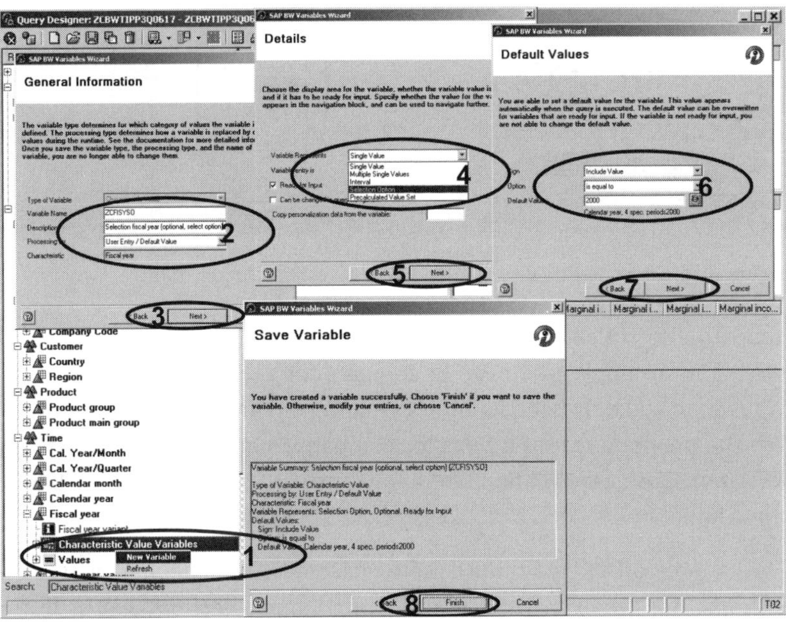

Figure 6.42 Characteristic Value Variable with Selection Option, Part 1

Selection option during query execution

In the selection screen that is displayed during query execution, you can also enter a value directly for the selection option variables, select a value by activating the drop-down box, or, for optional variables, make no selection. If, for the required restriction, several rows are required (in the example the values 1999 and 2000 are selected), then you must click on the **Insert Row** button (see Figure 6.43, Step 2). You can then select the required values and comparison conditions in the rows of the selection screen (see Figure 6.43, Step 3). After you click on the **Execute** button, the query result based on the selection conditions is displayed (see Figure 6.43, Steps 4 and 5).

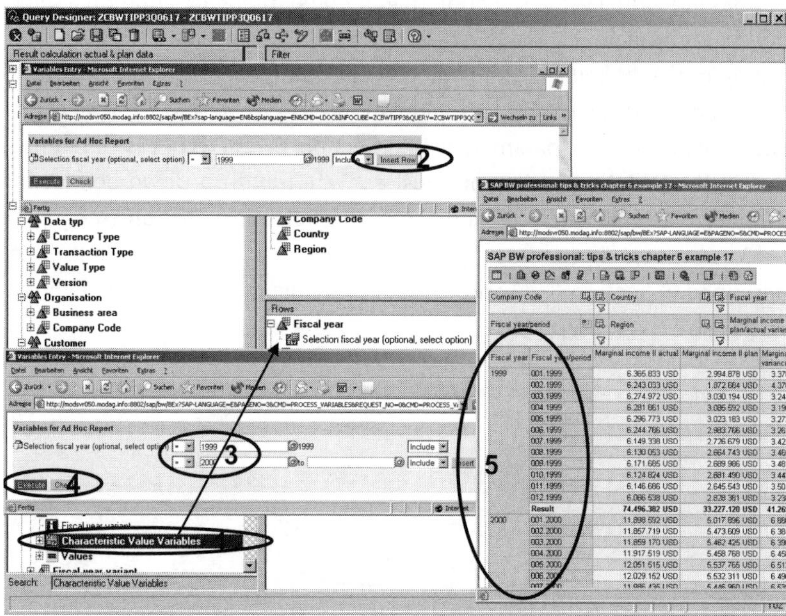

Figure 6.43 Characteristic Value Variable with Selection Option, Part 2

Variable offset

You can also "calculate" with characteristic value variables when necessary. If, for example, you need to compare the current year with the previous year, you only need to enter the current year as a variable. To establish the previous year as a basis for comparison in order to highlight any deviations, use a calculation operation. The variable *offset* is available for these situations.

For variable offsets, you must use a characteristic value variable (in the example, for the fiscal year) in a row or column selection. Similar to the description in Section 6.2.3, a new structure is created. Right-click on the new structure to open a context-sensitive menu and select the **New Selection** function (see Figure 6.44, Step 1). On the **New Selection** pop-up, the corresponding InfoObject is extracted from the (left) inventory frame (in the example: "Fiscal year") as well as the characteristic value variable (in the example: "Select fiscal year (optional)") and copied into the (right) selection frame (see Figure 6.44, Step 2). Click on the **OK** button to include the selection in the query definition (see Figure 6.44, Step 3).

If, in a second row or column, selection for the previous year should be compared, then you must establish the basis for this as well. You can either use the same procedure as you did previously, or copy the row or element. The acquisition of the previous year's selection then occurs via the configuration of the variable offset: right-click to display the previous year and select the **Edit** function in the context-sensitive menu that opens (see Figure 6.45, Step 1).

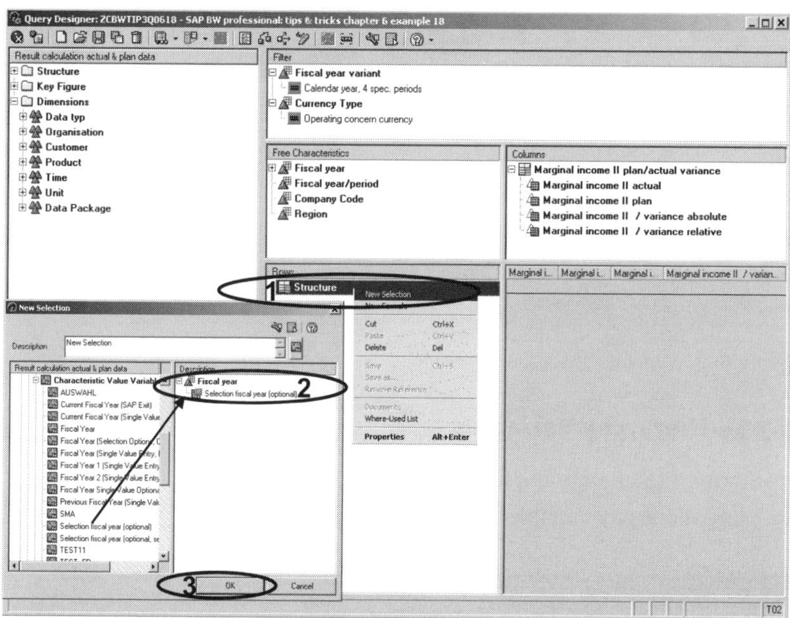

Figure 6.44 Selection with Variable for Fiscal Year

Right-click on the **Edit Selection** pop-up on the right frame on the characteristic value variable to open the context-sensitive menu and select the **Restrict** function (see Figure 6.45, Step 2). In the **Selection for ...** pop-up (in the example: "Fiscal year") on the characteristic value variable, open the context menu again via right-clicking and select **Specify Variable Offsets** (see Figure 6.45, Steps 3 and 4). Then, enter this offset again in the **Offset** input field on the **Enter Variable Offset** pop-up (see Figure 6.45, Step 5). The offset is acquired such that the absolute difference between the characteristic value entered in the characteristic value variable and the desired target value form the variable offset. With three clicks of the **OK** button, the entry is taken over into the query definition (see Figure 6.45, Steps 6 to 10).

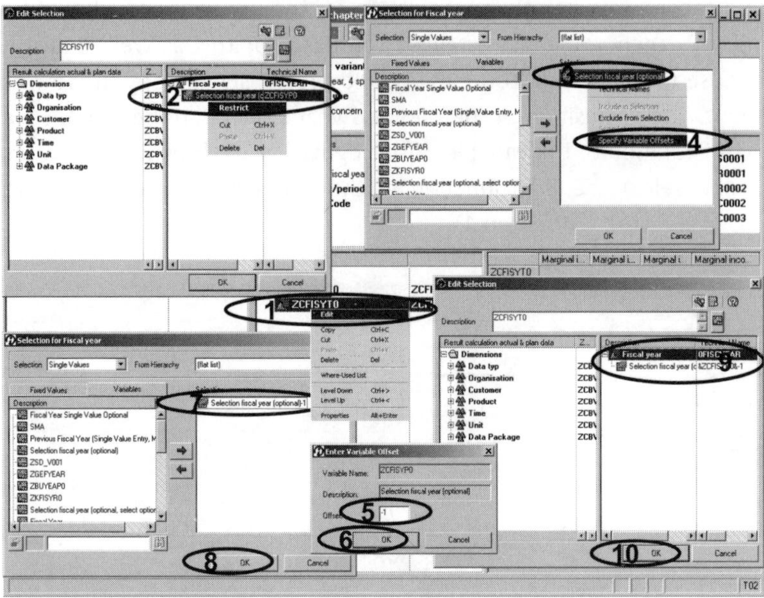

Figure 6.45 Variable Offset for the Previous Year's Selection

6.7.3 Hierarchy Variables

If you need to change the look of the hierarchy of queries, you can do so by using hierarchy variables.

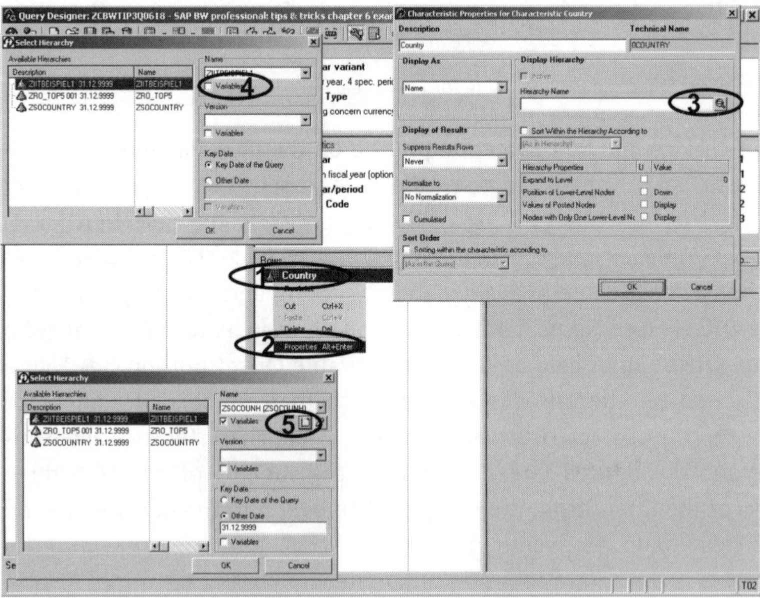

Figure 6.46 Creating a Hierarchy Variable, Part 1

To create a hierarchy variable, right-click on an InfoObject of the type "Characteristic," which is used in a query and bears hierarchies, to open the context-sensitive menu, and select the **Properties** function (see Figure 6.46, Steps 1 and 2). In the **Characteristic Properties for Characteristic ...** pop-up (in the example: "Country"), you must activate block presentation hierarchy, the drop-down box for hierarchy name (see Figure 6.46, Step 3). On the **Select Hierarchy** pop-up, activate the **Variables** option (see Figure 6.46, Step 4). Two additional buttons become visible; click on the **New Variable** button (see Figure 6.46, Step 5). Then, the screen sequence for maintaining variables (which is analogous to the definition of characteristic value variables) is called up. The only deviation is the default value acquisition (see Figure 6.47, Steps 1 to 9, and Figure 6.48, Step 1).

Creating a hierarchy variable

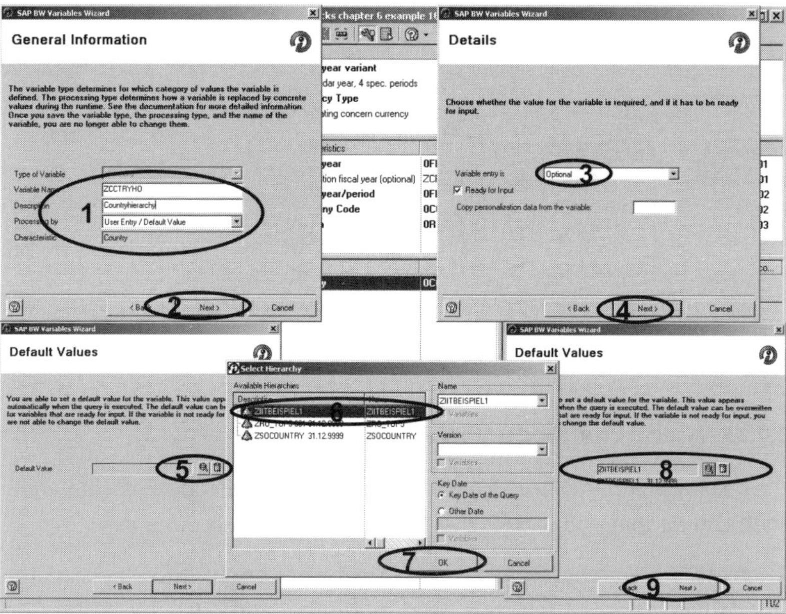

Figure 6.47 Creating a Hierarchy Variable, Part 2

After you save the variable, it is available on the **Select Hierarchy** pop-up and it can be taken over by clicking on the **OK** button (see Figure 6.48, Steps 2 to 4). With another confirmation by clicking on the **OK** button on the **Characteristic Properties for Characteristic ...** pop-up (in the example: "Country"), this variable is taken over into the query definition (see Figure 6.48, Steps 5 and 6).

Hierarchy variable during query execution After you save the query, during execution, the hierarchy variable appears first on the selection screen. In this screen, you can retain a value (if a default value exists), enter a value directly, or select a value from the list of available hierarchies (see Figure 6.48, Steps 7 and 8). To display the hierarchy in the query result, click on the **Execute** button.

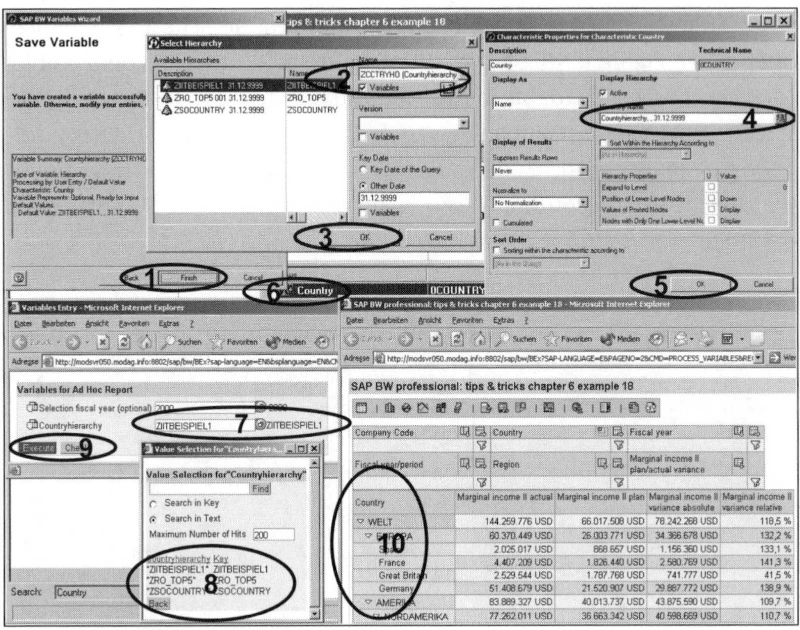

Figure 6.48 Creating a Hierarchy Variable, Part 3

6.7.4 Hierarchy Node Variables

The display of a partial tree from a hierarchy or the selection of a hierarchy node can be mapped in SAP BW using hierarchy node variables.

Creating hierarchy node variables To create a hierarchy node variable, right-click on an InfoObject of the type "Characteristic," which is used in a query and bears hierarchies, to open the context-sensitive menu, and select the **Restrict** function (see Figure 6.49, Steps 1 and 2). In the **Selection for...** pop-up (in the example: "Country"), right-click on a variable (or, if no variable exists, on the entry **No entries found**) in the **Variables** tab in the left frame to open the context-sensitive menu, and select the **New Variable** function (see Figure 6.49, Steps 3 and 4). Then, the screen sequence for maintaining variables (which is analogous to the definition of characteristic value variables) is called up. The only deviation is the default value acquisition (see Figure 6.49, Steps 5 to 9).

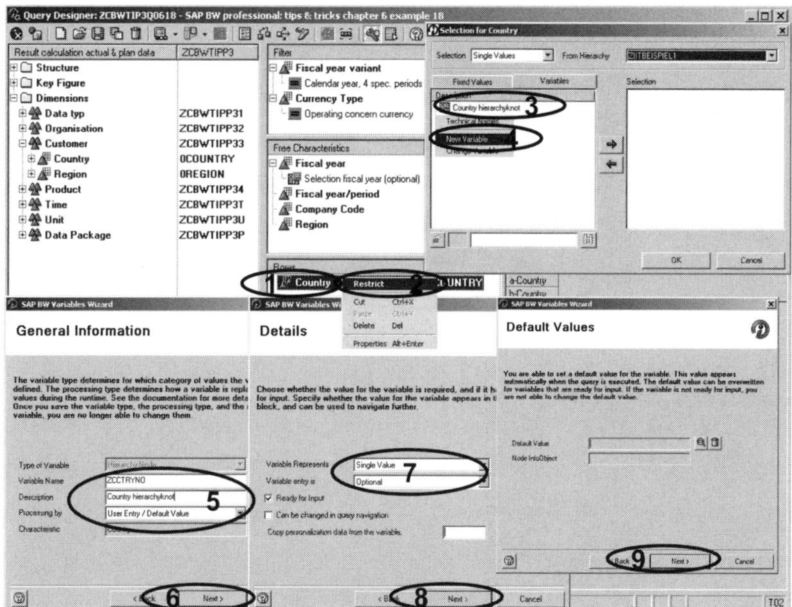

Figure 6.49 Creating a Hierarchy Node Variable, Part 1

Hierarchy node Variable during query execution

After completing the variable definition, click on the **Finish** button on the **Save Variable** screen (see Figure 6.50, Step 1). The hierarchy node variable is offered for selection on the left frame of the **Selection for...** popup (in the example: "Country"). To select it, highlight it and click on the **Add** button (see Figure 6.50, Steps 2 and 3). Click on the **OK** button; the hierarchy node variable is taken over into the query definition (see Figure 6.50, Step 4).

After you save the query, this variable is used during execution for the selection of a partial hierarchy: at the start, the selection screen is displayed (see Figure 6.51).

On the selection screen, the drop-down box on the hierarchy node variable is activated (see Figure 6.51, Step 1). Then, the selected hierarchy (in the example: "Geographic country hierarchy") is opened for selection of the node in a new screen. Right-click to select a hierarchy node or a characteristic value (see Figure 6.51, Step 2). The selected value is taken over on the selection screen (see Figure 6.51, Step 3). After you click on the **Execute** button, the query is executed and the selected partial hierarchy is displayed (see Figure 6.51, Steps 4 and 5).

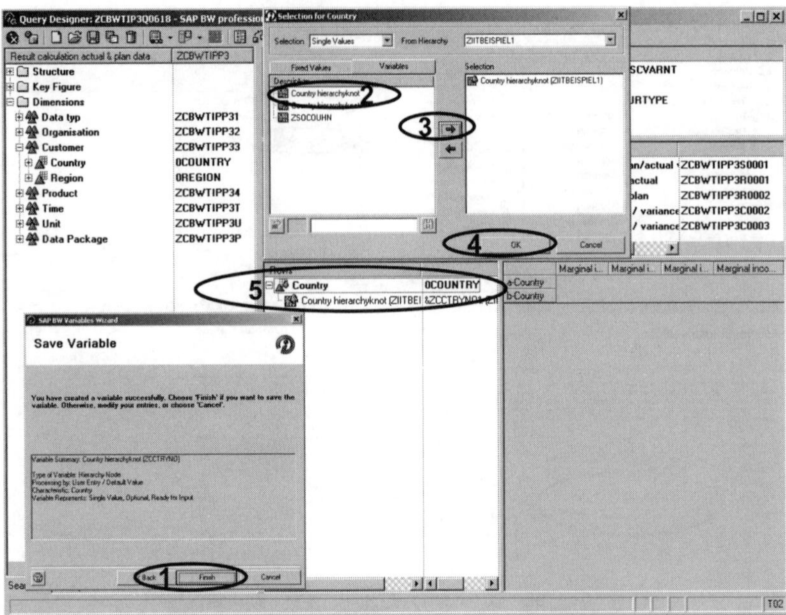

Figure 6.50 Creating a Hierarchy Node Variable, Part 2

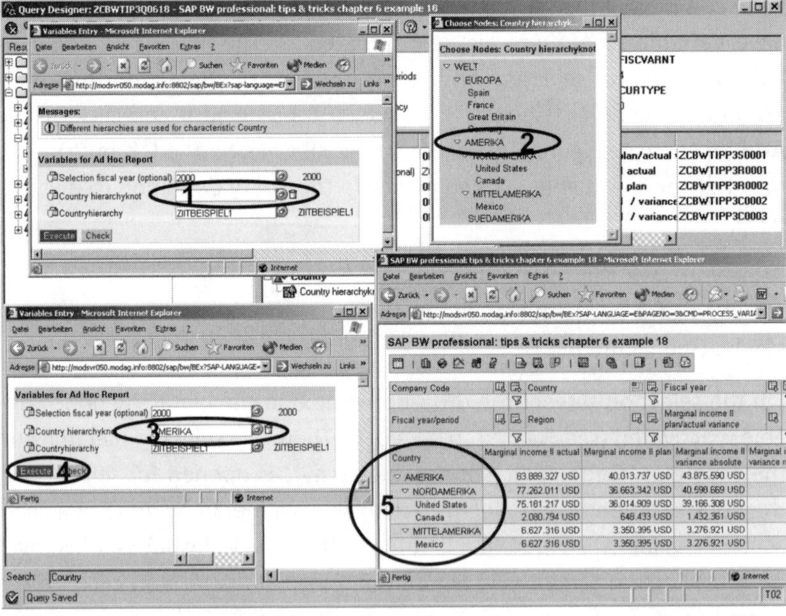

Figure 6.51 Executing Query with Hierarchy Node Variable

6.7.5 Text Variables

Dynamic column and row labeling

The naming of columns or rows during the listing of characteristic values for horizontal or vertical breakdown occurs dynamically using key values (characteristic values or hierarchy nodes) and the main data texts. As soon as selections are used (e.g., key with restriction to the fiscal year), the names are no longer acquired dynamically. For the mapping of dynamic labels for even more complex selections, text variables are available.

Creating text variables

A text variable can be created in different ways:

- By opening the context-sensitive menu on a structure and selecting **New Selection** (see Figure 6.52, Steps 1 and 2)
- By selecting a structural element by opening the context-sensitive menu and selecting the **Edit** function, or by selecting the **Properties** function

In the **New Selection** pop-up, by clicking on the **Text variable** button next to the Description input field (see Figure 6.52, Step 3), you can open the **Selection** pop-up. Right-click on the pop-up, select the **New** entry and click on the **OK** button (see Figure 6.52, Steps 4 and 5). Then, the screen sequence for maintaining variables (which is analogous to the definition of characteristic value variables) is called up (see Figure 6.52 and Figure 6.53). The only deviation is the other processing: in the **General Information** screen, for automatic replacement of the name with characteristic values, you must select **Processing by Replacement Path** (see Figure 6.52, Step 6).

On the **Characteristic** screen, select the characteristic whose data the text variable should replace. Activate the drop-down box, select the characteristic that you want, and confirm the selection by clicking on the **Next** button (see Figure 6.53, Steps 1 and 2). How the selected characteristic should be used in the text variable must be defined on the **Replacement Path** screen: you can define whether keys or text should be displayed, whether the replacement for intervals should occur via the From Value or the To Value, or whether a partial string should be displayed. In the example, the fiscal year is displayed whose values should be displayed K42000 or K41999 as 2000 or 1999. Confirm the definition by clicking on the **Next** button. Then, in the **Save Variable** screen, click on **Finish** to save the variable (see Figure 6.53, Steps 3 to 5).

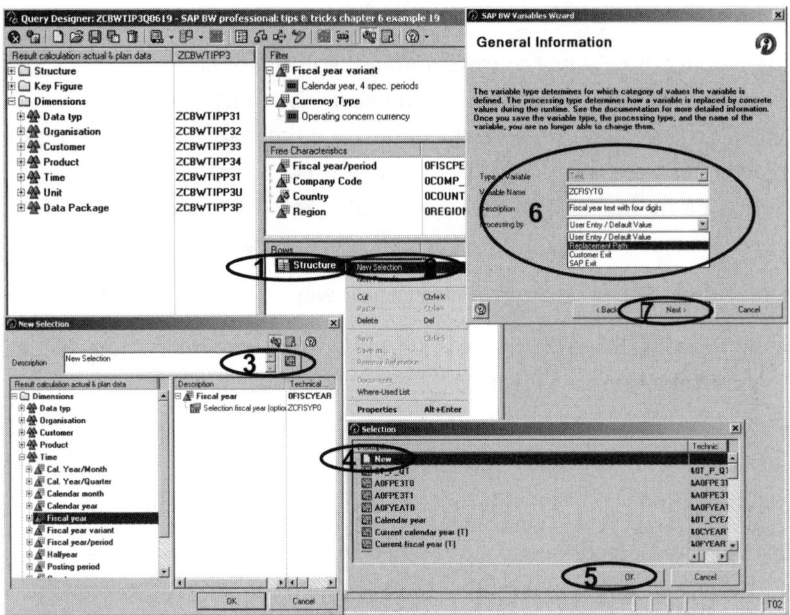

Figure 6.52 Creating a Text Variable, Part 1

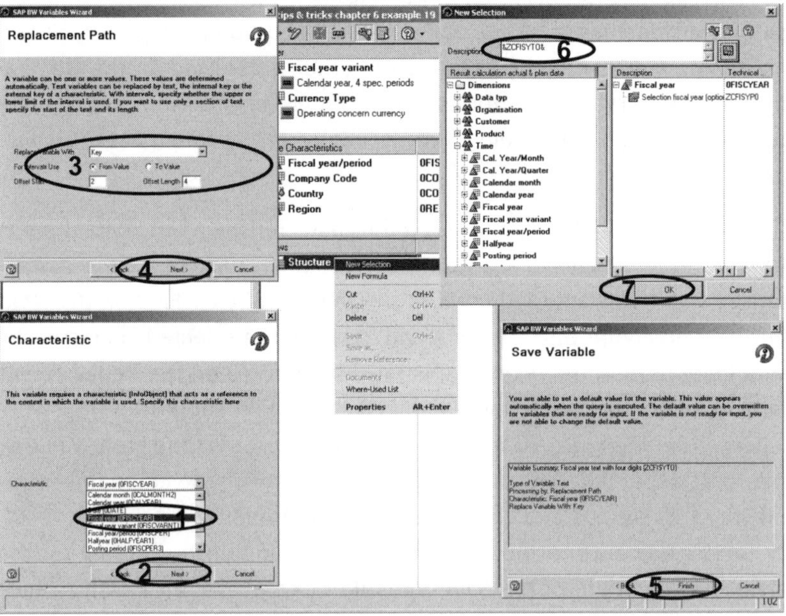

Figure 6.53 Creating a Text Variable, Part 2

After you have defined the variable, it is (identified via the in **&** incorporated technical name) taken over into the Description field. Click on the **OK** button; the definition is taken over into the query (see Figure 6.53, Steps 6 and 7).

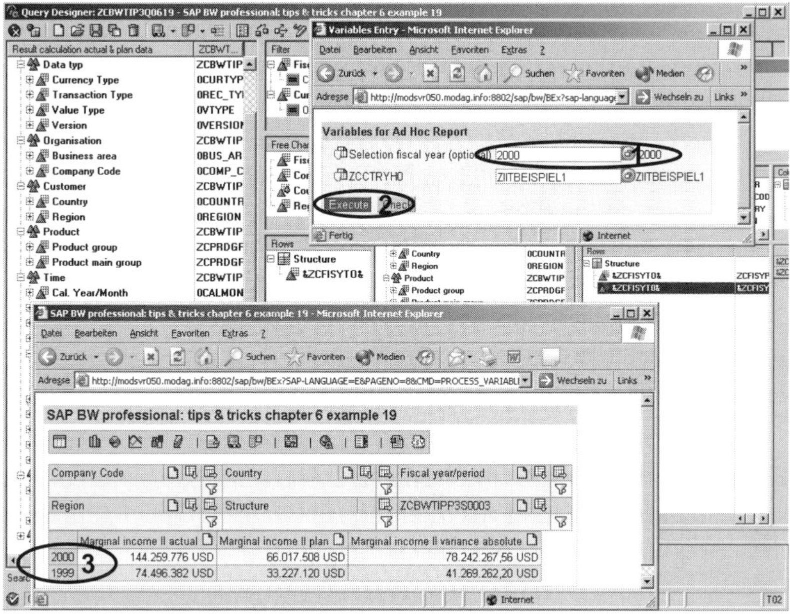

Figure 6.54 The Text Variable During Query Execution

Text variable during query execution

During query execution, the variable value is used in the column and row titles (see Figure 6.54). This also applies for calculations with variables using offsets: In the query used in Figure 6.54, row 1 contains the selection on the characteristic value variable for the fiscal year. With the offset -1, row 2 selects the data of the previous year. The technology of the replacement path acquires the correct title dynamically in both rows.

6.7.6 Formula Variables

All variables explained above select characteristics in some form (characteristic value variable, hierarchy variable, hierarchy node variable), or they process characteristic values (text variables). For various tasks, however, variables for work with keys are also required; for example, if in a formula, a prescribed value should flow into a calculation at query runtime, such a value must be consulted for exceptions.

For such demands, SAP BW makes available formula variables that represent numeric values. In the present example, the variable placement of threshold values for exceptions is demonstrated using formula variables.

Creating formula variable

Formula variables can be created from the exception definition, for example. Click on the **Exception** button in the Query Designer and select **New Exception** (see Figure 6.55, Steps 1 and 2). In the **Defining Exceptions** pop-up, you must make the specifications required for the exception definition: entry of a name, default, whether the exception should be active upon query start, and for which structural elements or characteristics the exceptions must be evaluated (see Figure 6.55, Steps 3 and 4). In order to be able to create the threshold values for the exception, you must click on the **New** button (see Figure 6.55, Step 5). While a lowest value must be specified (see Figure 6.55, Step 6), the upper value should be variable. Click on the **Variables Entry** checkbox (see Figure 6.55, Step 7). Then, the buttons for the new creation or maintenance of formula variables are displayed, of which the **New Variable** button must be clicked (see Figure 6.55, Step 8). This starts the variable maintenance.

In the screen sequence for the maintenance of variables, the procedure is similar to the definition of characteristic value variables (see Figure 6.55, Steps 9 to 12, and Figure 6.56, Steps 1 to 5).

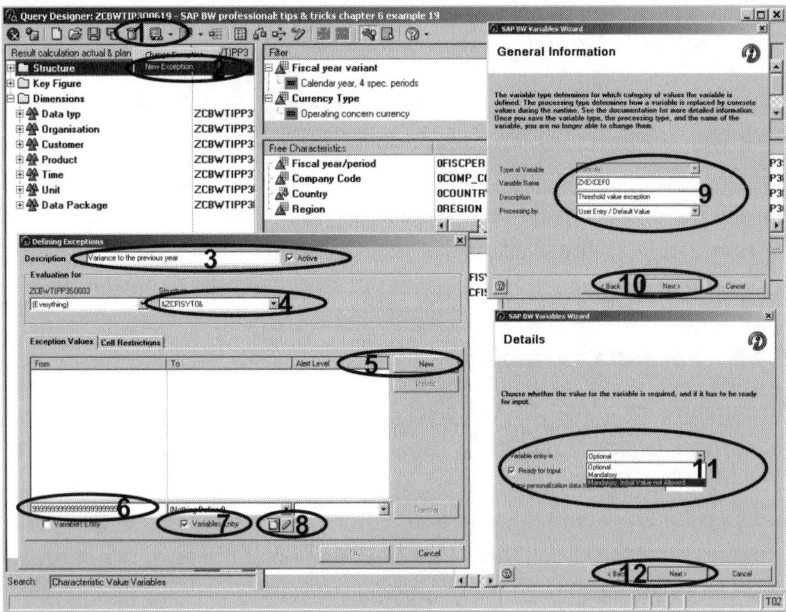

Figure 6.55 Creating a Formula Variable, Part 1

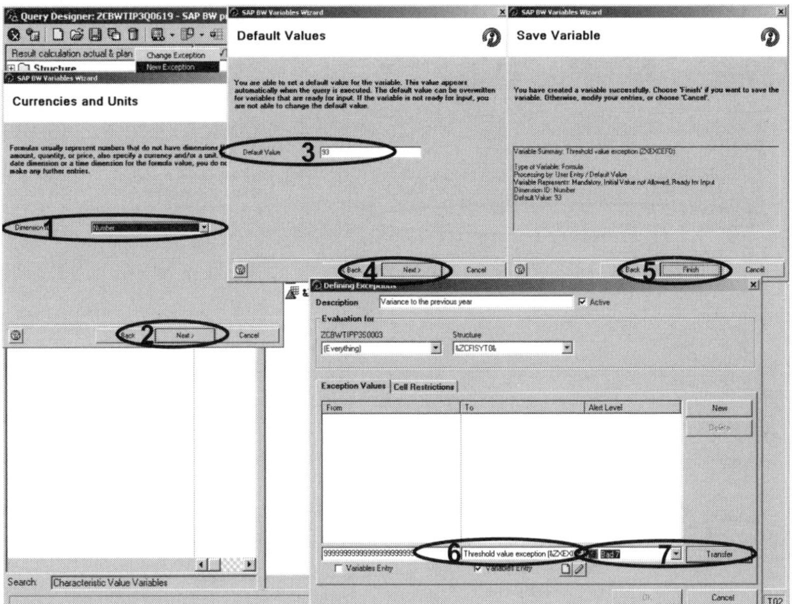

Figure 6.56 Creating a Formula Variable, Part 2

The deviation regarding the creation of characteristic value variables is the specification of the dimension indicator on the **Currencies and Units** screen: there, you must specify which type of keys (number, amount, price, quantity) the formula variable represents (see Figure 6.56, Step 1). If the variable definition in the **Save Variable** screen is completed by clicking on the **Finish** button, the formula variable is taken over in the exception definition as a threshold value (see Figure 6.56, Step 6).

The exception definition should be prepared as it was in Section 6.6 (see Figure 6.56, Step 7, and Figure 6.57, Steps 1 and 2).

Formula variable during query execution

If the query is started after saving the formula variable, the selection screen is started with the formula variables (in the example: "Threshold value exception"). Here, the threshold value must be taken over or entered (see Figure 6.57, Step 3). After you click on the **Execute** button, the exception is evaluated accordingly and the evaluation is displayed (see Figure 6.57, Steps 4 and 5).

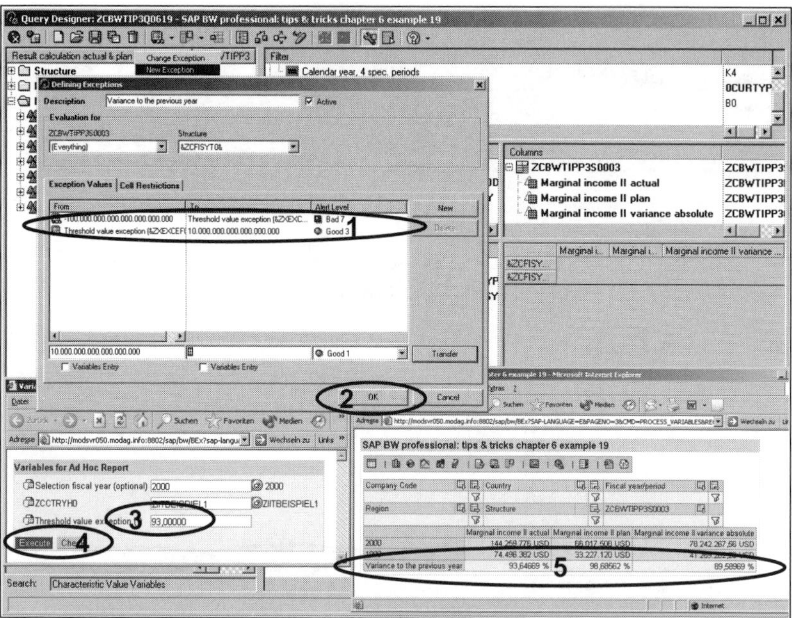

Figure 6.57 Exception with Formula Variables During Query Execution

6.8 Additional Selected Innovations in the Query Designer

6.8.1 Query Characteristics

The characteristics of the query

The query characteristics can be displayed and edited by clicking on the button with the same name. To display or change various characteristics, you must activate the corresponding tab:

- **General** tab (see Figure 6.58, Step 2)
  - **Description**
    The description of the query can be entered or changed. Text variables can be used in the description; to do so, click on the **Select text variable** button (see Figure 6.58, Steps 3 and 4).
  - **Key date**
    For time-dependent data, the key date determines exactly when the data is selected. The default value for the key date is the execution time of the query. Alternatively, you can enter the key date as a constant value or select a date variable. To do this, you must click on the **Values** button (see Figure 6.58, Step 5).

- **Sequence of the Entry Variables**
  By highlighting a variable and clicking on the ▼ or ▶ button, you can set the sequence in which the variables are displayed on the selection screen (see Figure 6.58, Steps 6 and 7).

- **Display** tab (see Figure 6.58, Steps 8 and 9)
  - **Display options**
    The display characteristics can be activated or deactivated. Since SAP BW 3.0, symbols (among other things) can be displayed for the incorporation of documents: if the **Display Document Links** option is activated, then the document symbol for jumping to the document display is inserted for relevant query elements during query execution (see Section 6.8.1).
  - **Numeric display**
    The display characteristics for numbers in the results table can be set (result position, sign display, as well as the handling of zeroes).

- **Specific** tab (see Figure 6.58, Step 10)
  - **Release for OLE DB for OLAP**
    If you activate this option, the query is enabled for the SAP SEM Balanced Scorecard and various third-party front-end tools.

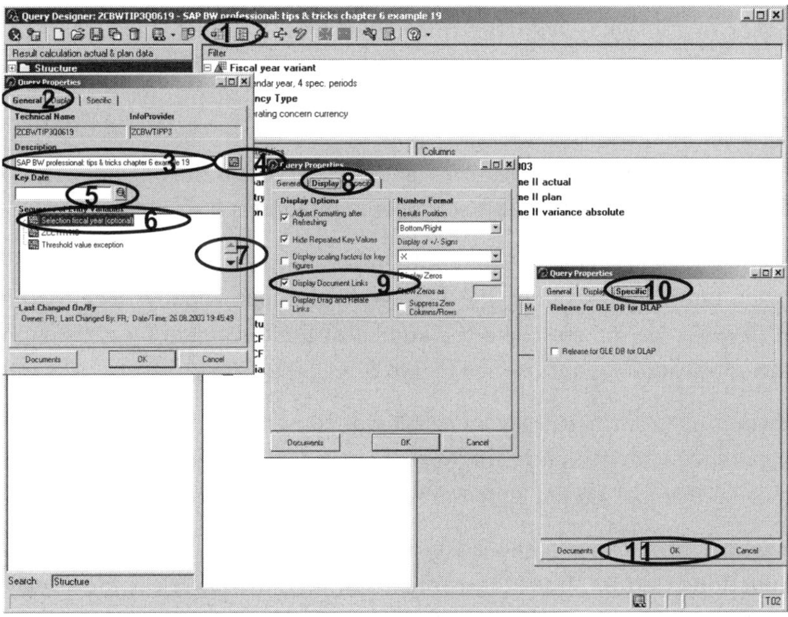

Figure 6.58 Setting the Query Characteristics

Setting up document links

To demonstrate how to use the query characteristics, we'll use the function for document incorporation as an example. This function has been available since SAP BW 3.0. The maintenance of the query characteristics occurs with a click of the button by the same name (see Figure 6.58, Step 1). After activating the **Display** tab (see Figure 6.58, Step 8), the document links are displayed during query execution by selecting the option with the same name (see Figure 6.58, Step 9, as well as the display and use of document links in Section 6.8.2).

6.8.2 Document Links

Since SAP BW 3.0, you can navigate from query execution directly to documents for metadata, main data, and motion data. Therefore, you can use query selection and the jump object, as well as the jump value, for document selection.

The display of the document link is configured in the Query Designer, in the query characteristics (see Section 6.8.1). After selecting the **Display Document Links** option, the query emerges during the query execution as follows.

Query execution with display of the document link

After you call up the query and (if input variables are present) click on the **Execute** button on the selection screen (see Figure 6.59, Step 1), the query is displayed. With the document links activated, the document symbols are displayed for all relevant elements (see Figure 6.59, Step 2). Simply by clicking on a document symbol, you display the **BW Document Browser** in a new window (see Figure 6.59, Step 3). The left frame contains links and function calls; the right frame contains the document contents. Upon display, the technical documentation is displayed first.

If an existing document is edited, then you must click on the Edit Document button. This opens the Change Document window (see Figure 6.59, Step 4). You complete the editing of the document by clicking on the corresponding button (see Figure 6.59, Step 5).

If you only want to display an existing document, you must click on the hyperlink with the name of the element (in the example: "Marginal income II actual") (see Figure 6.59, Step 6).

If you want to create a new document, you must click on the **Additional Functions** button. From the context-sensitive menu, select the **Create New Document** function (see Figure 6.59, Step 7). Then, the **Create Document** window opens and the title and contents are maintained. The entries (analogous to Figure 6.59, Step 5) are either saved or discarded.

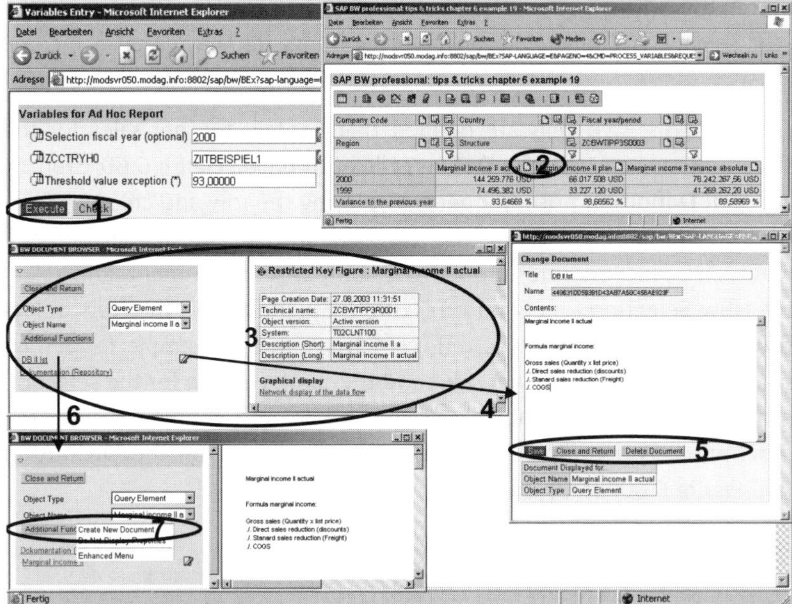

Figure 6.59 Document Display from a Query

6.8.3 Calculating with Cells Using the Example "Structure Percent"

Demand: calculations with individual cells

Calculations in reports can contain formulas via row elements or column elements, or combinations of cells with row or column elements.

Classic solution examples are balance sheets, profit and loss reports, and marginal income reports, which, in addition to the absolute amounts of individual positions, contain the relative shares of the individual positions with respect to a reference position. For balance sheets, this is the share of the stated position of the balance sheet total; in profit and loss statements or in coverage amount reports, often the relationships of the positions to net sales are stated. Since SAP BW 3.0, the definition of cells with restrictions and the function of the use of cells in formulas are available for these kinds of calculations.

Example

The setup of this function assumes a query with two structures. In the previous example, the relationships to net sales (here, gross sales/direct reductions of revenue) for the comparison of two years are stated in addition to absolute amounts of a coverage amount scheme. To illustrate this, we defined a query as an example, which contains the marginal income scheme in the rows (using the calculated keys for net sales and coverage amount) as one structure and the selection of a year and the previous year in the columns as another structure. Therefore, the columns with the year selections contain the absolute amounts for the marginal income keys.

Defining cells On this basis, two cells are defined that contain the net sales for the selected years: click on the **Define cells** button (see Figure 6.60, Step 1). The **Cell Definition** pop-up opens, displaying the row and column structures in the upper frame. In the lower frame, you can define the cells. Right-click on the frame to open the context-sensitive menu and select the **New Selection** function (see Figure 6.60, Step 2). In the **New Selection** pop-up, make the required restrictions: in the example for cell Nt sales year, select the key net sales and the same variable for the selection of the fiscal year that you selected in the column definition; enter the description, and complete the definition by clicking on the **OK** button (see Figure 6.60, Steps 3 and 4).

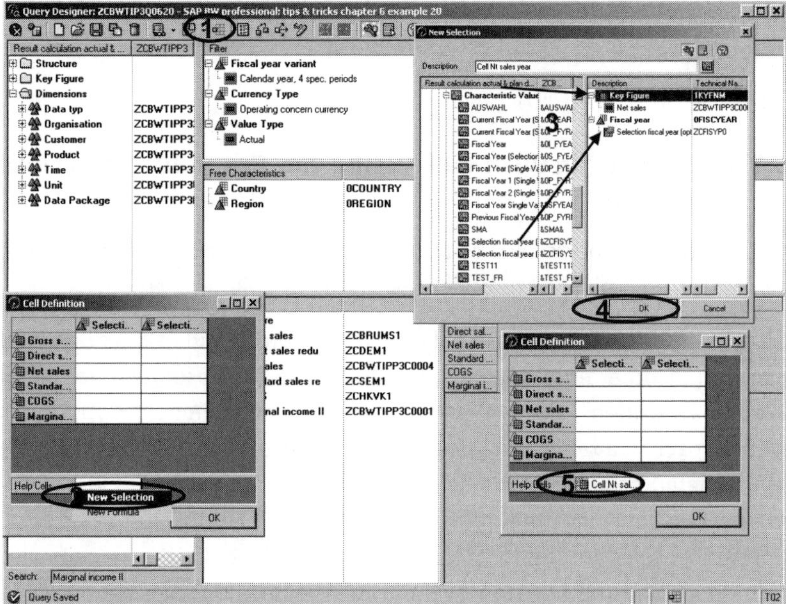

Figure 6.60 Defining Cells

As you did when defining the first cell (cell Nt sales year), define another cell for the previous year (cell Nt sales previous year). The selection of the previous year occurs by using the same variable that you selected in the first cell; however, this time, it has an offset of -1.

In the second step, the cells are used for formulas in the columns in order to display shares of the marginal income keys of net sales in the selected year: right-click on the column structure to open the context-sensitive menu and select the function **New Formula** (see Figure 6.61, Steps 1 and 2). In the **Edit Formula** pop-up, use the calculation to drag & drop the fiscal year selection and the cell Nt sales previous year (from the first column) and the function percentage share (from the second column) into the Formula input field (see Figure 6.61, Steps 3 to 5). Click on the **OK** button to ensure that the formula definition is copied into the query as an additional column (see Figure 6.61, Step 6).

Use of cells in formulas

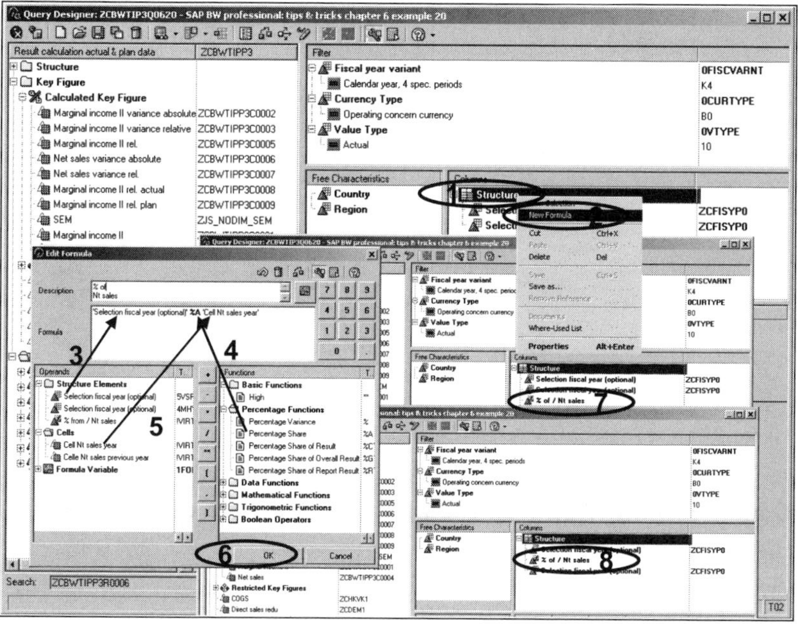

Figure 6.61 Use of Cells in Formula Definitions

The newly defined column is inserted at the end of the list and at the extreme right column. Since, however, the reference to the first column should be created, the second column (with the selection fiscal year – 1) must be moved using drag & drop "in front of" the newly created formula column (see Figure 6.61, Steps 7 and 8).

Using the cell Nt previous sales year and the second column (with the selection fiscal year – 1), the definition of another column, which states the shares in the previous year, occurs analogous to the creation of the column cell Nt sales year (see Figure 6.62, Steps 1 to 5).

During query execution (after you have previously saved the definition), and after you select the fiscal year in the variable entry (in the example "2000") and click on the **Execute** button, the result is acquired and displayed (see Figure 6.62, Steps 6 to 8).

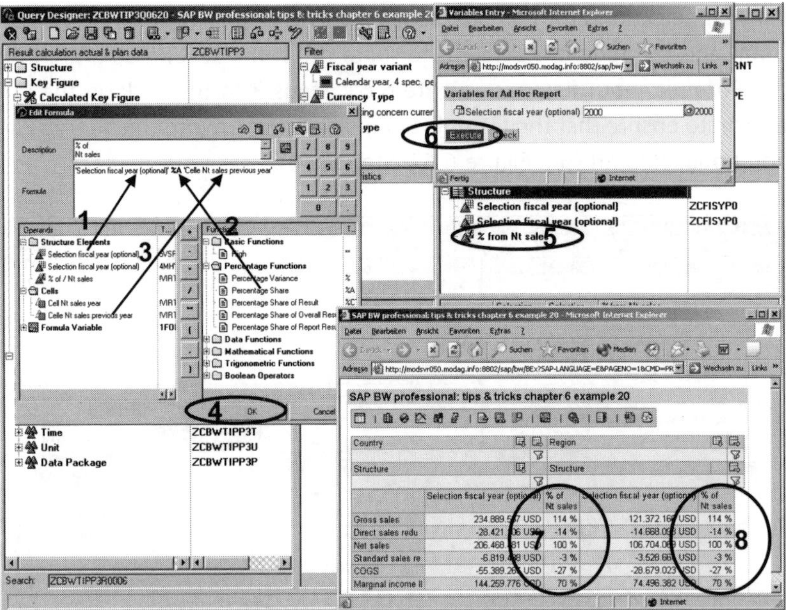

Figure 6.62 Execution of the Query with Cell-Based Formulas

6.8.4 Tabular Reporting Using the Example of Main Data Reporting

The tabular reporting approach

Business demands such as the need for multidimensional analysis of consolidated enterprise data—for example, using slice & dice to examine data from different points of view—characterize the functionality of OLAP reporting. SAP BW has offered this functionality for a long time. Since SAP BW 3.0, there is tabular reporting in addition to the OLAP reporting. As explained in the SAP BW documentation:

> *In tabular display, the characteristics and keys are displayed in the columns. In distinction to OLAP reporting, there are no free characteristics and no rows. In tabular display, you can use the filter and order characteristics, keys, and attributes freely in the columns. For example, you can place a key column between two characteristic columns. The column display is fixed and is specified at the time of design. With tabular reporting, the interaction possibilities are limited to "Filter," "Filter and drill-down*

according to," "Sort according to," and the navigation to hierarchies. Navigation functions that would change the geometry of tabular lists, that is, the number and arrangement of columns, such as "Exchange" or "Add drilldown," are not possible with tabular reporting – in contrast to OLAP reporting.

The tabular display of queries is especially suited for formatted and formula-based reporting (e.g., for list-like display of a list of materials). With formatted reports, the most important thing is a pixel-precise layout design and comfortable print options.

A first example shall be a motion data report, which is displayed as an OLAP report and as a tabular report: Different keys, such as "Sales quantity," "Net sales," and "Marginal income amount," must be displayed for the characteristic "Customer" with various attributes. The definition is similar to the previous explanations in this chapter (see Figure 6.63, Steps 1 and 2). The display attributes for the customer are listed for selection by opening the **Attributes** folder under the InfoObject "Customer" in the left frame and can be taken over into the query using drag & drop (see Figure 6.63, Step 3).

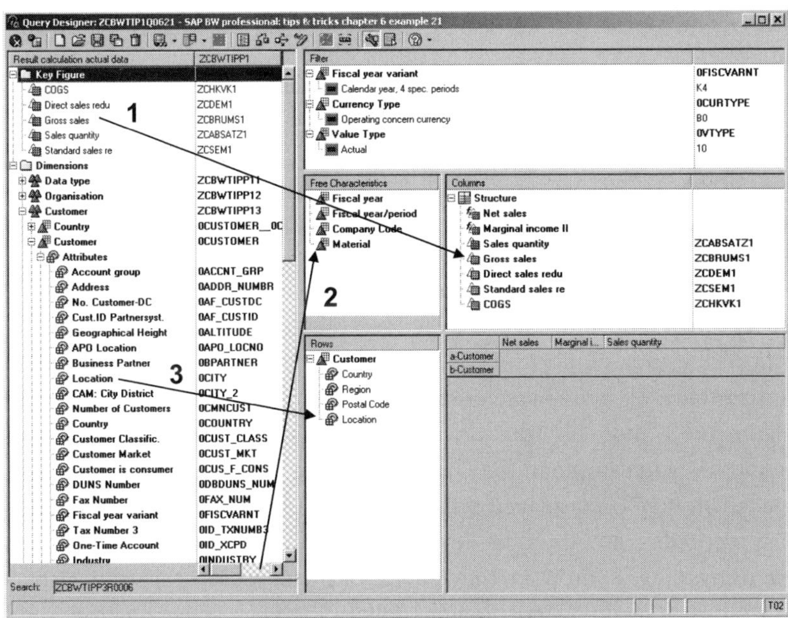

Figure 6.63 OLAP Report with Characteristic and Display Attributes

The OLAP report For the configuration of the query, an OLAP query is created by default (see the **Free characteristics** frame). The execution of the query also offers OLAP functionality. The attributes are listed as additional columns directly to the right next to the characteristic "Customer" (see Figure 6.64, Step 1); the navigation occurs as explained (see Figure 6.64, Steps 2 to 4).

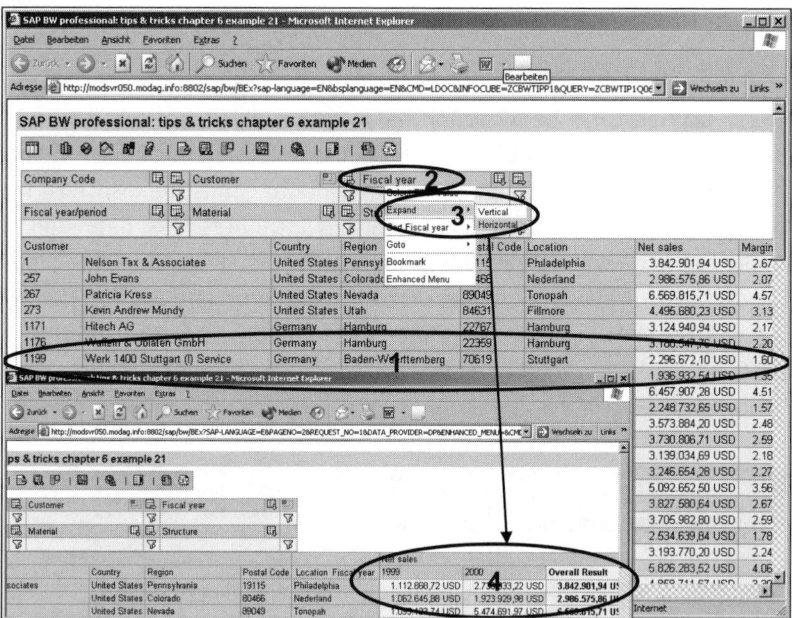

Figure 6.64 Display of the Customer with Selected Attributes and Horizontal Drilldown According to Fiscal Year

Tabular report By clicking on the **Tabular display** button, you can convert the OLAP query into a tabular display (see Figure 6.65, Step 1). Because the tabular report does not support functions such as **Add drilldown** or **Drill down horizontally**, all free characteristics are copied into the Filter frame (see Figure 6.65, Step 2). You can now customize columns in the tabular report. As you can see in the OLAP query, the list criterion (in the example "Customer") is displayed principally in column 1, followed by the display attributes, and then the key columns. You can adjust these columns by using drag & drop in the Query Designer, so that in the display attributes, "Country" and "Region" follow the keys "Sales quantity" and "Net sales." Only then are the actual list characteristic "Customer," the key "Marginal income II," and the display attributes "Postal code" and "Location" listed (see Figure 6.65, Step 3).

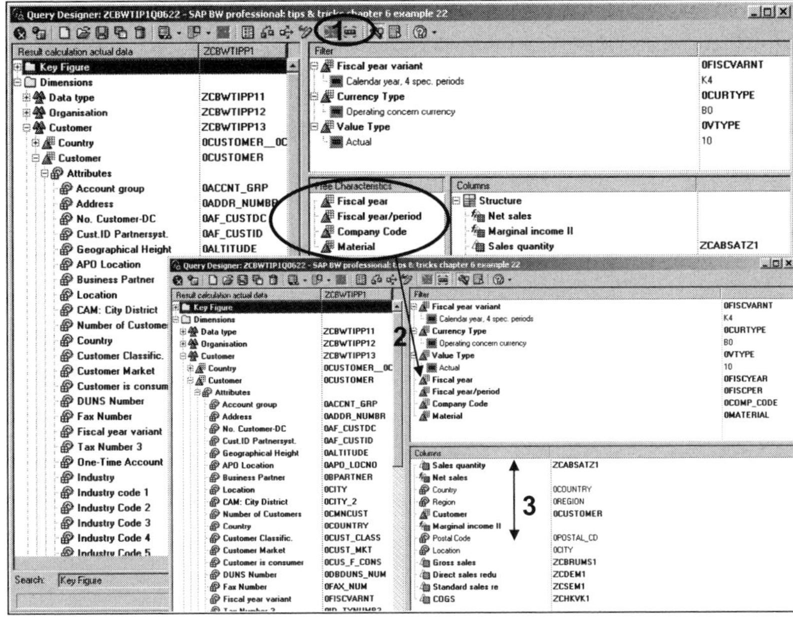

Figure 6.65 Switching to Tabular Reporting

Functions—such as set filter, sort, and exchange the list criterion—are also supported by tabular reporting (see Figure 6.66, Steps 1 to 3).

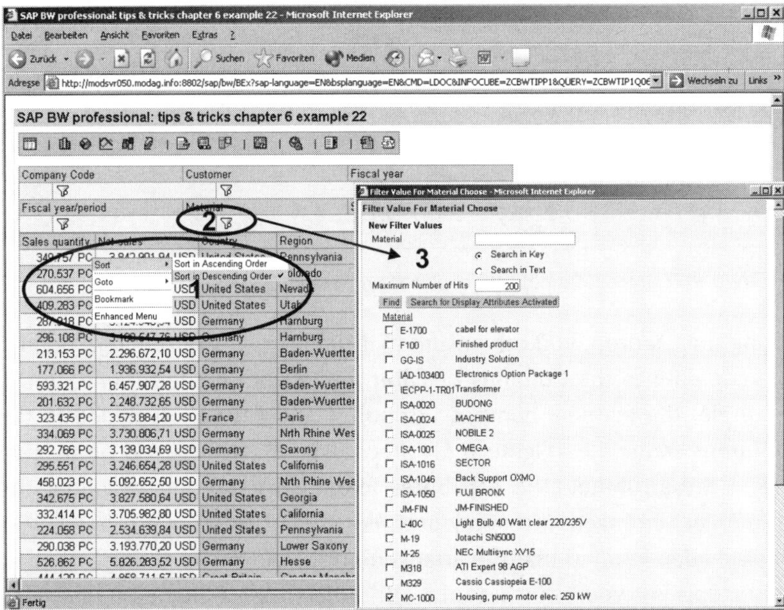

Figure 6.66 Execution of the Tabular Report

Main data reporting: defining query

Similar to OLAP reporting, the functionality of main data reporting using SAP Business Explorer, which has been available since SAP BW 3.0, is configured in the Query Designer.

In the Query Designer, you must click on the **New Query** button to select a main data InfoProvider (see Figure 6.67, Step 1). Then, the **New Query: Select InfoProvider** pop-up opens. There, right-click to highlight the InfoProvider that you want and select it by clicking on the **OK** button (see Figure 6.67, Steps 2 and 3). The elements of the InfoProvider are now available in the left (selection) frame in the Query Designer. Click on the **Tabular display** button to change the structure of the Query Designer accordingly (see Figure 6.67, Step 4).

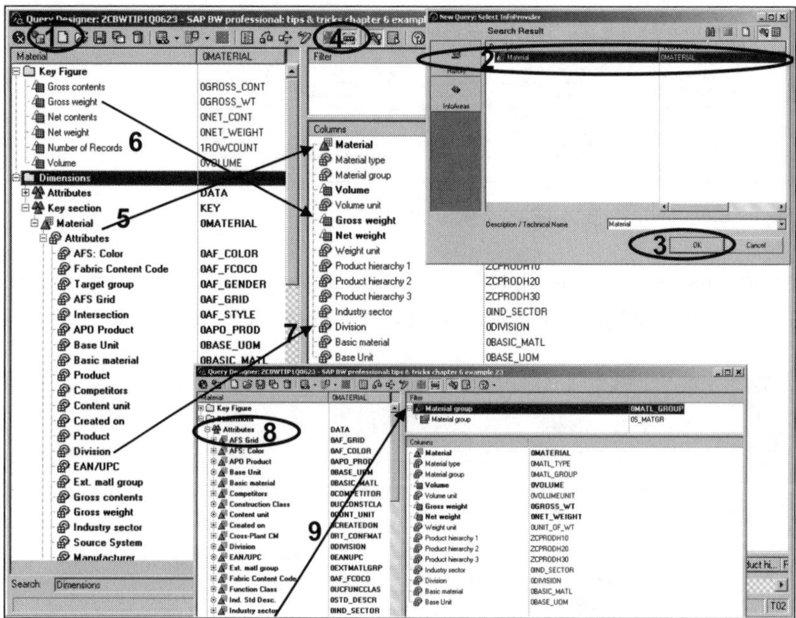

Figure 6.67 Configuration of the Tabular Main Data Query

Using drag & drop, you can ensure that the elements of the InfoProvider are copied into the **Columns** or **Filter** frame from the left frame. In the example, the material number, attributes, and keys are included in the **Columns** frame (see Figure 6.67, Steps 5 to 7). In order to be able to select the attributes, the **Attributes** folder must be opened under the InfoObject arranged in the **key part**. For the inclusion of attributes, you should keep in mind that the arrangement of the columns must occur in two steps. For you to include the attributes in the **Columns** frame, they must first be arranged directly in front of the key criterion (in the example: "Material") or existing attributes. Then, you can move these columns to any positions by using drag & drop.

Execution of a tabular main data query

In order to use attributes for navigation (e.g., "Place filter"), you must open the **Attributes** folder directly under the **Dimensions** folder. Using drag & drop, you can move these elements into the desired location (see Figure 6.67, Steps 8 and 9). After saving the query, you can execute it in the browser.

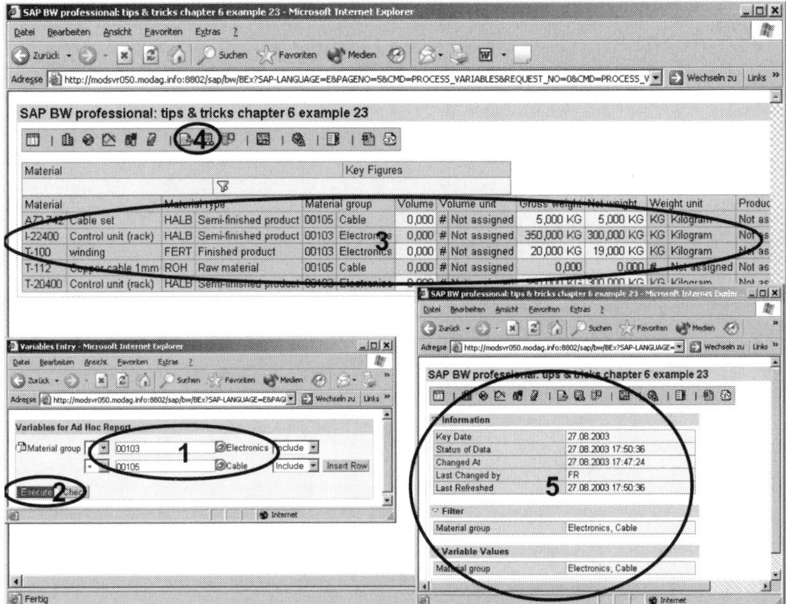

Figure 6.68 Executing a Main Data Query

If the filter variables are used, the selection screen for entering the desired variable values is displayed first (see Figure 6.68, Step 1). After you click on the **Execute** button (see Figure 6.68, Step 2), the result list is displayed (see Figure 6.68, Step 3). Click on the **Info** button (see Figure 6.68, Step 4) to display the text elements and, hence, the filter values (see Figure 6.68, Step 5).

7 Selected Functions of the SAP BW Web Application Designer in SAP BW 3.x

In addition to the SAP Business Explorer Query Designer, the SAP Business Explorer Web Application Designer is the central tool for creating reports in SAP BW. Since Release 3.0, SAP BW has used this winning combination to position itself as the best-practice data warehouse solution. The opportunity to integrate significant parts of Web publishing with the SAP BW development environment of the Web Application Designer substantially eases the professional development of reports right on through to Management Cockpits. This chapter will explain the functionality and basic components of this newest component of SAP BW—the Web Application Designer.

7.1 The Web Application Designer in the Framework of the SAP Business Explorer Components

Presentation of the information in earlier versions

In the SAP Business Explorer (SAP BEx) framework, queries created with the Query Designer form the basis of all presentations of information from SAP BW. Now, as before, you can evaluate these presentations with the Excel-based SAP BEx Analyzer. In the first versions of SAP BW, however, the limitations of the Excel basis were so apparent that many companies using SAP BW took refuge in third-party front-end tools.

Web Reporting since SAP BW 2.0

SAP BEx Web Reporting has been available since SAP BW 2.0. Unnoticed by many consulting companies and clients, SAP BW offered the chance to develop professional analytical applications. The problem (and perhaps a significant reason for the obscure existence of Web Reporting) was that the HTML coding for such presentations had to occur offline in HTML editors. The report developer, therefore, was faced with completely new and still greater demands.

Basis: Query Designer and default Web template

For SAP BW 3.0, SAP advanced the development of reporting as a whole, and, in particular, focused on the Web Reporting functionality. The queries created with the Query Designer are included by default, as is a Web template in the HTML browser. SAP's default Web template, which is delivered with the SAP BW 3.x versions, already possesses extraordinary capabilities and exceeds the capabilities of both the SAP Business Explorer Analyzer (SAP BEx Analyzer) and many third-party front-end tools as well—for example, SAP's default Web template can be expanded and customized to meet customer requirements.

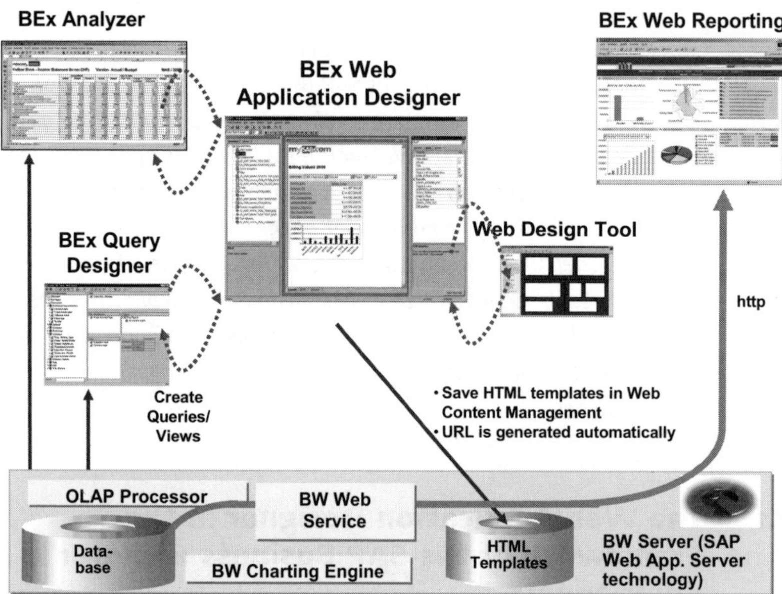

Figure 7.1 The Web Application Designer as a Development Interface for Web Reports

Role of the Web Application Designer

If data from one or several Business Explorer queries must be displayed differently, or with other functionalities than are available in the stored default Web template, it has been possible to create the corresponding HTML pages in the Web Application Designer since SAP BW 3.0. While Query Designer configures the functionality of the query and the data provision, Web Application Designer develops the functionality and the layout of the information presentation. The provision of this tool provides you with the opportunity to develop a multitude of powerful Web functions system-supported online based on SAP BW and without the need for HTML knowledge. In addition, the HTML coding can be done manually. Similarly, the export of the HTML code and the provision for any HTML editor is also supported. Even if the Web Application Designer does not yet represent a full-fledged WYSIWYG (What You See Is What You Get) development interface, according to the author's experience, when compared with *third-party front-end products* (such as inSight/dynaSight), the advantages of the SAP default functionality prevail, given the power it affords us to configure functions with simple tools and utilize the openness of the HTML code.

7.2 The Functionality of the Web Application Designer: Overview

7.2.1 Introduction

Web templates

The core function of the *Web Application Designer* application is the creation and editing of HTML pages, which are stored as *Web templates* in SAP BW. When they are called by a Business Explorer query, these Web templates present data provided in an HTML browser (such as Microsoft Internet Explorer).

Web items

The HTML pages created with the BEx Web Application Designer typically contain BW-specific content such as tables, charts, and cards. These objects (called *Web items*) draw their data from a data provider and make it available as HTML code in a Web application. The Web applications can be accessed via URL using the intranet or mobile end-user devices. In addition, the Web applications can be saved as iViews and integrated into a portal solution.

Therefore, a Web template serves to specify the structure and functionality of a Web application. With the assistance of the Web Application Designer, placeholders for Web items and data providers (in the form of object tags) and BW URLs are inserted into an HTML document. The HTML document with the BW-specific placeholders is designated a Web template and can be checked into the Web Application Designer and stored in SAP BW. The HTML page displayed in the Internet browser is called a *Web application*. A Web application can, depending on which Web items were inserted into the Web template, contain one or several tables, charts, cards, the Alert Monitor, and also HTML and program code (e.g., JavaScript), etc.

Web Application Wizard

An assistant, called the *Web Application Wizard*, is integrated into the Web Application Designer. It supports the creation of simple Web applications using an automatic step-by-step sequence and enables a simplified design procedure.

7.2.2 Web Items

Available types of Web items

Web items are objects that get data from data providers and make it available in a particular way as, for example, HTML. Web items have attributes such as title, width, height, frame type, etc. The attributes can be changed via programming or by calling up commands. If the data, the navigation state, or the attributes change, the HTML for the Web item is recreated. A Web item must always be assigned to a data provider.

In the documentation for the Web items in SAP BW, SAP lists the following Web applications:

- **Table**
  A table displays the result of a query in a concrete navigation state and in rows and columns.
- **Chart**
  A chart displays the result of a query in graphical form. In SAP BW, the following chart types are supported:
  - Bar chart
  - Area diagram
  - Line chart
  - Sphere, pyramid, and cylinder charts
  - Pie and ring (doughnut) charts
  - Net chart (radar)
  - Surface chart
  - Profile chart
  - Tachometer
  - Point chart
  - Step chart
  - Histogram
  - Portfolio
  - Quadrant
- **Drop-down box**
  The drop-down box makes available values (e.g., characteristic values) in the Web application for filtering a selection list that can be opened by right-clicking on it with the mouse. Precisely one value is selected.
- **Radio button group**
  The radio button group makes available characteristic values for filtering a group of selection buttons. Precisely one value is selected.
- **Checkbox**
  A checkbox is a Web item that places the characteristic values for filtering a group of boxes that can be checked. No value, one value, or several values can be selected.

- **Generic navigation block**
  The Web item generic navigation block is the most powerful Web item for controlling the query. It displays the navigation state of a query view in the form of a table. In the table, all characteristics and structures of the query view are listed and their filter values are displayed. Using generic navigation blocks, you can change the navigation state of a query. It is possible to place characteristics and structures on an axis (rows or columns) or to take them from the axis. You can also filter the query for individual values, or remove the filters once again.
- **Hierarchical context menu**
  The Web item that creates a context menu from the hierarchy of a characteristic or a structure. The hierarchy nodes appear as context-menu entries and can be set as filters. With the assistance of the hierarchical context menu, you can filter a query view according to hierarchy nodes.
- **Filter**
  The Web item filter displays the filter values created by navigation for a query view in the Web application.
- **Label**
  The Web item label allows the display of characteristic, attribute, or structural component names and the placing of a link on the context menu of this characteristic, attribute, or structural component.
- **Text elements**
  The Web item text elements show information about the query on which the query view, and consequently the Web application, rely. You can also select individual text elements. There are three different types of text elements available:
  - General text elements (e.g., description of the query, InfoProvider, author of the query)
  - Variables
  - Static filter values
- **List of exceptions**
  The Web item list of exceptions displays the state of the exceptions of a query view in the Web application in the form of a table. For each exception, the state of the exception (active/not active) is also displayed. The exceptions can be activated or deactivated. New exceptions can also be defined during the query execution.

- **List of conditions**
  The Web item list of conditions displays the state of the conditions of a query view in the Web application in the form of a table. All conditions that can be applied to the current navigation state of the query view are listed. For each condition, the state of the condition (active/not active/not applicable/not used) is also displayed. The conditions can be activated or deactivated. You can also define new conditions during the query execution.
- **Alert Monitor**
  With the assistance of the Web item Alert Monitor, an overview list—with the exceptions evaluated by the reporting agent—is displayed. From the Alert Monitor, it is possible to jump to query views.
- **Role menu**
  The Web item role menu displays the favorites or roles of a user in tree form. You can limit the role menu to the favorites and roles of a user, or to a particular role. If this particular role is not assigned to a user, no menu entries are displayed. The menu entries can be filtered according to various types. A menu entry is a URL for which, for example, a BEx Web application with the attribute "TARGET" can define the window for execution of the URL.
- **Ticker**
  The Web item ticker allows the contents of a table to be displayed as a ticker.
- **Card**
  The Web item card enables you to format and evaluate data with geographic reference (e.g., to characteristics such as "Customer," "Sales region," "Country"). The geo-relevant data is displayed graphically on a map. Via expanded navigation possibilities (*geographic drill-down*), regional references on various levels of granularity can be evaluated more easily. Because a map displays spatial proximity of places and regions, geographic relationships become clearer.
- **Individual document**
  This Web item enables you to display individual documents in the Web application.
- **List of documents**
  The Web item list of documents enables the calling up or creation of context-sensitive information about the motion data used in the Web application. If navigation occurs in the Web application (for example, a characteristic is limited to a particular characteristic value), then the list

of documents adjusts itself automatically. That is, only those documents appear that are relevant for the limited navigation state. In addition, new documents can be created in the Web application.

- **Ad-hoc Query Designer**
  The Web item that enables the ad-hoc creation and changing of queries in a Web application.
- **ABC classification**
  The Web item ABC classification that enables the classification of objects (e.g., characteristics such as "Customer," "Products," or "Employees") on the basis of a particular measurement value (sales or profit) with the assistance of particular classification rules.
- **Simulation prediction**
  The Web item simulation prediction enables the prediction in the dialog for an individual customer data set based on models that were defined with the assistance of services such as decision tree, scoring, and clustering.

7.2.3 Formatting

For the formatting of Web applications, the common capabilities of HTML are available in the Web Application Designer. To a limited extent, the immediate formatting of content is possible. The organization of data occurs in HTML with the arrangement of a page using tables. Style sheets offer the main functionality for formatting all components of HTML pages (including the Web items).

Cascading style sheets (CSS) represent an expansion of HTML and offer the greatest possibilities for formatting HTML pages. For example, it is possible to set fonts, colors, sizes, background colors, the display type of tables, and so forth.

Style sheet for Web applications

SAP BW makes available several style sheets for formatting. In the Web Application Designer, you can use a style sheet made available by SAP or a style sheet that you created.

Print style sheet

If a Web application should be printed out, a special style sheet, which is distinguished from the screen display, can underlie the printing.

7.3 First Steps in the Web Application Designer

7.3.1 Starting the Web Application Designer

The Web Application Designer can be started either from the Windows **Start** menu (see Figure 7.2, Step 1), or with the corresponding call in the command line (program wdbpwpub.exe in the BW folder, e. g., C:\Programs\SAP\FrontEnd\BW\). When you open the application, an SAP logon dialog box is displayed, in which you must enter your user name and password (see Figure 7.2, Steps 2 and 3). After logon, the Web Application Designer is displayed (see Figure 7.2, Step 4).

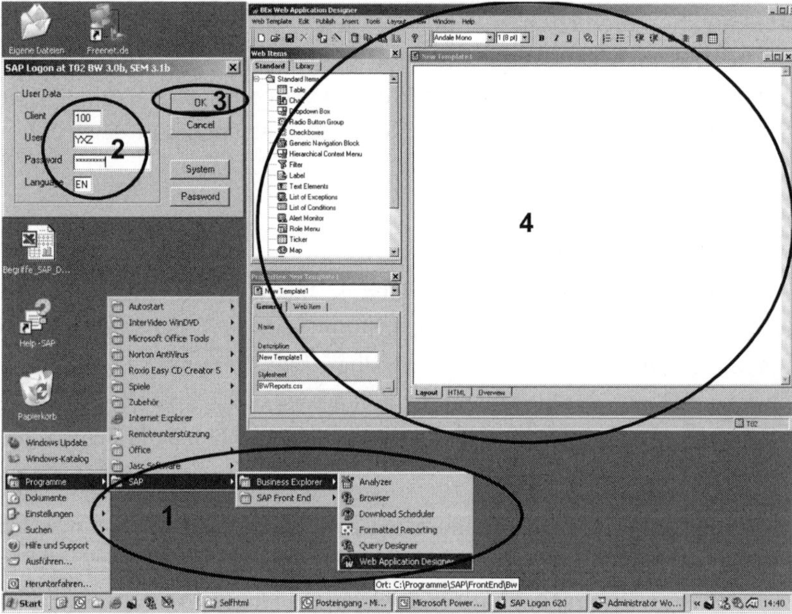

Figure 7.2 Starting the Web Application Designer

7.3.2 Creation of a Web Template Using the Web Application Wizard

Starting the Wizard

The Web Application Wizard can be started from the opened Web Application Designer. In the Web Application Designer, open the **Tools** pull-down menu and select the **Wizard...** command (see Figure 7.3, Step 1). The first time the wizard is called up, the start screen is displayed. This is purely informative and can be deactivated by activating the option **Do not display this page in future** (see Figure 7.3, Step 2).

Selecting a Web item

After clicking on the **Next** button (see Figure 7.3, Step 3), the **BEx Web Application Wizard** starts and the **Choose Web Item** screen is displayed. You can select a Web item (in the example: "Table") by highlighting it (see Figure 7.3, Step 4). Then, click the **Next** button (see Figure 7.3, Step 5).

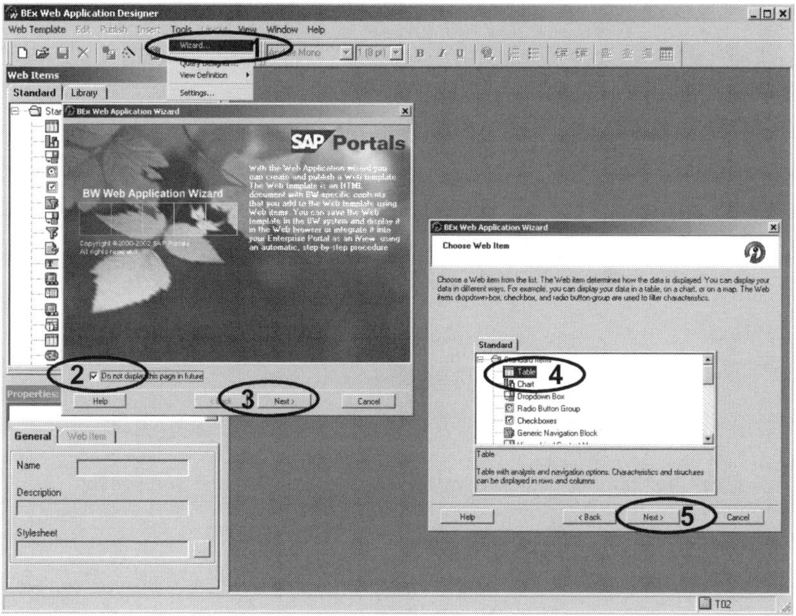

Figure 7.3 Starting the Web Application Wizard

Selecting a query or query view

On the **Choose a query or a query view** screen, you can select the desired data provider for the previously selected Web item. To do this, click the **Query** button (see Figure 7.4, Step 1). Then the **Open Query/View** pop-up opens, where the desired data provider can be selected. To do this, highlight the query or query view and click the **OK** button (see Figure 7.4, Steps 2 and 3). Then, the selection is taken over on the Maintenance screen (see Figure 7.4, Step 5).

Editing attributes

After you click on the **Next** button (see Figure 7.4, Step 6), the **Edit Attributes** screen is displayed. If desired, you can configure the display or functionality of the Web item here.

Overview

After you click on the **Next** button (see Figure 7.4, step 7), the **Overview** screen is displayed. Here, Web items inserted in the Web template are listed. If you want to insert additional Web items, click on the **Insert an item** button.

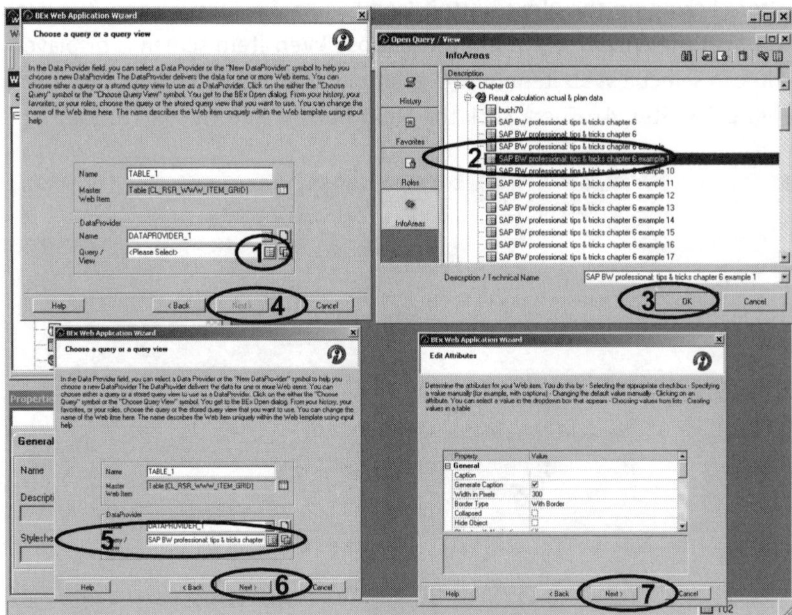

Figure 7.4 The Web Application Wizard: Selecting Data Providers and Editing Attributes

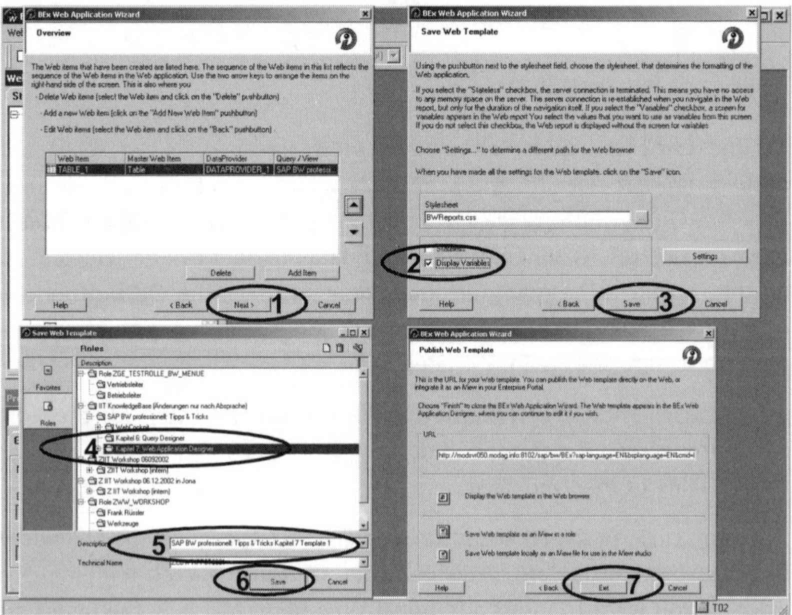

Figure 7.5 The Web Application Wizard: Saving and Publishing the Web Template

Saving Web templates

After you click on the **Next** button (see Figure 7.5, Step 1), the **Save Web Template** screen is displayed. There, you must establish the corresponding settings. You must activate the **Display Variables** option, particularly if variables are present (see Figure 7.5, Step 2). Then, click the **Save** button (see Figure 7.5, Step 3). On the **Save Web Template** pop-up, you must store the template in the favorites or in a role. To do so, highlight the role or the position in the favorites by right-clicking, then enter the description and technical name, and click on the **Save** button (see Figure 7.5, Steps 4 to 6).

Publishing the Web template

Then, the **Publish Web Template** screen is displayed. Here, the Web template can either be started for display in the browser or it can be stored as an iView. After you click on the **Exit** button (see Figure 7.5, Step 7), the Web template is displayed in the Web Application Designer (see Figure 7.6).

Execute Web template

With a click of the **Execute in the browser** button, the Web template is opened in the HTML browser (see Figure 7.6, Step 1). The variable display occurs according to the configuration displayed above. After you enter or select the variable value and click on the **Execute** button (see Figure 7.6, Steps 2 and 3), the query result is presented in the Web template (see Figure 7.6, Step 4).

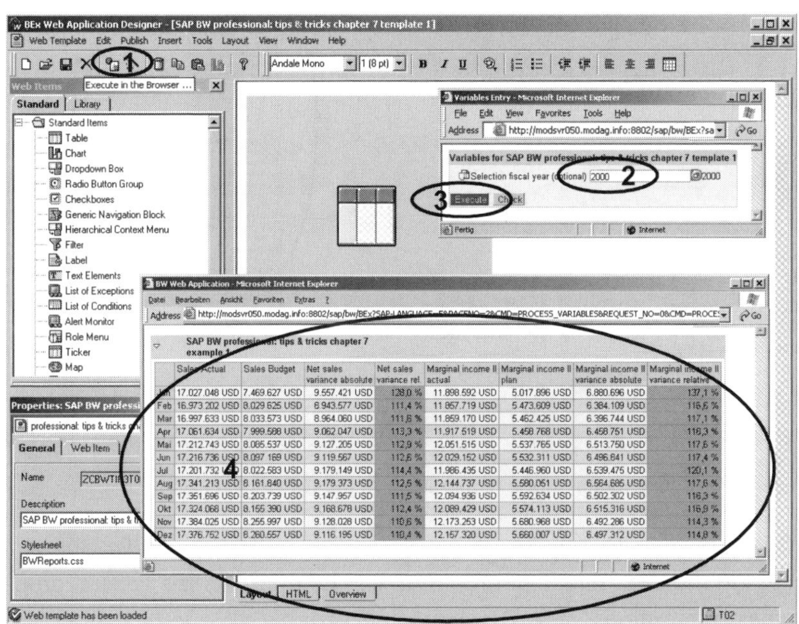

Figure 7.6 Displaying and Starting the Web Template

7.4 Web Items in the Web Application Designer

7.4.1 Properties of Web Templates and Positioning of Objects

Select style sheet

To select a style sheet, select the uppermost entry (that is, the Web template itself) in the object hierarchy in the Web Application Designer with an open Web template in the Properties frame (bottom left) (see Figure 7.7, Step 1). In this step, in the **General** tab, the general properties (title and style sheet) of the Web template are offered for maintenance. For the style sheet, you can select either one of the SAP templates, or you can specify an individual cascading style sheet (CSS) file (see Figure 7.7, Step 2).

Web Item-Related Properties

By clicking on the "..." button, the selection list of the available style sheets is displayed. When you activate the **Web Item** tab, you can configure the Web item-related properties (see Figure 7.7, Step 3).

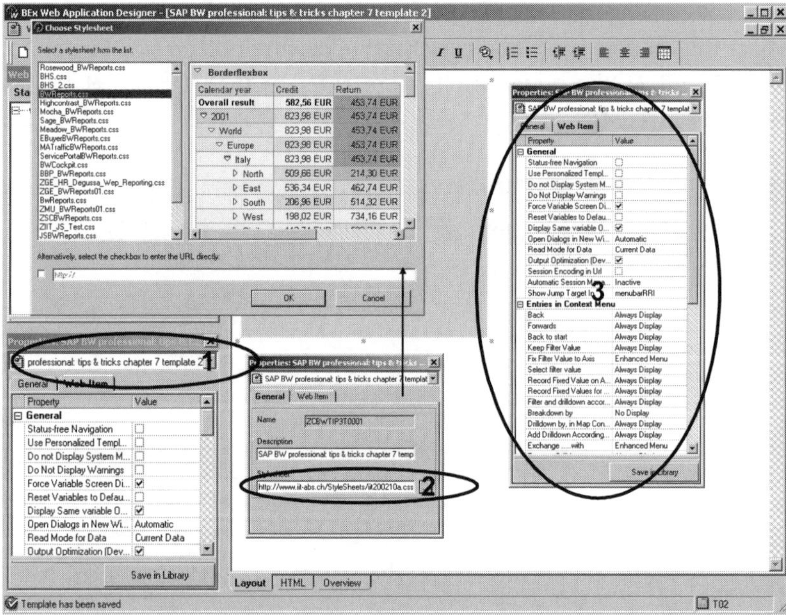

Figure 7.7 Configuration of the Properties of the Web Template

Of the settings that deviate from the default settings, the following settings in the Web template properties can be useful: in the general properties, for example, the **Display Same variable O...** setting is recommended; the entries in the context menu should be arranged according

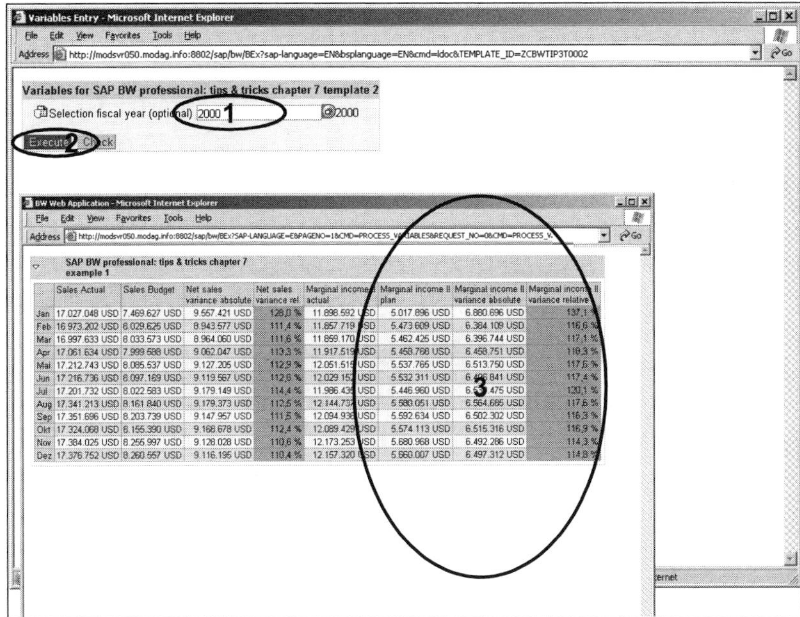

Figure 7.8 Web Template with Customer-Specific Style Sheet

to the demands and the target group of the Web template (see Figure 7.7).

Figure 7.8 shows the execution of a Web template with a customer-specific style sheet and changed context menu.

Web items in the template

Web items can be integrated into the Web template from the Web items selection list in the upper-left frame using drag & drop.

Positioning objects

The positioning of objects on HTML pages occurs primarily using tables. Generally, *blind tables* are used, that is, tables whose grid lines are invisible.

Inserting tables by clicking on a button with the table's respective name occurs on the **Layout** tab of the **Web Application Designer** (see Figure 7.9, Step 1). In the **Insert Table** pop-up, you must specify the number of lines, columns, and other attributes (see Figure 7.9, Step 2). After you confirm the entry by clicking on the **OK** button (see Figure 7.9, Step 3), the table is displayed in the layout (see Figure 7.9, Step 4).

When you use drag & drop, Web items are integrated into and therefore positioned in the table (see Figure 7.9, Step 5). A precise positioning is possible via a specification of the HTML coding.

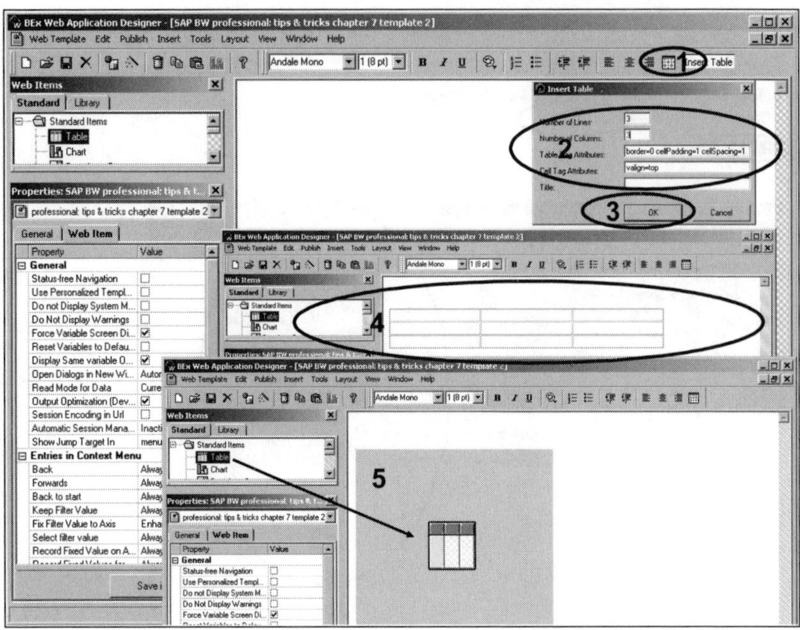

Figure 7.9 Positioning Objects Using Tables

7.4.2 The Table

Selecting data providers

The Web item **Table** relates to a data provider. The specification of the data provider to be used occurs after selection of the table item with a double-click. In the **General** tab, you can select the data provider by clicking on the **Select query** or **Select view** buttons (see Figure 7.10, Steps 1 and 2).

Properties of the Web item "Table"

After switching to the **Web Item** tab, you can edit the properties—this adjustment is generally recommended (see Figure 7.10, Step 3). For many applications, you won't need a title above the tables (it is often additional and the same for the query). Therefore, here, we suggest that you deactivate the option **Generate Caption** (see Figure 7.10, Step 4).

Similarly, in many cases, it is recommended that you limit the number of rows and columns displayed on a page so that the row criterion (that is, the "Leading column") and the column titles cannot scroll outside of the display. To impose this limitation, we recommend that the setting for the "Number of Data Rows Displayed at Once" (in the example: 20) correspond with the setting for the "Number of Data Columns Displayed at Once" (in the example: 4) (see Figure 7.10, Step 5).

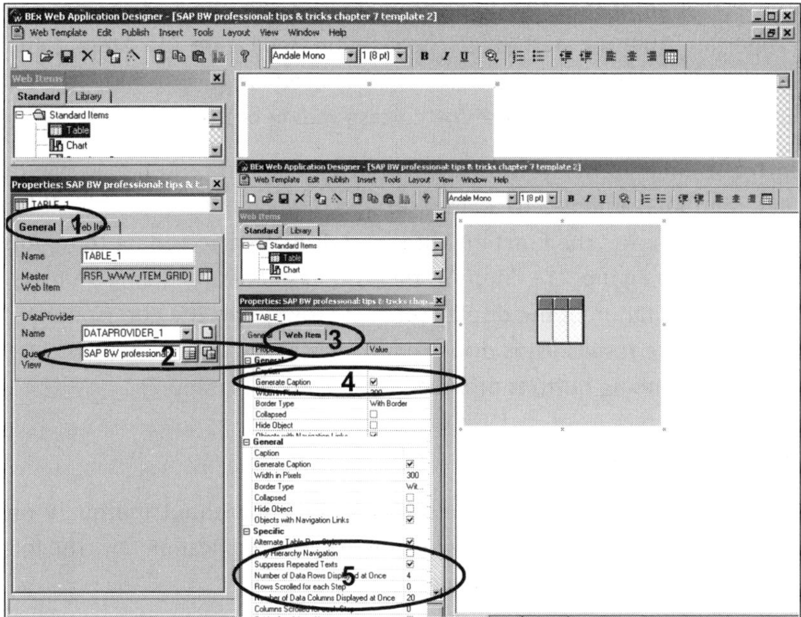

Figure 7.10 Selecting a Data Provider and Configuring the Properties of the Web Item "Table"

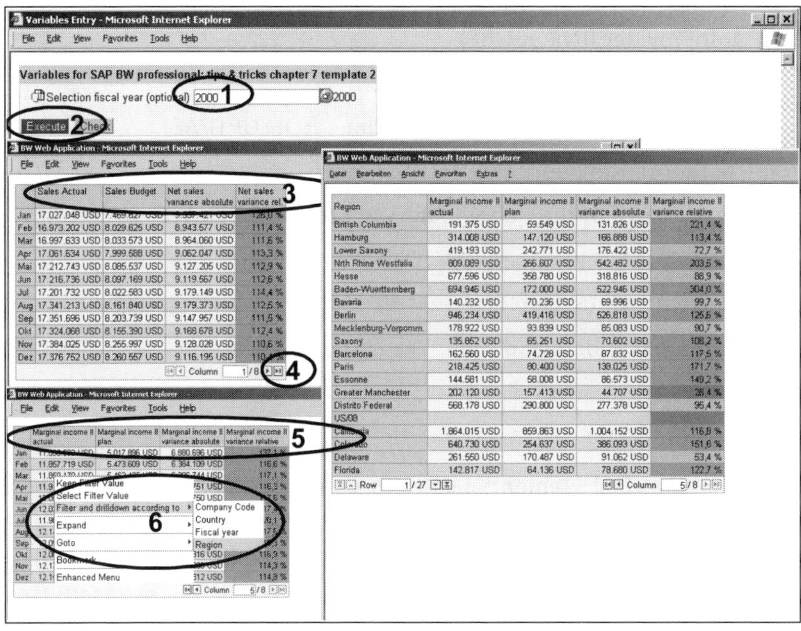

Figure 7.11 Web Template with Changed Table Properties

Execution of the Web template

The execution of the Web template illustrates the effect of the defined properties. After the start of query execution (see Figure 7.11, Steps 1 and 2), only four columns of the query are displayed (see Figure 7.11, Step 3). To display other columns, use the corresponding buttons available.

In the example, after you click on the **Last column** button (see Figure 7.11, Step 4), columns 5 to 8 are displayed (see Figure 7.11, Step 5). If for the period "June," the function **Filter and drilldown according to region** is called (see Figure 7.11, Step 6), then the results list contains 32 rows. With the limitation of the display set to 20 rows, only the corresponding portion of the results list is displayed. To navigate through the rows, use the corresponding buttons provided (see Figure 7.11, Step 7).

7.4.3 Text Elements

The Web item **Text Elements** displays information about the query on which the query view and consequently the Web application rely. The following text elements are available.

- General text elements:
  - Technical name of the query (REPTNAME)
  - Description of the query (REPTXTLG)
  - InfoProvider (INFOCUBE)
  - Cutoff date of the query (SRDATE)
  - Timeliness of the data (date and time, ROLLUPTIME)
  - Author of the query (AUTHOR)
  - Last change of the query (date and time, MODTIME)
  - Last editor of the query (MODUSER)
  - Current user (SYUSER)
  - Last refresh (date and time, SYUZEIT)
- Variables
- Static filter values

Selecting Data Providers

The Web item **Text Elements** relates to a data provider. The specification of the data provider to be used occurs after you select the text element item by double-clicking on it. The assignment of the data provider (generally, the one to which the table or graphical Web item is assigned) (see Figure 7.12, Steps 1 to 3) occurs in the **General** tab.

The change in the **Web Item** tab shows the properties of the Web Item **Text Elements** (see Figure 7.12, Step 4). If the text elements are used in the default form, you should change the Web item width (see Figure 7.12, Step 5).

Properties of the Web item "Text Elements"

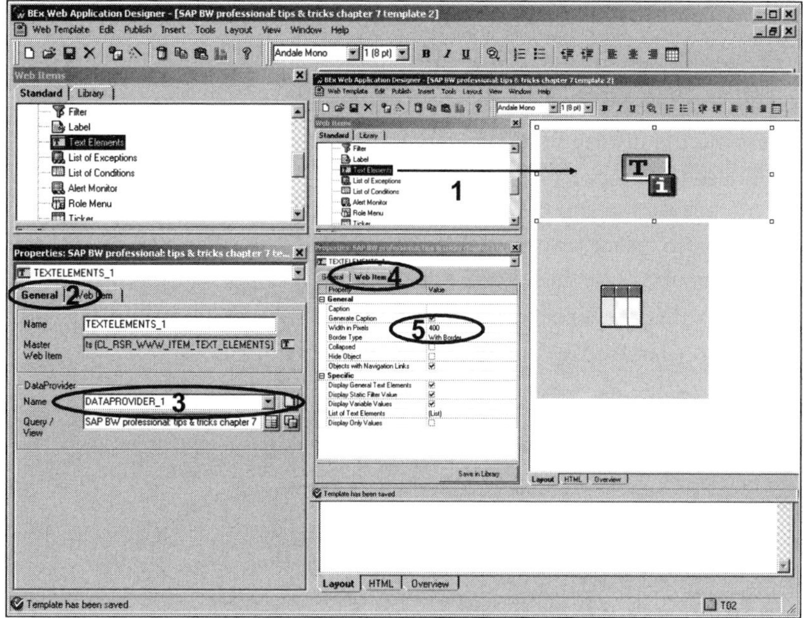

Figure 7.12 Properties of the Web item "Text Elements"

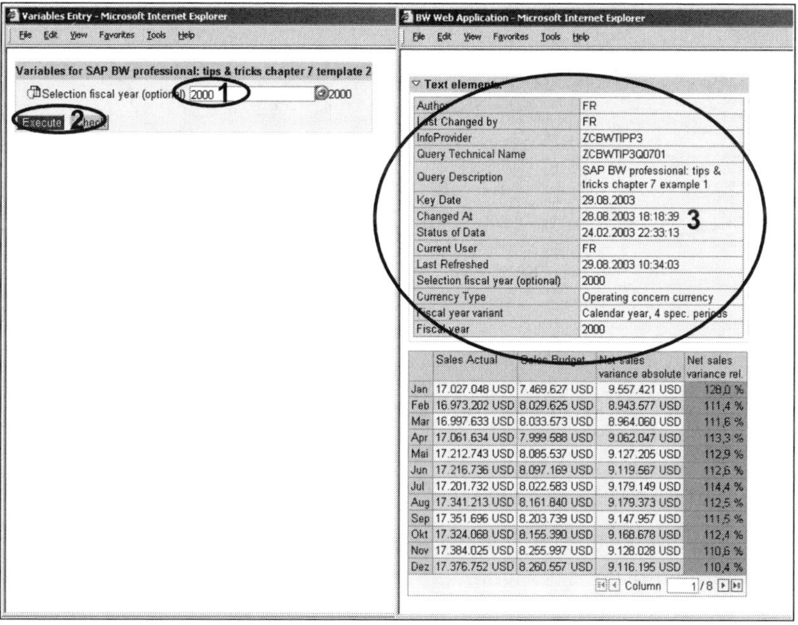

	Sales Actual	Sales Budget	Net sales variance absolute	Net sales variance rel.
Jan	17.027.048 USD	7.469.627 USD	9.557.421 USD	128,0 %
Feb	16.973.202 USD	8.029.625 USD	8.943.577 USD	111,4 %
Mar	16.997.633 USD	8.033.573 USD	8.964.060 USD	111,6 %
Apr	17.061.634 USD	7.999.588 USD	9.062.047 USD	113,3 %
Mai	17.212.743 USD	8.085.537 USD	9.127.205 USD	112,9 %
Jun	17.216.736 USD	8.097.169 USD	9.119.567 USD	112,6 %
Jul	17.201.732 USD	8.022.583 USD	9.179.149 USD	114,4 %
Aug	17.341.213 USD	8.161.840 USD	9.179.373 USD	112,5 %
Sep	17.351.696 USD	8.203.739 USD	9.147.957 USD	111,5 %
Okt	17.324.068 USD	8.155.390 USD	9.168.678 USD	112,4 %
Nov	17.384.025 USD	8.255.997 USD	9.128.028 USD	110,6 %
Dez	17.376.752 USD	8.260.557 USD	9.116.195 USD	110,4 %

Column 1/8

Figure 7.13 Execution of the Web Template with the Web Item "Text Elements"

Regarding the use of the text elements, note that there are additional options offered that enable you to use Web templates in professional design. For example, you can include those elements that are relevant to the application from the end user's point of view, such as using the name of the query for the title instead of inserting it in a text element table. You may also realize that you may not want to use such specific properties as " Display Static Filter Value" and "Display Variable Values."

Text elements: Display Only Values

To enable the display of a text element as a simple string (that is, not in a table) use the property Display Only Values.

Selecting text elements

You can also select text elements from among the three types—General text elements, Static filter values, and Variable values—in the properties. Based on this pre-selection and using the selection list of the text elements, you can display one or several elements in a Web item.

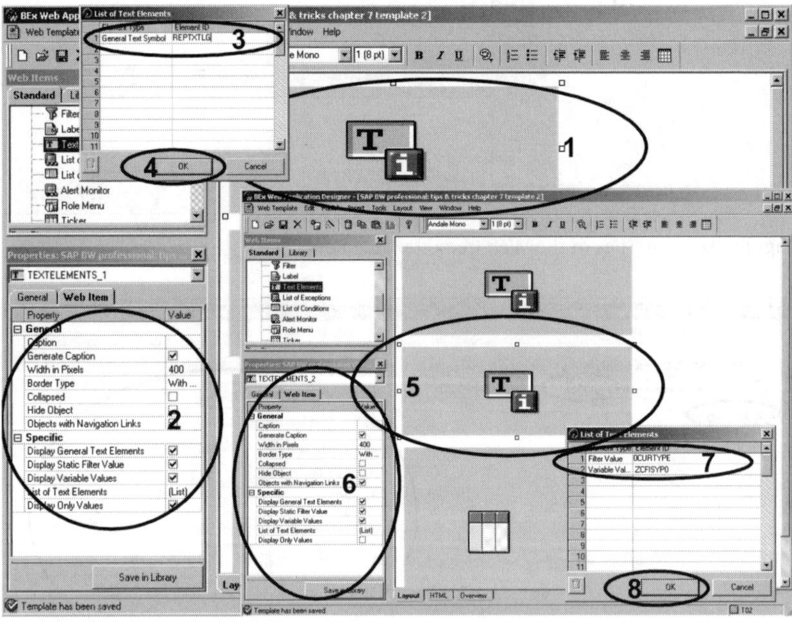

Figure 7.14 Display Only Selected Values of Text Elements

For example, in a Web template, the query name in the form of a simple string as title, as well as the filter value "Currency type" and the fiscal year selected via variable, should be displayed in a table.

Inserting title as string

To display these selected values, you must first insert a text element into the Web template (see Figure 7.14, Step 1), for which the general property "Generate Caption" is deactivated and the "Width in Pixels" is set to

400. In the "Specific" properties, only the "List of Text Elements" is activated. Right-click on the **List of Text Elements** drop-down box, and a pop-up with the same name opens (see Figure 7.14, Step 2). There, for the type of element General text symbol, enter the technical name of the query description (REPTXTLG) as the name of the element (see Figure 7.14, Step 3). Click on the **OK** button to drag and drop the entry into the template definition (see Figure 7.14, Step 4).

Inserting selected selection criteria as table

Then, insert another text element into the Web template (see Figure 7.14, Step 5), for which the general property "Generate Caption" is deactivated and the "Width in Pixels" is set to 400. In the "Specific" properties, activate "Display Static Filter Values" and "Display Variable Values." Right-click on the **List of Text Elements** drop-down box, and a popup with the same name opens (see Figure 7.14, Step 6). There, for the type of element Static filter value, enter the technical name of the InfoObject "Currency type" (0CURTYPE) and for the type of element Variable value, enter the technical name of the characteristic variable "Selection fiscal year (optional)" (ZCFISYP0) as the name of the element (see Figure 7.14, Step 7). Click on the **OK** button to drag and drop the entry into the template definition (see Figure 7.14, Step 8). After you save the definition, the template can be executed.

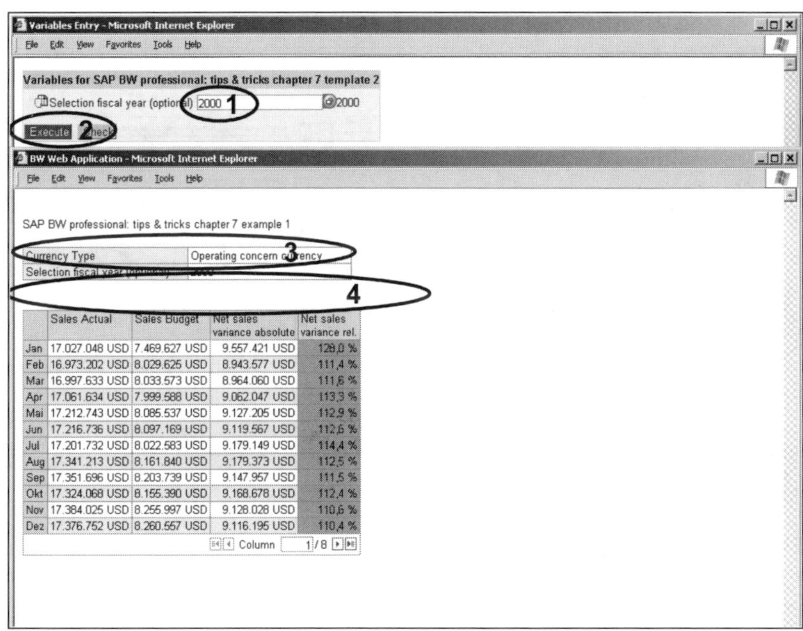

	Sales Actual	Sales Budget	Net sales variance absolute	Net sales variance rel.
Jan	17.027.048 USD	7.469.627 USD	9.557.421 USD	128,0 %
Feb	16.973.202 USD	8.029.625 USD	8.943.577 USD	111,4 %
Mar	16.997.633 USD	8.033.573 USD	8.964.060 USD	111,6 %
Apr	17.061.634 USD	7.999.588 USD	9.062.047 USD	113,3 %
Mai	17.212.743 USD	8.085.537 USD	9.127.205 USD	112,9 %
Jun	17.216.736 USD	8.097.169 USD	9.119.567 USD	112,6 %
Jul	17.201.732 USD	8.022.583 USD	9.179.149 USD	114,4 %
Aug	17.341.213 USD	8.161.840 USD	9.179.373 USD	112,5 %
Sep	17.351.696 USD	8.203.739 USD	9.147.957 USD	111,5 %
Okt	17.324.068 USD	8.155.390 USD	9.168.678 USD	112,4 %
Nov	17.384.025 USD	8.255.997 USD	9.128.028 USD	110,6 %
Dez	17.376.752 USD	8.260.557 USD	9.116.195 USD	110,4 %

Figure 7.15 Specific Use of the Text Elements

On the **Variables for...** selection screen, enter or select the desired fiscal year (see Figure 7.15, Step 1). Click on the **Execute** button (see Figure 7.15, Step 2) to display the query result. The title with the query description is displayed as a string (see Figure 7.15, Step 3); the configured selection information is displayed in a table (see Figure 7.15, Step 4).

7.4.4 The Generic Navigation Block

The Web item offers complex navigation possibilities via query elements:

- ▶ Drilldown into rows
- ▶ Drilldown into columns
- ▶ Remove drilldown
- ▶ Select filter value
- ▶ Remove filter value
- ▶ All functions of the context menu

Selecting data providers

The Web item **Generic Navigation Block** pertains to a data provider. You specify which data provider that you want to use after you select the navigation block item by double-clicking on it. The assignment of the data provider (as a rule the one to which the table or graphical Web item is assigned) (see Figure 7.16, Steps 1 to 3) occurs in the **General** tab.

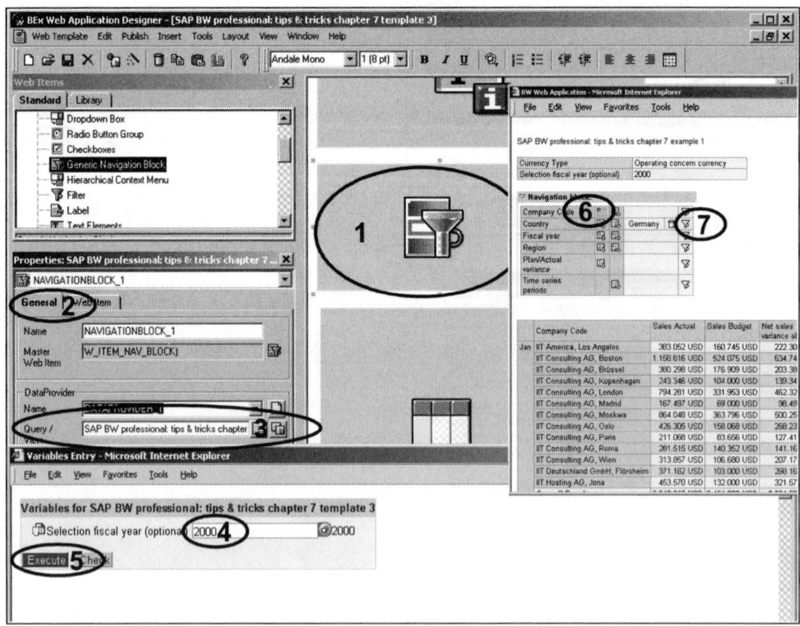

Figure 7.16 Selecting the Generic Navigation Block in the Web Application Designer When Executing the Web Template

Use for selection and drilldown

During the execution of the Web template, the generic navigation block is displayed with the query result after selection and execution (see Figure 7.16, Steps 4 and 5). By clicking on the corresponding buttons, for example, **Drilldown into lines** (see Figure 7.16, Step 6) or **Select filter value** (see Figure 7.16, Step 7), the respective function is applied to all assigned data providers and the Web items are assigned to them.

When using the navigation blocks, making the following properties adjustments are often recommended:

- Utilizing the available space by changing the width in pixels
- Arranging the entries next to each other
- Excluding elements that are not relevant to or practical for navigation

These properties can be adjusted accordingly for the generic navigation block in the Web Application Designer, on the **Web Item** tab.

Changing properties of the navigation block

To change the properties of the navigation block, highlight the icon for the generic navigation block on the layout, and right-click to select the **Web Item** tab in the **Properties** frame (see Figure 7.17, Steps 1 and 2).

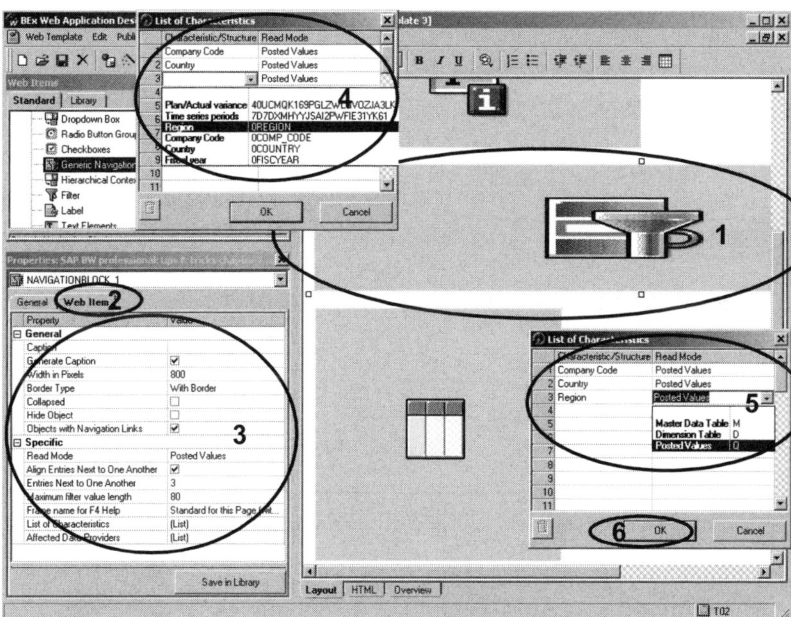

Figure 7.17 Changing the Properties of the Navigation Block

In the **General** folder, deactivate the property **Generate Caption** (see Figure 7.17, Step 3) and set the property **Width in Pixels** to one of the respective default resolution values (in the example: 800). For optimal use of the available width, activate the **Entries Next to One Another** property in the **Specific** folder and set it to "3". To ensure that only those query elements that are relevant to the user group—and the type of information that they want to display—are offered for navigation, activate the **List of Characteristics** drop-down box. In the **List of Characteristics** pop-up, after activating the drop-down box in the **Characteristic/Structure** column, use the selected elements integrated line by line to create a selection list (see Figure 7.17, Step 4). Then, in the **Read Mode** column, you must define whether the following elements or values should be offered during the execution of the Web template (for selection of the values in the generic navigation block): the **Master Data Table**, the **Dimension Table**, or the **Posted Values** (see Figure 7.17, Step 5). Click on the **OK** button to drag and drop the settings into the Web template (see Figure 7.17, Step 6). Then, save the Web template.

In the example, during the execution of the Web template, the changed settings are displayed: after you select the variable value ("Fiscal year 2000") and click on the **Execute** button (see Figure 7.18, Steps 1 and 2), the changed properties are reflected in the way that the navigation block works in the Web template (see Figure 7.18, Step 3).

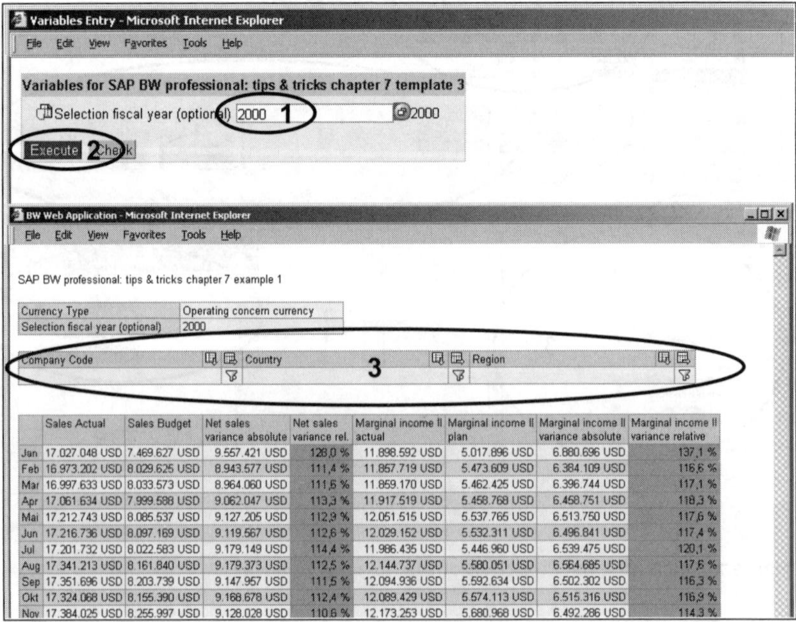

	Sales Actual	Sales Budget	Net sales variance absolute	Net sales variance rel.	Marginal income II actual	Marginal income II plan	Marginal income II variance absolute	Marginal income II variance relative
Jan	17.027.048 USD	7.469.627 USD	9.557.421 USD	128,0 %	11.898.592 USD	5.017.896 USD	6.880.696 USD	137,1 %
Feb	16.973.202 USD	8.029.625 USD	8.943.577 USD	111,4 %	11.857.719 USD	5.473.609 USD	6.384.109 USD	116,6 %
Mar	16.997.633 USD	8.033.573 USD	8.964.060 USD	111,6 %	11.859.170 USD	5.462.425 USD	6.396.744 USD	117,1 %
Apr	17.061.634 USD	7.999.588 USD	9.062.047 USD	113,3 %	11.917.519 USD	5.458.768 USD	6.458.751 USD	118,3 %
Mai	17.212.743 USD	8.085.537 USD	9.127.205 USD	112,9 %	12.051.515 USD	5.537.765 USD	6.513.750 USD	117,6 %
Jun	17.216.736 USD	8.097.169 USD	9.119.567 USD	112,6 %	12.029.152 USD	5.532.311 USD	6.496.841 USD	117,4 %
Jul	17.201.732 USD	8.022.583 USD	9.179.149 USD	114,4 %	11.986.435 USD	5.446.960 USD	6.539.475 USD	120,1 %
Aug	17.341.213 USD	8.161.840 USD	9.179.373 USD	112,5 %	12.144.737 USD	5.580.051 USD	6.564.685 USD	117,6 %
Sep	17.351.696 USD	8.203.739 USD	9.147.957 USD	111,5 %	12.094.936 USD	5.592.634 USD	6.502.302 USD	116,3 %
Okt	17.324.068 USD	8.155.390 USD	9.168.678 USD	112,4 %	12.089.429 USD	5.574.113 USD	6.515.316 USD	116,9 %
Nov	17.384.025 USD	8.255.997 USD	9.128.028 USD	110,6 %	12.173.253 USD	5.680.968 USD	6.492.286 USD	114,3 %

Figure 7.18 The Changed Navigation Block during Execution

The generic navigation block is the most powerful Web item, whereby navigation and the setting of the query or query element properties (such as type of display of a characteristic, sorting, etc.) are possible. However necessary, the associated complexity is not desired for the user group of Web reporting. For this, there are additional selection and navigation items available in the Web Application Designer (see Section 7.4.5 and the sections that follow).

Advantages and disadvantages of the generic navigation block

7.4.5 The Drop-Down Box

Selecting data providers

The **Web Item** drop-down box handles the selection of characteristic values and components of structures. It gets its data from a data provider. The data provider to be used is specified after the drop-down box is copied into the layout, or after the Web item has been selected by double-clicking on it (see Figure 7.19, Step 1). In the **General** tab, the data provider that is providing the values is selected (e.g., the one that is assigned to a table or graphical Web item) (see Figure 7.19, Steps 2 and 3).

Selecting a characteristic or structure

In addition, you must select the characteristic or structure whose values should be offered for selection by the drop-down box. To select a characteristic or structure, you must use branching to the **Web Item** tab. In the **Specific** folder, you must activate the drop-down box for the **Characteristic/Structure** property and select the value that you want (see Figure 7.19, Steps 4 and 5). In the example, two drop-down boxes are added to the Web template, with which the **Country** and **Region** can be selected. After you save the Web template, the settings are available during execution.

During execution of the Web template, the **Web Item** drop-down box is displayed in the example: after you have selected the variable value ("Fiscal year 2000") and clicked on the **Execute** button (see Figure 7.20, Steps 1 and 2), the activated drop-down box **Country** offers characteristic values for selection (see Figure 7.20, step 3).

Alternative properties

Some default properties of the drop-down box should be omitted or replaced with alternative properties because they are not desirable; for example, the default display places the name of the respective characteristic or structure in front of the actual drop-down box, thus using up valuable space.

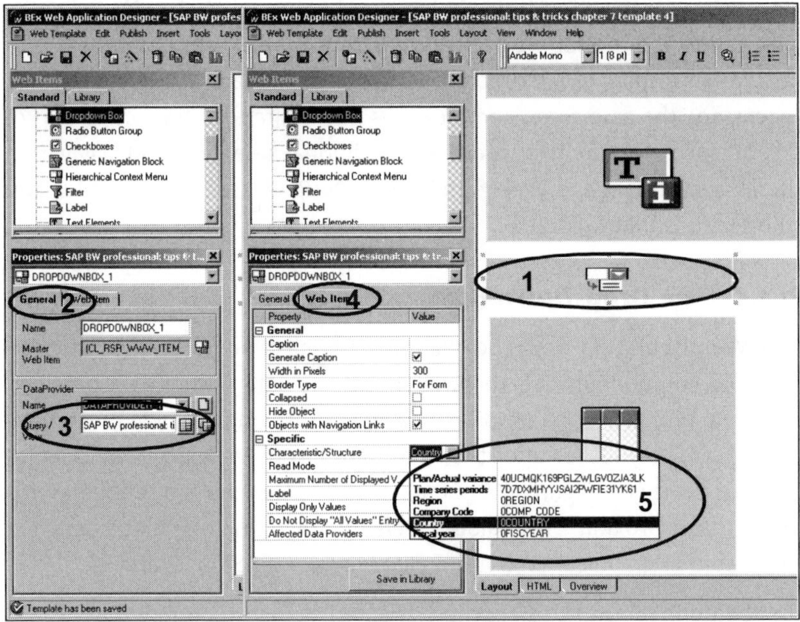

Figure 7.19 The Drop-Down Box in the Web Application Designer

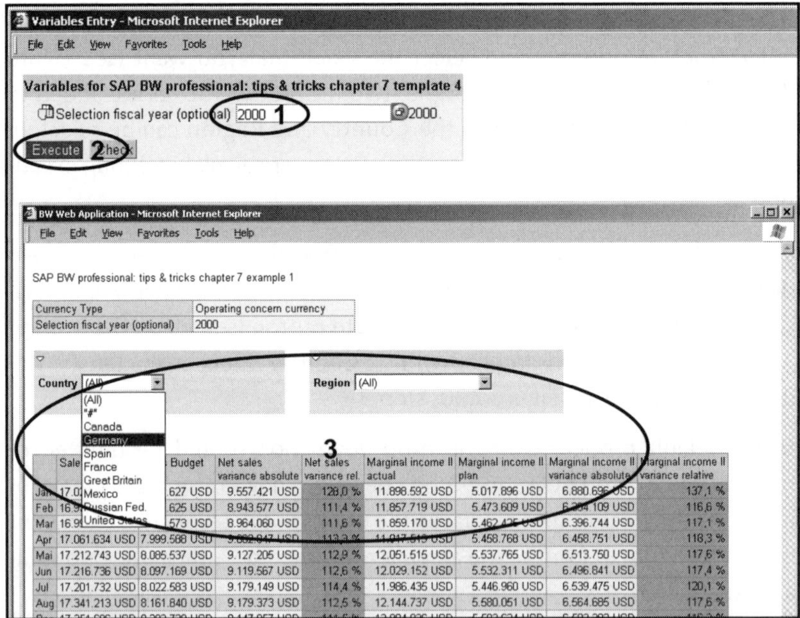

Figure 7.20 The Application of the Web Item "Drop-down Box" for the Selection of Characteristic Values

In the following examples, the default properties can create problems:

- If the dimension table contains invalid values (because of earlier data errors and the absence of cleansing the table after deleting the erroneous data), these values still appear in the selection list (see the value Country "#" in Figure 7.20 and Region "DE/#" in Figure 7.21, Step 1).
- If, in the Web template, several drop-down boxes are used (e.g., for the bracketing of connected characteristics **country** and **region**) and a selection has already occurred from the leading characteristic (in the example: "Country"), flawed entries can occur. Due to the default setting "Read Mode Dimension Table" and despite the selection of a country (e.g., "United States") in the drop-down box for the region, all regions contained in the dimension table, including the German federal states, are offered for selection. If, however, the selection for the country is "United States" and for the region is the German federal state "Baden-Wüerttemberg," the result quantity is empty; then such flawed entries for selection should be prevented (see Figure 7.21, Step 2).

Select the **Web Item** tab for the drop-down boxes (see Figure 7.22, Steps 1 and 2). In the **General** folder, deactivate the **Generate Caption** property (see Figure 7.22, Step 3). To ensure that only valid values are selected and flawed entries are avoided, in the **Specific** folder, set the **Read Mode** property to **Posted Values** (see Figure 7.22, Step 4). Then, save the Web template.

In the example, during the execution of the Web template, the changed settings are displayed. After you select the variable value ("Fiscal year 2000") and click on the **Execute** button, the changed properties are reflected in the way that the drop-down boxes in the Web template work:

1. During the selection of the country, only the values that exist in the InfoCube are offered.
2. If a country was selected, then in the drop-down box for the "Region" characteristic, only the states of this country are offered for selection (see Figure 7.22, Steps 5 and 6).

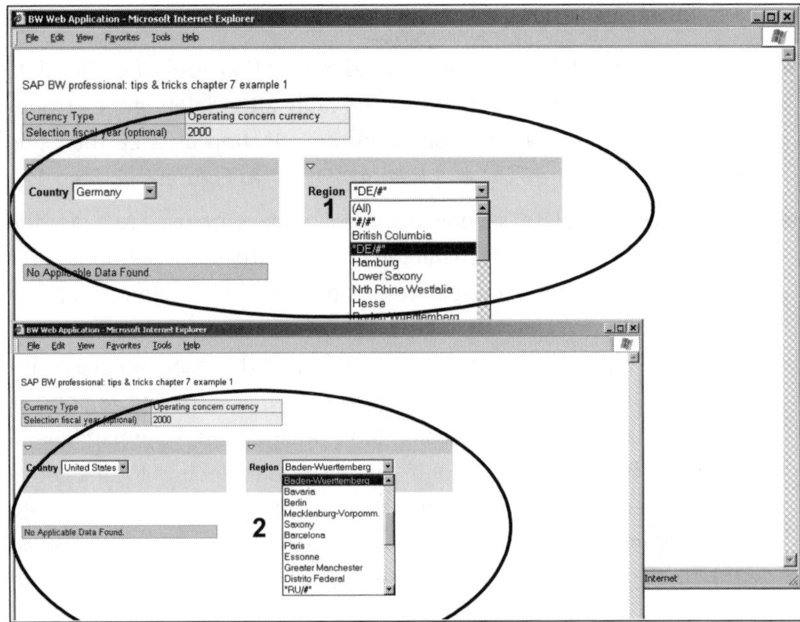

Figure 7.21 Problematic Effects Due to the Default Properties of Drop-Down Boxes

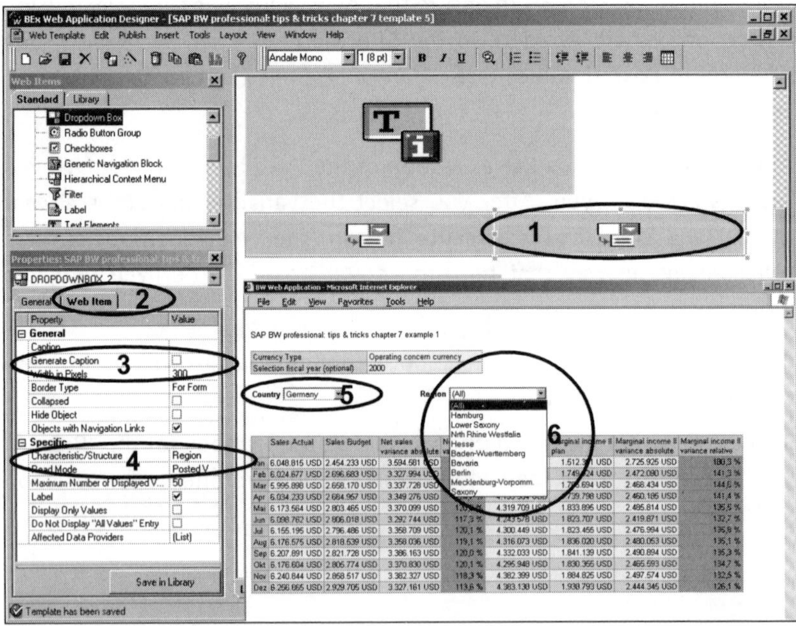

Figure 7.22 Avoiding Erroneous Entries by Using a Practical Setting for the Properties of Drop-Down Boxes

7.4.6 The Radio-Button Group

The Web item **Radio-Button Group** offers characteristic values and components of structures in a group of buttons from which to select. Here, you can select only one value. The radio-button group is most suitable when you have to choose from among a small number of values.

Selecting data providers

The Web item **Radio-Button Group** gets its data from a data provider. Specify the data provider that you want to use after dragging and dropping the radio button group into the layout, or after you select the item by double-clicking on it (see Figure 7.23, Step 1). In the **General** tab, select the data provider that provides the values (e.g., the one that is assigned to a table or graphical Web item) (see Figure 7.23, Steps 2 and 3).

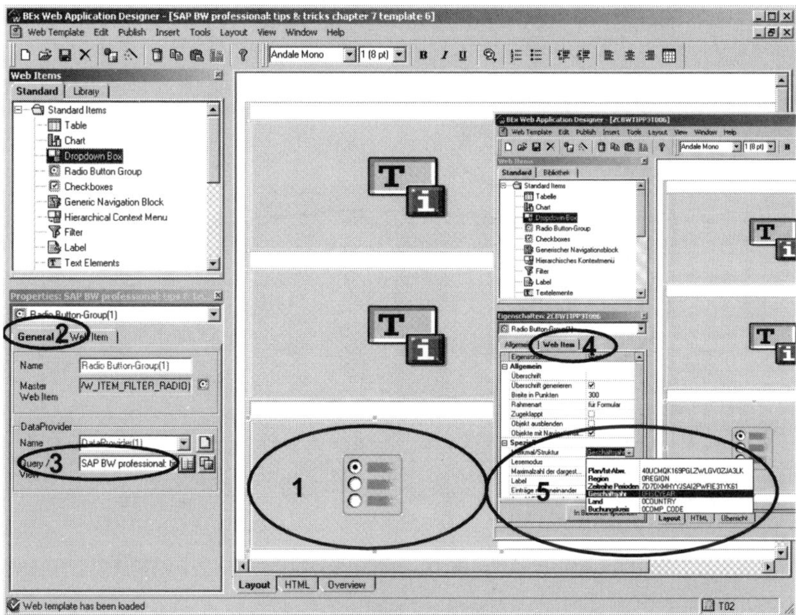

Figure 7.23 The Radio-Button Group in the Web Application Designer

Selecting a characteristic or structure

In addition, you must select the characteristic or structure whose values should be offered for selection by the radio-button group. To do this, you must use branching to the **Web Item** tab. In the **Specific** folder, activate the drop-down box for the **Characteristic/Structure** property and select the element that you want (see Figure 7.23, Steps 4 and 5). In the example, a radio-button group with which the fiscal year can be selected is added to the Web template. After you save the Web template, the settings are available during execution.

During the execution of the Web template, the Web item **radio-button group** is displayed in the example. There is no selection for the characteristic variable ("Selection fiscal year (optional)") and the **Execute** button is clicked (see Figure 7.24, Steps 1 and 2). The radio- button group offers the values of the fiscal year for selection. By clicking a selection button (in the example: K4/1999), the value is selected (see Figure 7.24, Step 3) and the result table is displayed accordingly (see Figure 7.24, Step 4).

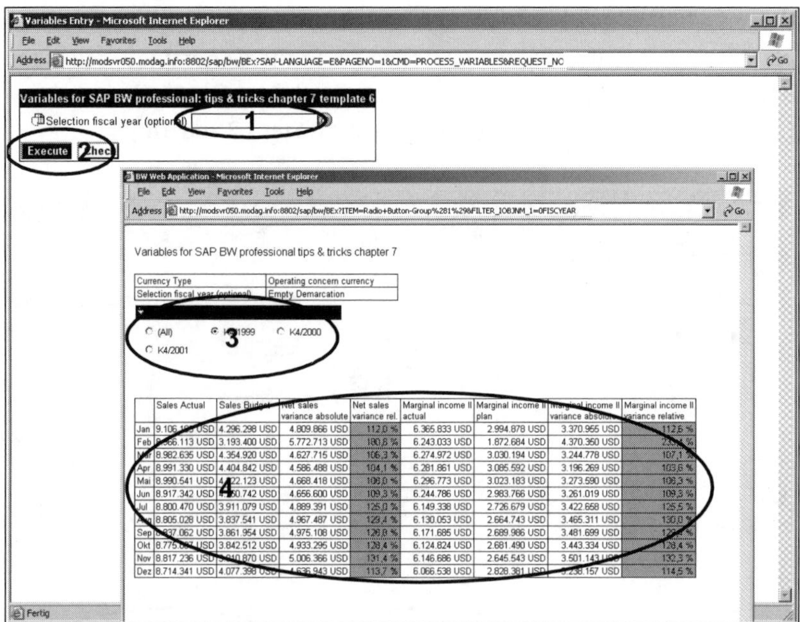

Figure 7.24 The Application of the Web Item "Radio-Button Group" for the Selection of Characteristics

Alternative properties

In some instances, some default properties of the radio-button group can be problematic:

1. The display of a frame for the title takes up space.
2. The multi-line display of the values also takes up space and can become overly complex.
3. Because the values in this Web item (e.g., in distinction to the drop-down box) can appear without an object name (in the example: "Fiscal year"), a title or a label may be necessary.
4. With the **radio-button group**, the display of all values of the dimension table, or of the master data table, can be problematic. Therefore, displaying the posted values makes sense in many instances.

Here are two additional ways to optimize the use of this Web item:

1. If a characteristic selection is offered in the radio-button group for selection, the use of a characteristic variable is not appropriate for this object.
2. The display of bracketed characteristics (like the bracketed fiscal year variant in the example) is not practical and even incomprehensible for certain user groups. In this case, the display of the characteristic values should be enabled and set in the corresponding form.

Adjustment of an InfoObject

To display characteristic values (in the example: "Fiscal year") without the bracketed characteristics (in the example: "Fiscal year variant"), the InfoObject must have the corresponding properties: in the example, the SAP Business Content InfoObject 0FISCYEAR is changed such that it contains language-independent short texts and short text is selected as the default display. You must generate and maintain the texts for the InfoObject.

To do this, the InfoObject "Fiscal year" (0FISCYEAR) is changed in the Administrator Workbench, **InfoObjects** view (Transaction RSA14): on the **Master data/texts** tab, the properties **With texts** and **Short text exists** are activated (see Figure 7.25, Steps 1 to 3). On the **Business Explorer** tab, the display is set to **Text** (see Figure 7.25, Steps 4 and 5).

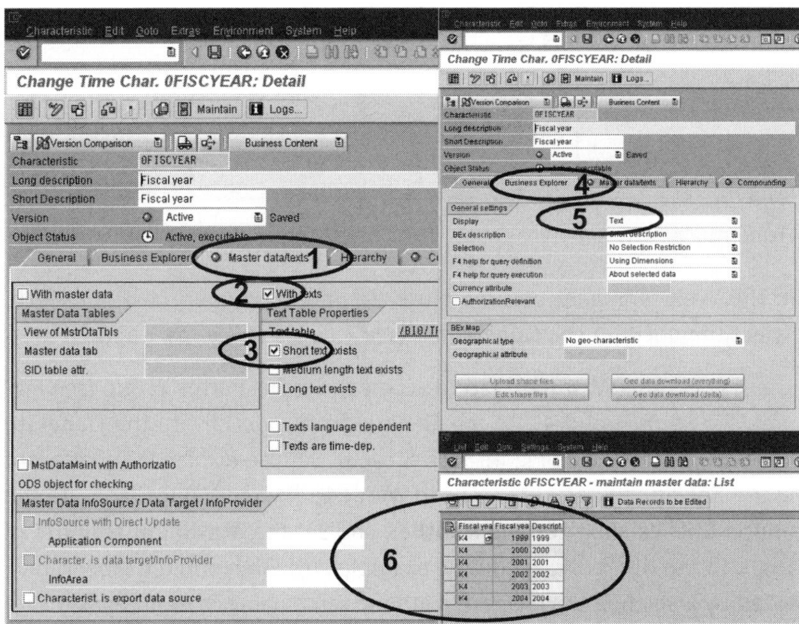

Figure 7.25 Adjustment of the InfoObject "Fiscal year"

The texts for the InfoObject "Fiscal year" must then be maintained, generated automatically, or loaded (see Figure 7.25, Step 6).

Use of the adjusted properties in the query

Then, you must use the settings for the InfoObject "Fiscal year" in the query. Alternatively, you must avoid using a characteristic variable for the same InfoObject.

To do this, create a query, which contains no variable for the characteristic to be set, using the radio-button group (in the example: "Fiscal year"). Then, display this as text in the query (see Figure 7.26, Steps 1 to 4).

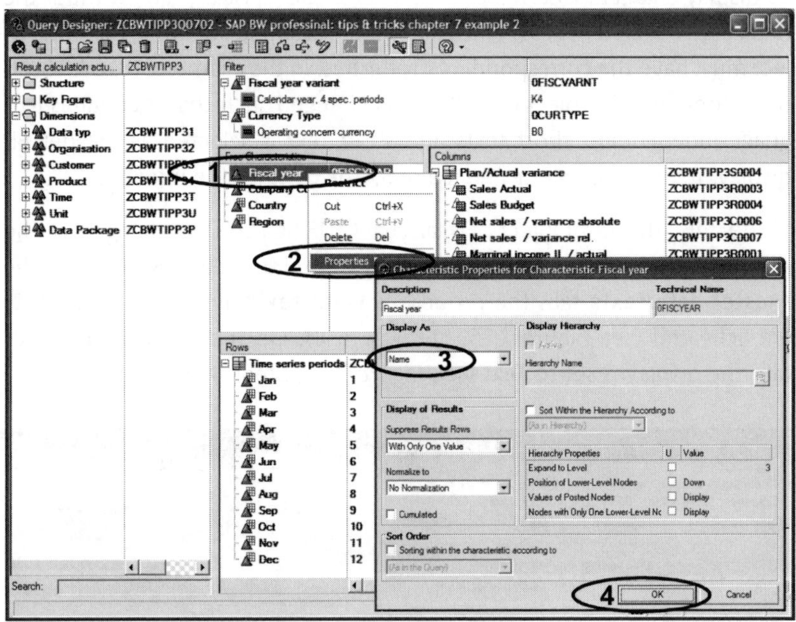

Figure 7.26 Adjustment of the Query

Adjustment of the Web template

In the Web template, you must use the modified query in Figure 7.26. Select the query in the **General** tab (see Figure 7.27, Steps 1 and 2).

Then, select the **Web Item** tab to access the radio-button group (see Figure 7.27, Steps 3 and 4). In the **General** folder, deactivate the **Generate Caption** property (see Figure 7.27, Step 5). Set the display that you want in the **Specific** folder: set the **Read Mode** to **Posted Values**, activate the option **Entries Next to One Another**, and set the **Maximum Number of Dis...** to the desired value (in the example: 10). The required label is provided by activating the property with the same name. If required, activate the property entry **Do Not Display "All Values"** (see Figure 7.27, Step 6). Then, save the Web template.

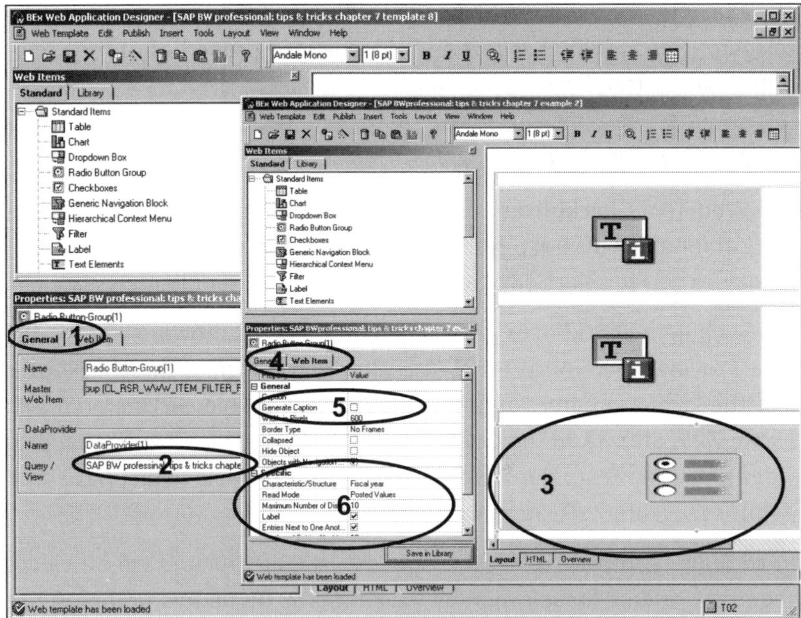

Figure 7.27 Adjustment of the Radio-Button Group

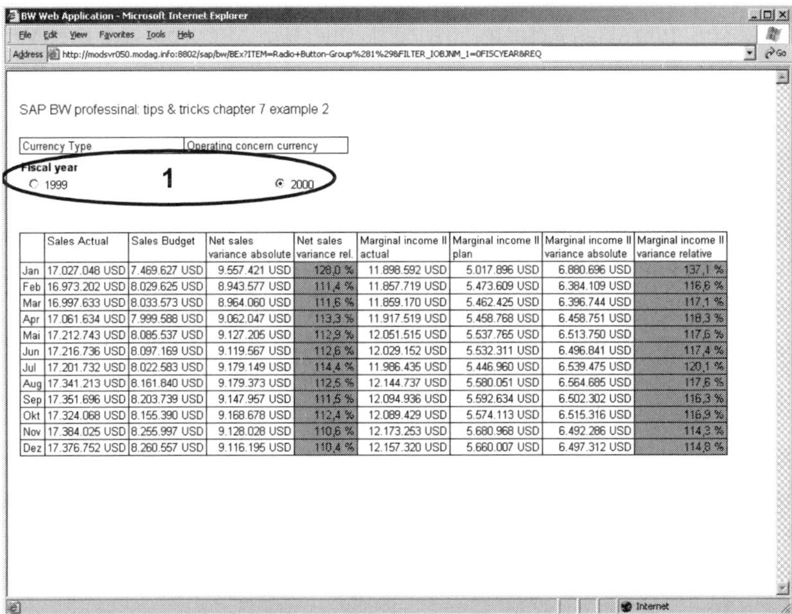

	Sales Actual	Sales Budget	Net sales variance absolute	Net sales variance rel.	Marginal income II actual	Marginal income II plan	Marginal income II variance absolute	Marginal income II variance relative
Jan	17.027.048 USD	7.469.627 USD	9.557.421 USD	128,0 %	11.898.592 USD	5.017.896 USD	6.880.696 USD	137,1 %
Feb	16.973.202 USD	8.029.625 USD	8.943.577 USD	111,4 %	11.857.719 USD	5.473.609 USD	6.384.109 USD	116,6 %
Mar	16.997.633 USD	8.033.573 USD	8.964.060 USD	111,6 %	11.859.170 USD	5.462.425 USD	6.396.744 USD	117,1 %
Apr	17.061.634 USD	7.999.588 USD	9.062.047 USD	113,3 %	11.917.519 USD	5.458.768 USD	6.458.751 USD	118,3 %
Mai	17.212.743 USD	8.085.537 USD	9.127.205 USD	112,9 %	12.051.515 USD	5.537.765 USD	6.513.750 USD	117,6 %
Jun	17.216.736 USD	8.097.169 USD	9.119.567 USD	112,6 %	12.029.152 USD	5.532.311 USD	6.496.841 USD	117,4 %
Jul	17.201.732 USD	8.022.583 USD	9.179.149 USD	114,4 %	11.986.435 USD	5.446.960 USD	6.539.475 USD	120,1 %
Aug	17.341.213 USD	8.161.840 USD	9.179.373 USD	112,5 %	12.144.737 USD	5.580.051 USD	6.564.685 USD	117,6 %
Sep	17.351.696 USD	8.203.739 USD	9.147.957 USD	111,5 %	12.094.936 USD	5.592.634 USD	6.502.302 USD	116,3 %
Okt	17.324.068 USD	8.155.390 USD	9.168.678 USD	112,4 %	12.089.429 USD	5.574.113 USD	6.515.316 USD	116,9 %
Nov	17.384.025 USD	8.255.997 USD	9.128.028 USD	110,6 %	12.173.253 USD	5.680.968 USD	6.492.286 USD	114,3 %
Dez	17.376.752 USD	8.260.557 USD	9.116.195 USD	110,4 %	12.157.320 USD	5.660.007 USD	6.497.312 USD	114,8 %

Figure 7.28 Execution of the Web Template with the Adjusted Radio-Button Group

The execution of the query shows the settings of the characteristic to be selected ("Fiscal year") as text and the changed properties of the radio-button group (see Figure 7.28, Step 1).

7.4.7 The Checkboxes

The Web item **Checkboxes** controls the selection of characteristic values and components of structures. What is special about this Web item is that it enables you to select one value or several values simultaneously.

Selecting data providers

The Web item **checkboxes** gets its data from a data provider. Specify the data provider that you want to use after you integrate the checkboxes into the layout, or after you select the item by double-clicking on it (see Figure 7.29, Step 1). In the **General** tab, select the data provider that provides the values (e.g., the one that is assigned to a table or graphical Web item) (see Figure 7.29, Steps 2 and 3).

Selecting a characteristic or structure

In addition, you must select the characteristic or structure whose values should be offered for selection by the checkbox. To do this, you must use branching to the **Web Item** tab. In the **Specific** folder, activate the drop-down box for the **Characteristic/Structure** property and select the element that you want (see Figure 7.29, Steps 4 and 5). In the example, the code structure "Plan Actual/Variance" is selected. After you save the Web template, the settings are available during execution.

During the execution of the Web template, the Web item **Checkboxes** is displayed in the example: after you select the variable value ("Fiscal year 2000") and click on the **Execute** button (see Figure 7.30, Steps 1 and 2), the checkbox offers the limited codes of the structure "Plan/Actual variance" for selection (see Figure 7.30, Step 3). Then, after you select the values that you want by checking the appropriate checkboxes (here: "Sales Actual" and "Sales Budget") and clicking on the **Filters** button (see Figure 7.30, Step 4), the display is updated with the values selected (see Figure 7.30, Step 5).

Editing the Web item "Checkboxes"

Similar to the explanations for the Web items previously described, a corresponding setting of the properties of the Web item **Checkboxes** is equally practical: in the example, the display of the title is omitted, the label is displayed, and four entries are displayed next to one another (see Figure 7.31, Steps 1 to 7).

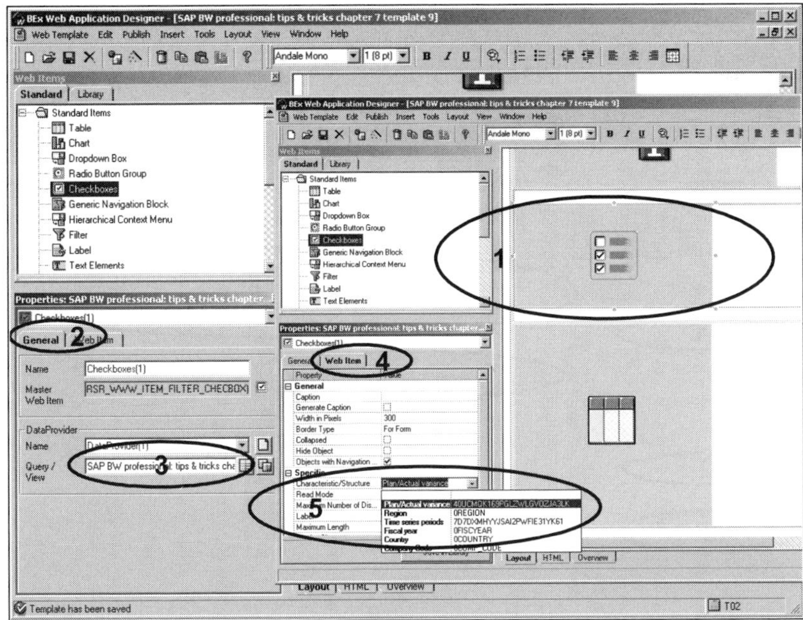

Figure 7.29 The Checkbox in the Web Application Designer

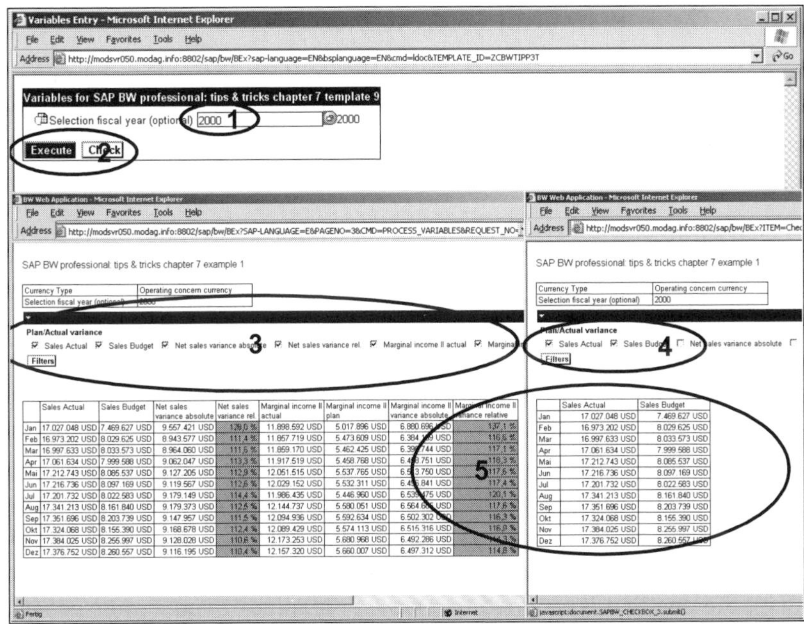

Figure 7.30 The Application of the Web Item "Checkboxes" for the Selection of Structural Components (e.g., Limited Identifiers)

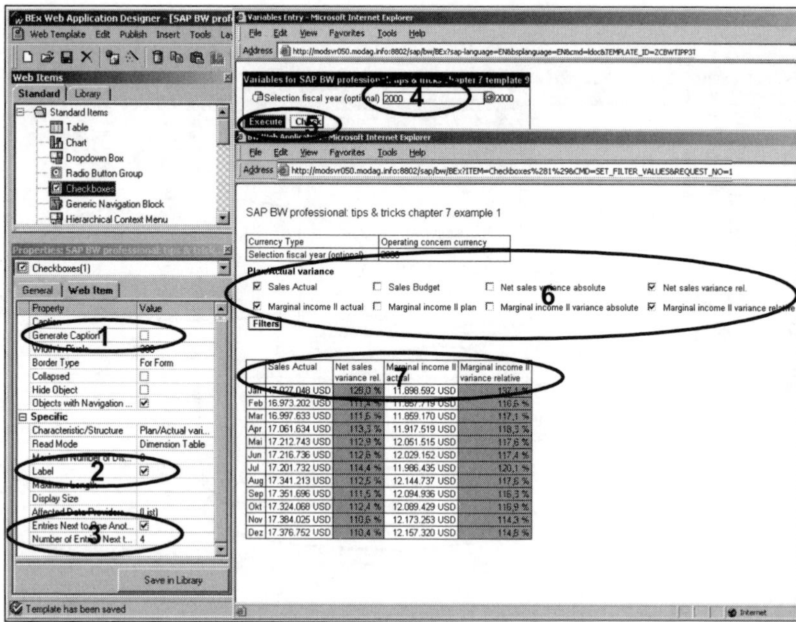

Figure 7.31 The Changed Settings of the Checkbox

7.4.8 The Hierarchical Context Menu

The Web item **Hierarchical context menu** controls the selection of hierarchy nodes or nodes of a hierarchical structure. The hierarchy nodes are displayed as context menu entries and can be set as filters during query execution.

Basis: query with hierarchy

A query with one or several hierarchies forms the basis of the hierarchical context menu. In the example, for the free characteristic "Country," a presentation hierarchy is selected (see Figure 7.32, Steps 1 to 6).

Selecting data providers

On this basis, the Web template can be created: using drag & drop, you must integrate the Web item **Hierarchical context menu** into the layout. The Web item **Hierarchical context menu** gets its data from a data provider. You specify that data provider that you want to use after you drag and drop the hierarchical context menu into the layout, or after you have selected the item by double-clicking on it (see Figure 7.33, Step 1). In the **General** tab, select the data provider that provides the selected hierarchy (e.g., the one that is assigned to a table or graphical Web item) (see Figure 7.33, Steps 2 and 3).

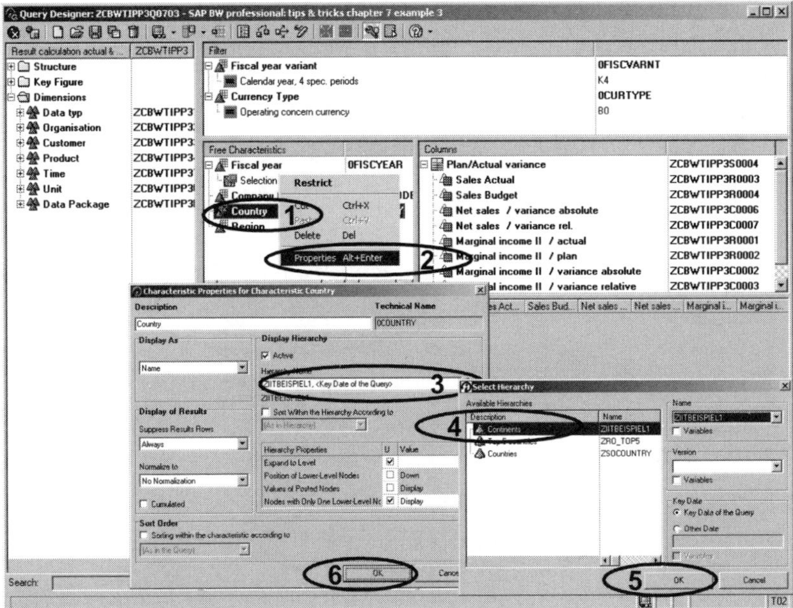

Figure 7.32 Query with Hierarchy as Basis for the Context Menu

Selecting a characteristic or structure and hierarchy

In addition, select the characteristic or structure whose hierarchy nodes should be offered for selection by the hierarchical context menu. To do this, use branching to the **Web Item** tab. In the **Specific** folder, activate the drop-down box for the **Characteristic/Structure** property and select the value that you want. In the example, the characteristic "Country" is selected. Then, you must select the hierarchy name for the selected characteristic (see Figure 7.33, Steps 4 and 5). After you save the Web template, the settings are available during execution.

During the execution of the Web template, the Web item **Hierarchical context menu** is displayed in the example: after you select the variable value ("Fiscal year 2000") and click on the **Execute** button (see Figure 7.34, Steps 1 and 2), the hierarchical context menu offers the nodes of the selected presentation hierarchy for selection (see Figure 7.34, Step 3). After you select the desired values by opening the context menu, the display is updated with the values selected.

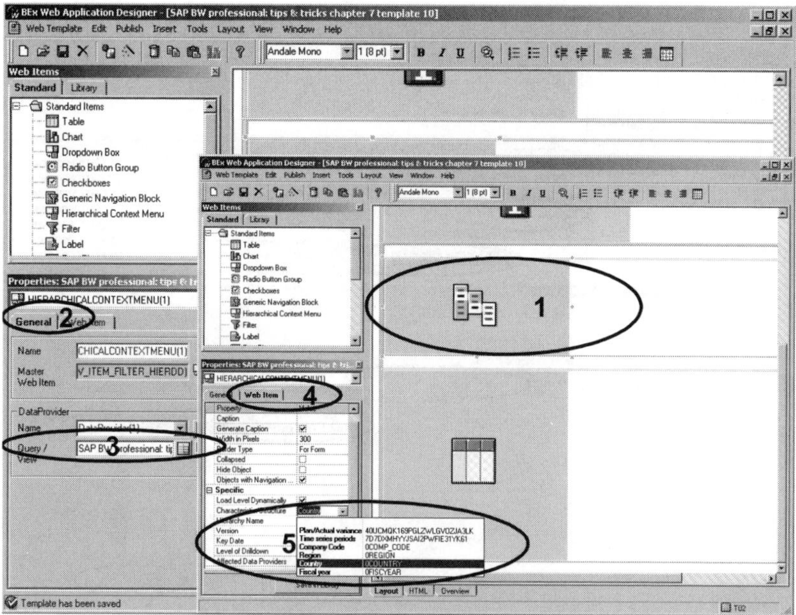

Figure 7.33 The Hierarchical Context Menu in the Web Template

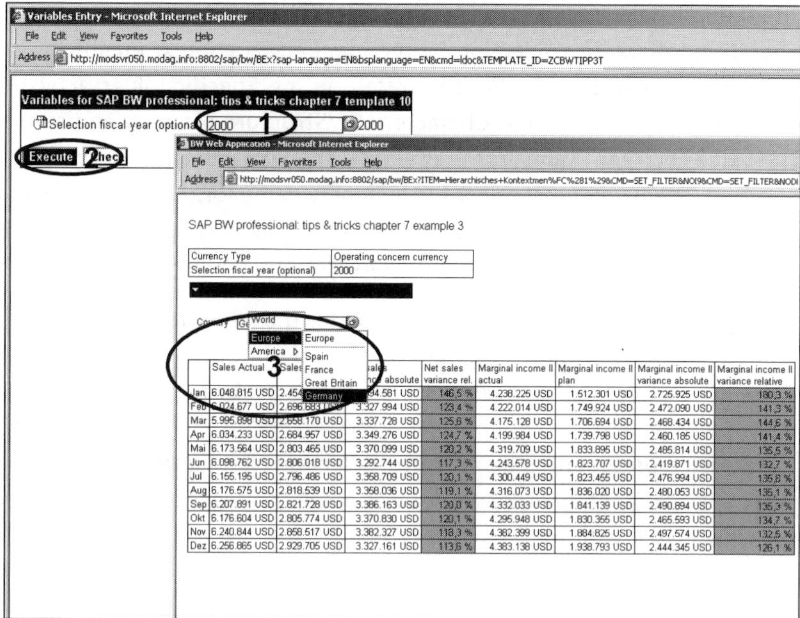

	Sales Actual	Sales	Net sales variance absolute	Net sales variance rel.	Marginal income II actual	Marginal income II plan	Marginal income II variance absolute	Marginal income II variance relative
Jan	6.048.815 USD	2.454 [illegible]	[illegible]94.581 USD	146,5 %	4.238.225 USD	1.512.301 USD	2.725.925 USD	180,3 %
Feb	[illegible]024.677 USD	2.696.683 [illegible]	3.327.994 USD	123,4 %	4.222.014 USD	1.749.924 USD	2.472.090 USD	141,3 %
Mar	5.995.898 USD	2.658.170 USD	3.337.728 USD	125,6 %	4.175.128 USD	1.706.694 USD	2.468.434 USD	144,6 %
Apr	6.034.233 USD	2.684.957 USD	3.349.276 USD	124,7 %	4.199.984 USD	1.739.798 USD	2.460.185 USD	141,4 %
Mai	6.173.564 USD	2.803.465 USD	3.370.099 USD	120,2 %	4.319.709 USD	1.833.895 USD	2.485.814 USD	135,5 %
Jun	6.098.762 USD	2.806.018 USD	3.292.744 USD	117,3 %	4.243.578 USD	1.823.707 USD	2.419.871 USD	132,7 %
Jul	6.155.195 USD	2.796.486 USD	3.358.709 USD	120,1 %	4.300.449 USD	1.823.455 USD	2.476.994 USD	135,8 %
Aug	6.176.575 USD	2.818.539 USD	3.358.036 USD	119,1 %	4.316.073 USD	1.836.020 USD	2.480.053 USD	135,1 %
Sep	6.207.891 USD	2.821.728 USD	3.386.163 USD	120,0 %	4.332.033 USD	1.841.139 USD	2.490.894 USD	135,3 %
Okt	6.176.604 USD	2.805.774 USD	3.370.830 USD	120,1 %	4.295.948 USD	1.830.355 USD	2.465.593 USD	134,7 %
Nov	6.240.844 USD	2.858.517 USD	3.382.327 USD	118,3 %	4.382.399 USD	1.884.825 USD	2.497.574 USD	132,5 %
Dez	6.256.865 USD	2.929.705 USD	3.327.161 USD	113,6 %	4.383.138 USD	1.938.793 USD	2.444.345 USD	126,1 %

Figure 7.34 The Hierarchical Context Menu for Query Runtime

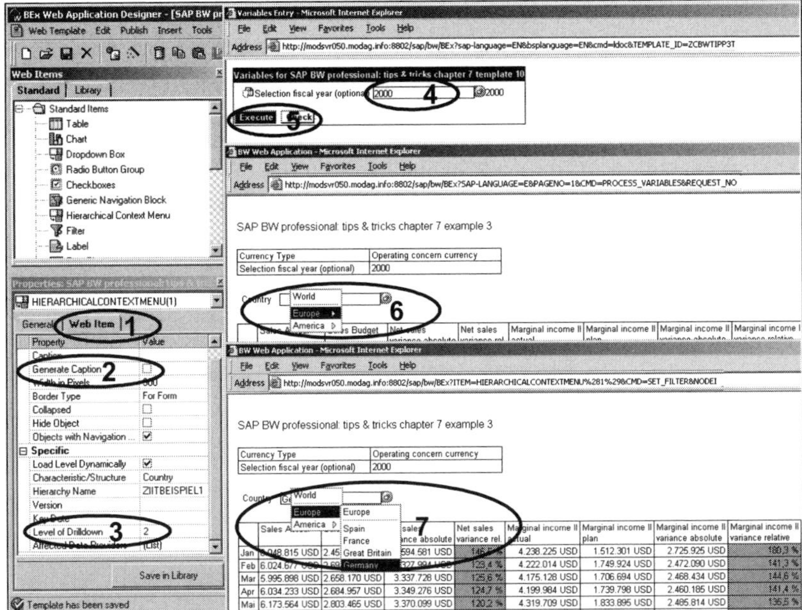

Figure 7.35 Editing the Hierarchical Context Menu

Editing the Web item "Hierarchical context menu"

Similar to the explanations for the Web items previously described, using a corresponding setting for the properties of the Web item **Hierarchical context menu** does make sense. In the example, the display of the title is omitted (see Figure 7.35, Steps 1 and 2). In addition, the **Level of drill-down** property is set (in the example: "2"): here it is set to how many hierarchy levels are read when the hierarchy is opened (see Figure 7.35, Step 3). Especially with large hierarchies, a loading step-by-step is optimal in order to minimize the response time.

During the execution of the Web template, the changed settings are applied (see Figure 7.35, Steps 4 to 7): when you open the **Hierarchical context menu** in the example, only the uppermost two hierarchy levels are read directly and offered. If the third hierarchy level is requested, it is read afterwards.

7.4.9 Filter

Selecting data providers

The Web item **Filter** displays the filter values that arise due to navigation during the execution of a query. It gets its data from a data provider. You specify the data provider that you want to use after you select the filter item by double-clicking on it. In the **General** tab, select the data provider that provides the selected filter (e.g., it is the one to which the table or graphical Web item is assigned) (see Figure 7.36, Steps 1 to 3). The other settings of the Web item **Filter** remain unchanged (see Figure 7.36, Steps 4 and 5). After you save the Web template, the settings are available during execution.

Use of the Web item "Filter"

During execution of the Web template, the Web item **Filter** is displayed in the example: After you select the variable value ("Fiscal year 2000") and click on the **Execute** button (see Figure 7.37, Steps 1 and 2), the Web item contains no values (see Figure 7.37, Step 3).

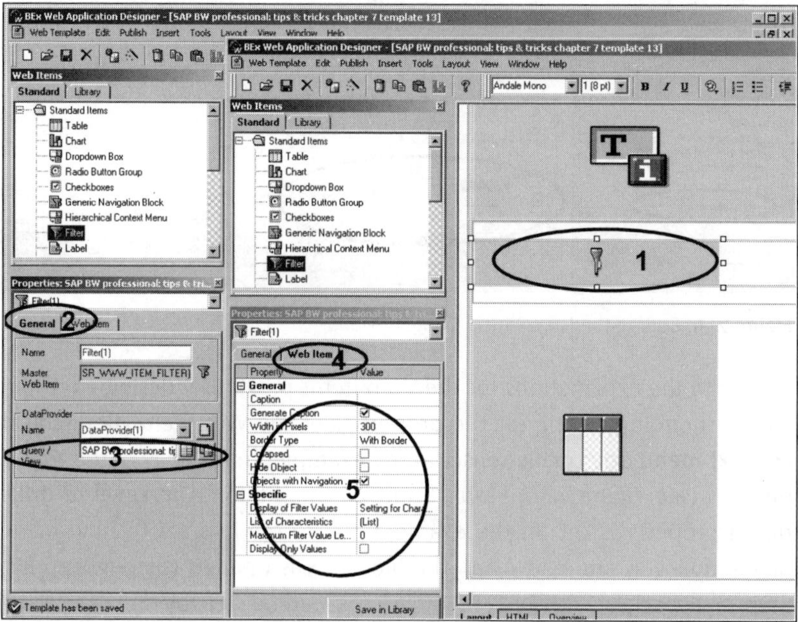

Figure 7.36 The Properties of the Web Item "Filter"

If during the query execution due to navigation a value is selected (in the example, by right-clicking on the value "May" of the characteristic "Accounting period") and the function **Filter and drilldown according to** causes a filtering and breakdown of an accounting sector (see Figure 7.37, Steps 4 and 5), then the selected value is displayed in the Web item **Filter** (see Figure 7.37, Step 6). If additional selections are undertaken (in the example: "filtering of an accounting sector and breakdown according to country"), the additional filters are added dynamically to the table with the filter values (see Figure 7.37, steps 7 to 10).

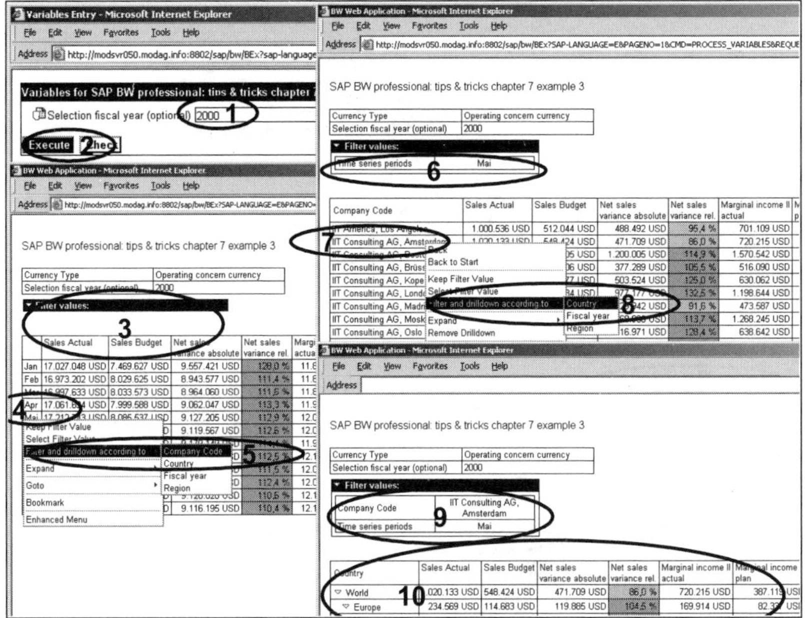

Figure 7.37 The Web Item "Filter" During the Query Execution

Editing the Web item "Filter"

Similar to the explanations of the Web items previously described, a corresponding setting of the properties of the Web item **Filter** does make sense. In the example, the display of the title is omitted. To reduce the display space required, the filters are displayed only next to each other, but in a specified sequence as values rather than in a table.

To modify the Web item **Filter**, in the list of Web items, select **Filter** by double-clicking on it (see Figure 7.38, Steps 1 and 2). In the **General** tab, deactivate the **Generate Caption** property (see Figure 7.38, Step 3). You can set the sequence as well as the display of the filter values in the **Specific** folder by activating the **List of Characteristics** drop-down box (see Figure 7.38, Step 4). In the **List of Characteristics** pop-up, you can then select the filter values (to be displayed in the Web item) in the desired sequence in the drop-down box of the column **Filter Characteristic/ Structure** of the line that is active at this moment (see Figure 7.38, Step 5). For each characteristic or each structure, the desired setting can be made in the active line, using the drop-down box in the **Display of Filter Values** column (see Figure 7.38, step 6). By clicking on the **OK** button, the settings are integrated as a Web item property (see Figure 7.38, Step 7). Then, activate the **Display Only Values** property (see Figure 7.38, Step 8).

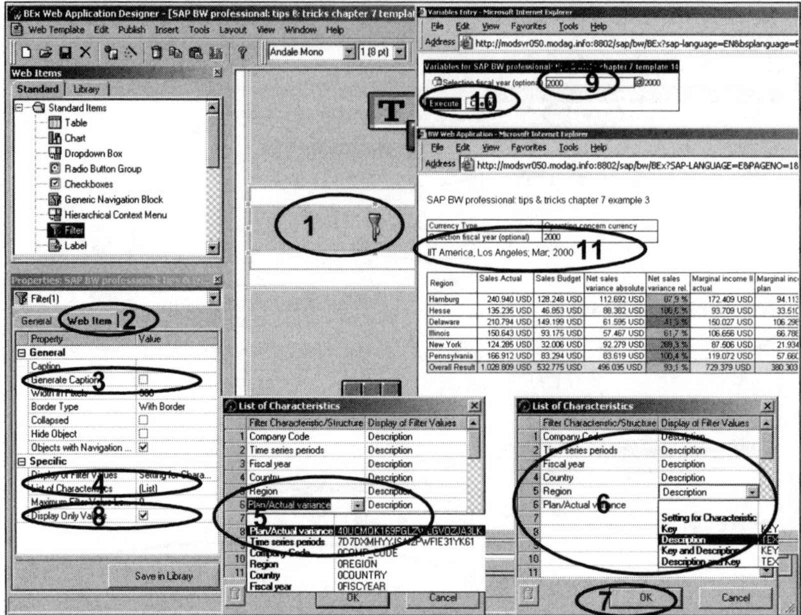

Figure 7.38 Adjustment of the Web Item "Filter"

After you save the settings, the changed properties are used during execution of the Web template: After you select the variable value ("Fiscal year 2000") and click on the **Execute** button (see Figure 7.38, Steps 9 and 10) and several applications of filter functions (e.g. through the function **Filter and breakdown according to...**), the selected values are listed in the configured sequence and display (see Figure 7.38, Step 11).

7.4.10 The Label

The Web item **Label** controls the display of characteristic, attribute, or structural component names and enables you to link to the context menu of this characteristic, attribute, or structural component. An important advantage of this Web item is that it does not contribute to any performance problems (in contrast, e.g., to the drop-down box).

Selecting data providers

The Web item **Label** gets its data from a data provider. You specify the data provider that you want to use after you drag and drop the label into the layout, or after you select the item by double-clicking on it (see Figure 7.39, Step 1). In the **General** tab, select the data provider that provides the values that you want (e.g., the values that are assigned to a table or graphical Web item) (see Figure 7.39, Steps 2 and 3).

Selecting a characteristic or structure

In addition, select the characteristic or structure that should be offered by the label. To do this, use branching to the **Web Item** tab. In the **Specific** folder, activate the drop-down box for the **Characteristic/Structure** property and select the element that you want. In the example, two labels with the characteristic "Country" (0COUNTRY) and "Region" (0REGION) are incorporated into the Web template (see Figure 7.39, Steps 4 and 5). After you save the Web template, all functions of the label are available during execution of the Web application (see Figure 7.40).

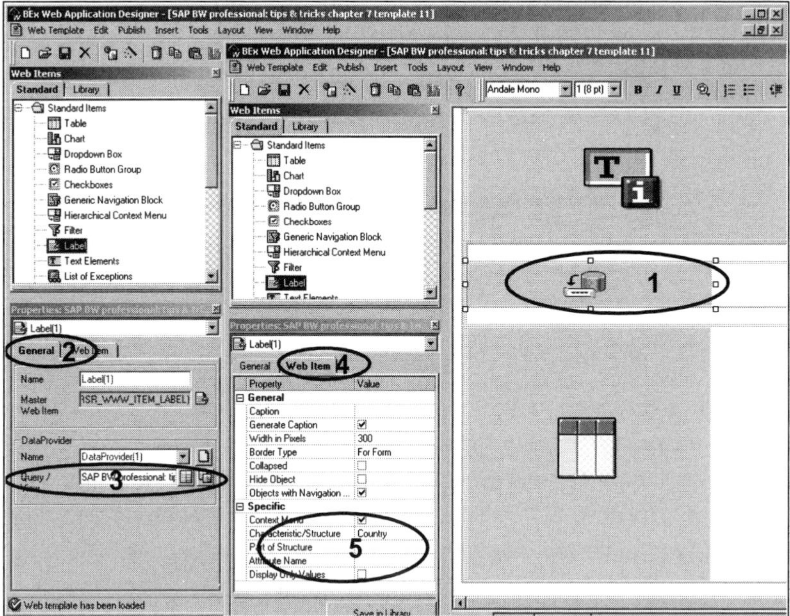

Figure 7.39 The Label in the Web Template

During the execution of the Web template, the Web item **Label** is displayed in the example: after you select the variable value ("Fiscal year 2000") and click on the **Execute** button (see Figure 7.40, Steps 1 and 2), the label offers various functions for selection (see Figure 7.40, Step 3). In addition to the general functions permitted in the Web template, you can select the following functions in the context-sensitive menu for the relevant object (in the example: characteristic "Company"):

- Select filter value
- Drilldown
- Sort

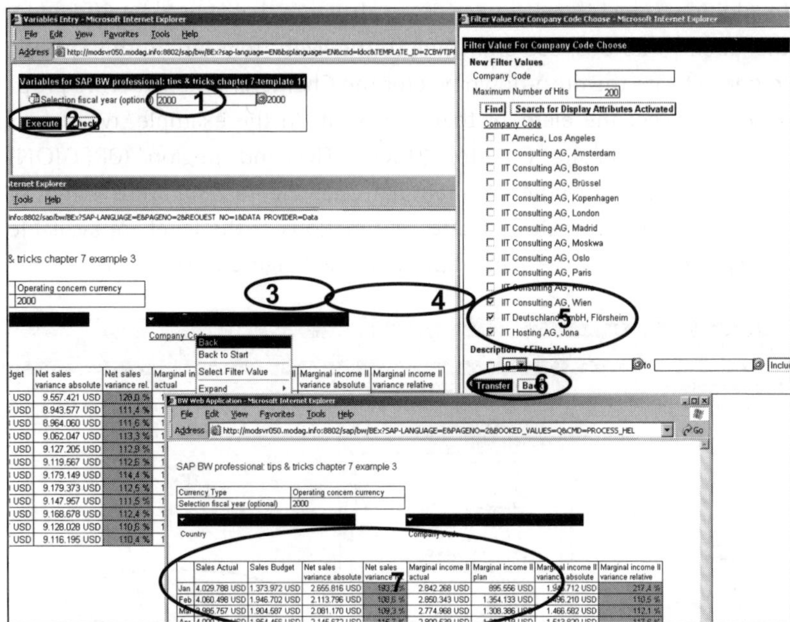

Figure 7.40 The Label During the Query Execution

After you select the function that you want by opening the context-sensitive menu and right-clicking on it (see Figure 7.40, Steps 3 and 4), the corresponding function is executed. In the example, the command Back is selected. To do this, the Filter Value for... pop-up opens. There, you must make the desired selections and confirm your selections by clicking on the Transfer button (see Figure 7.40, Steps 5 and 6).

A problem during filtering using the Web item "Label"

The display of the selected values occurs correctly (see Figure 7.40, Step 7); however, it becomes apparent immediately that to use the Web item Label in this way does require additional settings. As you can see in the example, you do not get corresponding information that the values were limited. In practice, this causes misinterpretations and is therefore not viable.

Combination of "Label" and "Filter"

Therefore, the combination of the Web items **Label** and **Filter** is useful: when you use the Web item **Label**, the corresponding functions are executed; when you use the Web item **Filter**, the selected values, if selections occur, are displayed.

The following example shows the corresponding settings: in a multi-line table, labels for the characteristics and structures to be offered for navigation are arranged in a line using the procedure explained in Figure 7.39.

In a line that falls below other lines, a Web item filter is arranged for each label positioned above.

For the label in the upper line of the first column (see Figure 7.41, Steps 1 to 4), a Web item **Filter** is inserted in the line below (see Figure 7.41, Step 5). In the **Web Item** tab, in the **General** folder (see Figure 7.41, Step 6) the property **Generate Caption** is deactivated (see Figure 7.41, Step 7).

Upon activation of the **List of Characteristics** drop-down box in the **Specific** folder (see Figure 7.41, Step 8), the **List of Characteristics** pop-up opens. In this pop-up, the same characteristic (in the example: "Country"), or the same structure as in the label above, as well as the desired display of the filter value, is selected (see Figure 7.41, Step 9). After you click on the **OK** button (see Figure 7.41, Step 10), the settings are copied and the **Display Only Values** property is activated (see Figure 7.41, Step 11). For the additional columns, proceed accordingly.

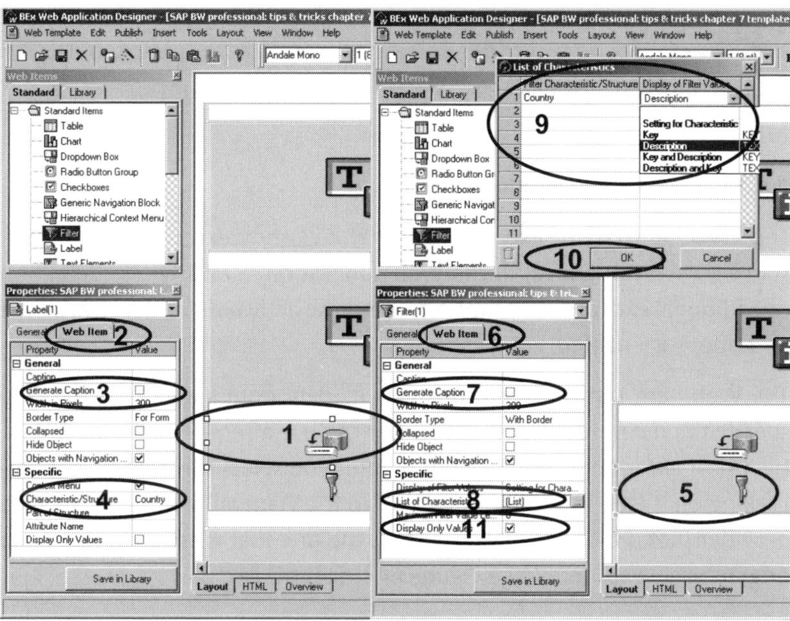

Figure 7.41 Combination of the Web Items "Label" and "Filter"

After you save the Web template, the changed properties are used during execution in the Web application: after you select the variable value ("Fiscal year 2000") and click on the **Execute** button (see Figure 7.42, Steps 1 and 2) and select the values (in the example for "Country" and "Accounting Sector"), the filters are displayed in the table above the query results (see Figure 7.42, Steps 3 to 10).

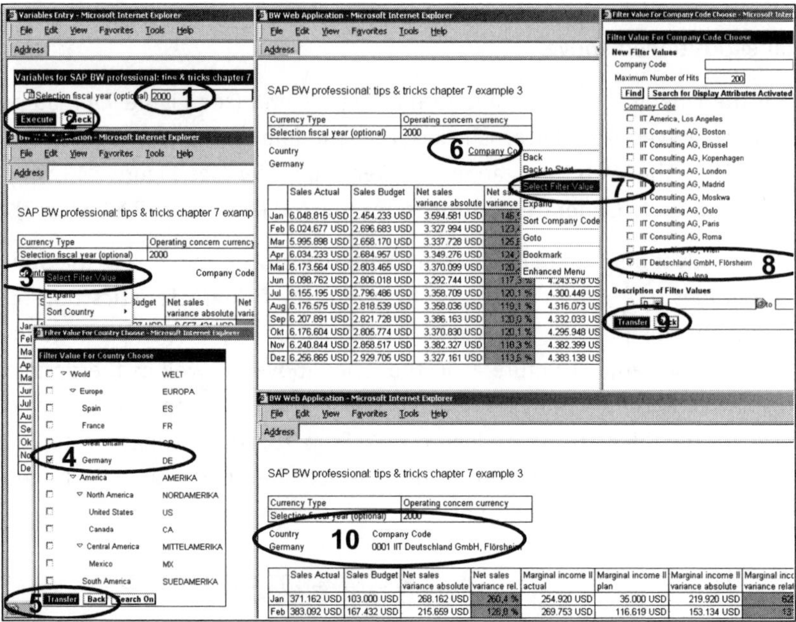

Figure 7.42 The Combination of the Web Items "Label" and "Filter" During the Query Execution

7.4.11 List of Exceptions

The Web item **List of exceptions** lists the existing exceptions with their states (active/not active) in the Web application. Similarly, the definition of additional exceptions is supported and the activation or deactivation of exceptions is enabled.

Selecting data providers

The Web item **List of exceptions** gets its data from a data provider. You specify the data providers that you want to use after they are copied into the list of exceptions in the layout or after you select the item by double-clicking on it (see Figure 7.43, Step 1). In the **General** tab, select the data provider that provides the values (e.g., the one that is assigned to a table or graphical Web item) (see Figure 7.43, Steps 2 and 3).

Because the **List of exceptions** has no special properties, you can use this Web item immediately. After you save the Web template, the functions of the **List of exceptions** are available during execution of the Web application. After you select the variable value ("Fiscal year 2000") and click on the **Execute** button (see Figure 7.43, Steps 4 and 5), the **List of exceptions** is displayed (see Figure 7.43, Step 6).

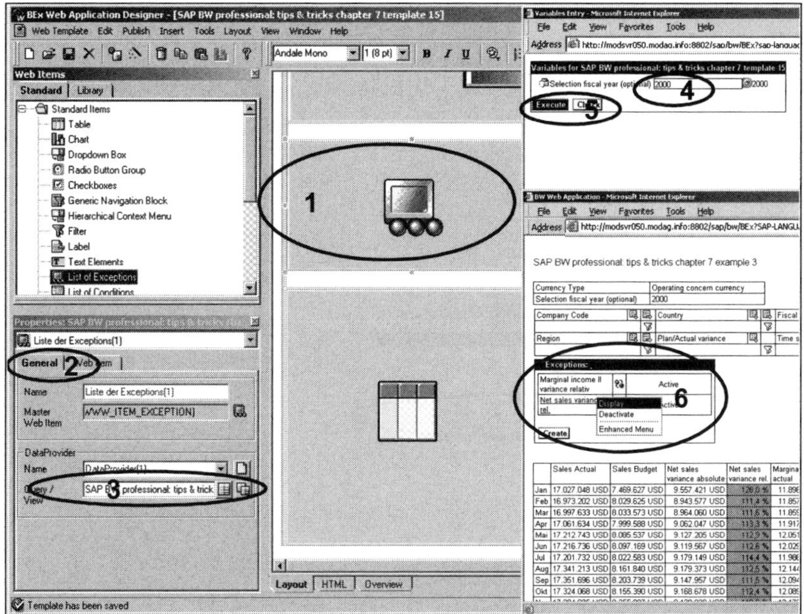

Figure 7.43 The Web Item "List of Exceptions"

You can switch on or turn off the conditions by clicking on the **Deactivate** or **Activate** button, or by opening the context-sensitive menu via right-clicking on a command.

Creating an exception

The **Create** button enables you to define exceptions during the execution of the Web application (see Figure 7.44, Step 1). Then, the **Define Exception** popup opens. There, you must specify the description and the state (active/inactive) of the exception (see Figure 7.44, Step 2) (in the example: "Sales Actual" as active exception for the structural element with the same name). In the **Exception Values** block, the quick values and the associated evaluations (see Figure 7.44, Step 3) are defined. In the example, the boundary between good and bad evaluation is specified at 17 million USD monthly. To avoid nonsensical evaluations, you can make the required definitions in the **Cell Restrictions** block: in the example, the evaluation occurs for "Everything Except for Results" (see Figure 7.44, Step 4). You must then confirm the specifications by clicking on the **Transfer** button (see Figure 7.44, Step 5). Then, the corresponding evaluation of the query results will occur (see Figure 7.44, Steps 6 and 7).

Special general properties can also be specified for exceptions, such as the omission of a generated caption and the width of the Web item. In this case, proceed as you would for the Web item described above.

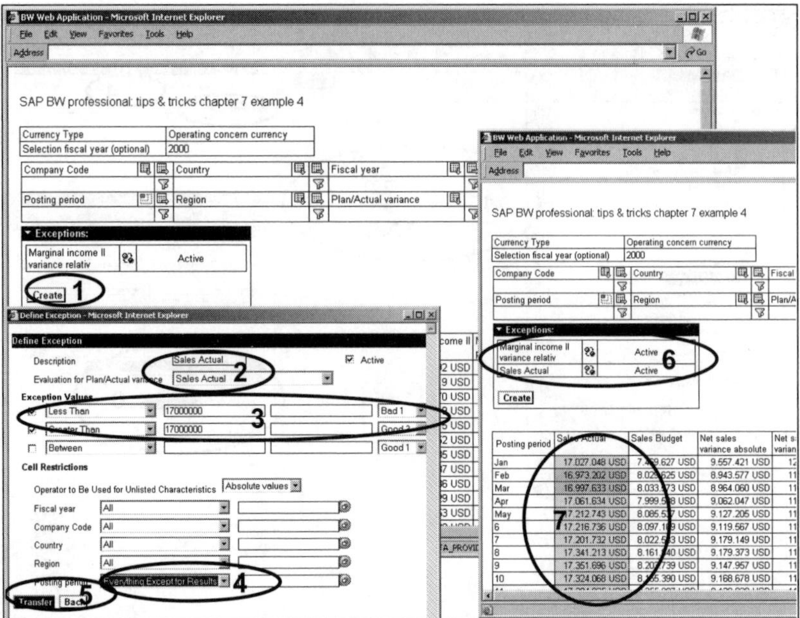

Figure 7.44 Definition of an Exception During Execution of the Web Application

7.4.12 List of Conditions

The Web item **List of conditions** lists the existing conditions with their states (active/inactive/not applicable/not used) in the Web application. Similarly, the definition of additional conditions is supported and the activation or deactivation of conditions is enabled.

Selecting data providers

The Web item **List of conditions** gets its data from a data provider. You specify the data provider that you want to use after takeover of the list of conditions into the layout, or after you select the item by double-clicking on it (see Figure 7.45, Step 1). In the **General** tab, the data provider that provides the values is selected (e.g., the one that is assigned to a table or graphical Web item) (see Figure 7.45, Steps 2 and 3).

Because the list of conditions has no special properties, you can use this Web item immediately. After you save the Web template, the functions of the list of conditions are available during execution of the Web application. After you select the variable value ("Fiscal year 2000") and click on the **Execute** button (see Figure 7.45, Steps 4 and 5), the list of conditions is displayed (see Figure 7.45, Step 6).

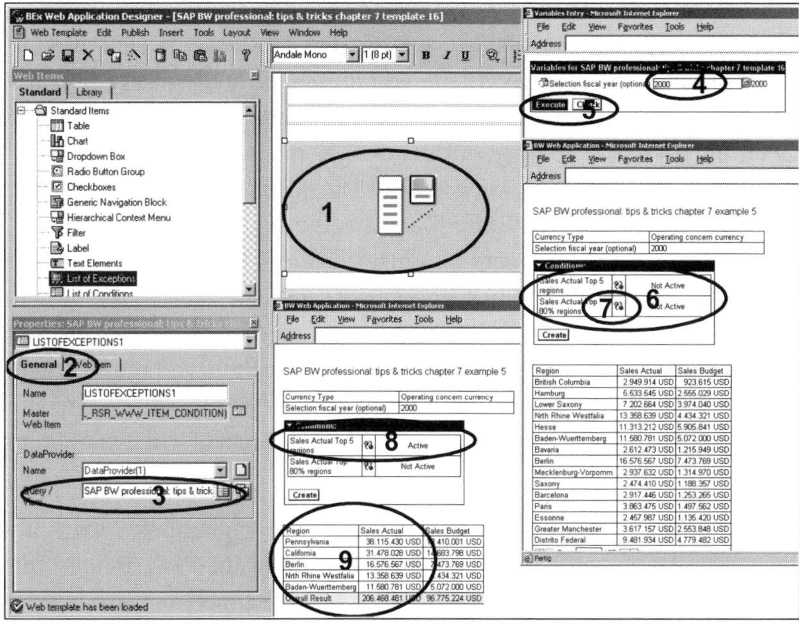

Figure 7.45 The Web Item "List of Conditions"

You can switch on or turn off the conditions by clicking on the **Deactivate** or **Activate** button, or by opening the context-sensitive menu via right-clicking on a command (see Figure 7.45, Steps 7 to 9).

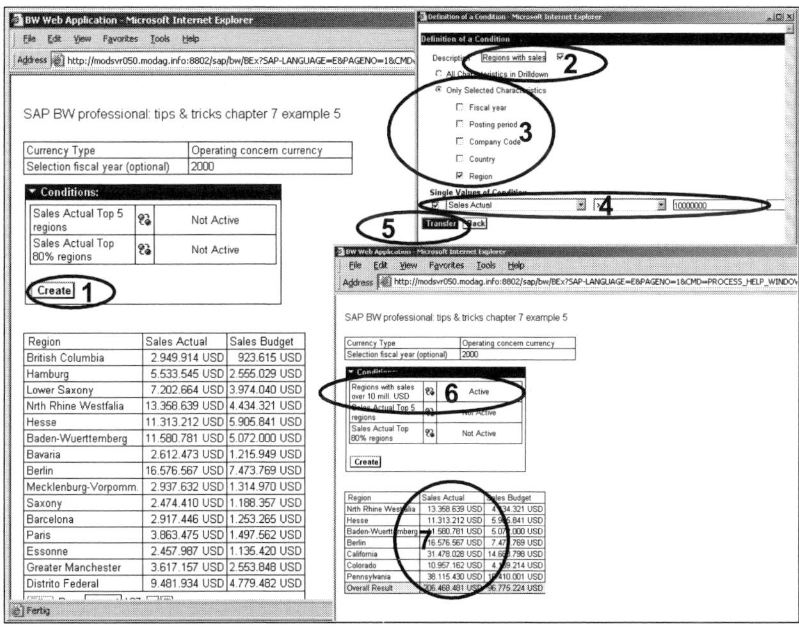

Figure 7.46 Definition of a Condition During Execution of the Web Application

Creating a condition

The **Create** button enables you to define conditions during the execution of the Web application (see Figure 7.46, Step 1). Then, the **Definition of a Condition** pop-up opens. There, you must specify the description and the start condition (active/inactive) of the condition (see Figure 7.46, Step 2) (in the example: "Regions with sales > 10 million USD" as active condition). The condition can be valid for all characteristics in the drilldown. Alternatively, you must specify the characteristics that you want in the **Only Selected Characteristics** block (see Figure 7.46, Step 3). In the **Single Values of Condition** block, you must specify the code or the desired structural element with the criterion (larger, smaller, top, last, etc.) and the limit value or values (see Figure 7.46, Step 4). Then, you must confirm the specifications by clicking the **Transfer** button (see Figure 7.46, Step 5); then the condition is applied to the query results (see Figure 7.46, Steps 6 and 7).

Special general properties can also be specified for conditions, such as the omission of a generated caption and the width of the Web item. In this case, proceed as you would for the Web item described above.

7.4.13 Ticker

The Web item **Ticker** displays the contents of the query results in a table in a ticker. The prerequisite for using the ticker is the enabling of the JavaScript function in the Web browser.

Selecting data providers

The Web item **Ticker** gets its data from a data provider. You specify the data provider to be used **after you copy** the ticker into the layout, or after you select the item by double-clicking on it (see Figure 7.47, Step 1). In the **General** tab, select the data provider that provides the values (see Figure 7.47, Steps 2 and 3).

You can then use the Web item **Ticker** immediately. After you save the Web template, the functions of the ticker are available during the execution of the Web application. After you select the variable value ("Fiscal year 2000") and click on the **Execute** button (see Figure 7.47, Steps 4 and 5), the ticker is displayed (see the change of the Web item over time in Figure 7.47, Steps 6a and 6b). The table underlying the ticker displays the cells of this table during execution in the sequence of the rows and columns. The delimitation of the cells in the ticker occurs via separators.

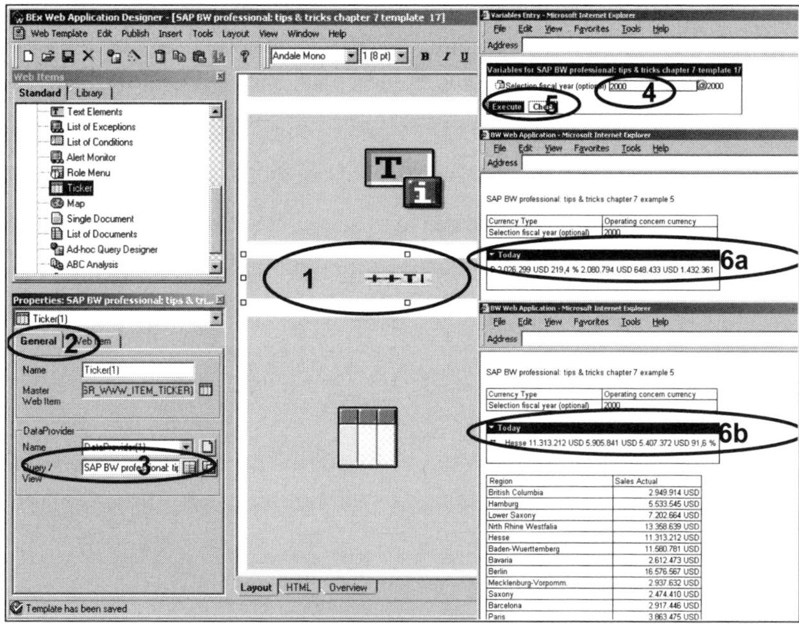

Figure 7.47 The Web Item "Ticker"

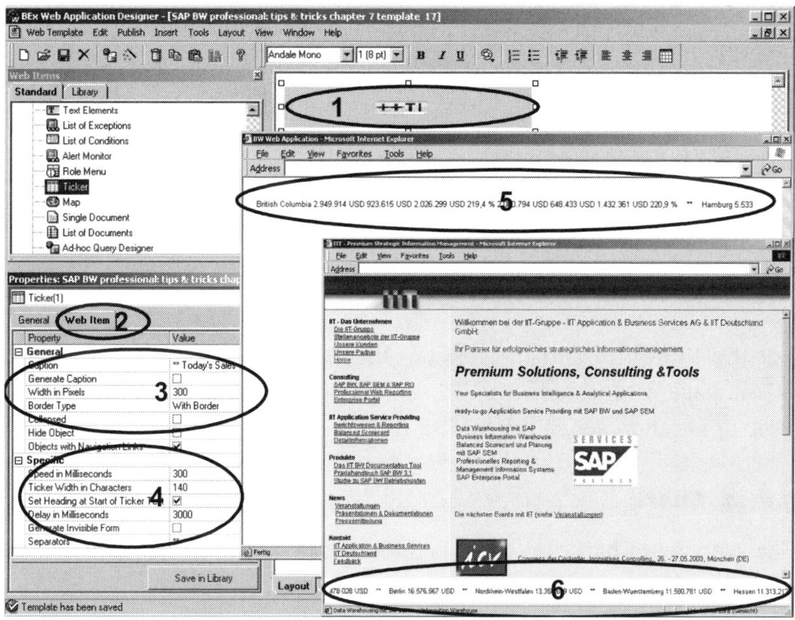

Figure 7.48 Ticker as Component of a Web Site

Editing the Web item "Ticker"

The Web item **Ticker** has general and special Web item properties. As described in the previous sections, here, general properties such as the generation of captions or the width can be adjusted to meet the requirements.

In the special properties, you can set the following:

- The separator for delimiting cells
- The delay in milliseconds before the running text "wanders" 1 character to the left (in the Web Application Designer, this is referred to as "*Speed in milliseconds*")
- The width of the ticker in characters: the length of the running text overrides the width of the Web item.
- As an option, you can place the title from the general Web item properties at the beginning of the text (without an explicit title, the long text of the query is used).
- The delay in milliseconds before the running text starts up

Incorporating a ticker into a Web site

Therefore, you can incorporate a ticker into a Management Cockpit or a general Web page. In the example, a title was defined that was placed in front of the text, the separator was changed to "**", and the width of the ticker was set to 140 characters (see Figure 7.48, Steps 1 to 4). Figure 7.48, Step 5, shows the execution of the Web application. This Web application can now be incorporated into a Web page using the following coding:

```
<frameset rows="65,*,50" border="0" frameborder="0">
  <frame name="Oben" scrolling="no" src="URLOben">
  <frame name="Mitte" src="URLMitte">
  <frame name="Unten" scrolling="no" src="URLUnten">
</frameset>
```

For the `URLOben` and `URLMitte`, the Web address of the respective HTML page is specified. The `URLUnten` is replaced with the URL of the Web application generated by SAP BW (see Figure 7.48, Step 6).

7.4.14 Chart

Selecting data providers

The Web item **Chart** displays the contents of a query result in a chart. The Web item **Chart** gets its data from a data provider. You specify the data provider that you want to use after you copy the chart into the layout, or you select the item by double-clicking on it (see Figure 7.49, Step 1). In the **General** tab, select the data provider that provides the values (see Figure 7.49, Steps 2 and 3).

You can then use this Web item immediately. After you select the variable value ("Fiscal year 2000") and click on the **Execute** button (see Figure 7.49, Steps 4 and 5), the chart is displayed (see Figure 7.49, Step 6).

Generally, charts produce only reasonable results with useful settings of the Web item properties. This is clear with a glance at the display of the data in the chart in the example: although the query result is suited for a graphical display (see the table display of the result in Figure 7.49, Step 7), the bars created by the SAP BW default settings are not grouped sensibly.

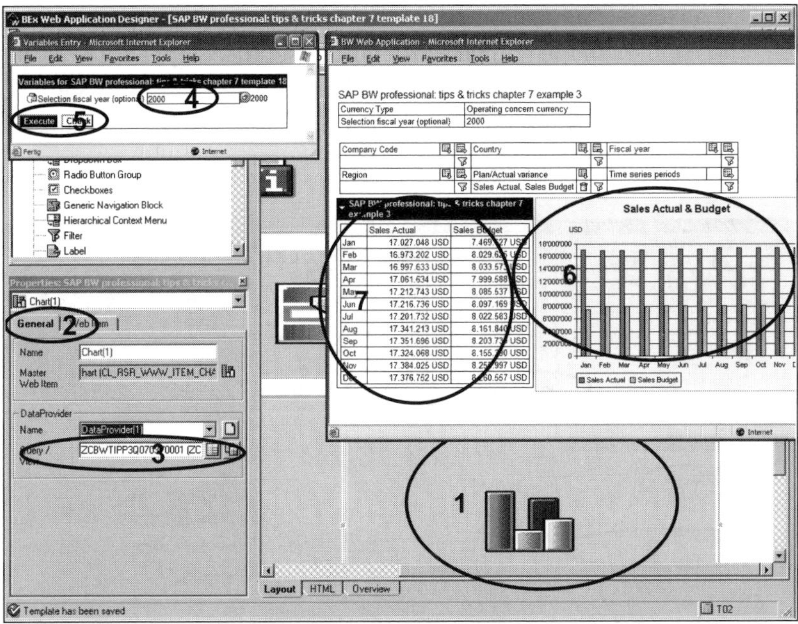

Figure 7.49 The Web Item "Chart": Basic Function

Sensible settings for bar charts

Below, various chart types with selected, often useful, graphical settings will be explained in examples. To create practical displays of charts, the Web item properties are specified. If a query result like the table in Figure 7.49, Step 7, must be displayed as a bar chart, you must adjust the settings accordingly, as described below.

Properties of the Web item "Chart (Bar Chart)"

After you change to the **Web Item** tab, the properties can be edited (see legend for Figure 7.50, Steps 1 and 2). Often, the display of headings using external frames is omitted. Similarly, many charts with the default setting in the size 300 are not legible. Therefore, the width of the chart in pixels is changed (in the example to 450) (see legend for Figure 7.50, Step 3).

In the **Specific** folder (Web item properties), you can activate the **Automatic Display of Units and Currencies...**, and enter a chart title (see legend for Figure 7.50, Step 4). With the specified table form (with the rubric "Period" in the rows and two codes as data rows in the columns), you must activate the **Swap Display Axes** property (see legend for Figure 7.50, Step 5). Concurrently, you can start editing the chart by double-clicking on the chart type (in the example: bars).

Editing graphic "Bar Chart"

Double-click on the **Chart Type** to open the **Edit Chart** pop-up. In the center of the chart, you can open the context-sensitive menu by right-clicking and selecting the function **Format Plot Area** (see legend for Figure 7.50, Step 6). In the **Format Plot** pop-up that then appears, select the fill color from the drop-down box (see legend for Figure 7.50, Step 7). Finally, you can copy the settings by clicking on the **OK** button (see legend for Figure 7.50, Step 8).

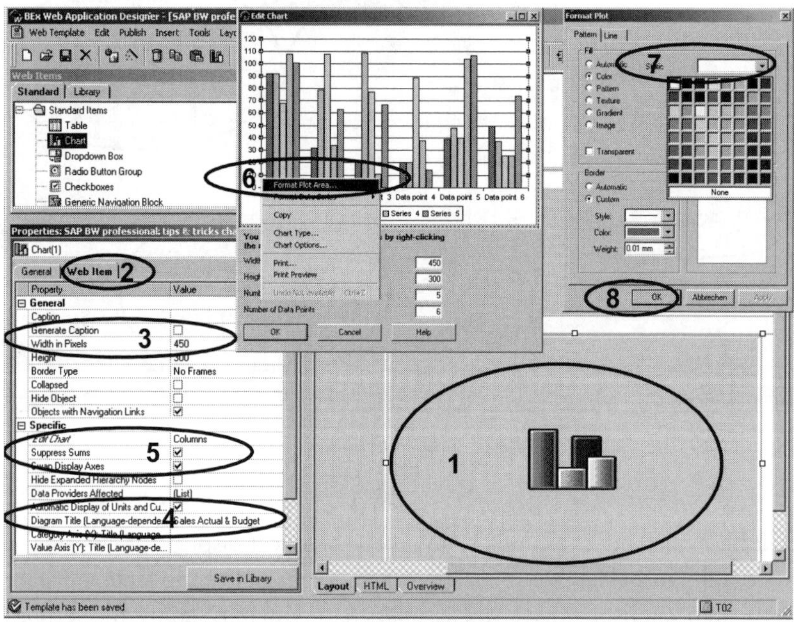

Figure 7.50 Web Item Properties of the Bar Chart, Part 1

Legend

In the **Edit Chart** pop-up, you can open the context-sensitive menu in the chart area (e.g., in the lower left corner) by right-clicking and selecting the function **Chart Options...** (see Figure 7.51, Step 1). In the **Chart Options** pop-up that opens, in the **Legend** tab, you can select the position of the legend (see Figure 7.51, Steps 2 and 3). The settings copied by clicking on the **OK** button (see Figure 7.51, Step 4).

Similarly, in the **Edit Chart** pop-up, you can call up the **Format axis** function by double-clicking on an axis (see Figure 7.51, Step 5) (in the example: Y-axis of the chart). After selecting the **Number** tab (see Figure 7.51, Step 6), you can select the desired formatting from the **Number formats** selection list by highlighting it (see Figure 7.51, Step 7). Click on the **OK** button in the pop-ups to copy these settings (see Figure 7.51, Steps 8 and 9).

Axis formatting

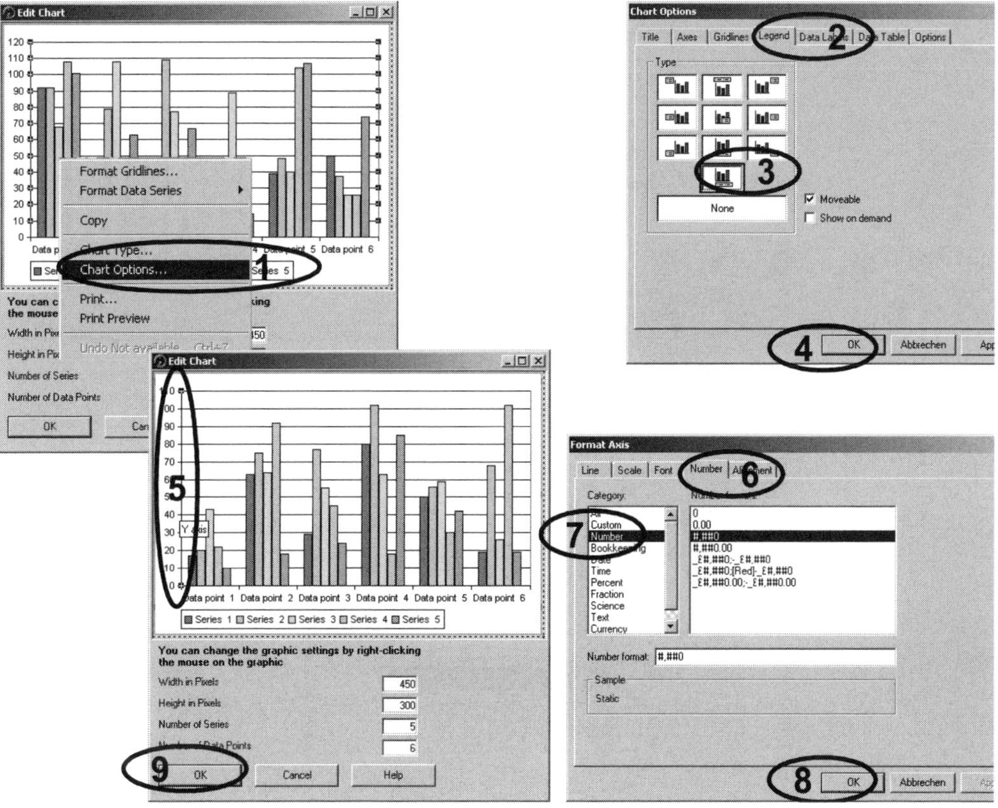

Figure 7.51 Web Item Properties of the Bar Chart, Part 2

In the **Edit Chart** pop-up, you can open the context-sensitive menu for the chart area by right-clicking (see Figure 7.52, Step 1) to call up the **Format Plot Area** function and set the type and color of the frame (see Figure 7.52, Steps 2 to 5). After you save the Web template, the execution of the Web application shows the changed chart settings (see Figure 7.52, Step 5).

Formatting chart spaces

If a query result should be displayed as a pie chart, then the general settings for a given result table (see Figure 7.53, Step 1) should be configured as explained above (see Figure 7.53, Steps 2 to 4). The Web item properties can be adjusted as displayed in Figure 7.54.

Practical settings for pie charts

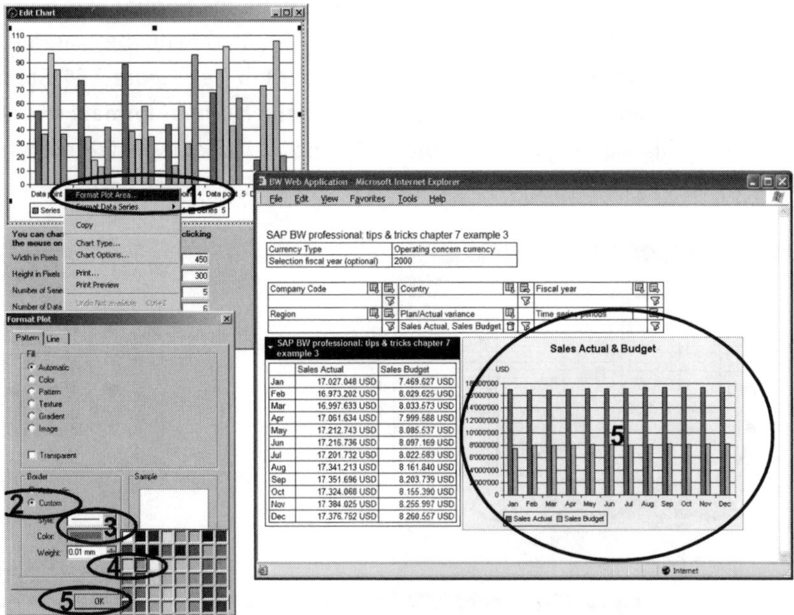

	Sales Actual	Sales Budget
Jan	17.027.048 USD	7.469.627 USD
Feb	16.973.202 USD	8.029.625 USD
Mar	16.997.633 USD	8.033.673 USD
Apr	17.061.634 USD	7.999.588 USD
May	17.212.743 USD	8.085.537 USD
Jun	17.216.736 USD	8.097.169 USD
Jul	17.201.732 USD	8.022.583 USD
Aug	17.341.213 USD	8.161.840 USD
Sep	17.351.696 USD	8.203.739 USD
Oct	17.324.068 USD	8.155.390 USD
Nov	17.384.025 USD	8.255.997 USD
Dec	17.376.752 USD	8.260.557 USD

Figure 7.52 Web Item Properties of the Bar Chart, Part 3

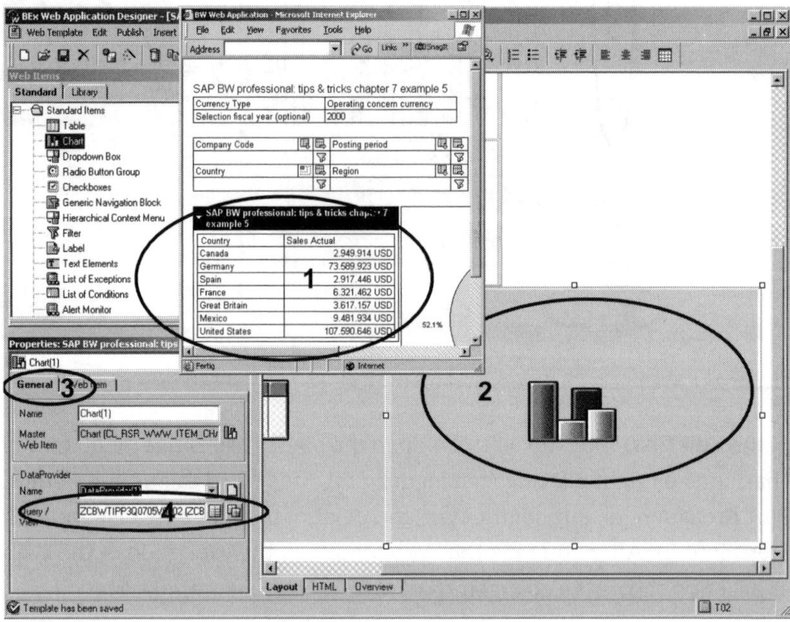

Country	Sales Actual
Canada	2.949.914 USD
Germany	73.589.923 USD
Spain	2.917.446 USD
France	6.321.462 USD
Great Britain	3.617.157 USD
Mexico	9.481.934 USD
United States	107.590.646 USD

Figure 7.53 Result Table for Pie Chart

Properties of the Web item "Chart (Pie chart)"

After you change to the **Web Item** tab, the properties can be edited (see Figure 7.54, Steps 1 and 2). Often the display of the title using exterior frames is omitted (instead the language-dependent chart title is used). Similarly, many charts with the default setting in the 300 dpi size are not legible. Therefore, the width of the chart in pixels (in the example 450) is changed (see Figure 7.54, Step 3).

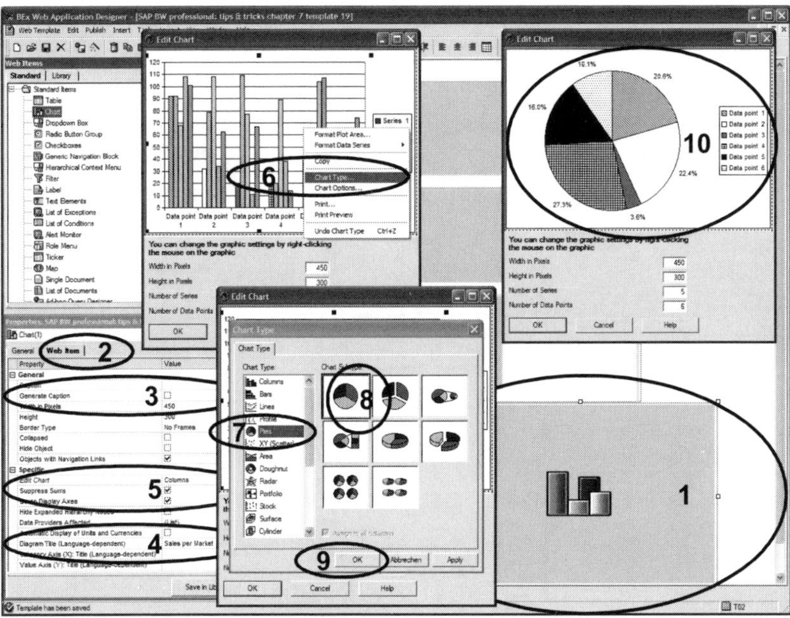

Figure 7.54 Web Item Properties of the Pie Chart, Part 1

In the **Specific** folder (Web item properties), the special property **Chart title** can be specified (see Figure 7.54, Step 4). With the specified table form (with the rubric "Country" in the rows and a code as data row in the columns), activate the function **Swap Display Axes** (see Figure 7.54, Step 5). Concurrently, double-click on the **Chart Type** (on the default characteristic **Edit bars for chart**) to activate the editing of the chart.

Change chart type

Then, the **Edit Chart** pop-up will open. On the chart, right-click on the context-sensitive menu and select **Chart Type...** (see Figure 7.54, Step 6). Then, the **Chart Type** pop-up opens. Right-click to select the desired type and subtype (see Figure 7.54, Steps 7 and 8) (in the example: chart type "Pies"). After you click on the **OK** button (see Figure 7.54, Step 9), the chart type is copied into the **Edit Chart** pop-up (see Figure 7.54, Step 10).

Changing color attributes

For pie charts, adjustment of the color attributes is often necessary. For this, primarily the **Number of Data Points** must be entered (see Figure

7.55, Step 1) for which colors and patterns should be defined. Then, with a double-click on a legend symbol to be adjusted (see Figure 7.55, Step 2), the **Format Legend Key** pop-up opens in which the desired combination of color and pattern can be set (see Figure 7.55, Step 3). After you click on the **OK** button (see Figure 7.55, Step 4), the color attributes are copied into the **Edit Chart** pop-up.

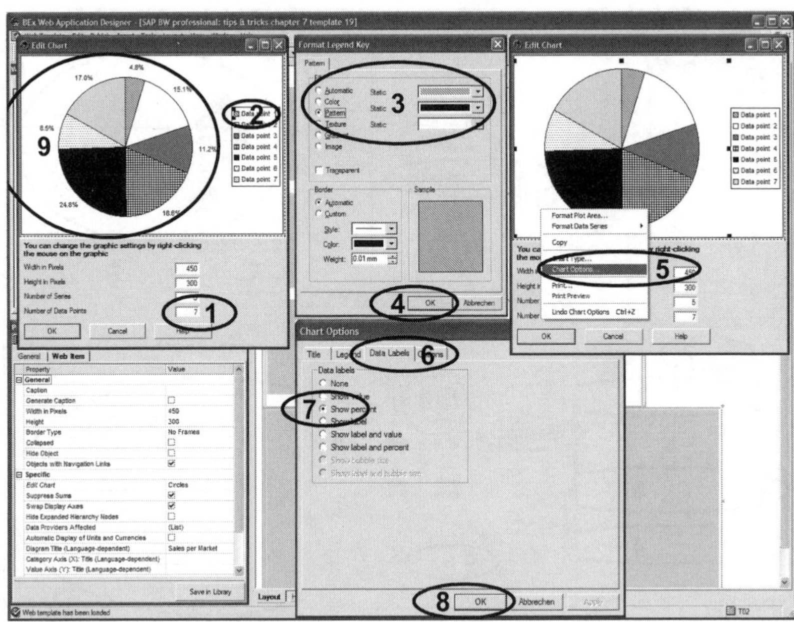

Figure 7.55 Web Item Properties of the Pie Chart, Part 2

Display Values in the chart

Furthermore, to improve the expressive properties of the pie chart, you can display a portion of the various characteristics as you desire. This setting can be undertaken in the **Edit Chart** pop-up by opening the context-sensitive menu and selecting the **Chart Options...** (see Figure 7.55, Step 5): In the **Chart Options** pop-up, on the **Data Labels** tab, the **Show percent** property is selected (see Figure 7.55, Steps 6 and 7). After you click on the **OK** button (see Figure 7.55, Step 8), the changed settings copied into the **Edit Chart** pop-up (see Figure 7.55, Step 9).

Formatting of the values in charts

If necessary, the default formatting in the chart must be adjusted. To do this, the **Format Data Labels** pop-up must be opened with a double-click on a title in the **Edit Chart** pop-up (see Figure 7.56, Step 1). There, for example, the **Number** tab can be selected (see Figure 7.56, Step 2) in order to change the default setting (in the example, the category "Percent") manually from two to one decimal place (see Figure 7.56, Step 3).

After you click on the **OK** button (see Figure 7.56, Step 4), the changed settings are copied into the **Edit Chart** popup (see Figure 7.56, Step 5). With another click of the **OK** button (see Figure 7.56, Step 6), all settings for the chart are copied into the Web Application Designer: the chart type bars is replaced in the special Web item properties by the type pie (see Figure 7.56, Step 7).

After you save the Web template, execution of the Web application shows the changed chart settings (see Figure 7.56, Step 8).

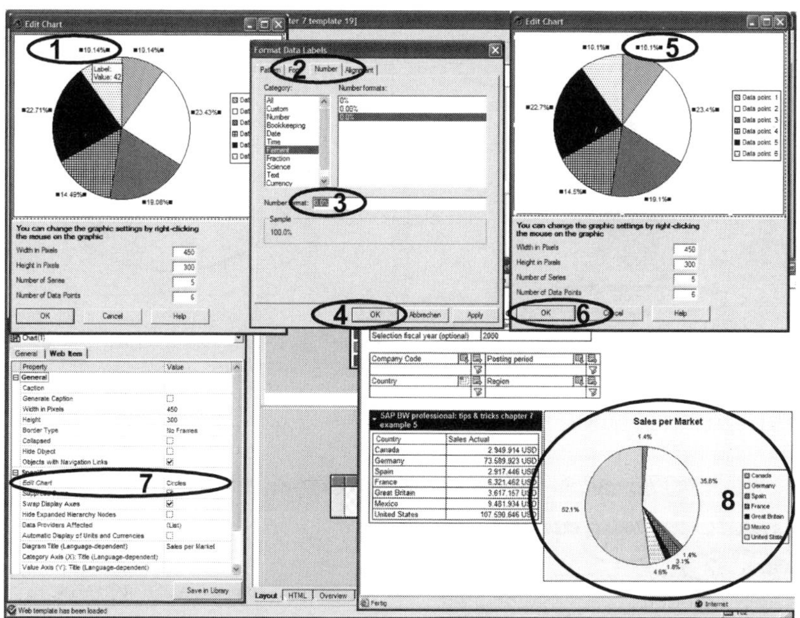

Figure 7.56 Web Item Properties of the Pie Chart, Part 3

7.4.15 Map (Map Chart)

The Web item **Map** displays the contents of a query result with a geo-relevant drilldown characteristic on a map chart. The general properties of the Web item **Map** can be set similarly to the properties you set for the previous Web items.

Selecting data providers

The Web item **Map** gets its data from a data provider. You specify the data provider that you want to use after takeover of the chart into the layout, or after you select the item by double-clicking on it (see Figure 7.57, Step 1). In the **General** tab, you select the data provider that provides the values for the corresponding map level (the first level is created automatically by incorporating the Web item into the Web template) (see Figure 7.57, Steps 2 and 3).

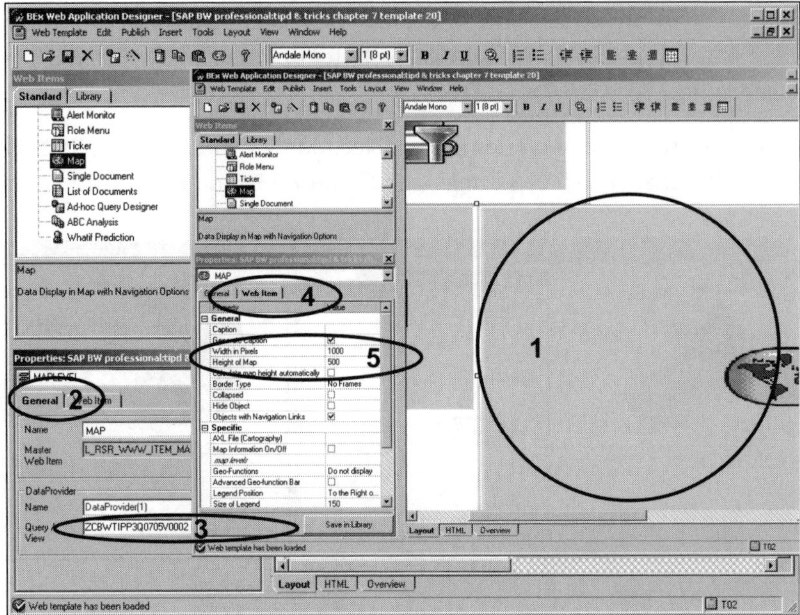

Figure 7.57 Basic Settings for the Web Item "Map"

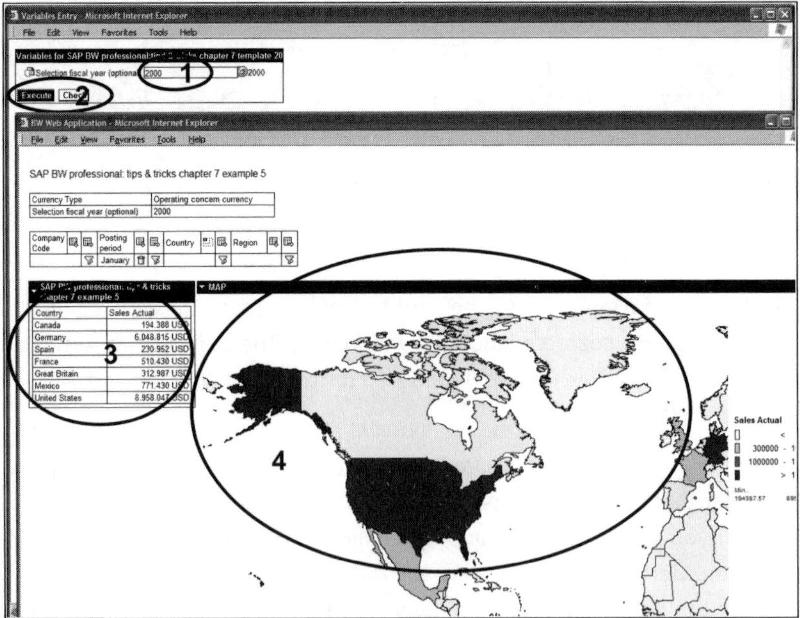

Figure 7.58 Basic Function of the Map (Map Chart)

Settings for height and width

Therefore, you can use the Web item map immediately. Because the legend provided automatically covers a majority of the surfaces provided by the default settings, however, the general Web item properties **Width in Pixels** (in the example: 1000) and **Height of Map** (in the example: 500 without automatic calculation) must often be adjusted (see Figure 7.57, Steps 4 and 5).

Already due to these simple settings, after you select the variable value ("Fiscal year 2000") and click on the **Execute** button (see Figure 7.58, Steps 1 and 2), the map is displayed. (See Figure 7.58, Step 4, for a tabular display of the data of the underlying data provider, Step 3.)

Geographic function bar

The advanced geo-function bar allows the following (note that in the default settings, this bar is not visible):

- Change of size ("Zoom") with the following buttons:
  - + for Zoom in
  - – for Zoom out
  - Globe for restore to full size
- Move the map section according to the point of the compass with the following buttons:
  - ← to move west
  - → to move east
  - ↑ to move north
  - ↓ to move south

After you change to the **Web Item** tab, this property can be changed (see Figure 7.59, Step 1). By selecting a position for the geographic function bar (see Figure 7.59, Step 2), after you save the Web template, it will be displayed during execution of the Web application (see Figure 7.59, Step 3). By clicking on the zoom and positioning buttons (in the example: + for enlarging and for moving to the north), the enlarged map section Europe is displayed (see Figure 7.59, Step 4).

Property "Visible map area"

Because you can use the explicit setting of **Visible map area property**, you can create a navigation that has a significant improvement in clarity. If the special property of the Web item map is set to **Data Only** (see Figure 7.60, Steps 1 and 2), then only that section of the map is displayed, that is, the section that contains data. Therefore, an automatic zoom occurs. Especially with the function **Filter and drilldown according to...** the zoom and positioning steps are omitted (see Figure 7.61).

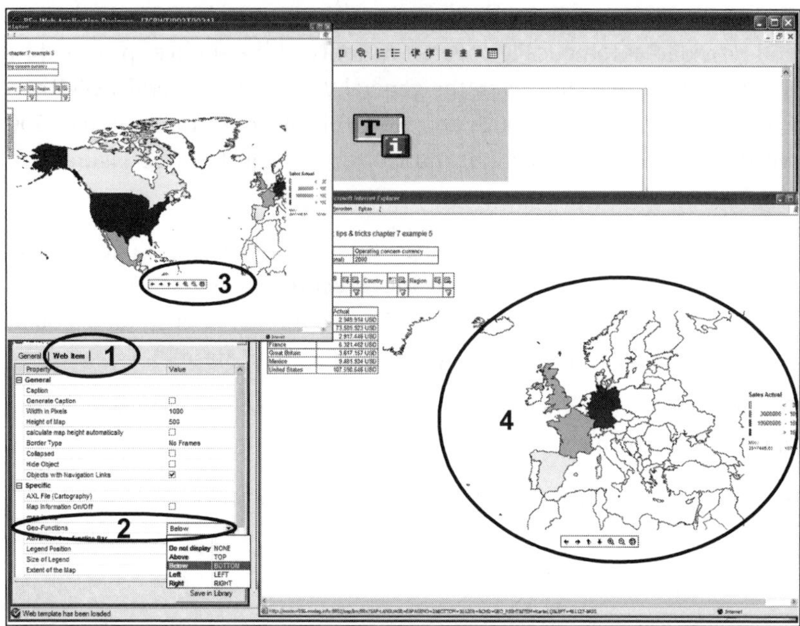

Figure 7.59 Using the Geographic Toolbar

Map level

A particularity of the Web item map are its map levels. The levels of a map contain various geographic or economic information. In the Web application, the individual levels are laid on top of one another to form the total view of the map. Per map level, there are corresponding properties available. Consequently, it is necessary in the selection list with the Web items to branch out into the class levels to be edited (see Figure 7.60, Step 3).

Property "Number of Classes"

In the example, the property **Number of Classes** will be set for the color shading to be generated based on the query result (see Figure 7.60, Step 4).

Individual values

Similarly, set the **Individual Values** property in order to set a more defined color for the shading. To do this, activate the drop-down box for this special property of the map level (see Figure 7.60, Step 5). In the **Individual Values** pop-up that opens, open the **Colors** pop-up by activating the drop-down box in the **Individual Color Values** column (see Figure 7.60, Step 6). Right-click on the color of shading that you want in order to select it (see Figure 7.60, Step 7). Click on the **OK** button to copy this setting into the **Individual Values** pop-up (see Figure 7.60, Step 8).

For the color values, the upper threshold value for the selected color value must be input into the column **Upper class limit** (see Figure 7.60, Step 6). Click on the **OK** button in order to copy the settings into the

Web template (see Figure 7.60, Step 9). After you save the Web template, the changed properties are applied in the Web application during execution.

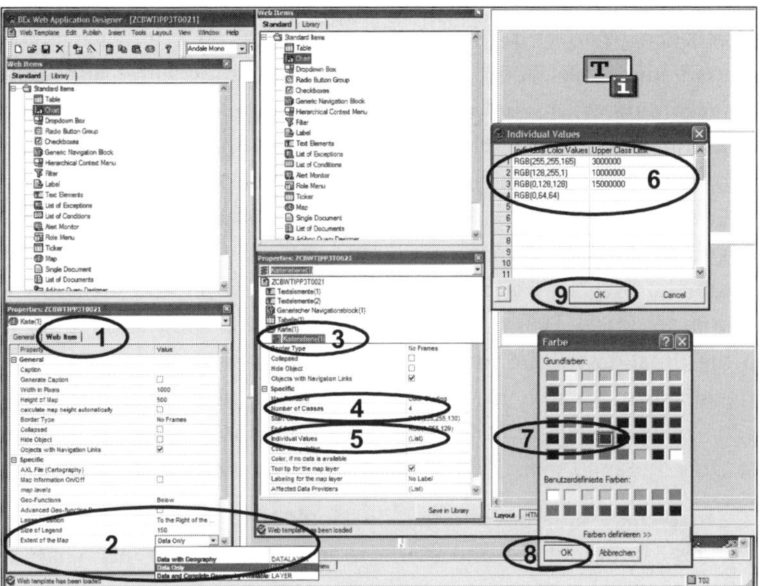

Figure 7.60 Adjustment of the Web Item "Map"

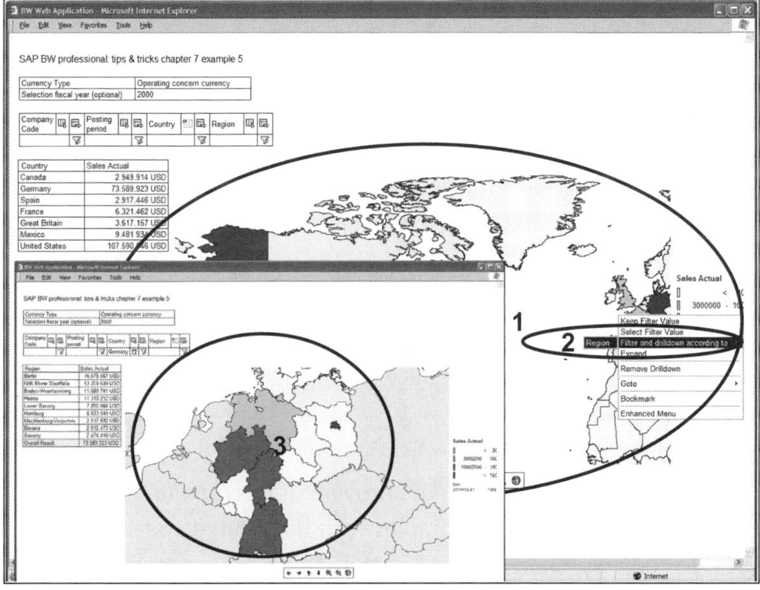

Figure 7.61 Execution of the Web Template with the Adjusted Map Chart

By setting the **Extent of the Map** property to **Data Only**, at the start of the Web application, only those countries from the world map section (for which data exist) are displayed. Similarly, the explicitly specified class limits and colors are applied immediately (see Figure 7.61, Step 1).

Navigation in the map chart

The Web item **Map** of the SAP BW Web application is interactive and supports various navigation possibilities. The function **Filter and drill-down according to...** is explained in the following example: if in the data provider underlying a map chart, there are additional geo-relevant drill-down characteristics available, by selecting a characteristic (in the example: "Country Germany") via right-clicking on it, you can open the context-sensitive menu and incorporate this geo-relevant characteristic (in the example: "Region") by selecting the function **Filter and breakdown according to...**, (see Figure 7.61, Step 2). In the Web application, there is then the **Breakdown due to drilldown** in the map on the selected geo characteristic. In the example, the sales of German federal states are evaluated in color (see Figure 7.61, Step 3). By setting the visible map range to **Data Only**, the map selection is optimized automatically once again.

Use of several map levels

If, on a map chart, different information should be displayed, then several map levels can be defined and used. As an example, on a map chart in addition to the color evaluation of the sales volume of the respective geographic drill-down characteristic, information about actual and planned sales is displayed simultaneously in the form of a bar chart.

Based on the previous example, the configuration occurs in the following steps:

Second map level

1. **Adding a second map level**
   After selecting the Web item **Map** by double-clicking on it, select the **Web Item** (see Figure 7.62 Step 1). By right-clicking on the **Specific** properties, the drop-down box for the "map levels" property is activated (see Figure 7.62, Step 2). This opens the **Map Layers for Map ...** pop-up, where by clicking the **Add Map Layer** button, the second map level is defined (see Figure 7.62, Step 3). After you click on the **Close** button, this setting is copied to the Web template (see Figure 7.62, Step 4).

Assigning data provider

2. **Data Provider**
   For map level 1, the required data provider is assigned (here, the query view used in the previous examples with the limited code "Actual net sales" in the column as well as the drill-down characteristic "Country" and the free characteristic "Region" is assigned) (see Figure 7.62, Step 5).

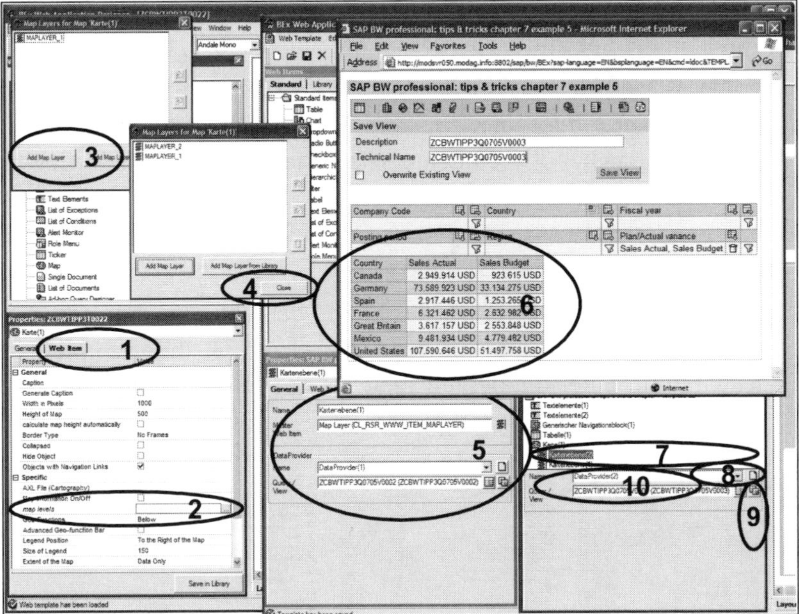

Figure 7.62 Configuration of a Map Chart with Two Levels, Part 1

For the second map level, a query or a query view is provided that contains the necessary codes for this level (in the example: limited code "Actual net sales" and "Planned net sales") as well as the necessary breakdown characteristic (in the example: characteristic "Country") and the required free characteristic (in the example: characteristic "Region").

In the example, for this a new query view is in from the Web Application Designer using the **Tools** pull-down menu, **Function view definition...** (see Figure 7.62, Step 6).

The assignment of this data provider occurs in the Web Application Designer, the list (hierarchy) of Web items is opened and map level 2 is selected (see Figure 7.62, Step 7). Then in the **General** tab, click the **New Data Provider** button (see Figure 7.62, Step 8). After this, by clicking on the **View** button (see Figure 7.62, Step 9), the required source can be assigned (see Figure 7.62, Step 10).

Assigning map renderer

3. **Map renderer**
   With a map renderer, you can specify how the BW data should be displayed on a map level.

   On map level 1, the data is displayed with color shading (see previous examples). To do this, open the list (hierarchy) of Web items, select the map level 1, and activate the **Web Item** tab (see Figure 7.63, Step 1). There, in the **Specific** properties, as described above, the attributes of the color shading are selected (see Figure 7.63, Step 2).

On map level 2, the data is displayed with a bar chart. To do this, open the list (hierarchy) of Web items, select the map level 2, and activate the **Web Item** tab (see Figure 7.63, Step 3). There, in the **Specific** property **Renderer of a Map**, activate the drop-down box and select the bar chart entry (see Figure 7.63, Step 4).

If necessary, the property bar height and bar width must be adjusted for the map renderer of the type "bar chart" (in the example: bar height 100). Enter the desired value for the respective property (see Figure 7.63, Step 5).

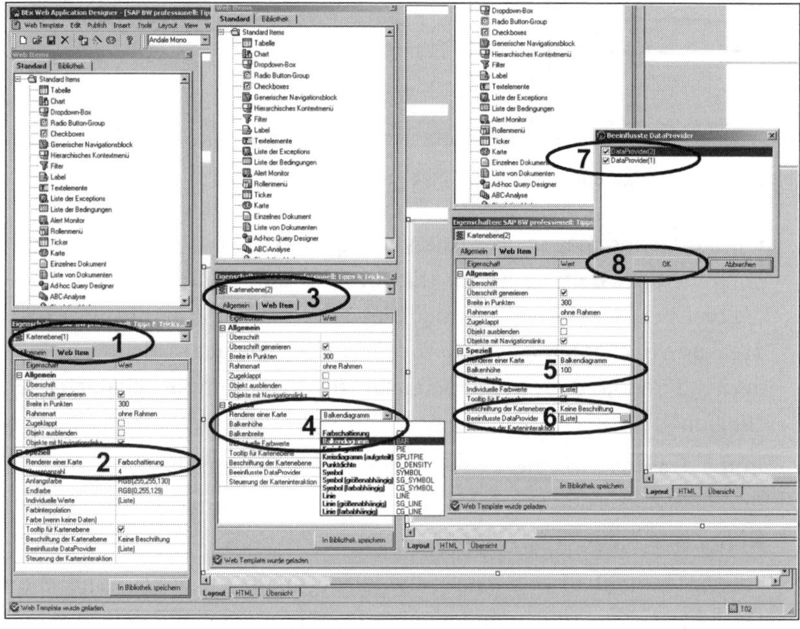

Figure 7.63 Configuration of a Map Chart with Two Levels, Part 2

Influenced data providers

4. **Influenced data providers**
So that during navigation (e.g., **Filter and drilldown according to ...**) the navigation is handed down to both map levels, the property **Influenced Data Providers** is edited: on each map level, the drop-down box of the property **Influenced Data Providers** is activated (see Figure 7.63, Step 6). In the pop-up with the same name, both data providers are selected (see Figure 7.63, Step 7). By clicking on the **OK** button, the settings are copied into the Web template (see Figure 7.63, Step 8).

After you save the Web template, the changed properties are applied in the Web application during execution.

Web application with several map levels

After you select the variable value ("Fiscal year 2000") and click on the **Execute** button (see Figure 7.64, Steps 1 and 2), the map chart is displayed with two map levels: with the map level 1 in the example, actual net sales is indicated in the chart with coloring of the map. At the same time on the map level 2 for each country, the actual and planned sales are displayed via a bar chart (see Figure 64, Step 3). In the legend, the limit values of the charts for both map levels are displayed (see Figure 7.64, Step 4).

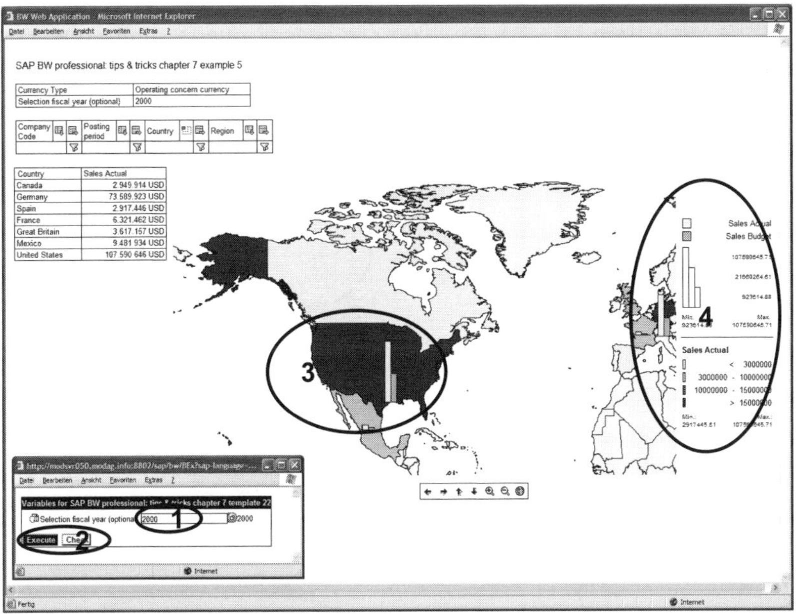

Figure 7.64 Execution of a Map Chart with Two Levels

7.4.16 The Alert Monitor

Based on exceptions by the reporting agent, the Web item **Alert Monitor** displays the alerts that were reported as a list or hierarchy with traffic-light symbols in the Web application. With the assistance of the Web item **Alert Monitor**, you can also jump into the query views ascertained by the exception reporting and the reporting agent in order to see at-a-glance conspicuous results that deviate from defined threshold values.

Because there is only one data source for the Alert Monitor, the Web item **Alert Monitor** must not be assigned a data provider during the definition of the Web template. The Web item **Alert Monitor** creates an appropriate data provider for itself automatically and forwards the filter operations to it automatically.

Requirements of the Alert Monitor

Prerequisites for the display of alerts in the Alert Monitor of the SAP BW Web application are exceptions defined in queries, which were evaluated as alerts in the reporting agent.

Basic settings of the Alert Monitor

After the Web item Alert Monitor has been copied into the layout, the activation of the **General** tab in the **Properties...** frame shows that no data provider assignment is necessary or possible (see Figure 7.65, Steps 1 to 3). To use the Alert Monitor in the Web application, as a minimum configuration, you must specify the source of the alert in the s properties on the **Web Item** tab: for this, you can specify queries, InfoCubes, or InfoAreas (see Figure 7.65, Steps 4 and 5).

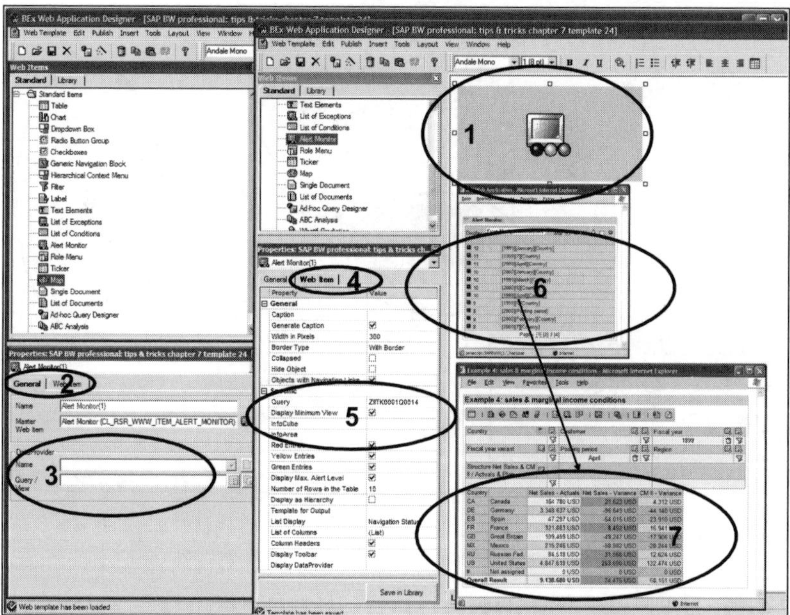

Figure 7.65 Basic Settings and Functions of the Alert Monitor

After saving the Web template, you can use the Alert Monitor in the Web application during execution. Starting the Web template with the Alert Monitor shows a list of traffic-light symbols and texts (see Figure 7.65, Step 6). If an alert is selected by right-clicking on it, the Web application generates a query view, which displays the underlying query precisely (with the underlying selection and the required drilldown) so that the selected exceptions are displayed (see Figure 7.65, Step 7).

Adjustment of the Web item "Alert Monitor"

With various settings in the reporting agent in the Administrator Workbench of SAP BW and also in the Web Application Designer, additional information and functions are available in this Web item.

Because the Alert Monitor contains no explanatory texts, without a descriptive title, you cannot deduce the meaning of the alerts. Therefore, using a title is often required. As for the other Web items, this is set by selecting the **Web Item** tab and activating the general property **Generate Caption** (see Figure 7.66, Steps 1 to 3).

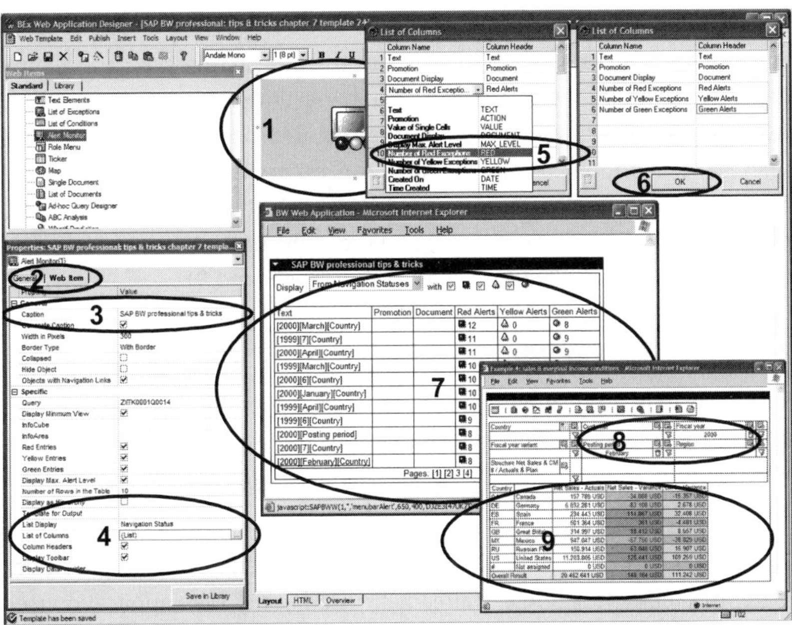

Figure 7.66 Adjustment of the Alert Monitor

The setting of the **Specific** property **List Display** (here a default list of individual cells makes sense) and the **Display Toolbar** property expand the flexibility of the Alert Monitor (see Figure 7.66, Step 4). In addition, the tabular display of the alerts offers additional information and functions. To do this, activate the property **Column Headers** and right-click to display the drop-down box of the **List of Columns** property (see Figure 7.66, Step 4). In the **List of Columns** pop-up, select the respective desired value by activating the drop-down box in the **Column name** column (see Figure 7.66, Step 5). Click on the **OK** button to copy the settings into the Web template (see Figure 7.66, Step 6).

Execution of the Web Application with Adjusted Alert Monitor

After you save the Web template, the Alert Monitor can be used in the Web application during execution: the start of the Web template with the Alert Monitor shows the list of traffic-light symbols and texts (see Figure 7.66, Step 7). With the toolbox, the desired display can be selected via the **Display of the Alert Monitor** drop-down box from various list forms. With the tabular display, there are also other functions (such as action and document links) and information available (for which the Alert Monitor entry shows how many alerts of which type—red, green, yellow—are present) in addition to the respectively highest alert level and the text description (see Figure 7.66, Step 7).

If an alert is now selected with a click of the mouse, the Web application generates a query view, which displays the underlying query precisely (with the underlying selection and the required breakdown) so that the selected exceptions are displayed: in the example, the selection of the alert "Germany [Region]" occurs. With the selection with a click of the mouse, the selection ("Germany") and the relevant breakdown ("Region") is applied automatically (see Figure 7.66, Steps 8 and 9).

7.4.17 The Role Menu

The Web item **Role menu** enables the calling of functions (e.g., Web applications) using the favorites or roles of a user in a tree display. For this Web item, no data provider must or can be assigned when defining the Web template.

With the incorporation of the Web item **Role menu** into the Web template, this menu function can already be used in the Web application (see Figure 7.67, Step 1). After saving the Web template, you can execute the Web application and display a Web page with the favorites and roles (see Figure 7.67, Step 2). After you select an entry by right-clicking (if necessary, after opening the role or favorite tree), the underlying function (in the example: starting a Web application with map chart) is executed (see Figure 7.67, Step 3).

For many application cases, explicit settings of the properties are required. The freely configurable properties of the role menu can be divided into various groups: properties for setting layout functions, of the SAP BW functionality, and for configuration of the browser properties.

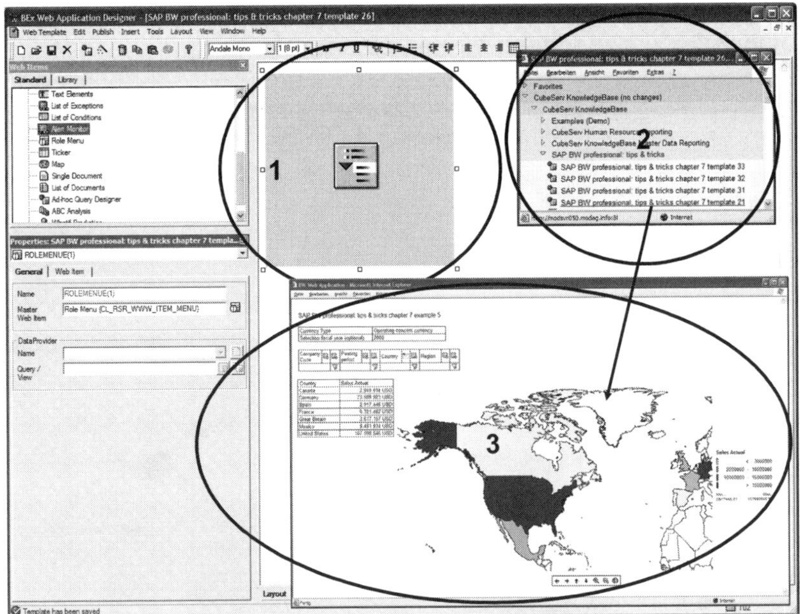

Figure 7.67 Basic Functions of the Web Item "Role Menu"

Layout functions

The following layout functions are available:

- Display the scroll bar
- Switch on/off the display of the current user and a logo icon
- Selection of the logo with the associated path
- Setting whether the menu is displayed with or without colors
- Setting whether the display of the menu occurs with or without icons

These settings occur in addition to the general properties in the **Specific** properties folder on the **Web Item** tab of the role menu: for this, highlight the symbol for the role menu on the layout and by right-clicking, change to the **Web Item** tab in the **Properties** frame (see Figure 7.68, Steps 1 and 2). In addition to setting the general properties (see Figure 7.68, Step 3), in the example, the property **Display Toolbar** must be left at the default value. If needed (see Figure 7.68, Step 4), the display of user and logo is activated, the display of the first level of the role menu (often not desired since it displays the technical descriptions of the SAP roles) is deactivated, and the **Display With Icons** (symbols for the various types of menu entries in the role menu) was left at the default value "Active" (see Figure 7.68, Step 5).

After you save the Web template, the settings are used during execution of the Web application (see Figure 7.68, Step 6).

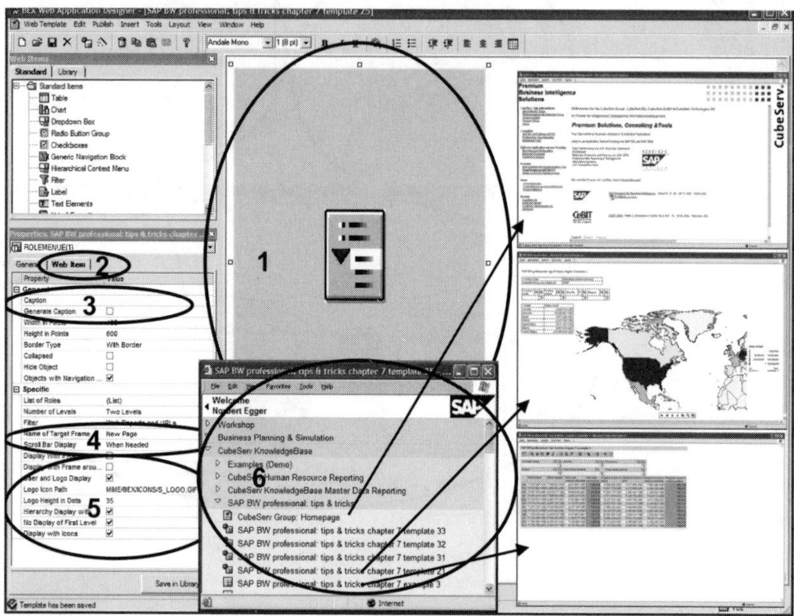

Figure 7.68 Adjustment of the Layout Functions of the Role Menu

SAP BW Functionality

The settings for SAP BW functionality contain the following:

- The selection of the roles to be displayed
- The setting for the number of levels of the role menu to be read initially
- The filtering of role menu entries

They also occur (in addition to the demonstration of alternative settings for the example layout) (see Figure 7.69, Step 3) in the special properties of the Web item role menu (in preparation, see Figure 7.69, Steps 1 and 2).

Selection of the Roles to be displayed

By activating the drop-down box for the property **List of Roles**, the pop-up with the same name is opened. There, a list of the roles to be displayed can be created, in that in the rows of the **Name of the Role** column, the drop-down box for role selection is activated (see Figure 7.69, Step 4) and the desired roles are taken over in the desired sequence (see Figure 7.69, Step 5). The settings are copied by clicking on the **OK** button in the Web template (see Figure 7.69, Step 6).

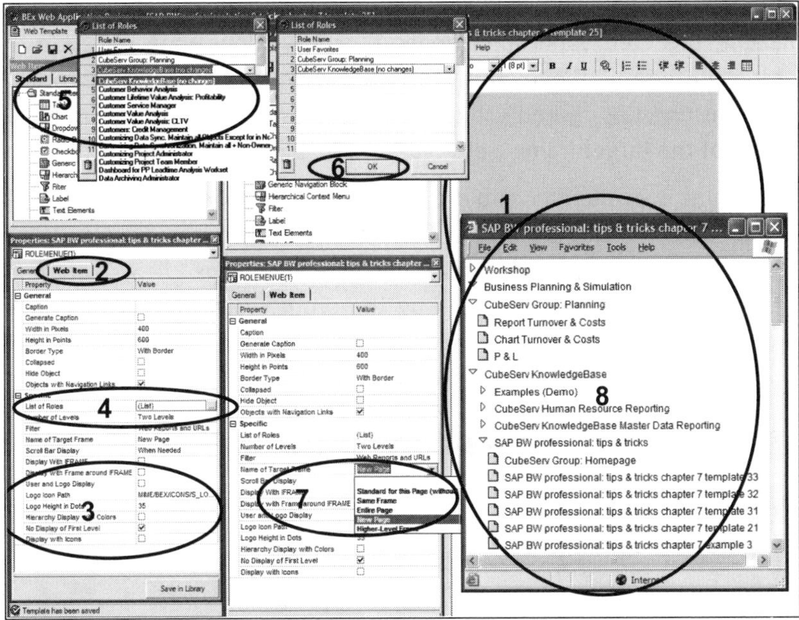

Figure 7.69 Adjustment of the Properties for SAP BW Functionality

Number of levels

If roles with many entries must be displayed, the construction of the role menu in the Web application can be time-consuming. To deal with this issue, the property **Number of Levels** is available. If, for this property, a value not equal to 0 is entered, then initially during the construction of the role menu, only the specified number of levels is read. The additional levels of the role menu are read only after opening (see Figure 7.69, Step 4). If the value 0 is specified, then initially all levels are read.

Filtering of role menu entries

By activating the drop-down box filters, the desired types of menu entries for display in the role menu in the Web applications can be selected (see Figure 7.69, Step 7). In the example, these are: "All Web Reports and URLs".

After you save the settings, the Web application displays the settings undertaken during execution (see Figure 7.69, Step 8).

Configuration of the browser properties

The settings for the browser properties contain the following points:

- Control of the target frame during execution of menu positions
- Alternative display in the iFrame
- Display with frame and iFrame

Target frame They occur in the special properties of the Web item **Role menu**. By default, the Web application opens a new window upon selection of entries in the role menu. This function can be configured by activating and selecting the desired value in the drop-down box for the property **Name of the target frame** (see Figure 7.69, Step 7).

The iFrame The iFrame is an alternative to the independent menu window. In the special properties of the Web item **Role menu**, the property **Display With IFRAME** must be activated for this (see Figure 7.70, Steps 1 to 3). If desired, this can be suppressed optically by the property **Display With Frame around IFRAME**. After you save the settings, the Web application displays the settings undertaken during execution (see Figure 7.70, Step 4).

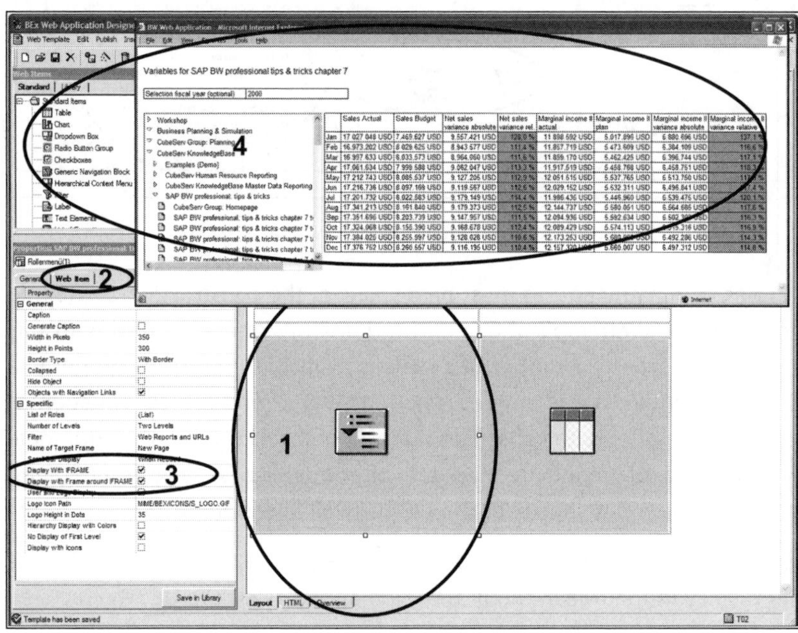

Figure 7.70 Use of the iFrame for the Role Menu

Problems when using iFrames The advantage of this functionality is the information that is provided when the SAP BW Web application first starts. In practice, this solution is generally insufficient: a Web application with iFrames will run only in browsers that support the iFrame technology.

Even if information is already displayed in addition to the role menu at the start of the Web application, during execution of entries from the role menu, either a new window must be opened, or the report must be displayed in the same frame (where the role menu once again would not be in the display), or the iFrame with the role menu must be incorporated in all reports (whereby the problem of menu entries like "normal" Web addresses would not be solved).

Combination of HTML and SAP BW functionality

A better solution can usually be accomplished with the combination of HTML with the SAP BW functionality. The role menu and the reports to be executed from it are embedded in a frameset. While the role menu is executed in a left menu frame, for example, all URLs started from here are displayed in a content frame arranged next door.

Defining a frameset

A frameset to be created using an HTML editor forms the basis:

```
<HEAD>
  <TITLE>IIT Application &amp; Business Services AG</
TITLE>
</HEAD>
<FRAMESET FRAMEBORDER="0" BORDER="FALSE" cols="420,*">
  <FRAME NAME="Daten" SRC="URL_Rollenmenue">
  <FRAME NAME="Text" SRC="URL_Startseite">
  <noframes>
    Ihr Browser kann diese Seite leider nicht anzeigen.
  </noframes>
</FRAMESET>
</HTML>
```

The placeholder for the URL with the role menu (in the coding: `URL_Rollenmenue`) can be replaced with the URL of the Web application, for example:

```
http://modsvr050.modag.info:8802/sap/bw/BEx?sap-langu-
age=DE&cmd=ldoc&TEMPLATE_ID=ZCBWTIPP3T0027
```

The placeholder for the URL with the start page of the content frame (in the coding: `URL_Startseite`) can be replaced with the desired URL, for example:

```
http://www.iit-abs.ch/IITHome.htm
```

Defining Web template with role menu

For the navigation frame, a corresponding Web template must be defined with the Web item role menu. The configuration occurs as explained in the following examples. Please note that for the property **Name of Target Frame**, that frame name is specified (see Figure 7.71, Steps 1 to 3) that was provided in the HTML coding as the content frame (in the example: `<FRAME NAME="Text" ...>`).

After you save the Web template and the HTML coding with the frameset, the Web application displays the settings undertaken during execution (see Figure 7.71, Steps 4 to 6). In the example, the start of the frameset occurs (see Figure 7.71, Step 4). In the right frame, the start content is displayed; in the left frame, the SAP BW Web application is executed (see Figure 7.71, Step 5). After you right-click to select a menu option, this Web application is executed in the right content frame (see Figure 7.71, Step 6).

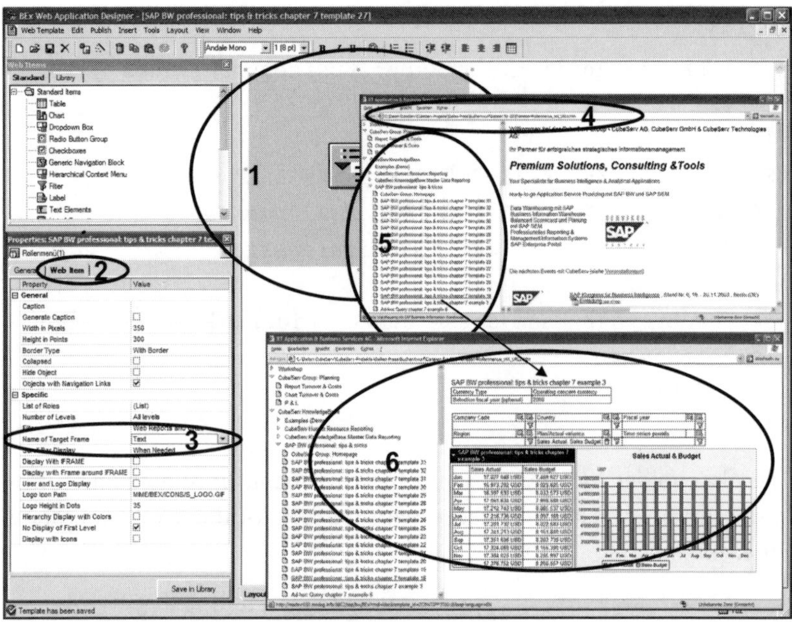

Figure 7.71 Web Template with Role Menu and Application of the Frameset Solution

Meaning of the role menu

The use of the Web item role menu enables the use of the authorization control and dynamic roles and thus enables professional menu control.

7.4.18 Individual Document

The Web item **Individual document** enables the display of individual documents that were created in the Administrator Workbench, in the main data maintenance or document processing in the Web application.

Characteristic Is document property

The settings in the Administrator Workbench and the main data are a prerequisite for using the documents. In the maintenance of the InfoObject in the Administrator Workbench (Transaction RSA 14), for the complete usability of the document incorporation even for movement data, the

InfoObject property **Characteristic Is Document Property** is activated (see Figure 7.72, Step 1).

Documents for main data

Assigning the documents in the main data maintenance to main data is another prerequisite. To create such documents, in the maintenance image, you must highlight a main data item by right-clicking on it and then click on the **Documents for Characteristic** button (see Figure 7.72, Steps 2 and 3). The documents listed in the **Display of Documents for Characteristic** specification are available for reporting in SAP BW (see Figure 7.72, Step 4).

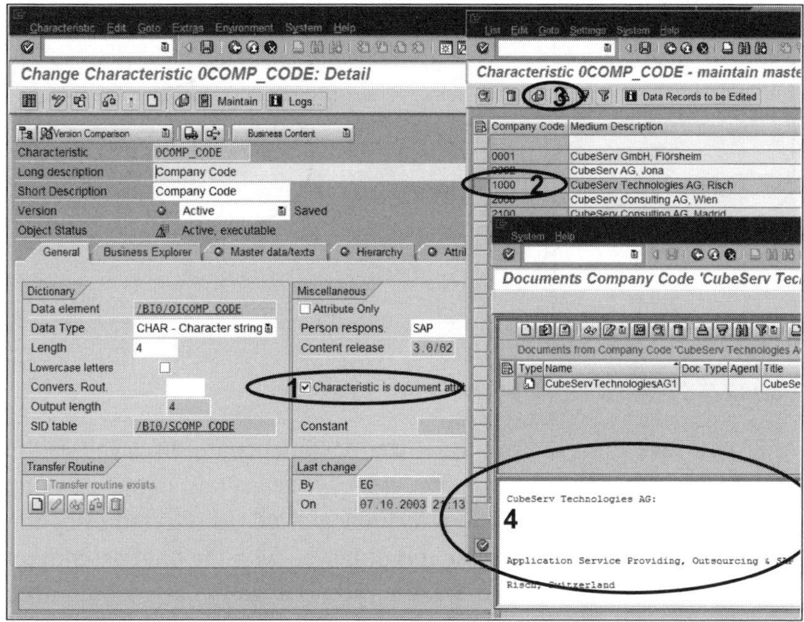

Figure 7.72 Configuration of the InfoObject and Document based on the Class "Main data"

Selecting data providers

The Web item **Individual document** gets its data from a data provider. You specify the data provider that you want to use after the Web item is copied into the layout, or after you select the item by double-clicking on it (see Figure 7.73, Step 1). In the **General** tab, you select the data provider that provides the values (this is analogous to the explanations for the data providers described above).

Selecting a characteristic

In addition, you must select the characteristic whose document should be displayed. To do this, you must branch out to the **Web Item** tab (see Figure 7.73, Step 2). In the **Specific** folder, activate the drop-down box for the property **Characteristic** and select the desired InfoObject (see Figure 7.73, Step 3).

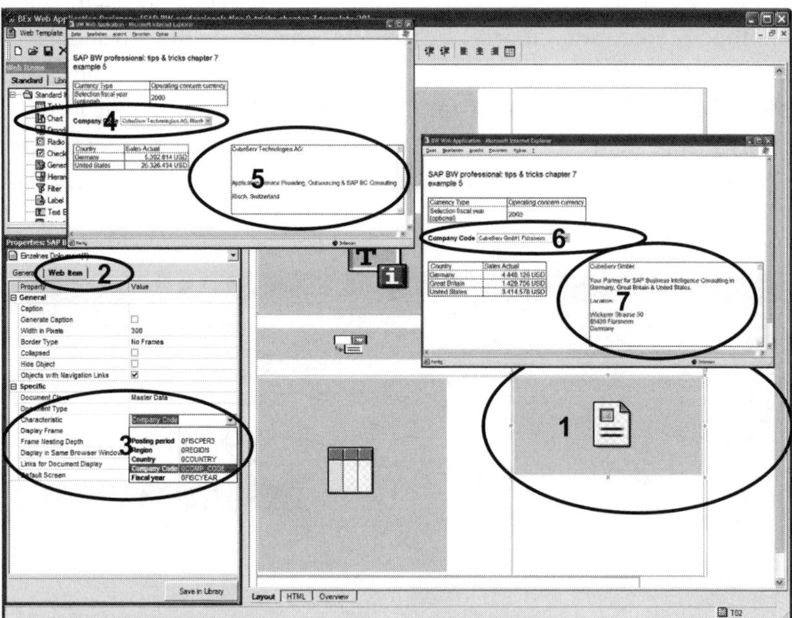

Figure 7.73 Individual Documents in the Web Application

After you save the Web template, the documents are displayed in the Web application depending on the respective selections: in the example, the accounting sector "CubeServ Technologies AG" is selected using the drop-down box and the document is displayed with the brief description (see Figure 7.73, Steps 4 and 5). After you change the selection (in the example: "CubeServ GmbH"), the data and also the document for the changed selection is displayed (see Figure 7.73, Steps 6 and 7).

Editing the Web item "Individual Document"

Analogous to the explanations for the abovementioned Web items, a corresponding setting of the properties of the Web item **Individual Document** may make sense to provide another type of information: in the example, the display of the title is omitted and the width is adjusted (see Figure 7.74, Steps 1 to 3). Instead of the direct display of the corresponding document, a selection-dependent link to the document display with simultaneous omission of display in the same browser window is selected (see Figure 7.74, Step 4).

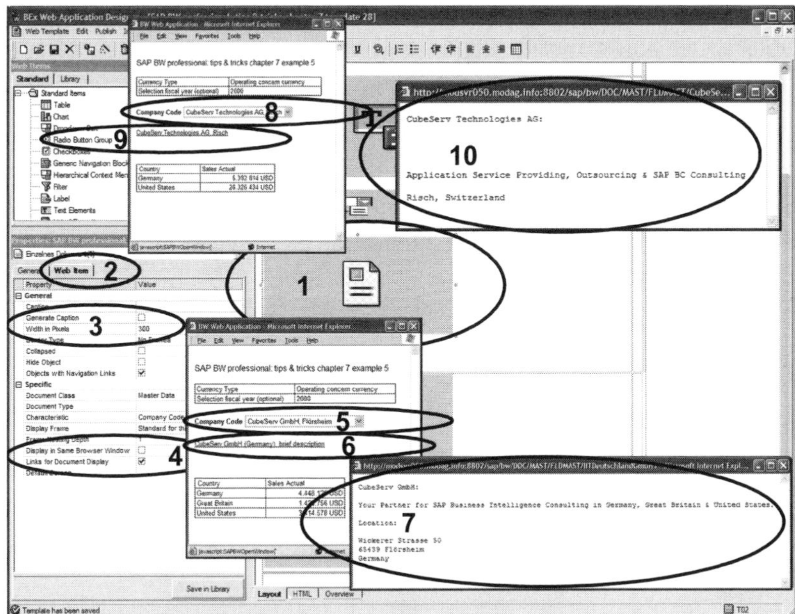

Figure 7.74 Selection-Dependent Links to Documents

After you save the Web template, the changed settings are applied in the Web application: in the example, the accounting sector "CubeServ GmbH" is selected using the drop-down box (see Figure 7.74, Step 5). This selection generates the selection-dependent hyperlink to the document (see Figure 7.74, Step 6). With a click of the mouse on this hyperlink, the document is opened in a new window (see Figure 7.74, Step 7). After you change the selection (in the example: "CubeServ Technologies AG"), the data and also the hyperlink for the changed selection are displayed and, after a mouse click on the hyperlink, the corresponding document is displayed in a new document (see Figure 7.74, Steps 8 to 10).

7.4.19 List of Documents

This Web item displays a list of documents in the Web application and even enables the creation of new documents in the Web application during execution time. In the list, the documents for each characteristic that was set as a document property in the Administrator Workbench appear automatically.

In the Web application, context-sensitive information about the motion data used in the Web application is displayed by the list of documents. If navigation occurs in the Web application (for example a characteristic is limited to a particular characteristic value), then the list of documents adjusts itself automatically. That is, only those documents appear that are relevant for the limited navigation state.

Characteristic is document property

With respect to the requirements for the use of documents, beyond the principles explained in Section 7.4.18, it applies that in the Web item **List of Documents**, the documents for motion data created in the Administrator Workbench or in the Web application are displayed.

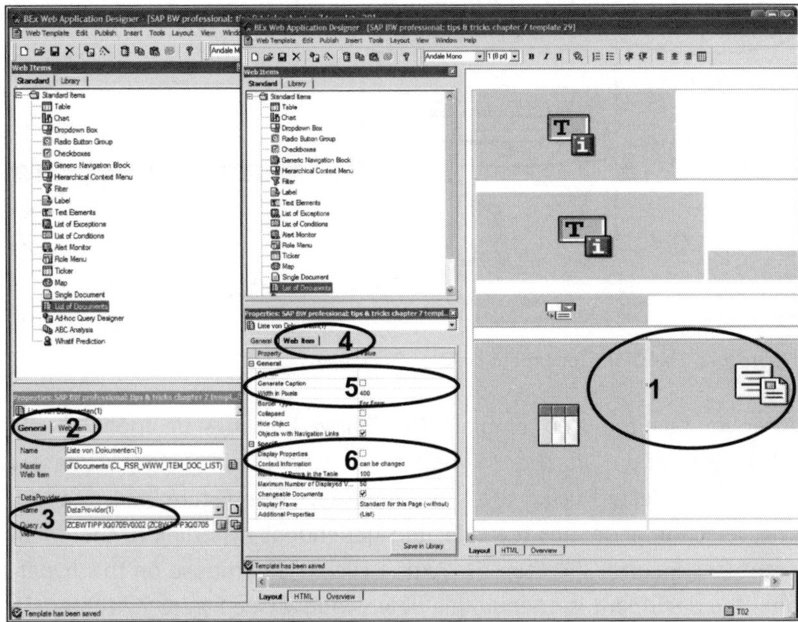

Figure 7.75 Configuration of the Web Item "List of Documents"

Selecting data providers

The Web item **List of Documents** gets its data from a data provider. You specify the data provider to be used after the Web item is copied into the layout, or after you select the item by double-clicking on it (see Figure 7.75, Step 1). In the **General** tab, select the data provider that provides the values (e.g., the one that is assigned to a table or graphical Web item) (see Figure 7.75, Steps 2 and 3).

Settings for "List of Documents"

If necessary, you can adjust the settings of the Web item **List of Documents**: in the example, after you select the **Web Item** tab, the property of the Web item **Width in Pixels** is set for better usability and the property **Generate Caption** is deactivated (see Figure 7.75, Steps 4 and 5). For more flexible use, the property **Context Information** is set changeably (see Figure 7.75, Step 6).

"List of Documents" in the Web Application

During execution of Web templates with the Web item **List of Documents**, the list of documents is displayed depending on the selection and the current navigation state. After you select the variable value ("Fiscal year 2000") and click on the **Execute** button (see Figure 7.76, Steps 1 and 2), the list of documents is displayed (see Figure 7.76, Step 3).

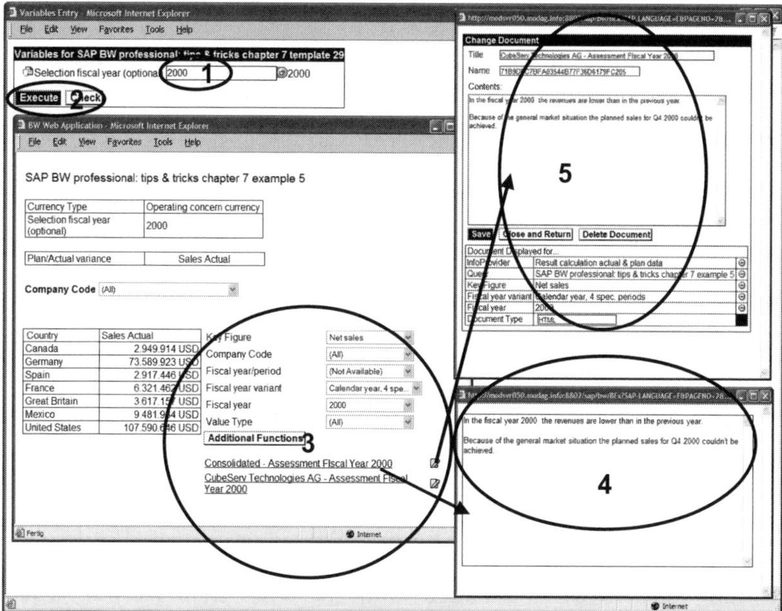

Figure 7.76 The Web Item "List of Documents" in the Web Application

Right-click on a document link to display the content of the document in a new window (see Figure 7.76, Step 4). By clicking on the **Edit Document** button to the right of the document link, the maintenance of the document is enabled in a new window (see Figure 7.76, Step 5).

7.4.20 The Ad-hoc Query Designer

Using the Web item **Ad-hoc Query Designer**, you can create and change queries in a Web application, that is, in the HTML browser and without local installation.

The SAP BW documentation describes the possibilities and restrictions of this Web item. It enables especially the following:

- The creation of queries through the arrangement of characteristics of an InfoProvider in the rows, columns, filters, and free characteristics, and the incorporation of codes of the InfoProvider into the code structure of the query

- The limitation/filtering of codes and characteristics
- The use of predefined code structures and limited or calculated codes in the query
- The setting/changing of query properties and of the properties of codes/characteristics in the query
- The creation/changing of conditions and exceptions.

Restrictions in the Ad-hoc Query Designer

Combined with the BEx Query Designer, there are restrictions during the creation or change of queries with the Web item **Ad-hoc Query Designer**. The following is not possible:

- The direct incorporation of variables into the query (variables can, however, be contained in reusable structures, limited or calculated codes that are used in the Ad-hoc Query Designer)
- The use of two structures in a query (one structure can be used, but it must be the code structure and be located in the rows or columns of the query)
- The definition of codes in the filter or of code structures in the filter
- The definition of exception cells (since this assumes two structures, which is not at all possible in the Ad-hoc Query Designer)
- The creation of reusable structures or limited or calculated codes

Existing queries can be edited with the Web item **Ad-hoc Query Designer** if they fulfill the restrictions listed above. The Ad-hoc Query Designer checks these requirements when loading a query. If the query is too complex, then it can be loaded into the Ad-hoc Query Designer, but it cannot be changed there. You will then receive the corresponding messages. A checking and execution of the query is possible, however.

Creating a Web template with the "Ad-hoc Query Designer"

For the Web item **Ad-hoc Query Designer**, no data provider must or can be assigned when defining the Web template. By incorporating the Ad-hoc Query Designer into the Web template, it is already usable in its complete scope in the Web application (see Figure 7.77, Steps 1 to 3).

Optionally, in the special properties of the Web item, limitations can be placed on an InfoProvider or a query (see Figure 7.77, Step 4).

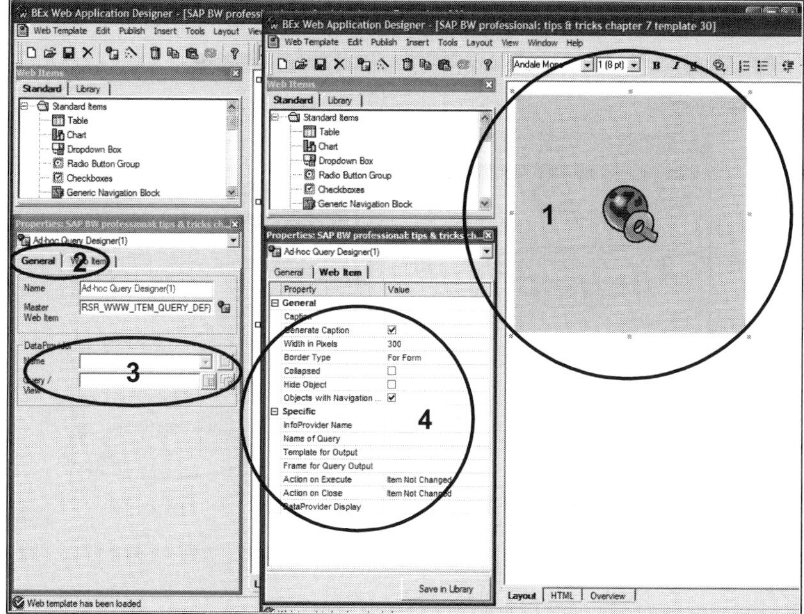

Figure 7.77 Web Template with the Web Item "Ad-hoc Query Designer"

Using the Ad-hoc Query Designer

After saving the Web template, you can create new queries with the Ad-hoc Query Designer. The first step is to click on the hyperlink **Create New Query** (see Figure 7.78, Step 1). In the **Choose an InfoProvider** pop-up, select the InfoProvider that you want from the history or from the Info-Provider hierarchy as displayed in the InfoAreas (see Figure 7.78, Step 2). After you click on the InfoProvider that you want (see Figure 7.78, Step 3), the Technical Name and Description are copied into the fields Selected Object and Description (see Figure 7.78, Step 4).

After you click on the **Transfer** button (see Figure 7.78, Step 5), the reporting-relevant components of the InfoProvider are copied into the definition environment of the Ad-hoc Query Designer (see Figure 7.79, Steps 1 and 2).

In the example, using the context-sensitive menu (warning: in the HTML browser, via left mouse click), "Sales Actual" are copied to the columns (see Figure 7.79, Steps 3 and 4). Due to the restrictions of the Ad-hoc Query Designer, the subsequent takeover of the code "Sales Budget" via context-sensitive menu can occur only in the (automatically created) structure (see Figure 7.79, Steps 5 and 6). For the takeover of characteristics, the drop-down box with the object types is set to **Characteristics** (see Figure 7.79, Step 7).

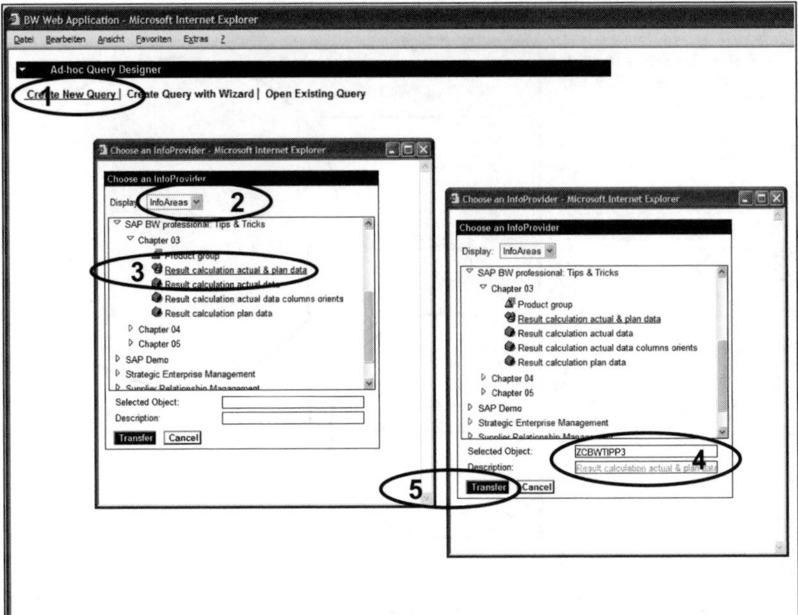

Figure 7.78 Creating a Query with the Ad-hoc Query Designer, Part 1

Then the dimensions and characteristics are displayed in the component inventory (see Figure 7.79, Step 8). Via context-sensitive menu, the characteristics are now copied into the rows (see Figure 7.79, Step 9 and Figure 7.80, Step 1).

When you use the context-sensitive menu, the characteristic **Fiscal year variant** can be copied as a filter (see Figure 7.80, Step 2). The selection of a filter value occurs, in turn, via the context-sensitive menu on the characteristic **Fiscal year variant** in the filter range and the selection of the function **Select Filter Values** (see Figure 7.80, Steps 3 and 4). In the **Filter Value For Fiscal year...** pop-up, select the filter value that you want by clicking on it (in the example: "Fiscal year variant/Calendar year, 4 spec. periods"). To save or retain it as a filter value (see Figure 7.80, Step 7), click on the **Transfer** button.

By re-opening the context-sensitive menu on **Caracteristics**, these can be copied as **Free Characteristics** (see Figure 7.80, Steps 8 and 9). Finally, click on the **Execute** button (see Figure 7.80, Step 10).

Then the **Choose a Folder to Save the Query** pop-up opens. There, the query (selectable via drop-down box) can be saved in favorites or roles (see Figure 7.81, Step 1). The desired folder must be selected with a click of the mouse (see Figure 7.81, Step 2).

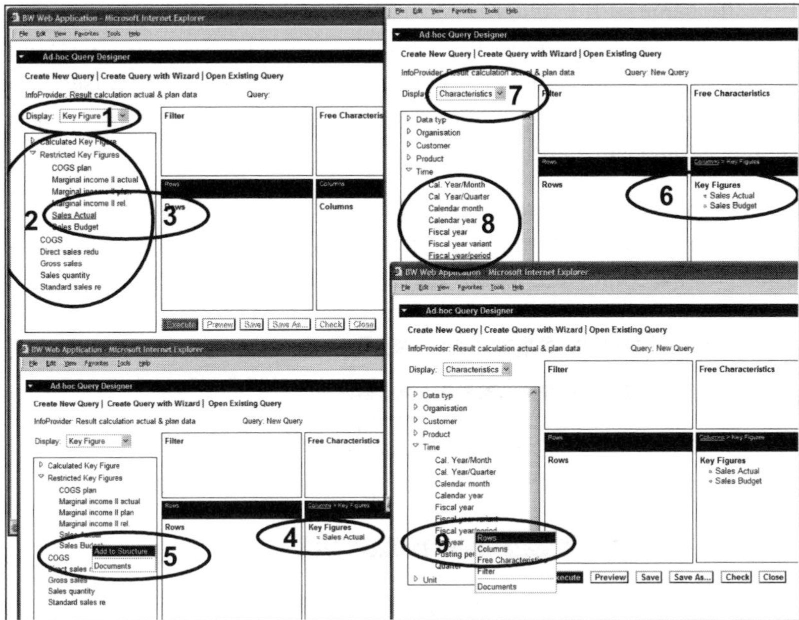

Figure 7.79 Creating a Query with the Ad-hoc Query Designer, Part 2

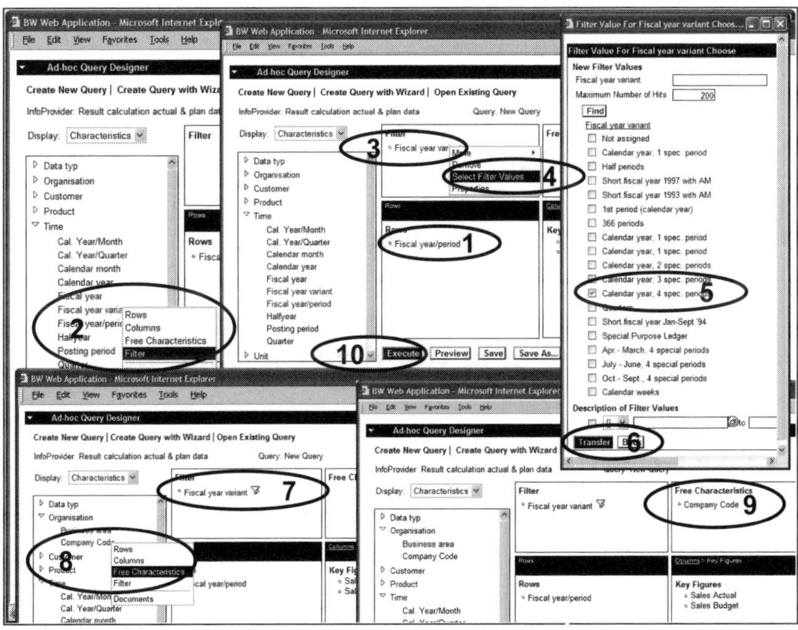

Figure 7.80 Creating a Query with the Ad-hoc Query Designer, Part 3

Thus the name of the folder is copied in the output field Save Query In. After entry of the Technical Name and Description (see Figure 7.81, Step 3), you can save the query after clicking on the **Transfer** button (see Figure 7.81, Step 4). The description is also copied into the Ad-hoc Query Designer (see Figure 7.81, Step 5).

Now the query can be started from the Ad-hoc Query Designer by clicking on the **Execute** button (see Figure 7.81, Step 6). The additional possibilities for executing queries are also available (see Figure 7.81, Step 7).

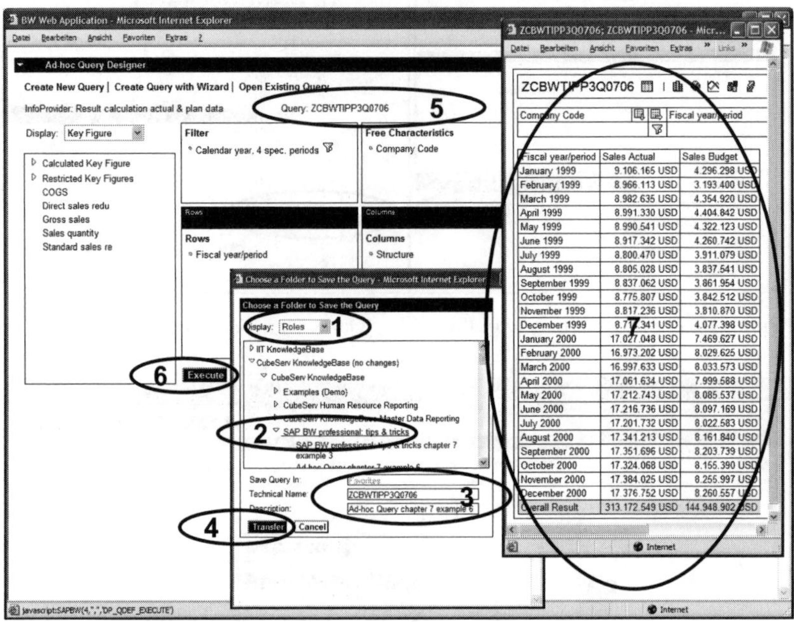

Figure 7.81 Creating a Query with the Ad-hoc Query Designer, Part 4

7.5 HTML Coding in the Web Application Designer

7.5.1 Introduction

The corresponding code that can be processed by the Web browser is generated from the Web items configured in the Web Application Designer and arranged in the layout. This applies to the SAP BW-specific objects such as tables and charts and also to the browser functionality such as positioning of the objects (e.g., using tables) and formatting.

HTML

The coding created in the SAP BW Web templates for processing by the Web browser is HTML code. HTML stands for Hyper Text Markup Language; it is a so-called markup language. Its task is to describe the logical components of a document. HTML is standardized by the W3 Consortium. The HTML coding used in the SAP BW Web templates contains generally valid and also proprietary code elements.

Tags

The content of HTML files is HTML elements. These are marked with so-called *tags*. The majority of HTML elements are marked by an introductory and a final tag. The content between the tags is the validity range of the corresponding element. Tags are written in pointy brackets (<...>).

A generally valid tag used in SAP BW Web templates is the document title that is, for example, displayed in the HTML browser:

```
<TITLE>BW Web Application</TITLE>
```

7.5.2 The HTML Code of the Web Template

Due to definitions of properties and Web items in the Web Application Designer, placeholders for Web items (in the form of object tags), data providers (in the form of object tags), and BW URLs are inserted into an HTML document (this is called the Web template).

HTML Code of a Web template

The Web Application Designer creates the code in a Web template that contains the query name as text and a table without title (see Figure 7.82), for example, the following HTML code (see Figure 7.83):

- An object tag precedes, which defines the origin of the data (in the example data provider query ZCBWTIPP3Q0706 from InfoCube: ZCBWTIPP3) (see Figure 7.83, coding section 1).
- In the header of the HTML code then come the abovementioned title tag with the link tag on the style sheet that defines the formatting (see Figure 7.83, coding section 2).
- The text body contains two object tags that contain the definitions for the text element (see Figure 7.83, coding section 3) and the result table (see Figure 7.83, coding section 4).

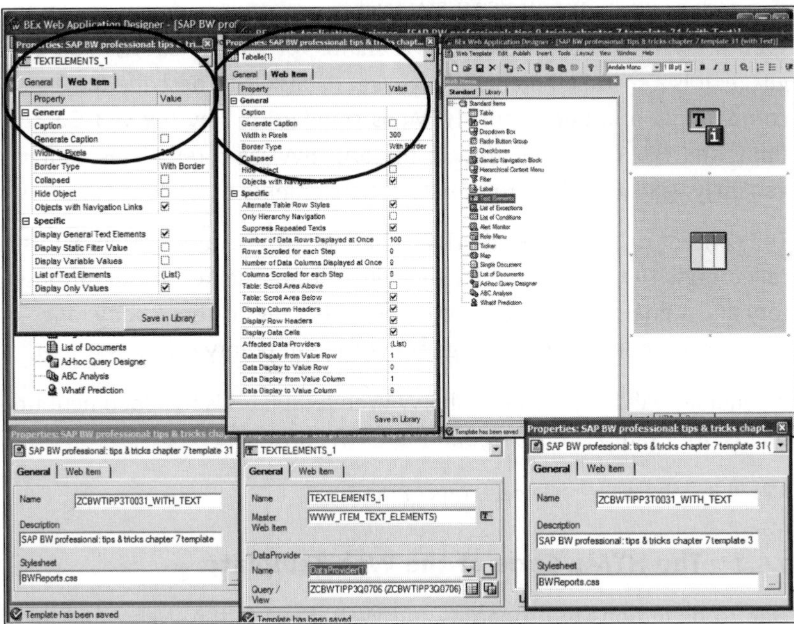

Figure 7.82 Sample Web Template

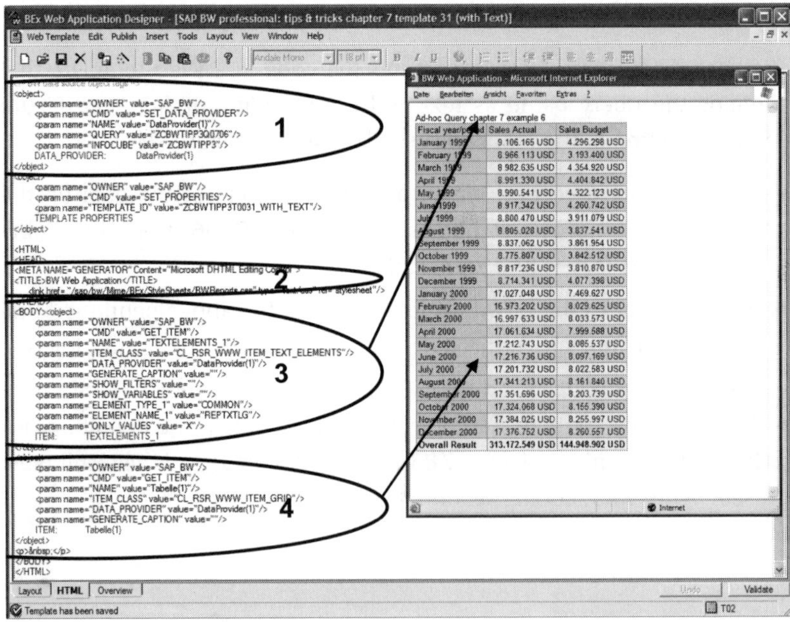

Figure 7.83 HTML Code of the Web Template from Figure 7.82

7.5.3 Manual Editing of the HTML Code in the Web Application Designer

Manual editing of the HTML code

The HTML code in the Web Application Designer can also be edited manually, for example:

- If a more expressive title should be defined, then the desired title can be entered between the tags `<TITLE>` and `</TITLE>` (see Figure 7.84, Step 1):

```
<TITLE>Norbert Egger (CubeServ Group) - SAP BW Profes-
sional: Tips &amp; Tricks</TITLE>
```

- If the query name should receive the format of the title-first order, then the tags `<object>` and `</object>` can be framed by the tags for the desired format (see Figure 7.84, Step 2):

```
<h1><object> ...
  ITEM:              Textelemente(1)
</object></h1>
```

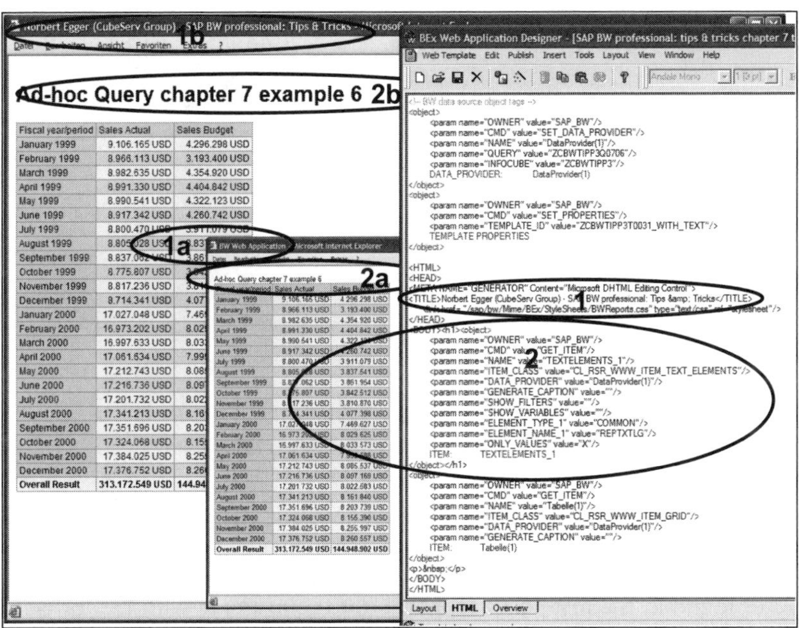

Figure 7.84 Manual Editing of the HTML Code

Language-dependent texts in SAP BW Web Applications

SAP BW makes various specific tags available. Central here is the tag for mapping language-dependent texts on the basis of ABAP/4 text elements (*<SAP_BW_TEXT>*). The prerequisite for this is a generated ABAP/4 program that contains translated text elements (see Figure 7.85, Steps 1 to

5). It is recommended that for this, a "program" used exclusively for this purpose be created. This program requires no ABAP/4 code.

The ABAP/4 text elements can be added with the syntax

<SAP_BW_TEXT PROGRAM='*[Program Name]*' KEY='*[Text-ID]*'>

into the HTML code of the Web template.

In the following, two examples are given:

- Instead of the (in practice often not optimally suited) query name, an ABAP/4 text element is used as a title (see Figure 7.86, Step 2).
- Below the result table, a hyperlink to a Web site is inserted (see Figure 7.86, Step 3).

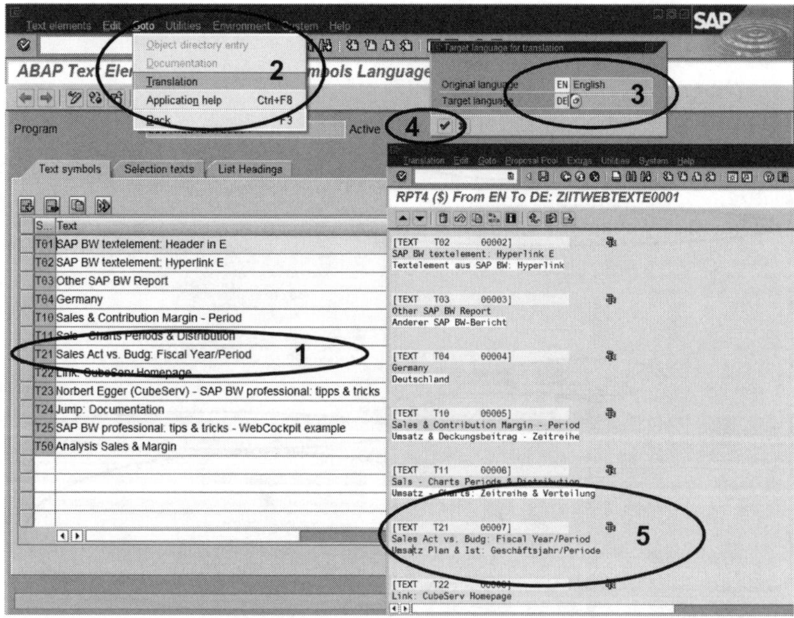

Figure 7.85 ABAP/4 Text Elements as Basis for Language-Dependent Texts in Web Applications

After logon in the respective language (in the example with DE for German or EN for English, see Figure 7.86, Steps 1a and 1b), the content of the ABAP/4 text elements is displayed depending on the logon language in the Web application (see Figure 7.86, Steps 2a and 2b, and 3a and 3b).

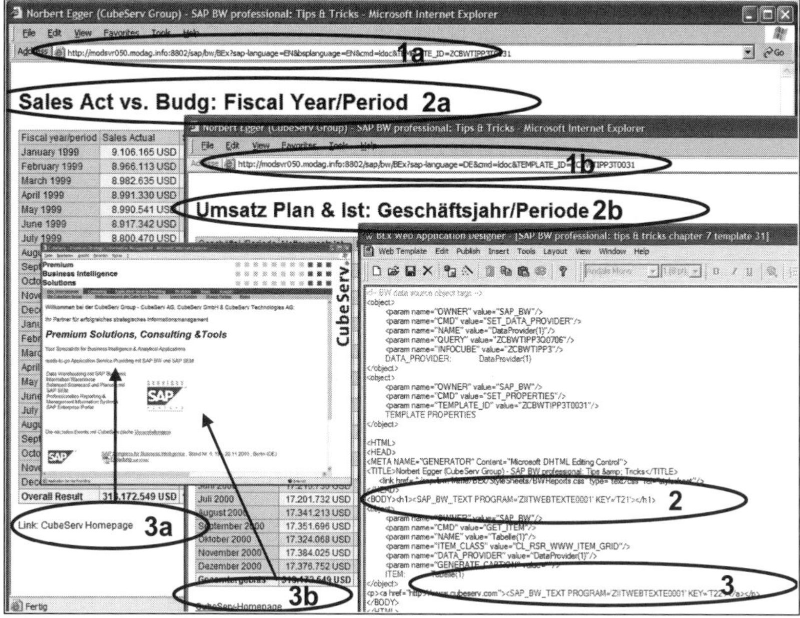

Figure 7.86 Language-Dependent Texts in Web Applications with the <SAP_BW_TEXT> Tag

SAP_BW_URL

A SAP BW-specific tab offers the function to deposit SAP BW-specific URLs. These serve as placeholders for URLs and are replaced upon generation of the HTML page with one of the following URLs. With command URLs, the following functions can be executed:

- Call up Web template
- Change Web template
- Personalize Web template
- Remove personalization
- Create bookmark
- Change icon index
- Enable Web template
- Call up variable image
- Variable preassignments for Web applications
- Variable value change
- Adjustment and expansion of the context menu
- Sequence of commands

For example, a selection is deposited in a hyperlink using the tag *<SAP_BW_URL>*. The HTML coding for this hyperlink in the Web template is:

```
<A href="<SAP_BW_URL DATA_PROVIDER='[DataProvider]'
FILTER_IOBJNM='[Characteristic]' FILTER_VALUE='[Value]'
>"> [Link Text]</a>
```

is added (see Figure 7.87, Step 1).

With a click of the mouse on the hyperlink with the SAP_BW_URL tag (see Figure 7.87, Step 2), the selection is applied. In the example, the Web template is completed with a filter Web item, which displays the selection after execution of the SAP_BW_URL (see Figure 7.87, Step 3).

Forms Additional HTML functionalities such as forms can also be used in Web templates (see Figure 7.88).

JavaScript In the HTML code of Web templates, there is also the possibility of executing commands or sequences of commands via JavaScript. In addition to self-coded functions, SAP BW-specific functions are also available, for example, for the expansion of the context menu with customer-specific entries, for depositing URLs, or for closing windows.

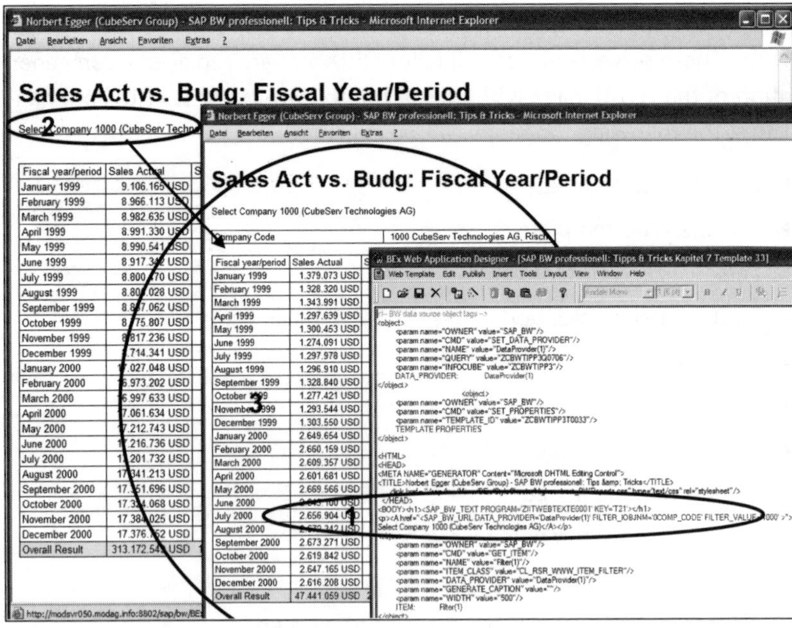

Figure 7.87 Example for the Application of SAP_BW_URL

In the example, using a button created using a form, the SAP BW JavaScript function is started for executing a URL in the same window.

In the header area, the variable is defined (see Figure 7.88, Step 1):

```
<script language="Javascript" type="text/javascript">
  <!--
    var sprungziel = "http://www.iit-abs.ch";
  -->
  </script>
```

The form with the call of the JavaScript function is created with the coding (see Figure 7.88, Step 2):

```
<form name="Eingabe1">
  <input type=button value="Mittels JavaScript- Funk-
tion SAPBWOpenURL zur IIT-Homepage abspringen"
  onClick="SAPBWOpenURL(sprungziel);">
</form>
```

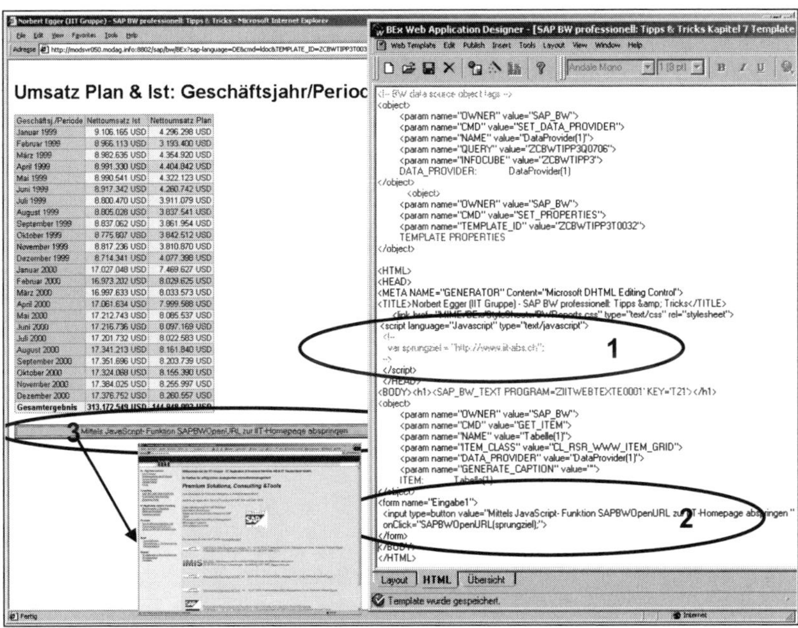

Figure 7.88 Use of Forms and JavaScript Functions

With a click of the button, the URL transmitted by the variable is executed (see Figure 7.88, Step 2).

7.6 Conclusion

A very capable tool

With the Web Application Designer (in combination with the Query Designer) in SAP BW, a very capable tool for creating professional analytical applications is made available.

The special feature of these products is that flexible and capable applications can be created even without programming knowledge. However, please keep in mind that at least basic knowledge of HTML and JavaScript is required for professional applications. It should also be noted that the effort required for creating and maintaining Web applications using coding-based technologies (if necessary, completed with ABAP/4 components on through to Web Design Application Programming Interface) grows out of proportion.

Capability versus WYSIWYG

Compared with the development interfaces of other front-end providers (for example, arcplan, Inc., the manufacturer of the products *inSight/dynaSight* that once dominated the SAP environment) the lack of a full-fledged WYSIWYG (What-You-See-Is-What-You-Get-) development interface is noteworthy. When compared with the other tools to be used with SAP BW, the Web Application Designer offers significantly superior functionality and integration possibilities.

8 Sample Solution for an Extendable Web Cockpit in SAP BW

By harnessing the possibilities of the Query Designer and the Web Application Designer in SAP BW, and adding a few minor adjustments, you can create a powerful SAP BW Web-Cockpit. In this chapter, we'll explain just how you can can create this sample solution.

8.1 Introduction

The Management Cockpit contains information from various different sources and displays an overview of the results in graphic form. In this chapter, we'll use a tutorial to show you how to develop a WebCockpit.

The contents of the WebCockpit

Four charts are displayed in the initial page of our example WebCockpit, presenting information from different data providers. The following charts are displayed for a selected fiscal year:

- A time series with the development of the actual and planned sales for the selected period.
- A time series showing the development of the relative marginal income over the selected period.
- A pie chart showing the distribution of the actual sales for the selected year per country.
- A map graphic with a color-coded appraisal of the actual sales and a bar chart showing the margins for the selected year.

Structuring a solution with framesets

The information appears in a frame-based solution, which contains the enterprise logo and a language-dependent title in the header area and displays the SAP BW role menu for direct report selection in a navigation frame.

8.2 Creating the Queries and the Query Views

8.2.1 "Time series" query

Content of example query 1

Based on the query creation methods explained in Chapters 6 and 7, a query "SAP BW professional: time series sales and margin (ZCBWTIPP3Q0801)" is created for the charts in the WebCockpit with the time series. Among other things, it determines the planned and actual sales and the relative marginal incomes and displays them using the posting periods of a fiscal year, which is selected by variables.

In addition to the definitions explained above, the relative marginal incomes are defined as calculated key figures as follows (see Figure 8.1, Steps 1 through 4):

- Marginal income II rel. actual = 'Marginal income II actual' %A 'Sales actual'
- Marginal income II rel. plan = 'Marginal income II plan' %A 'Sales plan'

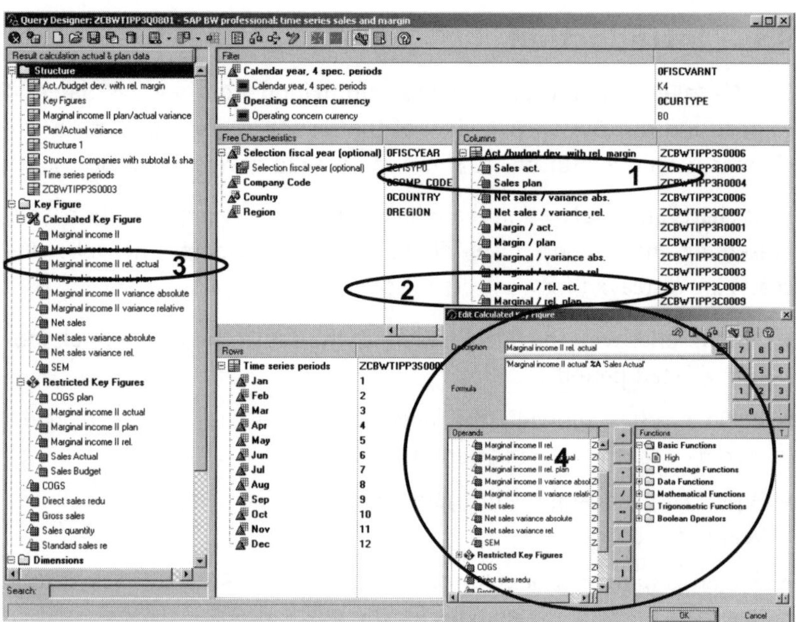

Figure 8.1 Defining the Query With Sales and Marginal Income II Development

Figure 8.2 shows the execution of the query from Figure 8.1, in which the variables are selected, the **Execute** button is pressed, and the query result is displayed (Steps 1 through 3).

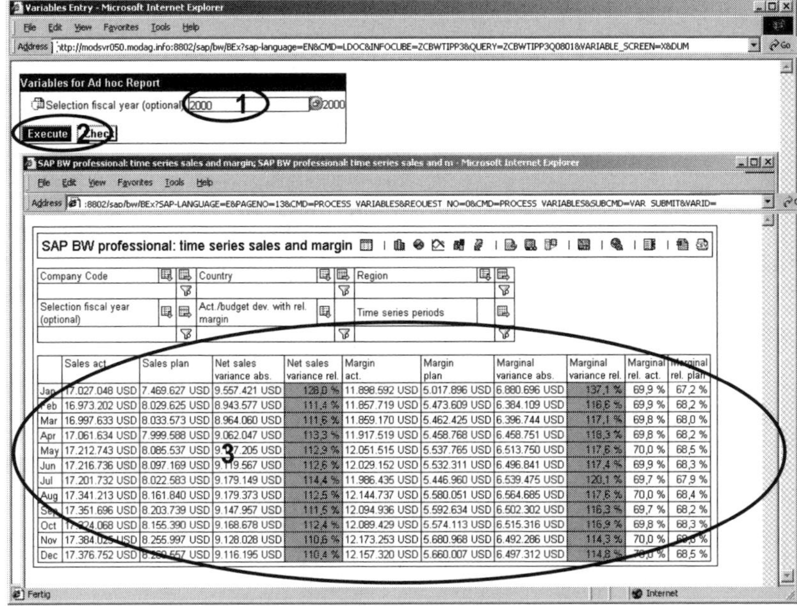

Figure 8.2 Execution of the Query with Sales and Marginal Income II Development

8.2.2 Query According to Countries and Regions

Content of example query 2

Based on the query creation methods explained in Chapters 6 and 7, a query "SAP BW professional: time series sales & margin/country & r. (ZCBWTIPP3Q0802)" is created for the pie charts and map graphs in the WebCockpit, which will determine, among other things, the planned and actual sales for a fiscal year selected by variables, and also the relative marginal incomes and list them per country. The characteristic "Region" is available as a free characteristic (see Figure 8.3, Steps 1 through 5).

8.2.3 Query View for the Chart "Sales Development (Plan/Actual Comparison)"

Defining the query view

The query view "ZCBWTIPP3Q0801V0001 comparison of plan/actual sales development" is created in the Web Application Designer. It is based on the query described in Section 8.2.1, "SAP BW Professional: time series sales and margin (ZCBWTIPP3Q0801)". Define the view as explained in Chapter 7 (see Figure 8.4).

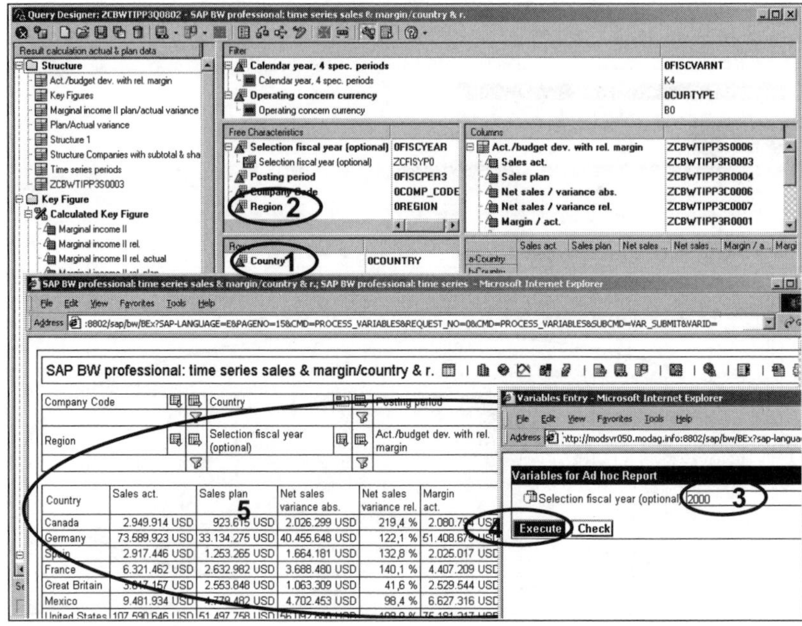

Figure 8.3 The Query with Actual and Plan Sales and Relative Margins Per Country and Free Characteristic "Region"

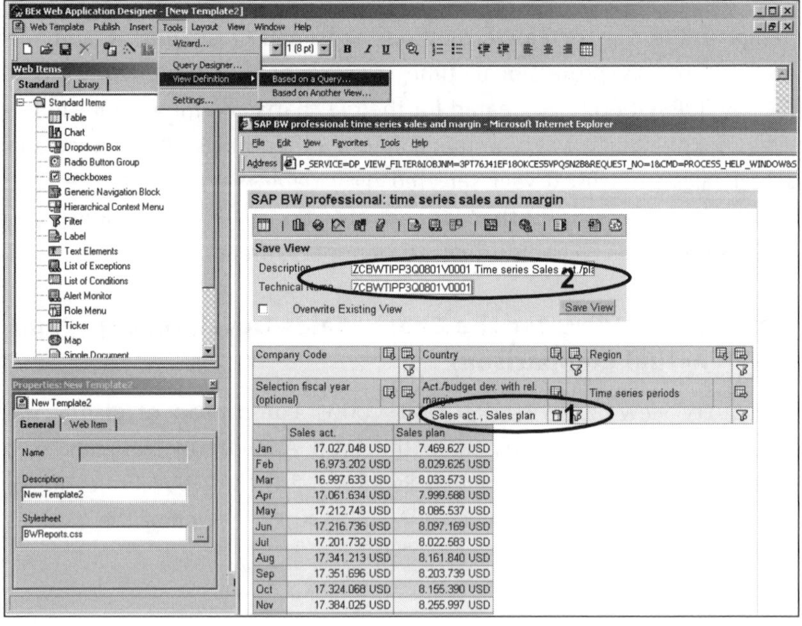

Figure 8.4 Query View for the Chart "Sales development (Plan/actual comparison)"

8.2.4 Query View for the Chart "Development of the Relative Margins"

The query view "ZCBWTIPP3Q0801V0001 time series margin" is created in the Web Application Designer, based on the query described in Section 8.2.1, "SAP BW Professional: time series sales and margin (ZCBWTIPP 3Q0801)". Define the view as explained in Chapter 7 (see Figure 8.5).

Defining the query view

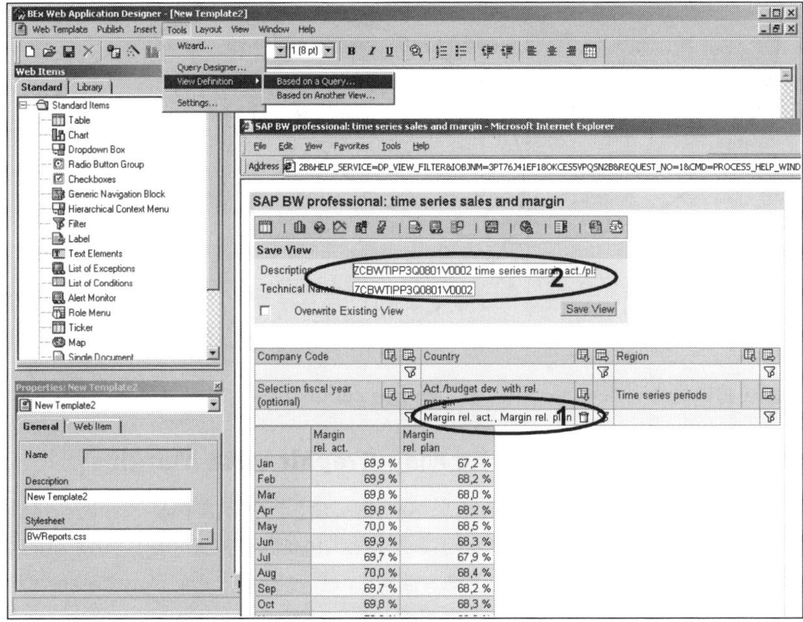

Figure 8.5 Query View for the Chart "Development of the Relative Margins"

8.2.5 Query View for the Chart and the Map Graphic "Distribution of Sales per Country"

The query view "ZCBWTIPP3Q0802V0001 distribution of sales per country" is created in the Web Application Designer, based on the query described in Section 8.2.2, "SAP BW professional: time series sales & margin/country & r. (ZCBWTIPP3Q0802)". Define the view as explained in Chapter 7 (see Figure 8.6, Step 1).

Defining the query view

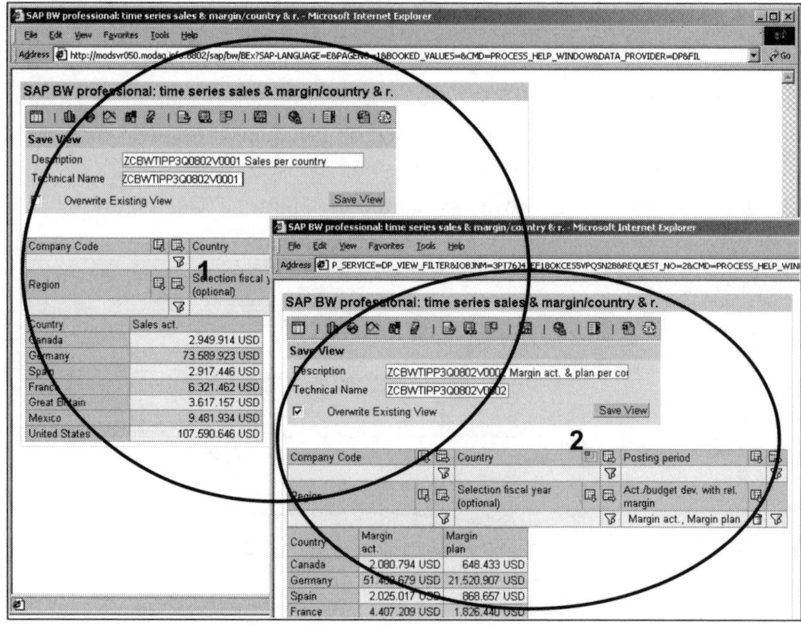

Figure 8.6 Query Views for Sales and Margins per Country

8.2.6 Query View for the Map Graphic with Margins

Defining the query view for the map layer 2

Based on the query described in Section 8.2.2, "SAP BW Professional: time series sales & margin/country & r. (ZCBWTIPP3Q0802)", the query view "ZCBWTIPP3Q0802V0002 Margin act. & plan per... " is created in the Web Application Designer. Define the view as explained in Chapter 7 (see Figure 8.6, Step 2).

8.3 Creating the Web Template with the Charts

8.3.1 General settings

General settings in the Web template

Based on the Web template settings described in Chapter 7, make the following general settings in the Web template (see Figure 8.7):

- Set the desired StyleSheet for the Web template as a general property (**General** tab)
- Activate the general properties (**Web Item** tab, **General** folder)
  - Display Same Variable Only Once
  - Force Variable Screen Display

▶ Configure the context menu (**Web Item** tab, **Entries in Context Menu** folder)

  ▶ Report/Report Jump Targets: Always Display

The Web template is saved as "SAP BW professional: Tips & Tricks: Web-Cockpit (ZCBWTIPP3T0034)".

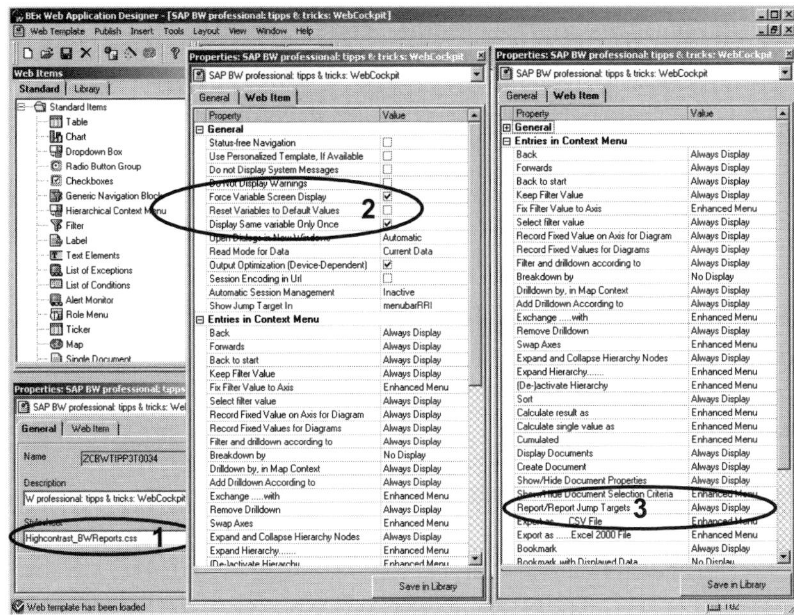

Figure 8.7 General Settings in the "WebCockpit" Web Template

8.3.2 Web Items and Positioning

Components of the WebCockpit

In addition to the four charts that show the data content in the Web-Cockpit, two other Web items are also inserted:

▶ A drop-down box that displays the selected fiscal year.

▶ A drop-down box that enables you to select company code.

HTML tables for positioning

Use HTML tables to position objects: The single-row, two-column table at the top contains the drop-down box for the characteristic "fiscal year" in the column on the left and the drop-down box for the characteristic "company code" in the column on the right.

The two-row, two-column table in the middle contains the following lines:

- In the column on the left:
  - In the first row, the time series with the development of the actual and planned sales for the selected period.
  - In the second row, the time series with the development of the relative marginal income over the selected period.
- In the column on the right:
  - In the first row, the pie chart showing the distribution of actual sales for the selected year per country.
  - In the second row, the map graphic with color-coded appraisal of the actual sales and a bar chart showing the relative margins for the selected year.

At the bottom, a one-row table with two columns contains a hyperlink to documentation in the column on the left and a hyperlink to the enterprise homepage in the column on the right. The tables are separated from each other with line breaks.

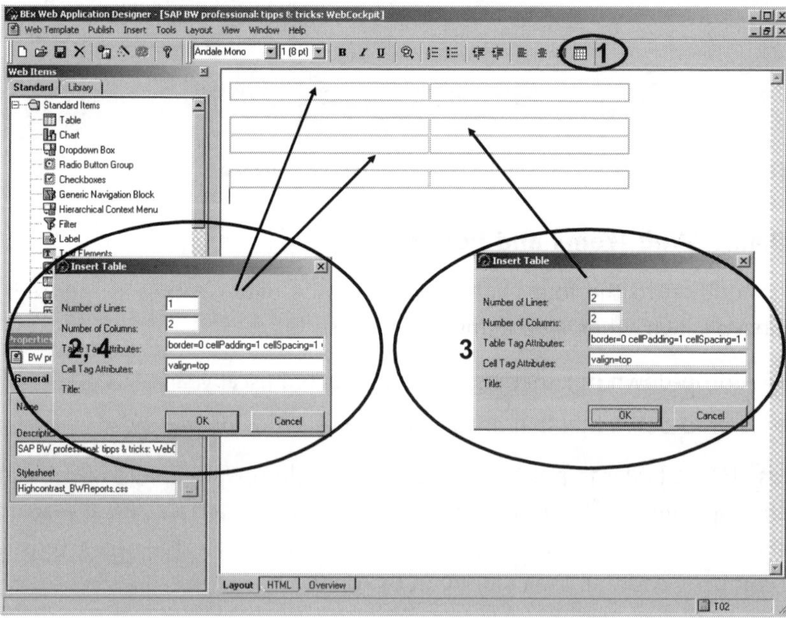

Figure 8.8 Creating the HTML Tables for Positioning the Elements

Implementation can be carried out in the layout view of the Web Application Designer. Click on the **Insert Table** button to insert each required table at the desired location (see Figure 8.8, Steps 1 through 4).

Implementation

The tables are stored in the HTML code between the tags *<BODY>* and *</BODY>* as follows:

```
<TABLE border=0 cellPadding=1 cellSpacing=1
width="75 %">
   <TR>
    <TD vAlign=top></TD>
    <TD vAlign=top></TD></TR></TABLE>
<br>
<TABLE border=0 cellPadding=1 cellSpacing=1
width="75 %">
   <TR>
    <TD vAlign=top></TD>
    <TD vAlign=top></TD></TR>
  <TR>
    <TD vAlign=top></TD>
    <TD vAlign=top></TD></TR></TABLE>
<br>
<TABLE border=0 cellPadding=1 cellSpacing=1
width="75 %">
   <TR>
    <TD vAlign=top></TD>
    <TD vAlign=top></TD></TR></TABLE>
```

You can then insert the Web items into this template. As explained in Chapter 7, insert the Web items into the tables at the top and those tables in the middle. Insert a **drop-down box** into each cell in the table at the top. Then, insert a **chart** into each row in the left column and a chart into the upper row on the right-hand side in the table in the middle. Lastly, insert a **map** Web item into the second row of the right-hand column (see Figure 8.9).

Insert Web items

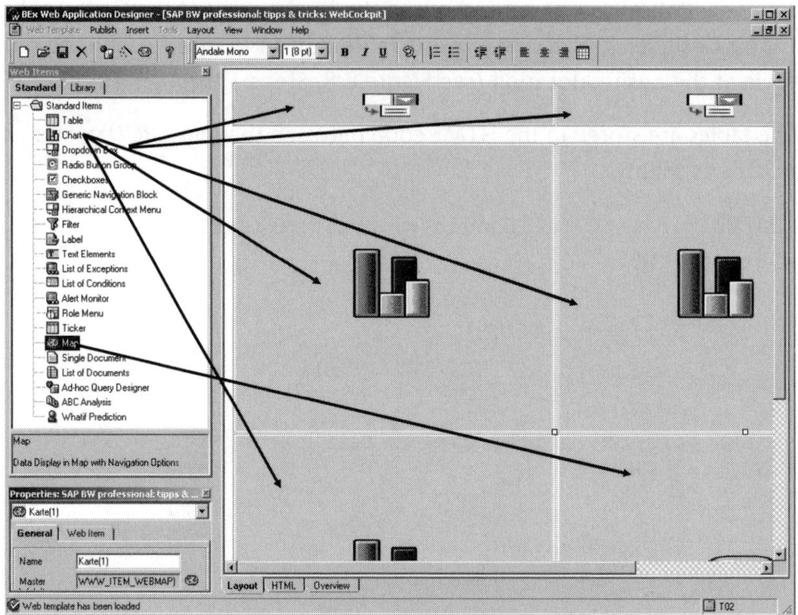

Figure 8.9 Inserting the Web Items in the HTML Table

8.3.3 Assigning Data Providers to Web Items

Assigning data providers

You must assign the necessary Data Providers to the Web items in the Web template:

- The query view "ZCBWTIPP3Q0801V0001 Sales development plan/actual comparison" is assigned as "Data Provider (1)" for the two **Drop-down box** Web items and the chart on the upper left in the middle table (see Figure 8.10, Steps 1 through 1c).
- The query view "ZCBWTIPP3Q0801V0002 Development of relative margins" is assigned as "DataProvider (2)" for the Web item **chart** in the column on the left, second row, of the table in the middle (see Figure 8.10, Steps 2 through 2a).
- The query view "ZCBWTIPP3Q0802V0001 Distribution of sales per country" is specified as a "DataProvider (3)" for the Web item **chart** and for "MapLevel(1)" for the Web item **map** (see Figure 8.11, Steps 1 through 1b).

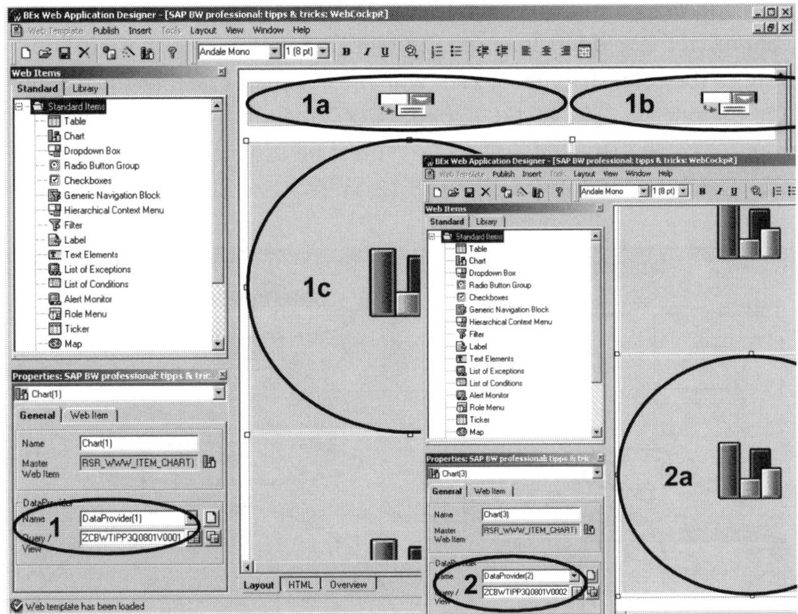

Figure 8.10 Assigning Data Providers 1 and 2

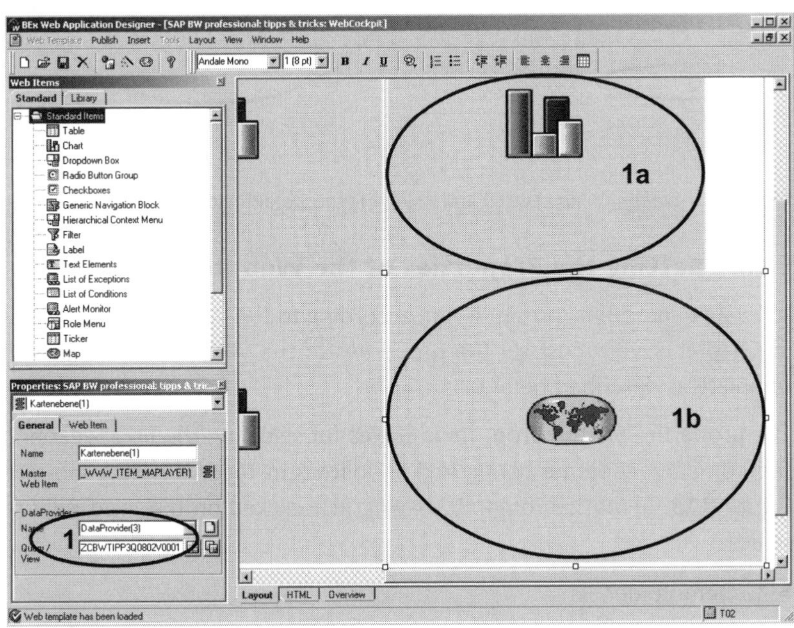

Figure 8.11 Assigning Data Provider 3

A "MapLevel(2)" must be created for the **map** Web item in the right-hand column of the middle table (see Figure 8.12, Steps 1 through 6), to superimpose the color shading for sales with the bar chart based on the margins. The query view "ZCBWTIPP3Q0802V0002 margin II actual and plan per country (ZCBWTIPP3Q0802V0002)" must be assigned to "MapLevel(2)" as a "Data Provider(4)" (see Figure 8.12, Steps 7 and 8).

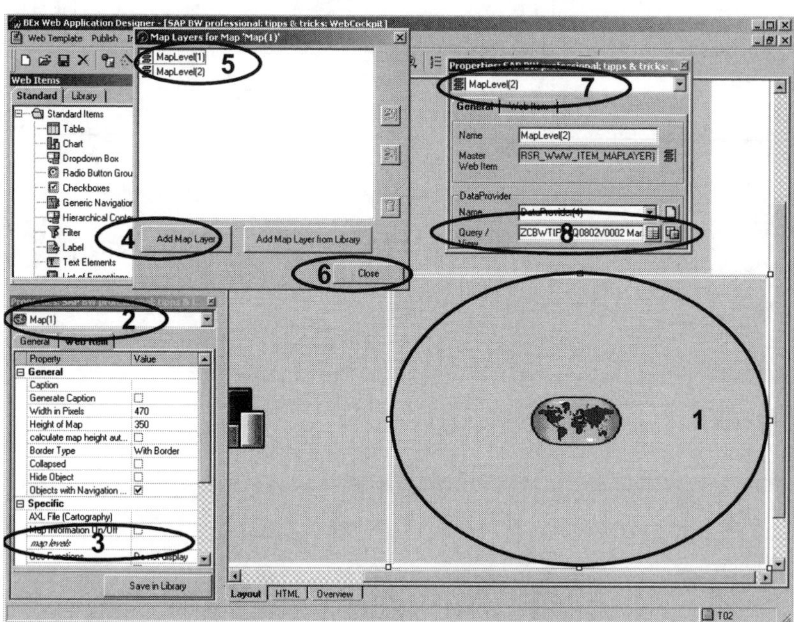

Figure 8.12 Creating Map Level(2) and Assigning the DataProvider(4)

8.3.4 Setting the Properties of the Web Items

Properties of the Web items

To ensure an optimal presentation, according to the instructions provided in Chapter 7, you must set the properties of the Web items in the Web template as described below.

Properties of the drop-down boxes

The properties for the drop-down boxes for selecting the fiscal year and the company code are configured as follows in the **Web Item** tab (see Figure 8.13, Steps 1 through 7), having first clicked on the Web item to select it:

- **General** folder
  - Deactivate the property **Generate Caption** (see Figure 8.13, Steps 2 and 8).
  - Set the **Width in Pixels** property to 400 (see Figure 8.13, Steps 2 and 8).

- **Specific** folder
  - For the property **Characteristic/Structure**, select the fiscal year (see Figure 8.13, Step 3) or the company code (see Figure 8.13, Step 9) from the selection list.
  - For the property **Affected Data Providers**, open the drop-down box (see Figure 8.13, Step 4 or 10) and select all three Data Providers (see Figure 8.13, Step 5 or 11) and confirm the entry by clicking on the **OK** pushbutton (see Figure 8.13, Step 6 or 12).

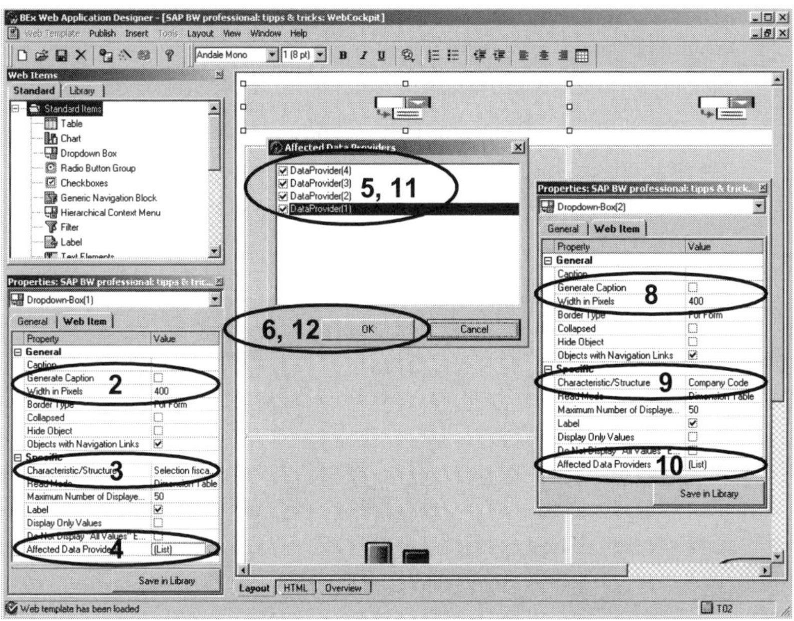

Figure 8.13 Configuration of the Drop-down Boxes

Properties of the line and bar (column) charts

The properties for the line and bar charts for presenting the sales and marginal income development are configured in the **Web Item** tab as follows (see Figure 8.14, Steps 1 through 7), having first selected the Web item by clicking on it:

- **General** folder
  - Deactivate the property **Generate Caption** (see Figure 8.14, Steps 2 and 8).
  - Set the **Width in Pixels** property to 400 (see Figure 8.14, Steps 2 and 8).
  - Set the **Height** property to 350 (see Figure 8.14, Steps 2 and 8).

- **Specific** folder
  - For the property **Edit Chart**, select the diagram type **Columns** (see Figure 8.14, Step 3) or **Lines** (see Figure 8.14, Step 9) from the selection list.
  - Activate the property **Swap Display Axes** (see Figure 8.14, Step 3 or 9).
  - Activate the drop-down box for the property **Data Providers Affected** (see Figure 8.14, Step 4 or 10) and select all three Data Providers (see Figure 8.14, Step 5 or 11). Confirm your entry by clicking on the **OK** pushbutton (see Figure 8.14, Step 6 or 12).
  - For the property **Diagram Title (Language-dependent),** indicate the desired descriptions (in the example: "Time series sales actual/ plan comparison or Time series marginal income", see Figure 8.14, Step 4).

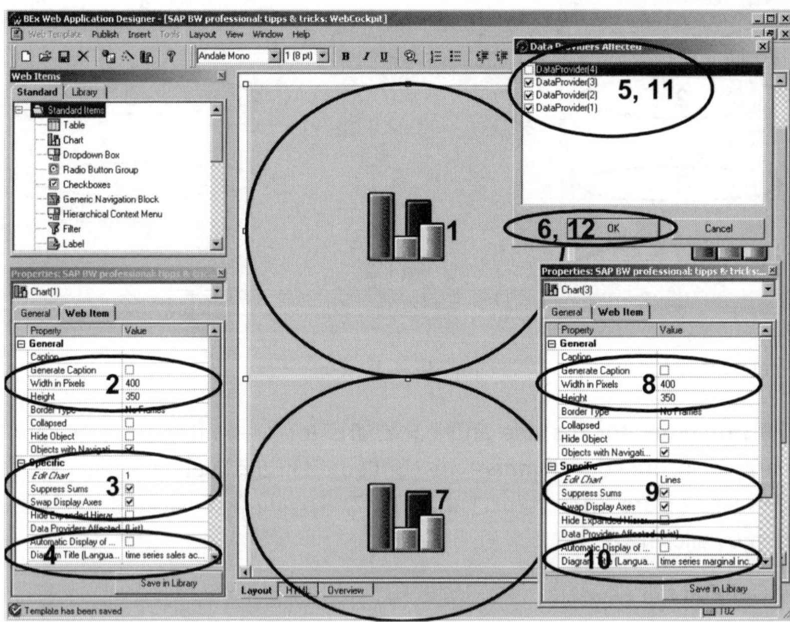

Figure 8.14 Configuration of the Bar and Line Charts

Detail properties of the bar chart

Use the context-sensitive menu in the **Edit Chart** popup to set the detail properties for the bar chart, according to the instructions in Chapter 7 (see Figure 8.15, Steps 1 through 3).

The example shows the following:

- Using the popup **Format Axis**, the numbers in the axis are presented with a thousand separator (see Figure 8.15, Step 5).
- In the **Format Chart Area** popup, you can add a border around the diagram (see Figure 8.15, Step 4).
- Using the **Format Plot** popup, you can set the background colors (see Figure 8.15, Step 6).
- Use the **Chart Options** popup to position the legend under the chart.

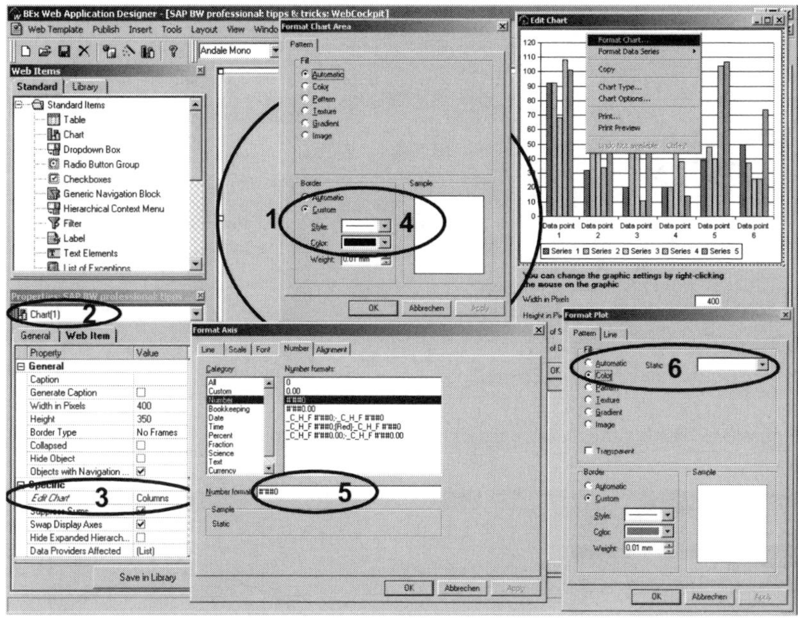

Figure 8.15 Editing the Detail Properties of the Bar Chart

Detail properties of the line chart

In accordance with the instructions in Chapter 7, set the Detail properties for the **line** chart using the context-sensitive menu in the **Edit Chart** popup (see Figure 8.16, Steps 1 through 3).

The example shows the following:

- In the **Chart Type** popup, select the chart type **Lines** (see Figure 8.16, Step 4).
- In the **Format Chart Area** popup, put a border around the diagram (as you did in Figure 8.15, Step 4).
- Using the **Format Axis** popup, you can present the numbers in the axis with one decimal place (as in Figure 8.15, Step 5).

- Using the **Format Plot** popup, you can set the background colors (same as Figure 8.15, Step 6).
- Use the **Chart Options** popup to position a legend under the chart (see Figure 8.16, Step 6).

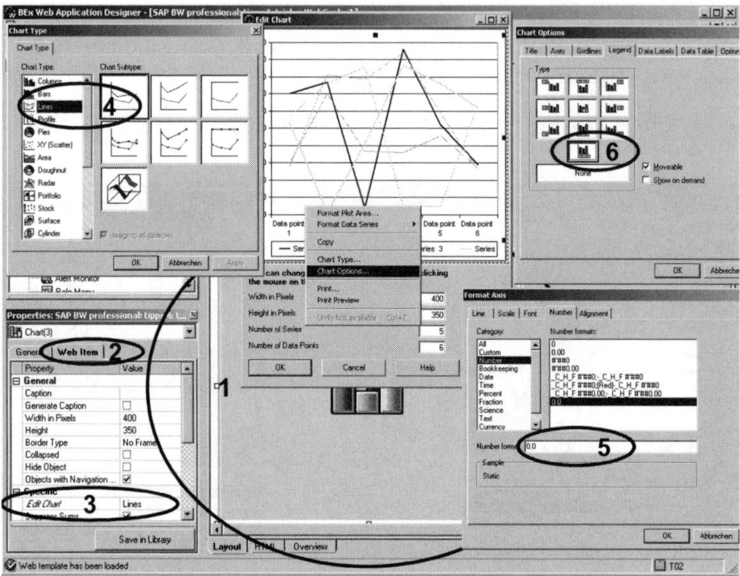

Figure 8.16 Editing the Detail Properties of the Line Chart

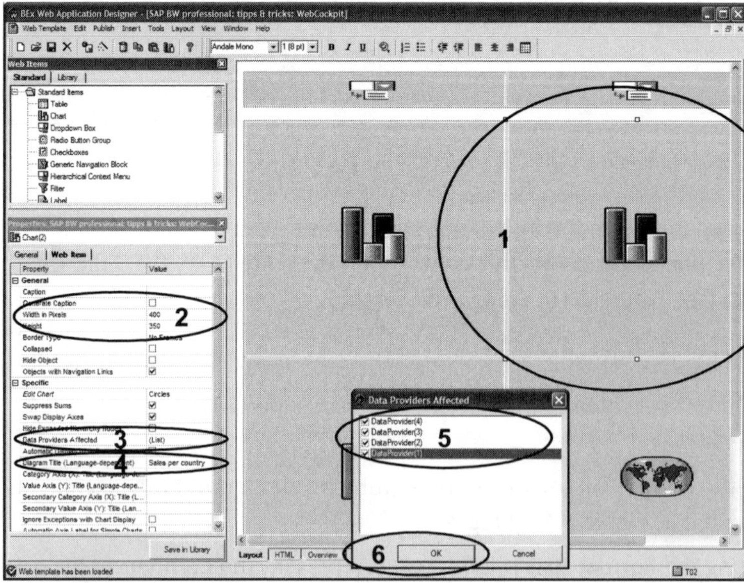

Figure 8.17 Configuring the Pie Chart

The properties for the pie chart for presenting the distribution of sales are configured as follows in the **Web Item** tab (see Figure 8.17, Step 1), after first clicking on the Web item to select it:

Properties of the Pie Chart

- **General** folder
  - Deactivate the property **Generate Caption** (see Figure 8.17, Steps 2 and 8).
  - Set the **Width in Pixels** property to 400 (see Figure 8.17 Steps 2 and 8).
  - Set the **Height** property to 350 (see Figure 8.17 Step 2).
- **Specific** folder
  - For the **Edit Chart** property, select the chart type **Pies** (see Figure 8.17, Step 3).
  - Activate the property **Swap Display Axes** (see Figure 8.17, Step 3).
  - For the property **Data Providers Affected**, open the drop-down box (see Figure 8.17, Step 4), select all three Data Providers (see Figure 8.17, Step 5), and confirm the entry by clicking on the **OK** pushbutton (see Figure 8.17, Step 6).
  - Indicate the desired descriptions for the property **Diagram Title (Language dependent)** (in the example: "Distribution of Sales", see Figure 8.17, Step 4).

Detail properties of the pie chart

In accordance with the instructions in Chapter 7, set the Detail properties for the pie chart using the context-sensitive menu in the **Edit Chart** popup (see Figure 8.18, Steps 1 through 3).

The example shows the following:

- In the **Chart Type** popup, select the pie chart (see Figure 8.18, Step 5
- In the **Format Chart Area** popup, you can put a border around the diagram (as in Figure 8.15, Step 4).
- Use the **Format Data Labels** popup to present the numbers with one decimal place (see Figure 8.18, Step 4).
- Use the Format Plot popup to set the background colors (same as Figure 8.15, Step 5).

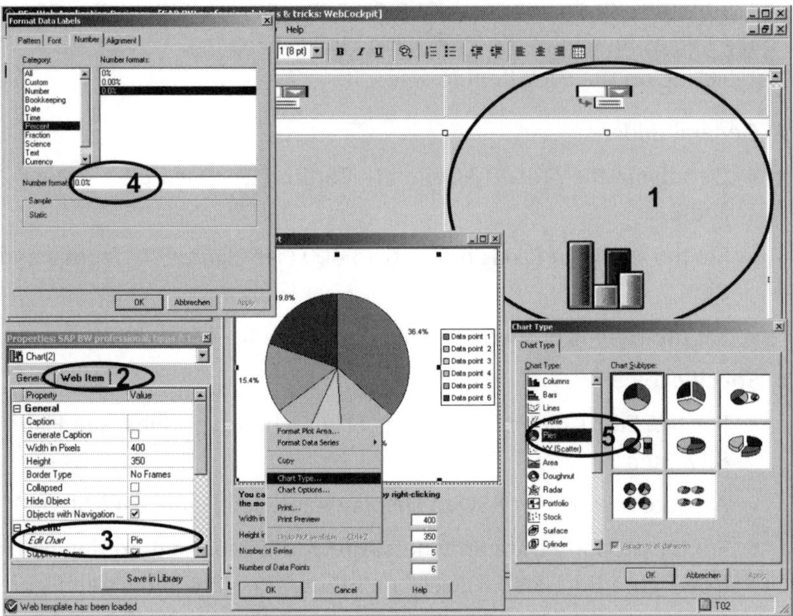

Figure 8.18 Editing the Detail Properties of the Pie Chart

Properties of the Web item "map"

The properties for the map chart for presenting sales and marginal income are configured in the **Web Item** tab as follows (see Figure 8.19, Step 1), having first clicked on the Web item to select it:

- **General** folder
  - Deactivate the property **Generate Caption** (see Figure 8.19, Step 2).
  - Set the **Width in Pixels** property to 470 (see Figure 8.19 Step 2).
  - Set the **Height** property to 350 (see Figure 8.19 Step 2).
- **Specific** folder
  - For the property **Extent of the Map**, select **Data Only** (see Figure 8.19, Step 3).

For MapLevel(1), the properties are configured as follows in the **Web Item** tab (see Figure 8.19, Step 4):

- **Specific** folder
  - Set the property **Map Renderer** to **Color Shading** (see Figure 8.19, Step 5).
  - Click on the drop-down box in the property **Individual Values** to open the **Individual Values** popup, then set the threshold values for visualizing the desired information and confirm your entries by clicking on the **OK** pushbutton (see Figure 8.19, Step 6 to 8).

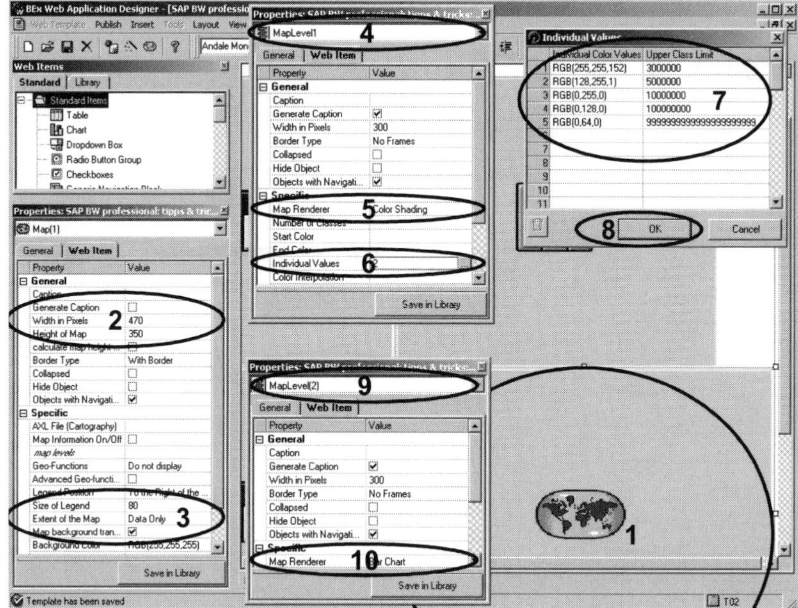

Figure 8.19 Configuration of the Map Chart

For MapLevel (2), the properties are configured as follows in the **Web Item** tab (see Figure 8.19, Step 9):

- **Specific** folder
  - Set the **Map Renderer** property to **Bar Chart** (see Figure 8.19, Step 10).
  - Set the desired column height to 70 (see Figure 8.19, Step 10).

Data providers affected

The chart is controlled from the drop-down boxes, which means that every selection for fiscal year and/or company code should be forwarded to all charts. For this reason, in all Web items the property **Data Providers Affected** must be configured in such a way that the drop-down boxes affect all Data Providers that are linked to the item.

8.3.5 Creating Hyperlinks

Hyperlinks

Hyperlinks to documentation and to the company homepage are created using SAP BW Text Tag. For this, you must add the necessary text elements to an SAP ABAP/4 program (see Figure 8.21, Step 1). The hyperlinks will then be inserted into the HTML code with a SAP BW Text Tag (see Figure 8.21, Step 2), as explained in Chapter 7. Figure 8.22 shows how the executed Web template, with the charts, is structured.

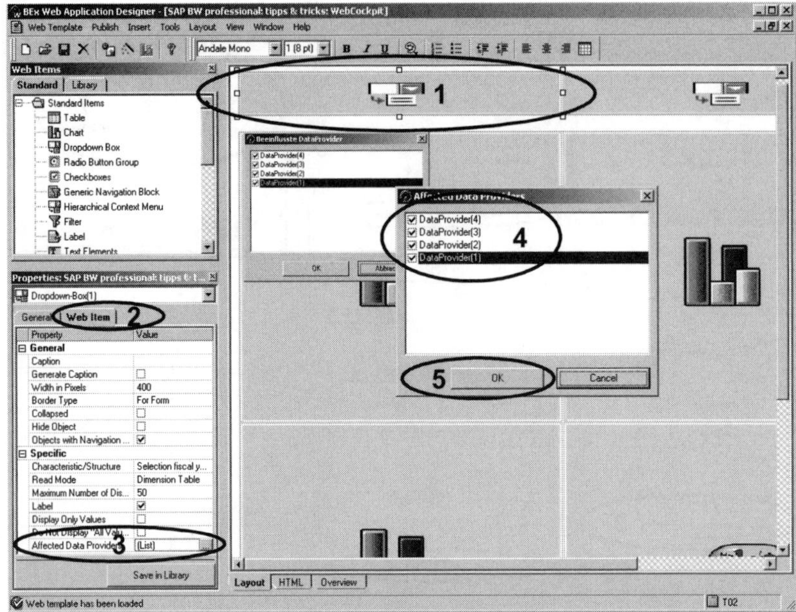

Figure 8.20 Controlling the Data Providers Using the Drop-down Box

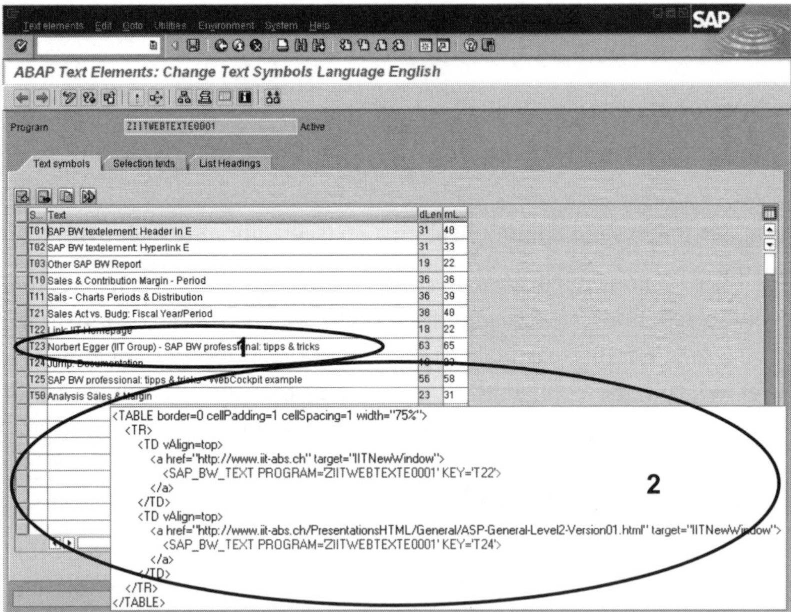

Figure 8.21 Adding Language-Dependent Texts to the Hyperlink

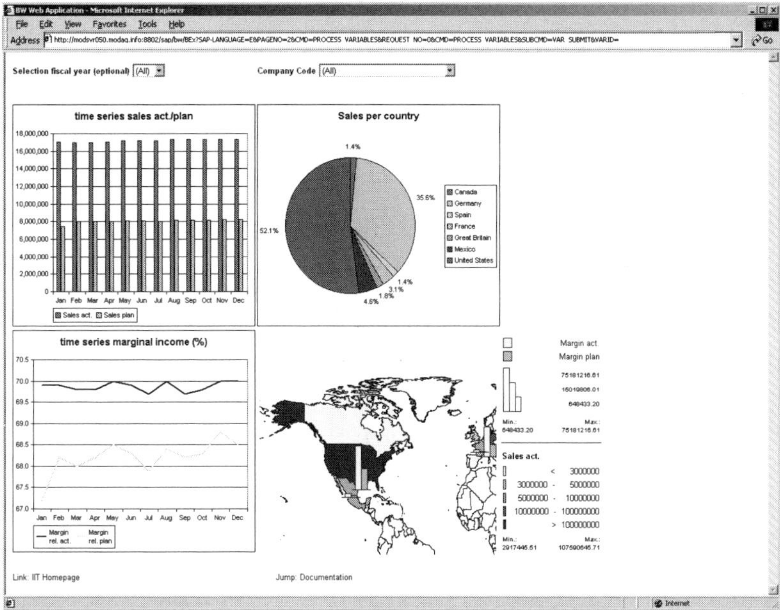

Figure 8.22 The Executed Web Template with Charts and Map

8.4 Creating the Web Template with the Role Menu

In accordance with the instructions in Chapter 7, you would create the Web template for the role menu (see Figure 8.23, Step 1) as follows:

- In the **General** tab, the style sheet **BWReports.css** is selected as a general property of the Web template.
- In the general properties, in the **Web Item** tab, deactivate the property **Generate Caption**.
- In the specific properties in the **Web Item** tab, the following applies:
  - The roles are explicit (in the example, only favorites) and the roles with Web templates for the WebCockpit are selected (by activating the dropdown box of the property **List of Roles** and selecting the relevant roles in the **List of Roles** popup, see Figure 8.23, Step 2).
  - The property **Name of Target Frame** is set to **ZielframeMC**.

Figure 8.23, Step 3, shows the Web template when the Web application is executed.

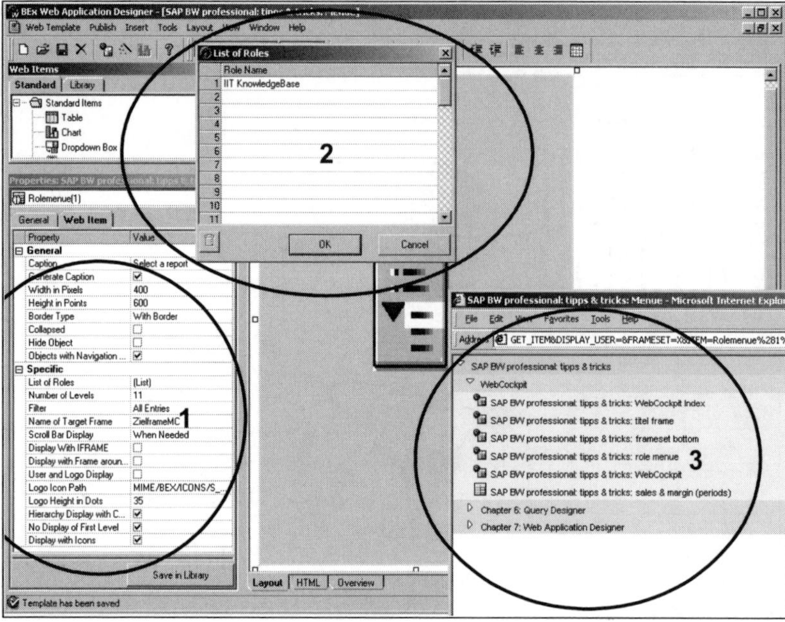

Figure 8.23 Web Template with Role Menu

8.5 Creating the Title Web Template

A Web template is created to display the header information, which may include, for example, the company logo, the company name, and the title of the application. In the body of the text in the following example, the name of the company is static and the name of the application is language-dependent:

```
<BODY bgcolor="#d4e2ee" topmargin="0" leftmargin="0">
<TABLE border=0 cellPadding=7 cellSpacing=0
width="100 %" bgcolor="#d4e2ee">
  <TR>
    <TD vAlign=center>
      <h3>
        <font face="Arial" size="4">
            IIT Application &amp; Business Services AG
        </font>
      </h3>
    </TD>
    <TD vAlign=center>
      <h3>
        <font face="Arial" size="4">
```

```
            <SAP_BW_TEXT PROGRAM='ZIITWEBTEXTE0001'
KEY='T25'>
          </font>
        </h3>
      </TD>
  </TR>
</TABLE>
</BODY>
```

In the **General** tab, the style sheet **BWReports.css** is selected as a general property of the Web template. Figure 8.24 shows the title Web template when the Web application has been executed.

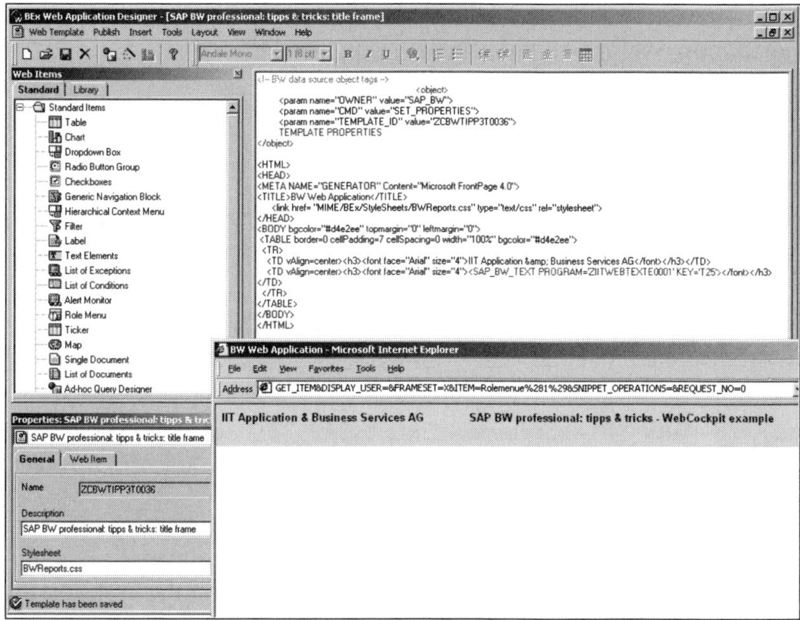

Figure 8.24 Title Web Template

8.6 Creating the Frameset

The components are finally united in a frameset. The tag <SAP BW-URL> is used in the following example for the sake of reusability. **The index**

The initial HTML document with the entire frameset contains the document with a frame at the top (with the title information) and a frame below (see below "Frameset with menu and cockpit").

```
<HTML>
<HEAD>
  <TITLE>IIT Application Services Demo-Area</TITLE>
</HEAD>
<FRAMESET FRAMEBORDER="0" BORDER="FALSE" rows="40,*">
<FRAME NAME="Logoframe" SRC="<SAP_BW_URL CMD='LDOC'
TEMPLATE_ID='ZCBWTIPP3T0036'>" scrolling=no bgco-
lor="#d4e2ee">
<FRAME NAME="Menuframe" SRC="<SAP_BW_URL CMD='LDOC'
TEMPLATE_ID='ZCBWTIPP3T0038'>">
</FRAMESET>
</HTML>
```

Frameset with menu and cockpit

The second HTML document contains the role menu in a frame on the left and the WebCockpit in a frame on the right:

```
<HTML>
<HEAD>
<TITLE>BW-Report</TITLE>
   <link href= "MIME/BEx/StyleSheets/BWReports.css"
type="text/css" rel="stylesheet">
</HEAD>
<FRAMESET FRAMEBORDER="0" BORDER="FALSE" cols="450,*">
<FRAME NAME="Daten" SRC="<SAP_BW_URL CMD='LDOC'
TEMPLATE_ID='ZCBWTIPP3T0035'>">
<FRAME NAME="ZielframeMC" SRC="<SAP_BW_URL CMD='LDOC'
TEMPLATE_ID='ZCBWTIPP3T0034'>">
</FRAMESET>
</HTML>
```

Figure 8.25 shows the frameset with the role menu and the WebCockpit as a Web application.

8.7 Linking with Other Reports Using the Report/Report Interface

To increase the flexibility of the WebCockpit, we can use transaction RSBBS ("Maintain Sender/Receiver Assignment") to configure the report/report interface (see Figure 8.26). Jump targets, such as queries or Web applications, are assigned for the desired InfoCube or InfoCubes (see Figure 8.26, Steps 1 through 4).

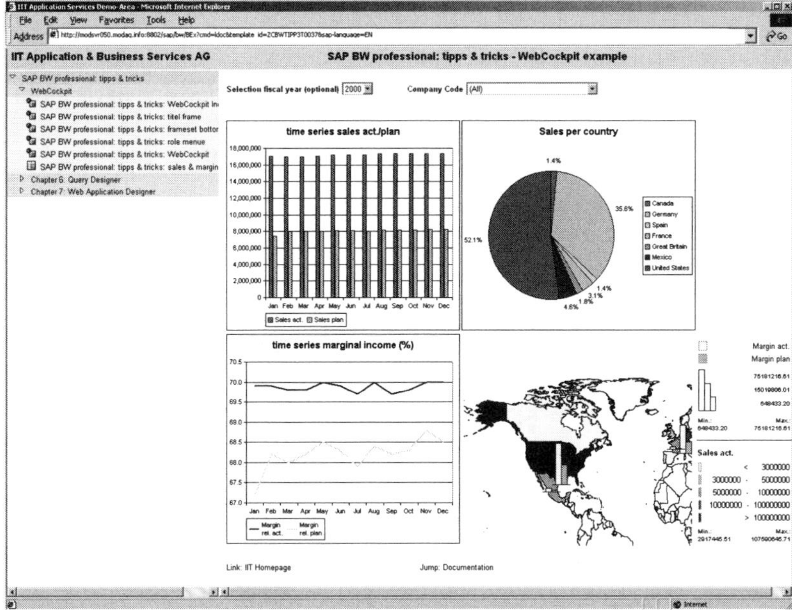

Figure 8.25 Execution of the Frameset with Title, Role Menu and the WebCockpit

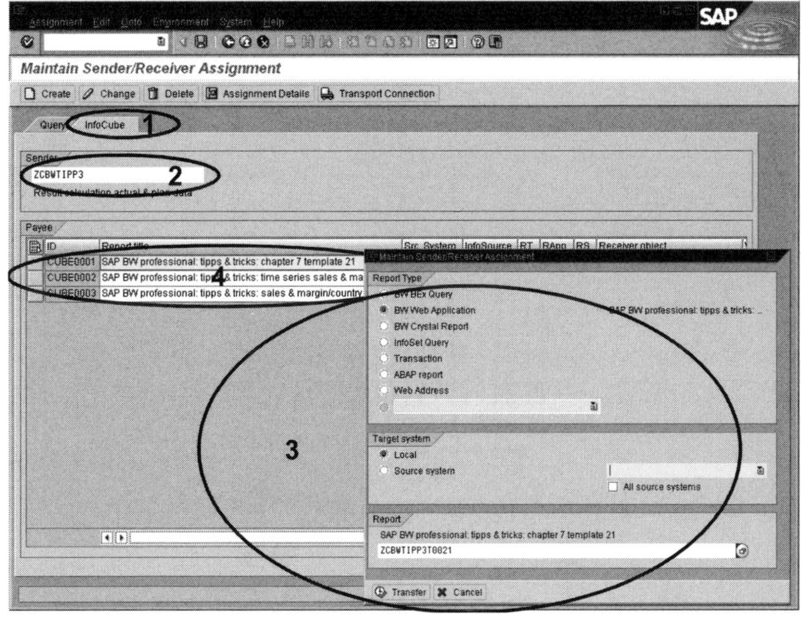

Figure 8.26 Maintaining the Report/Report Interface

8.8 Navigation in the WebCockpit

When you launch the WebCockpit, all functions of the individual linked Web applications are now available (for example, selection and navigation).

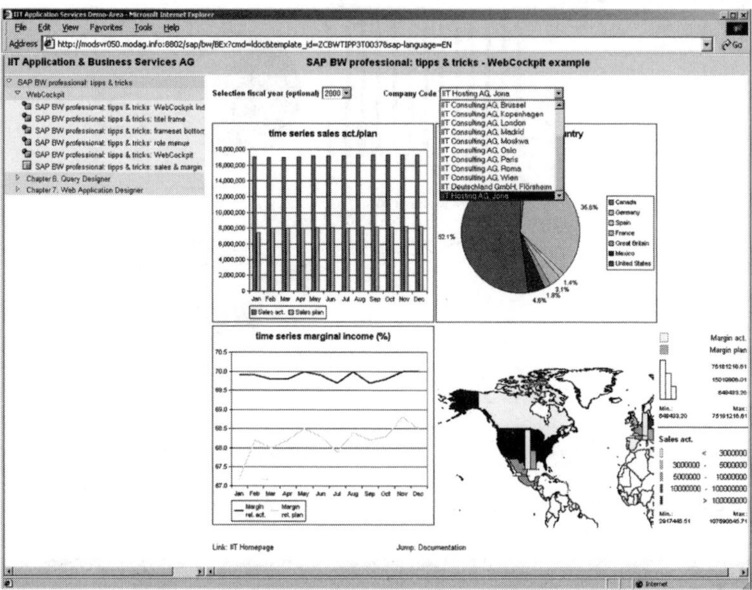

Figure 8.27 Display of the WebCockpit with "Company Code" Selection

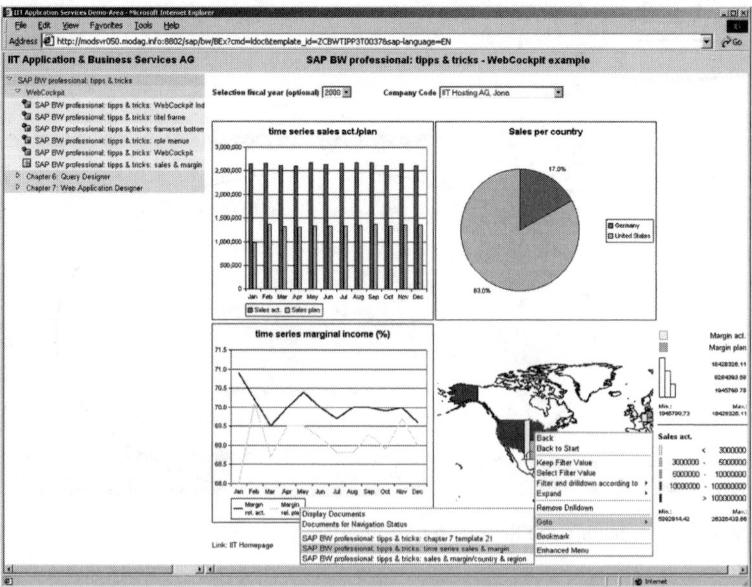

Figure 8.28 Result of the Selection and the Goto Detail Report

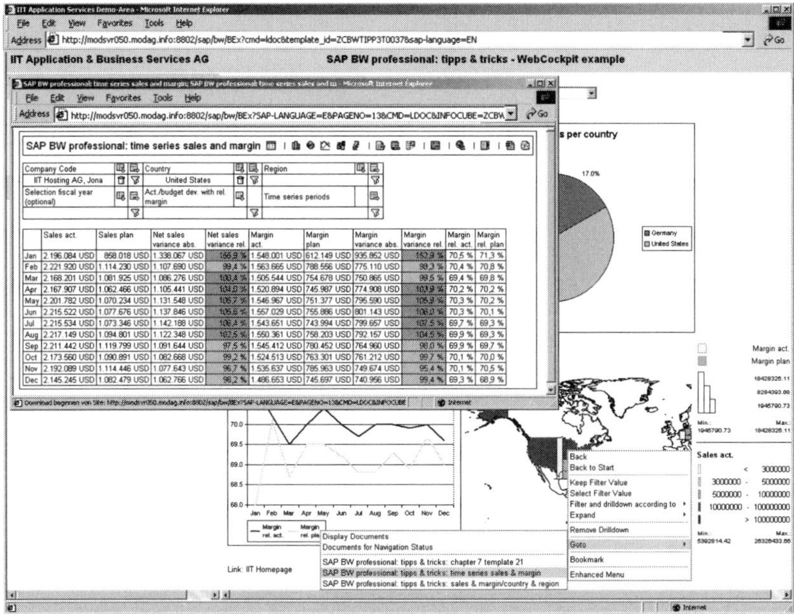

SAP BW professional: time series sales and margin

	Sales act.	Sales plan	Net sales variance abs.	Net sales variance rel.	Margin act.	Margin plan	Margin variance abs.	Margin variance rel.	Margin rel. act.	Margin rel. plan
Jan	2.196.084 USD	858.018 USD	1.338.067 USD	155,9 %	1.548.001 USD	612.149 USD	935.852 USD	152,9 %	70,5 %	71,3 %
Feb	2.221.920 USD	1.114.230 USD	1.107.690 USD	99,4 %	1.563.665 USD	788.556 USD	775.110 USD	98,3 %	70,4 %	70,8 %
Mar	2.168.201 USD	1.081.925 USD	1.086.276 USD	100,4 %	1.505.544 USD	754.678 USD	750.865 USD	99,5 %	69,4 %	69,8 %
Apr	2.167.907 USD	1.062.466 USD	1.105.441 USD	104,0 %	1.520.894 USD	745.987 USD	774.908 USD	103,9 %	70,2 %	70,2 %
May	2.201.782 USD	1.070.234 USD	1.131.548 USD	105,7 %	1.546.967 USD	751.377 USD	795.590 USD	105,9 %	70,3 %	70,2 %
Jun	2.215.522 USD	1.077.676 USD	1.137.846 USD	105,6 %	1.557.029 USD	755.886 USD	801.143 USD	106,0 %	70,3 %	70,1 %
Jul	2.215.534 USD	1.073.346 USD	1.142.188 USD	106,4 %	1.543.651 USD	743.994 USD	799.657 USD	107,5 %	69,7 %	69,3 %
Aug	2.217.149 USD	1.094.801 USD	1.122.348 USD	102,5 %	1.550.361 USD	758.203 USD	792.157 USD	104,5 %	69,9 %	69,3 %
Sep	2.211.442 USD	1.119.799 USD	1.091.644 USD	97,5 %	1.545.412 USD	780.452 USD	764.960 USD	98,0 %	69,9 %	69,7 %
Oct	2.173.560 USD	1.090.891 USD	1.082.668 USD	99,2 %	1.524.513 USD	763.301 USD	761.212 USD	99,7 %	70,1 %	70,0 %
Nov	2.192.089 USD	1.114.446 USD	1.077.643 USD	96,7 %	1.535.637 USD	785.963 USD	749.674 USD	95,4 %	70,1 %	70,5 %
Dec	2.145.245 USD	1.082.479 USD	1.062.766 USD	98,2 %	1.486.653 USD	745.697 USD	740.956 USD	99,4 %	69,3 %	68,9 %

Figure 8.29 Linked Report Containing the Selection

The screen sequence illustrates the functions: After executing the Web application with the WebCockpit (see Figure 8.27), a company code selection is made: all charts are updated. Then, from the map chart, you can go to a detail report using the report/report interface and adopt the selections (Figure 8.28). Figure 8.29 shows the result of the Goto query.

8.9 The Functions of the Sample WebCockpit

The sample WebCockpit has the following functions:

- SAP BW URL for the generic calling of cockpit components
- SAP BW Text for the language-dependent display of texts and hyperlinks
- Restricted role menu for targeted dynamic report selection
- Two-level map graphics and charts
- Several drop-down boxes that control Web items
- Report/report interface for jumping to detail analyses

The purpose of this example is to give you an idea of the options available in Web reporting in SAP BW in an easy-to-implement WebCockpit. You can also adapt this sample WebCockpit to meet your own needs, or customize it by replacing certain sections of code in the sample as necessary.

Appendix

A Structure of the InfoCubes from Chapter 3

A.1 InfoCube "Result calculation actual data (ZCBWTIPP1)"

```
InfoCube Data Model                                        Technical Name
------------------------------------------------------------------------
⊟- Result calculation actual data                          ZCBWTIPP1
 |
 ⊟- Data type                                              ZCBWTIPP11
 | |
 | |- Record type                                          0REC_TYPE
 | |- Value type for reporting                             0VTYPE
 | |- Version                                              0VERSION
 | |- Currency type                                        0CURTYPE
 |
 ⊟- Organization                                           ZCBWTIPP12
 | |
 | ⊞- Sales organization                                   0SALESORG
 | ⊞- Sales employee                                       0SALESEMPLY
 | ⊞- Cost calculation area                                0CO_AREA
 | | - Distribution channel                                0DISTR_CHAN
 | ⊞- Plant                                                0PLANT
 | ⊞- Company code                                         0COMP_CODE
 | | - Sales group                                         0SALES_GRP
 | ⊞- Business area                                        0BUS_AREA
 |
 ⊟- Customer                                               ZCBWTIPP13
 | |
 | | - Industry code                                       0INDUSTRY
 | ⊞- Material group                                       0MATL_GROUP
 | | - Division                                            0DIVISION
 | | - Customer group                                      0CUST_GROUP
 | | - Sales distribution                                  0SALES_DIST
 | ⊞- Customer number                                      0CUSTOMER
 | | - Sales office                                        0SALES_OFF
 |
 ⊟- Product                                                ZCBWTIPP14
 | |
 | | - Main material group                                 0MAINMATGRP
 | ⊞- Material                                             0MATERIAL
 |
 ⊟- Document information                                   ZCBWTIPP15
 | |
 | | - Item reference number                               0ID_ITMNUM
 | ⊞- Partner profit center                                0PART_PRCTR
 | | - Reference no. of the bus. ref. present              0REFER_ITM
 | | - Posting date on the document                        0PSTNG_DATE
 | | - Sales order item                                    0S_ORD_ITEM
 | | - Cancellation reference number                       ZASTOPOS0
 | | - Cancellation document number                        ZASTOBEL0
 | | - Reference no. of the document                       0REFER_DOC
```

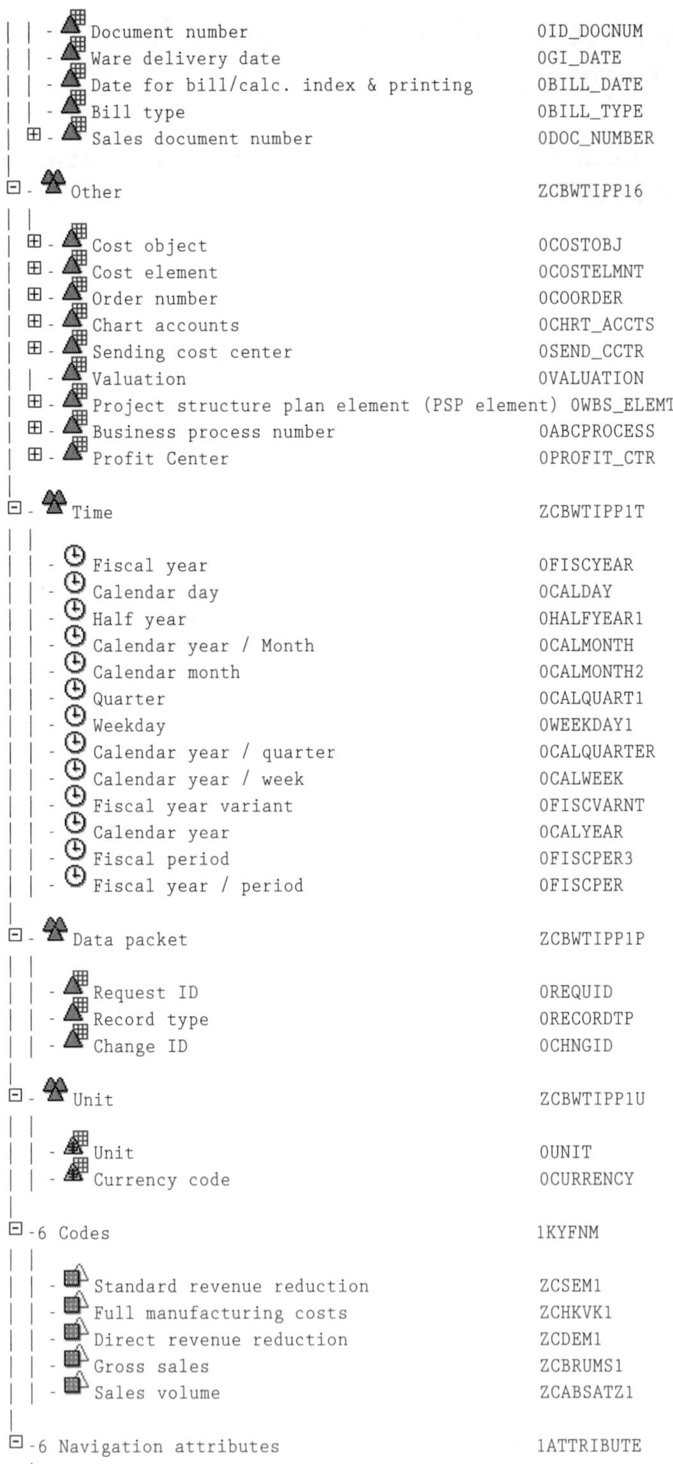

Name	Technical name
Document number	0ID_DOCNUM
Ware delivery date	0GI_DATE
Date for bill/calc. index & printing	0BILL_DATE
Bill type	0BILL_TYPE
Sales document number	0DOC_NUMBER
Other	ZCBWTIPP16
Cost object	0COSTOBJ
Cost element	0COSTELMNT
Order number	0COORDER
Chart accounts	0CHRT_ACCTS
Sending cost center	0SEND_CCTR
Valuation	0VALUATION
Project structure plan element (PSP element)	0WBS_ELEMT
Business process number	0ABCPROCESS
Profit Center	0PROFIT_CTR
Time	ZCBWTIPP1T
Fiscal year	0FISCYEAR
Calendar day	0CALDAY
Half year	0HALFYEAR1
Calendar year / Month	0CALMONTH
Calendar month	0CALMONTH2
Quarter	0CALQUART1
Weekday	0WEEKDAY1
Calendar year / quarter	0CALQUARTER
Calendar year / week	0CALWEEK
Fiscal year variant	0FISCVARNT
Calendar year	0CALYEAR
Fiscal period	0FISCPER3
Fiscal year / period	0FISCPER
Data packet	ZCBWTIPP1P
Request ID	0REQUID
Record type	0RECORDTP
Change ID	0CHNGID
Unit	ZCBWTIPP1U
Unit	0UNIT
Currency code	0CURRENCY
6 Codes	1KYFNM
Standard revenue reduction	ZCSEM1
Full manufacturing costs	ZCHKVK1
Direct revenue reduction	ZCDEM1
Gross sales	ZCBRUMS1
Sales volume	ZCABSATZ1
6 Navigation attributes	1ATTRIBUTE

```
|  - Region                                   0CUSTOMER__0REGION
|  - Country (customer)                       0CUSTOMER__0COUNTRY
|  - Main product group                       0MATERIAL__ZCPRDHGR1
⊞  - Product group                            0MATERIAL__ZCPRDGR1
```

A.2 InfoCube "Result calculation plan data (ZCBWTIPP2)"

```
InfoCube Data Model                                 Technical Name
---------------------------------------------------------------------
⊟ - Result calculation plan data                     ZCBWTIPP2
 |
 ⊟ - Data type                                       ZCBWTIPP21
 | |
 | | - Record type                                   0REC_TYPE
 | | - Version                                       0VERSION
 | | - Currency type                                 0CURTYPE
 | | - Value type for reporting                      0VTYPE
 |
 ⊟ - Organization                                    ZCBWTIPP22
 | |
 | ⊞ - Company code                                  0COMP_CODE
 | ⊞ - Business area                                 0BUS_AREA
 |
 ⊟ - Customer                                        ZCBWTIPP23
 | |
 | | - Region                                        0REGION
 | | - Country code                                  0COUNTRY
 |
 ⊟ - Product                                         ZCBWTIPP24
 | |
 | ⊞ - Product group                                 ZCPRDGR1
 |
 ⊟ - Time                                            ZCBWTIPP2T
 | |
 | | - Half year                                     0HALFYEAR1
 | | - Fiscal year                                   0FISCYEAR
 | | - Fiscal year variant                           0FISCVARNT
 | | - Calendar year / month                         0CALMONTH
 | | - Fiscal period                                 0FISCPER3
 | | - Fiscal year / period                          0FISCPER
 | | - Calendar month                                0CALMONTH2
 | | - Calendar year                                 0CALYEAR
 | | - Calendar year / quarter                       0CALQUARTER
 | | - Quarter                                       0CALQUART1
 |
 ⊟ - Data packet                                     ZCBWTIPP2P
 | |
 | | - Request ID                                    0REQUID
 | | - Change ID                                     0CHNGID
 | | - Record type                                   0RECORDTP
 |
 ⊟ - Unit                                            ZCBWTIPP2U
 | |
```

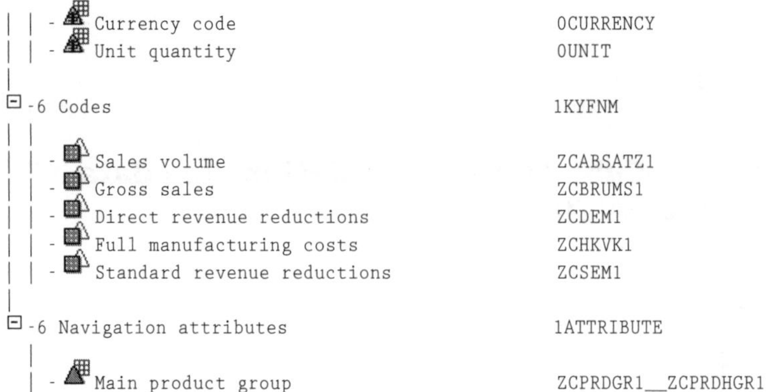

```
| | - Currency code                              0CURRENCY
| | - Unit quantity                              0UNIT
|
⊟-6 Codes                                        1KYFNM
| |
| | - Sales volume                               ZCABSATZ1
| | - Gross sales                                ZCBRUMS1
| | - Direct revenue reductions                  ZCDEM1
| | - Full manufacturing costs                   ZCHKVK1
| | - Standard revenue reductions                ZCSEM1
|
⊟-6 Navigation attributes                        1ATTRIBUTE
  |
  | - Main product group                         ZCPRDGR1__ZCPRDHGR1
```

A.3 Multiprovider "Result calculation actual and plan data (ZCBWTIPP3)"

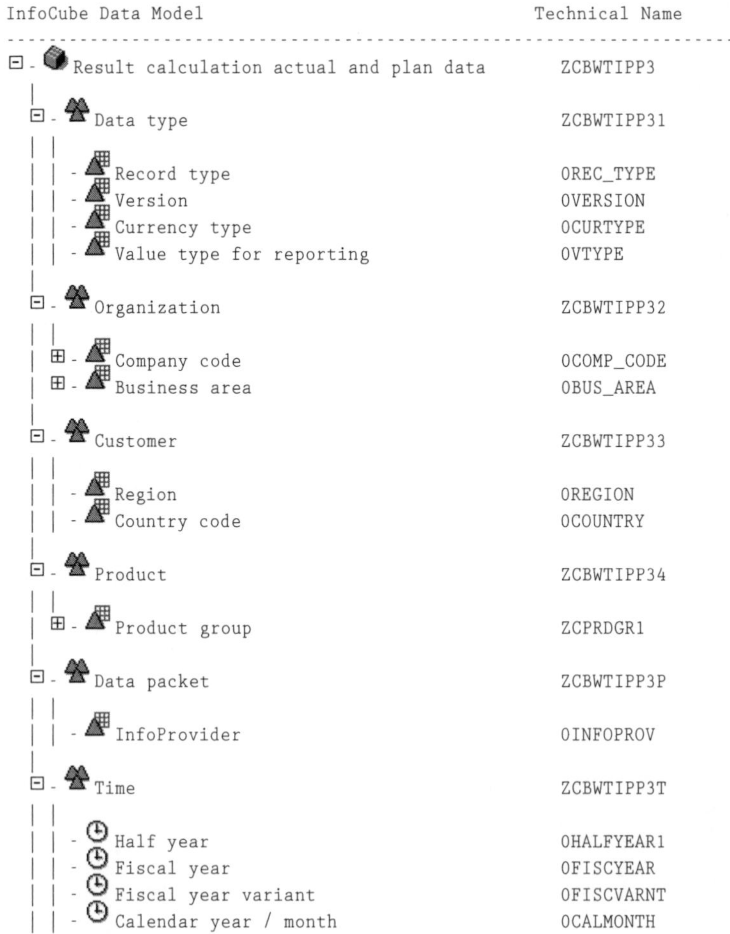

```
InfoCube Data Model                                    Technical Name
-----------------------------------------------------------------------
⊟ - Result calculation actual and plan data            ZCBWTIPP3
  |
  ⊟ - Data type                                        ZCBWTIPP31
  | |
  | | - Record type                                    0REC_TYPE
  | | - Version                                        0VERSION
  | | - Currency type                                  0CURTYPE
  | | - Value type for reporting                       0VTYPE
  |
  ⊟ - Organization                                     ZCBWTIPP32
  | |
  | ⊞ - Company code                                   0COMP_CODE
  | ⊞ - Business area                                  0BUS_AREA
  |
  ⊟ - Customer                                         ZCBWTIPP33
  | |
  | | - Region                                         0REGION
  | | - Country code                                   0COUNTRY
  |
  ⊟ - Product                                          ZCBWTIPP34
  | |
  | ⊞ - Product group                                  ZCPRDGR1
  |
  ⊟ - Data packet                                      ZCBWTIPP3P
  | |
  | | - InfoProvider                                   0INFOPROV
  |
  ⊟ - Time                                             ZCBWTIPP3T
  | |
  | | - Half year                                      0HALFYEAR1
  | | - Fiscal year                                    0FISCYEAR
  | | - Fiscal year variant                            0FISCVARNT
  | | - Calendar year / month                          0CALMONTH
```

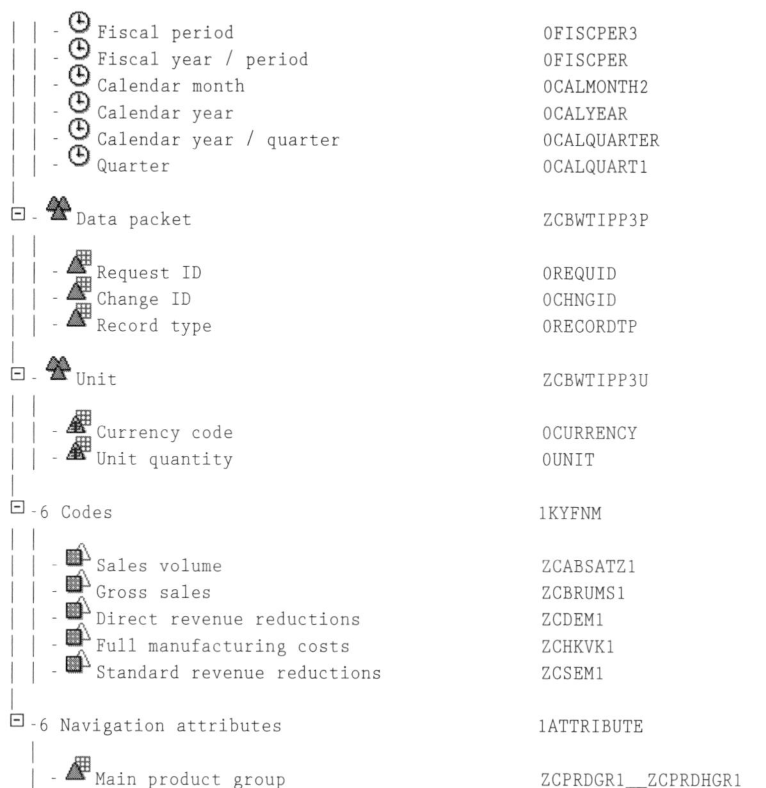

Description	Technical name
Fiscal period	0FISCPER3
Fiscal year / period	0FISCPER
Calendar month	0CALMONTH2
Calendar year	0CALYEAR
Calendar year / quarter	0CALQUARTER
Quarter	0CALQUART1
Data packet	ZCBWTIPP3P
Request ID	0REQUID
Change ID	0CHNGID
Record type	0RECORDTP
Unit	ZCBWTIPP3U
Currency code	0CURRENCY
Unit quantity	0UNIT
-6 Codes	1KYFNM
Sales volume	ZCABSATZ1
Gross sales	ZCBRUMS1
Direct revenue reductions	ZCDEM1
Full manufacturing costs	ZCHKVK1
Standard revenue reductions	ZCSEM1
-6 Navigation attributes	1ATTRIBUTE
Main product group	ZCPRDGR1__ZCPRDHGR1

B Structure of the InfoCubes from Chapter 4

B.1 InfoCube "Result calculation invoice data (ZCBWTIPP5)"

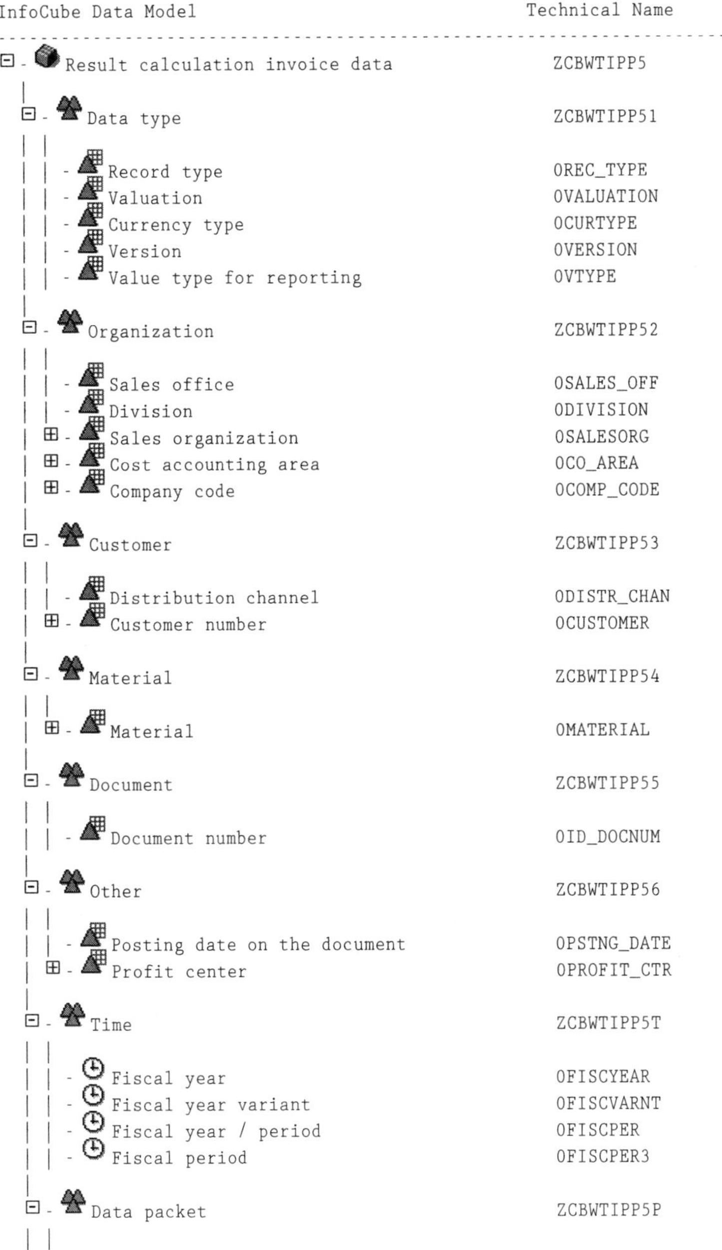

InfoCube Data Model	Technical Name
Result calculation invoice data	ZCBWTIPP5
Data type	ZCBWTIPP51
Record type	0REC_TYPE
Valuation	0VALUATION
Currency type	0CURTYPE
Version	0VERSION
Value type for reporting	0VTYPE
Organization	ZCBWTIPP52
Sales office	0SALES_OFF
Division	0DIVISION
Sales organization	0SALESORG
Cost accounting area	0CO_AREA
Company code	0COMP_CODE
Customer	ZCBWTIPP53
Distribution channel	0DISTR_CHAN
Customer number	0CUSTOMER
Material	ZCBWTIPP54
Material	0MATERIAL
Document	ZCBWTIPP55
Document number	0ID_DOCNUM
Other	ZCBWTIPP56
Posting date on the document	0PSTNG_DATE
Profit center	0PROFIT_CTR
Time	ZCBWTIPP5T
Fiscal year	0FISCYEAR
Fiscal year variant	0FISCVARNT
Fiscal year / period	0FISCPER
Fiscal period	0FISCPER3
Data packet	ZCBWTIPP5P

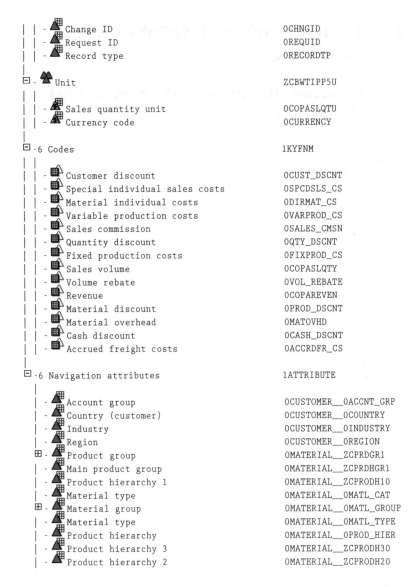

```
| | - Change ID                                OCHNGID
| | - Request ID                               OREQUID
| | - Record type                              ORECORDTP
|
⊟ - Unit                                       ZCBWTIPP5U
| |
| | - Sales quantity unit                      0COPASLQTU
| | - Currency code                            0CURRENCY
|
⊟ -6 Codes                                     1KYFNM
| |
| | - Customer discount                        0CUST_DSCNT
| | - Special individual sales costs           0SPCDSLS_CS
| | - Material individual costs                0DIRMAT_CS
| | - Variable production costs                0VARPROD_CS
| | - Sales commission                         0SALES_CMSN
| | - Quantity discount                        0QTY_DSCNT
| | - Fixed production costs                   0FIXPROD_CS
| | - Sales volume                             0COPASLQTY
| | - Volume rebate                            0VOL_REBATE
| | - Revenue                                  0COPAREVEN
| | - Material discount                        0PROD_DSCNT
| | - Material overhead                        0MATOVHD
| | - Cash discount                            0CASH_DSCNT
| | - Accrued freight costs                    0ACCRDFR_CS
|
⊟ -6 Navigation attributes                     1ATTRIBUTE
  |
  | - Account group                            0CUSTOMER__0ACCNT_GRP
  | - Country (customer)                       0CUSTOMER__0COUNTRY
  | - Industry                                 0CUSTOMER__0INDUSTRY
  | - Region                                   0CUSTOMER__0REGION
  ⊞ - Product group                            0MATERIAL__ZCPRDGR1
  | - Main product group                       0MATERIAL__ZCPRDHGR1
  | - Product hierarchy 1                      0MATERIAL__ZCPRODH10
  | - Material type                            0MATERIAL__0MATL_CAT
  ⊞ - Material group                           0MATERIAL__0MATL_GROUP
  | - Material type                            0MATERIAL__0MATL_TYPE
  | - Product hierarchy                        0MATERIAL__0PROD_HIER
  | - Product hierarchy 3                      0MATERIAL__ZCPRODH30
  | - Product hierarchy 2                      0MATERIAL__ZCPRODH20
```

B.2 InfoCube "Result calculation data proj./job accounting (ZCBWTIPP6)"

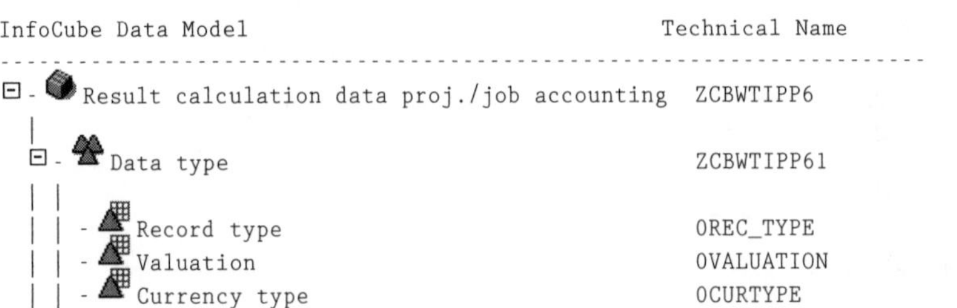

```
InfoCube Data Model                                      Technical Name
-----------------------------------------------------------------------
⊟ - Result calculation data proj./job accounting   ZCBWTIPP6
 |
 ⊟ - Data type                                     ZCBWTIPP61
 | |
 | | - Record type                                 0REC_TYPE
 | | - Valuation                                   0VALUATION
 | | - Currency type                               0CURTYPE
```

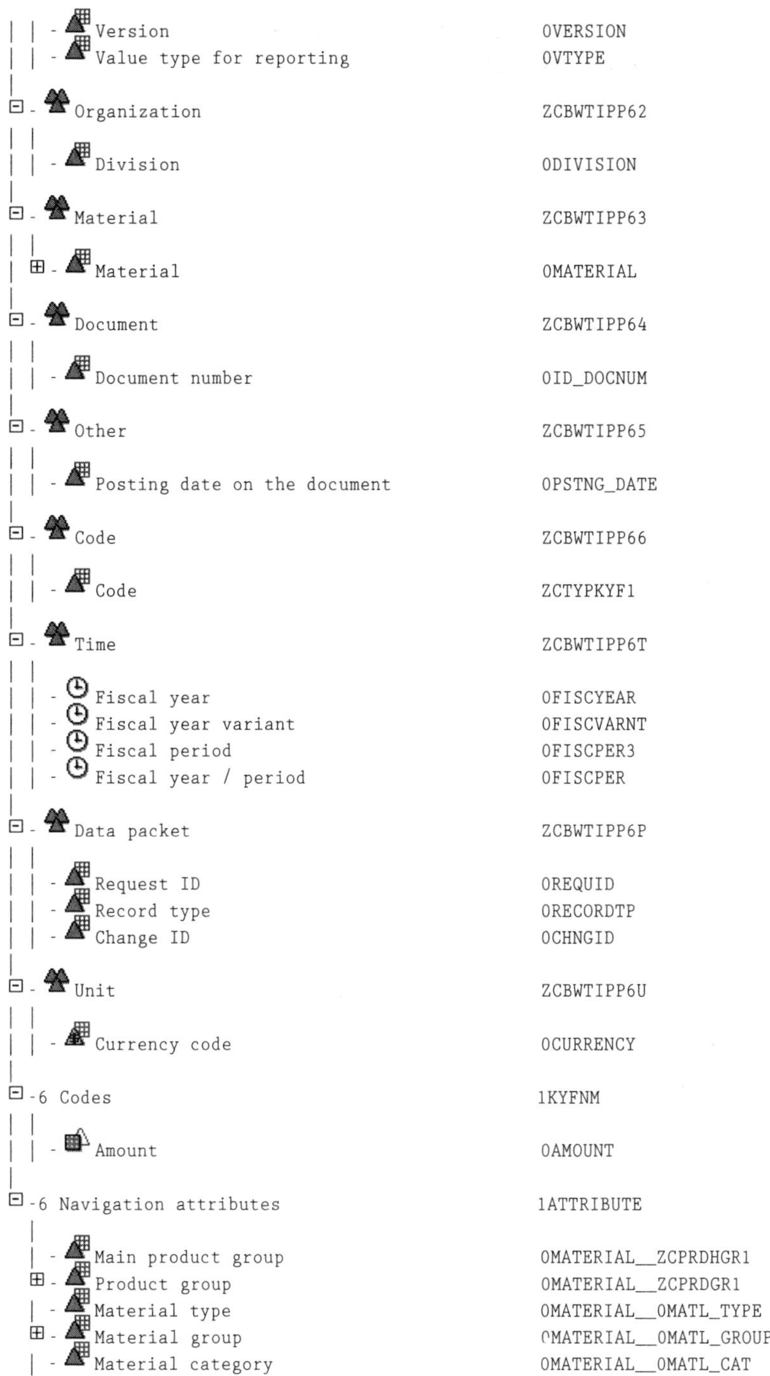
Version 0VERSION
Value type for reporting 0VTYPE
Organization ZCBWTIPP62
Division 0DIVISION
Material ZCBWTIPP63
Material 0MATERIAL
Document ZCBWTIPP64
Document number 0ID_DOCNUM
Other ZCBWTIPP65
Posting date on the document 0PSTNG_DATE
Code ZCBWTIPP66
Code ZCTYPKYF1
Time ZCBWTIPP6T
Fiscal year 0FISCYEAR
Fiscal year variant 0FISCVARNT
Fiscal period 0FISCPER3
Fiscal year / period 0FISCPER
Data packet ZCBWTIPP6P
Request ID 0REQUID
Record type 0RECORDTP
Change ID 0CHNGID
Unit ZCBWTIPP6U
Currency code 0CURRENCY
-6 Codes 1KYFNM
Amount 0AMOUNT
-6 Navigation attributes 1ATTRIBUTE
Main product group 0MATERIAL__ZCPRDHGR1
Product group 0MATERIAL__ZCPRDGR1
Material type 0MATERIAL__0MATL_TYPE
Material group 0MATERIAL__0MATL_GROUP
Material category 0MATERIAL__0MATL_CAT

B.3 InfoCube "Result calculation overhead costs (ZCBWTIPP7)"

```
InfoCube Data Model                                   Technical Name
---------------------------------------------------------------------
[-]- Result calculation overhead costs                  ZCBWTIPP7
 |
 [-]- Data type                                         ZCBWTIPP71
 | |
 | | - Record type                                      0REC_TYPE
 | | - Valuation                                        0VALUATION
 | | - Version                                          0VERSION
 | | - Value type for reporting                         0VTYPE
 | | - Currency type                                    0CURTYPE
 |
 [-]- Organization                                      ZCBWTIPP72
 | |
 | [+]- Cost accounting area                            0CO_AREA
 | [+]- Company code                                    0COMP_CODE
 | [+]- Sales organization                              0SALESORG
 |
 [-]- Customer                                          ZCBWTIPP73
 | |
 | | - Distribution channel                             0DISTR_CHAN
 |
 [-]- Document                                          ZCBWTIPP74
 | |
 | | - Document number                                  0ID_DOCNUM
 |
 [-]- Other                                             ZCBWTIPP75
 | |
 | [+]- Profit center                                   0PROFIT_CTR
 | | - Posting data on the document                     0PSTNG_DATE
 |
 [-]- Code                                              ZCBWTIPP76
 | |
 | | - Code                                             ZCTYPKYF1
 |
 [-]- Time                                              ZCBWTIPP7T
 | |
 | | - Fiscal year                                      0FISCYEAR
 | | - Fiscal year variant                              0FISCVARNT
 | | - Fiscal period                                    0FISCPER3
 | | - Fiscal year / period                             0FISCPER
 |
 [-]- Data packet                                       ZCBWTIPP7P
 | |
 | | - Record type                                      0RECORDTP
 | | - Change ID                                        0CHNGID
 | | - Request ID                                       0REQUID
 |
 [-]- Unit                                              ZCBWTIPP7U
 | |
 | | - Currency code                                    0CURRENCY
```

B.4 MultiProvider "Result calculation for all transaction types (ZCBWTIPP8)"

```
InfoCube Data Model                                  Technical Name
-----------------------------------------------------------------
⊟- Result calculation for all transaction types   ZCBWTIPP8
 |
 ⊟- Data type                                       ZCBWTIPP81
 | |
 | | - Record type                                  0REC_TYPE
 | | - Value type for reporting                     0VTYPE
 | | - Valuation                                    0VALUATION
 | | - Version                                      0VERSION
 | | - Currency type                                0CURTYPE
 |
 ⊟- Organization                                    ZCBWTIPP82
 | |
 | ⊞- Company code                                  0COMP_CODE
 | ⊞- Cost accounting area                          0CO_AREA
 | ⊞- Sales organization                            0SALESORG
 | | - Division                                     0DIVISION
 | | - Sales office                                 0SALES_OFF
 |
 ⊟- Customer                                        ZCBWTIPP83
 | |
 | ⊞- Customer number                               0CUSTOMER
 | | - Distribution channel                         0DISTR_CHAN
 |
 ⊟- Material                                        ZCBWTIPP84
 | |
 | ⊞- Material                                      0MATERIAL
 |
 ⊟- Document                                        ZCBWTIPP85
 | |
 | |- Document number                               0ID_DOCNUM
 |
 ⊟- Other                                           ZCBWTIPP86
 | |
 | ⊞- Profit Center                                 0PROFIT_CTR
 | | - Posting date on document                     0PSTNG_DATE
 |
 ⊟- Code                                            ZCBWTIPP87
 | |
 | | - Code                                         ZCTYPKYF1
 |
 ⊟- Data packet                                     ZCBWTIPP8P
 | |
 | | - InfoProvider                                 0INFOPROV
 |
```

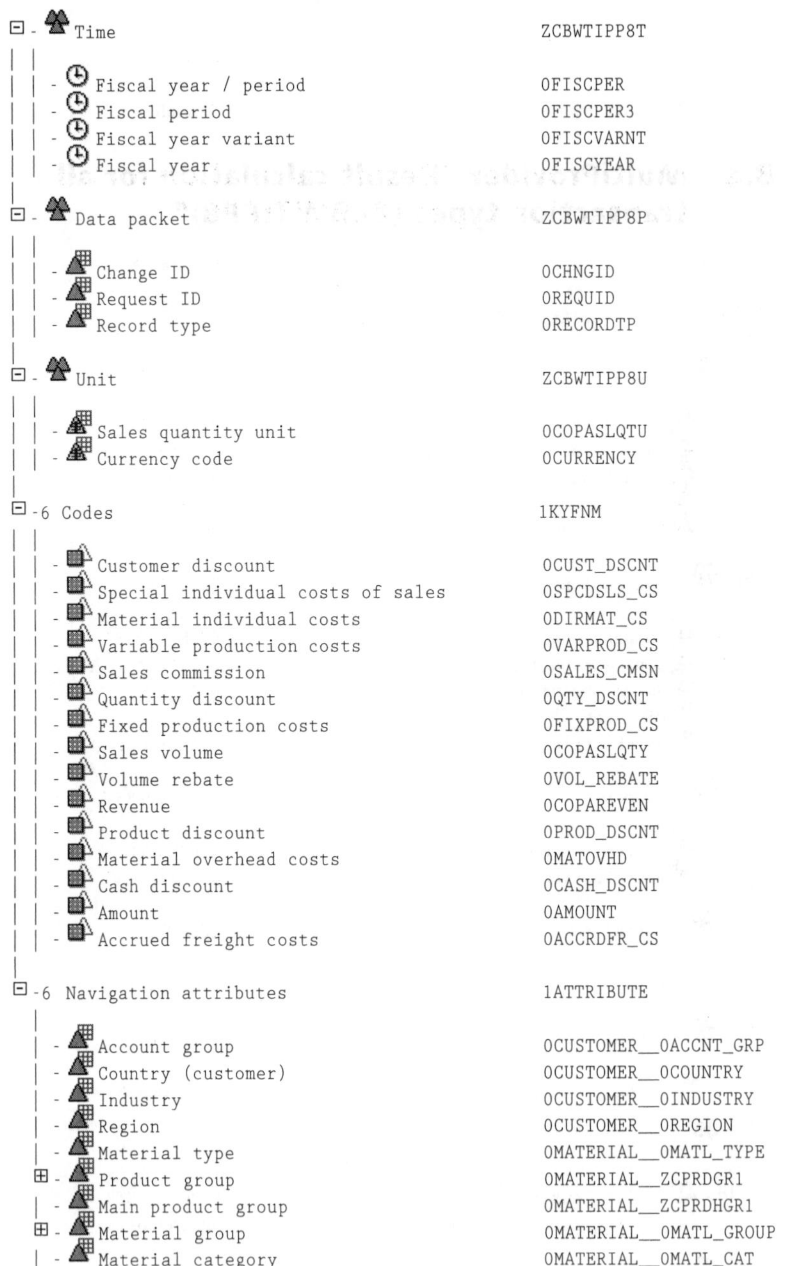
Time ZCBWTIPP8T
Fiscal year / period 0FISCPER
Fiscal period 0FISCPER3
Fiscal year variant 0FISCVARNT
Fiscal year 0FISCYEAR
Data packet ZCBWTIPP8P
Change ID 0CHNGID
Request ID 0REQUID
Record type 0RECORDTP
Unit ZCBWTIPP8U
Sales quantity unit 0COPASLQTU
Currency code 0CURRENCY
-6 Codes 1KYFNM
Customer discount 0CUST_DSCNT
Special individual costs of sales 0SPCDSLS_CS
Material individual costs 0DIRMAT_CS
Variable production costs 0VARPROD_CS
Sales commission 0SALES_CMSN
Quantity discount 0QTY_DSCNT
Fixed production costs 0FIXPROD_CS
Sales volume 0COPASLQTY
Volume rebate 0VOL_REBATE
Revenue 0COPAREVEN
Product discount 0PROD_DSCNT
Material overhead costs 0MATOVHD
Cash discount 0CASH_DSCNT
Amount 0AMOUNT
Accrued freight costs 0ACCRDFR_CS
-6 Navigation attributes 1ATTRIBUTE
Account group 0CUSTOMER__0ACCNT_GRP
Country (customer) 0CUSTOMER__0COUNTRY
Industry 0CUSTOMER__0INDUSTRY
Region 0CUSTOMER__0REGION
Material type 0MATERIAL__0MATL_TYPE
Product group 0MATERIAL__ZCPRDGR1
Main product group 0MATERIAL__ZCPRDHGR1
Material group 0MATERIAL__0MATL_GROUP
Material category 0MATERIAL__0MATL_CAT

C Bibliography

Balanced Scorecard Institute: *http://www.balancedscorecard.org*.

Codd, Edgar Frank et al.: Providing OLAP (Online Analytical Processing) to User-Analysts: An IT Mandate, 1993. White Paper by Arbor Software (Hyperion Solutions). *http://www.fpm.com/refer/codd.html.*

Inmon, William H.: Building the Data Warehouse, 3. Aufl. 2002 (eBook), Erstausgabe 1993.

Kaplan, Robert S. und Norton, David P.: The Balanced Scorecard. Translating Strategy Into Action. 1996.

Pendse, Nigel: The OLAP Report. What is OLAP? An analysis of what the increasingly misused OLAP term is supposed to mean, letzte Aktualisierung 27.7.2002, *http://www.olapreport.com/fasmi.htm.*

Rucker, Rudy: Dinosauriermaschinen und die Lust am Hacken, 23.12.1997. *http://www.heise.de/tp/deutsch/inhalt/co/2235/1.html.*

Scheer, August-Wilhelm: Business Process Engineering: Reference Models for Industrial. 2nd Revision edition 1994.

Auf der Suche nach der verlorenen Strategie. Expertenbefragung zur Balanced Scorecard. In: isreport 1/2003, S. 42 – 46.

D The Author

Norbert Egger is CEO of the CubeServ Group (CubeServ AG, CubeServ GmbH and CubeServ Technologies AG), which specialize in business intelligence solutions.

In 1996, he directed the construction of the first data warehouse in the world based on SAP. In the interim, he has implemented over 100 projects with SAP Business Information Warehouse (SAP BW) and SAP Strategic Enterprise Management (SAP SEM). He has many years of experience in the operation of SAP-based Business-Intelligence Solutions.

www.cubeserv.com

Index

J

K

M

N

O

P

Q

R

S

T

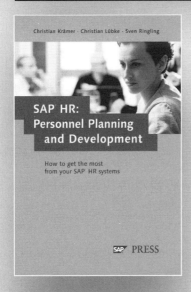

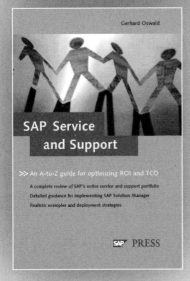

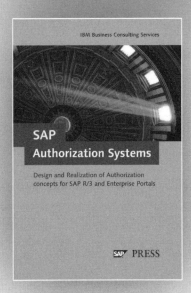

Recommended Reading by SAP PRESS

Business

N. Egger
SAP BW Professional

IBM Business Consulting Services
SAP Authorization System

G. Oswald
SAP Service and Support

Rickayzen, Dart, Brennecke, Schneider
Practical Workflow for SAP

R. Buck-Emden
mySAP CRM

Technical

M. Mißbach et al.
SAP System Operations

S. Hagemann, L. Will
SAP R/3 System Administration

Brochhausen, Kielisch, Schnerring, Staeck
SAP HR Technical Principles and Programming

T. Schneider
SAP Performance Optimization Guide

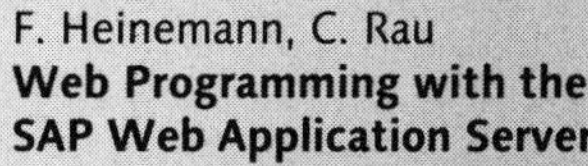

F. Heinemann, C. Rau
Web Programming with the SAP Web Application Server

L. Will
SAP APO System Administration

W.Hertleif, C. Wachter
SAP Smart Forms

H. Keller, J. Jacobitz
ABAP Objects – The Official Reference

H. Stefani (Ed.)
Archiving Your SAP Data